Employment Security and Labor Market Behavior

Interdisciplinary Approaches and International Evidence

Christoph F. Buechtemann, Editor

Cornell International Industrial and
Labor Relations Report Number 23

ILR Press
Ithaca, New York

331.12
E556

⁀Ρ   Library of Congress Cataloging-in Publication Data

Employment security and labor market behavior : interdisciplinary
approaches and international evidence / Christoph F. Buechtemann,
editor.
p.   cm.—(Cornell international industrial and labor
relations report ; no. 23)
Includes bibliographical references and index.
ISBN 0-87546-188-3
1. Job security—United States. 2. Job security—European
Economic Community countries. 3. Labor market—United States.
4. Labor market—European Economic Community countries.
I. Buechtemann, Christoph F. II. Series: Cornell international
industrial and labor relations reports ; no. 23.
HD5708.45.U6E47   1992
331.12′094—dc20   92-11308

Copies may be ordered through bookstores or directly from
ILR Press
School of Industrial and Labor Relations
Cornell University
Ithaca, NY 14853-3901

Printed on acid-free paper in the United States of America

5 4 3 2 1

Contents

France

Italy

Part III. The Future of Labor Market (De)Regulation in Industrialized Countries

Contents

Tables and Figures

Tables

Figures

Preface

On both sides of the Atlantic, employment security and job stability have become major concerns in academic labor market analysis and in the public debate about employment and labor market policy. Under the heading of labor market flexibility, employment protection and job security regulations have come to be viewed as possible sources of labor market "rigidities" inhibiting work force adjustment, increasing labor costs, strengthening "insider" bargaining power, and thus accounting at least in part for the long-term unemployment and sluggish employment growth in most countries of Europe as compared to countries such as the United States and Canada that have less elaborate or less comprehensive systems of labor market regulation. Inspired by the "American job miracle" and what they believed to be its driving forces, many European governments have selectively relaxed legal layoff and dismissal restraints during the 1980s to stimulate job creation.

These events contrast with recent developments in the United States in which policy advisers, many inspired by the Japanese model of cooperative labor relations and lifetime employment, have pointed out the beneficial effects of workers' rights and employment security on work commitment, technological innovation, and labor productivity. This change in perspectives has been accompanied by a gradual erosion of the prevailing employment-at-will doctrine through common-law court rulings, "concession bargaining" by unions involving far-reaching employment guarantees, and recent legislative changes that have established rudimentary layoff and dismissal protection.

So far, however, both theoretical arguments and empirical evidence on the allegedly detrimental or beneficial impact of employment protection and job security on worker productivity, labor market adjustment, and employment creation have been highly controversial on both sides of the Atlantic. With the quest for harmonization of national regulatory frameworks in the context of the completion of the European internal market in 1992 and in view of productivity problems and increasing competitive pressures facing the U.S. economy, employment security here and there is likely to remain one of the top priorities in the labor market policy agenda of the 1990s. Given the many theoretical and empirical questions involved, job stability and employment security will also remain central topics in academic labor market analysis and microeconomic theory.

The twenty-eight contributions to this book approach the issue from several disciplinary angles and national perspectives: In the introduction, Christoph Buechtemann develops an analytical definition of the issue, pointing out its many facets and links to other areas of concern; summarizes some of the core assumptions in the debate about employment security; provides an overview of the empirical evidence from major industrialized countries; and outlines some of the theoretical implications for future research.

Part I includes four chapters that focus on the economics of employment protection from a primarily theoretical and analytical perspective and provide contrasting conceptual frameworks for analyzing employment security policies. Robert Boyer's contribution views employment security policies in the larger context of changing modes of production and forms of industrial organization ("Fordism" and "post-Fordism") and offers a historically oriented macroeconomic framework for interpreting the questions involved. Daniel Hamermesh, in contrast, takes a decidedly microeconomic view and, extending standard assumptions of neoclassical labor market theory, develops a theoretical framework of how employment security policies, depending on the particular timing of their introduction, affect labor costs and the work force adjustment behavior (especially employment and hours substitution) of firms in different stages of the business cycle. Horst-Manfred Schellhaass complements Hamermesh's analysis by calling attention to the impact of employment security policies on the structure of labor demand and by discussing their potential effects on technological innovation by firms. Robert Flanagan focuses on the impact of legal layoff and dismissal restraints on hiring behavior in firms. He assumes that European employment security policies have shifted adjustment pressures primarily toward off-the-job screening of job applicants, thereby raising hiring costs, reinforcing the widespread hiring reluctance found among European employers, and contributing to the persistence of long-term unemployment.

Part II concentrates on the contrasting regulatory models of employment security in six major industrialized countries and provides empirical evidence of their respective impact on such key economic variables as total employment, unemployment, work force adjustment, firing and hiring behavior, "insider-outsider" segmentation, and the system of labor relations at large.

Part II is divided into five sections. The first section is devoted to the United States and includes comparisons with Japan. William Gould outlines recent legal developments in wrongful-discharge jurisdiction in the context of the wider legal framework of U.S. labor relations and compares it to that of Japan. Katharine Abraham and Susan Houseman show that Japan and the United States indeed exhibited significant differences in work force adjustment in the period from 1970 to 1985. Ronald Ehrenberg and George Jakubson view arguments for and against recent U.S. plant-closing legislation (WARN) in light of empirical evidence and find support for the contention that prenotification of dismissals has positive effects on the labor market. James Dertouzos and Lynn Karoly find significant repercussions of the recent erosion of the employment-at-will doctrine on overall employment levels and work force adjustment in the United States. Paul Osterman reports on experiences of major U.S. firms following "voluntary" employment security policies during the 1980s and points out institutional reform perspectives for improving the current state of employment security in the United States.

The second section deals with Germany. Rolf Birk provides an overview of the principles underlying German dismissal legislation. Friedrich Buttler and Ulrich Walwei present empirical evidence that supports their assumption that employment security regulation in the Federal Republic may well be compatible with or even enhance the allocative efficiency of labor markets. Their conclusion, that the German labor market is highly flexible despite an elaborate system of legal and collectively bargained dismissal restraints, is confirmed by the analyses of Wolfgang Franz and Kornelius Kraft on work force adjustment and employment elasticity in the German manufacturing sector. Christoph Buechtemann gives a detailed account of micro-level evidence on the range and impact of legal dismissal protection and reports findings on the effects of recent measures aimed at "deregulating" the hiring and firing behavior of German firms.

The third section focuses on the United Kingdom. Brian Bercusson outlines the basic constituents of British employment legislation and draws attention to the tight nexus and interaction between statutory regulation, collective bargaining, and special government measures in shaping recent developments in British labor relations. Richard Hyman argues that U.K. dismissal legislation has never put a severe restraint on firms' staffing policies but that employment security has been essentially provided through collective bargaining and firm-level worker representation. Thus, major changes in employment security during the 1980s had to be sought in the transformation of firm-level industrial relations rather than in legal deregulatory measures enacted by the Thatcher government. This conclusion is supported by Brian Towers, who contrasts assumptions underlying the British government's labor law deregulation agenda of the 1980s with empirical evidence showing that the impact of employment legislation on a firm's staffing practices frequently has been grossly overestimated in the current debate.

The fourth section contains three contributions on France. The paper by Antoine Lyon-Caen outlines recent trends in French labor legislation from a legal perspective and shows that during the 1980s France underwent a major reorientation from "legalistic" state regulation toward an emphasis on the role of collective bargaining in prenegotiating legislative changes. Contractual solutions were stronger as a result, and, at the same time, protective minimum standards were maintained through labor law. Guy Maurau and Alain Charraud each analyze the course of major policy changes in the area of employment security and "nonstandard" employment during the 1980s from an economic point of view. Both authors provide substantial evidence that even in a country with presumably rigid legal layoff and dismissal restraints, deregulatory measures enacted during the 1980s have had only a limited direct effect on actual hiring and firing behavior.

The fifth section is devoted to Italy. Tiziano Treu gives an account of the comparatively inflexible legal regulations governing both dismissals and hirings at the micro level. The adverse impact of rigid labor laws was strongly mitigated during the 1980s, however, by an increase in "collectively bargained flexibility" as quid pro quo for guarantees of employment security as well as by a significant expansion of supporting government measures. Leonello Tronti presents an economic analysis of the centerpiece of these supporting measures, the Cassa Integrazione Guadagni (Wage Compensation Fund), which has been essential in facilitating structural adjustment in core sectors of Italian industry. Peter Auer shows that the present coexistence of rigid hiring and firing regulations on the one hand and the high degree of internal adjustment flexibility provided through the Cassa in core sectors of industry on the other has strongly contributed to reinforcing industrial dualism and has resulted in increasing insider-outsider segmentation in the Italian labor market.

Part III consists of four chapters that focus on policy conclusions based on the evidence presented in part II and that outline scenarios for employment security in the decade ahead. Guy Standing diagnoses a continuing trend toward labor market fragmentation in major industrialized countries. This trend partly reflects explicit deregulatory measures by governments during the 1980s but is accounted for even more by the progressive differentiation of management practices and the work force. This process, which involves an increasing heterogenization and individualization of workers' status with regard to regulatory policies, threatens to undermine workers' potential for collective organization and calls for new and more comprehensive concepts of labor policy.

Claus Hofmann, by contrast, presents survey evidence from throughout the EEC showing that from both firms' and workers' perspectives there is still substantial unexhausted scope for enhancing labor market flexibility, the utilization of which may provide a way for European countries to cope in the 1990s with the joint problems of persistently high unemployment and an increasing labor supply.

Burkart Lutz emphasizes that the deregulatory policies of the 1980s rested on a mistaken diagnosis of the causes underlying labor market problems and are therefore unlikely to provide an answer to the challenges of structural change in the 1990s. The solution, Lutz says, is in a large-scale "professionalization" of labor markets based on broadly defined skill patterns of the work force and involving a high degree of functional labor mobility. This solution points far beyond the range of traditional employment security policies.

Günther Schmid concludes the volume by outlining further components of a comprehensive policy of coordinated flexibility that refrains from either narrowly focusing on or relinquishing the quest for employment security.

The contributors to this volume are internationally renowned experts who represent several academic disciplines—labor law, labor economics, industrial relations, and policy evaluation. They have long-standing experience in academic research dealing with employment security, labor market regulation, and related subjects. This volume is the outcome of a conference organized and held in May 1990 by the Social Science Center Berlin (WZB) in conjunction with the International Labour Office (ILO) and the International Institute for Labour Studies (IILS) at the ILO. Special thanks are owed to Gerry Rodgers (IILS) and Guy Standing (ILO), without whose encouragement and support the conference could not have been held. Generous financial support for the conference by the Fritz-Thyssen Foundation, Cologne, is gratefully acknowledged.

I would also like to thank all the contributors to this volume and all the assistants, particularly William Hungerbuehler, Kei Ishii, and Lothar Linke at the Social Science Center Berlin, who were very helpful in preparing the texts for publication. Last but not least, I would like to express my gratitude to Frances Benson, Erica Fox, and Patricia Peltekos of ILR Press for their support and commitment in the final publication process.

Employment Security
and Labor Market Behavior

Introduction:
Employment Security and
Labor Markets

Christoph F. Buechtemann

I t is natural enough that passions tend to be aroused by any model purporting to analyse employment security and stability." This statement, by the American economist Sherwin Rosen (1985:1145) in a review of recent developments in labor market analysis, pinpoints a major concern and increasingly controversial issue since the mid-1970s in both academic labor market research and the current debate on public labor policy.

The initial impetus for the interest in this issue came from empirical findings that real labor markets even in the absence of major institutional constraints (as, for example, in the U.S. nonunionized sector) exhibit a high degree of price and quantity adjustment inertia, deviating from the patterns and dynamics predicted by conventional labor market theory. These findings cast considerable doubts on previously held notions about the "optimal" behavior of economic agents, directed attention toward the role of market imperfections affecting economic behavior, and led to the development of influential new strands of economic theory, such as implicit contract theory, efficiency wage models, and, more recently, insider-outsider theory.[1]

The issue received additional fuel from the perception that there were widening discrepancies in labor market performance among major industrialized countries following the two worldwide oil price recessions of 1974–75 and 1981–82, which redirected interest toward the role of institutional factors in explaining cross-country variations in labor market adjustment behavior. Institutional wage-setting systems, social security provisions, rigid working-time regimes, and legal layoff and dismissal restraints imposed in many European countries came to be widely regarded as essential in causing labor-cost "stickiness" and employment inertia in adjusting to the more volatile economic environment of the later 1970s and 1980s (see, for example, OECD 1986b:91ff.).

Whereas recent research has cautioned against assuming that less regulated and more decentralized wage-setting systems (as, for example, given in the U.S.)

---

[1]An overview of the arguments characterizing these new approaches is given below.

necessarily imply a higher degree of medium and long-term wage flexibility (see Calmfors and Driffil 1988), the notion that employment security regulations account for a considerable share of the persistently high unemployment and slow employment growth in Europe has proved to be more pertinacious and consequential (see, for example, OECD 1989a). With an envious leer toward the "American job miracle" and under the influence of massive complaints from the business community, several European governments during the 1980s took legislative steps to stimulate employment growth, by selectively relaxing legal dismissal restraints and/or widening institutional "loopholes," thereby allowing an evasion of dismissal protection, for example, by the use of temporary workers or the conclusion of fixed-term contracts (see OECD 1990b).[2]

These changes are in contrast to recent developments in the United States, where legal restraints on dismissals and layoffs were virtually absent in the private sector until very recently and collectively bargained employment security provisions cover only a small part of the work force. The perception of increasing competitive problems faced by U.S. manufacturing, combined with a series of conspicuous new labor management experiments, particularly in the automobile industry, and a wave of concession bargaining since the late 1970s, showing that many workers value secure jobs more than wage increases, have led scholars and policy advisers alike, many inspired by the Japanese management model, to question the employment-at-will doctrine and to take a more favorable stance toward the introduction of basic employment security standards (see, for example, Bolt 1983; Piore 1986; Tarullo 1989; Dertouzos et al. 1989:125ff.).

Increasingly, employment security is seen as a basic prerequisite for enhancing worker productivity, improving product quality, and facilitating technological innovation through more cooperative labor relations (see, for example, Rosow and Zager 1984). The recognition that dismissals may cause substantial external costs in lasting income losses and immaterial hardships for the workers affected has been underlying recent court rulings at state levels, establishing judicial exceptions from employment at will and the recent enactment by the federal government of rudimentary procedural rules for worker displacements (see Addison 1989a).[3]

Last but certainly not least, the issue of employment security touches the core question of the trade-off between social equity and economic efficiency in labor market regulation. On the one hand, large-scale work force reductions in the

---

[2] In most European countries, the relaxation of legal layoff and dismissal restraints was part of a larger package of legislative measures aimed at increasing labor market flexibility. These measures frequently involved a shift of regulatory competences from the level of binding statutory standards (substantive regulation) toward the level of contractual agreements between the labor market parties (procedural regulation). For an overview, see Emerson 1988a.

[3] Recent developments in federal plant-closing and state-level dismissal legislation have to be seen in the wider context of a general tendency in the United States to strengthen the role of legislation in the labor market. The latter is manifested in a significant increase in labor-related bills brought before the U.S. Congress since the late 1970s (see Ehrenberg 1985; Addison 1989a).

wake of the two oil price recessions and massive industrial restructuring involving major displacements not only of blue-collar workers but increasingly of white-collar employees and managerial staff have naturally strengthened workers' concern about protection from job loss (see Struempel 1989). On the other hand, the experience of costly layoffs and their adverse impact on shop-floor labor relations have alerted employers to labor turnover costs and, in the face of growing economic uncertainties, have made them more wary of hiring additional staff as soon as the economy shows signs of recovery (see Flanagan 1988). Recent examples of labor law deregulation in Europe have to be seen as an attempt to shift the burden of adjustment from firms toward workers, particularly those workers entering the labor market or seeking reemployment after a spell of unemployment. At the same time, this shows that the equity/efficiency trade-off concerns not only the balance of interests between workers and employers but also the distribution of employment opportunities among workers themselves, namely between stably employed "insiders" and unstably employed or long-term unemployed "outsiders."

The purpose of this book is not to pique the passions but rather to substantiate the current academic and political debate about employment security by viewing its central arguments from different disciplinary as well as theoretical angles and by confronting them with the experiences during the 1980s of six major industrialized countries: France, Germany, Italy, the United Kingdom, the United States, and Japan. The purpose of this introduction is to provide an overview of the complexity and many theoretical as well as empirical facets involved in the issue of employment security. The next section presents an analytical definition of employment security and outlines some of the main arguments for and against employment security in the current debate. We then take a random tour through the empirical evidence from various countries that casts doubt on some of the widely held beliefs about the labor market impact of employment security policies. Finally, I discuss these doubts in light of recent developments in theoretical labor market analysis.

The Controversy over Employment Security Policies

Defining the Issue

In the current debate, *job* security and *employment* security are commonly used as synonyms to denote either job stability or protection from job loss or both. From an analytical point of view, however, job and employment security may in fact denote vastly different things that have different implications for labor market adjustment. It is therefore useful to start with a definition of what we mean by employment security.

Job security refers to a worker's probability of keeping a particular job, including the specific work tasks, skill requirements, compensation, and nonwage attributes (e.g., competences) associated with that job (see Gennard 1986:9). Job security, therefore, presumes, more or less, narrowly defined job categories or job descriptions that have been underlying the traditional system of work rules in U.S. collective bargaining agreements. These work rules have imposed serious restrictions on internal job mobility and have involved high transaction costs in the case of internal reassignments or changes in work tasks (see Piore 1986:147ff.; Osterman and Kochan 1990:159ff.).[4] Job security by definition always refers to the micro level.

Employment security, by contrast, has both a macro- and a microeconomic dimension (see Lindbeck and Snower 1988a:120ff.). *Macroeconomic employment security* refers to the availability of employment opportunities in the economy as a whole and can be defined as a worker's probability of staying in employment or finding new employment when first entering or reentering the labor market. In its broadest meaning, macroeconomic employment security denotes "an economic state wherein an individual worker is able to have continuity of work opportunity throughout the career that he wishes to be employed" (McLovell quoted in McKersie 1989:442). The degree of macroeconomic employment security is influenced primarily by macroeconomic policies and only very indirectly by labor legislation.

Microeconomic employment security refers to the worker's probability of not being unjustly or arbitrarily fired from his or her job and thereby relates to ongoing employment with a particular firm rather than to a particular job within that firm. Unlike job security, microeconomic employment security may involve internal reassignments as well as changes in work tasks and compensation (e.g., promotions), but also downgradings or horizontal job mobility (see Gennard 1986:9). Thus, microeconomic job security refers to the behavior of firms and commonly implies "not laying-off employees (temporary) or dismissing them (permanent) until all practical alternatives have been exhausted" (Rosow and Zager 1988:193). Microeconomic employment security in this sense lies at the very heart of the current debate on employment security.

Finally, *income security* refers to the provision of income through wage payments and nonmarket (wage-related or other) public or private wage-replacement benefits (such as unemployment, retirement, or maternity benefits). Income security is more or less independent of the availability of employment opportunities but may as such be an important complement to microeconomic employment security (see Rosow and Zager 1984:2ff.).

These distinctions make it clear that job security, macro- and microeconomic employment security, and income security are highly interrelated and interdependent. Macroeconomic policies, by smoothing demand fluctuations, may perform a vital role in facilitating the provision of microeconomic employment security by firms. In a more volatile macroeconomic environment (and all the more in the event of a macroeconomic shock), microeconomic employment security policies

---

[4]The concept of job security as outlined has been the organizing principle of what Osterman in this volume calls the "industrial model" of blue-collar work in U.S. unionized settings as opposed to the white-collar salaried model, which involves a higher degree of internal and functional flexibility in the framework of more stable employment relationships (i.e., employment security).

become more costly for firms and—given cyclical variations in the availability of alternative employment opportunities—more valuable for workers. This is all the more true since, when macroeconomic employment security is not guaranteed, workers' propensity to quit declines, thus increasing the costs of microeconomic employment security for firms (see Gavin 1986). The costs and benefits of microeconomic employment security thus can be seen to be highly dependent on the overall economic environment. In a setting of continuous economic growth and tight labor markets, as characterized the situation of major European economies such as Germany and France throughout most of the 1950s and 1960s, the provision of microeconomic employment security involves low costs for firms and little benefits for workers in that alternative employment can easily be found elsewhere. Even in a more volatile overall economic climate, a firm's costs of providing employment security may be substantially reduced if employment security is coupled with a higher degree of internal job mobility and functional flexibility, which lowers the transaction costs involved in that worker reassignments or job redefinitions involve low transaction costs. This has, in fact, been frequently assumed to be one of the core factors underlying the Japanese system of lifetime employment (on *shushin koyo*, see Hashimoto 1990b:23ff.) and shows that microeconomic employment security and job security tend to be inversely related.

Last but not least, measures providing income security (e.g., through unemployment benefits or early retirement schemes) may greatly reduce opposition to and ease acceptance of permanent job losses by workers and unions. Such measures—if publicly or collectively funded—may also exonerate firms from turnover costs involved with temporary work reductions, thereby enhancing employment security for the retained work force. Promoting microeconomic employment security by providing income guarantees while at the same time subsidizing labor hoarding by firms during cyclical downturns is the principle underlying short-time working compensation schemes common in many European countries.

Some countries, such as the United States, have institutionalized a direct link between income security and microeconomic employment security by experience rating firms' unemployment insurance contributions. Firms providing employment security pay less taxes to the unemployment insurance system; those who shed many workers pay higher taxes. In most other industrialized countries, this link is established only indirectly, namely through employment security regulations tying dismissals to certain objective conditions and criteria. The interrelatedness of job, employment, and income security makes clear that the issue of microeconomic employment security policies has to be seen in the wider institutional setting of labor markets and the system of labor relations at large.

Another important distinction is the one between *institutional* and *de facto* (or "natural") employment security. The term de facto employment security is commonly used to describe empirical findings that, even in the absence of legal or collectively bargained dismissal and layoff restraints, many workers enjoy a high degree of factual employment security involving long-term employment relationships extending through variable states of overall economic conditions and labor demand (see, for example, Addison and Castro 1987). The finding of considerable de facto employment security in the absence of external constraints suggests that both workers and firms may have endogenous interests in continuing employment relationships (see Rosen 1985:1144) and that microeconomic employment security is by no means necessarily opposed to microeconomic efficiency.[5]

In a way, however, de facto employment security is a misnomer: the mere de facto persistence of employment relationships over longer periods of variable economic conditions does not necessarily involve employment *security* in the sense that workers do not have to fear arbitrary and/or sudden job terminations. Even in an environment of de facto prevailing long-term employment relationships, individual workers may face severe uncertainty with regard to the continuation of their employment contract (see Osterman 1987:277ff.). It is, therefore, more precise to speak of de facto employment *stability*.

From mere de facto employment stability, we distinguish *institutional* employment security through explicit or implicit rules and provisions putting a restraint on the ability of firms to dismiss workers "at will." Such restraints may be endogenous, that is, the outcome of unconstrained, "efficient" contracting between firms and workers or exogenous, that is, imposed by law or collective agreements, as in most European countries as well as large parts of the U.S. public sector. Whereas endogenously evolved employment security standards and rules as we encounter them, for example, in various nonunion U.S. corporations that follow a voluntary "no-layoff" strategy (see Foulkes 1989) are generally considered unproblematic in economic terms,[6] the controversy over employment security has focused largely on institutional dismissal or layoff restraints imposed by law or collective agreements,[7] which, by raising the costs of economically necessary work force reductions and disciplinary dismissals, have been assumed to impair the allocative efficiency of labor markets and thus to result in losses of societal welfare.

As with de facto employment stability, the term *employment security* may also be misleading. In most cases,[8] institutional employment security does not mean absolute security against job loss in the sense of guaranteed employment. Such *absolute* protection seems to be incompatible with the prerequisites and dynamics of Western market economies. In market economies, employment security can for the vast majority of workers mean security only from ungrounded or arbitrary job terminations (i.e., involuntary job separations are tied to certain predictable standards, rules, and procedures, the concretization of which may vary between

---

[5]These endogenous interests are discussed below.

[6]Shapiro and Stiglitz (1984) and others have shown that they may, in the presence of market imperfections, well involve overall losses in socioeconomic welfare (e.g., in the form of persistently high unemployment in the presence of "efficient" matches between firms and stably employed insiders).

[7]The same criteria apply to collective bargaining agreements only as far as unions have acquired monopoly power through political regulation (see, for example, Posner 1984).

[8]Exceptions are, for example, civil servants enjoying lifetime appointments.

different groups of workers, from situation to situation, as well as from country to country). In this sense, microeconomic employment security policies are to be seen "as a continuum rather than a fixed point" (Rosow and Zager 1984:3), ranging from legal prenotification requirements, seniority rules for layoffs, and basic "fairness" criteria for disciplinary dismissals to rather comprehensive systems involving judicially enforced "just-cause" requirements, mandatory consultation with workers' representatives, and authorization procedures by public authorities, frequently coupled with diverse supporting measures such as early retirement schemes and short-time working subsidies or temporary layoff provisions.

Arguments and Assumptions in the Current Debate

For a long time, microeconomic employment security appeared to be uncontroversial and was generally considered beneficial in that it was assumed to increase social equity in firm-worker relations and to mitigate cyclical unemployment, thereby—via the income effects of more stable employment—promoting overall economic stability (on this stabilizer effect, see Keynes 1973:250ff.). The introduction and/or tightening of legal and collectively bargained dismissal restraints in many European countries during the 1950s, 1960s, and early 1970s did, in fact, encounter little more than symbolic opposition by firms and employers' associations, who, in the face of tight labor markets, were more concerned about reducing voluntary labor turnover than about dismissal costs. As Dornbusch noted, "During the 1950s and 1960s, when employment growth was much higher and sustained, firms could readily consent to demands for tenure and job security because growth in employment over time made any excess hiring in any particular month or quarter at most a mistake of a few weeks, months, or a year" (1986:14).

This situation changed dramatically when the first worldwide oil price recession (1974–75) put to a sudden end the era of nearly uninterrupted self-sustaining growth and initiated a new era characterized by a more volatile economic environment, increasing competitive pressures from newly industrialized countries, and growing economic uncertainties. Differences in the adjustment experiences of major industrialized countries, particularly the United States, Japan, and most European economies during the 1980s, have shifted the issue of employment security into the focus of the controversy over employment and labor policy.

By its critics, employment security regulations have been identified as an important source of labor market rigidity, hampering necessary work force adjustments, increasing labor costs, and thus accounting at least in part for the persistently high unemployment and sluggish employment growth in many Western European countries. By slowing down work force reductions in periods of declining labor demand, layoff restraints such as legally imposed prenotification periods, redundancy procedures, and mandated severance payments have been assumed to increase the shadow price of labor and thereby to have a depressing effect on overall employment. The underlying argument runs as follows.

Given the greater barriers to firing due to legal dismissal restraints and the procyclical decline in quit rates (attrition), the firm facing a sudden drop in demand will adjust its employment level more slowly to its new optimal level and thus has to bear considerable adjustment costs in terms of labor hoarding, severance pay, and worker "buyouts" (e.g., through early retirement plans). In the following recovery, the firm will anticipate the dismissal costs due in the next downturn and consequently hire less labor than it would in the absence of (legally imposed) dismissal restraints. Although adjustment costs may cause employment to be higher during the initial downturn (labor hoarding), the lower level of employment resulting from less hiring in the following recovery will persist throughout the subsequent business cycle. The medium-term net employment impact of dismissal protection is therefore negative (see Nickell 1978; Long and Siebert 1983; Joll et al. 1983:210ff.; Soltwedel et al. 1990:134ff.).

This classical argument has recently been subject to a series of revisions and criticism, particularly with regard to its underlying presumption of perfect information and certainty about the future of the economy. Thus, M. K. Gavin (1986) has pointed out that it is not so much the amount of dismissal or severance costs but their expected probability that influences firms' hiring decisions. In an environment of uncertain future demand, possible firing costs naturally become more important in the firm's hiring decision than in a stable environment of continuous employment growth. Yet, given uncertainty, the impact of firing costs is not a linear one as assumed by the basic model: "The firm knows that marginal workers may one day have a low MRLP [marginal revenue product of labor] and/or firing costs will have to be paid, but this possibility is heavily discounted since hiring occurs in good times, and bad times are far into the future" (Bentolila and Bertola 1990:393). Conversely, under conditions of uncertainty, current firing costs and expected future (re-) hiring costs may induce the firm to exercise additional caution in firing after a demand slowdown (Bentolila and Bertola 1990), so that the higher level of employment in the economic downturn and the lower hiring rate in the economic recovery may in fact just about level out (see also Layard 1986:59). Given the uncertain economic environment of the 1980s, the net impact of firing costs induced by dismissal legislation on overall labor demand may thus have been rather marginal (see Gavin 1986:43).[9]

A second argument assumes that employment security regulation, by reducing voluntary labor mobility and discouraging firing in bad times and hiring in good times, has a smoothing effect on overall employment fluctuations and on a firm's recourse to the external labor market, thereby diminishing the reemployment prospects of job seekers and contributing to unemployment persistence (see Flanagan 1988; Bertola 1990). In this view, employment security legislation, by protecting those in employment and reducing firms' willingness to hire, leads to increasing segmentation between stably employed insiders and increasingly long-

---

[9]Based on these arguments, S. Bentolila and G. Bertola (1990:398) caution against hopes that a partial deregulation of dismissal restraints will have a positive net impact on overall employment. Given hiring costs (for recruiting, screening, and training workers) that are not influenced by dismissal regulation, an unanticipated reduction in firing costs "should insignificantly increase firms' marginal propensity to hire, and strongly affect their willingness to fire," thus, in the short term at least, inducing a drop rather than an increase in employment.

term unemployed outsiders with all its self-reinforcing effects on the future reemployment prospects of the latter (on hysteresis, see Blanchard and Summers 1987). The declining substitutability between insiders and outsiders in turn raises the former's bargaining power for higher wages, thereby causing equilibrium unemployment to rise even higher (see Lindbeck and Snower 1988a:252ff.). Against this "negative spiral" scenario, Burgess (1988:84) has maintained that the higher firing costs imposed by employment security provisions may in fact be outweighed by lower hiring costs in the presence of high unemployment. Likewise, Burgess and Nickell (1990:309) have assumed that universally applying dismissal laws may have a positive effect on workers' quit propensity in that they "reduce the probability that the alternative job will be unexpectedly terminated," thereby encouraging job changes and partly offsetting the adverse impact of dismissal restraints on involuntary job terminations.

A third prominent argument against dismissal protection focuses on its impact on the *structure* of labor demand. Given the higher recruitment, screening, and training costs involved with hiring skilled labor, skilled workers can be assumed to enjoy a higher degree of de facto employment security (i.e., firms will be inclined to retain them through cyclical downturns regardless of legally imposed dismissal restraints) (see Joll et al. 1983:238ff.; Schellhaass 1990). By contrast, in the case of unskilled labor, the ratio of labor hoarding costs to firing plus anticipated rehiring costs will render dismissal the more attractive alternative for firms. This is all the more true if a cyclical decline in labor demand goes hand in hand with structural change toward higher skill requirements. In this situation, the firm faces only dismissal costs (since later rehiring is not expected) and will therefore lay off unskilled workers immediately (see Joll et al. 1983:238ff.). In other words, employment security regulations largely fail to protect those workers who need statutory protection most because they do not enjoy de facto employment security (see Soltwedel et al. 1990:136). Furthermore, given uncertainty, dismissal protection may likewise act as a disincentive toward hiring unskilled labor even in the absence of structural change. If firing costs are considerable, firms will prefer hiring such job applicants whose higher marginal value product permits a longer-term employment perspective even through bad times, thereby avoiding the incidence of dismissal costs altogether (see also Layard and Nickell 1986b:50).

Similar structural effects have been assumed to arise from differential dismissal protection for particular groups of workers, such as the severely handicapped, older workers, and women before and after childbirth. By raising dismissal costs for these groups (without affecting their marginal productivity), special employment security safeguards increase employers' reluctance to hire such workers, thereby inducing discrimination against the very groups such policies were originally designed to protect.

A fourth argument relates to the impact of dismissal legislation on firms' choice in the type of employment offered. Given selective exemptions from dismissal protection in small establishments, for example, or in the case of part-time, fixed-term, or temporary work, firms can be assumed to increasingly resort to "atypical" forms of employment or to subcontracting work to small firms not subject to dismissal restraints. In the medium term, dismissal legislation may thus lead to the relative growth of an unprotected sector and reinforce tendencies toward a two-tier labor market, "one with rigid job security requirements covering high-paid, senior full-time workers in large firms, the other more flexible, with part-time, low-paid, insecure workers in small businesses" (Hamermesh 1988:22).

A fifth argument emphasizes the potential adverse impact that employment security policies may have on the speed of technological innovation and structural change (for a discussion, see Schellhaass, chap. 3). Three main strands of reasoning underlie this argument. First, by raising costs for work force reductions in industries with declining markets (European iron and steel are frequently quoted as examples), employment protection regulations impede the flow of resources (capital and labor) into more promising growth sectors of the economy. Second, existing firms may be hindered from introducing advanced technologies (as well as new products dependent thereon) because high dismissal costs prevent them from adjusting their work force to the changing skills requirements involved with new technologies. This line of reasoning is based on the notion that skills adjustments to technological change can be managed best through external labor turnover (i.e., through firing workers with obsolete skills and hiring workers with more adequate, "modern" skills instead, assuming that the latter are readily available in the external labor market).[10] Third, dismissal regulation may discourage innovative entrepreneurs from setting up new firms in hitherto unexplored new markets or market niches involving a high risk of commercial (and consequently business) failure. All three alleged effects of dismissal protection may in the medium or longer term endanger international competitiveness (see, for example, Dichmann 1988; Walter 1988; Meyer 1989).

Against these propositions by the critics of employment security policies, its advocates have maintained basically five lines of arguments. The classical argument for employment security regulation stresses social justice and equity considerations. Dismissal protection is seen as a socially desirable transfer from firms to workers, introducing fundamental fairness standards into labor relations and conveying some basic sense of security into the lives of workers against being arbitrarily deprived of their basis of subsistence (see, for example, Gould 1987–88; Stieber 1984). This line of reasoning has been prevalent in large parts of the legal and sociological debate about employment security, frequently combined with the explicit assertion that in labor legislation social justice criteria should prevail over economic efficiency constraints.

A related, though somewhat more sophisticated, argument in favor of dismissal legislation is based on the assumption that in the absence of third-party interventions labor markets are characterized by a fundamental power asymmetry between

---

[10]Given that this argument presumes no scope for internal skills adjustment (through further training, retraining, reassignments, and so on), it seems to refer to job security involving strict work rules rather than to microeconomic employment security in the sense outlined above.

workers and firms (see, for example, Offe 1985; Buttler 1987). Labor markets are assumed to be not fully competitive since workers have fewer alternatives than firms (see Ehrenberg 1985:13ff.). In this view, legal regulation, including dismissal legislation, is needed to establish a balance between workers and firms and thus to create the preconditions for efficient market transactions (see also Selznick 1969:132ff.).

A third argument by the proponents of employment security legislation refers to the existence of market imperfections and the external costs resulting from merely private contracting between labor market parties (see, for example, Addison 1989b). Put simply, this strand of reasoning assumes that when making work force adjustment decisions, firms do not adequately take into account the full marginal costs involved with layoffs and dismissals for the workers affected as well as for the community at large. Dismissal legislation may force firms to endogenize at least part of these costs and thereby avoid externalities (see, for example, Hamermesh 1987).

A further line of argument emphasizes the economic efficiency advantages inherent in stable, long-term employment relationships (see, for example, Buttler and Walwei, chap. 11). According to this view, employment security involves "clear net cost advantages to employee and employer" (Rosow and Zager 1984:3) that basically consist in the encouragement of cooperative labor relations, a higher degree of internal (i.e., functional) flexibility and acceptance of technological change, incentives for commitment by workers and continuous investment in human capital by firms, the formation of cumulative skills and work competence, and an ensuing increase in overall productivity and competitiveness (see Rosow and Zager 1984:2ff.; Thurow 1985:175ff.). The argument, however, fails to explain why, given the alleged mutual advantages of employment security, the labor market parties do not by themselves devise and agree on termination rules and procedures through private contracting but need the legislator to impose employment security regulations (see Posner 1984). Nor does it explain why most employers, particularly in the United States, have traditionally been opposed to any encroachment upon the principle of *employment at will* (see Selznick 1969:213; Goldberg 1980:269; Troy 1990).

The last and most radical argument assumes that employment security legislation is needed to guide the economy onto more promising, future-oriented paths of development and to ensure international competitiveness in the medium and long term (see, for example, Piore 1989; Boyer, chap. 1). According to this argument, market transactions tend to have too short a time horizon for necessary investments (e.g., in human capital, the payoffs of which lie further in the future).[11] Markets need to be complemented, therefore, by politically imposed constraints (regulation[12]) as a means to "push American producers more up-

[11]For a discussion of time horizons with regard to U.S. corporate behavior, see Dertouzos et al. 1989:53ff.

[12]B. Mitnick (1980:5) defines regulation as "the intentional restriction of a subject's choice of activity by an entity not directly party to or involved in that activity."

market" and to "foreclose the possibility of competing with the developing world on the basis of wages comparable to their own" (Piore 1989:170). Employment security regulation has been considered one important element of a strategy forcing employers to adopt a longer-term time horizon for human resource development (see Piore 1986).

This brief summary shows that the core arguments in the current controversy over employment security ultimately rest on the competing notions of *market* versus *policy failure* (for an overview of this debate, see Wolf 1988). Whereas the proponents of legal dismissal protection stress the benefits of exogenously stabilized employment relationships and thereby reveal a high degree of trust in the ability of legislators and courts to devise and implement superior solutions to those of the market, the critics have pointed at its mostly unintended dysfunctional side effects and emphasized the superiority of unconstrained, voluntary contractual arrangements in terms of economic efficiency.

Given the broad spectrum of arguments proposed to support either of the conflicting positions and the complex questions involved with each of them, the following review of empirical evidence from major industrialized countries confines itself to the core issue of the alleged *employment impact* of employment security policies.

A Partial Look at the Evidence

To some extent, the current debate about the costs versus the benefits of employment security policies owes its longevity and persistence to the fact that, so far, the highly heterogeneous empirical evidence has been largely fragmentary, far from equivocal in its results, and thus hardly apt to lend stringent support to either of the controversial positions and conflicting policy recommendations derived from them. Yet a critical review of the evidence casts doubts on some basic notions and stereotypes underlying the current debate and calls attention to a series of theoretical questions that deserve to be dealt with in more depth in future international comparative research.

Employment Elasticity and Work Force Adjustment

On a fairly general and aggregate level, notions about the impact of employment security regulations have been inferred from studies comparing the relative speed of work force adjustment to changes in industrial output[13] in different countries (for an example, see the U.S./Japan comparison by Abraham and Houseman, chap. 6). Employment levels can be adjusted in two ways: by varying the number of workers (employment adjustment) and/or by varying the number of hours worked per worker (hours adjustment). Whereas the former assumes an at least temporary termination of the employment relationship between firm and worker,

---

[13]Because of difficulties in measuring output and the lack of comparable time-series data for service industries, these studies usually refer only to the manufacturing sector.

hours adjustment allows both parties to continue their relationship.[14] High dismissal costs imposed by employment security regulations are likely, all other things being equal, to shift firms' preferences from employment toward hours adjustments.

Several studies (for an overview, see Hart 1987:13ff.) have shown the mode of work force adjustment to demand variations to differ more or less strongly between countries. Though initially most countries tend to respond to a sudden drop in demand with a downward adjustment in hours rather than in employment (i.e., workers), the response patterns diverge as soon as the decline in demand proves to be more permanent. Whereas in the United States the initial shock is followed by a rather fast reduction in employment, in which the institution of temporary layoffs plays a prominent role, most European countries as well as Japan rely more strongly on hours adjustment. With the numbers of workers declining gradually over longer time periods, indicating a stronger commitment to employment security in these countries that may reflect endogenous factors (e.g., higher firm-specific training investments in workers; see Hashimoto 1990b:93ff.) as well as institutional factors, such as the existence of publicly subsidized work-sharing schemes and/or the impact of legal dismissal restraints. This pattern of strong hours and rather sluggish employment adjustment holds true for Japan, Italy, France, and the United Kingdom, yet, surprisingly, not for West Germany. Despite its highly elaborate system of employment protection (see Birk, chap. 10), the adjustment pattern found for Germany closely resembles that of the United States, in which the downward adjustment in employment is proportionally larger than the adjustment in hours (see also Hotz-Hart 1989:191ff.; Hamermesh 1986; Franz, chap. 12).

A more detailed analysis has been presented in a recent study by G. Maurau and J. Oudinet (1988) in which the authors compare long-term employment elasticities and the speed of work force adjustment (employment and hours) in five countries: France, Germany, Italy, the United Kingdom, and the United States. Using data for thirteen manufacturing industries over the period 1960–83, Maurau and Oudinet estimated long-term elasticities for employment (i.e., workers) and hours on the basis of an extended production function accounting for adjustment costs.[15] Both employment and hours elasticities were found to be largest in the United Kingdom (employment: 2.85/hours: 1.60), followed by the United States (1.27/1.13) and Germany (1.16/1.20), smaller in France (1.00/

---

[14]The institution of temporary layoffs as it is particularly prevalent in the United States somehow eludes this distinction. Although workers on layoff are not considered as employed by their firms anymore, they frequently retain certain collectively bargained rights concerning recall and postrecall compensation.

[15]Put simply, employment and hours elasticities indicate to what extent employment and hours are adjusted to variations in output or demand. Given fixed employment costs (e.g., for screening, hiring, and training workers) employment and hours adjustment will never be complete but follow the path of production and output at some distance. The degree of covariation (technically speaking, the coefficient) between labor input (workers and hours) and output is commonly referred to as employment or hours elasticity.

0.77), and smallest in Italy (0.84/0.28). Their findings reveal a wide dispersion of employment and hours elasticities not only between countries but between different industries within countries, which suggests an interaction of endogenous (i.e., economic) and exogenous (i.e., institutional) factors accounts for the observed differences in overall adjustment performance (see Maurau and Oudinet 1988:7ff.). As a second step, the authors calculated the speed of adjustment (i.e., adjustment rates) from a given to the desired (or optimal) level of employment and hours.[16]

The United Kingdom exhibits the largest employment and hours elasticities in the long run, indicating low fixed costs of employment. Because of a rather low adjustment speed in both employment and hours, however, these results were realized only over long adjustment periods. On average, the time required to reach optimal employment levels in the United Kingdom was 4 years for workers and 1.5 years for hours over the period under consideration (1960–83).

France, by contrast, is characterized by little long-term employment elasticity combined with a slow adjustment speed for both employment and hours. On average, it took 3.2 years for employment and 18 months for hours to adjust to their optimal levels.

Italy shows little long-term employment elasticity combined with a low speed of employment adjustment but a high speed of hours adjustment, reflecting the particular institutional setting of the Italian labor market (particularly the Cassa Integrazione Guadagni, see Tronti, chap. 22). On average, it took employment in Italy 2.57 years to adjust to its optimal level, whereas the average time lag for hours adjustment was a little over 6 months.

Germany displays a rather high degree of employment elasticity in the long run, suggesting a lower share of fixed employment costs than in Italy and France, which goes along with a relatively high speed of both employment and hours adjustment in the short run. Employment adjustment, on average, took about fourteen months and hours adjustment a little over six months to reach optimal levels, thus making it close to the pattern observed for the United States.

The United States shows the highest degree of long-term employment elasticity. Employment adjusted to its optimal level within a little more than one year and hours within less than six months.[17]

Both Germany and the United States, two countries with highly distinct institutional frameworks, thus emerge as having the most responsive labor markets among the countries investigated. By contrast, the United Kingdom, a country with a comparably low level of legal employment protection (see Emerson 1988a), exhibits the most sluggish pace of work force adjustment. This finding raises doubts about whether legal employment security regulations account for a significant share of cross-country variations in overall employment and job creation

---

[16]The speed of work force adjustment is measured by the time it takes employment and hours to reach their maximum degree of adjustment to production levels.

[17]For a detailed comparison of the United States and Japan, see the contribution by Abraham and Houseman (chap. 6).

performance. At the same time, the results show that countries face different options as to how to adjust labor inputs to variations in overall demand. Thus, the costs imposed by "rigid" legal dismissal restraints, as they have been frequently asserted, for example, for Italy (see Guigni 1987; Treu, chap. 21), may well be offset partly by supporting institutions, such as the Italian Wage Compensation Fund (Cassa Integrazione Guadagni), which allows fast adaptation through hours adjustments (see the contributions of Tronti and Auer in this volume). The importance of such supporting institutions in facilitating hours (instead of employment) adjustment is further underlined by the contrasting overall adjustment performance of Germany, on the one hand, which provides generous "short-time compensation," financed out of the unemployment insurance fund, and of France and the United Kingdom, on the other, where comparable measures ("chômage partiel" and "temporary short-time working compensation schemes") have been of limited range (see Szyszcak 1986:371ff.; Mosley 1991:26ff.).

The incidence of labor hoarding provides further evidence of the existence of employment adjustment costs. Though most of the data used are not comparable, there is empirical evidence that labor hoarding during economic downturns plays a major role in all the countries considered above (see for the United Kingdom, Burgess 1988:99ff.; Layard and Nickell 1986a:57; for France, Bloch and Puig 1986:11ff.; Elbaum 1988; for Germany, Friedrich and Spitznagel 1981:30ff.; for the United States, Fay and Medoff 1985; Fair 1985; Garber 1989). Both survey evidence from Germany (Friedrich and Spitznagel 1981) and the fact that labor hoarding is widespread even among nonunionized U.S. manufacturing firms, where neither legal nor collectively bargained layoff restraints exist, again suggest, however, that excess labor to a large extent reflects endogenous factors (e.g., turnover costs; see Schlicht 1978; Goldberg 1980; Okun 1981) rather than merely exogenously imposed (i.e., institutional) adjustment costs.

Job Stability, Turnover, and Dismissal Practice

Further indirect evidence concerning the impact of employment security policies on patterns of work force adjustment and external labor mobility has been inferred from international comparisons of *employment stability* and *job retention* based on tenure and job separation data (see OECD 1986b:50ff.; Bellmann and Schasse 1988; de Broucker 1988; Emerson 1988a:780ff.). As shown in table 1, job tenures, in fact, tend to be significantly shorter in the United States than in Japan and the more regulated European economies. Among the larger European countries, the United Kingdom is characterized by a higher share of short-tenured workers than both France and West Germany, with the latter's average current tenure (1985: 11 years) coming close to the one observed for Japan (1982: 11.7 years).

A similar picture emerges with regard to job retention rates. The probability that a newly hired worker will spend a substantial part of his or her lifetime with the same employer is considerably higher in Germany than in the United States, although, as shown in table 2, the differentials tend to narrow in the higher age

Christoph F. Buechtemann

TABLE 1. Employment Tenure of Employees in Selected Countries by Gender (in percent)

	Germany[a] (1985)			France[b] (1984)			United Kingdom[c] (1984)			United States[d] (1983)			Japan[e] (1982)
	Total	Male	Female	Total	Male	Female	Total	Male	Female	Total	Male	Female	Total
Tenure in present job													
up to 2 years	18.6	16.8	21.4	42.5	39.5	45.1	48.2	41.9	57.1	60.4	54.9	67.2	33.2
2–5 years	18.4	15.7	22.5										
5–10 years	20.9	18.9	23.9	21.5	20.2	22.2	22.0	21.5	22.7	12.4	12.2	12.5	18.8
10–15 years	17.1	18.4	15.2	25.3	26.0	23.6	19.4	21.9	16.1	10.9	11.7	10.1	26.1
15–20 years	9.7	10.4	8.6							6.4	7.5	5.0	21.9
More than 20 years	15.3	19.8	8.4	10.7	14.3	9.1	10.4	14.7	4.1	9.9	13.7	5.2	
Total 5 years and longer	63.0	67.5	56.1	57.5	60.5	54.9	51.8	58.1	42.9	39.6	45.1	32.8	66.8

[a] Socioeconomic Panel Study (SOEP), wave II, 1985.
[b] Enquete sur l'Emploi 1984.
[c] Labour Force Survey 1984.
[d] Seghal 1984:18.
[e] OECD Employment Outlook 1984.

TABLE 2. *Probability of Achieving an Eventual Job Tenure of Twenty or More Years in the United States and West Germany, 1979–84 (in percent)*

	Current tenure (years)											
	0 < 1		1 < 3		3 < 5		5 < 10		10 < 15		15 < 20	
Age Group	Male	Female	Male	Female	Male	Female	Male	Female	Male	Female	Male	Female
20–24 years												
U.S. total	5.6	1.9	13.3	5.2	29.4	9.2	19.4	12.4	—	—	—	—
Nonunion	4.6	1.8	12.2	5.3	29.7	9.5	—	—	—	—	—	—
Unionized	9.9	2.8	14.8	4.7	25.3	7.4	—	—	—	—	—	—
Germany	17.0	4.2	29.5	4.4	37.9	6.5	50.1	12.7	—	—	—	—
25–29 years												
U.S. total	12.8	2.6	24.7	5.5	33.3	7.9	36.7	20.3	60.3	30.9	—	—
Nonunion	9.8	1.9	21.1	4.2	29.1	6.7	41.8	24.3	81.7	—	—	—
Unionized	26.8	10.3	34.8	(13.4)[a]	43.1	(11.2)	(30.0)	11.3	(42.3)	—	—	—
Germany	30.3	14.7	41.4	14.7	44.9	13.0	62.2	14.6	50.0	15.3	—	—
30–34 years												
U.S. total	12.2	3.8	21.8	7.8	33.0	14.1	48.4	20.1	64.8	38.3	64.6	77.6
Nonunion	9.3	2.5	16.4	5.6	27.7	10.9	42.3	16.5	(76.0)	22.7	69.0	(—)
Unionized	24.1	(19.5)	43.3	(20.5)	43.7	23.9	49.7	22.4	(50.7)	44.5	(59.2)	(—)
Germany	36.5	15.0	59.9	23.0	38.6	25.5	72.3	30.8	70.3	26.7	66.0	28.3
35–39 years												
U.S. total	12.3	4.7	23.7	10.5	28.1	15.2	47.5	24.4	63.5	33.3	78.8	100.0
Nonunion	7.7	3.7	16.2	8.8	19.5	13.1	41.0	20.7	59.7	29.6	89.9	100.0
Unionized	31.9	15.5	45.3	20.9	(57.2)	23.2	(61.3)	32.3	(56.0)	(40.8)	67.3	100.0
Germany	40.4	14.3	59.7	15.2	45.7	25.4	83.5	31.4	64.5	40.8	100.0	4.6
40–44 years												
U.S. total	11.7	5.1	23.1	10.2	27.0	12.9	42.9	23.0	54.4	38.4	100.0	52.5
Nonunion	8.2	4.2	16.3	8.9	18.3	11.8	33.0	22.1	54.3	34.2	100.0	54.1
Unionized	22.9	16.7	44.4	22.2	60.4	19.5	61.7	25.2	55.3	(46.2)	100.0	53.3
Germany	(—)	5.2	(—)	4.2	(—)	3.1	84.7	35.1	75.4	43.2	94.6	74.3

Source: Bellmann and Schasse 1988:12; Addison and Castro 1987:397.
[a]Numbers in parentheses indicate small numbers of cases underlying percentages.

groups and become rather small when considering only the unionized sector in the United States. Despite their higher degree of overall job stability, workers in Europe, especially in lower-tenure categories, exhibit substantial job mobility. Nearly half (46 percent) of all newly started employment relationships in (West) Germany and 62 percent of newly started jobs in France have been found to end within twelve months (see Cramer 1986:265; Choffel and Garnier 1988:269). For the United States, Cohen and Schwartz (1980:10) found a comparable figure (70 percent). Although overall job mobility is lower in Europe than in the United States, the data seem to contradict popular conceptions, such as the one expressed by Dornbusch (1986:114), that in Europe "the risk of hiring an extra worker is to make a near irreversible investment."

Yet job stability or worker turnover rates alone do not allow any conclusions about the impact of employment security regulations. Cross-national variations in employment stability patterns may reflect differences in overall business conditions (especially cyclically varying hiring rates) or demographic developments (i.e., differing age patterns of the work force). Furthermore, cross-country variations in overall job stability and worker turnover may be accounted for by purely endogenous factors, such as differences in industrial structure and product market environments, differences in the relative share of large-firm employment, as well as differences in plant turnover due to varying business entry and exit barriers. Service sector jobs (outside banking and finance), which account for a much larger fraction of total employment in the United States than, for example, in (West) Germany, generally tend to be more unstable and short lived than manufacturing jobs.[18] Likewise, jobs in large firms generally have been found to be considerably more stable than those in smaller establishments (see Rebitzer 1986; Schasse 1991; Choffel and Garnier 1988; Hashimoto 1990a), and annual business closings have been shown to affect a larger part of the work force in the United States than, for example, in Germany or France (see OECD 1987:97ff.; Cramer and Koller 1988; Dunne, Roberts, and Samuelson 1989:70ff.; Davis and Haltiwanger 1991).

Last, but certainly not least, job stability patterns and worker turnover are determined by both involuntary (dismissals or layoffs) and voluntary job separations (quits by employees),[19] the ratio of which tends to vary strongly with the demographic (gender, age) and skill composition of the work force and is also influenced by institutional factors such as paid or unpaid leave-of-absence provisions or the availability of early retirement benefits. Women, youngsters, and low-skill blue-collar workers generally show a higher propensity to quit voluntarily than do skilled prime-age males. Higher turnover and job separation rates in the United States as compared to countries in Europe may thus well be explained by the higher percentage of females in the work force, the absence of European-type parental leave options, and the different patterns of labor market behavior among young workers, especially those still enrolled in school (on "job shopping," see Hall 1982; OECD 1988a:53ff.; Haber 1983:20ff.; OECD 1990a:142ff.). The scarce comparable data on worker turnover show that the higher overall job separation rates (and consequently lower job stability) in the United States (1978–79: 18.2 percent[20]) as compared to major European coun-

---

[18]In Germany, the average duration of employment spells completed in 1988 was found to be 8.3 years in energy and mining, 4.8 years in manufacturing, 8.3 years in banking and insurance, 2.6 years in other private sector services, 2.6 years in retail, 2.5 years in transportation, and 5.5 years in the public service. See Institut der deutschen Wirtschaft 1990:3; OECD 1989a:187.

[19]That quits and dismissals are distinct events in economic terms and that it is, therefore, useful to distinguish between them has been firmly established by recent empirical work (see Gottschalk and Maloney 1985; Dunne, Roberts, and Samuelson 1989; Burgess and Nickell 1990; Gerlach and Schasse 1990).

[20]Separation rates are based on longitudinal data from the PSID (Gottschalk and Maloney

tries (Germany: 13.9 percent; France 15.8 percent[21]), in fact, must be attributed largely to a higher quit rate among American workers (see also OECD 1986b:58).

Annual dismissal rates,[22] by contrast, tend to be rather low on both sides of the Atlantic. During the mid-1980s, annual dismissal rates amounted to not more than 4 percent of the work force in (West) Germany (1984–87: 3.5–3.7 percent), France (1984–87: 3.6 percent), and the United Kingdom (1984–89: 3.5–4 percent).[23] In Italy, given the system of internal layoff and recall through the Cassa Integrazione Guadagni, dismissal rates were even lower (1984: 3.1 percent).[24] These findings are consistent with results from the EC labor force surveys that show that the proportion of workers who were dismissed from their jobs and subsequently unemployed[25] hardly exceeded 1 percent of all persons in dependent employment in these countries (see table 3).

Not counting temporary layoffs with subsequent recall, overall dismissal rates in the United States do not deviate substantially from those in major European countries with highly elaborate employment protection regimes. According to longitudinal data reported by Gottschalk and Maloney (1985:118), the United States dismissal rate for male heads of household was 5.2 percent between 1978 and 1979. Taking into account that dismissal rates tend to be lower for women, Stieber (1985, quoted in Ehrenberg 1985:9) estimates that each year 4 to 5 percent of all American workers are discharged from their jobs (see also OECD 1986b:58).

Given the substantial institutional differences between Europe and the United States, the rather low dismissal rate for the latter as well as the similarity between the U.S. rate and the rates of major European countries contradicts stereotypes that there is uninhibited hiring and firing here and "Eurosclerosis" there. Even in the absence of statutory dismissal restraints, as it applies to the large majority of nonunionized workers in the United States, permanent discharges tend to be limited to a small minority of workers[26] whose share in the total work force does

---

1985:118). Not counted among separations are temporary layoffs with subsequent recall, which account for over 70 percent of all layoffs in the United States (see Lilien 1980).

[21]Sources: Germany—Socio-Economic Panel Study 1984/85 (see Schupp 1988:90ff.); France—Enquête sur l'Emploi (see Ministère du Travail, various volumes).

[22]Calculated as employer-initiated job terminations due to dismissal, permanent layoffs, or plant closings as a percentage of all employees at the beginning of the observation period.

[23]Sources: Germany—Gerlach and Schasse 1990 (longitudinal data from the Socio-Economic Panel Study); Buechtemann, chap. 13 (survey data from establishments employing five or more workers); France—Ministère du Travail, no. 6, 1990:54 (DMMO— data referring to establishments employing fifty or more workers); United Kingdom—estimate based on data reported in Bird 1990:451 (Labor Force Survey 1989) and Millward and Stevens 1987:186 (1984 survey of establishments employing twenty-five or more workers).

[24]Source: OECD 1986a:58 (based on data from establishments employing fifty or more workers).

[25]Defined as all unemployed persons who have been dismissed or made redundant by their employer during the six months preceding the survey.

[26]According to Stieber (1985) annual dismissal rates in the U.S. nonunionized sector were 5 to 6 percent (unionized sector: 2 to 3 percent).

TABLE 3. *Dismissals with Subsequent Unemployment in Selected EC Countries, 1985 (in 1000s)*

	West Germany			France			Italy			United Kingdom		
	Total	Male	Female	Total	Male	Female	Total	Male	Female	Total	Male	Female
(1) Total employees (excluding apprentices)	23,013	13,981	9,033	17,713	10,180	7,533	14,566	9,688	4,878	21,498	12,085	9,413
(2) Total unemployed	1,931.7	987.2	944.5	2,435.9	1,154.9	1,281.0	2,093.4	924.1	1,163.3	3,151.4	1,903.3	1,248.1
(3) Total unemployed after dismissal	645.2	410.2	235.0	615.1	391.1	224.0	204.8	120.7	84.1	637.2	481.5	155.6
Percentage of (2)	11.6	14.0	0.1	8.1	11.5	5.0	2.6	3.7	1.7	7.9	9.6	5.4
(4) Total unemployed who separated from previous job within past six months	404.0	223.2	180.7	524.5	299.8	224.7	170.6	91.7	78.9	701.3	260.6	268.3
Percentage of (1)	1.8	1.6	2.0	3.0	2.9	3.0	1.2	0.9	1.6	3.4	2.2	2.9
(5) Total unemployed dismissed from previous job during past six months	225.0	138.2	86.7	197.8	133.3	64.5	53.5	33.9	19.5	249.9	182.2	67.7
Percentage of (1)[a]	1.0	1.0	1.0	1.1	1.3	0.9	0.4	0.3	0.4	1.2	1.5	0.7
Percentage of (4)	55.7	61.9	48.0	37.7	44.5	28.7	31.4	37.0	24.7	35.6	69.9	25.2

[a]Dismissal rate.

Source: EC Labour Force Sample Survey 1985 (Buechtemann and Meager 1991).

not significantly exceed that observed for major European countries—at least during the periods for which comparable data are available.[27] This is consistent with other studies that have shown a high degree of de facto employment stability in the nonunionized sector of the United States (see Addison and Castro 1987). Employment security policies thus appear to account for only a small part of the Europe-United States differences in overall labor market dynamics and performance. This preliminary conclusion does not preclude the possibility, however, that the secular decline in voluntary quit rates, which has been considerably stronger in Europe than in the United States (see OECD 1986b:57), has shifted the pressure of employment adjustment to variable demand situations more toward involuntary job terminations and costly worker "buyouts" (e.g., through voluntary severance payments or early retirement schemes). This might also explain some of the alleged "hiring reluctance" among European employers (see Flanagan 1988) and their heightened concern about dismissal costs (see also Gavin 1986:33ff.; Blanchard and Summers 1988:186).

Impact of Employment Security Policies

The evidence reported so far permits only indirect inferences about the likely impact of different institutional environments on firms' work force adjustment behavior and workers' employment stability. The results indicate, however, that the genuine impact of employment security policies has been frequently overstated in the current debate on labor market flexibility. The strong cross-country variations in the speed of employment adjustment to demand fluctuations, particularly between the United States and Germany on the one hand and Italy, France, and the United Kingdom on the other, have shown that the mere existence of employment security legislation does not necessarily result in different adjustment patterns. To assess the genuine impact of employment security policies seems to require a closer look at the institutional micro-level structure and the particular modes of implementation of the policies and regulations in these countries.

The observed differences in the relative importance of hours versus employment adjustment further suggest that the effects of legal and collectively bargained dismissal restraints may be partly offset by other institutions, such as public short-time working subsidies, special temporary layoff schemes (e.g., the Italian Cassa Integrazione Guadagni or seasonal work practices commonly found in the construction industry), low premiums for overtime work, or the availability of early retirement schemes that allow a socially acceptable circumvention of strict employment safeguards for senior workers. Studies that narrowly focus on legal

---

[27]Most available data refer to economic recovery periods. For the United States there is evidence that involuntary permanent job separations tend to increase noticeably in recessionary periods (see OECD 1986b:58); for Germany, a comparable previous survey of private sector firms found an annual dismissal rate of 7.4 percent for 1978, a year of economic decline (1985–87: 3.5 percent; see Falke et al. 1981:61; Buechtemann, chap. 13). In France, annual dismissal rates in firms employing fifty or more workers were found to vary between a minimum of 2.3 percent (1980) and a maximum of 3.9 percent (1987; see Ministère du Travail, various volumes).

dismissal restraints (or only single components of them) and ignore their wider institutional setting are, therefore, likely to come to misleading conclusions about the overall impact of employment security policies. Thus, the hitherto unexplained long average tenures and small proportion of short-tenured workers in (West) Germany, despite its rather rapid external work force adjustments relative to other European countries, might be partly explained by a more even distribution of the adjustment burden between junior and senior workers made possible by early retirement programs, the costs of which are shared by all firms and workers of all age groups alike (see Mosley 1991). Conversely, it can be assumed (and empirically supported) that even in the absence of direct legal layoff restraints, the U.S. system of experience rating of employers' unemployment insurance contributions has exerted a smoothing effect on employment fluctuations (see Becker 1981:102ff; Hamermesh, chap. 2). A similar comment has been made about the 1974 Japanese Unemployment Insurance Law, which—by providing disincentives to external work force adjustments—has induced firms increasingly to recur to hours instead of employment adjustments (see Hashimoto 1990a:260ff.).

Finally, the evidence reported indicates that the impact of one and the same employment security "regime" may vary depending on the overall dynamics of the regulated area and the behavioral patterns prevailing therein. In a socioeconomic environment characterized by a high level of general vocational skills, little firm-specific human capital investments, a "culture" of high voluntary worker mobility, and consequently high work force attrition rates (as for example prevailing in the United States youth labor market and in some professional craft labor markets), legal layoff and dismissal restraints may be perceived much less as a "burden on business" than in a low-mobility labor market environment characterized by internal career labor markets and traditionally strong worker-firm attachments. The latter seem to function well only in an environment where other stabilizing mechanisms provide for a smoothing of demand fluctuations.

Another example is Japan, where legal regulations concerning unfair dismissal (though based purely on judge-made law) in many respects formally resemble those of (West) Germany (see Gould 1984a and Gould, chap. 5). Japan's ability to preserve stable, long-term employment relationships in its industrial core sector without incurring high unemployment despite a sharp decline in labor mobility has been attributed to a combination of high wage flexibility and internal functional mobility of the work force and a greater use of inventories and hours adjustments to buffer demand variations, a higher degree of production decentralization, and a widespread practice of "early retirement" of older workers into the small-firm sector (see Dore 1986; Aoki 1988b; Hashimoto 1990a).

Institutional variety. European countries cover a wide array of different employment security regimes, each of which has evolved more or less ad hoc from different labor market conditions, sociopolitical environments, and underlying policy motives rather than according to a coherent and consistent policy concept (for details, see the contributions by Birk, Bercusson, Lyon-Caen, and Treu in this volume). Some of these policy regimes (e.g., Germany and France) had their first foundations (mainly prenotification periods) laid as early as the 1920s, frequently in conjunction with the introduction of unemployment benefits, and were further expanded during the 1950s, 1960s, and 1970s. Some date back to the etatist regulation of labor relations under dictatorial regimes (e.g., Portugal and Spain). Others (e.g., Italy and the United Kingdom) are of more recent origin and reflect the socio-political conditions and worker unrest during the later 1960s and early 1970s. Some—depending on the overall circumstances and policy motives of their introduction—emphasize financial compensation for job loss and were originally designed as a mobility incentive (e.g., United Kingdom). Others (e.g., Germany and Italy) focus more on job preservation and reinstatement in cases of unjustified dismissal. Still others were introduced as special safeguards to prevent "moral hazard" behavior in the use of unemployment insurance benefits (e.g., France). Some are more "legalistic," centralized, and universal (e.g., France, Spain, and Portugal), while others (e.g., Italy and the United Kingdom) rely more heavily on contractual modes of regulation (i.e., corporatist regulation and collectively negotiated procedures and remedies).

Depending on the relative strength and importance of such contractual and collective elements in dismissal protection, a mere look at given statutory provisions may tell only part of the story. Whereas statutory dismissal restraints appear to be rather "lax" in the United Kingdom, for example, negotiated dismissal and redundancy procedures as well as informal worker opposition (e.g., threats of industrial action) at the firm level have been shown to play a major role in British firms' work force adjustment behavior (see Dickens et al. 1985:225ff.; Daniel and Stilgoe 1978:22; Daniel and Millward 1983:215). Finally, employment security policy regimes each operate within the wider institutional framework of the labor market (comprising vocational training, social security, the system of industrial relations, and public labor market policies), which in turn varies strongly from country to country and thus renders international comparisons of their potential impact a complex endeavor.

Despite their broad variety of historical roots, underlying policy motives, and institutional approaches, most European employment security regimes have many formal features in common, such as probationary periods with a lesser degree of dismissal protection, legal prenotification periods, "just-cause" requirements, mandatory consultation with workers' representatives, special administrative control or authorization procedures for larger-scale layoffs and plant closings, as well as mandatory severance payments to compensate for "unjustified" job loss and/or to cushion economic hardships resulting from work force reductions (see table 4). Only in a few instances do these common features reflect attempts by international bodies to achieve a harmonization of minimum standards across countries, such as ILO Recommendation no. 119/1963 on "termination of employment," which asserted the "just-cause" principle for dismissals and the worker's right of appeal against unjust dismissals, or the 1975 EC Directive 75/129, which requires prior notification to and consultations with workers' representatives and public labor market authorities in the event of mass layoffs. Given the strong national variations in legal casting, judiciary specification, and

TABLE 4. Components of Legal Employment Security Regulations in Europe, 1990

	Germany	France	Italy	Netherlands	U.K.	Spain	Portugal	Denmark
Legal rules for individual dismissals								
Written notification required	−/+	+	*	+	+	+	+	+
Information of/consultation with workers' representatives	+	+	+	*	−	*	+	+
Continued employment until court settlement	+	*	*	*	*	*	*	*
Permission by local authorities required	−	−	−	+	−	−	−	−
Severance payment in any case	−	+	+	+	−	+	−	−
Severance payment in case of unjust dismissal	+	+	+	+	+	+	+	−
Right to reinstatement	+	+	+	+	+	−	+	+
Minimum notice periods (months/weeks/years)								
Minimum tenure requirement	<5 years:	6–24 months:	−	−	1–24 months: 2+ years:	−	−	6 months–8 years
Notice period	6 weeks	1 month	2 weeks–4 months	1 week per year of tenure	1 week 3 months			1 month

Minimum tenure requirement							
Notice period	5–12 years: 3 months	24+ months: 2 months	—	max 13 weeks (age 45+: max. 26 weeks)	24+ months: 1 week per year of tenure (max. 12 weeks) (max. 12 weeks)	—	9 + years 6 months
Minimum tenure requirement							
Notice period	12+years: 6 months						
Shorter notice periods for blue collar workers	+						
Regulation through collective agreement							
Blue-collar workers	+	*	+	*	*	*	+
White-collar workers	+	*	*	*	*	*	
Legal rules for collective redundancies/ mass dismissals							
Narrow definition of "mass dismissal"	—	—	+	+	+	+	—
Cooperation of workers' representatives	+	+	+	+	+	+	—
Notice to labor office required	+	+	+	+	+	+	—
Minimum severance payments	—	*	*	+	+	+	—
Social plan required	+	(+)	—	—	—	—	—

Source: Kuechle 1990:409ff.
+ = yes, − = no, * = no information available.

factual implementation of employment security provisions, however, we can assume that national differences prevail over common formal characteristics. Given the lack of a uniform policy pattern, generalizations about the impact of European employment security provisions should be viewed with some skepticism.

This is all the more true if we include in the picture the wide array of direct supporting institutions and accompanying measures, such as unemployment benefits, work-sharing subsidies, early retirement schemes, and "active" labor market policies, that can be assumed to have an immediate (attenuating) impact on the level and distribution of institutionally imposed dismissal costs. Such supporting institutions and programs have played a major role in most European countries (as opposed to, for example, the United States) but show strong variations in objectives (facilitating *external* versus *internal* adjustment), mix, scope, and implementation across countries. Special early retirement schemes that allow an evasion of otherwise rather strict dismissal protection for older workers have been rather limited in the United Kingdom in terms of both funding and participants, but have played major roles in Italy, France, and Germany in cushioning cyclical downturns and industrial restructurings. Likewise, short-time working compensation schemes, which can be seen as public subsidies for firms' labor hoarding strategies, have acted as important "shock absorbers," facilitating work force adjustments in Germany and Italy, while their range in France and the United Kingdom has been very modest (see Mosley 1991:26ff.).

The United States, by contrast, has frequently been cited as the only highly industrialized country where institutional dismissal restraints (as well as supporting institutions) have been largely nonexistent, at least until very recently, and, consequently, has acted as a "reference scenario" in the debate about numerical labor market flexibility and "Eurosclerosis." This image is far from correct and has been getting less valid during the past decade, which has seen a progressive transformation of American labor relations as far as legal and collectively bargained safeguards against unjustified dismissals and layoffs are concerned (see Gould 1986:885).

It is true that the late nineteenth-century doctrine of "*employment at will,*" that employment can be terminated without notice by either side at any time and for any reason, "for good cause, for no cause, or even for cause morally wrong" (*Payne v. Western & Atlantic RR*, 81 Tenn. 507, 519–520, quoted in Stieber 1984:34), is in principle still the "law of the land" for some 60 million U.S. workers, that is, the overwhelming majority of the U.S. work force (see Ehrenberg 1985:8ff.). Legally binding and enforceable procedural rules for dismissals and layoffs have been largely confined to public sector employees[28] and to workers in the private unionized sector, which, however, has experienced a continuous decline over the past two decades. At the end of the 1980s, no more than 14 percent of the U.S. private sector work force were covered by union contracts (see Curme

---

[28]Federal civil service workers have been covered by legal provisions requiring "just cause" for dismissals since as early as 1912, state and local civil service workers since 1960.

et al. 1990:5ff.) Further, in the early 1980s, only a fraction of these contracts (15 percent) contained rudimentary provisions for layoffs and plant closings, such as (in most cases rather short) prenotification periods, due process requirements, or rules for union participation in layoff procedures (see Harrison 1984:41; Troy 1990).[29]

Nonetheless, under the impression of massive industrial restructurings involving major worker displacements and a major decline in the recall rates of workers on temporary layoff, the late 1970s and 1980s saw a surge in concession bargaining for greater job and employment security in exchange for wage concessions and greater internal job mobility, which indeed marked a major shift in U.S. union policies (see Kochan, Katz, and McKersie 1986:119ff; Capelli 1985). Some of the major agreements concluded during the 1980s contain rather extensive employment and income guarantees, including provisions for assistance for displaced workers, that seem to go far beyond the scope of European employment security laws (for a description, see Friedman and Fisher 1989). In the nonunionized sector, comparable employment guarantees have been limited to some thirty large leading firms, such as Delta Airlines, Hewlett Packard, Digital Equipment, IBM, and Eastman Kodak, which have voluntarily followed no-layoff policies (see Foulkes 1980; Osterman 1987; Brown and Reich 1989). But the fact that many of these firms were forced to revoke these policies or at least restrict their benefits to the core of their personnel in the face of the more volatile business conditions of the 1980s (see Foulkes 1989; Osterman, chap. 9) casts doubts on the feasibility of recent proposals for a strictly *voluntary* introduction of corporate employment security policies on a broader basis (as suggested for example, in Rosow and Zager 1984).

At the same time, the late 1970s and 1980s witnessed a progressive erosion of the employment-at-will doctrine as a growing number of state supreme courts recognized far-reaching exceptions to the doctrine (see Leonard 1988; Mendelsohn 1989; Weiler 1990:48ff.; Gould, chap. 5). The result was an unprecedented surge in wrongful-discharge litigation cases, many involving huge compensatory and punitive damage awards (see Gould 1987; Dertouzos, Holland, and Ebener 1988). Despite this increase in litigation, however, wrongful-discharge suits are still rare in the United States compared to unjust-dismissal suits in most European countries and have primarily involved higher-skill white-collar employees and managerial staff (see Gould 1986). Only very recently, after many bills to introduce further-reaching statutory protection had failed (see Addison 1989a; Ehrenberg and Jakubson 1988), did both state legislatures (e.g., Montana in 1987) and the U.S. federal government enact rudimentary statutory rules for worker displacements, such as a mandatory sixty-day prenotification period for plant closings

---

[29]It should be noted, however, that the experience rating of unemployment insurance (UI) taxes and the restriction of UI benefits eligibility to workers laid off through no fault of their own involves an implicit just-cause principle in that the UI administration requires basic information about the reasons underlying discharges when determining benefits eligibility. For details, see Becker 1972:126ff.

and major layoffs in larger enterprises through the 1988 federal Worker Adjustment and Retraining Notification Act (WARN) (see Ehrenberg and Jakubson, chap. 7).[30]

Moreover, in the United States, probably because of the lack of statutory protection against unjustified dismissals, employers' contributions to the unemployment insurance system are (unlike the case in most European countries) "experience rated," that is, dependent on the number of eligible persons made redundant by the firm. In principle, this is expected to exert a deterrent effect on employers' layoff decisions, but so far experience rating has been highly incomplete, and in some cases has even encouraged rather than prevented dismissals (see Topel 1983; Marks 1984). This situation has been exacerbated by the fact that—despite successful experiments—most state UI systems do not as yet provide any work-sharing (short-time working) benefits (see Schiff 1986).

Japan is another example that "the absence of regulations does not . . . mean the absence of judicial constraints" (Emerson 1988b:33). Although, except for a thirty-day notice period, there is no statutory dismissal protection in Japan, the courts have established just-cause requirements for all dismissals for economic as well as disciplinary reasons (see Hanami 1982; Gould 1984b; Gould, chap. 5). More important in shaping what is perceived as the "Japanese model" has been the collectively negotiated system of lifetime employment (on *shushin koyo*, see Koshiro 1984; Koike 1987b) in large enterprises. This system has also had significant spill-over effects on smaller firms (see Koike 1987a) and, supported by state subsidies and employment-stabilization incentives through the unemployment insurance system, has significantly contributed to the smoothing of employment fluctuations and the prevalence of long-term job attachments in the Japanese labor market (see Dore 1986:87ff.; Abraham and Houseman, chap. 6). Thus, the Japanese case provides another illustration of the fact that firm policies aiming to achieve employment stabilization may well reflect endogenous (i.e., efficiency-related) considerations rather than the mere effect of exogenously imposed dismissal restraints (see Koike 1987b; Hashimoto 1990a:277).[31]

International comparisons. Despite the complexities involved, several studies have attempted, using different methodological approaches, to assess the relative severity and restrictiveness of different employment security regimes.

Based on ratings by officials from national business associations, a study by the International Organization of Employers (IOE 1985, quoted in Emerson 1988a:791) concludes that the obstacles to the termination of employment contracts have to be considered as "fundamental" in France, Germany, Italy, the

---

[30]Some state legislatures (Maine, Wisconsin, Hawaii, and Montana) introduced broader legislation, partly to stem the tide of wrongful-discharge litigation, in recognition of exceptions from employment at will. The Montana law, for example, requires dismissals to be grounded on "good cause" but limits compensatory damages for successful plaintiffs to back pay (see Leonard 1988:668ff.; Krueger 1991; Mendelsohn 1989; Addison 1989a:238ff.).

[31]For a theoretical analysis of the economic rationale underlying the Japanese model, see the contribution by Boyer, chap. 1.

TABLE 5. Importance of Obstacles to the Termination of Employment Contracts

Obstacles are fundamental.	France
	Germany
	Italy
	Netherlands
	Portugal
	Spain
Obstacles are serious.	Austria
	Belgium
	Ireland
	Norway
	Sweden
Obstacles are minor.	Denmark
	Finland
Obstacles are insignificant.	United Kingdom

Source: International Organization of Employers (IOE) 1985, quoted in Emerson 1988a:791.

Netherlands, Spain, and Portugal, whereas obstacles are only "minor" in Denmark and even "insignificant" in the United Kingdom (see table 5).

Comparing legal provisions in a series of countries, Kuechle (1990:392ff.) found that Spain, Portugal, and the Netherlands have the most restrictive dismissal regulations, while the United Kingdom and Greece are at the other end of the spectrum, with Germany, France, Italy, and Belgium (along with other European countries) ranking somewhere in between.

In a firm survey conducted in 1985 in ten European countries on behalf of the EC Commission, "too little flexibility in hiring and shedding labor" was rated as a "very important" reason for not increasing the work force beyond current levels by 68 percent of the Italian, 48 percent of the French, and 23 percent of the German manufacturing firms, but by only 7 percent of the manufacturing firms in the United Kingdom. This ranking was confirmed in a follow-up survey undertaken in 1989 (see table 6).

Using evidence reported by Emerson (1988a), a similar ranking of countries was compiled by Bertola (1990:853) in which Italy, Belgium, and France headed the list as the most restrictive; the Netherlands, Denmark, and the United States were classified as the least restrictive; and Germany, Japan, and the United Kingdom were somewhere in the middle.

Bertola confronted these ratings with various aggregate data on labor market performance and found a weak correlation between job security rating and employment stability during economic downturns (1972–75), as well as unemployment persistence. High job security countries tend to recur more to hours than work force adjustment, which explains their more sluggish postrecession decline in unemployment (Bertola 1990:863ff.). Bertola concludes that "by themselves, job security provisions . . . neither bias the firm's labor demand towards lower

TABLE 6. *Barriers to Hiring More Personnel as Perceived by Industrial Firms in the EC, 1985 and 1989 (in percent)*

Question read as follows: *"Following is a list of reasons which employers have given for not being able to employ more people. In relation to employment in your firm, could you say whether each reason is very important, important, or not (so) important."*

Reasons	France 1985	France 1989	Germany 1985	Germany 1989	Italy 1985	Italy 1989	United Kingdom 1985	United Kingdom 1989
Present and expected levels of demand for your products								
Very important	37	25	43	37	62	46	65	53
Not important	25	28	25	35	8	15	8	14
Insufficient flexibility in hiring and shedding labor (i.e., necessary redundancies and dismissals and new recruitment may be difficult and costly)								
Very important	48	32	23	21	68	45	7	9
Not important	15	26	39	38	17	22	58	54
Shortage of adequately skilled job applicants								
Very important	8	21	25	25	3	13	17	27
Not important	60	33	43	30	58	25	50	37
Insufficient profit margin due to nonwage labor cost level (e.g., employers' social security contribution, payroll taxes, allowances, etc.)								
Very important	42	32	28	33	46	25	9	6
Not important	23	17	28	15	8	16	50	56

Source: Nerb 1986:71; *European Economy* 47 (March 1991).

average employment at given wages, nor bias wage determination towards higher wages and lower employment" (877). He recommends that "job security provisions should not be too quickly blamed for the poor employment performance of European countries" (878).

A quite different conclusion emerges from a recent comparative analysis by Lazear (1990) of the impact of statutory notice periods and severance payments on employment and unemployment in twenty-two countries. Using aggregate data for a twenty-nine year period, statutory notice periods and severance payments due in the case of discharge of a worker with ten years of service were computed from national legal sources and were used as a proxy indicator of the relative severity of legal dismissal restraints. The ranking of the countries according to these two criteria resembles the one used by Emerson (1988a) and Bertola (1990). Italy, Spain and France head Lazear's list; Germany and Sweden ranked somewhere in the middle; and the United Kingdom and the United States (where both notice periods and severance payments were coded as "zero") were positioned at the bottom of the list (Lazear 1990:710).

Using an admittedly "parsimonious, reduced-form specification" estimation model, the author found that from a cross-sectional, cross-country comparative perspective severance payments (more than notice periods) "have a depressing effect on employment rates, labor force participation rates, and hours of work" (717), though, probably due to discouragement effects, only a weak impact on unemployment levels. On the basis of the coefficients obtained, Lazear estimates that "a three months increase in severance pay would decrease the employment population ratio by about 1.08 percent. In the US that would cost just over a million jobs" (719). Furthermore, in countries that have experienced a marked increase in the amount of statutory severance pay over time, the ensuing increase in dismissal costs was found to explain a substantial proportion (in France, for example, as much as 59 percent, in Italy more than 200 percent) of the overall increase in unemployment over the period 1956–59 to 1981–84 (720), although Lazear cautions with regard to the question of causality.

Lazear's analysis has been quoted at length because to our knowledge it is so far the only empirical study to conclude that employment security policies have had a strong adverse impact on employment. Most other empirical studies using aggregate data have failed to establish such an immediate relationship (see, for example, Nickell 1982; Burgess 1988; Burgess and Nickell 1990; Bertola 1990) and concluded that at present it is best to "remain agnostic on this question" (Layard and Nickell 1985:59).[32]

Lazear's study is at the same time a good illustration of the problems inherent in analyses departing from more or less "global" country classifications based on partial information about the legal regulations in each country and which, therefore, barely permit any inferences about the relative "severity" or "rigidity" of the underlying employment security regimes. Such global classifications necessarily neglect both the institutional "subtleties" of employment security regulations and their overall political and institutional context, which may be essential in determining the amount of restrictions and costs imposed on firms' firing behavior.

In Italy, for instance, a country ranked at the very top of Lazear's rigidity list, until 1990 most statutory dismissal restraints applied only to firms employing fifteen or more workers and thus excluded large parts of the work force (see Treu 1982; Treu, chap. 21).[33] Moreover, severance payments in Italy consist largely of the "indemnita anzianata," a seniority-graded, lump-sum payment due with any

---

[32]A further exception may be the study by Houseman (1991) on industrial restructuring in the European steel industry. Controlling for a wide array of intermediary variables, Houseman concludes that "job security had profound and pervasive impacts on restructuring in the EEC steel industry affecting employment levels, work hours, and productivity performance" (141ff.). In that the European steel industry is highly cartelized and politically regulated, the results hardly allow any further generalizations regarding other industries or European economies at large.

[33]According to OECD statistics, firms with less than ten workers accounted for 43.4 percent of all employment in Italy in 1981 (see OECD 1985:71).

voluntary or involuntary job separation, which, consequently, has to be regarded as a delayed variable wage component rather than as a tax on dismissals raising the fixed costs of labor. Finally, Lazear's analysis ignores the compensating impact of supporting institutions and accompanying measures such as the Italian Cassa Integrazione Guadagni ("CIG"), which has strongly reduced the fixed costs of work force reductions in the Italian industrial and construction sectors (see Garonna 1989; Tronti, chap. 22). If Italy is to be blamed for having an overall low level of worker turnover (see, for example, Emerson 1988a:780), then this is accounted for to a large extent by temporary layoffs through the CIG that do not show up in turnover statistics as the employment relationship is formally upheld (see Ministero del Lavoro 1987:170ff.; Auer, chap. 23).

Furthermore, legal severance payments in many European countries are due mostly in cases of unjustified (i.e., unlawful) dismissals. The extent to which severance pay provisions raise the costs of work force reductions depends therefore (1) on the legal and judiciary definitions of "just cause," (2) on the extent to which firms would "unfairly" dismiss workers in the absence of legal regulation, and (3) on the number of "unjustly" discharged persons who actually sue their employer through an industrial tribunal or labor court. In (West) Germany, for instance, not more than 9 percent of all dismissals in private industry in the period 1976–78[34] were found to involve any severance payments by the employer (see Falke et al. 1981). Projected to all employees in the private sector, all severance payments taken together accounted annually for less than two hours gross wages per employed worker, hardly an amount that is sufficient to account for the large employment impact asserted by Lazear. These few examples make clear that "wholesale" approaches that neglect the regulatory details and wider institutional setting of employment security regimes are likely to miss the issue at hand.

National micro-level evidence from European countries. A more differentiated picture emerges from a review of the scattered empirical evidence of various national studies that were conducted in major European countries during the 1970s and 1980s. In sum, this evidence also tends to cast doubt on the assumption that employment security regulations (and, conversely, recent deregulatory measures in the area of dismissal restraints) have had a strong genuine impact on firms' work force adjustment behavior, which could explain the persistence of high unemployment and sluggish employment growth (for an overview with a similar conclusion, see Gennard 1986).[35]

All of these studies found a widespread reluctance among firms to dismiss workers for economic reasons and a strong preference for alternative measures of "soft" work force adjustment through natural wastage (attrition) and hiring stops, incitations to quit ("voluntary redundancies"), worker buyouts involving voluntary severance payments, early retirement schemes, and hours adjustments (on overtime variation and short-time working, see Schultz-Wild 1978; Pick 1988; Hotz-Hart 1989; Daniel and Stilgoe 1978; Wood et al. 1988; Bacot et al. 1977;

---

[34]Not including dismissals due to business closedowns.
[35]Most of the available evidence relates to Germany, France, and the United Kingdom.

Vrain and Ardenti 1988; Auer et al. 1991; Treu 1982). This common dismissal-as-last-resort policy is consistent with the overall low dismissal rates in the European countries reported above. Whereas the large majority of firms were characterized by highly stable work forces (see Millward and Stevens 1987; Choffel and Garnier 1988; Buechtemann and Hoeland 1989), dismissals tend to be strongly concentrated among a minority of "hire-and-fire" firms (see Deaton 1984; Elbaum 1988; Buechtemann, chap. 13), indicating that legal layoff and dismissal restraints have by no means rendered external work force adjustment prohibitively costly, let alone impossible (see Daniel and Stilgoe 1978:48; Dickens et al. 1985:270). Likewise, most studies have shown dismissals to be more frequent among smaller enterprises (see Falke et al. 1981:74ff.; Daniel and Stilgoe 1978:60ff.; Bessy 1987:44), reflecting the smaller scope for "soft" work force adjustment measures (attrition, hours adjustment) in small firms and indicating that industry- and firm-specific factors rather than merely institutional constraints account for the high degree of employment stability observed in the majority of firms.

Moreover, dismissals have been found to be largely concentrated among low-tenured workers (see Falke et al. 1981:97ff; Millward and Stevens 1987:186; Choffel and Garnier 1988), reflecting the prevalence of the selection principle of last in/first out in collective redundancies, as well as the importance of involuntary job separations in the job-matching process. The importance of early terminations in the job-matching process is reaffirmed by the fact that disciplinary dismissals (including those for personal incapacity, shirking, and high absenteeism) account for a large and increasing proportion of all worker dismissals by firms in the countries investigated (see Bacot et al. 1977; Lewis 1981; Falke et al. 1981:99ff.; Dombois 1986; Ministère du Travail, various volumes.).

At the same time, however, the evidence justifies skepticism as to whether the observed patterns can be attributed to employment protection legislation and whether the latter has had any significant genuine impact on firms' dismissal behavior. Indeed, in those countries for which detailed firm survey data are available (Germany and the United Kingdom), the overwhelming majority of firms attributed hardly any influence to employment security legislation on their firing decisions (see Daniel and Stilgoe 1978; Daniel 1981; Clifton and Tatton-Brown 1979; Evans et al. 1985; Falke et al. 1981:151ff; Friedrich and Spitznagel 1981; Buechtemann and Hoeland 1989). This was particularly true with regard to dismissals for economic reasons, which in the major European countries (France may be an exception) are restrained little by employment legislation.

If there has been any immediate impact, it is rather in the area of disciplinary discharges, in that dismissal protection has led to a more careful performance screening, especially of newly hired workers (see Bacot et al. 1977; Millward and Stevens 1987; Dombois et al. 1982). These changes have been accompanied by increasingly widespread implementation of formalized disciplinary and dismissal procedures (see Daniel and Stilgoe 1978:48ff.; Advisory, Conciliation and Arbitration Service (ACAS) 1988b; Evans et al. 1985), frequently involving a centralization of dismissal decisions from the level of foremen and immediate supervisors to the level of the personnel department (see Dickens et al. 1985:246), thus reinforcing a trend that already prevailed before the introduction and further extension of legal dismissal protection (see Mackay et al. 1971:226ff.; Mumford 1975; Brown et al. 1981:102ff.). For the majority of firms "which use carrots more than sticks in dealing with their workforces, where the right to dismiss is already exercised in the way characterized by the bureaucratic control model, there will be little difficulty in complying with the requirements and implications of unfair dismissal provisions" (Dickens et al. 1985:267).

The overall weak impact of dismissal protection laws on firms' dismissal behavior also has to be seen in the context of the fact that actual *direct dismissal costs* have been found to be considerably lower than commonly assumed. In the United Kingdom, for example, less than half of all redundancies involve redundancy payments,[36] which in 1986, on average, amounted to no more than two months' full-time wages (see Root 1987), and are partly paid out of the collectively financed Redundancy Fund (see Anderman 1986). With regard to disciplinary dismissals, the evidence shows that only 10 percent of dismissed workers enter claims under the Employment Protection (Consolidation) Act (EPCA),[37] of which only a minority (23 percent) prevail at the industrial tribunal; and only in very few cases (0.08 percent of all dismissals) is the industrial tribunal's decision followed by reinstatement of the worker. Most successful claimants merely receive financial compensation for the job loss, the median amount of which in 1981 was equivalent to less than eight full-time weekly wages (see Dickens et al. 1984). The direct impact of unfair dismissal legislation on total labor costs can, therefore, be assumed to be very low (see Daniel and Stilgoe 1978:51ff.).

The evidence for West Germany shows that in the overwhelming majority of cases dismissals intended by management encounter no objections from works councils (see Hoeland 1983). Likewise, only a minority (9 percent) of all worker dismissals (including those for economic reasons) have been found to involve voluntary or mandatory severance payments, which in 1978, on average, did not exceed two months' full-time wages. Only a fraction of all dismissals ended up in a labor court, and, again, in most of these cases, successful plaintiffs received financial compensation and were not reinstated in their old jobs (see Falke 1983; Buechtemann, chap. 13).

A detailed analysis of the mandatory procedures for France in cases of economically motivated dismissals (see Elbaum and Tonnerre 1986) found that of all 300,000 to 400,000 *licenciements économiques* per year, one-third did not require any administrative authorization and another third required only a verification of the grounds for dismissal by the authorities. While only one in three involved more thorough administrative control of procedural compliance, in 87 percent of these cases, the dismissals were approved by the authorities, the majority within

---

[36]Workers with less than two years of service as well as workers entering retirement are not entitled to redundancy pay (see Anderman 1986).

[37]According to Millward and Stevens (1987:187ff.), in 1983, no more than 7 percent of all U.K. firms were involved in an unfair dismissal suit by a dismissed employee.

less than fifteen days after notification. In only 13 percent of the cases did the authorities refuse to grant permission for the dismissal. In 1986, these refusals resulted in an estimated sixty thousand *sureffectifs* (surplus labor) in French firms, plus twenty thousand due to administrative delays. Studies conclude, therefore, that the adverse impact frequently attributed to administrative procedures of managers and employers' associations appears to have been largely psychological in nature (see Ministère du Travail 1988:53; Tiano 1988:142ff.).

If dismissals are, nonetheless, avoided by the overwhelming majority of firms in the countries investigated, then this seems to be accounted for largely by economic considerations, such as the retention of skilled personnel and the avoidance of turnover (not dismissal) costs, the maintenance of morale among the work force and of cooperative relations with workers' representatives, as well as the prevention of adverse reputational effects on future job applicants and customers alike (see Bacot et al. 1977). This conclusion is affirmed by the fact that most firms were already following an employment-stabilizing, low-dismissal policy *before* the introduction or extension of dismissal protection legislation (see Lutz and Weltz 1966; Mackay et al. 1971). Viewed from a historical perspective, the enactment of stricter employment security legislation in the later 1960s and 1970s indeed frequently appears to have been an *ex post codification* of de facto practices that already prevailed in large parts of the economy (see Daniel 1985:78ff.; Marsden 1986:35; Lutz, chap. 26).

Nor is there much reliable evidence to support the view that employment protection legislation has had a strong deterrent impact on firms' *hiring* behavior (see Daniel and Stilgoe 1978; Daniel 1981; Clifton and Tatton-Brown 1979; Evans et al. 1985; Falke et al. 1981:155ff.; Buechtemann and Hoeland 1989:272ff.). At least in Germany and the United Kingdom, hiring decisions have been found to be primarily determined by demand expectations and the expected medium-term utilization of newly hired workers (see Clifton and Tatton-Brown 1979; Evans et al. 1985; Friedrich and Spitznagel 1981; Koenig and Zimmermann 1985; Nerb 1986). If there has been any impact on firms' hiring behavior, it has been primarily on the quality of recruits rather than on the overall quantity of hires, notably inducing firms to conduct more careful productivity-oriented screenings of job applicants so as to avoid mismatches and premature terminations during probationary periods (see Daniel and Stilgoe 1978:50; Daniel 1985:80; Bacot et al. 1977; Buechtemann and Hoeland 1989; see also Flanagan, chap. 4). Together with the proceduralization and centralization of personnel decisions, the prime impact of dismissal protection legislation seems to have been in encouraging more careful firm-level human resource management practices, the overall effects of which have been considered beneficial rather than detrimental to company performance by interviewed personnel managers (see Daniel and Stilgoe 1978:50ff.; Millward and Stevens 1987:184ff.; ACAS 1988b; Pick 1988).

France here again may be an exception. French studies have found a noticeable change in firms' recruitment behavior from the mid-1970s on, when the mandatory administrative authorization of dismissals for economic reasons was introduced. The evidence shows a weakening of the correlation between firms' hiring behavior and economic variables such as expected demand, production costs, and productivity (see Dormont 1988:170). Likewise, studies have found that, unlike Germany or the United Kingdom (see Buechtemann and Hoeland 1989; Evans et al. 1985; Hakim 1990), in France, legislative restraints on economically motivated dismissals have had a substantial impact on firms' use of "atypical" job arrangements, particularly temporary work contracts ("contrats a durée determinée" and "intérim"), which currently account for more than two-thirds of all hires by French firms (see Bacot et al. 1977; Auer and Buechtemann 1990; Charraud, chap. 20).

Last but not least, the impression that dismissal laws have by and large been only a minor deterrent in hiring and firing behavior has been affirmed by empirical evidence on the effects of recent deregulatory measures in the area of employment security. Evans et al. (1985) found that, although a majority of firms in the United Kingdom welcomed the 1979–80 extension of the waiting periods for statutory unfair dismissal protection through the Thatcher government, firms did not alter their hiring and firing behavior in the following years, and were not "using the extended service qualification to adopt 'hire-and-fire' policies" (Evans et al. 1985:65) or to prolong probationary periods for newly hired employees. This finding conforms with the results of an earlier study by the Confederation of British Industry (CBI), according to which hardly any firms expected to increase their work force in response to a hypothetical abolition of redundancy payments or a mitigation of workers' unfair dismissal rights (see Layard 1986:58ff.). The latter finding is also consistent with the more general finding that the ensemble of deregulatory measures enacted by the Thatcher government during the 1980s—contrary to expectations—had little effect on firms' actual adjustment behavior in coping with structural change (see Brown and Wadhwani 1990; Wood et al.1988:21; Stewart 1991; Hyman, chap. 16).

A similar conclusion emerges with regard to the facilitation of temporary (i.e., fixed-term) employment through the German Employment Promotion Act of 1985. During the first years after its enactment, the overwhelming majority of firms in the private sector made no use of the new temporary work regulations. Where the new options were used (by not more than 4 percent of all enterprises in the private sector), the prevailing motive for doing so was to prolong the probation of newly hired employees. The facilitation of external work force adjustment through hiring and firing or the substitution of additional workers for overtime work by the core work force played, by contrast, hardly any role at all. Nor was there evidence that firms modified their hiring behavior because of the legal change, so that the net employment effect of the act has been estimated to be negligible (see Buechtemann, chap. 13).

In 1986, the French government gave in to massive complaints by the employers' confederation and abolished the heavily criticized *autorisation administrative* for economically motivated dismissals and relaxed legal restraints on the use of temporary workers. Studies have found, however, that the impact of these measures on firms' personnel policies has been hardly notable (see Maurau, chap. 19). After an initial increase in the number of redundancies, particularly of older workers, the number of dismissals soon resumed its previous trend and since 1987 has declined to its lowest levels since the early 1980s (see Genthon and Maroni 1989). The empirical evidence likewise casts doubt on the results of earlier firm surveys, such as one conducted by the EC in 1985 (see Nerb 1986), which reported a high willingness by firms to increase hiring if major institutional restraints on hiring and firing were removed. A follow-up survey of the same firms two years later found that French firms that had originally attributed to dismissal protection a negative impact on their hiring propensity showed no signs of intensified hiring activities in the twelve months following "deregulation." Those firms that reported strong employment increases in fact had already intensified their hiring activities before the new dismissal regulations went into effect (see Elbaum 1988:19ff.). Nor was there a notable decline in the use of fixed-term and temporary job arrangements after the administrative restraints on economically motivated dismissals were abolished in 1986. At best, deregulation may have had a symbolic and psychological effect; in real terms, its net employment impact has been considered nil (see Elbaum et al. 1986; Boyer in this volume).

To summarize, the empirical micro-level evidence presents quite a different picture from the one drawn in the current debate about "Eurosclerosis." Given that the actual direct dismissal costs imposed by legislation have been found to be considerably lower than commonly assumed, it is no surprise that the genuine deterrent impact of employment security regulations on firms' hiring and firing behavior appears to have been rather marginal in most of the countries investigated. If legal dismissal protection has had any major impact at all, it is primarily of a structural kind, namely, reinforcing a widespread trend toward more careful, systematic, and forward-looking human resource management policies that already prevailed before the introduction or extension of statutory dismissal and layoff restraints in the late 1960s and 1970s. This trend, to a large extent, appears to reflect *endogenous* factors, such as growing turnover costs due to the spread of internal labor markets, increasing firm-specific human capital investments, and corporate endeavors to elicit a high degree of commitment and work effort from the work force, rather than the genuine impact of *exogenously imposed* institutional constraints.

Evidence from the United States. Given the short time since their introduction, the recent statutory changes in the United States at state (e.g., Montana) and federal levels (WARN) hardly permit a reliable assessment of their labor market impact and overall economic costs and benefits. Considering the limited range of the new legislation, its many exceptions and exemptions, and the very rudimentary protection and restraints it has introduced (see Ehrenberg and Jakubson, chap. 7), the impact is likely to be small. Nonetheless, there is some evidence suggesting that the introduction of mandatory prenotification periods for major layoffs and plant closings, as in WARN, may have a beneficial impact, particularly of reducing the external effects of firms' work force adjustment behavior that have been encouraged rather than discouraged by the incomplete experience rating of the U.S. unemployment insurance system. Thus, studies have found that prior notification of dismissals, by providing workers with early information about imminent job loss, may prevent inefficient human capital investments (see Hamermesh 1987); by inducing timely job search efforts, prenotification reduces workers' postlayoff unemployment experience (see Addison and Portugal 1987a; Podgursky and Swaim 1987a; Swaim and Podgursky 1990); and, by reducing the incidence and duration of postlayoff unemployment, indirectly mitigates workers' earnings losses after reemployment (see Addison 1989a:255). In contrast, empirical evidence about the alleged adverse impacts of prenotification, as they have been emphasized by the opponents of plant-closing legislation, has so far been rather scarce (see Ehrenberg and Jakubson, chap. 7). Here again, however, the change in firms' behavior immediately induced by the legislation must be assumed to be limited. Studies conducted before the enactment of WARN have shown that most firms in the size band covered by the legislation voluntarily provided advance notification of impending layoffs to their workers. Even in the nonunionized sector, 58 percent of the larger enterprises gave prior notice to blue-collar workers and 69 percent to their white-collar workers in the case of major work force reductions (General Accounting Office 1987; see also Addison 1989a).

More difficult is an assessment of the labor market impact of the recent erosion of the employment-at-will doctrine and the ensuing surge in wrongful-discharge litigation. According to estimates (see AFL-CIO 1987; National Conference of Commissioners on Uniform State Laws 1990:23), the total number of wrongful discharges in the United States that would entitle the worker to a claim under a just cause regulation does not exceed 150,000 to 200,000 per year. Projected onto all 60 to 70 million U.S. workers not covered by union contracts or special legal provisions, this means that roughly 1 out of 400 can be expected to be wrongfully discharged each year. The Bureau of National Affairs (1989, quoted in Troy 1990:5) has estimated that in 1989 a total of 25,000 wrongful-discharge suits were pending in the U.S. state and federal courts, twice as many as in the early 1980s. Even recent steps taken by the courts to put a "cap" on the exorbitant damage awards involved in many of these cases by ruling out punitive damages and limiting compensatory damage awards to the amount of actually lost earnings and benefits (as in the famous 1988 *Foley v. Interdata* verdict of the California state supreme court) have not been able to stem the tide of wrongful-discharge litigation (see Pristin 1991).

Based on an analysis of 120 jury verdicts in California in the period 1980–86, Dertouzos, Holland, and Ebener (1988) have shown that the punitive and compensatory damage awards amounted, on average, to $650,000 per successful plaintiff.[38] The authors concluded, however, that total aggregate *direct* costs of wrongful-discharge litigation must be considered trivial in that the overall incidence of suits by wrongfully dismissed employees is low: "Even after we include estimates of payments and legal fees for the 95 percent of all cases that settle without going to trial, the total expense per employed worker still amounts to

---

[38]Two-thirds of all plaintiffs were found to prevail in court (see Dertouzos, Holland, and Ebener 1988; Mendelsohn 1989).

only $12.25" (ix). The largest part of these direct costs, however, was found to be accounted for by mere legal transaction costs. In fact, the median postsettlement sum remaining for the successful plaintiff after deducting attorneys' fees did not exceed $30,000: "Many of the trial participants would probably have benefitted from an early resolution of the dispute. Considering legal fees, most defendants would be better off paying the initial demands rather than going to trial" (viii).

Distinct from the *direct* costs are the *indirect* economic costs of wrongful-discharge litigation in terms of its impact on employers' firing and hiring behavior. Based on industry-specific employment data for all fifty U.S. states, Dertouzos and Karoly (chap. 8) found a significant negative impact from recent wrongful-discharge jurisdiction on aggregate employment performance in those states that had adopted the furthest-reaching common-law exceptions to the employment-at-will doctrine. Especially in the nonmanufacturing sectors, "wrongful termi-nation doctrines have resulted in a reduction in equilibrium employment and have changed the employment mix in favor of part-time workers." Furthermore, the courts' recognition of a tort cause of action has been found to have had a depressing effect on the overall speed of work force adjustment in response to changes in economic conditions (Dertouzos and Karoly 1990:x), a finding reaf-firmed by Hamermesh (chap. 2).

Given the overall low *direct* costs of wrongful-termination litigation, these results seem surprising. One explanation frequently proposed by both legal experts (see Gould et al. 1984; Gould 1986; Leonard 1988) and economists (see Krueger 1991; Mendelsohn 1989; Troy 1990) refers to the high degree of legal uncertainty created by ex post court rulings that vary from state to state and to the unpre-dictability of the size of damages awarded by juries. As a consequence, employers have been found to take precautions against wrongful-discharge litigation by increasing their selectivity in hiring, adopting formalized rules and procedures for employee discipline, offering severance payments, and voluntarily imposing due process as well as just-cause restrictions on employee terminations (see Bureau of National Affairs 1985a; Leonard 1988:634ff.; Mendelsohn 1989:13ff.; Troy 1990).

Qualitative evidence reported by Reuter (1988) supports the conclusion that the grown risk of wrongful-discharge claims by fired employees and the huge amounts of damages involved in most of these cases have led firms to be more wary in their hiring and firing behavior ("managers have become gun-shy," 23).[39] A recent survey by the Conference Board of larger firms (Troy 1990) shows that, although the total number of wrongful-discharge suits may still be rather small, the number of firms immediately affected appears to have been growing steadily. Not less than 80 percent of the 216 firms surveyed had some experience with wrongful-discharge litigation by dismissed employees during the 1980s; 50 per-cent of the total 644 litigation cases reported by the firms related to discrimination

---

[39]Such responses have been reinforced by other recent developments in common-law court rulings, such as the courts' recognition of a tort of "negligent hiring" (see Shattuck 1989), as well as, of course, by antidiscrimination legislation (see Troy 1990; Weiler 1990).

issues, whereas the other half involved common-law violations such as "breach of covenant of good faith and fair dealing" (30 percent), "breach of implied contract" (18 percent), and "violation of public policy" (1 percent).[40] In a recent survey by the Bureau of National Affairs (1990), 27 percent of 255 responding firms reported that they had been sued by dismissed employees for wrongful termination. Most of the cases (80 percent) reported in the Conference Board's study (Troy 1990) were, in fact, settled out of court, which may explain why, despite the relatively small numbers of court cases, the impact of wrongful-discharge litigation seems to have been substantial.

Given, on the one hand, the rather limited range of remedy of wrongful-discharge litigation in terms of the kind of abuses covered[41] and the type of employees likely to bring suits[42] and its perceived adverse impact on firms, on the other hand, William Gould IV (1986:905) concludes that "the law, while fashioning proper incursions upon the 'terminable-at-will' principle, has given us the worst of both worlds." This appears to be all the more true since the personnel policies that have rendered firms vulnerable to wrongful-discharge litigation can easily be revoked by firms through changes in implied contract terms. The study by the Conference Board (Troy 1990:11ff.) found that, urged by corporate attorneys and human resource consultants, the overwhelming majority (90 percent) of firms had indeed reviewed their employment practices during the 1980s by explicitly stating the at-will nature of employment or by even making employees sign written at-will agreements, thereby reducing the risk of being sued on grounds of breach of implied contract.[43] Likewise, of the few firms in the sample that at one time had followed a voluntary no-layoff policy, half reported that they had discontinued this policy during the 1980s (see Troy 1990:12; see also Foulkes 1989). In other words, despite the judicial erosion of the employment-at-will doctrine, "the practical locus for decisions on job security and job rights has remained that of the collective and individual bargain" (Addison 1989b:132) with all the insecurities involved, particularly for the vast majority of workers in nonunionized settings (see Osterman, chap. 9).

In the face of these unintended side effects of the current system, commentators have, in fact, called for the introduction of dismissal legislation modeled on the

[40]Eighty percent of the cases reported were, in fact, settled out of court, which is consistent with the findings of Dertouzos, Holland, and Ebener 1988.

[41]Varying from state to state, these comprise violations of public policy (i.e., firing employees for refusing to engage in unlawful activities), breach of implied contract (i.e., firing employees contrary to promises of employment security), and breach of covenant of good faith and fair dealing (i.e., firing employees despite previous promotions and positive performance evaluations (for details, see Gould, chap. 5). Not covered by wrongful-discharge jurisdiction are most cases of dismissal for alleged misconduct (see Stieber 1984) as well as most dismissals for economic reasons (see Levine 1989).

[42]These have been found to be mostly high-salary employees from upper managerial and executive ranks (see Gould 1986; Dertouzos, Holland, and Ebener 1988).

[43]This led Wachter and Wright (1990:104) to conclude that the present debate over wrongful discharge "is not of great import for the long run, unless the courts were to decide that their default settings were nonwaivable by the parties."

European example (see Summers 1976; Gould et al. 1984; Letts 1989; National Conference of Commissioners on Uniform State Laws 1990), including "just-cause" requirements, the establishment of a governmentally enforced arbitration system, and statutory rights to reinstatement or financial compensation (severance pay) for unjustified termination, as a quid pro quo for a legal limitation of employers' financial liabilities. Such moves have recently gained support not only from unions (see AFL-CIO 1987), which usually have been opposed to statutory labor regulation,[44] but also from business associations (see Krueger 1991) and have led to the 1987 passage of "just-cause" legislation in Montana and the introduction of similar bills in as many as eight other U.S. state legislatures (California, Colorado, Connecticut, Michigan, New Jersey, Pennsylvania, Washington, and Wisconsin). If we follow the Conference Board's survey results (Troy 1990), however, most firms would rather see a restoration of *employment-at-will*, whereas only a tiny minority would vote for the introduction of mandatory arbitration procedures, reflecting the general preference of U.S. employers for voluntary rather than statutory approaches (see also Selznick 1969:213; and Rosow and Zager 1984).[45]

The voluntary provision of basic employment security has, in fact, been far more widespread in the United States than popular conceptions of uninhibited hiring and firing in a country devoid of any further-reaching statutory dismissal restraints would suggest. As reported above, studies have found a high degree of de facto employment stability even in the nonunionized sector of the U.S. economy (see Addison and Castro 1987).

Historical evidence collected by Jacoby (1984) shows that certain elements of modern employment security policies (namely, notice periods and formalized procedures, seniority rules, and "fairness" standards for job terminations) were first adopted by large U.S. companies as early as the 1910s, 1920s, and 1930s, with the aim of reducing worker turnover and absenteeism and limiting abuses by foremen under the so-called drive system. Thus, Henry Ford's famous introduction of the "five-dollar day" in 1914 was accompanied by measures restricting the foremen's "ability to discharge workers arbitrarily . . . by centralizing authority over hiring and firing in the Employment Department" (Raff and Summers 1987:67). This was followed by a propitious fall in labor turnover and dismissal rates as well as a steep increase in worker productivity (Raff and Summers 1987:73ff.).

The years after the enactment of the National Labor Relations Act (1935) witnessed a steady diffusion of voluntarily adopted dismissal procedures and measures aimed at stabilizing employment also among nonunionized firms, though frequently spurred by the threat of unionization. By the mid-1960s, 25

[44]Underlying this opposition have been fears that statutory regulations of employment and working conditions would be detrimental to unionizing efforts (see Neumann and Rissman 1984). In Europe such fears with regard to legal dismissal protection have been found to be ungrounded (see Dickens et al. 1985:224ff.; Anderman 1986:432).

[45]That this preference is not necessarily shared by U.S. workers is shown by survey results reported in Selznick 1969:186ff.

percent of all U.S. wage earners were eligible for severance pay, and 43 percent were employed in firms having formalized dismissal rules (see Jacoby 1984, 1990a:172). In a survey of two hundred firms conducted in the early 1980s, Abraham and Medoff (1983:21) found that "80 percent of private sector non-agricultural, non-construction employment is located in settings where senior workers enjoy substantial protection against losing their jobs."

The combined effect of these developments is evident in the substantial increase in the overall de facto job stability of American workers since the beginning of the century (see Carter 1988). Given the absence of exogenously imposed statutory constraints and collectively bargained employment security provisions for the large majority of the U.S. work force, this high degree of de facto employment stability appears to be at odds with the traditional view that uninhibited external work force adjustment is optimal in terms of adjustment efficiency: "If a 'you're fired' was forthcoming at every deviation from required productivity, currently employed workers would hardly be expected to average an eighteen year job tenure in their current job" (Akerlof and Main 1981:1008ff.).

Some Theoretical Implications

Taken together, the empirical evidence summarized above presents a puzzling picture that runs counter to most commonly held views in the current debate about employment security policies and raises a series of theoretical questions that demand further attention. Until now, large parts of the political debate have been strongly guided by two mostly implicit underlying assumptions. The first assumption is based in a rather simplistic or archaic notion of the functioning of labor markets as in principle akin to that of the classical spot-market type in which short-term transactions and the perpetual renewal (rather than continuation) of exchange provide optimal results in terms of allocative efficiency and in which any external intervention is likely to decrease rather than to enhance efficiency (see also Cohen and Wachter 1989:245).

The second assumption is based on a rather crude notion of the functioning of labor market regulation according to a simple *stimulus-response* model that does not distinguish and account for any interaction between *exogenously* imposed institutional constraints (of the social engineering type) on the one hand or institutions as *endogenously* or "spontaneously" evolved behavioral patterns and regularities on the other (for such a distinction, see Schotter 1986:116ff.).

Both these notions have been strongly called into question by the reported empirical evidence. Even in the absence of exogenously imposed statutory or union constraints, modern labor markets have been found to generate a high degree of de facto job stability. Where legislators have imposed legal rules and procedures for employment terminations, these were frequently congruent rather than in opposition to firms' own work force adjustment preferences, as manifested in the prevalence of similar endogenously evolved practices, rules, and procedures before the introduction or tightening of employment security laws.

Endogenous versus Exogenous Factors in Accounting for Labor Market Outcomes

The first theoretical question raised by the findings, therefore, refers to the relative importance and specific interaction of endogenous factors versus exogenously imposed (legal) constraints in accounting for observed labor market outcomes. In recent international comparative approaches, cross-country differences in economic and labor market performance have frequently been "explained" by merely pointing at differences in the institutional framework given in the countries analyzed. This reasoning underlies much research in the "flexibility" debate of the 1980s (see OECD 1986b). Though they may mark an improvement as compared to models that banished institutional factors altogether into the realm of mere "externalities," such approaches necessarily fail to explain the many similarities in labor market performance and outcomes between countries with highly distinct institutional settings, such as the prevalence of long-term job attachments and the overall low incidence of dismissals and permanent layoffs in both the United States, a largely "unregulated" labor market setting, and parts of Europe, which compared to the United States have highly regulated labor market settings.[46] If the latter are not accounted for by *exogenously* imposed constraints (legal rules for dismissals and layoffs), then the question arises as to which and what kind of *endogenous* factors[47] should be taken to account for the observed similarities.

In fact, since the mid-1970s, developments in theoretical labor market analysis (for a critical appraisal, see Jacoby 1990b) have been strongly inspired by the empirical finding of long-term job attachments and the high degree of inertia of employment (as well as wages) in adjusting to demand fluctuations. Various theoretical explanations for these empirical deviations from the patterns and dynamics predicted by the classical market model have been proposed; indeed, they appear to account for a large part of the similarities in employment adjustment observed in both the U.S. and European labor markets. Common to most of these explanations is the notion of market frictions due to asset specificity and idiosyncratic exchange: that is, exchanges between workers and firms, as opposed to transactions in classical commodity markets, involve specific irreversible investments (sunk costs) that generate economic rents for both sides (dual monopoly) as long as the exchange between the parties continues, thereby establishing a mutual interest in long-term employment relationships.

The first set of such explanations focuses on the existence of turnover costs that arise in the event of a discontinuation of employment relationships involving sunk costs due to prior investments by the contracting parties. Such investments

---

[46]Such (unexplained) similarities despite institutional differences have also been found with respect to interindustry wage differentials (see Fels and Gundlach 1990).

[47]Endogenous factors are commonly considered those that are the outcome of unconstrained voluntary exchanges between rational, utility-maximizing individuals or collective agents (e.g., firms).

have been assumed to take place at various stages of the evolving employment relationship.

When hiring workers, firms incur *search, screening, and other hiring costs* that vary with the specificity of skills supplied and demanded as well as with the cost of equipment needed for the particular job for which the workers are hired (see Barron and Bishop 1985).[48] Increasing skill requirements due to the introduction of new, more complex technologies and the reintegration of work tasks ("post-Fordism"), combined with an increasing capital intensity of jobs (i.e., general tendencies observed for advanced industries in most highly industrialized countries) (see Boyer, chap. 1), can be assumed to raise overall hiring costs and thus reinforce firms' (and workers') interest in longer-term employment relationships. Empirical evidence for both the United States and European countries suggests that hiring costs do in fact play a major role in firms' employment decisions (see, for example, Barron, Bishop, and Dunkelberg 1985; Holzer 1990; Friedrich and Spitznagel 1981).

Further costs are incurred in the course of the *job-matching* process (see Javanovic 1979). Given imperfect information, both sides (worker and firm) require some time to gather information about the actual productivity of the worker and the nonwage attributes of the job. This process of "job watching" usually takes place during an initial probationary period.[49] During this period workers and firms "shop" for the best fit and separate in the case of mismatches. The notion of job/worker matching is consistent with international evidence that both quits and noneconomic dismissals tend to be concentrated during the very first months after hiring and then decline to rather low levels (see Osterman 1987:277; Garen 1988; Bellmann and Schasse 1988). Depending on the number of unsuccessful attempts necessary to achieve a good match, successful matches will reinforce both parties' interest in longer-term employment relationships. In that each mismatch implies that search and hiring costs have to be incurred once again, firms will make all the more effort the higher the turnover costs involved to reduce mismatches by intensifying prehiring applicant screening. According to Robert J. Flanagan (chap. 4), this may indeed explain some of the widespread reluctance to hire among European employers.

Turnover costs are further increased by job- or firm-specific *training investments* (see Becker 1975; Schlicht 1978; Hashimoto 1981). With increasing investments in job-specific skills and firm-specific experience acquired in the work process, the worker's productivity and wages in a particular job are assumed to rise and consequently both voluntary and involuntary job separations to decline: "Where workers acquire imperfectly transferable skills, the firm and the worker have an

---

[48]Workers likewise incur costs in a job search (going through interviews, gathering information about the particular job offered, and so on) that can be expected to vary with their skill level as well as with the specifics of the jobs offered and the production equipment involved. Thus, the argument is symmetrical and its consequences can be assumed to apply to both parties alike.

[49]Such probationary periods are common among both European and U.S. employers (see, for example, Evans et al. 1985; Holzer 1987) and usually involve very short notice requirements for terminations as well as exemptions from unfair dismissal protection.

interest in devising a governance structure to assure a continuing, co-operative relationship between them" (Wachter and Williamson 1978:556). Again, the basic assumption that the amount of sunk investment in specific human capital raises employment stability seems to be supported by empirical evidence of a strong concentration of short-term employment spells and dismissals among lower-skilled workers and a widespread practice of labor hoarding during economic downturns, particularly in the higher skill categories.

Another source of turnover costs has recently been proposed by the *insider-outsider theory*. Lindbeck and Snower (1988a:44ff.) distinguish between "production-related" turnover costs (i.e., search, screening, matching, and training costs) on the one hand and "rent-related" turnover costs on the other. The latter result from the threat by incumbent workers that they will refuse to cooperate with or train newly hired workers from "outside" who have gained their jobs by accepting lower wage offers ("underbidding"). If the firm wants to hire workers from the external labor market, it therefore has to take into account not only market wages plus costs for hiring, screening and training novices but also the potential costs of noncooperation (and reduced work effort) by the incumbent work force. This increase in turnover costs, in turn, raises the insiders' bargaining power for pay increases or more employment security guarantees (Lindbeck and Snower 1988a:109ff.). These assumptions appear to be consistent with ample evidence from both sides of the Atlantic of a growing hysteresis in unemployment and a high degree of segmentation between a majority of stably employed insiders and a growing number of unstably employed or increasingly long-term unemployed outsiders, even in the absence of any major skill-specific mismatches in the labor market.

These examples make clear that, given turnover costs, the labor market ceases to function like an auction market, and what at first appear to be rigidities, such as sluggish work force adjustment or wage stickiness, may well be the outcome of efficient transactions between workers and firms: "Fixed costs, firm-specific investments or match-specific capital create the equivalent of market frictions that render significant value to enduring employment relationships. Maintenance of existing employment attachments creates shared rents which introduce a wedge between the value of a current job and outside opportunities" (Rosen 1985:1147; see also Schultze 1985:2). Thus, turnover costs are likely to explain a large part of the similarities (and, inasmuch as turnover costs differ between countries, also much of the differences) in labor market performance between countries with distinct institutional settings, such as the high degree of de facto employment stability, the overall prevailing pattern of work force reductions through less hiring, and the use of dismissals as a measure of last resort.

The prevalence of long-term employment relationships and U.S. firms' practice of temporary (rather than permanent) layoffs in periods of declining labor demand have been the object of a second set of explanations commonly referred to as *implicit contract theories.* According to these theories, workers are more risk averse than firms and therefore accept lower than current market wages in good times in exchange for stable employment and a continuous income stream through bad times as well. Contract wages thus embody a compensation and an insurance component (i.e., implicit payments of insurance premiums by workers in favorable states and the receipt of indemnities in more adverse states) (see Rosen 1985). In exchange for employment security, workers do not accept the next best alternative wage offers, thereby reducing the firm's turnover costs (see Rebitzer 1989). Whereas implicit contract models may be applicable to more recent developments of concession bargaining in U.S. unionized industries (see Capelli 1985), their explanatory potential with regard to other, particularly European labor markets has been thought to be rather limited (see, for example, Marsden 1986:32ff.; for the United States, see Brown and Ashenfelter 1986).

A further set of explanations for the phenomena at hand is provided by *efficiency wage* or *effort regulation* models, which have focused on the existence of informational asymmetries in labor markets and on the costs involved in monitoring work effort in employment relationships (for overviews see Akerlof and Yellen 1986; A. Weiss 1990). The starting point of these models is the fact that firms do not pay workers merely for time spent on the job but for productive accomplishment in the job. After hiring workers for a specified time period, the firm faces the problem of devising and implementing a governance structure that ensures productive utilization of their labor. In that actual worker productivity is difficult to measure and work effort may be costly to monitor, the firm may devise special compensation schemes to elicit maximum work effort and thus to guarantee an efficient use of resources.

Earlier models, frequently quoting empirical evidence from the 1930s, assumed firms pay wages above market-clearing levels so as to increase workers' earnings losses should they be found to be shirking and subsequently be dismissed (on so-called stick and carrot models, see Shapiro and Stiglitz 1984). More sophisticated models, namely the one developed by Lazear (1981), have tried to explain the existence of seniority-wage profiles that do not necessarily reflect a higher productivity of senior (i.e., tenured) workers. In these models, firms pay senior workers higher than market wages as a reward for past effort and as an incentive for junior workers to increase current effort: "Senior workers are paid a high wage not because they are more productive at this point in time, but rather because paying high wages to older workers induces young workers to perform at the optimal level of effort in hopes of growing old in that firm" (Lazear 1981:615).

Such delayed compensation schemes offer an explanation for long-term job attachments that is complementary to explanations based on turnover costs: "Even in the absence of any on-the-job training or investment in human capital, it pays to enter into long-term wage-employment relationships which pay workers wage rates less than their value of marginal product (VMP) when they are junior, and more than their VMP when they are older employees" (Lazear 1981:607). Delayed compensation systems, which can take the form of seniority wages or of firm-specific pension benefits or severance pay entitlements for tenured workers, at the same time have the advantage of reducing turnover costs for the firm. Junior workers leaving the firm for higher wage offers elsewhere would forfeit what their present firm owes them in deferred payments for past work effort. Like the earlier models, the model proposed by Lazear rests on the condition that firms can dismiss shirking workers before they reach seniority. It is consistent with empirical observations that dismissals strongly decrease with tenure (layoff by "reverse seniority") and that premature terminations of senior workers (i.e., before retirement age) mostly involve severance payments or early retirement benefits.

Internal labor market theories, commonly referring to the evolution of particular employment practices in large firms, often combine several of the above assumptions to explain the observed dualism of work force adjustment inertia and wage stickiness in some parts of the economy and more rapid market adjustments involving external labor turnover and a high degree of wage flexibility in others (see Goldberg 1980; Okun 1981:26ff.; Wachter and Wright 1990; Siebert and Addison 1991). According to these theories, internal labor markets "develop as technological considerations require firm-specific investments and asymmetric information necessitates the monitoring of work effort: workers make sunk investments in training and monitoring by accepting deferred compensation. At the same time the firm makes sunk investments in shared training costs and in intangibles such as reputation in the labor market" (Cohen and Wachter 1989:245).

Even in the case of highly standardized ("Fordist") work patterns (i.e., in the absence of mutual investments in firm-specific skills), the development of internal labor markets offering a high degree of de facto employment stability may be optimal for the firm. Attempts by firms to make quitting expensive for workers through deferred payment schemes may take an important "ransom" out of workers' hands, namely, the threat to quit and thereby to disrupt the production process. In addition, by making job loss costly to workers, firms gain the disciplinary device of being able to threaten to dismiss (see Goldberg 1980:258ff.). Likewise, firms may pay higher than market wages and provide employment security for their workers in order to have a queue of applicants ready to be hired as soon as labor demand increases (see Okun 1981:65; Krueger and Summers 1988:280ff.).

Finally, more systematic approaches that attempt to explain why certain firms have adopted personnel strategies involving internal or career labor markets with high wages and a high degree of de facto employment security while others have continued to rely more heavily on the "classical" mechanisms of wage adjustments and external labor turnover ("casual labor strategy") have directed attention toward explanatory variables that lie beyond the range of traditional labor market analysis. Recent studies of the possible reasons underlying the observed persistence of interindustry wage differentials (see Bulow and Summers 1986; Krueger and Summers 1988; Katz and Summers 1989; Rebitzer and Robinson 1990; Fels and Gundlach 1990) have found industry affiliation to have a sizeable independent impact on both relative wages and employment stability (turnover) even after controlling for a wide array of supply- and demand-side intermediary variables as well as turnover costs. Firms in the export-intensive durable goods manufacturing industries and in the chemical industries (as opposed to industries largely confined to domestic markets, such as wholesale, retail, and services) tend to pay significantly higher wages and to offer considerably higher employment security, reflecting the substantial economic rents shared by the workers in these industries.

These findings lead us to focus more than hitherto on the particular product market environment in which firms operate and on the implications arising thereof with regard to the choice of personnel policies. Such an interrelationship between firms' product market and labor market strategies has been suggested by Okun's (1981:134ff.) concept of "customer markets," whose functioning and economic rationale bear close resemblance to those underlying internal or career labor markets. Like firms may have an interest in long-term employment relationships; they may also reap economic gains from stabilizing demand in their product markets by developing "clientele relationships" with their customers involving recurrent transactions induced by brand-name strategies, customer pricing policies, repair and maintenance contracts, and so on. As in the case of labor markets, given imperfect information, such customer relationships enable both parties (firms and buyers) to economize on a variety of transaction and information costs (see Okun 1981:150ff.). The economic rents created thereby and the concomitant stabilization of product demand are at the same time necessary conditions for establishing and maintaining "career labor markets" involving little wage fluctuations and a high degree of de facto employment stability for workers (see Okun 1981:108). Conversely, the feasibility of a strategy involving stable customer-supplier relationships presumes that the firm under typical circumstances maintains capacity reserves in terms of inventories, working-time variability, and job applicant queues to allow a flexible response to changing customer demands (Okun 1975:365; see also Bruno 1987). To operate successfully in an environment of rising and more rapidly shifting customer preferences regarding the quality of products can also be assumed increasingly to involve the firm-level availability of skills reserves and the keeping of "inventories" of innovative competences accumulated by the work force in the course of longer-term employment relationships (see Piore 1986; Boyer, chap. 1).[50]

To sum up, recent developments in labor market analysis provide many arguments to explain the prevalence of long-term employment arrangements and sluggish work force adjustment without recurring to the notion of exogenously imposed institutional constraints on individual maximizing behavior. Endogenous factors reflecting efficient behavior by firms and workers can be taken to account for a large part of the hitherto largely unexplained similarities in labor market outcomes across countries with highly distinct institutional labor market settings. Likewise, insofar as the relative importance of endogenous factors such as turnover costs due to specific search, matching, and training investments,

---

[50]Another more general explanation of adjustment inertia and adjustment lags relates to the fact that economic agents themselves are "imperfect" and prone to decision errors: to minimize costly decision errors (e.g., "panic layoffs"), "the imperfect agent may either start adjusting soon but very slowly compared to the optimal agent or start adjusting with a noticeable delay compared to the optimal agent" (Heiner 1988:256). This may explain lags in employment adjustment to demand variations irrespective of whether there are any information, search, or other (i.e., institutionally imposed) costs of adjustment.

deferred compensation schemes, and product market environments can be assumed to vary from country to country (as well as from industry to industry), they are also likely to explain part of the cross-country (as well as interindustry) variations in observed labor market outcomes. This brings us to the next question, whether employment security can be achieved merely through private transactions between firms and workers or whether public regulation and third-party enforcement are needed to ensure or enhance overall socioeconomic efficiency. Or, put differently, if firm-worker transactions in modern labor markets endogenously create a mutual interest in stable long-term employment relationships, why should there be a need for public employment security policies?

Private Contracts versus Public Regulation

Labor market transactions have been shown to deviate from transactions in "classical" commodity markets. In labor markets, immediate market transactions (hiring) and actual exchange (the productive employment of labor in the production process) are distinct events. Mutual investments in match-specific information gathering and specific training and the exclusive rents resulting thereof were seen to create a mutual interest in the continuation of exchange between the parties. Employment arrangements thus emerge as open-ended relationships between parties sharing a dual monopoly. This temporal nature of the exchange between workers and firms implies that labor market transactions are characterized by a high degree of uncertainty.

Incomplete information on both sides involves the existence of informational asymmetries. When hiring, the firm does not know about the actual productivity (and therefore the "true" value) of the worker. Nor does the worker have complete knowledge of the nonwage job attributes (e.g., the occupational health hazards involved with doing a particular job). Even after hiring, the firm may have difficulty in monitoring the worker's effort just as the worker may have difficulty getting a clear picture of the relative security of the job or the "fairness" of his or her wage in relation to the firm's profitability.

The existence of informational asymmetries implies the risk of opportunistic behavior[51] by either party both at the time of hiring and during the subsequent employment relationship. Workers cannot necessarily rely on employers to represent their undertaking's overall economic situation (e.g., expectations of layoffs in the near future) when offering jobs or when demanding work effort with the prospect of future rewards. Nor can firms rely on workers to expound their actual productivity when applying for jobs or to exert appropriate work effort once they are hired. Firms offering employment security may attract less motivated workers who would soon be fired for shirking or malperformance in other firms practicing a strict at-will employment policy (on adverse selection, see Levine and D'Andrea-

---

[51] According to a frequently quoted definition by Williamson (1975:58), opportunistic behavior means "self-interest seeking with guile" involving "strategic manipulation of information or misrepresentation of intentions."

Tyson 1990; Levine 1991). Likewise, firms offering deferred compensation schemes may fire workers shortly before they reach seniority (on moral hazard, see Wachter and Cohen 1988:1379).

Furthermore, both parties share a lack of information or uncertainty about the contingent states of the world in the future into which their relationship has to continue if the future gains from their initial shared investments are to be captured. The worker may be forced to reduce his or her work hours or to quit altogether because of health problems or other unforeseen (supply-side) events and thus depreciate or even invalidate the firm's (and his or her own) sunk investments. The firm may be forced to reduce its work force (or to lower wages) and to relinquish its promises of employment security (or of regular wage increases or seniority compensation) in the event of an unforeseen major decline in the demand for its products.

The coexistence of sunk investments, informational asymmetries, and uncertainty about future contingencies of the economic environment raises the dual question of mutual trust and risk sharing: how can both parties devise and implement an open-ended arrangement that (1) insures each side against opportunistic behavior by the other side and (2) ensures a sufficient degree of flexibility to cope with contingent future events? With increasing sunk investments and the resulting increase in the length of the period needed to retrieve the mutual rents thereof, the arrangement required to meet these two criteria is likely to become more complex and delicate.

The market answer to this question is private contracting. Following Rosen (1985:1145), a contract can be defined as a "voluntary ex-ante agreement that resolves the distribution of uncertainty about the value and utilization of shared investments between parties. The contract specifies precisely the amount of labor to be utilized and the wages to be paid in each state of nature that is conditional on information . . . observed by the parties." The mere specification of hours and wages, however, does not yet tackle the problem of informational asymmetries and the risk of opportunistic behavior inherent therein (see Okun 1981:84ff.). Nor does it account for the problem of uncertainty about future states of the world that cannot be foreseen when the contract is concluded (see Hall and Lazear 1984; Booth and Chatterji 1989). Both problems indeed seem to be intricately interwoven.

The best safeguard against opportunistic behavior by a firm offering deferred compensation for current work effort (seniority wages) appears to be an explicit contractual arrangement guaranteeing workers continued employment until retirement age. This, however, would bereave the firm of all its flexibility to respond to an unexpected sudden decline in demand by reducing its work force through layoffs and thus could possibly jeopardize the economic survival of the undertaking as a whole. Conversely, if the firm were to retain its full freedom to dismiss workers in the event of a deterioration in its market environment, the workers would have to fear that the firm would be inclined to dismiss first those workers who otherwise would be entitled to higher seniority wages (see A. Weiss 1990:11). Likewise, the firm could pledge to follow a no-layoff policy even if this involves a serious deterioration of profitability in the case of an unforeseen worsening of market conditions and the workers abuse their high degree of employment security by reducing their work effort even in good times, thus debasing total firm performance (for further examples, see Okun 1981:86ff.).

The multiplicity of situations in which there is the potential for opportunistic behavior as well as the infinite randomness and unpredictability of possible future states[52] affecting firm-labor relations render the negotiation and precise contractual specification of all the behavioral quid pro quos involved impossible or, if all possible future states were known, at least excessively costly. Rather, the feasibility of open-ended, contingent employment contracts allowing the rents from mutual sunk investments to be reaped over a contingent future, and therefore the willingness of the parties to make such investments in the first place, depends on whether a contractual arrangement can be reached that not only specifies hours and wages but, by setting up general (or "universalistic") standards, rules, and procedures for dealing with unknown future events, generates trust between the parties and at the same time preserves their ability to respond to future contingencies. Given that all (even the most casual) labor market transactions involve some transaction costs and sunk investments by both sides, firms and workers can be assumed to have a common interest in the establishment and maintenance of such general rules, standards, and procedures, which dispell distrust in the face of an uncertain future (see Okun 1981:84).

Whereas hours and wages (or alternatively piece rates) are in most cases expressly specified (see Hall and Lazear 1984), the general standards, rules, and procedures for coping with contingent future events can be of an implicit or explicit nature (and in the real world commonly comprise a mixture of both). *Implicit rules* (recall Okun's famous "invisible handshake") can take various forms ranging from "logical" expectations (e.g., firms' training investments reassure workers "that the firm seriously intends to employ them for a substantial period of time"; see Okun 1981:85) and culturally shared "fairness" criteria (see Akerlof's [1984b] concept of "labor contracts as a partial gift exchange") through intangible bonding (e.g., the firm that unjustly dismisses workers forfeits its reputation as an "honest" employer and thus will not be able to attract "good" workers anymore and will have to face the adverse effects on motivation and work effort by its remaining work force [see Wachter and Cohen 1988; Lindbeck and Snower 1988b]) to behavioral ostentations of fair dealing (e.g., in the form of regular promotions and pay increases for deserving employees) and nonbinding statements of intentions (e.g., to practice a no-layoff policy as long as economic conditions allow).

The existence of such implicit rules creating mutual trust may explain why, for example, many firms, even in the face of a substantial change in their economic environment (e.g., a transition from tight labor markets to persisting high unemployment), may not be willing to deviate from "an established pattern built

---

[52]Langlois (1986) in this context distinguishes between "parametric" and "radical" uncertainty. Whereas the former denotes an unknown distribution of known future states or events, the latter involves a lack of knowledge about the nature of possible future states of the world.

into its management practices and communicated to its workers" (Okun 1981:105).[53] Even in a major cyclical downturn, a "career–labor market" firm will therefore, given somehow fixed wages, resort to layoffs only after all alternative "soft" adjustment measures (building inventories; instituting a hiring freeze; engaging idle workers in maintenance tasks or further training; reducing hours; canceling subcontracting arrangements) are exhausted. If dismissals are nevertheless unavoidable, the firm will take great care to dismiss the visibly least productive and least committed (shirking) junior workers first in order to maintain the incentive patterns for those retained and to preserve its reputational capital (see Okun 1981:107ff.).[54]

At the same time, however, implicit arrangements and reassurances necessarily tend to be latently fragile. They do not offer any definite safeguards against deceitful (or at least negligent) behavior by the other side and, being legally nonbinding in most cases,[55] do not provide any ex post remedy or compensation for individual losses due to such behavior. Moreover, in particular situations, the trust-creating mechanism of implicit contracts is likely to fail. When a firm is closing down altogether, for example, it may no longer be concerned about losing its reputation as a fair employer and thus forfeit workers' sunk investments without facing the penalty of the loss of reputational capital (see Addison 1989a:246ff.). This may indeed be one reason for the recent introduction of U.S. federal legislation dealing particularly with plant closings (as well as the rather early enactment of similar regulations in many countries in Europe).

These inherent shortcomings of implicit arrangements can be circumvented by setting up *explicit rules and standards* ranging from individual agreements on mutual obligations (regarding information disclosure or confidentiality toward third parties) and conditions for contract terminations (separation penalties, maximum retirement age) through unilateral express statements of firm policy (e.g., regarding profit sharing) all the way to collectively negotiated standards and procedures for hiring, changes in working conditions (job reassignments; modifications of hours arrangements), and contract terminations (last in/first out; severance payments for senior workers), worker participation in decision making, and firm-level conflict resolution (arbitration procedures). By institutionalizing "voice," such explicit procedural rules create a mechanism to maintain trust and prevent costly "exit" options through varying circumstances and situations that are not predictable and specifiable ex ante (see Freeman and Medoff 1984).

Unlike implicit arrangements, explicit standards and procedures establish binding and enforceable legal entitlements and thus generally provide a less volatile

---

[53]These reasons may also explain why most firms in Europe have not made use of the increased options for external work force adjustment provided by recent measures of labor law deregulation.

[54]This is consistent with empirical evidence for European countries that firms have shifted their dismissal practices from dismissals for economic reasons toward disciplinary dismissals (see above). For the United States, Bishop (1990) has found layoffs to be strongly correlated with perceived worker productivity (supervisor ratings).

[55]Antidiscrimination legislation as well as the recognition of a covenant of good faith and fair dealing by U.S. state courts have altered this situation.

basis for mutual trust. Yet, because they require express specification of the kind, the holders, and the conditional requirements of the rights involved, explicit rules and guarantees usually imply higher transaction (negotiation and implementation) costs and frequently provide less behavioral flexibility than informal, implicit norms. The degree of flexibility to cope with varying situations tends to be larger the more abstract and general the explicitly agreed-on rules and procedures are. A high degree of generality, in turn, is likely to involve some incompleteness and ambiguity with regard to particular situations and therefore implies the risk of costly external, case-by-case litigation if conflicting interpretations by the parties cannot be settled internally. This was the case when U.S. state courts began to recognize company statements regarding employment security as binding and enforceable contractual commitments and thus initiated the recent surge in wrongful-discharge litigation.

The economic benefits inherent in the establishment and maintenance of explicit and/or implicit standards, rules, and procedures protecting mutual sunk investments and dispelling distrust in the face of future contingencies seems to offer a powerful explanation of why implicit practices and explicit rules concerning disciplinary procedures, prenotification requirements, selection for layoffs, and severance pay entitlements are quite common in more advanced industries even in the absence (or prior to the introduction) of exogenously imposed legal constraints.[56]

Assuming it were feasible to set up efficient private contracts between workers and firms (or their collective representatives) establishing mutually binding standards, rules, and procedures to cope with future contingencies while protecting both parties' sunk investments, one would have to conclude that "workers' rights in jobs do exist as a result of voluntary exchanges" (Addison 1989b:136), that is, without the need for any third-party intervention (legislation). This has indeed been the view taken by the proponents of a radical "laissez-faire" in labor relations who postulate that, given clearly defined and assigned property rights,[57] unconstrained voluntary negotiations between private parties produce optimal results

[56]This is not to say that unions did not have a genuine impact on the adoption of these practices and procedures but acted merely as the executants of microeconomic efficiency constraints: "The objective of unions is to shift the allocation of the surplus in favor of the worker." This implies, of course, that "they are constrained by the problem of preserving the joint surplus" (Okun 1981:122). The literature in fact provides rival interpretations as to whether voluntarily agreed-on (explicit) rules and procedures found in nonunionized settings reflect spillovers from unionized sectors (on the "union threat" model, see Freeman and Medoff 1984; Jacoby 1990b) or whether union activities are to be seen as "formalizing and institutionalizing the conventions of the non- union career labor market, not only in determining the wage structure, but also in developing understandings about hirings, layoffs, promotions, firings, and the environment of the workplace" (Okun 1981:122). With regard to the relationship between union policies and economic efficiency, see Addison and Hirsch 1989; Levine and D'Andrea-Tyson 1990.

[57]Such property rights "establish the initial distribution of rights, the exclusivity of the rights, and the mechanisms under which transfers of property rights are effected and recognized" (Spulber 1989:48). Without the assignment of clearly defined, exclusive property rights, market transactions cannot take place.

and who, therefore, have opposed any further legislative interventions into the labor market (see, for example, Posner 1984:990ff.; Fishel 1984; Epstein 1984).

In this view the role of the legislator should be confined to the assignment of exclusive, tradable property rights and the establishment of rules and procedures for the public enforcement of private explicit contracts (see Lazear 1988:60; Soltwedel et al. 1990:148ff.). Against recent proposals to introduce European-type just-cause legislation in the United States to overcome the deficiencies of present wrongful-discharge litigation, these authors have upheld that the current problems, particularly the considerable legal and financial uncertainties involved and their adverse impact on firms' employment decisions, have resulted from the blurring of property rights assignments by recent common-law court rulings rather than from a lack of legal regulation (see, for example, Krueger 1991). Changes in the assignment and distribution of property rights through the judicature that interfere with ongoing private contracts necessarily result in market inefficiencies (for a general discussion, see Coase 1983; Demsetz 1972)—a dictum that, of course, also applies to the introduction of legislation altering rights in ongoing employment relationships (see Hamermesh, chap. 2). Any further legal interventions beyond the ex ante assignment of property rights and the ex post enforcement of privately negotiated contractual arrangements would most likely produce further market inefficiencies and consequently would result in a loss in overall socioeconomic welfare.

Such arguments rest on the central assumption that freely negotiated, private contracts are capable of providing efficient solutions to the dual problem of opportunistic behavior and future contingencies inherent in labor market transactions. Conversely, any plea for or defense of employment security legislation would have to provide evidence that purely private contracting in labor markets produces inefficiencies that can be avoided or minimized by third-party interventions. Past research both on labor law regulation (see Ehrenberg 1985; Buttler 1987; Wachter and Cohen 1988; Schwab 1989; Leslie 1989) and on regulation in other fields (for an extensive overview, see Spulber 1989) has in fact pointed out various situations in which market failures are likely to occur and in which market regulation (e.g., legislation) may produce superior results.

One situation in which public regulation may enhance efficiency is when the private negotiation and monitoring of contingent private contracts involves very high or even insurmountable transaction costs that may be reduced by the establishment of general standards and rules by an external agency. With increasing sunk investments, increasing time horizons to reap the mutual rents thereof, and an overall increasing volatility in the economic environment (i.e., uncertainty), the transaction costs for privately negotiating individual contracts between firms and workers are likely to rise (see Spulber 1989:62). In this situation, just-cause legislation for dismissals, by supplying general norms and procedures for contract terminations and by providing a universally applying default setting, may reduce actual transaction costs, since it frees workers and firms from having to negotiate individual just-cause agreements (see Savarese 1980). Transaction costs may also become prohibitively costly when a large number of possibly difficult to identify parties are involved in the transaction or are affected by the consequences and spillovers of economic behavior. Such a situation is given, for example, in the case of air pollution, but in principle also in the case of major redundancies and mass layoffs which may affect a whole community through reduced tax revenues, increased social costs for income maintenance programs, and declining real estate prices.

A further situation in which there are efficiency gains through public regulation occurs when private parties (e.g., firms and workers) produce external costs for third parties not involved in the initial bargain ("externalities"), pointing to the fact that real markets frequently are not fully competitive (see Ehrenberg 1985:13). Insider-outsider theory provides many illustrations of how "efficient" bargains between two parties (insiders and firms) may produce costs for nonparticipating outsiders and thus reduce overall labor market efficiency (see Lindbeck and Snower 1988a). Such externalities of private maximizing behavior may further be induced by the existence of "external" institutions, such as the provision of unemployment benefits without (as in most of Europe) or with incomplete (as in the United States) experience rating of unemployment insurance contributions (see Lazear 1988). In the absence of legal safeguards (e.g., controls of the causation of job loss and of the economic necessity and inevitability of dismissals), such institutions create incentives for parties deliberately to negotiate terms involving costs for nonparticipating third parties (e.g., excess layoffs as they have been frequently diagnosed for the United States; see Hall and Lazear 1984). Externalities may also be the outcome of unintentional behavior (e.g., if individual workers and firms lack sufficient information about the health hazards involved with doing particular jobs and therefore produce deferred consequences for one of the parties or for third parties) involving costs not considered in the initial bargain (see Spulber 1989:393ff.). In these cases ex ante legal regulation forcing the parties to internalize the costs of future damages and potential costs to external parties may be efficiency enhancing (see Wittman 1977; Shavell 1984).

Legislation may further increase overall efficiency if the enforcement of private contracts is very costly and legal regulation could provide enforcement at a lower cost. This is the case if contractual noncompliance is difficult to monitor, damages through noncompliance are difficult to measure, and causation of damages or harms is difficult to establish (see Rose-Ackerman 1991). In such instances contract enforcement is likely to entail costly information gathering by third parties (external arbitrators) in the course of lengthy case-by-case investigations. This scenario poignantly describes the problems resulting from the recent surge in common-law liability litigation in the United States, which has not been confined to wrongful discharge issues but has also occurred in other areas (particularly industrial relations and environmental and product liability law; see Litan and Winston 1988; Huber and Litan 1991; Schuck 1991).

The current U.S. "litigation explosion" (Flanagan 1987b) may in fact be a manifestation of increasing market failures in bringing about efficient private bargaining solutions in the face of grown sunk investments in employment relationships and increasing harm resulting from breaches of contracts. Critics of litigation have, therefore, argued that, given the greater complexity and contingencies involved in individual employment relationships, the latter progressively cease to "fit comfortably into the traditional common law scheme" (Leonard 1988:636; see also Savarese 1980) with its underlying assumption that all their terms are the result of conscious bargaining between parties:[58] "Rather than resorting to costly litigation in each instance of breach, it may be preferable to have standard penalties for breach that are established and enforced by a regulatory agency" (Spulber 1989:60).

The surge in common-law litigation may also reflect the fact that, to manage the grown complexities and contingencies involved, privately negotiated employment contracts increasingly contain rather abstract formulas and general clauses for handling hypothetical future situations which give rise to conflicting interpretations once such situations have occurred. In these cases, if a settlement among the parties cannot be reached, jurisdiction of the civil courts is called upon to establish case-by-case ex post liability rules. Such ex post establishment of liability rules, however, produces a high degree of legal uncertainty. If the behavioral rules and standards arising from individually tailored contracts are determined by ex post and retrospectively applied court rulings, then "there appears to be no possibility for individuals to determine a priori what standards they must meet. Precedents may not apply to their particular situation, or precedents may be contradictory" (Spulber 1989:405; see also Krueger 1988:5). Inasmuch as they fail to give clear signals to agents as to how to adjust their behavior, uncertain legal standards are likely to lead either to *under*compliance or *over*compliance in that agents do not respond at all or they modify their behavior beyond the point that would be socially optimal (see Craswell and Calfee 1986). In such instances, legislation setting ex ante standards and rules for individual behavior may indeed be superior, in that it contributes to reducing behavioral uncertainties by clearly defining individual rights and remedies for violations (see Spulber 1989:60ff.; Kolstad et al. 1990).[59]

Moreover, there are situations in which private contracting may fail to rule out the dual problem of adverse selection and moral hazard inherent in open-ended employment relationships involving sunk cost investments. As long as, for example, the negotiation of just-cause requirements for dismissals is left exclusively

---

[58]For a general treatment of the differences between common law and civil law, see Cooter and Ulen 1988:72ff.

[59]This does not mean that by legal regulation all ex post litigation is avoided. Most laws also contain general clauses that may lead to conflicting interpretations to be settled by the judicature. This ex post setting of retrospectively applying standards by labor courts has indeed been the focus of recent criticism of legal dismissal protection by German employers (see Soltwedel et al. 1990:28ff.). Given, however, that dismissal protection laws also clearly specify remedies for unjust dismissals (e.g., fixed maximum amounts for severance payments) and that specialized labor courts (as established in Germany) provide for speedy conflict resolutions, the threat to firms resulting from litigation by dismissed employees can be assumed to be incomparably smaller than the one resulting from common-law litigation in the United States.

to the discretion of private parties, firms offering such benefits are more likely to attract workers who in other firms would face a higher risk of being fired. For the individual firm, such adverse selection of job candidates and the ensuing risk of shirking once the workers are hired may be an incentive to discontinue offering just-cause standards for dismissals, thus, of course, also negatively affecting the lot of nonshirking workers. By contrast, if "just-cause were universal, then these poorly motivated workers would be distributed evenly across firms. . . . Under these circumstances, the efficiency gains of just-cause policies are more likely to outweigh the burden imposed by shirkers" (Levine and D'Andrea-Tyson 1990:219; see also Levine 1989). Likewise, motivated workers may lack sufficient information about the past behavior and the reputational capital of firms promising employment security and therefore make investments in the "wrong" firm or prefer to queue up for jobs in firms having a more visible "honesty" record (see Shapiro and Stiglitz 1984). The examples show that, by universalizing rules and standards for individual behavior, legislation may be able to dispel distrust and solve typical *prisoner's dilemma* situations, thereby increasing overall efficiency.

Likewise, in the presence of market imperfections, legislation may act as an incentive and supporting structure for efficient private contracting by granting special inalienable negotiation and joint-decision rights to private parties, thereby facilitating "voice" solutions and rendering particular issues negotiable that would otherwise not get included in private bargaining agendas. This is particularly true of collective labor law, which, by establishing industry- or firm-level bargaining "arenas" and providing procedural rules for collective negotiations, is assumed to have played a vital part in promoting industrial peace (see Schwab 1989), preventing inefficient "exit" options (e.g., industrial action; wildcat strikes), and overcoming mutual distrust, especially in settings with previously adversarial labor relations and impaired confidence in the other side's observance of fairness criteria (see Freeman and Medoff 1984; Cohen and Wachter 1989:250). There is indeed ample evidence from various countries that the legal endorsement of collective "voice" mechanisms has greatly contributed to dispersing mutual fears of opportunistic behavior and thereby, for example, reduced opposition to the introduction of productivity-enhancing and labor-saving new technologies (see, for example, Warnken and Ronning 1990; Levine and D'Andrea-Tyson 1990:204ff.).

To summarize, there seem to be many instances in which labor regulation in general and dismissal legislation in particular fosters efficient contracting between firms and workers and thus enhances labor market efficiency. With regard to employment security policies, this implies that the direct economic costs imposed by dismissal legislation, which have been the focus of the current political debate, need to be carefully weighed against the alternative costs of private contracting and—if the latter should fail—the socioeconomic welfare costs of forgone sunk investments. As shown by current skill problems and the comparatively poor productivity performance of the U.S. economy (see Dertouzos et al. 1989:81ff.), these economic welfare costs may, in fact, be substantial.

Which Employment Security Policy?

That employment security legislation may be efficient and improve welfare in some cases does not yet answer the crucial question of which type of regulation is optimal to achieve this goal. There certainly is no abstract, universal answer to this question. As shown by the strong differences in work force adjustment behavior and overall labor market performance both among countries with rather strict legal layoff and dismissal restraints (e.g., Sweden[60] and Italy or France) and among countries with few exogenously imposed restrictions (e.g., Japan and the United States), the decision as to which policy is optimal is largely determined by the overall socioeconomic setting and wider institutional framework in which it is to operate. Nor, as several contributors to this book (Birk; Bercusson; Lyon-Caen; Treu) argue, were the employment security regulations in major European countries designed abstractly and then enacted in a social engineering manner. Rather, the policies evolved over time more or less incrementally as a result of different economic conditions, historical exigencies, sociopolitical pressures, and different underlying policy motives. Even if a model for an "optimal" policy could be designed, it would still have to face the crucial test of merging into a given socioeconomic and wider institutional setting and the behavioral rationalities or "opportunity structures" (Selznick 1969) prevailing therein.

In contrast to widespread conceptions of regulation as operating as a simple stimulus-response mechanism, external regulatory impulses directed toward economic behavior "are filtered according to special selection criteria into the respective system structures and adapted to the autonomous logic of the regulated system. . . . Legal regulations are accepted as triggers for internal developments which are no longer controllable by law" (Teubner 1987:20). The case for employment security legislation and the appropriate form that legislation should take therefore "depend crucially on the empirical nature of labor markets" (Ehrenberg 1985:36) given in each country.

Yet, despite national differences in labor market settings and their historically evolved wider institutional frameworks, the quest for employment security has, as a common feature across countries, been closely associated with the spread of internal labor markets[61] and their typical concomitants of capital-intensive production; economies of scale; a high degree of division of labor; the depreciation of transferable, craftlike skills; high costs of labor turnover; and continuing worker-firm attachments (see the detailed account by Boyer, chap. 1). In such a setting both workers and firms have been shown endogenously (i.e., without external

---

[60]For evidence on Sweden, see Bjoerklund and Holmlund 1987.

[61]The concept of internal labor markets has become rather vague. With Wachter and Wright (1990:89), we use the term to denote all labor market settings where firms and workers incur substantial sunk cost investments and therefore have a mutual interest in continuing ongoing relationships. In external labor market settings, which range from very low-skill and casual to rather high-skill trade and professional labor markets, both parties make little specific investments in the relationship; skills, as far as present, are transferable between firms; and job separations (quits or dismissals) can occur at little cost to either side.

constraint) to develop an interest in devising and implementing a governance structure between them that protects their mutual sunk investments, mitigates distrust, promotes work commitment, and minimizes costly production disruptions while at the same time providing the degree of flexibility needed to cope with future contingencies in a more or less uncertain economic environment.

Such a governance structure involves, as we have further seen, the establishment of explicit and/or implicit standards, rules, and procedures for both parties' behavior in contingent future situations that cannot be foreseen at the time of the initial employment contract. Given their dual objective of generating mutual trust in order to enable mutual sunk investments and of providing a basis for risk sharing in the face of a contingent future, an essential part of these standards, rules, and procedures is concerned with specifying more or less general conditions and criteria for the termination of employment contracts (or the ex post modification of their explicit terms). Mutual trust is created by the establishment of standards and rules that provide safeguards against opportunistic behavior by the other side. This implies that firms cannot fire workers or alter contract terms arbitrarily, thereby depriving workers of their share in the rents from mutual sunk investments, and workers cannot lower the firm's returns from such investments by shirking without facing dismissal. Risk sharing implies that neither of the parties can be forced to maintain its contractual commitments if, because of unpredictable changes in the economic environment, this would involve a serious jeopardizing of their initial goals for engaging in labor market activities (in the case of the firm, the yielding of sufficient profits to secure the medium-term survival of the undertaking and in the case of the worker the grasping of opportunities for maximizing lifetime income).

Efficient contracts, therefore, contain clauses tying individual disciplinary dismissals to the requirement of objectifiable just-cause criteria such as malperformance, shirking, or misconduct by the worker, and, at the same time, allow unilateral contract termination if changed economic conditions, such as a decline in labor demand or better wage offers elsewhere, obviously require either party to do so. In the case of workers quitting to accept better wage offers elsewhere, the economic reasons for doing so do not seem to need any further proof, whereas dismissals by firms for economic reasons require a substantiation of their necessity in order to prevent opportunistic behavior on the side of the firm. Insofar as firms offer deferred compensation schemes to elicit work effort and worker commitment, efficient contracts will also contain clauses detailing that junior workers are to be laid off first (layoff by reverse seniority). If layoffs of senior workers are inevitable, they will involve severance payments or firm-specific early retirement benefits as compensations for past work effort.[62]

---

[62]In this sense, Osterman and Kochan (1990:163) correctly observe that instead of offering a job guarantee by prohibiting terminations, it is essential "that an employment security policy be perceived by the labor force as representing the 'best efforts' of the firm. That is, the firm should be seen as making every effort to avoid layoffs; it is the degree of effort (or cost), not the ultimate absense of layoffs that represents the key test."

These criteria describe exactly the basic structure and characteristics of actual legal employment protection regulations in such major European countries as France, Germany, and the United Kingdom. In their basic components the real models established in these countries appear to be largely congruent and consistent with theoretically derived criteria for efficient contracting in labor market settings involving sunk investments, information asymmetries, and economic uncertainty (see also Goldberg 1980:270). This may also explain why firms in countries without dismissal legislation, such as Japan and the United States, frequently have voluntarily adopted implicit or explicit dismissal practices resembling those of European firms and why in many European countries existing legal layoff and dismissal restraints (as well as their partial deregulation during the 1980s) have failed to have a major impact on firms' work force adjustment behavior. In fact, in those countries for which historical evidence is available (Germany and the United Kingdom), many of the rules and procedures required by dismissal legislation had already become common practice in large and growing parts of the economy *before* legislation was introduced or extended in the later 1960s and 1970s (see for the United Kingdom, Mackay et al. 1971:366ff.; Mumford 1975:1ff.; Marsden 1986:35; for Germany, Lutz and Weltz 1966; Boehle and Lutz 1974:24ff.; Buechtemann and Stille 1992).

Does this mean, as Jacoby (1990a:171ff.) critically puts it, that "economic efficiency incentives are sufficient to account for observed institutional outcomes"? This question certainly cannot be answered generally in the affirmative. There are many instances in which labor market institutions, such as the very rigid hiring regulations in Italy (see Auer, chap. 23), but also the lack of adequate supporting institutions for firms' employment security policies in the United States (see Osterman, chap. 9) may be associated with a loss in overall economic efficiency. In several instances, however, dismissal legislation appears to be highly compatible with and indeed the outcome of efficient microeconomic behavior, namely, in those cases (as exemplified by Germany and the United Kingdom) in which legislation was to a large extent the mere legal codification of widespread de facto practices that had evolved endogenously in dominant and advanced sectors of the economy.[63] This policy mode involves several advantages.

First, by fashioning labor law principles according to sunk cost rules underlying efficient private contracting in modern labor market settings, it provides a supporting structure and incentive for sunk investments and the overall economic efficiency gains inherent therein (see Wachter and Cohen 1988:1382).

Second, "by adopting the rule that the majority of the labor market bargainers would reach if they bargained over the issue, [it] will save those majoritarian bargainers the costs of crafting a tailor-made rule" (Leslie 1989:230).

Third, by legally codifying the implicit or explicit terms of the majority of

---

[63]Selznick (1968:55) in this context speaks of "incipient law." Some U.S. authors have argued that the generalization of "efficient," endogenously evolved "best practices" was also the policy intention underlying the enactment of the National Labor Relations Act (NLRA) in 1935 (see Cohen and Wachter 1989:250; Osterman and Kochan 1990:179ff.).

ongoing employment relationships, it largely avoids the efficiency losses incurred from a redefinition and reassignment of existing property rights that interferes with ongoing market exchanges (see Hamermesh, chap. 2).

Fourth, by merely universalizing what the majority of firms practice in the absence of any exogenously imposed constraints, it produces little additional costs in that its immediate impact is confined to a minority of idiosyncratic firms whose personnel practices deviate from the predominant pattern (see Levine and D'Andrea-Tyson 1990:219) and, therefore, can be assumed to encounter little political opposition (see Goldberg 1980:252).

Fifth, by drawing immediately on efficient practices in advanced sectors of the economy, it avoids the problems and risks of regulatory failure resulting from legislators' information deficits about the functioning of real labor markets and overcomes the crucial regulatory problem of the "structural coupling" (Teubner 1987) between policy, law, and the sphere of economic action.

Taking into account the other potential efficiency advantages of legislation mentioned above, the legal codification of common practices that have evolved from unconstrained private bargaining between workers and firms (or their collective representatives) in advanced sectors of the economy emerges as an efficient way of introducing dismissal legislation, which—by increasing the scope for sunk investments and cooperative labor relations—may result in substantial gains in overall socioeconomic welfare. As such, legislation may also act as a viable policy model for solving current problems facing the U.S. common-law system and the U.S. labor market at large.[64] Given the high degree of de facto employment stability already enjoyed by a large part of the U.S. work force and the prevalence of voluntary layoff and dismissal procedures in larger U.S. enterprises, it would seem that the economic costs of converting de facto protection to de jure protection would be outweighed by its benefits.[65] By replacing the currently prevailing "strict liability" rule with a general *negligence* rule that establishes a legal standard of behavior and "imposes liability only on people who fail to comply" (Cooter 1991:13), unjust dismissal legislation would greatly reduce the legal uncertainties and inequalitites of the attorney- and jury-driven ex post litigation system. To a large extent then, the efficiency of the legislative approach depends on the accuracy

---

[64]A similar policy concept seems to underly the recommendation by the MIT Commission on Industrial Policy that the U.S. federal government should endorse and seek to diffuse new management and labor relations practices that have developed in leading companies by "adopting a national labor policy that encourages continuous innovation and strengthens cooperation in labor-management relations" (see Dertouzos et al. 1989:153).

[65]A starting point for the introduction of unjust dismissal legislation in the U.S. could be that most state unemployment insurance laws, by restricting benefits eligibility to workers who have lost their jobs through no fault of their own, indirectly require some control of the reasons underlying dismissals. Such a proposal was recently made by Ehrenberg (1985:16): "One wonders why pressure for reform does not take the form of devising ways to have state unemployment insurance systems more rigorously examine 'dismissals for misconduct' and to encourage them to award benefits without extra waiting periods in cases in which the dismissal was deemed excessive." The viability of this proposal would, however, presume a reform of the incomplete experience-rating system (see also Bellace 1983).

of the behavioral standards imposed. Defining the latter with reference to prevailing norms of "reasonable cause" and majoritian practice can be assumed to provide efficient results because such norms and practice have evolved from repeated interaction (see Cooter 1991:22). Moreover, transaction costs would be reduced because everyone claiming liability damages would have to prove negligence by the other party in complying with the established behavioral standards.

Finally, by conveying to privately negotiated standards and procedures of fair dealing the status of inalienable legal rights, a legislative policy universalizing common best practices would at the same time overcome the typical prisoner's dilemma faced by firms voluntarily offering employment security: whether in the event of an economic downturn to maintain their self-imposed commitments and thereby forgo short-term profits or whether to follow their "firing" competitors and relinquish their employment security promises, thereby, of course, triggering the vicious circle of forfeited trust and declining work commitment by workers, rising labor turnover, latently or overtly adversarial labor relations, and decreasing sunk investments in the medium term.

The higher degree of irreversibility of rules and procedures introduced by a legal codification of common practices may thus have an overall beneficial impact in the medium term. In the long run, however, the higher inertia inherent in legal regulation as compared to private bargaining may involve a loss in adjustment efficiency. To ensure, nonetheless, a sufficient degree of flexibility for adjusting to changing economic conditions, legislation would have to be restricted to setting minimum standards (substantive regulation) and besides focus on strengthening individual and collective "voice" mechanisms (procedural regulation) that allow a more flexible tailoring of rules and procedures to local circumstances and varying economic situations (see, for example, Ichniowski and Lewin 1987).

The costs of a legal codification of common best practices are largely borne by those (idiosyncratic) firms whose employment practices for various reasons deviate from those of the majority of firms in the more advanced sectors of the economy.[66] Some of those firms that pursue a casual labor market strategy involving frequent hiring and firing are forced by legislation to alter their personnel practices under the threat of the costs of unjust dismissal litigation by employees. Similar to a sudden increase in minimum wages, this will, as shown by the European evidence summarized above, induce some firms to adjust to the new situation "by making additional investments in trying-out, screening, and training of workers," thus enhancing efficiency and offsetting tendencies toward underinvestment in human capital due to market imperfections (Okun 1981:123). Where such a "forward" adjustment is not feasible because of particular conditions in product markets or given patterns of labor supply, legislation is likely to lead to efficiency losses. The latter can be mitigated, however, by granting selective exemptions to very small firms lacking the scope to develop organizational structures akin to the internal

---

[66]Empirical evidence from the United Kingdom and Germany shows that firms adhering to an intensive hiring and firing personnel policy are those that complain most about the costs imposed by dismissal legislation (see Daniel and Stilgoe 1978:48; Buechtemann and Hoeland 1989:272ff).

labor market model or by allowing under certain conditions the use of atypical employment arrangements that are not subject to statutory dismissal protection. Such exemptions are highly common in European countries and in Japan (see Hanami 1982). Evidence from Germany and the United Kingdom shows that, given a competitive labor market setting without excessive legal layoff restraints, firms are unlikely to use such atypical job arrangements strategically to evade employment security provisions since they would thereby forgo the efficiency gains inherent in stable, long-term employment relationships (see, for example, Evans et al. 1985; Buechtemann, chap. 13).

Last but not least, the European experience shows that the feasibility of effective job security policies depends to a large degree on the existence of a wider institutional framework that provides the right incentives to stabilize employment and a supporting infrastructure that enables firms to benefit from the efficiency advantages inherent in internal work force adjustments and long-term employment relationships. Such incentives can take the form of a more complete experience rating of employers' unemployment insurance contributions, forcing firms to endogenize the costs of worker displacements, or a reduction in overtime premia[67] and the provision of short-time working compensation as an alternative to unemployment benefits, thereby increasing the scope for hours instead of employment adjustments and lowering the costs of labor hoarding during cyclical downturns. The lack of a publicly provided supporting framework frequently has been blamed for U.S. firms' difficulties in sustaining voluntarily adopted employment security policies through adverse times (see Osterman, chap. 9). At the same time, however, the European experience of an increasing segmentation between a majority of stably employed insiders enjoying a high degree of de facto employment security and a grown margin of unstably employed or long-term unemployed outsiders suggests that employment security policies need to be complemented by policies aimed at reducing turnover costs by providing the incentives and prerequisites for voluntary job mobility. This can be achieved, for example, by providing workers with broad, transferable, and regularly updated professional skills that can be productively employed in variable settings without long periods of on-the-job training (see Lutz, chap. 26).

In all this it should be remembered that labor markets do not exist for their own sake and that microeconomic employment security first of all depends on the relative stability and time horizons prevailing in the wider product and capital market settings in which firms operate. Industrial policies providing incentives to shift investment into less volatile markets, allowing the development of stable customer-supplier relationships based on quality rather than mere price competition, as well as policies aimed at easing pressures on firms to sacrifice longer-term investment perspectives for maximizing short-time returns, will ultimately determine whether employment security policies can work. Inducing firms to

---

[67]In the United States overtime premia are substantially higher than in most European countries or Japan (see Tachibanaki 1987). For a detailed discussion of the wider impact of overtime premium policies on workforce adjustment, see Ehrenberg and Schumann 1982.

follow the example of those that have already developed more careful and forward-looking human resource management practices is likely to be an important step in that direction.

To devise optimal employment security policies and render existing ones more effective still requires that a great deal of research be done. In that the clue to better policies is found not in textbooks but rather where such policies are to be implemented and practiced, this first of all requires more empirical information about the actual functioning of real labor markets in contrasting socioeconomic and institutional environments. Based on evidence from six major industrialized countries, the contributions in this book provide a solid platform from which to work toward that goal.

Part I

The Economics of
Employment Protection

1

The Economics of Job Protection and Emerging New Capital-Labor Relations

Robert Boyer

M any observers have compared European and American job creation performance. A common view is that excessive social regulation has prevented the adaption of jobs in number and quality to meet the changing pattern in world competitiveness and technological advances. In the early 1980s, wage rigidity was at the forefront of many international comparative studies. Both inflation and unemployment rates were supposed to be closely related to an index measuring nominal or real wage rigidity. Throughout the period, many reforms were undertaken to soften previous legislation, although workers more and more preferred job preservation to wage increases.

The debate has now shifted to new topics. Job creation resumed in the second half of the 1980s in Europe, and wage moderation has been obtained in most European countries. Consequently, the role of workers' protection and the impact of general education and training are now considered key factors in labor market dynamics. This paper relates these issues to a broader question: what are the tranformations occurring in the capital-labor relations inherited from World War II? Basically, a long-term historical and international comparative approach will locate the role of the so-called Fordist compromise in the growth regime that used to characterize most highly industrialized countries. This approach points out the core institutional factors governing the viability of any job security regulation, studies their transformations during the last two decades, and finally outlines some new principles that are shaping work organization, wage formation, and skills. From the results I will derive some consequences with regard to employment adjustment.

The reasoning will follow five steps. First, it will be argued that a form of partial job security was roughly consistent with increasingly mild business cycles from the 1950s to the 1960s. Yet the very success of the new institutional forms elaborated after 1945, which launched the Fordist growth regime, led to major and converging imbalances during the 1970s. Consequently, after a period of reinforced employment protection (at least in countries like France), the strengthening of competition and international pressures called for a reversal of previous social regulations. The search for job flexibility was and still is part of this general trend reversal. Nevertheless, in the early 1990s, the focus of the flexibility debate has shifted. People are now asking, What are the key features of the genuine capital-labor relations that can overcome the Fordist structural crisis? They have tentatively been labeled "Toyotism" and "Volvoism," according to two contrasting variants. Job security therefore has to be consistent with these new principles rather than with the older ones.

Given this general framework, the rest of this paper is more analytical. On the one hand, the new microeconomic theories about wage-labor relations suggest that, even without public regulation, maximum flexibility in employment adjustment is generally not optimal. On the other hand, most macroeconometric analyses conclude that the long-term impact of labor market deregulation on employment trends is generally small, sometimes positive, sometimes negative. Finally, it is argued that employment flexibility plays only a small part in any global strategy that tries to implement the new principles of labor management. Furthermore, many different institutional settings might be appropriate for coping with such an objective. Deregulation of employment protection is not a fatality; nor does it seem to be the most efficient strategy in the long run for coming to terms with the new competitive pressures facing highly industrialized countries.

Some Job Preservation Was Viable within Fordist Capital Relations

It is necessary, first, to locate the role of employment adjustments and related public regulations in the general configuration for the capital-labor relations (CLR) inherited from World War II. The contemporary debate about deregulation will thus become clearer.

Post–World War II: An Unprecedented Configuration

Now, in the early 1990s, the main features of the Fordist capital-labor relations are easier to characterize. In contrast to the 1980s, the roaring 1960s were built on four founding principles.

A deepening of the division of labor. This has been a distinctive feature of the post–World War II era. On the one hand, a clear distinction between conception and execution, production and sales, and marketing and finance allows an unprecedented technical and social division of tasks within the original domain of Fordism (i.e., the manufacturing sector) but also in all production-related tertiary sectors. Within the firm, specialized equipment is designed to embody the largest technical knowledge possible; assembly tasks require a very low level of education and skills. Basically, the Fordist principle of highly standardized mass products sets the pace in industrial organization (see fig. 1-1).

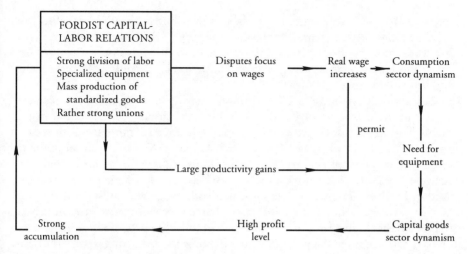

FIGURE 1-1. Fordist Hypothesis

Standardized mass production is the modern method for reaping increasing returns to scale in Adam Smith's tradition, given the technical opportunities and social compromise of the post–World War II era. Labor productivity has therefore experienced an unprecedented growth rate in most OECD countries, with the exception of the United States, where strong economic growth has been prevailing for more than a century (Maddison 1982). During the last Fordist boom, from 1969 to 1973, even the United Kingdom exhibited very high productivity and growth rates. But this achievement had its price: in most countries, increasing capital intensity led to an accelerating decline in the output-capital ratio (Glyn 1988).

A compromise about productivity sharing. This principle guides wage formation, in contrast to previous competitive mechanisms, according to which labor scarcity and the general price level were the major factors in real wage dynamics. First, pressure by unions and workers for wage indexation with respect to consumer prices is actually taken into account, either by explicit clauses within collective agreements or by the formation of expectations about inflation, which is now a permanent feature of Fordist growth (Benassy, Boyer, and Gelpi 1979). Conceptually, the wage is no more a pure market variable since it incorporates a minimum standard of living not only for low-wage earners but for each category of worker. Second, wages are adjusted according to general productivity increases. During the golden years, most government officials, even the most conservative, called this sharing the dividend of progress.

The miracle is precisely that this broad vision of the world inspired the actual wage policies of firms. With uneven lags, all countries exhibited a perfect long-term wage indexation with respect to consumer prices. This was far from a fact of nature; in the nineteenth century the corresponding elasticity was about 0.1 to 0.2 (Boyer 1979).

Productivity sharing is a little more complex to investigate. The best evidence relies on the noticeable constancy of labor's distributive share (adjusted for the shift toward salaried activities) in the medium run. In the short run, econometric studies seem to confirm this productivity sharing, either as instantaneous (Germany and Japan) or as occurring over a multiperiod labor contract (United States and probably France).

Collective bargaining. This institutional setting created strong complementarities in the evolution of Fordist capital-labor relations, which started in the highly unionized leading sectors and progressively spread to more atomistic sectors and finally to the civil service (Piore 1988; Coriat 1988). The innovation with respect to the previous century or even the interwar period is far-reaching. Labor struggles used to create wage differentials between skills, sectors, or regions. Within Fordist capital-labor relations, successful wage demands are setting the pace for average nominal wage increases. Three mechanisms at least contribute to this: a rather high degree of centralization in collective bargaining at the sectoral or even national level, the voluntary mobility of workers moving toward the best-paying jobs, and finally, in some countries, minimum wage policies by governments.

Most indexes for wage dispersion confirm the extensive stability of wage differentials under Fordism, a feature that has even withstood periods of crisis (OECD 1985, chap. 5). Nevertheless, within this new historical configuration, some national specificities emerge: the conventional opposition between primary and secondary jobs (Doeringer and Piore 1971) and the persisting competitive wage formation legacy explain why wage differentials played a role in the United States even during the Fordist golden years. With some minor exceptions, more homogeneity prevails in OECD countries; wage differentials in absolute and relative terms are kept fairly low, particularly in countries with social-democratic governments.

A Keynesian welfare state. The fourth pillar of Fordist capital-labor relations, consisting of the basic social compromise and new conceptions about the role of the state, induces and legitimizes an impressive redistribution of income via the Keynesian welfare state. Interpersonal and intergenerational solidarity, which used to operate through family ties, is now transferred to more collective and horizontal institutions. The welfare state system is therefore a key component of the new deal between citizens and the state. The recognition of the social wage, general access to health care, basic education, and the provision of pension funds for the poor and of unemployment benefits during cyclical downturns explain the surge of redistributive mechanisms established by the state or by collective agreements between unions and employers.

Again, this introduces a far-reaching innovation in CLR and regulation mode at large. On the one hand, the disciplinary role of firings and unemployment is weakened (with possible adverse impacts on work intensity), and real wage increases are more stable, smoothing the cycle. On the other hand, the variety of public transfers create built-in stabilizers, given their financing through taxes and social security contributions. Nevertheless, this Keynesian-Beveridge state is unequally developed in different advanced capitalist countries. Just before the oil shock, the share of collective redistribution was higher in social democratic countries such as Sweden and Austria than in the countries in the European Community, although redistribution was a major element of policy here too (e.g., in Italy). Public welfare programs are least important in the United States and Japan, where family solidarity and private pension funds constitute prevailing alternatives to the provision of public welfare.

Effects of the Weakening of Recessions

Business cycles are milder. Previous historical and statistical studies (Benassy, Boyer, and Gelpi 1979) have shown that the emergence of these institutional features of the Fordist regime have promoted a progressive shift from one set of dynamic adjustments to another (i.e., from competitive to monopolist *régulation*). In this new configuration, the Fordist compromise of productivity sharing allows some kind of synchronization between production and effective demand; the major discrepancies that used to characterize the interwar period and that led to the 1929 structural crisis are avoided. This is the first and the major factor accounting for the smoothing of business cycles after World War II and it is closely related to the new rules of wage formation. Another factor is the increasing role of public spending and fiscal redistribution. Even more, the success of Keynesian principles promotes countercyclical policies that enable a further reduction of cyclical fluctuations.

Statistical evidence confirms this smoothing of conventional business cycles after World War II. Major depressions turned into mild recessions (see Zarnowitz 1985:528). During the early 1970s, some experts were therefore induced to think that the business cycle had become obsolete. Downward employment adjustments became less frequent and less steep than during the 1920s or 1930s. In a sense, quite independently of any public regulation, employment flows had become stabilized. This was a silent and unnoticed form of employment protection. As long as growth was buoyant, stable, and predictable, there was no need for general work force reductions and consequently no perception of any built-in rigidity.

Structural inertia in employment. A series of other factors specific to employment decisions and institutional settings contributed to reinforcing employment stability. First, in mature manufacturing sectors, mechanization and automatization led to high capital-output ratios, which created built-in rigidity within the production process itself. Second, and closely related to the Fordist social and technical division of labor, the ratio of indirect labor (administrative work) to direct labor (productive work) has been increasing. Consequently, it has become less and less possible to vary total employment continuously since overhead costs are now very important; the other side of the coin about dynamic, increasing returns to scale is a high degree of rigidity with regard to varying the volume of labor and equipment. Third, the ongoing success of rapid and stable growth affects the formation of firms' expectations: why adjust the employment level downward if the post-World War II recessions have become milder and milder? The expectations that recessions will be short and transitory brings

TABLE 1-1. Speed of Employment Adjustment in the 1930s and 1970s

	France	United Kingdom	United States
1930s	0.70	0.87	0.76
1970s	0.24	0.22	0.55

Comparison of the Two Recessions, 1930 and 1975
Estimates for the parameter λ in the following equation:

$$N_t = (1 - \lambda) N_{t-1} + \lambda N_t^* \qquad 0 \leq \lambda \leq 1 \text{ Adjustment speed}$$

N_t = effective employment N_t^* = efficient employment

Source: Boyer and Mistral 1978:198.

in another source of employment stability. Finally, the new Keynesian countercyclical policies reinforced the belief in the stability of long-term economic growth.

As a direct consequence of these expectations and beliefs, large firms, especially in Europe and Japan, implemented job tenure schemes that became functional within the Fordist regime. They enhance workers' commitment, a form of social armistice, and allow learning-by-doing effects to be captured within the firm. This may explain why the inherent Fordist rigidity and the loss of external flexibility did not show up before the breakdown of the international order and the emergence of imbalances within American manufacturing. Further, from a macro point of view, a slowdown in employment adjustments adds to the global stability of the Fordist regime (Boyer and Mistral 1978).

Some crude statistical estimates confirm the reduction in employment adjustment speed (table 1-1). It has been shown that this structural change, linked to technological and institutional transformations, might have contributed, at least in part, to preventing the first oil shock from triggering a cumulative depression. This could be one of the major differences between the 1970s and the late 1920s.

Contrary to the conventional belief of the early 1980s, a form of job tenure, often mitigated by labor segmentation and external mobility within the secondary sector, might have had a positive impact on growth, on welfare (by dampening the business cycle), and correlatively on the stability of the political and social compromise, which was at the heart of the Fordist era. But precisely this was not granted for eternity: the very success of this unprecedented regime has been unwinding the roots of a genuine structural crisis. In this emerging new context, labor flexibility is at the core of political debates and corporate strategies.

Pressures on Job Preservation and the Breakdown of Fordism

Having outlined the functional complementarity between significant employment inertia and Fordist growth, I will first investigate the underlying structural factors that might explain its demise and then derive from this analysis some insights about labor market flexibility.

The Roots of the Structural Crisis of the Growth Regime

Social malaise. A series of tensions progressively emerged within the Fordist model. The first evidence of increasing tensions occurred at the end of the 1960s, when low-skilled blue-collar workers in the automobile industry began to rebel against the monotonous character of assembly-line tasks. Wildcat or organized strikes challenged Fordist production methods, and in some countries, such as Italy, led to a new law giving more power to workers and unions in controlling work organization and work intensity. In France, similar demands were converted into wage increases after large-scale strikes in May 1968. In the United States, the Fordist malaise took a more subtle form via a rise in absenteeism and turnover, declining product quality, and finally a slowdown in productivity. Social unrest against Taylorism and Fordism, even if rather contained, was the first warning of the limitations of this model.

More deeply, better educational opportunities for the broad mass of the population led to an increasing rejection of basic Fordist axioms, according to which work requires only physical and mechanical abilities, and little personal initiative or intellectual creativity. Consequently, most OECD countries experienced rising difficulties in recruiting workers who would accept the more monotonous manufacturing jobs. As migration from agriculture to industry slowed down, most European countries had to rely on migrant workers to fill the gap. They now represent an increasing proportion of the workers in manufacturing and construction employment. The second root of the Fordist crisis lies precisely in this discrepancy between the tendency of scientific management toward deskilling on the one hand and the rising expectations of the young about the quality and initiative of work on the other (Tarentelli 1973).

Productivity and rigidity problems. The creeping social crisis was complemented by considerable strains on the core economic mechanisms of post–World War II growth. As a consequence of workers' dissatisfaction, firms tried to push further ahead with mechanization. In the late 1960s and early 1970s, one observes a rising capital-output ratio that did not convert into more productivity. The puzzling decline of apparent as well as total productivity growth in the U.S. economy and in many other countries' manufacturing sectors well before the first oil price shock is indirect but significant evidence of the post–World War II crisis of productive organization. Nevertheless, with the exception of the United States, the productivity slowdown did not occur until the 1970s for most OECD countries. This is further evidence of the specificities of national trajectories and of the close marriage of American methods with national institutions, cultures, and specialization.

With the 1974–75 recession, another limitation became apparent: productivity underwent the most severe slowdown or decline in most typical Fordist industries. Given the large indivisibilities associated with assembly lines or even continuous processes, labor can no longer be varied continuously, whereas low-capacity utilization implies a slowdown in total productivity. In the medium run, the employment level somehow has to be adapted to its optimal level given the volume of demand and the underlying trends in productivity. Thus, a new but basic complaint about Fordist organization is its excessive rigidity in the face of unexpected variations in demand. The previous historical analysis suggests, however, that the rigidity problem is more a consequence than a cause of the crisis (Flanagan 1988). The need for a significant revision in engineering principles therefore, comes to the surface (Piore and Sabel 1984).

Product quality and world competition. The inertia of mass production refers not only to the quantity of standardized goods but also to the quality and versatility of products. In durable consumer goods (e.g., automobiles), for example, when the market turns from prime users to largely replacement demand, the quality and differentiation of products appear to be critical in the new competitive environment: in a buyers' market, consumers become more choosy and sensitive to quality, not only to cosmetic quality but quality in terms of servicing, durability, user costs, and so on. Again, the very large lag between the perception of new demands, the conception of alternative products, and their production at low cost impairs the adaptability of Fordist organization. The required flexibility is mainly internal and obtained from the polyvalence of skills and the good knowledge of managerial routines. Nevertheless, subcontracting and short-term employment contracts are used to gain external flexibility. Managers and academics alike then rediscover that within the conventional product/process matrix, craft production and diversified quality production are economically efficient and rational in such a context.

Worldwide competition progressively destabilized Fordist oligopolistic competition, which used to operate on each national market. From the mid-1960s until the 1980s, external trade developed faster than domestic markets, potentially breaking down the very smooth and peaceful path of competition. Since production capacities are generally underutilized, price wars take place, during which speed in reacting to market opportunities plays a key role. Fordist methods get outperformed by more flexible hybrids, such as those operating in West Germany, Italy, Sweden, and Japan. Simultaneously, the Fordist macroeconomic virtuous circle is challenged by export-driven strategies and rising uncertainties about the world financial and trade system. Consequently, the need for downward adjustment of employment becomes stronger for the less competitive firms, sectors, and economies.

Far-reaching innovations. Another destabilizing factor is related to the progressive exhaustion of the very cluster of innovations that launched Fordist dynamics. One observes a decline in the efficiency of research and development expenditures for mature industries such as mechanical engineering, chemistry, and aerospace (Patel and Soete 1987; OECD 1987). But concurrently, sunrise industries are exploding and partly replacing older ones: research and development in electronics and software is booming and is being converted into a new generation of products and processes. All these innovations seem to delineate a possible shift in paradigmatic organization, due to the potential impact of information technologies (Freeman 1989; Sundquist 1988). Somehow, employment flows have to follow these new patterns, in terms of employment patterns, work volume, and skills.

These innovations may have far-reaching consequences for the fate of Fordist methods and products. On the one hand, the large assembly line used to suffer from imbalances between the various tasks and from the very significant costs and lags associated with the retooling of equipment in cases of model changes. Numerically controlled machines, robots, the integration of various equipment via electronic networks, and the ease with which electronic equipment can be reconfigured all introduce significant technical flexibilities. The same equipment can now be used to manufacture different products from the same base product. This is one way to "fight" a typical deficiency of Fordism: the decline in the output-capital ratio (Ayres 1985; Boyer and Coriat 1986). On the product side, the versatility of equipment and/or workers allows faster reactions to qualitative shifts in both final and intermediate demand. This gives a premium to more flexible organizations in the new context of increased international competition. Again, internal and functional labor flexibility (polyvalent workers) outperforms external and numerical flexibility (layoffs and dismissals).

Though very important, information technology is not the only explanation for the general search for flexibility. Technical flexibility is merely one of a spectrum of different flexibility strategies. For example, multiskilled workers can in some cases replace heavy mechanization or even informatization, let alone more traditional flexibilities. Variations in working hours, work force reductions, and wage adjustments are each alternative strategies that, depending on their specific combination, may form quite distinctive national management styles (see Boyer 1987:108a).

Mobility and Numerical Flexibility: Priorities in the Eyes of Business and Governments

In this section I focus more specifically on worker mobility and labor market deregulation. Most of the features of the 1970s and 1980s have exerted strong pressure on previously established employment arrangements, whether formalized by law or by collective agreements. It was not at all surprising, therefore, that most countries during the 1980s experienced a significant, if not dramatic, revision of their conceptions of labor mobility.

Fordist rigidity revealed. Labor mobility between sectors and between regions used to be easier, faster, and more predictible the higher the growth rate. When production became sluggish and demand uncertain after the two oil shocks, jobs had to be cut to an extent far exceeding the scope of turnover. Correlatively, a stiffening of international competition had made labor saving a key objective of management. Consequently, in most OECD countries, there were major job reductions in mature industries. It is in this context that the rigidity of Fordism was revealed: firms, governments, and specialists realized that downward adjustments were hard to implement. Logically, the heyday of the flexibility debate took place in the early 1980s, when the world economy was quasi-stagnating, and induced purely defensive strategies. Again, this is indirect evidence that labor rigidity was a manifestation and consequence of the structural Fordist crisis and not necessarily its cause and driving factor.

Initially, these adjustments in employment were thought to be purely transitory. As time elapsed, however, it became apparent that far-reaching structural transformations were affecting work organization, skill requirements, the spatial distribution of jobs, and the relative size of various sectors. Generally, advanced capitalist countries experienced some form of deindustrialization, since a continuously rising share of employment shifted toward service activities. Even if these sectors were quite heterogeneous, they generally have weak unions, smaller firms, and therefore higher worker mobility than manufacturing. Within manufacturing, sunrise activities have not necessarily compensated for the job losses occurring within the old and mature industries. Labor mobility has therefore taken on a new significance with respect to the roaring 1960s: it is the means for transforming one configuration of industrial economies into another, largely new one.

Both short-term macroeconomic trends and long-term transformations have become far more unpredictable than during the Fordist era. The conventional business cycle is transformed, so that firms face major difficulties in forecasting demand, inflation, interest, and exchange rates. Furthermore, the large strategic errors made after the first oil shock induce managers to be more and more cautious in any decision affecting long-term variables.

In that job tenure was the implicit ideal to be followed, the legacy of the 1960s diffuses the view that labor has become a quasi-fixed factor. When demand becomes uncertain in volume and composition, firms logically react by restricting access to primary labor markets. Consequently, atypical employment has been spreading in most OECD countries: part-time employment, fixed-term work contracts, state-subsidized employment, and the like. These new forms provide flexibility and reversibility. The 1980s thus experienced a return to the ideal of secondary markets (Boyer 1988a). Similarly, subcontracting and short-term employment contracts are appealing to firms and sectors undergoing rapid and sometimes uncertain technical change. When long-term views are blurred by radical uncertainty, firms' rational behavior is to prefer liquidity to productive investment (Amendola and Gaffard 1988), secondary jobs to employment tenure.

Far-reaching structural change. At the end of the 1970s, the massive surge in unemployment in Europe and North America once again raised a major question about the status of labor markets. The apparent inability of previous Keynesian policies to counteract unemployment gave some credibility to more classical views about the self-regulating properties of markets in the absence of public regulation and monopoly power. There was apparently inescapable evidence: if labor markets were totally flexible, mass and long-term unemployment could not occur. This view was first applied to wage formation (OECD 1986a), the rigidity of which was said to impede the adjustment to trends in productivity. But during a second phase, the institutional obstacles to hiring and firing were blamed as the direct culprit, particularly with regard to Western Europe (Flanagan 1988; Layard and Calmfors 1987). Now a more balanced view prevails, but in the mid-1980s most analysts and governments considered mass unemployment direct proof of excessive labor market rigidity in terms of both wage formation and employment regulations.

Effective deregulation in the early 1980s in product and financial markets have made labor flexibility more necessary than ever. On the one hand, the import penetration of most domestic markets and correlatively the generalization of aggressive export strategies call for faster and usually larger adjustments in employment by skills, sectors, regions, and so on. On the other hand, unprecedented high real interest rates trigger much more active management policies by firms, which are eager to see legal constraints removed, particularly those on labor markets. Simultaneously, unions have undergone a steady and strong decline in most, though not all, OECD countries. During the 1980s, the initiative shifted from workers and unions to managers. This is another key factor in explaining the implementation of policies aimed at social deregulation. In July 1986, for example, the conservative government in France had to concede to impatient and vocal managers significant flexibility in hiring and firing procedures (see Maurau, chap. 19).

All these factors converge toward a significant revision in labor legislation and the content of collective bargaining. Indeed, atypical labor contracts make up the large part of all jobs created during the past fifteen years (OECD 1988b). Nolens volens, implicitly or explicitly, by negotiation or by a drastic shift in bargaining power, Europe and North America, with the significant exception of the Scandinavian and some other social democratic countries, witnessed diverse forms of labor market deregulation (Rowthorn 1990). This defines an important caveat with respect to previous analyses: they are relevant for North America and the European community but not necessarily for Japan and the other more advanced Asian economies, Sweden, Finland, and Austria. Previous research has shown the existence of contrasting national trajectories (Boyer 1990). But before returning to this key issue—what have been the consequences of labor market deregulation?—I will investigate a more basic question: do more flexible employment arrangements provide better results for firms and national economies?

Uncertain Impact of Employment Flexibility on Unemployment Levels

Labor rigidity: Cause or consequence of unemployment? From a theoretical point of view, Keynesian macroeconomic theory was developed in reaction to the common view according to which employment and wage levels in labor markets are determined by the same regulating mechanisms as any other commodity market (i.e., by price and quantity adjustments). The General Theory had convincingly argued that such an extrapolation from micro- to macroeconomics might be invalid. Imagine, for example, that financial markets, in conjunction with open market policies, govern interest rate formation and long-term views about the profitability of productive investment. In an effective demand model, the level of employment will be set according to the interaction of product and financial markets, without any role for the labor market itself. Remember the arguments expounded by Keynes in his *General Theory*: if mass unemployment is the result of insufficient effective demand, wage flexibility will not have any automatic role in restoring equilibrium in the labor market (Favereau 1989; Boyer 1988a).

Mutatis mutandis, the same reasons may explain why apparent employment rigidity may be only a consequence of macroeconomic imbalances, sometimes exacerbating them but not necessarily causing them. Incidentally, modern disequilibrium theory (Benassy 1982) and the related econometric estimates suggest that in France, for example, most unemployment is Keynesian (i.e., linked to insufficient effective demand); on the contrary, productivity or adverse terms of trade shocks would imply only transitory classical unemployment, associated with wage levels exceeding marginal productivity. In other words, the Keynesian message is not necessarily obsolete and might explain more stylized facts than alternative neoclassical or classical models that rely on competitive supply only. An assessment of the likely impact of European integration in 1992 seems largely to confirm this view (Boyer 1990a).

The respective chronologies about labor flexibility and the general directions of macroeconomic policy show close interactions and similarities. In the early 1980s, restrictive fiscal policies and rationing of public expenditures, as well as major international imbalances, were probably the main determinants of the surge in European unemployment (Fitoussi and Le Cacheux 1989). Wage rigidity is now attributed a significant but limited role in the persistence of this European "disease." During the second half of the 1980s, the buoyant American boom, prolonged by the softening of monetary policy after the October 1987 Wall Street crash, alleviated unemployment problems, even in Europe, and consequently shifted the emphasis from previously defensive flexibility (lower wages, easier firings) to a more offensive approach. For example, recent OECD reports (e.g., OECD 1989a) have emphasized skill requirements and general education as major components of labor market flexibility.

To summarize, neoclassical causality has been replaced by a Keynesian one. Both causalities can be reconciled within a synthetic diagram that distinguishes between initiating factors on the one hand and propagative mechanisms on the other (fig. 1-2). The roots of the crisis are seen as mainly macroeconomic, whereas labor market rigidity belongs to the second category.

Employment rigidity, not only the result of regulation. From a methodological standpoint, one has to consider whether public regulation of hiring and firing is the main factor behind employment rigidity. Research conducted in the context of the *régulation* approach suggests a balanced view (fig. 1-3). Three features of the Fordist regime imply a significant inertia of employment adjustments, especially downward ones.

Many structural and organizational features are responsible for such a novelty with respect to competitive capitalism. First, Fordism is built on static and

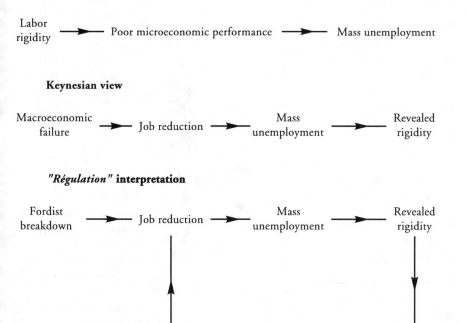

Conventional neoclassical view

Labor rigidity ⟶ Poor microeconomic performance ⟶ Mass unemployment

Keynesian view

Macroeconomic failure ⟶ Job reduction ⟶ Mass unemployment ⟶ Revealed rigidity

"Régulation" **interpretation**

Fordist breakdown ⟶ Job reduction ⟶ Mass unemployment ⟶ Revealed rigidity

Defensive flexibility strategies ⟵ Microeconomic imbalance

FIGURE 1-2. Three Conceptions of Labor Rigidity

dynamic increasing returns to scale, which imply strong indivisibilities for most manufacturing sectors (the assembly line of the automobile industry, continuous process production in steel production, electricity generation, heavy chemicals, the petrochemical industry, and so on). The putty-clay character of most equipment is associated with an increase in indirect labor in relation to typical blue-collar production work. Consequently, it is no longer possible during a severe recession to vary continuously and proportionally workers and equipment: good productivity performance in the past now has a clear cost, namely, a large inertia in adjusting to unexpected disturbances.

Second, a significant part of plant efficiency derives from in-house training and on-the-job learning by technicians, engineers, and professionals, often involving job- or firm-specific skills. The firm is therefore more reluctant to dismiss these workers. Simultaneously, training and hiring costs logically induce any rational firm to dampen employment adjustments to demand variations. The so-called productivity cycle is the normal outcome of such inertia, quite independent of any legal constraints imposed on firms (Soderstrom 1972).

Third, and finally, for some large Fordist firms, implicit employment security provides an efficient incentive to extract loyalty and commitment from workers.

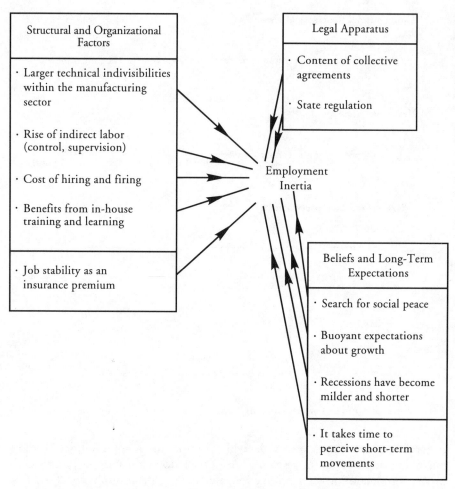

FIGURE 1–3. Factors Governing Inertia in Employment Adjustment

Similarly, implicit contract theory could be extended so that the insurance premium given to workers bears on continued employment and no more on the maintenance of nominal wages. Again, this is a rational form of behavior, quite apart from any union demand or public regulation.

Similarly, beliefs and long-term expectations shape firms' behavior in the face of disturbances emanating from the international economy, the financial sector, economic policies, and so on. Throughout the 1960s and early 1970s, for example, most politaicians and experts thought that French society would not accept more than half a million unemployed because social peace would be at stake. These views have been drastically revised, but they played a role in smoothing the surge in unemployment in France, which was at odds with what was observed in the United States, the United Kingdom and Germany.

Likewise, optimistic expectations about the sustainability of a fast growth track were used to reduce layoffs and dismissals during minor recessions, because the latter were interpreted as purely transitory in nature. Since the 1970s, however, macroeconomic evolutions have become erratic, and flexible and reversible strategies have come to be preferred to more efficient but largely irreversible ones.

Finally, on a more micro level, it takes time for firms to diagnose the onset of a recession or depression. This lag between information, decision, and effective behavior governs investment decisions but also partly applies to hiring and firing decisions. Again, all these mechanisms are independent of any direct public interventions concerning employment security.

The constraints imposed by state regulations and collective agreements merely reinforce these structural and institutional factors. Nevertheless, employment security legislation is prevalent mainly in Europe, not to any large extent in North America or Japan, although endogenous structural influences can be assumed to apply generally. Similarly, legislation does not impede employment variations but rather places procedural requirements, delays, and/or extra costs on firing. To stem long-term and youth unemployment, many OECD countries have also subsidized firms that hire such categories of workers. This is a countervailing mechanism with respect to employment security regulation.

Finally, collective agreements provide another set of partial job security or layoff regulations. If negotiated within a stable environment, both intuition and optimal contract theory suggest that the final agreement will mutually benefit workers and managers. The standard American procedure for layoffs belonged to this category, at least until the 1980s. When the environment drastically changes, however, the previous arrangements can turn into rigidities, at least in the eyes of managers. In some instances, highly sophisticated firing rules can even exacerbate the initial financial problems of the firm. Nevertheless, firing rules generally are not at the root of these difficulties, which are linked to foreign competition, the poor quality of products, insufficient product and process innovations, and other forms of mismanagement.

National trajectories. From a purely logical point of view, the legal apparatus cannot be the only factor to blame for employment inertia; the very institutional, technological, and economic bases of Fordism imply such a structural rigidity when the economy faces a severe or unexpected recession. A set of international comparisons (table 1-2) seems to support this preliminary conclusion. Roughly speaking, there are strong contrasts between countries with regard to the relative severity of employment protection regulations.

Italy seemed to represent the prototype of a highly regulated labor market, at least until the mid-1980s. Not only were public regulations severe, but also firms perceived them to be major obstacles to employment variations (see Emerson 1988a). This implies sluggish movement in hirings and separations. The employment stability rate of Italy is the highest in the whole sample (table 1-2), and, consequently, the standardized unemployment rate is the highest among OECD countries after Ireland and Spain. At the same time, the share of long-term unemployment is high compared to North America or social democratic countries. More institutionally oriented investigations (Mire 1989) confirm this

TABLE 1-2. Job Stability and Unemployment across Countries

Countries	Average new hires and separations (%)	Instability index (% workers with tenure of fewer than two years)	Standardized unemployment rate (1988) (%)	Share of long-term unemployment (%)	Active labor market policy measures (% of GDP)
Belgium	—	18	10.2	45.5	1.27
Denmark	—	27	8.6	29.6	1.13
Ireland	—	22	16.7	65.8	1.48
Italy	11	13	11.8	55.0	0.67
France	14	18	10.1	45.5	0.74
Germany	25	19	6.2	48.1	0.95
Greece	—	—	7.7	45.8	0.43
Netherlands	—	28	9.5	55.6	1.12
Portugal	—	—	6.0	56.6	0.50
Spain	—	—	19.1	61.9	0.65
United Kingdom	20	24	8.3	45.2	0.80
Average for EEC	18	19			
Japan	18	19	2.5	20.2	0.19
Sweden	18	—	1.6	8.2	1.96
United States	40	39	5.4	8.1	0.26
Finland	35	—	4.5	19.0	0.88
Norway	—	—	3.2	5.0	0.51
Canada	—	—	7.7	9.4	0.58
Austria	—	—	3.6	10.8	0.31

Sources: First two columns: Emerson 1988a:781, 782. Other three columns: OECD 1990c:90, 94.

statistical analysis. Productive decentralization, subcontracting, and drastic reorganization of firms, facilitated by the Italian Wage Compensation Fund (on *Cassa Integrazione Guadagni,* see Tronti, chap. 22), have aimed to relax the constraints on institutional labor mobility imposed after 1968–69 (Wolleb 1988).

The United States belongs in the opposite category: soft or nonexistent public regulations provide a high degree of freedom for firms, manifest in the highest employment instability rate of all OECD countries (table 1-2). Consequently, labor market adjustments are very pronounced, which also explains the prevalence of rather short unemployment spells. Finally, the U.S. unemployment rate regained its previous long-term level by the end of the 1980s, contrary to the persisting and long-term unemployment prevailing in most EC countries. Significantly, active public labor market policies played a very subordinate role in the United States, suggesting that such policies might complement highly regulated labor markets such as in Sweden or other European countries.

The United Kingdom apparently contradicts this crude model in which there is employment flexibility and low unemployment on the one side and rigidity and persisting mass unemployment on the other. As far as public regulations are concerned, they do not seem very restrictive, and U.K. firms do not perceive any strong institutional obstacles to fast employment adjustments. Surprisingly, long-term unemployment and average unemployment rates move at the European average and differ from those of North America or Scandinavian countries. The correlation between employment flexibility and low unemployment is contradicted by this evidence. Other rigidities, in skills, job rules, or wages, may explain the British case.

Small social democratic countries provide further exceptions: public regulations are significant, whereas mobility is collectively organized and/or negotiated by unions. Nevertheless, long-term unemployment and total unemployment are the lowest within all OECD countries (table 1-2). This provides an important lesson: by themselves, institutions governing capital-labor relations are not necessarily rigid; they appear rigid, though, when their specific setting is inadequate with respect to technological trends, external competition, and macroeconomic dynamics. Efficient labor market institutions (and macroeconomic policies) can be designed to resist even a severe worldwide structural crisis. Although now challenged, the Swedish model is not without merit. The relatively less satisfactory performance of Austria would suggest that active employment policies are central for such a process to be efficient (for their relative efforts, see table 1-2).

An indirect and partial impact of job stability on unemployment. A more systematic cross-national comparison reconfirms the previous analysis. One does not find any close and direct relationship between the unemployment rate and the share of long-term unemployment on the one hand and any index of institutional constraints and perceived obstacles to employment adjustments on the other hand. A closer look suggests some indirect and mediated influence, however (fig. 1-4). First, the qualitative analysis of the legal and institutional system is not without a link to the perception by firms of obstacles to mobility, whatever index we choose (hiring, layoffs, or global assessment). Second, the perceptions by firms across Europe are associated with effective mobility measures, such as the importance of hirings and separations and job instability, captured by the share of workers who have been with the firm for less than two years. Third, one notes a simultaneity between employment stability and high, long-term unemployment, whereas frequent hiring and firing is associated with lower levels of long-term unemployment. Fourth, and finally, the closest relation emerges between the overall unemployment rate and the share of long-term unemployment. Nevertheless, causality is an open question. Either job protection hinders hiring and job creation, thereby raising unemployment, which in turn tends to perpetuate itself, or a high unemployment rate triggers cautious behavior on the side of workers, who become reluctant to quit because they see few job opportunities elsewhere. Reduced turnover implies that the unemployed also experience difficulties getting a job, and this mechanism turns out to be a vicious circle. In this scenario, too, long-term unemployment would be a consequence, not a cause.

To conclude, it should be emphasized that the above results are clearly shaky.

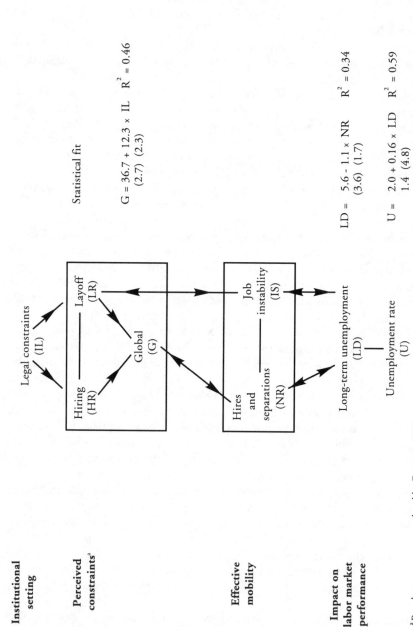

Statistical fit

$G = 36.7 + 12.3 \times IL \quad R^2 = 0.46$
$\quad\quad (2.7) \quad (2.3)$

$LD = 5.6 - 1.1 \times NR \quad R^2 = 0.34$
$\quad\quad (3.6) \quad (1.7)$

$U = 2.0 + 0.16 \times LD \quad R^2 = 0.59$
$\quad\quad 1.4 \ (4.8)$

Institutional
setting

Perceived
constraints[a]

Legal constraints
(IL)

Layoff
(LR)

Hiring
(HR)

Global
(G)

Effective
mobility

Job
instability
(IS)

Hires
and
separations
(NR)

Impact on
labor market
performance

Long-term unemployment
(LD)

Unemployment rate
(U)

[a] Based on assessments updated by Emerson 1988.

FIGURE 1-4. *Influence of Employment Security on Job Stability and Unemployment: A Cross-sectional Analysis*

First, the statistical indexes are partial, imperfect, and not available for all OECD countries, which leads to a number of caveats in interpreting the partial correlations in figure 1-4. Second, if the notion of national trajectories were valid, no general model would work at a cross-national comparative level. Job mobility might depend on very different factors in the United States and Germany, in the United Kingdom and Italy (Flanagan 1988).

With all these caveats, the following provisional hints emerge. Roughly speaking, constraints on mobility may play some role in long-term and total average unemployment, but the exact extent to which they act as an initiating or pure propagating factor remains an open question. To overcome this uncertainty, I shall analyze what the place of employment security should be in the potential successors to the Fordist regime, and whether it is possible to construct more analytical micro and macro models that capture the contradictory effects of labor mobility on employment and economic stability.

New Principles for Capital-Labor Relations and the Need for New Job Regulations

As we have seen, the model of implicit employment security, which was consistent with the Fordist growth regime, has been challenged during the past two decades. Many institutional, technological, and financial changes have taken place since the first oil price shock. Thus, in conformity with the historical approach taken by *régulation* theory, the basic question here is the following: is a new regime in labor management emerging, and, if so, what would be the role of labor mobility in this new regime?

Phase of Purely Defensive Flexibility Seems Over

Throughout the 1970s and 1980s, managers, engineers, and academics experimented in a process of trial and error. Business fads emerged, generated enthusiasm, and, when implemented, often delivered poor and disappointing results. Nowadays, converging views seem to be emerging as far as management is concerned. Of course, management practices are still rather different across industrialized countries: a comparison of five national studies conducted to illustrate the report presented at the Helsinki OECD Conference exhibits very distinct effective strategies in the United States and Japan and in France and West Germany; the Swedish model is largely original. To sum up the central message: a possible successor to Fordism can now be delineated and given a fairly coherent theoretical basis.

Initially, firms, sectors, and nations explored rather conservative strategies at the margin of Fordism. Some exported conventional Fordist methods to new geographical areas (for example, credit and direct investment to Latin American countries in the 1970s). Others maintained previous management practices but implemented defensive flexibility, for example by lowering wages, to preserve obsolete Fordist or create new tertiary jobs. Still others used the opportunities raised by new information technologies to keep alive Fordist principles (strong division of conception and execution, intensified monitoring of labor, control of labor intensity by new computerized machine tools). Finally, the rise of the service sectors and the deepening of labor market segmentation have also been widely used to compensate for the crisis within the Fordist manufacturing sectors (Boyer 1988a).

Nevertheless, international comparisons (Schmitter et al. forthcoming) suggest that these four strategies will not necessarily solve the crisis of the forgone management model, even if they can ease the passage from one regime to another. For example, the rather defensive strategy that has been adopted in North America along traditional Fordist principles seems to have delivered poorer results than the more innovative management style worked out by Japanese managers. Similarly, the very sluggish adaptation of British manufacturing has given the Japanese a lot of opportunities to direct investments to some key sectors, such as automobiles and consumer electronics. The rather defensive strategy used by English managers has been outperformed by the surprisingly successful introduction of new and different management principles.

The same result seems to emerge from a systematic statistical analysis of firms' trajectories during the 1970s and 1980s. In the case of France, it has been convincingly shown that sticking to old Taylorist principles of deskilling has usually led to very disappointing results (Choffel, Cuneo, and Kramarz 1988). First, small or medium size firms with high technical knowledge and sufficiently skilled workers have succeeded in gaining access to new external markets, which have replaced the domestic market. Second, of the large firms, only those that have mitigated or abandoned the deskilling of blue-collar workers inherent in Fordism have succeeded in limiting job destruction. A large majority of firms still following Taylorist strategies have incurred serious difficulties. Consequently, even within the same country, alternative strategies have led to greater or lesser success.

Twelve Principles for an Alternative to Fordism

From my compilations of several research projects, elaborated by specialists of management, technical innovation, industrial relations, and comparative political science, twelve common principles emerge (Boyer 1990). These principles can be elaborated into a coherent new management style that is capable of coping with the new features of the world economy in the 1990s (table 1-3).

Global optimization and continuous integration of innovations within production. *Global optimization of productive flows* (P1), once a traditional objective of scientific management, was progressively "forgotten" by Fordist management practices. Heavy mechanization and large inventories were conceived as methods for counterbalancing workers' lack of discipline and production disruptions caused by strikes. Consequently, during the 1960s in the automobile industry, for example, very costly and specialized equipment was underutilized, resulting in a decline in the productivity of capital. The new management model takes into account that the full optimization of productive flows has to deal symmetrically with labor, intermediate products, and equipment. In other words, if Taylorism was fighting against workers' laziness and underutilization, the new system fights against equipment underutilization and excessive inventories caused by idle working process. Just-in-time production has precisely this objective, very much in line, indeed, with original scientific management strategies. Total factor productivity, including the rotation circulation speed of capital, has replaced labor productivity as a major index of technical efficiency.

Fully integrated research, development, and production organization (P2) is the second major principle. In typical Fordist mass production, the sequence was clearly oriented from design, through production, and ultimately to marketing. The division in charge of conceiving new products did not really integrate any clear vision about the methods for manufacturing them; nor did they reflect on the needs and the demands of customers or buyers. Consequently, the lag between design and mass production of a new model used to be about six to seven years in the automobile industry. Furthermore, the product could turn out to be a failure if market trends changed in the meantime (for example, from large cars to more fuel-efficient ones). Moreover, in the 1970s and 1980s, the versatility of demand showed the process of design and innovation in conventional Fordist organizations to be very sluggish.

It is not surprising, therefore, that management theory now stresses the need for a fuller integration between these stages. The sequential relation between design and manufacturing is replaced by pooled or reciprocal coordinating mechanisms. All the national studies point out many experiments of plant integration in which microelectronics allow a closed and fast connection between design, production programming, quality control, and planning. This is, for example, the case in the German capital-goods industry (Pries and Trinczek 1989). In Japan, the management style seems to rely more on engineers' and technicians' mobility between the research and development department and the production site, back and forth (Watanabe 1989).

High quality and versatility at reasonable cost. *Closer relationships between producers and users* (P3) marks a third breakthrough with respect to typical Fordism. Previously, the marketing division was trying to find out how to launch and sell the product elaborated by the production department, itself inspired by scientific organization principles. The matching of new products to consumers' needs was therefore an ex post and sometimes costly process. Now the more successful firms seem to have elaborated a two-way flow of communications between the people conceiving new products and the users themselves. This is especially so for sophisticated capital goods and for consumer durables. Again, the Japanese firms provide a good example of a better integration of the R & D department, production, and the marketing division. It has been suggested that such a strategy reduces the risk of failures in, for example, the automobile industry since a sample of potential consumers have helped design the final product. The needs and proposals of final users are also a large source of innovation in the computer industry. In this sector, as in the machine tool industry (Watanabe

TABLE 1-3. From Fordism to a New Model: A Synoptic Presentation

Fordist principles	Challenges of the 1970s and 1980s	Principles of a new model
F1: Rationalization of labor is the main target, mechanization is the means	C1: Underutilization of equipment; large inventories of work in process	P1: Global optimization of the whole productive flows
F2: First design and then manufacture and organize work process	C2: Lags and large costs in passing from innovation to effective production	P2: Tentative full integration of research, development, and production
F3: Indirect and mediated links with consumers via marketing studies and strategies	C3: Losing touch with choosy consumers; failures in launching new products	P3: Close and long-lasting ties between producers and users; capture learning by using effects
F4: Low cost for standardized products is the first objective, quality the second	C4: Ex post quality controls cannot prevent a rising defect rate; consumers more selective about quality	P4: High quality at reasonable costs, via a zero-defect objective at each stage of the production process
F5: Mass production for stable and rising demands, batch production for unstable demands	C5: Even mass consumers' demands become uncertain: the Fordist production process appears rigid	P5: Insert the market demand into the production process to get fast responses
F6: Centralization of most decisions about production in a special division of a large firm	C6: Sluggish and inadequate reaction of headquarters to global and local shocks	P6: Decentralization as far as possible of production decisions within smaller and less hierarchical units
F7: Vertical integration, mitigated by circles of subcontractors	C7: Given radical innovations, even large firms can no more master the whole techniques needed for their core business	P7: Networking (and joint ventures) as a method for reaping both specialization and coordination gains
F8: Facing cyclical demand, subcontractors are used as stabilizing device to preserve large firms' employment	C8: During the 1970s, bankruptcies and/or loss of competence of subcontractors, now confronted with international competition	P8: Long-term and cooperative subcontracting as far as possible to promote joint technical innovations

TABLE 1-3 (continued)

Fordist principles	Challenges of the 1970s and 1980s	Principles of a new model
F9: Divide and specialize at most productive tasks; main source of productivity increases	C9: Excessive labor division might turn counterproductive: rising control and monitoring costs; built-in rigidity	P9: To recompose production, maintenance, quality control, and some management tasks might be more efficient, technically and economically
F10: Minimize the required general education and on-the-job training of productive tasks, according to Babbage's and Taylor's principles	C10: New technical opportunities (IT); more competition and uncertain demands challenge most of the previous very specialized tasks	P10: A new alliance between a minimal general education and effective on-the-job training to maximize individual and collective competence
F11: Hierarchical control and purely financial incentives to manufacture an implicit consent to poor job content	C11: Young generations, better educated and with different expectations, reject authoritarian management styles; too much control becomes counterproductive	P11: Human resource policies have to spur workers' competence and commitment and work out positive support for firms' strategy
F12: Adversarial industrial relations converge toward wage demands; collective agreements codify a provisional armistice	C12: Firms' employment might be hurt by the lack of cooperation and an exclusive concern for wage; a contrario, concession bargaining does not necessarily provide any advantage for wage earners	P12: An explicit and long-term compromise between managers and wage earners is needed to reap general support for this model: commitment versus good working conditions and/or job tenures and/or a fair sharing of modernization dividends

Source: Boyer 1989b:6.

1989), the closeness and cumulative nature of the links between final users and designers enhance the effects of learning by doing (Von Hippel 1988; Lundvall 1989).

High quality at reasonable cost (P4) can now be reached within the new management system. In the past, mass production of cheap but low-quality products was complemented by craft and customized production of top-quality luxury goods. Under the old system, a clear trade-off had to be made between low cost and high quality. This feature turned out to be quite detrimental to many Fordist industries. In the automobile industry, for example, when the buoyant market of new buyers shifted toward mere replacement demand, more sophisticated consumers became aware of quality and much more choosy than before. Typical American mass producers were consequently challenged by Japanese, German, and Swedish models, which integrated a concern for servicing, durability, fuel efficiency, and so on. Traditionally, however, high quality was associated with small or medium-size runs. The electronification of equipment goods, in particular, the computerization of design and manufacturing, has provided both a reduction in costs (since changing a model may take only a few minutes rather than a whole day or week) and greater precision in metal cutting, melting and assembling. The Toyota system therefore provides, via a fragile and lean system, in contrast to the robust and buffered one typical of Fordist production, both higher productivity and better quality.

The *insertion of market demand into the production process* (P5) defines another new principle. Again, within Fordist methods, the production capacities of large firms were set in order to satisfy the lower demand levels of the cyclical pattern characterizing the 1960s. By definition, the ideal was to immunize the assembly line against any perturbation from the environment. Subcontractors or second-rank producers were given the role of coping with uncertainty and demand variability (Piore and Sabel 1984).

This arrangement broke down when even mass-production consumer demand became uncertain in volume and composition. Given a significant internationalization of markets, demand could now be satisfied by imported goods, providing much more diversity. This is essentially the well-known problem of technical rigidity inherent in conventional Fordism. This new context initiated a genuine adaptation of scientific management. Given the new flexibility allowed by electronic machine tools, production can now be determined according to effective orders rather than oriented toward building inventories of goods to be sold later. Consequently, even fluctuating demand can be met by flexible, automated production and, symmetrically, small or medium-sized firms can master a segment of the market. The traditional division between large and smaller firms is therefore blurred; both have to cope with more variability in demand.

Networking, cooperation, decentralization. More *decentralization of production decisions* and smaller plant size (P6) are the direct consequences of the above principles. During the golden 1960s, labor management could be centralized within a specialized department and each plant given limited autonomy to implement the sophisticated rules associated with internal labor markets. Now, the variety of local and sectoral situations calls for each plant to have more autonomy. Even more, one observes on a large scale a trial-and-error process for finding out new modes of eliciting workers' commitment and determining pay. Theoretical models have clearly shown that when demand is uncertain (but not too great) and rapidly shifting from one product to another, decentralization might be more efficient than complete centralization (Aoki 1988b). Given the new context of the 1980s and 1990s, the same objectives of scientific management would now be fulfilled by a quite different internal organization of the large firm: the "J-firm" (the Japanese model) would replace the Fordist (or American) firm and its division into vertical departments, which are integrated only at the top of the hierarchy. At the same time, international comparative data exhibit a decline in average plant size, which may be evidence of a progressive implementation of this sixth principle.

Networking and joint ventures (P7) define a seventh feature. During the 1960s, vertical integration, to some extent mitigated by circles of subcontracting, was the usual way to reap the dynamically increasing returns to scale associated with R & D expenditures, high fixed investment costs, and learning by doing. This configuration evolved progressively during the 1970s and 1980s under the pressures of increasing instability and competition. Even large firms are no longer necessarily able to master the whole set of techniques needed to be efficient in their core business. For example, combining information processing and telecommunications completely shifted the boundaries between these two industries, inducing some struggles and joint ventures to gain control of the more crucial innovations. Simultaneously, considerable uncertainty prevails regarding the main feature of the emerging new sociotechnical system.

Even in mature industries such as automobile manufacturing, the electronification of consumer and capital goods calls for genuine competence, brought into the enterprise via joint ventures or networking to get the benefit of innovations. Networking might therefore be the code word of the 1990s. With various configurations, it seems to be the emerging organizational structure of the more dynamic part of the Italian economy, as well as most sectors of Japanese manufacturing. Even multinational firms are evolving from a centralized hub toward integrated networks: every unit, whatever its specialization, has potential links with other units belonging to the same firm. From a more theoretical point of view, networking is the contemporary method for reaping gains in both specialization and coordination.

Long-term and cooperative subcontracting (P8) is another consequence of the same trends, according to which institutionalizing complementarities between firms might enhance their joint productivity. In the Fordist era, large firms used subcontracting to cope with fluctuations in demand and/or to maintain oligopolistic pricing practices. During the past two decades, this has led to numerous bankruptcies of subcontractors and a loss of their know-how as large firms aimed to reduce their unit costs. In the United States, for example, this trend among machine tool producers seems to have been the consequence of arms-length relations between producers and users and between large and small firms (Dertouzos et al. 1989). A similar development has taken place in France, where a harsh and short-sighted subcontracting policy by large automobile manufacturers has finally led to a loss of competence and expertise in small and medium-sized firms (Lafont, Leborgne, and Lipietz 1982).

The need for competent and innovative subcontractors is now widely recognized, and a new model is emerging: the key reference is again the Japanese organization of subcontracting. The larger firm commits itself to multiyear contracting and helps the subcontractors modernize and buy modern electronic equipment. Some international comparative studies suggest that this long-term and cooperative strategy brings better results than the short-term, cost-minimizing Fordist strategy (Leborgne 1987).

A new compromise: polyvalence and commitment to employment stability.
A reduction in the division of labor within the firm (P9) is also a key feature emerging
from both the limits of Fordism and the new opportunities opened up by information technologies. If confirmed by subsequent developments, this may be a major change, if not a total novelty, in long-term trends in scientific management.
Managers now realize that, contrary to conventional Taylorist methods, allocating
a larger scope of the tasks to each worker can benefit productivity. Production work
is therefore combined with management tasks at the shop-floor level, for example,
in maintenance, repair, inventories, and orders. Quality is improved and break-
downs are more easily diagnosed and repaired when some shop-floor-level management is done by skilled workers and not by outside controllers or special
maintenance workers. Increases in productivity as a result of the better use of human abilities is the best response to economic uncertainty and a major source of innovation. Consequently, one observes in many OECD countries a redefinition of
the hierarchy toward a reduction of the layers of middle management.

On-the-job training and general education are brought into a new alliance (P10).
The Fordist system used to rely on highly skilled technicians, engineers, and
managers with a high degree of general education on the one hand and on a larger
fraction of the work force being trained mainly on the job and having a poor
general education on the other. The shift in manufacturing tasks from those that
are purely physical to those that are predominantly intellectual and monitoring
activities calls for adequate literacy and numeracy in typical blue-collar jobs.
Similarly, in the tertiary sector, computerization calls for fairly good abilities to
master abstraction, routines, and procedures (i.e., skills that used to be the logical
outcome of a successful general education system).

A converging set of evidence suggests that the balance is now shifting toward
the need for a higher level of general education for the majority of blue- and
white-collar workers. Greater polyvalence calls for initiative, commitment, and a
problem-solving orientation among assembly-line workers as well. The performance of firms depends more and more on adequate behavior and initiatives by
workers to bring about efficient decentralization and centralization of management and production. Learning by doing and learning by communicating with
other workers or departments are key factors.

Consequently, *skills* have to be enhanced *as a way of increasing commitment,
competence, and productivity* (P11). Again, during the Fordist era, Taylorist principles implied that engineers should conceive equipment and plant organization
with the aim of minimizing skills (i.e., by permanently downgrading the competence required of blue-collar workers). In the 1980s, managers saw the limits
of this strategy. A new motto, more than a business fad, is therefore emerging:
the quality and commitment of the work force are essential components in
achieving a competitive edge in the firm, sector, or country. This new principle
is clearly at odds with previous trends in labor management and has tremendous
consequences for labor markets, education, training, and retraining. Maximizing
skills and then extracting from them the maximum know-how and competence
might be one of the genuine features of the Japanese model investigated by Aoki
(1988b). Convincing analyses suggest that the Japanese system of employment

security in large firms is not only a legacy of Confucian or paternalistic values but a rational strategy, given the important learning-by-doing effects and the importance of the support of the firm by its employees (Koike 1987a).

More commitment also means advantages for wage earners: good wages and/ or more employment stability (P12). No doubt, this new model requires much more commitment from workers and that they each manage a broader range of work tasks. Such commitment and flexibility cannot be reaped by the firm unless wage earners are offered an explicit advantage. The theoretical analysis of Japanese firms by Aoki (1988b) suggests that a principle of dynamic surplus sharing is needed to induce workers to consent. It can be fulfilled either through explicit (quasi-) employment security or through a wage system that rewards individual commitment, linked to firm, sectoral or national performance. OECD countries exhibit various mixes of these two types of rewards.

In the long run, the principle of dynamic surplus sharing has important implications regarding the viability of such a new management style, since it is hard to imagine well-educated, strongly committed workers being underpaid and recurrently laid off during cyclical downturns. Such a compromise is not easy to negotiate in countries where adversarial labor relations have a long tradition. The opportunities of a purely defensive strategy are not without appeal, especially when unions are disoriented, union membership is declining, and initiative has shifted toward the employers' side. Nevertheless, most experts in the United States now realize how essential such a new compromise is: commitment versus some kind of employment stability. In contrast, the German and Swedish cases suggest that strong unions and a continuous process of negotiation might promote the diffusion of new technologies. This was a key message of the Sundquist report (1988).

The Job Tenure Ideal: An Essential Component of the New Management Model

The place of employment protection and job stability in the post-Fordist regime now has to be discussed in more depth. This is not easy, since the diffusion of this new regime is rather recent. Nevertheless, comparative studies and theoretical models suggest five hypotheses.

Job instability might hinder the viability of the new management style. Facing recurrent disturbances and grown uncertainties about economic developments and policies, it has been rational for firms to value flexible employment contracts (i.e., contracts implying short tenures and easily revised wage rates). The stiffening of international competition and deregulatory policies have triggered efforts to curb labor costs. There is no doubt that the freedom to adjust employment levels has contributed to static efficiency (i.e., the optimal reaction to varying demands and relative prices). This type of flexibility might explain why the employment share of large firms declined to the benefit of small or medium-sized enterprises in almost all OECD countries. If long-term optimal management were to result from a series of short-sighted decisions, numerical employment flexibility would be the ideal to be pursued.

Nevertheless, the long-range effects of this strategy might be to inhibit or even contradict the implementation of Toyotism or Volvoism as successors to Fordism. In fact, employment instability might be detrimental to most of the twelve founding principles listed in table 1-3. How are high-quality standards to be attained if sophisticated plants are run by temporary workers who cannot capture the learning effects associated with complex modern production organization (P4)? Of course, global optimization (P1) and swift reactions to demand (P5) can be obtained by firing and hiring workers according to the level of inventories, demand, and profitability. But then management should not ask workers to be loyal and committed to a firm they work for only temporarily. Similarly, in-house training policies will be largely wasteful and irrational if, because of high turnover, newly trained workers have to look for another job and/or are systematically fired when there is a recession. Principles P9, P10, and P11 collapse.

Likewise, any long-term compromise between managers and wage earners is devoid of meaning if workers do not benefit from long-term employment contracts or at least implicit employment security. Of course, higher wages could compensate for employment instability, at least from a theoretical standpoint. But all empirical studies suggest that high employment instability and low wages are closely linked for secondary jobs, whereas the primary sector exhibits the opposite features. Consequently, complete freedom in hiring and firing might put firms, sectors, or countries on the wrong track as far as the new industrial organization is concerned. Comparative research suggests that the more flexible the labor market, the more severe the Fordist nostalgia (Boyer 1989a). On the contrary, a collectively bargained or legal constraint on employment can induce much more innovative strategies. Why not convert this employment rigidity into an advantage and look for high internal flexibility? Remember the Japanese "flexible rigidities" (Dore 1987).

Job tenure or employment inertia may be an inducement to organizational flexibility. Basically, the new management model looks for global optimization in the use of human resources, equipment, raw materials, and information. These are mainly internal issues that cannot be solved by pure market transactions; they call for a strong cooperative climate between engineers and marketing specialists, foremen and blue-collar workers, banking and finance, stockholders and managers. Within capital-labor relations, a minimum stability of employment is a prerequisite for adhesion to this new model.

Consequently, some dismissals and financial losses can be incurred in the short term if an unexpected and severe recession makes part of the work force redundant. But this institutionalized rigidity maintains the morale and the incentive among wage earners in a manner such that the long-term trajectory may turn out to be quite original. The cumulative competence associated with learning by doing, learning by using new equipment, and learning by reassignments within the firm promotes high product quality (P4), versatility in switching from one job to another (P9), and a strong aptitude to respond to technical innovations and new market opportunities. The Toyotist or Volvoist models need more informational exchange, sophisticated control procedures, and equipment as new sources of productivity, which can be reaped only when there is a core of highly stable workers. Of course, subcontracting can be used to dampen fluctuations in demand, but even then, the Italian or Japanese systems suggest that it might be efficient in the long run to codify stable, long-term relationships between large firms and their network of subcontractors. Contract termination is the measure of last resort, not the first one in this new model: varying bonuses, wages, hours, shifting workers from one job to another, launching new products, or implementing new processes usually provide sufficient scope for adaptation, at least as long as recessions do not become cumulative depressions.

This shift in the organizational paradigm is not without precedent. A retrospective of the U.S. automobile industry over one century suggests that job stability was an initial objective of Henry Ford himself (Raff 1988; Boyer and Orlean 1990). The assembly line for the Model T generated a surge in labor turnover: this was the origin of Ford's famous five-dollar-day policy. During the interwar period, competition shifted from price competition toward product differentiation. The annual model changes promoted by General Motors (GM) led to a reorganization of the assembly line precisely to achieve this new objective (Houndshell 1984). Broadly speaking, high wages and ongoing product innovations were two means for promoting a minimum of employment stability, which was considered beneficial to both workers and managers. Simultaneously, a complete network of subcontractors, closely linked to GM, was organized. In a sense, the J or the S (i.e., Swedish) models are the modern and contemporary followers of this key objective, constantly pursued by scientific management. Employment stability is far from being contradicted by this long history of industrial organization and technology. But then how are short-term quantitative disturbances to be coped with?

Actual economies are mixing job tenure and labor mobility. Much historical research suggests that leading industrial models do not cover the whole spectrum of activities and firms. In the long-run, various organizational forms coexist and usually have rather similar economic performance. For example, even if the Fordist era had exhibited a clear tendency toward homogenization of capital-labor relations, the opposition between primary and secondary jobs would still have existed and played a functional role in coping with economic fluctuations and uncertainty (Boyer 1981). Probably the same disparity will prevail within the fully developed Toyotist/Sonyist model.

For simplicity's sake, let me define two configurations of the capital-labor relation and its response to flexibility. *Secondary jobs* are usually characterized by short tenures, atypical work contracts, strong hierarchical control, and conventional equipment. Rather low wages are highly sensitive to external economic developments and labor market imbalances. This could be labeled defensive flexibility. *Primary jobs* benefit from long-term employment relationships, conventional (i.e., permanent, full-time) employment contracts, significant work autonomy, and modern equipment, whereas wages reflect institutionalized career patterns and internal procedures linking income to individual and collective performance. This can be termed offensive flexibility (Boyer 1988b).

A French survey (Bué 1989) allows us to estimate the relative scope of these two categories (table 1-4). Professionals and technicians, women more than men,

TABLE 1-4. Patterns of Flexibility in French Firms, 1988

Work force characteristics	Offensive flexibility	Defensive flexibility
Professionals	3%	15%
Technicians	9	33
White collars	44	41
Workers	42	10
Total	100%	100%
Men	53%	45%
Women	47	55
Total	100%	100%
Age 15 to 24 years	42%	4%
25 to 29 years	38	58
40 to 49 years	11	23
50 to 59 years	7	15
More than 60 years	2	1
Total	100%	100%
Number of employed	1,500,000	850,000

Source: Bué 1989:35.

and workers between twenty-five and thirty-nine years are the main beneficiaries of offensive flexibility, including some job stability. By contrast, young workers under twenty-five and blue-collar workers usually obtain only short-term employment contracts and therefore suffer from a high degree of employment instability. Seemingly, only one-third of the total work force benefits from offensive flexibility.

The basic issue then is the following: which of the two configurations determines the overall evolution of average wages, total employment, and average productivity? During the 1960s, the primary sector, formalizing a Fordist compromise, was clearly setting the norms. Wage increases were diffusing from leading sectors to the rest of the economy; since quasi-full employment prevailed, the secondary sector benefited from similar increases. Macroeconomic stability tended to promote implicit job security, even in the secondary sector but, of course, less complete than within large Fordist firms in the primary sector.

Nowadays, under the pressure of persistent mass unemployment, the mechanisms might be partially reversed: the fear of losing a good job in the primary sector is leveling off wage demands. Similarly, the high degree of employment security enjoyed by some insiders is balanced by very high turnover in the secondary market. One unintended effect of a universalized and inadequately institutionalized employment security regime could therefore be to foster labor market segmentation and sharpen social inequalities among wage earners.

A large variety of adjustments to tasks, hours, or wages can cope with job stability. Conventionally, employment stability can be expressed by the adjustment speed term within an econometric equation linking effective employment

TABLE 1-5. Work Force Adjustment and Institutional Rigidities

| Countries | Employment adjustment | | Hours Adjustment | | Institutional | Firms |
	Adjustment speed (δ)	Average lag (d)	Adjustment speed (δ)	Average lag (d)	obstacles to employment variations	perceiving rigidities
Italy	0.28	2.57	0.65	0.54	***	83
France	0.24	3.17	0.57	0.75	***	81
Germany	0.43	1.33	0.65	0.54	***	56
United Kingdom	0.20	4.00	0.40	1.50	0	26
United States	0.49	1.04	0.67	0.49	*	—

Source: Columns 1–4 from Maurau and Oudinet 1988: 4–17.

If N_t^* is optimum employment, the effective level N_t is set according to

$$\frac{N_t}{N_{t-1}} = \left(\frac{N_t^*}{N_{t-1}}\right)^\delta$$

where δ = adjustment speed

and $d = \dfrac{1-\delta}{\delta}$ average lag for adjusting effective to optimal employment.

to its past level and efficient employment (table 1-5). It takes three years in France and two and a half in Italy to adjust manufacturing employment, whereas American and German manufacturing needs only one year. This hierarchy does not fit with existing institutional obstacles to employment variations: in spite of the absence of any strong legislation, British industry is the slowest. Similarly, Germany and the United States are rather close from an econometric point of view in spite of the highly regulated system in the former and the largely free and decentralized system in the latter. Again, the looseness of the connection between labor laws and the precise features of the *régulation* mode is apparent.

Further, for a given average lag, the same ex post flexibility in total hours worked can be reached by varying weekly working time, according to the level of demand and inventories. It is striking to observe a strong convergence in the estimates for average lag when adjusting total hours (table 1-5). The only exception is the United Kingdom, where sophisticated job rules seem to put severe constraints upon this flexibility mechanism. The sharp contrast to the perception of rigidity by firms is interesting. The British system, usually considered very flexible, might well be the most rigid, at least as far as econometric studies are apt to distinguish between rigid and flexible systems.

Wage flexibility is another method for preventing fast employment adjustments. Theoretical models have attempted to show that an adequate wage formula (basic wage plus profit sharing) would ensure stable, full employment (Weitzman 1985). Large Japanese firms are often assumed to be the perfect example of such a complementarity of employment stability and wage flexibility. Most econometric studies indeed confirm that employment adjustment lags in the Japanese manufacturing sector are considerable compared to the United States, even if some econometric problems are pending (table 1-6) (see also Abraham and Houseman, chap. 6). Finally, sectors sheltered from foreign competition, such as conventional services, might exhibit an opposite property: employment is adjusted to the current unemployment rate according to a compensating mechanism with respect to the manufacturing industries.

Here again we note strong national specificities that do not seem to have declined during the 1980s. This strong exception to the common view about the convergence of industrial relations and management deserves some explanation.

A whole spectrum of institutional arrangements can provide job security. A genuine theory of the firm has recently emerged from quite contrasting traditions (Teece 1989; Aoki 1988b; Favereau 1989; Harvard Business Review 1986; OECD 1988b). Basically, the enterprise is seen as the locus of a collective process of learning by doing, which converts external innovations into new opportunities in order to build up or preserve some monopoly power. The viability of any firm thus depends on the sophistication of such a process. Nevertheless, the effective implementation of this model varies greatly according to national traditions, culture, and institutional settings. A recent research project has yielded a detailed account of such diversity (Boyer 1990a). I will therefore limit this short description to the job security issue.

The United States is the traditional land of large external stability (see table 1-2). Nevertheless, for a decade now, many experts have recognized that this might lead to a loss of expertise and should be corrected by an explicit accord between labor and capital (*Business Week* 1980). Even the automobile industry, which uses recurrent layoffs, has experimented with new compromises based on selecting more efficient workers and providing them with a form of employment guarantee and good wages. The SATURN project has had precisely this objective. In spite of this innovation, defensive flexibility still constitutes the dominant strategy: layoffs, geographic mobility of capital and workers, and more generally a widening of wage differentials and an increasing heterogeneity in employment contracts (Rosenberg 1989a) have served to prolong the life of the American model of decentralized defensive flexibility.

Japan shares some features with the United States, such as the role of large firms, the decentralized nature of collective bargaining and rather weak and declining unions. Nevertheless, Japan seems to explore a more offensive flexibility. The internal mobility of workers from one task to another, permanent retraining within the firm and the flexibility allowed by profit sharing make dismissals a measure of last resort usually undertaken only after more than two years of bad economic performance (Koike 1987a). Paradoxically, small and medium-sized firms do not dismiss workers more frequently than larger ones. This may be indirect evidence of the impact of the job tenure ideal within the whole economy. Simultaneously, large flexibility in working hours allows fast reactions to unexpected variations in demand or relative prices. In the long run, enhancing the competence of core workers and continuously launching new products and new processes are the best guarantee of lifetime employment.

TABLE 1-6. Sectoral Patterns of Work Force Adjustment

	Manufacturing				Sheltered sectors			
	Short-term elasticity	Average lag of employment (years)	Share employment/ hours	Elasticity with respect to relative costs	Short-term elasticity	Average lag of employment (years)	Share employment/ hours	Elasticity with respect to relative costs
Italy	0.26	8.3	41%	0.4	0.43	6.6	31%	0.1
France	0.28	3.8	74	—	0.31	2.2	100	—
Germany	0.58	1.6	66	—	0.52	2.1	62	0.2
United Kingdom	0.32	2.6	87	0.20	0.43	1.3	100	—
United States	0.75	0.7	71	0.15	0.54	1.2	84	0.35
Japan	0.13	19.0	38	0.7	0.55	0.5	70	—

Source: MIMOSA 1990:151.

Sweden and to some extent Austria provide a second configuration of offensive flexibility. Contrary to the two previous cases, strong and unique unions bargain at a centralized level over wages, employment, social welfare, job subsidies, and so on. Such an integration and centralization of the quasi-totality of the capital-labor nexus leads to genuine adjustments. First, job creation is the main objective of active labor market policies, rather than the mere relief of unemployment as in most EC countries. Second, retraining and mobility are organized by collective agreements between unions, firms, and public agencies. Third, in the long run, dynamism in process and product innovations is considered the best method for providing secure and well-paid jobs. Fourth, and finally, the commitment to full employment provides strong incentives for the adoption of such offensive flexibility.

France and Italy (like most EC countries) are following a hybrid model, between social democratic flexibility and decentralized defensive strategies. Generally, unions are stronger than in the United States but weaker or more divided than in Sweden or Austria. Similarly, the level of bargaining is between that of a totally decentralized and a highly centralized system. Welfare policies have favored wage compensation rather than active job creation as their main objective, even if new trends have emerged since the mid-1980s. Consequently, adjustments take place with the help of a new segmentation of labor markets: significant employment stability in large firms is compensated for by high instability among young workers and alternating periods of unemployment and short-term employment. Since European firms traditionally experience some difficulties in launching successful new products, they generally have reacted to a structural crisis by drastically rationalizing their production process.

Is there an optimal form of flexibility that would minimize the unemployment rate and average duration of unemployment spells? Table 1-2 suggests that the same quasi-return to full employment has been obtained both by decentralized offensive strategies (Japan) and the social democratic configuration (Sweden and to a lesser extent Austria). The U.S.-style decentralized defensive flexibility provides a return to standard unemployment rates, even if it sharpens social inequalities and performs poorly in terms of productivity and competitiveness. The worst case corresponds to the hybrid European model; of course, social inequalities are lower, but long-term and high youth unemployment remains a challenge for the 1990s (Rowthorn 1990).

One could imagine a U-shaped relationship between employment security and unemployment: at both extremes strong incentives propel the economy toward quasi-full employment. In a mixed system, however, unemployment can persist in the long run and even destabilize previous homogeneous labor legislation. Mutatis mutandis, one finds a parallel with the influence of the degree of decentralization on macroeconomic performance (OECD 1990c; Calmfors and Driffill 1988; Bowles and Boyer 1990).

A central conclusion emerges. Employment security per se does not induce unemployment. Only its inadequate institutionalization or incompatibility with the prevailing modes of *régulation* has such a negative impact.

The Economics of Workers' Protection: Preliminary Insights

The findings reported so far have provided the institutional and economic background necessary for a more analytical approach. I will now provide a brief survey of some basic models of job stability and employment adjustment speed. As far as possible, empirical data will be brought into the debate. Six provisional results are proposed for discussion and further investigation.

French Employment Deregulation Experience

Since the early 1980s, French managers had been complaining about excessive state interventions into dismissal procedures. Dismissals for economic reasons had to be approved by the Inspection du Travail, a branch of the Ministry of Employment and Social Affairs. The conservative government elected in 1986 decided to satisfy these very vocal demands from the employers' association (CNPF). Very crude and unconvincing surveys suggested that the abolition of these dismissal restraints would create about 400,000 jobs. The impact seems to have been grossly overstated, as becomes clear from a short summary of the statistical analyses made ex post to assess the effective impact of the 3 July 1986 and 1 January 1987 laws that abolished the administrative authorization of dismissals (see also Maurau and Charraud, chaps. 19 and 20).

The short-term impact was clear enough, although more moderate than expected: dismissals seem to have increased by some forty thousand. This represents less than 0.2 percent of total employment. This minor short-term impact might explain why this episode seems almost forgotten today. In addition, many other measures (training subsidies to firms, fixed-term contracts) have been affecting the French labor market, making it difficult to disentangle the effects of a single legal change and public intervention. Ironically, the deregulatory measures have also halted the gathering of statistical time-series data on dismissals by firms, thereby rendering direct econometric studies impossible.

The long-term effects, if there were any at all, were apparently minor as well. The cyclical pattern of the number of workers dismissed for economic reasons changed only briefly; the declining numbers of dismissals after 1987 was induced by the general economic recovery and the ensuing job creations (see Maurau, chap. 19). It would be excessive to attribute all the newly created jobs to the deregulation laws. Significantly, the most recent official assessments of French labor market policies do not even mention them (INSEE 1989). Moreover, the improvement in the employment outlook seems to have outpaced even the rather optimistic expectations of firms. It has been shown elsewhere that the recovery of the world economy is the main factor responsible for the improvement in job creation performance in France and the rest of Europe at the cost of some slowdown in productivity relative to past regularities (Boyer 1990a). This apparently contradicts the premises of labor market deregulation (fig. 1-5).

The assessment of the medium-term impact calls for an explicit micro-modeling

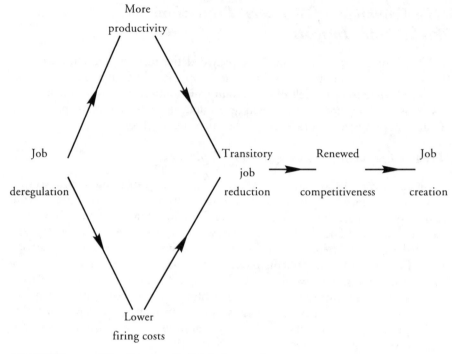

FIGURE 1-5. The "Dream" of Job Deregulation

of the employment behavior of firms. According to conventional wisdom, the relation of wage costs to productivity is supposed to be the main determinant of hiring decisions. Within this model, job deregulation is reducing severance payments, shortening adjustment lags, and hence lowering unit labor costs. The final impact on the employment level is therefore proportional to the long-term elasticity of total labor costs (table 1-7). Various simulations exhibit quite moderate impacts.

First, labor market deregulation has only a once-and-for-all effect on the long-term employment level. In the absence of dynamic increasing returns to scale, this is quite a conventional result. In the long-term, the employment variations are determined by technical change and demand trends.

Second, the positive impact is finally smaller than expected by the proponents of deregulation. In the most favorable case, the gains in employment would be around 2 percent, the central estimate shows around 0.5 percent. For the French manufacturing sector, in the absence of any significant real-wage elasticity, the effect would be nil. This does not necessarily contradict the previous statistical analyses; after a transitory acceleration of dismissals, they recover their previous dynamic.

Of course, this finding does not pretend to be of universal validity. It may be largely specific to the French or European economies. While price elasticities are quite high in Japan, they are not significant in Germany and in France, and the

TABLE 1-7. Employment Gains from Job Deregulation: Alternative Estimates

Cost of dismissal $\delta \cdot (d + s)$	High dismissal rate ($\delta = 0.2$)		Low dismissal rate ($\delta = 0.1$)	
β Elasticities	High cost $(d + s) = 1/6$	Low cost $(d + s) = 1/12$	High cost $(d + s) = 1/6$	Low cost $(d + s) = 1/12$
High (0.6)	2%	1 %	1 %	0.5%
Average (0.3)	1%	0.5%	0.5%	0.25%
Nil (0)	0	0	0	0

$(d + s) = 1/6$ corresponds to an average two months' lag in dismissal or two-month severance payment; $(d + s) = 1/12$, to one month.

results vary for the manufacturing sectors and the sheltered services (table 1-6). Nevertheless, it is consistent with the cross-national statistical analysis and with other approaches to be presented below.

The Microeconomics of Employment Regulation

Let us now address the central issue from a more theoretical point of view: should totally rational firms instantaneously adjust their employment and hours to orders, demand, and relative prices? The standard neoclassical model, assuming no adjustment costs, perfect information, and the assimilation of labor with its services, unambiguously answers in the affirmative. But if any of these three assumptions is abolished, an optimum reaction lag exists, which is positive. Consequently, even in the absence of public regulation or restraints imposed by collective agreements, firms should not adapt their activity levels instantaneously. After all, this was precisely the case during the nineteenth century and the interwar period. The speed of adjustment was significant but not infinite (see table 1-1). At least three arguments can explain such a spontaneous employment inertia.

Significant private hiring and firing costs are to be taken into account when a firm has to make an employment decision within an uncertain environment. If, for example, a firm observes a decline in its sales, it is not immediately possible to interpret this as a forthcoming recession; the firm has to wait for further information to be sure that the decline is not merely transitory. In the case of a premature and wrong decision, managers would incur the extra costs associated with hiring and firing procedures. It has been shown both theoretically and empirically that this factor alone is sufficient to generate a productivity cycle by a delayed adjustment of employment to demand (Soderstrom 1972). A priori, the average lag would increase with the length of firm-specific training, the costs of searching for new job candidates, and with the uncertainty about the macroeconomic environment (for this last influence, see Flanagan 1988). These two factors could explain why employment adjustments were so sluggish following the two oil shocks: labor was more highly skilled than during the 1930s, and it took time for managers to adjust their previously optimistic expectations to the reality of the Fordist structural crisis. If this interpretation is correct, a significant proportion of employment rigidity would derive from the very rational behavior of private firms, reinforced by the features of modern capitalism. Public regulation would add or shift, but not create, job rigidities.

According to a second theory, job security might correspond to a form of insurance for workers. Implicit contract theory has delivered precisely such a message and explains nominal wage rigidities accordingly. Since firms can diversify their assets and are therefore less risk-adverse than their workers, they will accept a wage level independent of their financial performance, as long as it is lower than the Walrasian equilibrium wage. The difference would correspond to a kind of insurance granted to workers by rational firms. Therefore, the employment contract would be intertemporal in nature and involve two components: an exchange of labor services against a wage and an insurance against adverse situations (Azariadis and Stiglitz 1983; Cooper 1987).

Elaborating on this basic model, one can imagine that workers may prefer wage cuts in exchange for keeping their jobs. By definition of the equilibrium concept used to solve the confrontation between firms and workers, it would be rational for managers to accept such a contract, which, on average, provides the same profits over a whole cycle. From an empirical standpoint, this model captures some of the basic features of modern employment contracts (Boyer and Reynaud 1988). Nevertheless, it implies a choice between the relative stability of wages and unemployment. Such a trade-off might be observed in international comparisons: job tenure seems to decrease from Japan, through Europe to the United States and Canada (see table 1-2). For a given national economy, however, this trade-off is not always evident: the primary sector exhibits good and rather stable wages combined with significant job stability, whereas the opposite configuration prevails in the secondary sector. Again, this rigidity might depend on public regulations, the unemployment benefit system, and collective agreements, since it is not the exclusive outcome of explicit job regulation. It can be mutually advantageous for managers and wage earners to keep employment as stable as possible.

Finally, efficiency wage theories argue that job security might induce workers' commitment and loyalty. In fact, labor cannot be considered a pure service or commodity. First, the disposition over labor services is purchased in the market, and, then the firm has to extract the maximum effort from a given time unit of labor services. To monitor this power relation within the production process, firms usually mix various methods: effort monitoring through supervisors and automatic equipment and indexing of wages to individual and collective performance, where the latter can be measured unambiguously. In modern capitalist processes with work teams and assembly lines, built-in complementarities and rigidities make work effort difficult to control. For conventional efficiency theory (Solow 1979), the payment of a wage in excess of Walrasian equilibrium levels is the method for stimulating productivity among workers. But this framework can easily be extended to employment security (Aoki 1988b). Managers and workers can agree on a long-term compromise: lower wages and higher work effort against employment security. The threat of a noncooperative strategy that would destroy this equilibrium is all the more unlikely the more important the learning effects within the firm. Consequently, the asset specificity of human resources plays an important role in job tenure (Williamson 1985). This feature fits with the stylized facts derived from research on the German system (Streeck 1991; Buechtemann 1989a).

Contrary to conventional labor market theory, modern micro-foundations of employment relationships imply some inertia in employment adjustments. This derives from purely rational decisions of managers facing uncertainty, human resources specificity, learning-by-doing effects, and the commitment or loyalty dilemma. Such implicit employment security can occur without any regulation or collective agreement about employment protection. Thus, labor law deregulation does not remove this component of employment inertia. This could explain the weak effects of the French 1986–1987 laws.

Macroeconomic Aspects of Employment Security

Let us now turn to the macroeconomic consequences of micro-based or institutionalized employment rigidities. Again, the conventional wisdom suggests that maximum flexibility should be optimal for full employment and innovation. While there can be no doubt that the breaking down of the Fordist growth regime has challenged most of its institutional forms, it is nevertheless important to question whether maximum flexibility is optimal at the macroeconomic level. Three major arguments support such a conclusion.

A lesson from the renewal of classical dynamic macroeconomic theory. Recent research has delivered stimulating models for long-term capitalist growth (Dumenil and Levy 1986, 1989). In a decentralized economy, each firm reacts according to its perceived disequilibriums: capital capacity utilization, ratio of inventories to sales, and possibly excess labor. The related decision of each firm leads to a new macroeconomic equilibrium, characterized by new imbalances for each firm. In this model, the consumption of wage earners and investment in circulating capital are endogenous, contrary to the Keynesian tradition. What will be the stationary states and the dynamic behavior of such an idealized system?

First, a multiplicity of equilibria may emerge: the normal equilibrium, an overheating one, and a stagnating Keynesian one, depending on whether capacity utilization is standard, above, or below normal. Paradoxically, a high speed of adjustment to perceived disequilibria may trigger the coexistence of all three equilibria. In a sense, the dynamics of the economy are simpler and easier to control if adjustment speed is moderate (see appendix to the chapter).

Second, some of these equilibria may become unstable if the adjustment speed is superior to some threshold that itself depends on the whole set of macroeconomic parameters of the model. For example, the economy can be pushed into a cumulative depression, resulting in a complete collapse. An excessive sensitivity by firms to disequilibria will trigger such global instability. The sum of totally rational individual behavior leads to a macroeconomic breakdown.

This surprising but convincing result puts a severe caveat on the motto of the mid-1980s, according to which it was desirable for governments to push for maximum flexibility. Since then, many researchers (Calmfors and Driffill 1988; OECD 1988b; Rowthorn 1975; Bowles and Boyer 1990) have cast doubts on such an extremist view. What has been learned about wage formation probably has to be extended and adapted to the issue of employment security.

1929: Almost complete employment flexibility but a complete collapse. Historical studies on the basis of the *régulation* approach provide a further condition (Boyer and Mistral 1978). The 1929 crash cannot be attributed to any excessive rigidity since all the markets for products, finance, and labor were characterized by extremely fast adjustments and very few limiting institutional factors at that time. Econometric analyses of price and wage formation as well as employment adjustments clearly show major differences with respect to the contemporary monopolist *régulation* mode.

The nominal wage reacted to the variation in industrial production indexes through rather competitive mechanisms, although less so than in the nineteenth century (Boyer 1979). Unions were unable to stop the deflation of wages, whereas public regulations were embryonic, at odds with neoclassical views of this period.

Similarly, prices were highly sensitive to excess capacity and competition, in constrast to the stability of the era of mark-up price formation, which is typical of the Fordist era. Consequently, a cumulative deflation followed the stock market since distress sales fed a vicious circle of depression and deflation. Again, cartels and collusive behavior were unable to stop this decline.

Employment was adjusted quite rapidly to declining demand and profitability. The comparison with 1973–74 is illuminating with regard to the magnitude of the differences between the two capital-labor nexuses (table 1-1). Simultaneously, hours were adjusted downward. It is therefore hard to point to any severe rigidity since job security regulations were nonexistent.

Nevertheless, the constellation that marked these three flexibilities did not stop the cumulative depression. Quite the contrary, the constellation seems to have propagated it from product markets to the labor market, from the basic to the industrial system in a dramatic spillover. Few contemporary economists could imagine that the severity of the depression was not linked to excessive rigidities but to insufficient safety nets (Fisher 1933). Simulations of a simple *régulationist* model suggest that wage indexing, oligopolistic competition, and sluggish employment adjustments prevented 1973 from becoming a repetition of 1929 (Boyer and Mistral 1978; Boyer 1988a).

The simultaneity of wage and employment flexibility may have devastating consequences for the stability of the labor market. This is a possible conclusion drawn from a standard neoclassical model. On the one hand, the employment level is supposed to vary in accordance with the past level of wages. On the other hand, wages react with a one-period lag to the level of employment, here equivalent to unemployment. Again, maximum flexibility does not stabilize the labor market per se.

First, wage and employment flexibilities are substitutes and not complementary strategies. This point has been clearly recognized by empirical studies (Emerson 1988a; Metcalf 1987b; Boyer 1988b) but is rarely taken into account by policy recommendations. Most conservative governments have been pushing for all forms of defensive flexibility simultaneously.

Second, combining wage flexibility with rapid employment adjustments may lead to structural instability in the labor market. This argument can be reinforced by a complete Keynesian model of effective demand: up to some threshold, any initial job cuts trigger a further weakening of demand, which through spillover effects induces further employment reductions (Boyer 1988b).

Modern theories, both micro and macro, significantly revise the conventional view derived from general equilibrium theory. In modern economies with major uncertainties, large indivisibilities, important learning-by-doing effects, and commitment problems, some degree of employment security might be optimal. Furthermore, as long as they are not excessive, the related frictions have a favorable impact on macroeconomic stability. Moderate flexibility seems better than maximum flexibility. Of course, more sophisticated models are needed to lend support to such a general statement. Two will be put forward below.

External Flexibility May Hinder Innovation and Long-Term Efficiency

Capitalist market economies are supposed to be characterized by both *static* and *dynamic efficiency*. The first relates to the short-term allocation of scarce resources to competing uses to satisfy unlimited needs. Most earlier analyses have addressed this issue. But what about dynamic efficiency—the ability of capitalism to push entrepreneurs constantly to innovate, improve productivity, and satisfy new needs in order to survive? In other words, does employment security spur or hinder technological and organizational innovation? The abundant literature on the determinants of the intensity of technical change suggests a rather optimistic view: employment security might well stimulate product and process innovation and therefore promote long-term economic growth (see also Schellhaass, chap. 3).

Innovation diffusion and the adjustment dilemma. On the one hand, if labor were totally immobile with respect to work tasks, skills, firms, regions, and so on, most of the dynamism associated with innovation would be blocked. By definition, technical change shifts relative opportunities, creates new products, finds new locations, and drastically changes the skill content of mass-produced goods. Accordingly, it can be argued that in societies where job rules are very detailed and inflexible, the diffusion of new technologies will be more sluggish than in societies with a high level of internal flexibility. Compare, for example, the British with the German manufacturing sector or the American with the Japanese (Boyer 1989a).

On the other hand, if adjustment is too fast, some neo-Schumpeterian applied models exhibit a less known but apparently serious opposite danger: the economy collapses. If technical change is by nature uncertain, firms cannot know the exact distribution of its returns. If they myopically optimize their choice of technique and production, they can go bankrupt when a series of major disturbances manifest the absence of any stationarity of their distribution (Heiner 1988). At the macro level, a fast adoption of the best available technology will first stimulate productivity, competitiveness, and hence growth. But the excessive homogenization of production techniques makes the economy highly sensitive to any sharp deviation in relative prices or sectoral demand. Because of insufficient productive variety, the output can totally collapse under an adverse disturbance (Eliasson 1989).

This suggests, once more, that employment adjustments and the adoption of new technologies should be gradual. An instantaneous change (if it were possible) would be optimal for neither the firm nor the economy at large.

Is technical change Schumpeterian or Leibensteinian? This question has far-reaching implications when discussing employment mobility. In fact, two broad contrasting conceptions seem to govern theorizing on technical change. The first, in its most radical version, assumes that technology can be altered only by the entry and exit of firms, each of which have different production sets that cannot be altered or modified once they are installed. Put differently, in these putty-clay models, the scrapping of obsolete equipment and its replacement by up-to-date equipment are the only methods available for increasing average productivity. Labor mobility is a prerequisite for technical change dynamism. According to this view, productivity increases should be higher in the United States and Canada, where firm and labor turnover are significantly higher, than in Japan, France, or Germany. A rough comparison of actual productivity figures (table 1-8) refutes this view (table 1-9). Nevertheless, the Schumpeterian mechanism may have been important during the 1970s and the 1980s, even if combined with other determinants of technical progress internal to each firm. Productive systems have been drastically transformed by the relative decline of old activities and the rise of new ones, according to a process inherent in any structural crisis.

An alternative view postulates that the efficiency of each technique can be continuously increased by incremental innovation and learning by doing and using or by permanently combining old equipment with new. In genuine neo-classical growth theory (Solow 1956), each factor, either capital or labor, sees its unit productivity increase as time elapses. In more sophisticated theories about endogenous technical change, cumulative production or the output of the capital goods sector governs experience effects and induces a cumulative productivity increase. In contrast, X-efficiency theories (see Leibenstein 1976) argue that firms are never on their production frontier but at some distance from it. This slack depends on the degree of competition, the profit rate, the growth of demand, and so on. According to this last conception, employment security might trigger product innovation and productivity increases, which in turn enable firms to comply with and satisfy the requirements of legal regulations and clauses in collective bargaining agreements.

Consequently, labor mobility exerts contradictory influences on technical change: positive if the neo-Schumpeterian mechanism is dominant, negative if a

TABLE 1-8. Macroeconomic Performance Indexes (annual percentage changes)

Countries	GDP growth		Real wage (GDP price)		Employment		Productivity		External trade/GDP	
	1971–80	1981–90	1971–80	1981–90	1971–80	1981–90	1971–80	1981–90	1971–80	1981–90
Belgium	3.2	1.9	4.5	0.7	0.3	0.1	2.9	1.8	-0.1	-0.2
Denmark	2.2	1.9	1.6	0.4	0.7	0.7	1.5	1.2	-2.9	-3.1
Ireland	4.5	2.8	4.0	1.1	0.9	-0.3	3.6	3.1	-6.3	-3.8
Italy	3.1	2.5	3.3	1.6	0.5	0.6	2.6	1.9	-0.2	-0.8
France	3.3	2.1	3.6	0.9	0.4	0.1	2.9	2.0	0.3	-0.5
Germany	2.7	2.1	3.0	0.8	-0.1	0.2	2.8	1.9	0.7	2.8
Greece	4.7	1.6	4.4	1.3	0.7	0.9	4.0	0.7	-1.9	-3.8
Netherlands	2.9	1.8	3.0	0.1	0.2	0.2	2.7	1.6	1.2	2.8
Portugal	4.5	2.7	6.3	0.1	-0.4	0.1	5.3	2.6	-3.2	-3.9
Spain	3.5	2.9	4.5	0.5	-0.6	0.9	4.1	2.0	-0.8	-1.0
United Kingdom	2.0	2.4	1.8	1.9	0.2	0.4	1.8	2.0	-0.6	-0.8
Average for EC	2.9	2.3	3.1	1.1	0.2	0.4	2.7	1.9	0	0.3
Japan	4.6	4.1	0.7	2.6	0.7	1.1	3.9	3.0	0.6	2.5
Sweden	2.0	2.2	—	—	0.9	0.6	1.1	1.4	—	—
United States	2.7	3.0	5.1	1.2	2.0	1.9	0.7	1.1	0.2	-1.9
Finland	4.3	3.2	—	—	0.3	0.9	4.0	2.3	—	—
Norway	4.9	3.3	—	—	1.6	1.3	3.3	2.0	—	—
Canada	4.9	3.4	—	—	3.2	2.0	1.7	1.4	—	—
Austria	4.3	1.7	—	—	0.3	0	4.0	1.7	—	—

TABLE 1-9. *Impact of Job Security on Technical Change and Long-Term Growth*
(*Correlation matrix [R] between variables*)

Variables	1970–80			1980–90		
	Growth (Q)	Productivity (PR)	Real Wage (RW)	Growth (Q)	Productivity (PR)	Real wage (RW)
Institutional constraint (IL)	0.12	0.48	0.40	−0.29	0.14	−0.34
Layoff constraint (LR)	0.43	0.59	0.71	−0.11	−0.12	0.26
Hiring constraint (HR)	0.39	0.60	0.69	0.14	0.25	0.23
Global perception of rigidity (G)	0.62	0.73	0.85	0.16	0.28	0.19
New hires (NR)	0.09	−0.17	0.14	0.28	−0.32	−0.32
Job instability (IS)	−0.34	−0.72	0.24	0.04	−0.52	−0.25

Leibensteinian logic prevails. Only empirical research can assess which impact finally emerges for a given firm, sector, country, and period.

Three national trajectories: U.S., Japanese, and Western European. Comparative studies of national systems of innovation (Nelson 1989; Freeman 1989) suggest contrasting organizational forms for governing technical change and diffusing it to the productive system. Basically, three major trajectories can be distinguished. For each of them, employment instability or job tenure interact with the intensity and the direction of technical change.

In the United States, many federal agencies play a role in subsidizing and orienting basic research and development, whereas university research leads to numerous patents in high-tech activities. For average manufacturing, old Fordist principles manifest a high level of inertia, and detailed job rules reinforce this long-term trend. Furthermore, flexible real wages might be a substitute for labor saving innovations. A long-term econometric study about U.S. manufacturing productivity shows that the quasi-stagnation of real wages during the last fifteen years has leveled off average increases in productivity (Dumenil and Levy 1989). High employment instability exacerbates wage flexibility, since enterprise-specific knowledge and experience are lost when workers move too often. In other words, U.S. manufacturing does not suffer from any lack of basic innovations, but, because the labor market is excessively flexible, from their inadequate implementation and diffusion.

In Japan, basic research has traditionally lagged behind American and European universities. Nevertheless, a much more centralized state and a very high degree of concentration in manufacturing and banking have promoted coherent innovation policies, which in the past aimed at adapting foreign devices to the Japanese style. Similarly, it has been argued that in Japan innovation has been governed much more by *techné* (experimenting and learning by doing) than by *epistemé* (deriving useful techniques from basic scientific advances).

Given this context, the objective of long-term stability of employment relationships, prevalent not only in large but also in medium-sized firms (Koike 1987a), channels the pressure to innovate in two directions. First, Japanese firms invest in human capital and experience in order to get a polyvalent and committed work force, a condition for the fast adoption of new technologies (Mansfield 1988). Second, the ability to conceive and produce new products at low costs and to transfer workers from one activity to another are related to implicit employment stability. In a sense, this second trajectory is quite complementary to the American one.

In the European Community, most national systems of innovation are between the North American and the Japanese systems. Basic and applied research are combined, as are public and private R & D expenditures. Consequently, specialization is strong for medium tech products. Significant real-wage inertia (see table 1-8) has triggered a large variety of rationalization strategies. Labor saving has been a leading objective in investment and innovation decisions, even if a shift seems to have occurred after 1979 (Boyer 1989a). Simultaneously, more complete job regulations might have reinforced this inducement to productivity.

Contrary to Japan, however, the ideal of long-term employment contracts in Europe has not fostered as much product innovation and/or reassignments of labor from one activity to another within the same conglomerate. Again, the configuration of the capital-labor compromise and public regulation contributed to the systemic coherence of this socioeconomic trajectory. A cross-national statistical analysis seemingly confirms these hypotheses.

On average, short-term numerical flexibility is detrimental to long-term productivity. A systematic correlation analysis has been run confronting the employment stability variables (tables 1-1 and 1-2) with indicators of long-term macroeconomic performance: average growth of gross domestic product (GDP) during the 1970s and 1980s and labor productivity and real wages during the same periods (table 1-8). Of course, the inherent shakiness of such an analysis has to be reiterated. Difficulties in measuring labor mobility, statistical discrepancies between countries, and the unequal availability of data all introduce some bias. Nevertheless, many controversies about labor market flexibility in the past have referred to cross-national comparisons. Therefore, the only purpose of this crude statistical analysis is to test conventional views and to confront them with more sophisticated analytical models. Three major but preliminary conclusions emerge (table 1-9).

During the 1970s, institutional and legal constraints on employment termination, as well as constraints on labor mobility as perceived by firms, seem to have been positively correlated with long-term increases in productivity but less so with growth. Thus, job stability would seem to foster more labor-saving innovations than pure product innovations. This conclusion is not rejected by more sophisticated productivity equations, including increasing returns to scale. Employment security is apparently an inducement to productivity increases.

During the same period, given the same productivity trends, job stability helped workers get higher real wage increases. Therefore, contrary to implicit contract or efficiency wage theories, there is no trade-off between high wages and employment stability. Institutionalist models of labor market segmentation are more consistent with such a finding: for economies in which micro corporatism or strong unions negotiate good-capital labor agreements, workers can, on average, get both better employment conditions and higher wage increases. This sheds some light on an argument already made for the United States: unions both foster good wages and stimulate technical change (Freeman and Medoff 1984). Alternatively, this positive correlation between high wages and employment stability could also provide comfort to insider-outsider theorists (Lindbeck and Snower 1988a).

Surprisingly, all of these relations vanished during the 1980s. First, the institutional constraints no longer seemed to exert pressure toward productivity (table 1-9). Some of these constraints may have been relaxed by governments, as, for example, in France. But, alternatively, basic uncertainty about the emerging new sociotechnical system, either Toyotism or Volvoism, and difficulties in its implementation may explain the blurring of most previous macroeconomic relations. Second, employment instability still has a negative impact on technical change, though at a very low level of significance. Third, the shift in bargaining power to the benefit of firms might explain why real wage increases have become relatively independent of productivity dynamics. The 1980s were indeed the decade of massive restoration of profits.

To conclude, job stability and employment security regulations used to be positively correlated with technical change. By restraining purely defensive flexibility, these regulations partly influenced the direction and intensity of innovations and the diffusion of technical change. The 1980s experienced the breakdown of this symbiotic relationship. The future will tell if this was a path-breaking change or only a transitory disruption, in that the new productive model is bound to bring a renewal of the ideal of employment security. Let me address this last issue.

A Return to Fast and Steady Growth Would Help Employment Adjustments

Too often, analyses of labor market flexibility point out the microeconomic consequences of inadequate public regulations but do not study feedback from macrodynamics on perceived and effective mobility. This issue is indeed important.

The new macroeconomic and institutional context of the 1990s. The heyday of the flexibility debate took place in the mid-1980s, after half a decade of continuous decline in average growth rates in most of Europe. The need for downward adjustments in employment was perceived all the more strongly by firms the more aggregate demand was stagnant and the more uncertainty prevailed concerning relative prices, real interest, and exchange rates—not to mention public policy makers who vocally proclaimed.a free market ideology and actually adhered to a bastard Keynesianism (in the United States at least).

I argued above that employment rigidity was much more a consequence and amplifying factor than the cause of structural and long-term unemployment. Conversely, the unexpected and long-lasting boom initiated in 1983 has significantly shifted both the debate as well as actual personnel management practices. Even European countries are now creating large numbers of new jobs, though still less than the puzzling American job machine (see Buechtemann 1991). Simultaneously, most managers seem to have softened their demands for labor market and social deregulation; in France, for example, this theme has virtually vanished. Finally, recent surveys point out a new and unexpected danger: the scarcity of skilled workers as a possible barrier to the ongoing economic boom (OECD 1989b). In some countries, such as the United Kingdom, this could explain the nominal wage explosion and the renewed inflationary pressures.

The persistence of long-term unemployment is nevertheless worrying, although it does not contradict our general interpretation. Young people who entered the labor market in the most dire period were denied access to the productive system and therefore lost incentives, expertise, and, indeed, the ability to work. As a consequence, unemployment seems to reproduce itself in a vicious circle. Further, firms assume that the long-term unemployed are less efficient than other workers, which exacerbates their relative situation and frequently leads to a permanent exclusion from jobs. Both theoretical and empirical arguments might support this view.

Optimal growth with labor as a quasi-fixed factor. Conventional investment theory (Jorgenson and Stephenson 1967) used to assume complete flexibility of equipment in deriving the optimal strategy for the capital formation of an individual firm. But this assumption implicitly relied on the existence of a second-hand equipment goods market. If such a market does not exist, then there is an irreversibility constraint in that net capital cannot be reduced below its normal replacement rate. The same framework can be extended to labor: in modern economies, labor has become a quasi-fixed factor (Oi 1962). This means that in an economy where complete employment security is implemented, the only way to reduce employment is by natural attrition. Capital and labor problems then become equivalent.

This line of analysis has been followed by Nickell (1974, 1979) and provides suggestive hints. First, the optimal pattern of hiring is altered, in accordance with conventional intuition. Imagine a roughly cyclical macroeconomic evolution. As the boom proceeds, firms are more cautious since they expect it to come to an end. Conversely, during a recession, employment will be kept at higher levels than in the case of a spot market for labor. This is consistent with the stylized facts about the U.S. business cycle in this century.

The second conclusion is somewhat trivial but important for the employment security debate. There always exists an average long-term growth rate for which labor rigidity is not binding. Basically, if OECD countries could again reach a 5 to 6 percent GNP growth rate, it is likely that most of the complaints about excessive labor market rigidity would disappear; all the more so if economic fluctuations again became more predictable than during the past two decades. There can be no doubt that the functioning of the labor market is closely linked to the features of the overall growth regime.

Labor mobility increases with job opportunities. The previous theoretical model can now be made a little more complex. In fact, workers separate from their jobs for many different reasons: voluntary quits when attracted by better offers elsewhere, early or standard retirement, layoffs, and dismissals. Quit decisions are made in view of alternative wage offers, job vacancies, career prospects, and so on. Thus, all of these variables are highly sensitive to macroeconomic fluctuations. American and French data confirm this hypothesis.

In the United States, both hiring and quit rates were found to be strongly procyclical, that is, highly correlated with capacity utilization (see Osterman 1987) and, therefore, indirectly related to GDP growth. Consequently, if growth accelerated, voluntary mobility would once again soon represent the larger part of total worker turnover. A contrario, if a severe recession were to take place, dismissals would increase and labor rigidity would again emerge as a major problem.

In France, quit rates drastically declined during the 1970s and early 1980s. The decline in job openings elsewhere was the main factor responsible for this decrease in voluntary mobility. A contrario, the renewal of significant growth rates after 1986 mechanically induced a substantial rise in voluntary job separation rates. The relative rise in quit propensity has been positively related to firm size (see Bertrand 1989:104).

Clearly, turnover is a highly endogeneous variable and not one determined solely by fixed institutional factors.

Contradictory factors shape voluntary job mobility. A recent international survey (Bertrand 1989) points out three main determinants of this variable. One, the size of firms is negatively correlated with turnover. Even if the size varies procyclically, the hierarchy is rather stable: roughly speaking, firms employing between 50 and 199 workers exhibit a turnover rate twice as high as firms with more than 500 workers. During the last two decades, larger firms have been increasingly replaced by smaller ones in all OECD countries, regardless of sector, region, or skill level. This would imply a larger average labor turnover rate in each of the broad firm-size categories. Consequently, contemporary economies would now be and would remain more flexible than during the post–World War II era, lending some support to the thesis put forward by Piore and Sabel (1984).

Two, skill composition exerts a definite impact upon voluntary mobility. All data for European countries seem to confirm the behavior observed for France. In conformity with capital investment theory, when firm-specific training is important, firms are reluctant to dismiss or lay off workers who are essential to the firms' efficiency and adaptability. While blue-collar workers without any previous training have a high turnover rate (14 percent in 1988), technicians, at the opposite end of the scale, are quasi-immobile; their turnover rate is only 2.5

percent. If the Toyotism-Volvoism model is to diffuse across industrialized countries, it will call for more trained workers. This would, ceteris paribus, reduce average turnover, even if hiring and firing in each skill category continue to conform to the same behavioral equations.

Third, at least in France but possibly also in other countries such as the United Kingdom, fixed-term employment contracts have now become so widespread that they offer firms a high degree of freedom with regard to downward employment adjustments (see Maurau, chap. 19). This new built-in (numerical) flexibility would probably make adaptation to a new recession easier than during the 1970s. The new regulations concerning temporary and part-time work tend to reinforce this new pattern. Maybe this is the underlying reason the French business association has become all but silent on the issue of employment security regulations; numerical flexibility is institutionally guaranteed to most enterprises.

To sum up, the most severe episode of labor market deregulation is probably over unless, of course, a new and unexpected recession sets in. In any case, contemporary economies have regained a lot of flexibility. The potential effects of this regained flexibility, however, may be counterbalanced or even offset by the countervailing effects of ongoing structural transformations, such as the shift away from Fordism or the changing skill composition of employment. The overall effect of all these changes is an empirical question and cannot be assessed from a purely theoretical point of view.

Only Detailed Empirical Research Can Disentangle the Issue of Workers' Protection

Conventional neoclassical theory is often invoked to argue that labor flexibility has an unambiguously positive impact on employment, always and everywhere. The theory relies on crude and irrelevant hypotheses about the employment relationship, which have been rejected by recent theories of capital-labor relations. Labor market flexibility is optimal for employment and welfare only if labor can be assimilated to its services and if labor is hired in a spot market where no adverse selection problems occur or commitment and loyalty issues are at stake. By contrast, when we recognize the separation of contracting labor from its actual utilization, the long-term character of most modern employment relationships, and the key importance of work effort and loyalty to the firm, then the basic neoclassical model collapses. New and more sophisticated models provide evidence of numerous contradictory effects that the impact of employment security can no longer be assessed on a priori grounds. Let us develop this view, which seems to be a core issue in recent research on employment security policies (Emerson 1988a; Flanagan, chap. 4; Metcalf 1987b; Hamermesh 1988; Gennard 1986).

Even in the short run, employment security may promote job creation. A whole spectrum of mechanisms interferes with hiring and firing decisions (fig. 1-6). At the first level, two broad conceptions of macroeconomic equilibrium can

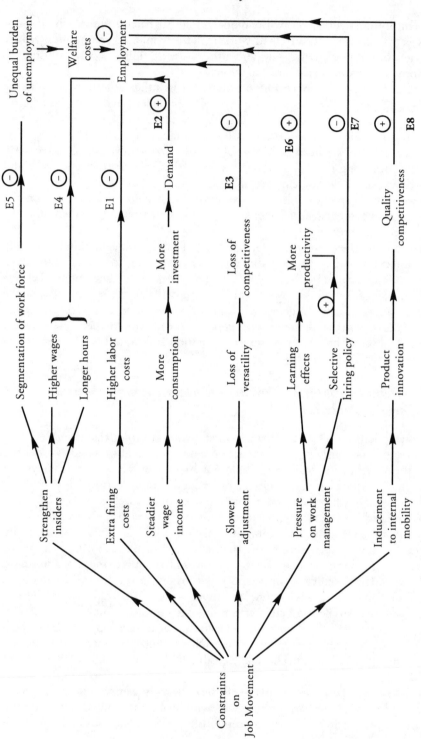

FIGURE 1-6. Effects of Employment Security

be opposed. First, the expectation of the extra costs associated with firing (time lags between the firm's firing decision and its administrative authorization, mandatory severance payments, and so on) will induce a rational firm to employ fewer workers. The standard neoclassical employment function (see table 1-7) predicts that the impact of employment security policies on the employment level will be negative (mechanism E1).

Second, in modern economies, wage earners represent the dominant part of the active population. Employment stability therefore provides a form of income security that tends to smooth cyclical adjustments in effective demand. This higher income feeds a larger consumption, which in turn enhances investment via an accelerator mechanism. Globally, effective demand generation has to be taken into account according to Keynesian macroeconomic theory: the impact of job security would then be positive (mechanism E2).

This analysis has to be extended when the economy is largely open to foreign trade and competition. Since a continuous trend in the internationalization of trade, production, and finance has taken place during the last two decades, two other complementary mechanisms have to be considered. One, employment regulation may induce slower adjustments and therefore imply a loss of adaptability to changing patterns of world demand. Simultaneously, the extra costs associated with firing provisions increase national production costs: the corresponding loss in external competitiveness will negatively affect employment to the extent that the industry is a price taker (mechanism E3). This has been a leading argument put forward by business associations and governments in promoting defensive flexibility strategies (Boyer 1988a). Two, this negative impact is not a fatality. It has already been shown that the constraints imposed on firms' management have an impact on the speed and direction of technical change (see table 1-9). Higher productivity might compensate for extra costs due to sophisticated job security legislation (mechanism E8). Further, the firm can use the cumulative competence of wage earners to react quickly to new international opportunities. More specifically, product innovation dynamism might be related to job tenure in large conglomerates.

Again, the net impact can be either positive or negative. Two other mechanisms have to be taken into account. One, in accordance with insider-outsider theory, job security might enhance the bargaining power of employed wage earners and weaken unemployed outsiders. On the one hand, unit labor costs will be higher (mechanism E4) but eventually compensated for by larger productivity (mechanism E6). This is the more commonly considered mechanism that is supposed to have a negative impact on employment. But that effect E4 will outperform effect E6 is not a fatality but a matter of empirical investigation. For example, large Japanese firms do not seem to suffer from any loss in competitiveness because of the bargaining power of insiders. Two, long-term unemployment will probably be the outcome of such a segmented labor market. Consequently, where the welfare state has institutionalized unemployment benefits, social security has incurred extra costs, to be covered eventually by new taxes levied on workers' wages or firms' profits (mechanism E5). Again, if the sector or national economy are price takers, this might reduce external competitiveness and result in lower employment.

In the long run, public regulations shape technical change and innovations. A long-term history of French industrial relations has tentatively shown that any advance in the institutionalization of a new capital-labor relation (for example, banning of night shifts and child work, limitations on weekly working time, institutionalization of a minimum wage, and so on) might generate new organizational forms, inventions, and innovations in engineering and machine tools design (CEPREMAP-CORDES 1977). An acceleration of technical change is a possible but by no means granted response to the challenge posed by advances in social regulation. Contradictory mechanisms still combine and shape the ex post trends in technical change.

Learning by doing and cumulative experience about the core business of the firm might be a major advantage in stimulating long-term productivity. Similarly, highly skilled workers play a major role in elaborating new products and processes as well as proposing incremental improvements. Clearly then, job tenure has a positive impact on productivity (mechanism E6). Furthermore, constant product innovation might help in renewing monopoly power and getting a competitive edge on international markets (mechanism E8).

Selective hiring policies might have counterbalancing effects. Large firms usually screen job applicants in order to hire those workers who appear most fitted to the firms' objectives. Consequently, managers will be very choosy in hiring and partially exacerbate labor market segmentation: by definition, primary jobs suppose secondary ones with higher employment instability (mechanism E5). Some authors have argued that the global impact will be negative: persistence of long-term unemployment and rising inequalities both between primary and secondary jobs and between employed and unemployed workers.

It is necessary to sum up and combine all these eight mechanisms before deriving any definite conclusion about the costs and benefits of employment security regulations. Sophisticated empirical studies are needed to reduce this basic uncertainty. My conclusion, not unsurprisingly, is very similar to that of Gennard (1986): "On the one hand, the regulations might curb employer flexibility to the extent that particular avenues and means for adjustment are foreclosed and degrees of adaptation reduced. . . . But on the other hand, regulation may be required to open up paths and space for flexibility which would not be available in its absence" (quoted by Metcalf 1987a:66).

The previous sections have provided components of such a general model, but they have to be combined and refined, which is not an easy task. Furthermore, adequate statistical indexes need to be collected over a sufficiently long period to capture the specificities of each national trajectory, especially the interaction between innovation and the system of industrial relations. These configurations might be specific to a given period, sector, country, or even region. Without detailed investigations, a cautious approach to job security deregulation is required.

Preliminary Conclusions

The debate about labor flexibility frequently supposes that maximum social deregulation would be optimal from an economic point of view. Conventional models in which labor is a commodity like any other inescapably lead to this conclusion. Modern micro theories of the capital-labor relation and the employment relationship challenge and question this optimistic view. When the quality of workers is uncertain, learning effects are important, and commitment is a central issue, then some inertia in employment adjustment might be optimal. Conversely, instantaneous variations in wage and employment are not necessarily optimal.

Macroeconomic modeling and international comparative studies tentatively conclude that employment flexibility should not always and everywhere be maximal. Employment security, provided by legislation or collective agreements, triggers a series of contradictory mechanisms that ex post may or may not be beneficial to productivity, the standard of living, employment, labor market homogeneity, and so forth. Only detailed empirical studies will be able to measure and assess the overall impact of these various mechanisms. A survey of the existing literature and the presented econometric tests, crude as they are, suggest a cautious approach to labor market deregulation. The advantages may be small, if they are positive at all.

Nevertheless, the employment security dilemma should not be denied. On the one hand, the complete immobility of labor within and outside firms will inhibit adjustment to varying international conditions and to technological and organizational innovations. Statistical evidence suggests that some job regulations in European countries have unintentionally reinforced long-term unemployment and labor market segmentation. On the other hand, the absence of any constraints on hiring and firing as well as complete flexibility in wage formation may hinder labor-saving and both product and process innovations. The most flexible labor markets were found to be associated, at least during the 1970s, with a sluggish adaptation to technical change and poor productivity performance. Again, regulations per se are not to be blamed but only an inadequate institutionalization of employment security through legislation or collective agreements.

Too often, economists and politicians prepare to win the last war but lose the next one because it exhibits new and unexpected features. The labor flexibility debate is a good example of such inertia of perceptions. The "flexibilization" strategies implemented by governments and firms during the 1980s have restored a higher degree of freedom in personnel adjustment. At the same time, many of the typically Fordist rigidities have been removed or "deactivated." The crucial issue now is which capital-labor compromise and form of public regulation will spur the emergence of an alternative to Fordism—Toyotism (i.e., micro corporatism and labor market segmentation) or Volvoism (i.e., macro corporatism and labor homogeneity)? The breakdown of most previous econometric regularities between macroeconomic variables and labor market characteristics as well as qualitative and institutional studies provide some support for this hypothesis. From this perspective, new forms for implementing the ideal of employment stability and voluntary and/or collectively negotiated mobility are on top of the agenda.

More precisely, within this new management model the status of employment stability is at the crossing of numerous and contradictory determinants. On the one hand, the emphasis on well-educated workers, commitment and loyalty, learning by doing, and the upgrading of skills calls for more sluggish employment adjustments, if not complete employment security for all workers. On the other hand, productive decentralization, union decline (at least outside Scandinavian countries), the continuous rise in tertiary employment, disturbances linked to international investment mobility, and finally the stiffening of international competition call for significant speed in employment and/or wage variations. The provisional prognosis is that a return to fast and steady growth will help in implementing the minimum stability that is at the core of Toyotism and Volvoism. Any catastrophic and unexpected recession, however, would delay the path toward this new management model and spur a new rush into purely defensive flexibility strategies.

These principles—alternatives to the decaying Fordist conceptions—do not imply a one-best-way model. Quite the contrary, the same functional properties can be obtained through a variety of national institutional forms. Given its past sociotechnical trajectory, the industrial relations atmosphere, and its cultural values, each society has to develop a genuine and unique articulation between job regulations, collective agreements, and employment contracts. It is important to recall that Japan seems to exhibit the most sluggish employment adjustment, whereas its economy is highly competitive and quasi-full employment is prevailing in the early 1990s. In contrast, Sweden has managed to be technically innovative and economically competitive with low wage differentials, active employment policies, and strong unions. Unfortunately, most of the EC countries exhibit rather disappointing results: their hybrid institutions between a purely decentralized system and a full-fledged social democratic compromise has brought moderate successes in innovation but quite disappointing performances in job creation. Maybe the opportunities opened by the European integration will induce a renewal of rapid growth and might prolong the positive employment trend that has been prevailing since 1985.

Needless to say, these are provisional and probably shaky results. Given the importance of the issues at stake, too daring or ambitious employment regulations should not be designed and decided on until more sophisticated and detailed empirical studies become available. This paper, however imperfect and lacunary, will have achieved its aim if it stimulates intelligent and thoroughly documented research.

Appendix to Chapter 1: Relationship between Maximum Flexibility and Macroeconomic Performance

General Macro Model

Let us follow Dumenil and Levy 1986 and imagine that firms react with a one-period lag to perceived disequilibria in both capacity utilization of fixed capital (u_t) and the ratio of inventories to output (s_t). The dynamics of the related economy can be captured by the following system:

$$u_{t+1} = U(u_t, s_t)$$

$$s_{t+1} = S(u_t, s_t)$$

which is supposed to have at least one stationary equilibrium such that (u^*, s^*). It can be shown that more than equilibrium exists: normal equilibrium: (N); overheating, when capacity utilization is above normal: (O); stagnating growth, or a Keynesian situation, when capacity utilization is below normal: (K); and depression, when the economy collapses toward zero (D). What is the influence of the speed of reactions on the existence and stability of equilibria? Consider, for example, the following parameter ε:

$$\varepsilon = \partial U / \partial s_t$$

which measures the intensity of reaction of firms to scale their level of capacity utilization up or down in response to changes in their inventories.

This discussion can be summarized by the following diagram:

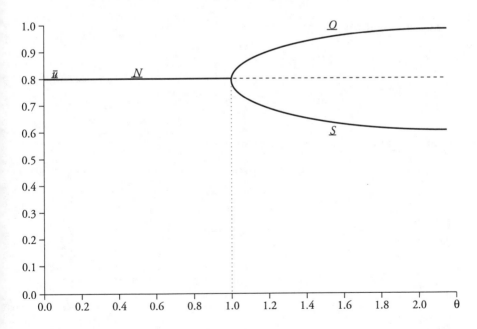

It follows that for moderate adjustment speeds a normal equilibrium exists but that up to a threshold ϵ^*, only overheating or depression equilibria exist of which one is stable. Consequently, from a macro point of view, the speed of adjustment should be kept moderate. In other words, maximum flexibility does not lead to an optimum. Mutatis mutandis, this would probably apply to labor market adjustments.

Specific Model for the Labor Market

Let us transpose the previous model to employment (N_t) and wage (w_t) adjustments. Suppose a one-period lag between the perception of disequilibrium and decision for the ongoing period:

$$N_{t+1} = N(N_t, w_t) \tag{I}$$

$$w_{t+1} = W(N_t, w_t) \tag{II}$$

To be more specific, the two relations will be assumed to be linear

$$N_{t+1} = \lambda N_t - \sigma w_t + n \qquad \text{with} \qquad \lambda \in [0, 1] \text{ adjustment speed}$$
$$w_{t+1} = \mu w_t + \theta N_t + w \qquad \qquad \qquad \text{for employment}$$

$\lambda \in [0, 1]$ adjustment speed for employment
$\mu \in [0, 1]$ adjustment for wages
σ: elasticity of employment with respect to employment
θ: elasticity of wage with respect to employment

The dynamic system associated

$$\begin{bmatrix} [N_t]_{1} \\ [w_t]_{1} \end{bmatrix} = \begin{bmatrix} +\lambda & -\sigma \\ +\theta & \mu \end{bmatrix} \begin{bmatrix} N_t \\ w_t \end{bmatrix} + \begin{bmatrix} n \\ w \end{bmatrix}$$

can be represented by the following diagram.

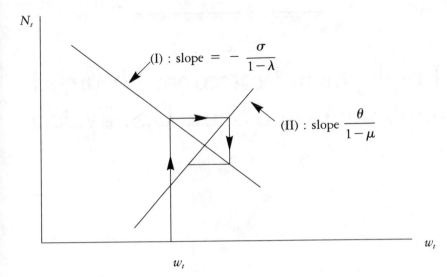

The labor market will converge toward the long-term equilibrium—here supposed to be unique—only if the adjustment speed $(1 - \lambda)(1 - \mu)$ is sufficient given the two elasticities σ and θ.

$$(1 - \lambda)(1 - \mu) > \sigma \theta \qquad \textbf{Stability condition}$$

One derives some important consequences. First, rapid wage adjustment and high-speed employment adjustment are substitutes, provided that no absolute inertia prevails ($\lambda = 1$ or $\mu = 1$). In the flexibility debate, this means that both strategies do not necessarily have to go together. Second, combining structural reforms increasing wage flexibility (higher θ) with rapid employment adjustments ($\lambda \mapsto 0$) might push the economy into an unstable condition. In other words, maximum flexibility strategies may be destabilizing.

2
Employment Protection: Theoretical Implications and Some U.S. Evidence

Daniel S. Hamermesh

E mployment protection covers a wide range of policies, from the provision of unemployment insurance by a central government in Western Europe to the loose and variable case law covering employment at will in the United States. For purposes of discussion here, I view employment protection (EP) as any explicit or implicit policy designed to increase employers' reluctance to lay off workers or to spread work at times of decreased product (and hence labor) demand. This very broad definition requires us to generalize about EP so that the theory essential for analyzing its effects need not be altered with each minor variation in policy. One of the main purposes of this paper is to set forth two general models of the potential impacts that describe EP policy.

EP policy affects the dynamics of employment partly because it affects the path of employers' hiring and laying off of workers. It also affects employment in a static framework, in that it can change the cost of labor relative to other inputs into production and the cost of employees relative to that of hours. Equally important, the timing of the introduction of EP policy affects its initial, and possibly intermediate-term, outcomes, so that the analysis I provide requires more than just standard comparative statics or dynamics.

My second purpose here is to examine how employment adjustment in the U.S. labor market has changed during the past twenty years and to study the United States's comparatively paltry policy efforts aimed at employment protection. Much of what the United States has done in the past twenty years involves changes in the case law dealing with the employment-at-will doctrine, which generally describes EP outside the small and shrinking unionized sector. I discuss this change, which has perhaps taken its cue from policy in the unionized sector, and the generalized impact of changing EP policies. I then briefly summarize evidence on the potential effects of two specific policies: premium pay for overtime work and the system of unemployment insurance. The former may affect EP by reducing hours and increasing employment; the latter has profound effects on EP because of the way it is financed.

Likely Effects of Archetypal EP Policies

Throughout the discussion in this section I follow the standard approach of economic analysis, assume that the policies are imposed on a competitive economy, and compare their effects to what would be observed under competition. This is obviously nonsense. It may well be that the policies are second-best efforts that move a labor market back toward a social optimum. It may just as well be that they are "first-worst" policies that enhance departures from competitive optima. Without any evaluation of the initial departure, I cannot evaluate which possibility is closer to the truth. All I can do is point out the costs and benefits imposed by the policy in comparison to what would exist if nothing else in today's labor market were altered. Whether the EP policies viewed from this standpoint hinder the functioning of the labor market and improve or reduce workers' well-being is left to the reader.

Policies That Restrict Firing

There is no "typical" EP policy that reduces employers' willingness to lay off workers. Clearly, increased experience rating of unemployment insurance taxation in the United States, the imposition of requirements for severance pay in Western Europe and extensions of their coverage, requirements for advance notice that a job is terminated, and changes in case law that somewhat restrict American employers' rights to end employment relationships at will can all be viewed as raising the cost to the employer of laying off workers. Thus, the archetypal EP policy does not exist. Nonetheless, an entire class of EP policies can be analyzed, recognizing that the major economic change they impose is an increase in the cost of downward adjustments in employment other than by attrition.

It is important to be clear about the dual nature of the change in labor costs that is imposed by such an EP policy. The change occurs whether or not a layoff ever takes place: by affecting employers' choices about their labor inputs, employers are induced to deviate from the economywide output-maximizing path of employment.[1] Its first effect is thus on the average cost of labor—on the cost of worker-hours used in conjunction with other productive inputs to generate intermediate and final products. Because the cost of an additional worker-hour over the worker's expected tenure with the employer is increased by the EP policy, the number of worker-hours demanded is reduced. There is abundant evidence

---

[1] This need not imply a departure from the set of Pareto optimal paths, since some workers may be made better off by the imposition of the EP policy. It need not even imply a reduction in social welfare, depending on how society weighs the reduced variability of some workers' employment against the efficiency costs of the program.

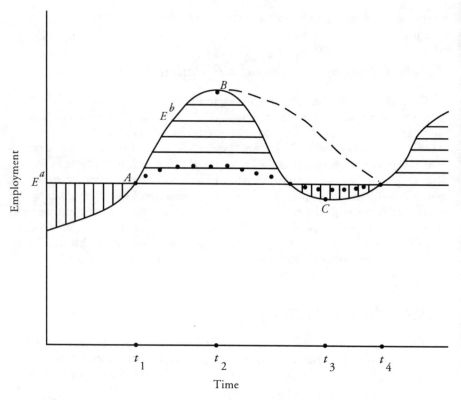

FIGURE 2–1. *Adjustments to a Draconian Employment Protection Policy*

(summarized in Hamermesh 1989a: chap. 3), covering numerous countries, that higher labor costs reduce employment. Ignoring employee-hours substitution, we may infer that the number of employees is reduced, on average, over the business cycle. The second effect, the one that the programs aim to achieve, is to change employers' incentives to reduce employment in response to negative demand shocks, in other words, to alter fluctuations in worker-hours around their average rate.

An artificial policy. To understand the issues generated by a more realistic archetypal policy, consider the following reductio ad absurdum: a policy that mandates and enforces a rule that any employer found guilty of laying off a worker will be punished by death. Let us first examine its impact on an existing firm, whose path of labor input before the policy is imposed is shown by the sinusoidal curve labeled E^b in Figure 2–1. I assume that the pattern of shocks to product demand is unchanged by the imposition of the policy. I also assume for the moment that the employers' choice between workers and hours is not changed by the policy, so that I concentrate on the demand for workers. The policy guarantees that the firm will never lay off workers. Indeed, it converts the variable factor labor into a fixed factor: once workers are hired, they will remain as long as they wish. This means that in the new steady state, employment will be constant at E^a. There is no question that this most draconian policy reduces employment fluctuations in existing firms.

The more interesting question is what the policy does to the average level of employment in the typical firm. With the conversion of labor from a variable (or quasi-fixed) to a fixed factor, the firm does not incur any costs in laying off workers that the policy would impose. Its optimal (and constant) rate of utilization will depart from the average over the path E^b only to the extent that $\Sigma \, [MP_L - W]$, the deviation over the expected tenure at the firm of the additional worker's marginal product from that worker's labor cost, W, differs when the path switches from E^b to E^a. The firm forgoes the profits that it might reap in good times from hiring additional workers beyond E^a and incurs losses in bad times on some of the workers that the EP policy induces it to retain. Taken together, these effects mean that the sum of the horizontally shaded areas in Figure 2–1 exceeds the sum of the vertically shaded areas: the average level of employment over the cycle falls.

This conclusion is strengthened if we relax the assumption that firms cannot substitute workers for hours. The EP policy raises the cost of an additional (necessarily permanent) worker relative to that of adding an additional hour to the workweek of current employees. The policy induces the constrained profit-maximizing employer to maintain a smaller work force and to vary its hours more over the cycle of product demand. Because the price of reducing hours per worker is somewhat lower than decapitation, employers will increase their reliance on fluctuations in hours.

The conclusion is weakened if we assume that some workers quit the firm voluntarily if wages are not fixed or if labor can usefully be hoarded during the downturn. In the first case, employers can increase employment beyond E^a during booms and still not face decapitation if they are certain that sufficient workers will quit as the downturn approaches to allow them to avoid layoffs. If wages are not fixed, the employer can allow some of the output shocks to be reflected in fluctuations in wages. Employers will lower wages during downturns, inducing some workers to quit and reducing the loss of profits. If workers can do something useful around the plant when product demand is down, perhaps repair machinery, the potential loss of profits when layoffs are avoided is less severe.

This extreme example also points out other perverse incentives that an EP policy can create. There are substantial profit opportunities for employers who can somehow employ temporary workers during good times and yet avoid beheading when the workers are laid off in bad times. Outright bribery to officials to ignore violations of the law is one possibility. Far more likely are lobbying attempts to ensure that not all workers are covered by the EP policy. Indeed, the growth of the market for temporary and so-called noncontract workers in Western Europe can be viewed as a response to these exemptions and the changes in profit opportunities produced by EP legislation.

If firms are noncompetitive in the product market, the results are not changed substantively. EP policy alters the amount of rents available for sharing, but there is no reason to presume that it changes the relative bargaining strengths of organized workers and the monopolistic employer. Similarly, assuming that the costs of adjusting employment lead to lagged responses to output shocks does not qualitatively change figure 2–1 (though it does slow and dampen responses to output shocks). Only if complete job security somehow shocks workers into becoming more productive is it possible to reverse the negative conclusion about the average level of employment over the business cycle. This might occur, for example, through increased teamwork by a more secure work force, but there is no evidence for this, and it is a very weak reed on which to rely.

A final argument against the possibility of long-term effects is that any costs of an EP policy will be offset by lower wages (i.e., will be borne by workers). This is equivalent to assuming that labor supply to the market is completely inelastic. Though there is substantial evidence that a large proportion of the imposed increases in labor costs are borne by workers (Hamermesh 1989a:chap. 5), the shifting is probably not complete, and it is certainly slow given the very long lags in adjustment of labor supply. Even if it were complete, it would mean that workers are trading off income for greater employment stability for some members of the group.

This discussion compares steady states before and after the policy is imposed. The more interesting question, and the one whose answers are more likely to inform policy evaluation, is, What is the path of employment from the time the policy is imposed?[2] Consider what happens if the policy is instituted at t_1, when employment happens to be equal to E^a and product demand is increasing. Assume workers do quit the firm voluntarily, albeit at rates insufficient to allow the employer to maintain the previously optimal path E^b. The employer can take advantage of some of the opportunities provided by the positive shock and move from A along the dotted line in figure 2–1. If workers quit voluntarily and independently of variations in wages, imposing the policy at t_1 generates a path of employment that fluctuates, though less than the prepolicy path and around a lower average level of employment. (If no quits occur, the employer will hold employment at E^a; the result is generated solely by the assumption of a positive quit rate.)

What if the policy is imposed at t_2? Unless the quit rate is sufficiently high, the EP policy will be successful: employment will move along the dashed path from point B in Figure 2–1. Until employment eventually reaches E^a, it is higher than it would have been without the policy. A researcher who evaluates the policy's impact on firms that existed before t_2 and that continue to exist through t_4 will correctly conclude that the policy has maintained employment. The final case is the imposition of the policy at t_3. In that instance employment just follows the path E^b until t_4, at which time and henceforth it follows the new steady state. The policy has no impact on employment between t_3 and t_4.[3]

---

[2]The imposition of the policy must be unexpected, or at least not fully expected, for this discussion to be relevant. If the policy is expected, employers will adjust optimally toward the steady-state path before the policy is imposed.

[3]Imposing the policy at points between A and B or between B and C leads to conclusions that are intermediate between these extremes.

This discussion may generate a sanguine view of EP policy: even a most draconian measure could, if it is an appropriately timed surprise, truly protect jobs. Is this a typical case of economists' paying too much attention to the long run (in which even economists are all dead) and ignoring the possibilities for clever policy makers to do wondrous things for the labor market?

It is true that EP policies of this sort can generate very favorable results in evaluation studies if they are a surprise to workers and employers. They can reduce firing and raise employment. The difficulty is that most evaluation studies deal with continuing firms, and the standard analysis presented above is based on the representative, infinitely lived firm. In reality, a substantial part of the fluctuations in employment is due to fluctuations in the rates of births and deaths of firms.[4] Evidence on the sensitivity of these rates to increases in labor costs is quite sparse; but evidence exists that the elasticities are not that different from standard labor-demand elasticities for continuing operations (Hamermesh 1989a:chap. 4). We have already seen that an EP policy reduces profit opportunities. This means that an EP policy will generate a reduction in the birth rate of new firms. Since some firms cannot survive the losses they would bear if they follow the dashed path from B in figure 2–1, the death rate of existing firms will rise. In the short run, the view implied above is too optimistic, for it ignores the changes in employment that occur through the dynamics of the entry and exit of firms.

In the long run, the birth rate of new firms will be lower than in the previous steady state. The reduced ability to use labor as efficiently during future business cycles as prospective employers envisioned before the policy was imposed reduces the number of potential firms that choose to enter the market. In the long run, plant closings are also reduced. By definition, in the steady state, deaths of plants must equal births, and births are reduced. The draconian EP policy will reduce the ability of new firms to generate additional competition in the product market.

The final issue is the timing of the policy. Might it not be imposed at the appropriate time so that the reduction in jobs generated by new firms could be more than offset by the gains in existing firms? It is possible, but it requires, as the analysis above shows, that the policy be imposed during booms. In fact, legislative pressures for EP policies are greatest during recessions. Assuming the policy is a surprise, the effect on employment in continuing firms will more than likely be negative. Any hysteresis effects on the labor market just compound the problem. If the policy is not a surprise, then the only impacts are the reduction in employment fluctuations and average employment in continuing firms and the decline in the rates of entry and exit of potential and existing firms.

A more realistic policy. Only the most ardent supporter of job guarantees would propose that governments execute employers who lay off workers. The more realistic archetypal policy can be stylized so that it raises the cost of firing workers without changing anything else. For this approach we can use Nickell's (1986) model of linear adjustment costs of hiring and firing to analyze EP policies.

---

[4]See recent evidence for the United States by Dunne, Roberts, and Samuelson (1989) and by Davis and Haltiwanger (1989) and the summary of these and a large variety of international evidence in Hamermesh 1989a:chap. 4.

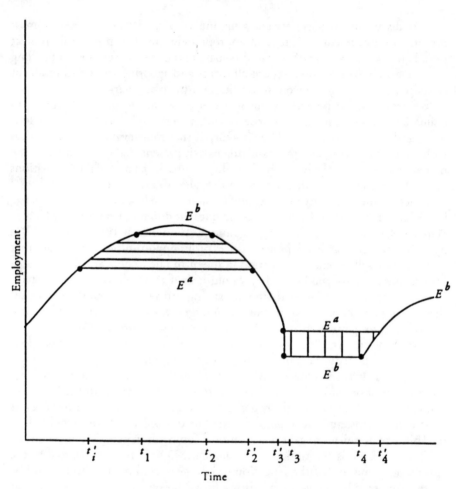

FIGURE 2–2. Adjustment to a Typical Employment Protection Policy

Consider a firm facing a decline in product demand. If it lays off the marginal worker, it must incur some additional costs beyond the wage cost of keeping him or her on the job. Similarly, if product demand increases and the employer considers hiring an additional worker, it must incur the amortized cost of hiring. Both costs impose a wedge between the worker's marginal revenue product and the current wage and benefit costs of employment. Both lead the employer to hold employment fixed in response to small shocks near cyclical peaks and troughs. The path of employment in the presence of linear hiring and firing costs is shown by E^b in figure 2–2.

Having analyzed the draconian policy, we can fairly readily infer the effect of the realistic policy. An increase in the costs of firing enlarges the wedge between the worker's marginal revenue product and the cost of changing employment. That the EP policy induces employers to avoid some layoffs, and thus hold employment constant for longer during a downturn in product demand, is fairly obvious. That it also induces employers to refrain from some hiring that they would have otherwise done, and thus keep employment unchanged for longer during a boom, is less obvious. The reduction in hiring can be understood by noting that any worker hired is a candidate for layoff in the future. The rise in firing costs raises the present value of the costs of a hire and thus reduces hiring. The new dynamic equilibrium path of employment is shown in figure 2–2 as E^a.

With an archetypal EP policy, employment fluctuates less than without the policy (though unlike the draconian policy, some fluctuations still occur even if there is no quitting). Because the present value of labor costs is raised by the increase in firing costs, average employment over the cycle is reduced: the reduction in employment that occurs near the cyclical peak is not made up by the jobs that are retained when product demand declines. For the typical employer the vertically shaded area in figure 2–2 is smaller than the horizontally shaded area.

As in the draconian case, the timing of policy may alter the conclusions, and the results of a properly conducted evaluation study may differ from the implications resulting from a comparison of dynamic equilibria before and after the EP policy is imposed. Because this EP policy is more subtle than the one depicted in figure 2–1, there are more transition cases to analyze. In discussing the cases I assume throughout that the representative firm stays in business. The seven cases involve imposing the EP policy as follows:

1. $t < t'_1$, $t'_2 < t < t'_3$. Employment proceeds along the new steady-state path E^a from the time the policy is imposed. There is no immediate effect of the policy, but eventually it produces a steady-state decline in employment fluctuations and lower average employment.

2. $t_1 < t < t_2$. Employment proceeds along the old path E^b until some time between t_2 and t'_2, at which time firing begins. The policy has no immediate impact.

3. $t_3 < t < t_4$. Like case 2 but with the reverse result: hiring begins between t_4 and t'_4. There is no immediate effect of the EP policy.

4. $t'_1 < t < t_1$. Employers will stop the hiring they had been doing. At some time between t_2 and t'_2 firing will start. The immediate effect of the policy is a reduction in hiring and a smaller expansion of employment.

5. $t_4 < t < t'_4$. Employers will delay hiring. For the observer, the result is a temporary reduction in hiring.

6. $t_2 < t < t'_2$. Employers will delay firing workers who otherwise would have been let go. Eventually, firing will begin and the firm will be on the new path E^a. The immediate result is the desired reduction in firing and the protection of jobs.

7. $t'_3 < t < t_3$. Firing will cease because of the policy. Employment will be held constant at a higher level than along E^b until hiring resumes between t_4 and t'_4. The observer will see the policy as successful in reducing firing and maintaining employment.

These cases show that an EP policy may reduce firing, reduce hiring, or have no impact on the firms whose behavior is examined. It depends on the timing of the imposition of the policy (and whether its imposition is expected) relative to the firm's expectations about the future path of its prices and product demand and thus its steady-state labor demand. The caveats discussed in the draconian case—the importance of expectations and timing, the strengthening of the results once we allow for worker-hours substitution, the weakening of the results when wage flexibility is allowed, the incentives for creating a second tier of unprotected workers, the transitional reduction in the birth rate of new firms, the transitional increase in the rate of plant closings, and the eventual detrimental effect on average employment all apply to this archetypal policy.

This plethora of possible effects will show up in any evaluation study. We know (Leonard 1987) that the diversity of employers' experiences is immense, even during times when aggregate demand is falling and even within narrowly defined industries. An evaluation of the immediate effects of an EP policy will thus present a highly varied picture of its effects. It should not be surprising if there is little evidence that an EP policy, or its removal, has the expected steady-state effect on employment or hiring.[5] Moreover, the immensity of differences among employers means that gross effects will dwarf any net negative impact on employment growth during good times or net positive effect in reducing layoffs during bad times. With aggregate data, the detrimental long-term effects of EP policy will not be discernible to the evaluator unless the EP policy is sufficiently stringent or sufficiently unexpected and imposed during a cyclical upturn.

Policies That Alter the Employee-Hours Mix

The variety of policies that affect employers' choices of workers and hours per worker is as great as the variety that affect the pattern of layoffs and hiring over the cycle. Among them are policies that reduce the length of the standard workweek; that require premium pay for hours worked beyond the standard workweek; that require employers to provide benefits, often fixed per worker, for persons working less than full-time schedules; and others. For purposes of analyzing their impact, the only common themes of these policies are that they raise labor costs and tilt employers' relative demand toward workers and away from hours.

The theory of reductions in standard hours has been analyzed with great care by Hart (1987). Since the policy has not been analyzed in the U.S. context, I ignore it in the remainder of this paper. Some theoretical analysis of the effect of the overtime pay premium has been offered. Since the policy raises the variable costs of worker-hours while leaving fixed, per-worker costs unchanged, it should increase the ratio of employment to hours. I examine the empirical evidence on this later and extend it in two directions.

One policy that has not been analyzed but that is likely to attract increased

[5]For example, Buechtemann (1989b) finds little evidence that the German Employment Promotion Act, essentially a relaxation of earlier EP policies, raised hiring. The discussion here makes it clear that the effect of such a policy cannot be inferred in the absence of a very well-specified counterfactual.

attention during the 1990s is mandatory coverage of part-time employees for certain employee benefits. Such coverage has been proposed in several recent congresses and usually applies to health and pension benefits.[6] The European Community has urged member states to offer part-time workers the same access to employee benefits (and job security) that they offer full-time employees (Disney and Szyszcak 1984). Proposals have also been put forth that would require Canadian employers to prorate benefits for part-time workers (Reid and Swartz 1982). Even broader are proposals to finance a comprehensive national health system by an expanded payroll tax.

Insofar as the hourly labor costs of part-time workers differ from those of full-time workers, these proposals merely raise the cost of part-time workers and induce employers to shift away from using part-time worker-hours. As such, they protect the worker-hours of full-time employees. To the extent, though, that the benefits proposed for mandated coverage of part-timers represent fixed costs to the employer, the proposals would also change the relative number of hours per part-time worker compared to full-time workers. That is, they would reduce the "part-timeness" of part-time work by providing employers with incentives to lengthen the part-time workweek. There is abundant evidence for numerous economies (OECD 1983) that the hourly earnings of part-time workers are below those of other workers. Other evidence demonstrates that part-time workers are less likely to receive employer-paid medical benefits, sick leave, and life insurance.[7] Since health coverage is a fixed cost, these proposals mandate policies that would increase the fixed costs of employing a group of low-wage workers. They would have less effect on the variable costs of employing part-time workers and less or no effect on any of the costs of employing full-time workers.

We know little about employment-hours substitution (Hamermesh 1989a: chap. 3) and nothing about the substitution of hours of one group of workers for employment in another group. Thus, we are unable to infer anything about the likely impact of such a policy on employers' relative demand for employment and hours of different types of workers. This inability to analyze the policy is compounded when we recognize that imposing mandatory benefits will surely change the supply behavior of part-time workers and thus change their wages and equilibrium employment.

The policy should be analyzed in a partial-equilibrium model that allows for supply responses of both part-time and full-time workers. The theory yields no useful predictions on this policy, other than that it reduces the total demand for worker-hours by raising labor costs. There is also no instructive empirical work

---

[6]The proposed Part-Time and Temporary Workers Protection Act, 101st Congress, H.R. 2563, would provide the pension protection under ERISA, the basic U.S. legislation covering private pensions, and the health insurance requirement under a new system of protection.

[7]A survey of larger firms showed that the likelihood of coverage by benefits increases with the number of hours worked per week (U.S. Chamber of Commerce 1990). For example, in 1989, 99 percent of the full-time workers in the survey had medical benefits but only 25 percent of the part-time workers did. Comparable figures for retirement plans were 89 and 36 percent; for paid vacations, they were 96 and 35 percent.

on this issue. I therefore ignore it in what follows, though it should be high on the list of labor market policies that attract the attention of economists during this decade. It is both an EP policy and one designed to protect the interests of women workers, who constitute the great majority of part-timers in most countries (OECD 1983).

Empirical Effects of EP Policies on Adjustment

Until the passage of the Worker Adjustment and Retraining Notification Act (WARN) in 1988, the United States had no national policy, and only a very few state policies aimed directly at minimizing layoffs or plant closings. For that reason there is none of the detailed analysis of specific policies that has been provided for Western Europe. We have, though, seen an erosion of the long-standing employment-at-will common-law doctrine that had given nonunion employers free rein to terminate workers with long tenure.[8] Given the inchoate nature of these changes, it is impossible to undertake a standard evaluation of one or several particular policies. Thus, the evidence I present is only suggestive of the impact of these myriad small changes.

My work is motivated by a series of studies that have examined changes over time, or differences across countries, in the lagged response of employment demand to shocks to product demand. Nickell (1979) used this approach to show that British firms slowed their adjustment of employment levels over the period 1955–76. Abraham and Houseman (1989a) find that U.S. employers adjust more rapidly to output shocks than their Japanese counterparts and observe (Abraham and Houseman 1989b) the same difference between the U.S. and West German economies. Hamermesh (1988) shows that the average lag of employment behind output shocks appeared to lengthen in many OECD countries in the 1970s. All of these results are interpreted as providing generalized evidence of the effects of EP policies in dampening employment fluctuations, as predicted by the theory discussed above.

I have severe problems with this literature for several reasons, and I am not sure we have learned anything from it. First, attributing a structural change in a time series involves artificially ruling out any contemporaneous causes of the change other than the particular item of interest, in this case the growth of EP policies. Second, and perhaps more important, all of these studies rely on the assumption that the costs of adjusting employment are quadratic and symmetric in the size of the adjustment. I have provided (Hamermesh 1989b) evidence that this assumption is not universally applicable. In light of this evidence, one

---

[8]See Krueger 1991 for an interesting discussion of this erosion and how it is leading states to begin legislating EP policies. A leading scholar of labor law (St. Antoine 1985) noted, "The most significant development in the whole field of labor law during the past decade was the growing willingness of the courts to modify the traditional doctrine of employment-at- will. . . . Judges in some thirty jurisdictions declared their readiness to blunt some of the worst rigors of the rule that an employment contract of indefinite duration can be terminated by either party at any time for any reason."

cannot use aggregated data to infer changes or differences in adjustment costs unless one holds constant for the structure of shocks to product demand among units in the aggregate (Hamermesh 1990a). These concerns simply suggest that this generalized literature must be taken with heaping tablespoonsful of salt.

Despite my difficulties with this literature, I carry it a step further and examine whether employment adjustment in the United States has been affected by the changing common-law interpretation of the employment-at-will doctrine and other still more diffuse changes. I provide two wrinkles on the literature: (1) the estimates cover only the period 1973–88 so as to avoid confusing changes in adjustment that might be caused by changing EP practices with the effects of any structural changes that occurred suddenly in the early 1970s; (2) I estimate the adjustment model separately for each major industry. I assume that interindustry differences in changes in adjustment paths are related to differences in the incidence of changes in the application of the employment-at-will doctrine. Given the lack of any information on the distribution of output shocks below the level of an industry, I assume throughout that there is no change in that distribution. Thus, while I do not circumvent my own criticism of this literature, I recognize the problem and improve slightly on previous work by disaggregating at least down to the level of major industries.

Let us assume that the relaxation of the employment-at-will doctrine had no impact on heavily unionized industries, since unionized workers in those industries are protected by their contracts, and it is possible that such protection spilled over to nonunion workers in the industry. If the predictions above are correct, and making the major assumption that we can ignore aggregation problems, we should observe a trend toward slower adjustment in the least unionized industries relative to the more unionized ones. This assumes that the effects that I attribute to changing EP policy are not attributable to changes in the extent of unionization or the magnitude of spillover from union firms.[9] The average incidence of union membership by major industry during 1979–81 is shown in the first row of table 2-1 for construction, mining, durable and nondurable manufacturing, transportation, public utilities and communications, retail and wholesale trade, and finance and services.

To measure the speed of adjustment, I estimate:

$$E_t = \alpha E_{t-1} + \alpha' \, t \, E_{t-1} + \beta \, t + \sum_{i=0}^{4} \gamma_i \, Y_{t-1} + \sum_{i=0}^{4} \gamma_i' \, t Y_{t-i}, \quad (2\text{-}1)$$

where α, β, and γ are parameters, E and Y are the logarithms of total employment and real output, and t denotes time. The equations are estimated for each of the nine major industries from the fourth quarter of 1973 through the third quarter

---

[9]In 1975, 25.5 percent of nonagricultural employees were members of unions. By 1988, the figure had fallen to 17.0 percent.

TABLE 2-1. *Unionization by Major Industry, 1979–81 (annual averages)*[a], *and Lag Parameters at Selected Points, 1973–88*

	Industry								
	CON	MIN	DUR	NON	TPU	RET	WHO	FIN	SER
	34.2	33.3	38.6	31.8	51.2	10.4	13.3	4.7	18.5
Quarter	Lag parameters, $\alpha + \alpha' t$								
1973.4	0.771	0.770	1.039	1.073	0.987	0.709	1.145	0.638	0.573
1981.1	0.767	0.708	0.994	0.818	0.817	0.765	0.828	0.859	0.616
1988.3	0.764	0.646	0.950	0.563	0.647	0.822	0.511	1.081	0.659

[a]Based on Kokkelenberg and Sockell's 1985 tabulations from Current Population Surveys.
CON=construction, MIN=mining, DUR=durable manufacturing, NON = nondurable manufacturing, TPU=transportation, public utilities, and communications, RET=retail, WHO=wholesale trade, FIN=finance, and SER=services.

of 1988.[10] Because I include interaction terms with the time trend, the estimated speed of adjustment can vary over time. It can be measured at time t as the inverse of $a + a' t$, or by simulating the impact of a steady-state increase in output demand on the path of employment.[11]

The estimates of $\alpha + \alpha' t$ are presented in table 2-1 for each industry at the beginning, middle, and end points of the sample period. Many of the changes over this period are insignificant. But in the five most heavily unionized industries (unionization in 1979–81 above 30 percent), the estimated lagged adjustment parameter fell during the sample period, indicating that the adjustment of employment to output shocks became more rapid during the 1970s and 1980s. In three of the four industries with unionization below 20 percent, the opposite change occurred: the adjustment parameter increased, indicating a slower response of employment changes to output shocks.

The simulations of the effects of a permanent 1 percent shock to output, presented in table 2-2, are less relevant to the issue of adjustment but are worth examining. They tell a less clear story. The distinction between heavily and less unionized industries is not discernable. There is, however, a general trend in all but wholesale trade toward smaller adjustments to permanent output shocks. This is consistent with, though hardly proof of, the proposition that workers have become more insulated from shocks to product demand because of changes in EP policies, particularly the decline of employment at will.

[10]The employment data are taken from CITIBASE and are averaged from the monthly establishment surveys. The nominal output data are national income by sector. For transportation, wholesale trade, retail trade, and mining, these data are deflated by the GNP deflator. For the other industries, sector-specific deflators are used. A diskette containing this data file is available on request from the author.

[11]A test of whether the parameters α' and γ'_i are jointly significant yields $F(6, 46) = 6.34$, 1.30, 1.74, 2.12, 2.27, 1.52, 1.50, 6.31, 1.76, different from zero at the 90 percent confidence level in four of the nine industries.

TABLE 2-2. *Responses of Employment to a Permanent 1 Percent Shock to Output*

Period	CON	MIN	DUR	NON	TPU	RET	WHO	FIN	SER
					Time of shock: 1973.4				
0	0.755	0.730	0.505	0.377	0.189	0.105	0.013	0.231	0.247
1	0.985	0.784	0.764	0.668	0.380	0.294	−0.010	0.299	0.457
2	1.107	0.724	0.925	0.801	0.623	0.410	−0.074	0.399	0.571
3	1.171	0.762	1.059	0.987	0.713	0.439	−0.265	0.414	0.628
4	1.412	0.842	1.139	1.151	1.269	0.585	−0.526	0.528	0.689
5	1.597	0.903	1.223	1.326	1.447	0.689	−0.821	0.602	0.724
6	1.740	0.951	1.309	1.512	1.622	0.762	−1.157	0.650	0.744
7	1.851	0.987	1.398	1.709	1.793	0.814	−1.537	0.681	0.756
8	1.936	1.015	1.491	1.920	1.961	0.852	−1.969	0.701	0.763
9	2.001	1.036	1.587	2.144	2.126	0.878	−2.459	0.714	0.766
10	2.051	1.053	1.687	2.383	2.288	0.897	−3.015	0.722	0.769
					Time of shock: 1981.1				
0	0.532	0.514	0.326	0.221	0.338	0.106	0.143	0.065	0.185
1	0.693	0.568	0.545	0.367	0.399	0.303	0.252	0.113	0.356
2	0.741	0.517	0.631	0.427	0.566	0.423	0.317	0.153	0.431
3	0.838	0.592	0.709	0.497	0.862	0.437	0.347	0.195	0.548
4	0.972	0.667	0.729	0.504	1.040	0.501	0.328	0.211	0.596
5	1.075	0.721	0.749	0.509	1.186	0.550	0.313	0.224	0.625
6	1.153	0.759	0.769	0.513	1.305	0.587	0.300	0.236	0.643
7	1.214	0.785	0.789	0.517	1.402	0.616	0.289	0.246	0.654
8	1.260	0.804	0.808	0.520	1.481	0.638	0.281	0.255	0.661
9	1.296	0.818	0.828	0.522	1.546	0.654	0.273	0.262	0.665
10	1.323	0.827	0.847	0.524	1.599	0.667	0.267	0.268	0.667
					Time of shock: 1988.3				
0	0.302	0.292	0.141	0.060	0.491	0.108	0.277	−0.106	0.121
1	0.392	0.371	0.334	0.136	0.368	0.313	0.440	−0.155	0.246
2	0.365	0.348	0.363	0.242	0.467	0.439	0.510	−0.266	0.275
3	0.498	0.472	0.407	0.298	1.010	0.437	0.620	−0.319	0.445
4	0.523	0.544	0.394	0.261	1.128	0.415	0.633	−0.527	0.478
5	0.541	0.591	0.381	0.241	1.205	0.398	0.639	−0.752	0.500
6	0.555	0.621	0.369	0.229	1.255	0.383	0.642	−0.995	0.515
7	0.566	0.640	0.357	0.223	1.287	0.371	0.644	−1.258	0.524
8	0.574	0.653	0.346	0.219	1.308	0.361	0.645	−1.542	0.531
9	0.581	0.661	0.336	0.217	1.321	0.353	0.645	−1.849	0.535
10	0.586	0.666	0.326	0.216	1.330	0.347	0.646	−2.180	0.537

CON=construction, MIN=mining, DUR=durable and nondurable manufacturing, TPU=transportation, public utilities, and communications, RET=retail, WHO=wholesale trade, FIN=finance, and SER=services.

These regressions provide some evidence that the apparent relaxation of the employment-at-will doctrine has had an effect on nonunion employers' willingness to lay off and hire workers. Given all the difficulties I have noted, however, the analysis is best viewed as only suggestive. Only with a thorough econometric examination of microeconomic data will we be able to produce convincing evidence of the impact, or lack thereof, of a panoply of EP policies.[12]

Evidence on Overtime Pay and Unemployment Insurance

Overtime Pay Premium

As noted above, the 50 percent premium for overtime work in employment covered by the Fair Labor Standards Act of 1938 should generate an increase in the ratio of employment to hours at each input of worker-hours. Substantial previous work has demonstrated that this does in fact occur. Perhaps the best estimate is that if we were to raise the premium to 100 percent, employment would rise by .5 to 2 percent at a fixed total demand for worker-hours (Ehrenberg and Schumann 1982).

Though these results are interesting, they do not answer the question that should concern the analysis of overtime pay premia in the context of job security, namely, the effect on the total demand for employees. The overtime pay premium raises the cost of labor. It is likely that workers and hours are jointly p − substitutes for capital, so that a higher overtime pay premium will induce firms to substitute capital for labor, thus reducing the demand for worker-hours. Exactly analogous to the archetypal EP policy, a higher overtime pay premium will protect employment but possibly reduce total employment through the higher labor costs it produces.

Even accounting for capital-labor substitution is not sufficient to allow one to infer the effects of changing the premium on equilibrium employment. One must also consider changes in the supply of labor induced by changes in the policy: the higher overtime premium raises the returns to working and induces an increase in labor supply. To embody these effects and the standard employee-hours substitution, I simulate a partial equilibrium model involving homogeneous labor whose hours of work can be varied. The crucial assumption throughout is that the supply elasticity of hours per week equals that of workers—the worker-hours distinction is unimportant on the supply side of the labor market.[13]

In the simulation I assume that the net change in employment can be parti-

---

[12]For a different approach to assessing the employment impact of recent exceptions from the employment-at-will doctrine, see Dertouzos and Karoly, chap 8.

[13]This assumption is clearly incorrect. On theoretical grounds, we know that income effects that change interior solutions to the worker's choice of utility-maximizing hours do not operate on the decision about whether to enter the labor force. The distinction is confounded by the importance of fixed costs of entering the labor force.

TABLE 2-3. Percentage Change in Employment Due to an Increase in the Overtime Premium

Labor-supply elasticity	Labor-demand elasticity					
	−.15	−.30	−.75	−.15	−.30	−.75
0	.16	−.18	−1.20	1.66	1.32	.30
.10	.30	−.01	−1.00	1.80	1.49	.50
.50	.42	.24	−.52	1.92	1.74	.98

tioned into the effect on the ratio of employees to hours at a given input of worker-hours and the effect on the total demand for worker-hours. In calibrating the simulation, I assume that we are evaluating the impact of increasing the overtime premium by one-third, from time and a half to double time. Using reasonable estimates of the amount of overtime worked, this implies a 2.3 percent increase in labor costs.[14] Following the massive evidence summarized by Hamermesh (1989a:chap. 3), I assume that the labor-demand elasticity takes on the values [−.15, −.30, −.75]. I assume that the supply elasticity of worker-hours takes on the values [0, .10, .50]. For both parameters, the middle value is the "best-guess" estimate. Finally, I assume that the effect of the one-third increase in the overtime premium on employment at a fixed total-labor input lies between .005 and .02, the range obtained in studies of this effect.

The results of the simulations are presented in table 2-3 for the three sets of parameters. They show very clearly the importance of considering capital-labor substitution in evaluating the impact of changing the rate of premium pay. If labor supply is quite inelastic, raising overtime premia will reduce total employment if the employee-hours substitution that it produces is near the low end of the range of estimates. At the middle of the range of estimates and with the "best guesses" about the elasticities of labor supply and demand, there is a negligible effect on total employment. Using the best available estimates of the extent of substitution along the various margins of labor demand, it seems clear that higher overtime pay will not expand employment unless labor supply is far more elastic than the huge array of estimates suggests.

One might argue that these negative conclusions are unfair, in that one purpose of mandatory overtime premium pay is to spread work in a recession. The policy, though, is permanent, and for this reason it has permanent impacts on equilibrium outcomes—employment, hours, and wages. The policy may generate short-term gains during cyclical declines, and the simulation shows that it can increase equilibrium employment, though even that is by no means certain. These effects

[14]Ehrenberg and Schumann (1982:46) infer from Current Population Survey (CPS) data that 69.8 million hours of overtime were worked in the reference week in May 1978. During that same week, total hours worked were 3.66 billion (*Employment and Earnings*, June 1978). Combining these figures, remembering that overtime hours cost 1.5 times regular hours, and assuming that wages equaled 80 percent of labor cost yields a share of overtime costs in total labor cost of 2.27 percent.

must therefore be offset by the negative impact on total worker-hours and the reduction in living standards that it generates by raising employment costs.

Unemployment Insurance

As the discussion so far has made clear, EP policy in the United States is a poor cousin of the policy in Western Europe and even Canada. I should not end, though, without discussing a uniquely American policy device that does function more or less like the archetypal EP policy. Though unemployment insurance was not intended to be primarily for employment protection, this program, which paid $13 billion in benefits in 1988, does protect employment. As massive amounts of evidence show, our unemployment insurance (UI) system probably generates greater fluctuations in employment than would arise in its absence.[15] A more fruitful way of looking at UI, however, asks what would occur if we financed benefits through flat-rate payroll taxes, as is done in most of Europe, instead of through partly experience-rated taxes. Viewed this way, one sees that the American UI system does stabilize employment, compared to one with the same rules on eligibility and benefit levels but financed by general payroll taxes (or out of general revenue) with the same tax ceiling as UI.

Cyclical fluctuations in employment in the United States are well known to be greater than those in Western Europe. The conventional wisdom is that the American UI system is responsible for employment fluctuations that would not otherwise exist. This is correct, though the nonrating of European systems suggests that the difference is due to subtle structural causes and/or to the very low tax base in the U.S. system (that biases employers against relying on variations in hours). Institutionally, the relevant counterfactual is not what the U.S. economy would look like in the absence of UI but what would occur if the United States abolished experience rating and adopted a European system of financing. By that criterion, UI, as long as it stays mainly experience rated, protects employment from output shocks. It would offer still more protection if experience rating were improved further and if the ceiling on the tax base were not so low. Moreover, because experience rating provides incentives to stabilize employment, it reduces benefit costs (and taxes), thus lowering labor costs and increasing average employment compared to what might otherwise occur. Though not formally a substitute for EP policies, continued and improved experience rating of UI benefits in the United States will do more to protect and create jobs than policies whose formal goal is employment protection.

Conclusions—Do We Know Anything about EP Policy?

The answer to this question is yes, but not much. Most important, we know that any policy that raises the per-period cost of labor will eventually reduce the

---

[15]See Topel 1985 and Hamermesh 1990b for discussions of the evidence on the effects of UI financing on employment fluctuations and levels.

total amount of labor—workers times hours—employed. We know this not from the study of any particular EP policy but from the massive literature on labor demand more generally. The reduction may not be immediate; but the effect will eventually be felt. How much depends on the stringency of the EP policy—how strictly it is enforced and the magnitude of the increment to the costs of labor. In the United States the weak enforcement and minuscule size of most EP policies means they cannot have had much effect on the labor market. Only continuing changes in the application of employment at will are likely to have much effect. We saw some slight reflection of this effect in the estimated decrease in the speed of adjustment of employment to output shocks in nonunion industry during the 1970s and 1980s.

This reduction in employment need not be detrimental with respect to overall social goals. It may be desirable to reduce variations in employment among those fewer workers who have jobs. It may be possible, though the opposite seems more likely, to impose policies at a time when they actually forestall reductions in employment that would otherwise occur during a cyclical downturn.

The theory of EP policy provides a cautionary note to those wishing to discern the detrimental effect of policy behind every rise in unemployment and for those who see the apparent absence of any effect as proof that such policies lack negative side effects. While its long-term effects—smaller employment fluctuations and lower average employment—are clear, EP policy can reduce hiring, reduce firing, or have no impact at all in the period after its introduction. The initial effect depends on employers' expectations about product demand and labor costs and their relation to the timing of the introduction of the policy. Evaluating EP policies requires more than examining their aggregate and immediate effects. One must study their initial and eventual impact on a broad sample of employers whose experiences cover the full range of exogenous shocks to labor demand.

3

The Economics of Employment Protection: A Comment to Daniel S. Hamermesh

Horst-Manfred Schellhaass

Daniel Hamermesh's paper in this volume is a fine example of an economic analysis of law. He uses the traditional microeconomic assumption of constrained profit maximization to examine the impact of employment protection policies on firms' incentive structure with respect to hiring and firing. He defines the scope of his research very broadly to include any explicit or implicit policy designed to increase employers' reluctance to lay off workers. This definition includes the traditional legal protection rules as well as financial disincentives through severance payments or through experience rating of employers' unemployment insurance contributions.

Impact on the Level of Employment

Hamermesh's most important assumption for his short-term analysis is that the introduction of layoff restrictions come as a surprise; in other words, enterprises do not have the chance to adjust the size of their staff or equipment to a restrictive policy in advance. Thus, the time of imposition is critical in determining whether the employment protection policy reduces firing or delays hiring immediately or whether it has no effect at all. This diversity of employers' reactions, however, makes it very difficult to conduct an empirical evaluation of immediate impacts.

The interesting aspect of the long-term effects is whether higher employment during a recession compensates for lower employment during a boom. Hamermesh argues that this is not so. In fact, this is only correct if one assumes, as Hamermesh does, that firms bear the costs of employment protection. Of course, it is difficult or even impossible to pass the costs of employment protection on to consumers or workers during a recession because the excess capacity precludes price increases and there may be obstacles to wage reductions (e.g., in the form of collective wage agreements), even if firms are operating at a loss. At the same time, the unbalanced growth of profits and wages during a cyclical upturn shows that firms may be successful in that period in passing on the costs of employment protection. Here, employment protection must be financed by the insured workers via sacrifices of potential income increases. In this setting firms act like insurers, partially covering the risks of income loss to their workers due to job loss. As direct wage costs are substituted for fringe benefits, total labor costs on average remain constant over the business cycle.

Under such circumstances it is doubtful whether employment protection policy necessarily reduces average employment over the cycle. Nickell (1978:339) has analyzed the conditions under which total employment decreases or increases. If the sum of irreversible wage costs and fixed costs in a recession is greater than gross profit per machine earned in a boom, average employment is reduced. Such a result does not appear to be unlikely, but other results are also possible.

Impact on the Structure of Unemployment

Even if the costs are borne by workers, financial compensation of the firms' expenditures for employment protection is only realized on average, not for every subgroup of workers. Actual collective agreements do not charge the true costs of employment protection to each group. Thus, groups such as the severely handicapped that are protected by special laws are expensive relative to their productivity and therefore have the greatest difficulties finding a job. In my opinion, the impact of traditional employment protection policies on the structure of unemployment is much more important and a larger social burden than any negative impact it may have on the level of employment.

Fortunately, the negative impacts of employment protection policies are not unavoidable. The German *Sozialplan* ("social plan"),[1] for example, does not discriminate between worker groups based on personal characteristics; the amount of severance payments is determined predominantly by tenure. In this way the amortized annual costs of the Sozialplan are nearly equal for skilled employees, who usually have longer job tenure, and for unskilled workers, who bear a higher risk of dismissal because of their lack of firm-specific human capital. In that neither group has a cost disadvantage at the time of hiring, the severance pay approach to employment security policy is unlikely to affect the structure of unemployment.

Impact on Technological Innovation

Hamermesh calls our attention to the fact that while standard analysis deals with continuing firms, a substantial proportion of the fluctuations in employment

---

[1]According to the 1972 Amended Works Constitution Act, the works councils in Germany can demand that a social plan be negotiated between management and workers' representatives in case of work force reductions or work reorganizations affecting a large part of the work force. Social plans are designed to cushion the socioeconomic impact of such changes on the workers and usually involve rules for seniority-graded severance payments, early retirement schemes, relocation allowances, and wage guarantees in the case of reassignment.

is due to births and deaths of firms. He finds that the birth rate of new firms in the new equilibrium will be lower than in the previous steady state. Hence, employment protection policy reduces the ability of new firms to compete in product markets. In a dynamic setting, competition is weakened when the rate of innovation slows down. In the following section I analyze whether employment protection policies may have such an impact.

There are two ways in which the costs of employment protection may influence the cost-benefit ratio of innovations. A direct impact results from the fact that for existing firms the introduction of innovations requires some adjustments in equipment and staff, which in general imposes costs on incumbent employees. The indirect impact lies in the anticipation that future severance payments will fall due when the newly introduced technology becomes obsolete. Undoubtedly, the direct and indirect costs make it more costly for an enterprise to adopt new technologies, thus reducing its profit expectations compared to the situation when there are no employment protection policies. Nevertheless, the costs of employment protection do not threaten the kind of path-breaking innovations that are most important for maintaining the competitiveness of an economy. The rate of return for those initiatives, even net of employment protection, should still be higher than for alternative projects.

With regard to moderate innovations, it is useful to distinguish between product innovations and process innovations. Typical of moderate product innovations are "me-too" products that improve aspects of a given product but do not incorporate real technological breakthrough. Since their payoff tends to be small, the costs of employment protection policies may push their rate of return below the critical margin. As a consequence, some "me-too" innovations will not be realized.

The economic consequence of a smaller number of "me-too" products is that there is less competition between innovators and imitators. Employment protection policies hinder the diffusion of product innovations, which, in turn, slows down the erosion of profits of the original innovators. The stronger position of the innovator does not lead to the conclusion, however, that the impact of employment protection policies on the rate of product innovations is necessarily negative.

The impact of employment protection policies on process innovations is different. They impede the continuous adaptation of technologies, as each adjustment requires severance payments to dismissed or transferred employees. With each technological process left unused, however, the profit incentives for a subsequent technological innovation increase since a larger cost reduction can now be realized by making only one major change in production technology. The main impact of employment protection policies on process innovations is that they reduce the number of discrete steps used to realize a given technological change. In that the rate of technical progress is measured by realized product and process innovations, however, and not by the required number of intermediate steps to achieve it, it cannot be unambiguously stated that employment protection policies negatively influence the rate of technical innovation.

Nevertheless, situations exist in which employment protection impedes the adoption of innovations. In practice, the internal financing of employment protection by gains from good times is threatened by potential breaches of the implicit wage contract. In Germany, firms are forbidden from charging reserves for future redundancy payments against current costs, with the consequence that wage reductions, which are in fact risk premiums to the firms, are shown as profits. If the income policy of the unions is governed by actual profits, it cannot be ruled out that risk premiums are transformed into wages during the profitable expansion period of a product. This would be a partial expropriation of the returns to the investor. In this event, internal financing of employment protection policies breaks down, eliminating the opportunity simultaneously to finance employment protection and product diversification programs to develop new markets in times of declining demand. Because of insufficient liquidity, the enterprise has no choice but to continue to produce its old products with its given staff in that diversification would require costly work force adjustment measures that cannot be financed in a period of stagnation.

For the economy as a whole, however, it is not important that innovations are introduced by a particular firm but that they are introduced at all. It can be argued that managers, who are unable to avoid the period of stagnation, may not be the most efficient innovators. Hence, employment protection policies that eliminate enterprises with structural adjustment problems through unaffordable severance payment plans may actually enhance the rate of technical progress by concentrating innovations within the more flexible firms.

Conclusions

On the one hand, there are strong theoretical reasons for employment protection policies to protect human capital investments or seniority wages. On the other hand, there are many examples of restrictive rules that reduce the efficiency of the economy or, even worse, put at a cost disadvantage the very groups that the rules were meant to protect. Obviously, we do not know enough about the equilibrium between social needs and economic efficiency. As Hamermesh says, we need further research to determine the optimal conditions for enacting employment protection policies. Whatever the kind and size of the policies we choose, we must be aware that insured employees will have to finance them through some reduction in their money incomes. How much employment protection we can afford, therefore, partly depends on workers' preferences. For this reason, different employment security policies may be optimal in different countries.

4

Hiring Behavior and Unemployment

Robert J. Flanagan

The analysis of hiring behavior discussed in this paper began with an interest in the influence of job protection arrangements and other institutional developments in labor markets on the increase in unemployment in Europe during the 1970s and early 1980s. Much of this increase, along with the more recent decline in unemployment in Europe, reflects cyclical developments and is not the focus of this paper. The nonaccelerating inflation rate of unemployment (NAIRU)—often regarded as a definition of equilibrium unemployment—also increased in Europe during this period, as it did in the United States (Coe 1985). The increase was more modest in the United States, however, and was followed by a reversal in the second half of the 1980s (Adams and Coe 1989). As a result, and in contrast to earlier periods, the NAIRU during the 1980s appeared to be higher in Europe than in North America.

This paper focuses on the influence of institutional changes in European labor markets on the increased equilibrium level of unemployment and finds that changes in job protection arrangements by themselves are unlikely to explain significant changes in equilibrium unemployment. The paper does not present a parallel analysis for labor markets in the United States, although the recent growth of wrongful-termination litigation discussed in other papers in this volume (see Gould and Dertouzos and Karoly) must be troublesome for those who wish to attribute higher unemployment to job protection policies. The U.S. NAIRU has declined during the period in which successful wrongful-termination litigation increased. Those who wish to link unemployment developments over the past fifteen years to job protection policies must explain why such policies raised unemployment in Europe and reduced it in the United States.

This paper first discusses the key facts regarding European unemployment that indicate the importance of changes in hiring incentives. It then turns to the evidence regarding the specific incentives that have changed and concludes by considering the relevance of some alternative theories of labor market behavior.

Why Emphasize Hiring Incentives?

That something important happened in European labor market behavior during the late 1970s and early 1980s seems clear from the outward shift in the Beveridge curve reported for many European countries. For a given labor market structure, this curve describes the negative cyclical relationship between the aggregate unemployment and job vacancy rates. Shifts in the curve reflect changing structural factors and are usually interpreted as reflecting changes in structural or frictional unemployment. Shifts can also be induced by changes in structural or frictional job vacancies, however, an interpretation that becomes important in discussions of hiring incentives. Increasing structural maladjustment of labor supply to labor demand and inadequate labor mobility to produce matching could cause an outward shift in the Beveridge curve, but empirical evidence does not support increasing "mismatch" in European labor markets. Instead, the relationship between unemployment and vacancy rates appears to have shifted out in all sectors.[1] Therefore, the key research question is, Why was a given job vacancy rate associated with more unemployment in virtually all sectors by the early 1980s? What incentives, common to all sectors, were at work?

The major clue to the answer to this question is found in the nature of European unemployment flows. Changes in the stock of unemployment equal the difference between flows into and out of unemployment. Flows into unemployment come from layoffs, quits, and labor force entry or reentry from school or housework, while outflows from unemployment occur when jobs are offered and accepted or when workers withdraw from the labor force. A key fact is that the growth of the equilibrium unemployment rate in several major European countries largely reflects a decline in the likelihood of leaving unemployment.

This intriguing fact has several fertile implications. First, certain differences in the unemployment experience in Europe and the rest of the world are traceable to differences in flows. Research on unemployment flows in the United States, Japan, and Australia finds that changes in unemployment in these countries are dominated more by changes in inflows (Darby, Haltiwanger, and Plant 1986; Gregory and Foster 1982). Thus, the duration structure of unemployment in Europe is quite different than in these other countries. In countries in which the odds of exiting unemployment are low, the duration of unemployment is quite long. Fewer people experience relatively long spells of unemployment, so that unemployment tends to be concentrated in a relatively small proportion of the labor force. This is the typical experience in Europe. In countries where inflows account for most of the variation in equilibrium unemployment, the duration of joblessness is shorter and unemployment experience is spread more broadly across the labor force since more people experience comparatively short spells of unemployment. This pattern typifies North America and, to a lesser extent, Australia and Japan. The differences are quite dramatic. In 1987, for example, about half the unemployed in the European Community had been out of work for a year or

---

[1] See Flanagan 1987b:178–84 for a review of the evidence on these points.

more, whereas only 8.1 percent of the unemployed in the United States had been jobless for more than a year. Comparable figures for other major non-European countries are Canada, 9.4 percent; Australia, 18.7 percent; and Japan, 20.2 percent (OECD 1989b:217).

Second, the pattern of unemployment flows that typifies major European countries indicates why job protection (dismissal) legislation may not reduce unemployment. While such legislation may reduce the flow into unemployment (by limiting dismissals), it may also produce reductions in the flow out of unemployment for reasons discussed below.

Third, and most important, the nature of the unemployment flows guides the search for specific labor market factors contributing to the growth of European unemployment. Reduced outflows can be traced to the increased reluctance of employers to hire workers from the pool of unemployed (more extensive employer search) and/or the increased reluctance of unemployed workers to accept job offers (more extensive worker search). My emphasis on changes in hiring behavior follows in large part from the failure of the alternative explanations of declining flows out of unemployment. The hypothesis that the European unemployment flow patterns indicate that workers have become more reluctant to accept available jobs has been undermined by evidence that changes in employee job search behavior and/or in the effectiveness of job matching in labor markets are not the primary sources of the structural component of increased unemployment. For example, several studies have noted that during the early 1980s, many European countries altered unemployment insurance regulations in ways that should have increased workers' willingness to accept jobs—by instituting stricter eligibility rules, reductions in the fraction of the average wages paid out in benefits, and taxation of unemployment benefits (Burtless 1987; Chan-Lee, Coe, and Prywes 1987). Nevertheless, the average of unemployment duration rose dramatically in Europe during this period.[2] By default, attention turns to the hypothesis that European employers have become more reluctant to hire in exchange for a given degree of cyclical pressure.

Hiring Incentives

Any institutional change affecting the structure of labor costs will influence hiring behavior by rational profit-maximizing employers. Such change is more or less ubiquitous in labor markets through the outcomes of legislative and collective bargaining decisions, but for the problem at hand the question is whether institutional changes have moved in sufficiently different directions on different continents to contribute importantly to observed differences in unemployment.

Understanding the role of hiring behavior in unemployment requires a consid-

---

[2]In addition, the failure of studies of several European economies to find evidence of increasing mismatch in the labor market during the 1970s and early 1980s indicates that allegations of less effective job-matching processes also have limited explanatory power (see the studies reviewed in Flanagan 1987b:178–84).

eration of the personnel strategies available to employers. Research on labor markets has shown that labor turnover is costly and employers therefore have economic reasons for preferring long-term employment relationships. Yet employers approach a hiring decision with considerable uncertainty regarding the quality and future productivity of their applicants. In many cases, this can be determined only during a period of on-the-job observation of performance. Rational employers thus seek to minimize hiring costs, subject to institutional constraints, by choosing among alternative personnel strategies. Three such strategies are analyzed in this section.

The first is the traditional trial-and-error strategy, in which unsatisfactory employees are fired after an initial period of observation on the job. The second is the self-selection strategy, in which employers adopt compensation systems that will be accepted only by workers who intend to be stable, high-performance employees. The third is the preemployment screening strategy, in which employers incur substantial search and screening costs before making a hiring decision in order to determine which applicants are most suitable for the enterprise. (A fourth strategy, the payment of efficiency wages, seems less applicable to the European situation and is discussed later in this paper.) Employers are not "locked into" any one strategy, a priori. Their choice of strategy depends on the particular structure of incentives they face.

Trial and Error Strategy

The trial-and-error strategy is the personnel policy implicit in the most simple textbook models of labor markets. Textbook labor market analysis also describes a relatively simple incentive structure in which labor is paid per unit of labor input, as in wage per hour. Common institutional impacts on labor markets alter this incentive structure by adding a fixed charge per employee per pay period, which is independent of the number of hours actually worked, or a fixed "adjustment" charge incurred upon the hiring or termination of a worker. Contributions for social insurance provide an example of the former, while the requirements of job protection (dismissal) legislation provide an example of the latter. Neither of these institutional impacts on hiring incentives appears to provide an adequate explanation of unemployment developments in the 1970s and 1980s, however.

An increase in fixed labor costs—costs incurred per worker rather than per hour of work—encourages firms to work fewer employees for longer hours (in a sense to favor employed insiders over potential new hires [outsiders]), to substitute skilled workers for unskilled workers, and to substitute capital for labor. Increased fixed labor costs therefore provide a case for reduced labor input and relatively large employment reductions for unskilled and inexperienced workers. The incentive effects of growth of fixed labor costs is unlikely to explain recent unemployment differences between the United States and Europe, however. In 1978, the fixed component of labor costs was similar in the United States and in the major countries of Europe, and between 1978 and 1981 there was virtually no change in the ratio of fixed to variable labor costs in these countries (OECD 1986a:102).

The trial-and-error approach may well be the cheapest personnel strategy in an economy that is free of institutional constraints on hiring and firing. Dismissal (job protection) legislation raises the cost of this strategy for employers by introducing procedural requirements or monetary costs to implement dismissals. To avoid these costs, employers must either shift to alternative personnel strategies or implement an alternative version of the trial-and-error approach by hiring temporary, part-time or other categories of workers who may be exempted from the provisions of dismissal legislation. This last option is unlikely to be viable across all skill and occupation levels, however.

Most European countries have some form of statutory dismissal (employment protection) legislation. Broadly speaking, the protections provided by such legislation increased during the 1970s and diminished during the early 1980s. To the extent that job protection legislation raises the costs of employer-initiated job separations, employers may reduce layoffs and hoard more labor during cyclical downturns, thus reducing the flow into unemployment. This direct effect is apparently what those who argue that dismissal legislation reduces unemployment have in mind.

There is an important indirect effect, however. Rational employers seeking to maximize the present value of their future stream of profits will recognize the higher costs of potential future dismissals and reduce their hiring. Thus, the reduction in the flow into unemployment will be counterbalanced by a reduction in the flow out of unemployment as hires are reduced. The unemployed and new labor force entrants will find it harder to obtain jobs. In summary, by themselves, changes in dismissal legislation seem unlikely to have major effects on the level of unemployment and hence are unlikely to have stimulated either the relative increase in European unemployment in the 1970s or the more recent decrease. Dismissal legislation can affect the composition of the unemployed, however, by tending to favor the future employment prospects of employed insiders and to disadvantage the future prospects of unemployed outsiders.

Changes in job protection legislation also fail to explain why the European unemployment experience of the past two decades has been so different from that of the United States. European observers sometimes conclude that the absence of statutory dismissal regulation in the United States denotes an absence of policy. In fact, policies exist at the state level through actions of the judiciary. During the 1980s, the judiciary in most large states increasingly found exceptions to the common-law employment-at-will doctrine that had previously prevailed.[3] Under various circumstances, which still vary by state, dismissals can now be challenged in the court system.

The odds of an employer being challenged by litigation over a dismissal are still probably lower in the United States than in most European countries, par-

---

[3]For a discussion of the grounds or legal theories for prohibiting certain dismissals, see Gould, chap. 5.

ticularly if blue-collar workers were dismissed. The monetary consequences of a successful suit are much greater in the United States, however. In Europe, successful challenges to dismissals produce compensatory monetary awards and/or reinstatement. Successful litigants in the United States also obtain compensatory damages, but courts permit compensation for longer periods of time. In reviewing damages permitted under European laws during the first half of the 1980s, I found ceilings on compensatory awards ranging from $2,200 (in Sweden) to normal earnings for a twelve-month period (in Germany). During the same period compensatory awards in the state of California averaged $344,000 (Flanagan 1987b:195–97). The major difference between the potential monetary costs of dismissals in Europe and the United States is the availability of punitive damage awards for certain categories of unjust dismissals in the United States. These awards can be quite large, since they are meant to punish. (The standard instruction to juries is to "consider an amount that will make the defendant [firm] take notice.") Punitive damage awards in California averaged $557,300 during the first half of the 1980s. Significant interstate variations in policy remain, but the situation just described is typical for most large industrial states. That unemployment insurance is experience rated in the United States but not in Europe also produces higher marginal dismissal costs for American employers. On balance, it seems that differences in dismissal incentives between the United States and Europe have been overstated.

By themselves, the direct effects of job protection policies appear ill suited to explain either increases in equilibrium unemployment or European-American differences in unemployment experience during the 1970s and 1980s. The ultimate effect of job protection legislation on unemployment will be determined by the costs of alternative personnel strategies to which employers may shift when dismissal legislation forecloses the trial-and-error strategy. Other institutional developments have foreclosed some options to European employers that remain available to American employers.

Self-Selection Strategy

Under the self-selection strategy, employers establish compensation systems in which pay rises rapidly with job tenure. Workers are paid wages that are lower than their marginal product early in their career in exchange for wages that exceed their marginal product late in their career, as long as their performance meets standards. (Pay and marginal product over a career are thus equal in an expected value sense.) The initial low wages are effectively a "performance bond" posted by the worker in the expectation that good performance will lead to continued employment, wage increases, and high relative wages late in the career. Workers effectively share the risk inherent in the initial recruitment decision. Workers who do not have desirable performance characteristics or who do not desire a long-term job attachment would be less inclined to accept employment at a firm offering such a compensation plan, and self-selection would substitute for employer screening (Lazear 1981; Salop and Salop 1976).

The self-selection strategy is circumscribed by institutional constraints on the payment of substantial wage differentials between low-tenure and high-tenure personnel. Legislative and collective bargaining developments in several European countries produced considerable pay compression during the 1970s, thereby circumscribing the use of this strategy. Legislative actions included revisions of national indexation and minimum wage systems in France and Italy. Collective bargaining outcomes included increased emphasis by unions on pay equality in France, Italy, and Scandinavian countries (Flanagan 1987a:202–6; Flanagan 1988:131–32). No parallel move toward greater pay compression occurred in the United States during this period.

Thus, institutional constraints developing during the 1970s reduced the attractiveness of the first two of the three broad personnel strategies to European employers.

Preemployment Screening

Under the third strategy—preemployment screening—employers incur greater screening costs than under the other strategies. Screening costs are a function of the gross change in a firm's employment. As such, these costs have a direct impact on the speed of employment adjustment in the short run. Because higher screening costs also raise the average cost of labor over a business cycle, they should reduce average labor input. Unlike fixed employment costs of the fringe benefit variety, screening costs are not generally recorded in official statistical measures of labor costs and thus have not entered previous comparative analyses of unemployment.

There is another potential reason for the greater reluctance among European firms to hire. It is highlighted by the unusually long duration of unemployment in most European countries cited earlier. Long periods of unemployment can produce skill depreciation. As important, employers may believe that long-duration unemployment signals skill depreciation and become reluctant to hire the long-term unemployed. Long-term joblessness then feeds on itself.

Evidence on the Hiring Incentive View

I now consider some evidence on the empirical implications of the "reluctance-to-hire" view of European unemployment. I consider first direct evidence of changes in employer search strategies, screening costs, and hiring behavior. This category of evidence is supportive but sparse.

During the 1970s and 1980s, hiring rates declined rapidly in European countries (OECD 1986b:57). Cyclical influence accounts for at least some of the decline, but the reluctance-to-hire view implies that there was also a structural component to the reduced hiring as employers shifted to a more extensive search for and screening of employees before filling vacancies. Data on employer search and screening costs are not available, but data on the duration of job vacancies exist for some countries. In the raw data, vacancy durations move inversely with the unemployment rate, reflecting cyclical variations in the availability of qualified workers. This cyclical component must be removed before testing for structural influences on the duration of employer search. When this is done, there is evidence of an increase in job vacancy durations in Germany (Franz 1989), consistent with the hiring incentive argument. Parallel analyses for other countries would be useful.

A different type of evidence is available from surveys of businesses regarding factors influencing their hiring plans. While what agents do is more revealing than what they say and while survey questions rarely present respondents with choices as they face them in a real market setting, surveys nonetheless can point to the factors influencing business decisions. In late 1985, the European Community conducted a special survey of some eight thousand industrial firms on employment issues. When asked why their employment levels were not higher, the respondents stressed (after cyclical factors) the high level of nonwage labor costs and insufficient flexibility in hiring and dismissing ("shedding") labor (Nerb 1986:27; see also the contribution by Hofmann in this volume, chap. 25). Unfortunately, the survey makes no distinction between different nonwage labor costs, so it is not clear whether respondents referred mainly to the increased search and screening costs emphasized in this paper or to more traditional (and more frequently recorded) nonwage labor costs. Wage and salary levels received much lower weight in the survey responses.

When asked to rank potential changes in labor market policies according to their expected impact on future employment at their firms, employers gave heaviest weight to "shorter periods of notice and simpler legal procedures in case of redundancies and dismissals." As argued earlier, constraints on dismissals feed back into hiring decisions.

The next three factors received about equal emphasis: "More frequent use of temporary contracts, better trained job-seekers, and introduction of wider wage differentials according to skills and working conditions." The pattern of responses is clearly consistent with the view of hiring incentives sketched earlier in the paper. Moreover, it reinforces the argument of the previous section that hiring reluctance has been fostered by a particular combination of institutional restraints that have foreclosed certain personnel strategies.

One of the stronger implications of the reluctance-to-hire view is that employers increasingly preferred to utilize employed insiders more intensively than to hire unemployed outsiders. Overtime hours constitute an important measure of the intensity of utilization of labor resources within a firm, while unemployment measures the utilization of outsiders. In the absence of changes in hiring incentives, there is a stable negative relationship between the unemployment rate and overtime hours, reflecting a tendency to work employees longer as qualified applicants become scarce in a general expansion of demand. Counterclockwise "loops" in the data around the average relationship trace out the normal tendency of employers to adjust to surprises in demand in either direction by varying hours worked before employment. This is exactly what one observes in the data for the United States. Changes in hiring incentives favoring insiders over outsiders will shift the overtime-unemployment relationship outward to the right, so that more overtime will be worked at a given unemployment rate: as insiders become more preferred to outsiders, the amount of overtime worked at any given unemployment rate will increase. Exactly such a shift occurred in several European countries in the early 1980s (Flanagan 1988:134–41).

The reluctance-to-hire view also has implications for wage determination. In a competitive labor market in which all labor costs are variable, insiders and outsiders are on an equal footing. Exogenous increases in productivity or product prices shift the labor demand curve and increase the employment of outsiders but have no effect on wages. Insider-outsider models raise the possibility that some or all of the gain in productivity may be captured by employed insiders in the form of wage increases, thereby diminishing the firm's incentive to expand employment and output.

The existence of screening, hiring, and dismissal costs discussed in this paper creates "economic rents" that can be divided between firms and their workers through formal or informal bargaining processes. To the extent that insiders have sufficient bargaining power to capture some of these rents, they will receive a higher wage than unemployed workers would accept, but firms will not hire the unemployed as long as the wage premium paid to the insiders is lower than the costs of hiring outsiders (Lindbeck and Snower 1988a). The balance between insider and outsider forces in wage determination is therefore important to the implications for unemployment.

There is both macro and micro evidence on this issue. At the macro level, there have been studies of the influence of insider and outsider variables on aggregate wage adjustments. These studies show that unemployment (a measure of the availability of outsiders) outperforms measures of insiders, such as employment, overtime hours, and business surveys of anticipated employment utilization (Grubb 1986; Flanagan 1988). The macro studies can easily be criticized for providing a rough indication at best of the firm-specific influences on wages that are crucial to assessing the arguments advanced above. To date, studies of this issue at the micro level (using individual firms as the unit of observation) appear confined to the United Kingdom. They generally accord much greater, although by no means exclusive, weight to the influence of internal firm factors in wage determination (Nickell and Wadhwani 1989; Blanchflower, Oswald, and Garrett 1990). This is another area in which micro studies of other European countries are needed.

Documenting the presence of insider influence on wage determination is easier than identifying the particular insider mechanism(s) that are at work. To date, the micro studies of wage determination in firms in the United Kingdom have been able to test only for the effects of insider influence exercised through unions. One micro study found insider effects associated with closed-shop arrangements, but these arrangements covered a rather small proportion of the sample firms (Blanchflower, Oswald, and Garrett 1990). Another study found no general relationship between insider power and the degree of unionization across industries but did find a tendency for insider power in wage setting to emerge in decentralized bargaining structures (Nickell and Wadhwani 1989).

The rather aggregative evidence on the effects of institutional pay compression provides mixed support for the hypothesis advanced earlier in this paper. Direct information on changes in earnings-tenure or earnings-experience profiles between 1970 and the mid-1980s are not available. Instead, one must rely on related measures of earnings differentials by skill level or occupation (on the grounds that some of the steepness in earnings-tenure profiles occurs via promotions). These measures show considerable pay compression for some, but not all, European countries during this period. Compression was particularly notable in France, Italy, and the Scandinavian countries (CERC 1989:57; Flanagan, Soskice, and Ulman 1983:chaps. 6, 9, and 10). In the United Kingdom, a period of pay compression during the 1970s gave way to widening differentials in the 1980s. In Germany, no clear trend emerges. Within the limitations of relatively aggregative data, there is evidence of a connection between pay compression and reduced employment in France (Flanagan 1988). Further progress seems unlikely until more firm-level empirical analyses are possible.

Alternative Theories of Unemployment

The explanation for the relationship between hiring incentives and European unemployment advanced in this paper differs from the efficiency wage approach to unemployment analysis. At a superficial level, similar considerations motivate both theories, notably employers' efforts to address their inherent uncertainty about employee ability and performance. Under efficiency wage theory, firms establish wages above market-clearing rates in order to provide performance incentives to workers whose work cannot be continually monitored. Although there are variants on the basic model, the idea is that this policy creates positive performance incentives in that workers who are caught malingering and dismissed will receive significantly lower wages in another job. An important and interesting feature of efficiency wage theories of unemployment is that firms will be unwilling to hire workers who are willing to work for less than the current wage because lowering the wage would erode the performance incentive. In principle, this wage policy could be added to the list of personnel strategies available to firms.

The bare facts of post–1970 unemployment and wage developments in Europe seem to resist an efficiency wage interpretation. The comparatively large increase in unemployment during this period raises this question: what changes during the 1970s and 1980s could have induced European employers—but not employers in North America—to adopt higher efficiency wages? It is difficult to formulate a coherent response to this question. Moreover, since the increase in unemployment during this period would have to be explained by an increase in efficiency wages, there is also a basic empirical question of whether efficiency wages in fact increased. A precise answer to this question raises unresolved conceptual issues regarding the measurement of efficiency wages.[4] Nevertheless, an increase in efficiency wages for workers whose performance is difficult to monitor would seem to imply an increasing dispersion of wages, and, as we have seen earlier in the paper, no such tendency toward greater wage dispersion developed in European countries during this period. On the contrary, in most countries, measurable wage dispersions narrowed. Indeed, in the presence of the institutional developments discussed above, it should have been increasingly difficult to pay efficiency wages in many European countries.

On the issue of wage dispersion, there is an important difference between efficiency wage theory and the ideas advanced in this paper. Under the career-wage profile ("bonding") story outlined earlier, pay compression in the presence of job protection legislation should produce more unemployment. Under efficiency wage theory, pay compression resulting in a reduction of above-market-clearing wages should produce less unemployment. Moreover, in economies with job protection legislation, paying efficiency wages is unlikely to be an attractive personnel policy since the credibility of an efficiency wage strategy rests on the ability to dismiss malingering employees. To the extent that job protection legislation makes dismissals costly, there would be nothing gained from paying efficiency wages. Turning this argument around does provide a case in which job protection legislation might reduce unemployment: in economies in which many employers follow an efficiency wage policy, legislation constraining dismissals might reduce unemployment by inducing employers to abandon efficiency wages. On balance, however, efficiency wage theory appears to offer little power in explaining unemployment developments in Europe since 1970.

Conclusion

There is considerable evidence that increases in the structural component of European unemployment reflect changes in hiring behavior. This observation is supported by the reduced probability of exiting unemployment, the inability of research to explain this development in terms of increased worker reluctance to accept job offers, and the increased preference accorded insiders over outsiders when firms increase their labor input.

The exact mechanisms and changes in hiring incentives that account for this result are more difficult to trace and may not be the same in all countries. It appears, however, that the effect of statutory or judicial job protection policies on the unemployment level has been overemphasized. Job protection policy may alter the composition of unemployment but by itself should not have a major impact on the level of unemployment. Its ultimate effect on the unemployment level depends on the extent to which the policy, in combination with other institutional changes, forces employers to adopt costlier search and screening strategies. I have suggested and presented some evidence that institutionally driven

---

[4]This issue has received considerable attention in U.S. literature recently. For a representative sample of the debate, see Katz and Summers 1989 and the accompanying comments and discussion.

pay compression is one such aggravating institutional change in some European countries. Other mechanisms are also at work. For example, long-duration unemployment in and of itself may breed hiring reluctance by signaling skill depreciation among the unemployed.

In interpreting the rather aggregative data that are available, one must realize that ceteris is not in general paribus; hiring incentives are not the only factors at work. Sweden, which has had a favorable unemployment experience despite considerable institutionally driven pay compression, provides a case in point. While shifts in the overtime-unemployment relationship in Sweden indicates the presence of hiring disincentives, their effect may have been overbalanced by other forces. For example, one still controversial hypothesis attributes superior macroeconomic performance to centralized collective bargaining structures (Calmfors and Driffill 1988). Alternatively, labor market mechanisms and outcomes may be obscured by a measurement error, to the extent that some enrollment in Swedish labor market programs is a form of disguised unemployment.

We have noted that long-duration unemployment, once started, tends to feed on itself. This begs the question of why long-duration unemployment spells become a characteristic of some labor markets in the first place. Why are European labor markets more inclined to generate "class" unemployment—to create comparatively long periods of joblessness among a relatively small percentage of the labor force—while labor markets in other economies distribute a given amount of unemployment more broadly and more briefly?

Part II

Regulatory Frameworks and Effects of Employment Protection: International Evidence

United States

5
Employment Protection and Job Security Regulation in the United States and Japan: A Comparative View

William B. Gould IV

T he law of job security in the United States has changed enormously during the past decade and, in some respects, has begun to move toward or converge with some of the rules in Japan. There is, however, one significant difference between the two countries regarding recent legal developments: for the most part, the American reforms have taken place in the context of individual dismissals through, most particularly, the common law of wrongful discharge, which has emerged over the past decade. By contrast, Japan has adopted a similar stance regarding both collective and individual dismissals.

The pattern of both law and practice as it relates to job security has indeed had an impact on so-called collective dismissals in the United States. The best examples of this are the Worker Adjustment and Retraining Notification Act (WARN) of 1988,[1] and state legislation of a similar nature enacted before and after its passage, designed to provide for notification in connection with plant closings or substantial layoffs so as to facilitate the retraining and relocation of workers. Similarly, in the shrinking organized sector of the economy in the United States, unions, particularly the United Auto Workers (UAW), have enhanced job protection guarantees in their collective bargaining agreements with the Big Three as well as other companies. Some nonunion companies have also provided guarantees to their workers.[2] Nonetheless, the law relating to the protection of workers in connection with collective dismissal remains antiquated by European and Japanese standards. The best example of this can be found in the National Labor Relations Act of 1935, which remains the basic statute pertaining to the labor-management

---

[1]29 U.S.C. .§§2101–2109 (1988); see also Ehrenberg and Jakubson, chap. 7.
[2]But see Wilke, "Firms Oust 'No Layoff' Tradition," *Wall Street Journal,* April 13, 1990:B1.

relationship in the United States. Essentially, there are three areas in which the antiquated nature of the act is most evident.

The first example is the law relating to strike replacements. Since 1938, the U.S. Supreme Court has established a rule that permits employers to replace strikers permanently and thus to deprive them of their jobs even though the strike is protected under federal labor law. The practical significance of this rule is that employees are supposed to be immunized against employer discharge and discipline.[3] This problem has assumed more considerable significance in the 1980s as major employers, such as United Airlines, Phelps Dodge, International Paper Company, Trans World Airlines, and most recently the Greyhound Bus Lines, have used the permanent replacement tactic against strikes, a phenomenon often thought attributable to President Ronald Reagan's dismissal of unlawfully striking air controllers in 1981.

The second manifestation is the Supreme Court's 1981 holding in *First National Maintenance v. NLRB*,[4] in which the Court held that employers are not obliged to bargain about their decision to close an operation but are obliged to bargain about its effects upon the workers. Through dicta, the Court indicated that employers would be mandated to bargain notice for other job protection features and collective bargaining agreements of the kind the UAW has negotiated in advance of the closing itself.

The third example relates to so-called successorship issues, which currently arise in the context of mergers, acquisitions, and sales of an enterprise. Here the Supreme Court, in a trilogy of decisions in the 1960s and 1970s, has made it impossible for a union to impose the features of a previously negotiated collective bargaining agreement on the successor employer and difficult to establish a union's representative status as exclusive bargaining agent unless the employer hires a majority of the predecessor's work force.[5] It hardly needs to be noted that this produces an obvious incentive for the employer who does not want to recognize the union not to hire the predecessor's employees, notwithstanding the prohibition and the statute against discrimination on account of union membership. In essence, the rule, like so many others in the American labor law arena as it relates to job security, is a problem for the unwary employer who operates without competent counsel. All of these developments, of course, contrast very vividly with the labor law terrain in Japan as well as that of Europe, where job security is promoted.

As noted above, the wrongful-discharge litigation and consequent discussions about the prospect for wrongful-discharge legislation have assumed center stage

---

[3] *NLRB v. Mackay Radio*, 304 U.S. 333 (1938); *TWA v. IFFA, 57 L.W. 4283 (1989)*.
[4] 452 U.S. 666 (1981).
[5] *Wiley & Sons v. Livingston*, 376 U.S. 543 (1964); *NLRB v. Burns International Security Services*, 406 U.S. 272 (1972); *Howard Johnson Co. v. Detroit Local Joint Executive Board, Hotel & Restaurant Employees International Union*, 417 U.S. 249 (1970).

and the scope of changes that have flowed from judge-made law in this arena makes it particularly worthy of our consideration.

Wrongful-Discharge Litigation and Legislative Proposals

Thus far, the American law of wrongful discharge, that is to say, the law involving the propriety of discharge of individual employees, has been judge-made common law promulgated by the courts, albeit with instructions to jurors, rather than devised by the state legislatures or Congress. The abiding principle of American wrongful-discharge law is that the contract of employment is terminable at will. That is to say, absent explicit reasons prohibited by federal or state statutes, such as those relating to discrimination on account of race, sex, or union activity or absent a collective bargaining agreement that protects workers against dismissal, the employer may dismiss the employee at any time for any reason under any circumstance. The law here has changed considerably during the past decade, but the principle that the contract of employment is terminable at will remains intact.

What has changed is that numerous judge-made exceptions have emerged and juries have fueled litigation through large damage awards, sometimes involving compensatory and punitive damages amounting to multimillion dollar judgments. This contrasts dramatically with the position of employees in the organized sector of the economy who are covered by collective bargaining agreements, which frequently limit but rarely ever prohibit layoffs. These agreements provide a measure of security through the seniority principle when layoffs are instituted (last hired/first fired), but also contain a just-cause provision that requires employers to demonstrate that they have cause—just cause or good cause—to dismiss workers in disciplinary matters.

The law of wrongful discharge applies to workers who have the protection of collective bargaining agreements as well as to nonunion employees, although the latter have disproportionately used the available theories. What is particularly important here, however, is the issue of remedy. The employee who is dismissed under a collective bargaining agreement in violation of a just-cause provision is entitled to reinstatement and back pay (sometimes with interest) if he or she prevails. In the courts, however, juries operating within the context of judicially devised instructions can formulate damage awards that dwarf the remedies available from an arbitrator, although the common-law tradition precludes the award of a reinstatement remedy.

Juries have a decidedly different approach to dismissal cases than do arbitrators. For instance, arbitrators, while generally adhering to the principle of progressive discipline in discharge cases (ie., counseling and possible suspension of the employee before the ultimate sanction of discharge is imposed), frequently adhere to management's view that a first offense can automatically mean discharge, where, for instance, the offense involves dishonesty, drunkenness on the job, and the like. Juries, functioning outside of the arbitral common law, may take a different view of such matters, as well as of the employer's discretionary authority to lay off workers for economic reasons. Juries often impose liability and large damage awards according to their own standards of fairness rather than the legal instructions provided by the judge, let alone the arbitral common law. Part of the explanation for this behavior is juror awareness of bad experiences that have been endured by the public at the hand of corporations with high visibility, such as utilities and banks, and a widespread perception that employers have deep pockets to pay out large damages. Although juries were thought to be unsympathetic to plaintiffs in racial discrimination cases, even those involving job discrimination in the 1960s and 1970s, age discrimination cases, which surfaced in the 1970s, have changed the dynamics. Jurors, many of whom were elderly, could identify with growing old. The same thing seems to be happening in connection with wrongful-discharge cases. Jurors can easily identify with the worker who has received a "pink slip."

These very different dynamics have placed a strain upon the collective bargaining system, have required unions to reassess the relatively limited remedies available in it, and have begun to induce some discussion about legislation that might provide for more attractive remedies in the arbitration system or integrate the union and nonunion sectors in a way that has long been true in both Europe and Japan.

Why has the new law of wrongful discharge so recently enhanced the position of workers protesting discharge in the United States? The first reason is the decline of the unions themselves. Unions now represent less than 17 percent of the work force. The need for some form of legal protection for the work force has therefore become more important.

The second factor in the erosion of the terminable at-will principle is the rash of corporate mergers that were smiled upon benignly by the pro-market buccaneers of the Reagan administration. These policies squeezed managers, particularly mid-level managers. This no doubt accounts in part for the disproportionately high number of managerial and professional employees who have instituted dismissal actions in the courts. Because of the subjective nature of the work involved in jobs at this level, their suits have proved particularly vexatious and ill suited to resolution by both judge and jury.

A third reason for these developments is that the anti-discrimination protests of the 1960s and 1970s have increased the awareness of issues related to fairness and due process in the workplace and, in so doing, have raised expectations and created challenges in employer decision making. One immediate consequence has been that, whatever the content of Title VII of the Civil Rights Act of 1964, both minority and female employees, as well as applicants whose complaints have been deemed unmeritorious for lack of proof, have nevertheless frequently challenged personnel unfairness that had nothing whatsoever to do with race and sex discrimination. Further, they have sometimes been successful in prompting policy changes for all employees. Moreover, the result of the Civil Rights Act of 1964 decisions that condemned nonjob-related tests and qualifications has benefited all employees in the work force, not just minorities and women.

The fourth reason is that one of the developments that has laid the groundwork for these changes is the rise of reverse discrimination litigation. As harmful as this development has been to the societal fabric of the United States, it has nonetheless been a basic attack on unfairness and inequity in the workplace. It has served to require employers to justify their conduct.

Finally, the fifth reason is that both the National Labor Relations Act and collective bargaining agreements, negotiated within the framework of the duty to bargain in good faith, have themselves provided for incursions on the principle that the contract of employment is terminable at will. The idea that employer discretion is limited has proved to be contagious.

A number of theories have been used to create new exceptions to the terminable at-will principle.[6] In the first place, most jurisdictions throughout the United States have accepted the principle that an employer may not discharge an employee for reasons that are inconsistent with public policy.[7] Public policy takes a variety of forms, the classic example being the situation that arose in the Supreme Court of California decisions of *Petermann v. International B'hd. of Teamsters*[8] and *Tameny v. Atlantic Richfield Co.*,[9] in which it was alleged that the employers dismissed the employees because the employees insisted on complying with the law. The reporting of criminal activity to public authorities, as well as the disclosure of illegal, unethical, or unsafe practices, has been deemed to be part of the public policy exception to the terminable at-will principle. Justification for the public policy cases has been articulated by Justice Tobriner of the Supreme Court of California in *Tameny*:

In the last half century the rights of employees have not only been proclaimed by a mass of legislation touching upon almost every aspect of the employer-employee relationship, but the courts have likewise evolved certain additional protections at common law. The courts have been sensitive to the need to protect the individual employee from discriminatory exclusion from the opportunity of employment whether it be by the all-powerful union or employer. [citation omitted] This development at common law shows that the employer is not so absolute a sovereign of the job that there are not limits to his prerogative. One such limit at least is the present case. The employer cannot condition employment upon required participation in unlawful conduct by the employee.[10]

---

[6]A total of forty-four states have developed one or more common-law exceptions to limit the terminable at-will principle. See Employment at Will, State Rulings Chart, 9A *Lab. Rel. Rep.* (BNA) 505:51–52 (1989) (hereafter State Rulings Chart).
[7]The courts in thirty-nine states—Alabama, Alaska, Arizona, Arkansas, California, Connecticut, Hawaii, Idaho, Illinois, Indiana, Iowa, Kansas, Kentucky, Maryland, Massachusetts, Michigan, Minnesota, Missouri, Montana, Nebraska, Nevada, New Hampshire, New Jersey, New Mexico, North Carolina, North Dakota, Ohio, Oklahoma, Oregon, Pennsylvania, South Carolina, South Dakota, Tennessee, Texas, Virginia, Washington, West Virginia, Wisconsin, and Wyoming—have adopted a public policy exception to the terminable at-will doctrine.
[8]174 Cal. App. 2d 184 (1959).
[9]27 Cal. 3d 167 (1980).
[10]27 Cal. 3d 167 at 178.

The California Supreme Court has held in *Foley v. Interactive Data Corp.*,[11] a landmark decision in a number of respects, that a "substantial public policy" violation is not to be found in an employer's discharge of an employee for reporting relevant information concerning other employees to his or her employer. The court indicated, however, that the question of whether the reporting was done to a public authority as opposed to a private employer was not necessarily dispositive of the public policy issue. Chief Justice Lucas said, writing for the majority:

> The absence of a distinctly "public" interest in this case is apparent when we consider that if an employer and employee were expressly to agree that the employee has no obligation to, and should not, inform the employer of any adverse information the employee learns about a fellow employee's background, nothing in the state's public policy would render such an agreement void. By contrast, in the previous cases asserting a discharge in violation of public policy, the public interest at stake was invariably one which could not properly be circumvented by agreement of the parties.[12]

Other courts, such as the Supreme Court of Oregon, have concluded that the public policy exception is applicable if an employer requires an employee to choose between a public duty, such as serving on a jury, and being employed with the employer.[13] Moreover, the Court of Appeals for the Third Circuit has concluded that discharge for the expression of views in accordance with one's own conscience is similarly a public policy violation.[14]

But the court in *Foley* did not resolve the scope of the public policy exception in California. Said the court:

> We do not decide in this case whether a tort action alleging a breach of public policy under Tameny may be based only on policies derived from a statute or constitutional provision or whether nonlegislative sources may provide the basis for such a claim. . . . We must . . . inquire whether the discharge is against public policy and affects a duty which inures to the benefit of the public at large rather than to a particular employer or employee.[15]

The public policy exception is significant because it is rooted in tort and punitive and compensatory damages are therefore available in jury trials for its violation. The difficulty, however, is that most employees, particularly those who are not within the managerial and professional ranks, are not able to avail themselves of it inasmuch as they are not in the position to possess information about which they could complain. Although the doctrine has been extended to unionized employees covered by collective bargaining agreements under grievance arbitration machinery and thus provides them with considerable more relief than back pay and reinstatement by virtue of the U.S. Supreme Court's decision in *Lingle*

---

[11]47 Cal. 3d 654 (1988).
[12]47 Cal. 3d at 670, n12.
[13]Nees v. Hocks 536 P. 2d 512 (Ore. 1975).
[14]Novosel v. Nationwide Insurance Co. 721 F.2d 894 (3d Cir. 1983).
[15]47 Cal. 3d at 669.

v. Norge,[16] the same practical obstacles to judicial access exist. Again, as a practical matter, the scope of the doctrine is limited. For defined theories that have a potentially broader scope one must look elsewhere.

A legal theory that has potentially broader application involves the contractual relationship between employer and employees where management attempts to dismiss and is attacked by workers who rely upon oral representation, employee handbooks, or personnel manuals that are distributed.[17] Frequently, such manuals advise employees that they will be treated fairly and will not be dismissed unfairly. Ironically, such policies are frequently made to ward off union organizing campaigns. A number of courts have taken the position that such a promise is part of the contract of employment, albeit a relatively unconventional unilateral contract, and enforceable in court.

A second theory is based on other employer behavior and imposes restrictions on management based on the view that the contract is implied in fact. This position has been explicitly accepted by the Supreme Court of California in *Foley.* Said the court:

> In the employment context, factors apart from consideration and express terms may be used to ascertain the existence and content of an employment agreement, including "the personnel policies or practices of the employer, the employee's longevity of service, actions or communications by the employer reflecting assurances of continued employment, and the practices of the industry in which the employee is engaged" [citation omitted]. . . . The presumption that an employment relationship of indefinite duration is intended to be terminable at will is . . . "subject, like any presumption, to contrary evidence. This may take the form of an agreement, express or implied, that . . . the employment relationship will continue indefinitely, pending the occurrence of some events such as the employer's dissatisfaction with the employee's services or the existence of some "cause" for termination.[18]

The court noted that employment security agreements are not "inherently harmful or unfair to employers" because, notwithstanding the fact that the employer would not receive a comparable guarantee of "continued service," the employer would benefit from the "increased loyalty and productivity that such agreements may inspire." Said the court, "we see no sound reason to exempt the employment relationship from the ordinary rules of contract interpretation which permit proof of implied terms."[19]

But contractual theories contain limits as well. In the first place, the damages awarded are those that are attributable to the breach of the contract itself, appar-

---

[16]486 U.S. 399 (1988).

[17]The courts in thirty-three states, plus the District of Columbia, have adopted an implied contract exception to employment at will. These include Alabama, Alaska, Arizona, Arkansas, California, Colorado, Connecticut, District of Columbia, Georgia, Hawaii, Idaho, Illinois, Kansas, Maine, Maryland, Michigan, Minnesota, Montana, New Hampshire, New Jersey, New Mexico, New York, Ohio, Oklahoma, Oregon, South Carolina, South Dakota, Texas, Utah, Vermont, and Washington. States Ruling Chart at 505:51–52.

[18]47 Cal. 3d at 680.

[19]47 Cal. 3d at 681.

ently not punitive damages, although the court in *Foley* did not resolve the measure of damages question in a wrongful-discharge action based on breach of contract. As Judge Peckham of the Northern District of California has held in *Mosely v. Metropolitan Life Insurance Co.*,[20] damages attributable to emotional distress may be part of a contract violation case. The same decision held that workers' compensation statutes do not preempt such a wrongful-discharge action theory.

The court in *Foley* acknowledged another limitation—although it did not confront the issue inasmuch as it was not presented in that case—that an express written provision could preclude enforcement of an implied in-fact modification of the terminable at-will principle. This means that employers who are sufficiently unperturbed by the possibility of a union organizing campaign, or a decline in employee morale by virtue of such conduct, can simply obtain a written waiver of the implied contract. Nonetheless, its ability to do so in connection with incumbent employees may be more problematic than is the case with applicants.

A minority of jurisdictions has taken the view that, at least under some circumstances, employers owe employees a covenant of good faith and fair dealing in the employment relationship.[21] Again, California has taken this position through the *Foley* decision. But, unlike the other jurisdictions that have adopted the theory, the Supreme Court of California has taken the position that the covenant is rooted in contract and not tort, thus precluding more expansive remedies of the type that are available in the public policy arena. The court declined to provide this significant remedy because it did not view the three characteristics that the law requires to trigger the covenant (i.e., inequality in bargaining power, a fiduciary duty to employees, and a quasi-public entity status for employers) to be present in employment relationships. The court rejected the view that there was a conflict between the employer and the employee in the employment relationship: "The interest of employer and employee are most frequently in alignment. If there is a job to be done, the employer must pay someone to do it."

The dissenting opinion of Justice Kaufmann seems to me to be more persuasive, however:

It is, at best, naive to believe that the availability of the "marketplace", or that a supposed "alignment of interests," renders the employment relationship less special or less subject to abuse than the relationship between insurer and insured [an area in which the covenant has been recognized as imposing tort liability]. Indeed, I can think of no relationship in which one party, the employee, places more reliance upon the other, is more dependent upon the other, or is more vulnerable to abuse by the other, than the relationship between employer and employee. And, ironically, the relative imbalance of economic power between employer and employee tends to increase rather than diminish the longer that relationship continues. Whatever bargaining strength and marketability the employee may have at the moment of hiring, diminishes rapidly thereafter. Marketplace? What market is there for the

[20] 4 IER Cases 1744 (N.D. Cal. 1989).
[21] Twelve state jurisdictions have recognized such an exception, namely, Alabama, Alaska, Arizona, California, Colorado, Connecticut, Idaho, Iowa, Massachusetts, Montana, Nevada, and New Hampshire. See State Rulings Chart at 505:51–52.

factory worker laid off after 25 years of labor in the same plant, or for the middle-aged executive fired after 25 years with the same firm?[22]

All this had led to a focus on legislation that has not yet been realized. A number of proposals have been put forward to remedy the law in this area. The California State Bar Committee on Wrongful Discharge and Termination At-Will (which I chaired) issued a 1984 report that advocated the enactment of a statute on the ground that the existing common law is harmful to both employers and employees, as well as the public, notwithstanding the fact that the judge-made exceptions to the terminable at-will principle are infinitely preferable to the status quo.[23]

The committee advocated that employees be protected against discharge under a "just-cause" standard of the type that generally prevails in unionized sectors of the economy. The committee argued that both justice and predictability would be served by such a standard, the latter because the arbitral common law, particularly as it relates to progressive discipline, is well established and could be incorporated into a wrongful-discharge statute. Although the committee advocated a statute that would be applicable only to nonunion employees, in 1987 the AFL-CIO Executive Council took the position that such a statute should be enacted and seemed to support the view that uniform standards should apply to both union and nonunion employees alike.

The arguments in favor of a comprehensive statute providing uniform standards and remedies, at least as a floor for the unionized sector, proceed on three assumptions: (1) all employees should have a guarantee of just-cause protection, so as to avoid the vagaries of common law, state legislation, or weak collective bargaining agreements; (2) if unionized employees are guaranteed a just-cause standard, those grievances that the union does not pursue to arbitration under the collective bargaining agreement can nonetheless be heard by the arbitrator or some other tribunal if the employee is willing to bear whatever expense is involved, and the prospect of unimpeded access for the employee will eliminate duty of fair representation liability for the labor movement, a not inconsiderable problem at this juncture; (3) the discrepancy between relief available in the unionized arbitration setting and under a wrongful-discharge statute might diminish disparities between the two sectors. A statute might enhance damages relief available in the unionized sector (reinstatement and back pay are all that is currently provided) and limit the expansive jury-devised damages that have become a central feature of contemporary wrongful-discharge litigation.

A second major feature of the California State Bar recommendation consists of the provision of arbitration rather than mandating the courts to handle such actions. As noted above, arbitration is already provided in the organized sector. A presumed virtue in substituting arbitration for the courts in the nonunion sector is the availability of a more expert, economical, and expeditious procedure through which to address dismissal and bear dismissal claims.

A third major feature relates to the relief itself. The committee was of the view

[22]47 Cal. 3d at 718 (Kaufmann, J. dissenting).
[23]See Gould et al. 1984; Gould 1984b, 1984c:A21.

that traditional labor law remedies should take the place of punitive and compensatory damages. While the new judge-made law has produced protection for employees, it has also resulted in erratic jury-imposed judgments that sometimes have little to do with the standards of law issued in the judge's instructions. Moreover, average employees seem to be screened out of the existing contingency fee arrangement through which lawyers receive a percentage of the award (i.e., 25 to 35 percent) because the lawyers are more likely to take cases involving employers who have higher salaries. This perhaps accounts for the disproportionate number of wrongful-discharge plaintiffs who were managerial and professional employees. The problem is exaggerated and compounded by *Foley*, which has made lost wages a larger part of the total recovery or award, given the unavailability of punitive damages in cases other than those involving public policy theory.

Thus far, comprehensive wrongful-discharge legislation has not been enacted in any state except Montana.[24] That statute does not oblige employers to proceed to arbitration, however. The Virgin Islands and Puerto Rico have severance pay statutes that are applicable to wrongful discharge actions. The reason for the almost universal absence of legislation is that employers prefer to litigate and take the risk of liability, especially in California now that *Foley* has diminished their exposure, rather than proceed to arbitration with a larger group of employees but limitations on liability. Similarly, plaintiffs' attorneys prefer to receive a contingency fee for a smaller group of workers, rather than traditional labor law remedies for a larger class. Legislation is sensible and right, but it lacks politically potent allies.

In Japan, despite the absence of explicit statutory or constitutional authority, the courts have imposed a just-cause substance of limitation on employers' right to dismiss workers.[25] If an employer does not have just cause to dismiss a worker, the dismissal vote will be regarded as invalid. The fact that the just-cause obligation applies to economic dismissals or layoffs attributable to a business decline as well as to disciplinary actions makes the Japanese situation quite different from that in America. In the United States, the seniority provisions that unions have negotiated generally provide for the last-hired/first-fired concept and govern the criteria relating to the selection of the employees to be laid off. Additionally, the negotiation of compensation or salary obligations to be met in the event of layoffs may deter them altogether in some circumstances. Moreover, moratoria on plant closings have been negotiated in the automobile industry, a promise that seems to have been eroded by an arbitral ruling that management is free to "idle" clients, even though it is obliged not to close plants altogether.[26] In Japan, a burden is

---

[24]Mont. Code Ann. §39.2.901 et. eq. (1987). Under the Montana statute, employees may not be discharged (1) without "good cause" (as defined therein); (2) in retaliation for refusing to violate or reporting a violation of public policy; or (3) in violation of the express provisions of an employer's own written personnel policy. Employees who are wrongfully discharged may be awarded lost wages and fringe benefits for up to four years, as well as punitive damages in cases where there is evidence of actual fraud or actual malice by the employer, 9A *Lab. Rel. Rep.* (BNA) 505:521 (1989).

[25]Much of the material contained in this section is based on Gould 1984a.

[26]"Patterson GW Wins Arbitration," *Wall Street Journal*, March 30, 1990:A3.

placed on management— similar to the burden utilized in American grievance arbitration cases in the organized sector of the economy relating to disciplinary matters—to explain the reason for a layoff attributable to economic considerations and to meet a just-cause test even though discipline is not involved.

The Japanese courts resolve the question of whether the employee is temporary or permanent. In the latter instance, the employee is covered by just-cause protection, and the courts generally require four prerequisites as indispensable to dismissals for economic reasons. First, the employer must show that there is simply no economic alternative to the dismissal and that dismissals are indeed the most effective way to remedy the employer's economic difficulties. In this connection, payment bonuses and wage increases at the time of the layoffs have convinced courts that the first prerequisite has not been fulfilled.

Second, once it has been established that the economic problem is indeed serious, the employer must show that there is no reasonable and suitable way other than dismissal to deal with the problem. Generally, the courts require that the employer make an effort to transfer the worker to another job or, in the case of large companies, to a subsidiary. Sometimes the courts have insisted that the employer first attempt to obtain voluntary resignations or to encourage early retirement through the use of the "tap on the shoulder," or *katatataki*, before dismissing the complaining workers.

In a sense, some of the recent collective agreements negotiated between the UAW and Japanese-owned companies on joint ventures replicate the standards of Japanese labor law. Illustrative of this trend is the agreement between New United Motor Manufacturing (NUMMI), the General Motors–Toyota joint venture, and the UAW, which states:

> The Company agrees that it will not layoff employees unless compelled to do so by severe economic conditions that threaten the long-term financial viability of the Company.
> The Company will take affirmative measures before laying off any employees including such measures as the reduction of salaries of its officers and management, assigning previously subcontracted work to bargaining unit employees capable of performing this work, seeking voluntary layoffs, and other cost saving measures.[27]

Significantly, the quid pro quo for this contractual promise is the union's adherence to such programs as the team concept and to goals such as superior quality and regular attendance. This, of course, has been a feature of Japanese industrial relations, albeit within the context of enterprise unionism, that is absent from the American scene.

Third, dismissals because of redundancy must be based on objective and reasonable criteria as to which employees are to be laid off. Here, the focus is similar to that of the subject matter addressed by the seniority provisions in American

---

[27]Article III, Job Security, of Collective Bargaining Agreements between New United Motor Manufacturing, Inc. and International Unions, the UAW, and Its Affiliated Local Unions, p. 4 (July 1, 1988).

collective bargaining agreements or the "social criteria" required by German labor law as it relates to collective dismissals.

Fourth, and finally, the employer is obliged to give employees complete information about planned dismissals or other measures and the necessity for them. The employer must consult with the union or with some other appropriate representative about the number of workers to be dismissed and the criteria on which the selection of those to be dismissed is based.

Disciplinary dismissals are handled similarly by the Japanese courts. Falsification, unsatisfactory work performance, chronic lateness, absence from work, refusals to obey orders, and embezzlement or theft, violence, or threats against other workers have been approved as just cause, although it is difficult to identify the criteria with specificity. This problem is similar to that experienced in both the organized and unorganized sectors of the U.S. economy. Of course, the overriding feature of Japanese industrial relations is *shushin koyo* or permanent employment—a practice adopted by larger Japanese firms that represents an informal understanding with unions and workers that is not contained in either law or collective agreements. Juxtaposed with permanent employment is early retirement at ages fifty-seven or fifty-eight to sixty. Nonetheless, this arrangement represents more reticent behavior by Japanese companies in comparison to American corporate conduct where layoffs are concerned.

Plant-Closing Legislation

Although a number of states[28] enacted statutes both before and after the passage of the Worker Adjustment and Retraining Notification Act of 1988, the federal statute is the major law in the area of plant closing.[29] The act obliges employers who employ more than one hundred employees to provide sixty days' notice before a plant closing or mass layoff to representatives of the employees or, in the event that there is no representative, to each "affected employee" and to state and local representatives. A plant closing is a shutdown that results in an employment loss for fifty or more employees at a single site of employment during any thirty-day period. A mass layoff notification obligation is triggered by the loss of employment for at least 33 percent of the employees or at least five hundred employees.

There are numerous limitations and exceptions in the statute. Only employers with one hundred or more employees are covered and thus only about half the work force in the United States. Part-time employees are excluded and are defined as employees who work fewer than twenty hours per week or who have been employed for fewer than six of the twelve months preceding the date on which notice is required. Temporary employees hired with the "understanding" that

---

[28]These are Connecticut, Hawaii, Maryland, Massachusetts, Michigan, Minnesota, Oregon, South Carolina, Tennessee, and Wisconsin. See 9A *Lab. Rel. Rep.* (BNA) 507:102 (1990); Gould 1988.

[29]29 U.S.C. §§2101–2109 (1988).

their employment would be limited to a specific duration are not covered. Moreover, the sixty-day period is, of course, an abbreviated one in any event—one which is inferior to all European labor law that addresses the same subject.

Another limitation in the statute is the reduction of the notification period and substitution of notice that is "practicable" where (1) the employer had to shut down before the sixty-day period and was "actively" seeking capital or business that would have enabled the employer to avoid or postpone the shutdown if the employer had a good-faith belief that the notice would have precluded the needed capital or business; (2) a premature closing (i.e., before sixty days) was caused by business circumstances that were "not reasonably foreseeable" at the time that notice would have been required; (3) the failure to give notice was attributable to a "natural disaster, such as a flood, earthquake or the drought currently ravaging the farmlands of the United States," or (4) the closing or layoff constitutes a strike or lockout not intended to evade the requirements of the act.

The act provides for civil actions against employers that violate the notice provisions and back pay for employees for each day of violation, at a rate of compensation not higher than the average regular rate received by the employees during the last three years of the employees' employment or the final regular rate received by such employees.

Aside from the strike-replacement cases noted at the beginning of this paper, the leading case under the act in the area of job security is *First National Maintenance v. NLRB*,[30] in which the Supreme Court, by a 7–2 vote, held that decisions to institute partial plant closings, and by inference complete closings as well, are not mandatory subjects of bargaining under the National Labor Relations Act and therefore not issues over which employers are obliged to bargain with unions to the point of impasse. The Court viewed certain subjects as properly beyond the act's duty-to-bargain obligation inasmuch as they can be characterized as "management problems." Said Justice Blackmun, speaking for the Court:

> In establishing what issues must be submitted to the process of bargaining, Congress had no expectation that the elected union representatives would become an equal partner in the running of the business enterprise in which the union's members are employed. Despite the deliberate open-endedness of the statutory language, there is an undeniable limit to the subjects about which bargaining must take place. . . . Some management decisions, such as choice of advertising and promotion, product type and designs and financing arrangements, have only an indirect and attenuated impact on the employment relationship [citation omitted].
>
> Other management decisions, such as the order of succession of layoffs and recalls, production quotas, and work rules, are almost exclusively "an aspect of the relationship" between employer and employee [citation omitted]. . . . The present case concerns a third type of management decision, one that had a direct impact on employment, since jobs were inexorably eliminated by the termination, but had as its focus only the economic profitability of the [commercial] contract . . . concern under these facts wholly apart from the employment relationship. . . . At the same time, this decision touches on matter of central and pressing concern to the union

[30]452 U.S. 666, 676 (1981).

and its member employees: possibility of continued employment and the retention of the employees' varied jobs.

. . . Management must be free from the constraints of the bargaining process [footnote omitted] to the extent essential for the running of a profitable business. It also must have some degree of certainty beforehand as to when it may proceed to reach decisions without fear of later evaluations labeling its conduct an unfair labor practice. Congress did not explicitly state what issues of mutual concern to union and management it intended to exclude from mandatory bargaining [footnote omitted]. Nonetheless, in view of an employer's need for unencumbered decision-making, bargaining over management decisions which have a substantial impact on the continued availability of employment should be required only if the benefit, the labor-management relations and the collective-bargaining process, outweighs the burden placed on the conduct of the business.[31]

The Court concluded that the burden of bargaining about the decision partially to close outweighs any benefits that might flow from the collective bargaining process. But with regard to other management decisions that have an impact on job security, such as the contracting out of work, relocations, sales, and the introduction of automated equipment, the NLRB and lower courts have determined that the question of whether the decision is bargainable depends on whether it is triggered by labor cost considerations or not. If labor costs are the major factor, the NLRB and the courts are of the view that the decision making is amenable to the collective bargaining process because unions could make proposals that would induce a reassessment on the part of management.

Continuity in the relationship may be imposed by either the collective bargaining agreement or the statutory duty to bargain when sales, mergers, or relocations are involved and when a successor's clause obliges the employer not to enter into a transaction that will allow another employer not to assume the collective bargaining agreement. But a motion for preliminary injunction must be filed against the predecessor employer in this instance.[32]

Further, continuity may exist if the successor employer hires a majority of the employees from the predecessor's work force. Quite obviously, the latter consideration creates an incentive on the part of the successor employer not to hire the predecessor's work force even though the National Labor Relations Act prohibits discrimination on the basis of union membership. Moreover, the rules put the job security of the predecessor's work force all the more at risk.

The rules relating to job security in the economic or collective dismissal arena in Japan stand in vivid contrast to those in America, as has been noted above. Somewhat analogous to the plant-closing legislation is Article 20 of the Labor Standards Law which obligates an employer to provide thirty days' notice before dismissal or to pay the equivalent of thirty days' average wages.

---

[31]452 U.S. at 676–79.
[32]See, for example, *Local Lodge No. 1266 v. Panoramic Corp.*, 668 F.2d 276 (7th Cir. 1981); *Lever Bros. Co. v. International Chem. Workers Local 217*, 554 F.2d 115 (4th Cir. 1976).

Conclusion

American labor law has been slow to protect the job security interests of workers, especially when one compares the American system with that of Japan. In the past decade numerous incursions have been made into the terminable at-will principle that have expanded the rights of individual employees. The difficulty is that the incursions are largely theoretical, given the narrow scope of some of the exceptions coupled with the practical obstacles to adequate relief through the judicial process.

In the area of collective dismissals, the Workers' Adjustment Retraining and Notification Act of 1988 provides some form of notice for workers with a view toward assistance and retraining, but most of the managerial decisions of organized employers remain unencumbered by the collective bargaining process. Only labor law reform in the United States through Congress and the state legislatures can change this.

6
Job Security and Work Force Adjustment: How Different Are U.S. and Japanese Practices?

Katharine G. Abraham and Susan N. Houseman

R elative to most European countries, the United States and Japan provide workers with little legal protection against layoff. Despite the absence of regulation in this area common to both countries, private sector practices regarding the adjustment of work force levels to cyclical and structural changes in demand have evolved in radically different ways. Japanese workers, on average, have much greater job security than American workers. There are, however, significant differences within each country in the degree of employment security enjoyed by various groups of workers. This paper focuses on employment and hours adjustment in the manufacturing sectors of the United States and Japan and on the implications of the differences both across and within countries for who bears the costs associated with economic change.

Workers can be provided with job security in a variety of ways. Employers can refrain from laying off workers during downturns without loss of profits if workers, as a group, are willing to accept shorter hours of work and lower compensation. Alternatively, employers may offer job security only to a core group of workers and use "peripheral" groups—such as temporary, part-time or subcontracted labor—to buffer the core group. Finally, employers may accept lower profits in

This paper is a revised version of a paper with the same title prepared for the NBER-TCER-CEPR Conference "Labor Relations and the Firm: Comparative Perspectives," held January 7–8, 1989, in Tokyo and published in the *Journal of the Japanese and International Economies* (December 1989):500–521, © 1989 by Academic Press, Inc. We have benefited from comments on earlier drafts of the paper made by Dan Hamermesh, Takatoshi Ito, Konosuke Odaka, Machiko Osawa, Eiko Shinozuka, and participants in the conference and in a seminar at the University of Maryland. Eiji Shiraishi of the Japan Ministry of Labour and Kazuyuki Matsumoto of the Japan Development Bank helped us with the Japanese data used in our analysis. Carolyn Thies, T. J. Grubbs, Steven Fagin, and Kelly Eastman provided excellent research assistance during the course of the paper's preparation. Support for this research was received from the School of Public Affairs at the University of Maryland and the University of Maryland Computer Center.

the short term if they believe that by providing job security for their workers they, in turn, will reap substantial benefits, such as greater employee commitment to the company or greater flexibility in job definition and job assignment. In this last case, the provision of job security may result in higher labor productivity and higher average profits for the company in the long run. Each of these practices is used to varying degrees by U.S. and Japanese employers. The extent and nature of employers' job security practices have clear implications for the distribution of the costs of adjustment to changing economic circumstances.

The empirical work in this paper addresses two sets of issues. We look first at the overall elasticities of employment: average hours and total hours with respect to changes in demand in the two countries. A key question in this part of the analysis is whether total labor input adjusts less in Japan than in the United States or whether greater flexibility in hours compensates for lower employment elasticities.

The second set of questions we address concerns differences in adjustment patterns across groups of workers within countries. To the extent that labor input is adjusted to changes in demand, are some groups within each country dispro-portionately affected? If so, are these groups the same in the United States as in Japan? And is the degree to which the employment of particular groups responds to changes in demand similar in the two countries?

The remainder of this paper is organized into five sections. The first section sketches the institutional context for our results and surveys previous empirical research. We discuss the model and the data underlying our analysis next, and then turn to the empirical results. Finally, we summarize the conclusions that can be drawn from our analysis concerning the overall dynamics of employment and hours adjustment and the relative job security of various groups in each country and outline directions for future research.

Background

Japanese workers are widely perceived as having greater job security than American workers. To a large degree, this stereotype is valid. Japanese and American researchers have consistently found faster adjustment of overall employment levels in the United States (see, for example, Shinozuka and Ishihara 1976; Shimada, Hosokawa, and Seike 1982; Shimada et al. 1982–83; Sterling 1984; U.S. Department of Labor 1985; Tachibanaki 1987; Hashimoto and Raisian 1988). Our results confirm these findings.

Previous studies have generated conflicting evidence concerning the adjustment of total labor input, which is a product of employment levels and average hours worked by employees. The prevailing wisdom seems to have been that in Japan, hours worked per worker are sufficiently responsive to changes in output to compensate for the lack of employment adjustment. Shinozuka and Ishihara (1976), for example, found that, while the adjustment of employment is slower in Japan, the adjustment of total labor input in the two countries is about the same. Shimada et al. (1982–83) also suggested that employment adjustment in

Japan is slower than in the United States but that the adjustment of total hours in the two countries is roughly comparable. The basis for this claim is unclear. Tachibanaki (1987), comparing standard deviations of employment and hours measures for Japan, the United States, and European countries, concluded that while Japan has the lowest adjustment of employment, it has the greatest adjustment of average hours. In contrast, Hashimoto and Raisian (1988), who related changes in labor input to changes in output using annual data for manufacturing, found slower adjustment in total hours in Japan. Using a more flexible functional form and somewhat different data to estimate labor elasticities than has been adopted in previous work, we present evidence that both employment and total hours adjustment is significantly greater in U.S. manufacturing than in Japanese manufacturing and that adjustment of average production-worker hours is about the same in the two countries.

While the average Japanese worker enjoys considerably greater job security than the average U.S. worker, industrial relations practices governing hiring, promotion, and layoff vary considerably in each country. Certain groups of workers tend to be insulated from demand fluctuations, while other groups are more vulnerable to layoff or contract termination during downturns. In analyzing the distribution of the burden of adjustment across groups of workers in each country, we make three comparisons. For both the United States and Japan, we compare adjustment patterns by broad occupational category (production versus nonproduction workers) and by sex. In addition, for Japan only, we look at differences in adjustment by establishment size.[1]

In the United States, industrial relations practices covering blue-collar workers tend to differ from those affecting white-collar workers. In particular, layoffs are much more common among blue-collar than among white-collar workers. The different treatment of the two groups is often rationalized on the grounds that, compared to white-collar workers, blue-collar workers have duties that are tied more directly to the level of production and they possess less firm-specific human capital. Job security for white-collar workers also has been rationalized as part of an interrelated set of labor practices. In contrast to the situation of blue-collar workers, employers generally can exercise considerable discretion in redefining white-collar jobs and in assigning workers to those jobs. In return for this flexibility, employers may give white-collar workers an implied promise of job security.[2]

The greater responsiveness of production employment compared to nonproduction employment in the United States is a well-established fact that has been explained on the basis of these economic and institutional factors. It is interesting that, in Japan, the so-called lifetime employment system covers blue-collar as well as white-collar workers. In turn, Japanese management tends to have considerable

[1]Unfortunately, available data do not permit parallel comparisons for the United States by establishment size.

[2]For a discussion of the differences in industrial relations practices applying to blue- and white-collar workers in the United States, see Osterman 1988a.

flexibility in deploying its work force within the firm. Our results indicate that production employment elasticities also exceed nonproduction employment elasticities in Japan but that the difference between the two groups is much smaller than that in the United States.

In the United States, workers typically are selected for layoff by inverse order of seniority. Because women's job tenure is, on average, shorter than men's, women may be more vulnerable to being laid off in the event of a reduction in force.[3]

In Japan, while both blue-collar and white-collar employees may be covered by the lifetime employment system, lifetime employment practices apply primarily to regular employees in large enterprises.[4] Insofar as women are less likely than men to hold regular, full-time positions and less likely to be employed in large firms, they may be more vulnerable to layoff or contract termination. In 1987, only 80 percent of women employed in manufacturing held regular positions, while 20 percent were employed as temporary workers or day laborers. In contrast, 97 percent of men employed in manufacturing held regular positions; only 3 percent were employed as temporary workers or day laborers.[5] In addition, about 22 percent of women employed in manufacturing held part-time positions. Virtually all (about 93 percent in 1987) part-time workers are women.

Women are also underrepresented in large establishments and overrepresented in small establishments. In 1984, only 21 percent of female employees in manufacturing worked in establishments with five hundred or more employees; 34 percent were employed in establishments with fewer than thirty employees. The corresponding figures for men were 41 percent and 24 percent.[6] These facts lead us to expect employment elasticities for women to be greater than those for men. In studies of the adjustment of employment levels by sex, Shinozuka (1980) and Nakamura (1983, 1984) found greater adjustment of female than of male employment in Japan. Our estimates support these results. We also find evidence of higher employment elasticities for women than for men in the United States, although the differences between the two groups are much less pronounced than those in Japan.

Insofar as the lifetime employment system is stronger in large firms than in small firms, one might expect to find systematic differences in the responsiveness

---

[3]For evidence on these points, see Abraham and Medoff 1984 and Hall 1982.
[4]For discussions of work force reductions in Japanese industry, see U.S. Department of Labor 1985 and Shimada 1986.
[5]In the Japanese Labour Force Survey, the monthly household survey from which these numbers are derived, temporary employees are defined as "employees employed for a period of not less than a month but not longer than a year" and day laborers are defined as "employees employed daily or for a period of less than a month."
[6]The data we use to estimate employment and hours elasticities, described later in the paper, exclude day laborers and employees of establishments with fewer than thirty employees. Among manufacturing employees who are either regular or temporary employees, only 83 percent of women but 98 percent of men are regular employees. Among manufacturing employees in establishments with thirty or more employees, only 31 percent of women but 53 percent of men are employed in establishments with five hundred or more employees.

of employment to changes in output by establishment size. It is also widely believed that small Japanese enterprises provide a production buffer for larger firms. By subcontracting work during expansions and terminating contracts during recessions, large firms may shift cyclical risk onto smaller companies. Others argue, however, that the links between large and small Japanese firms are more complex than this simple characterization would suggest (see, for example, Aoki 1984). Shinozuka (1980), using aggregate data by establishment size, found greater adjustment of small than of large establishment employment, but Sterling (1984) found no correlation between the proportion of an industry's employment in small establishments and the magnitude of employment adjustment in the industry. Our results reveal only a weak relationship between employment adjustment and establishment size.

Estimating Framework

The objective of the empirical work described in this paper is to characterize the process whereby U.S. and Japanese employers adjust employment and hours in response to short-term changes in the level of production. Given our comparative focus, it is important that our estimating equations be sufficiently flexible to capture any differences in the pattern of adjustment that might exist between the two countries.

Much previous work on employment adjustment, including almost all previous studies using Japanese data, has used the Koyck specification.[7] Although the Koyck specification is appealingly parsimonious and the Koyck parameters are amenable to precise structural interpretation, this approach requires very strong assumptions that are unlikely to be satisfied in practice. In particular, it assumes that adjustment costs are quadratic, so that adjustment to a given shock declines geometrically over time, and that the current level of labor demand is expected to persist indefinitely into the future. We have chosen to estimate employment elasticities using a distributed lag model that is flexible enough to capture employment dynamics and demand environments that are different from those presupposed by the Koyck model. Our basic estimating equation is of the following form:

$$\Delta \ln E_t = \alpha + \sum_{i=0}^{13} \beta_i \Delta \ln P_{t+1-i} + \theta t + \mu_t \qquad (6\text{-}1)$$

where E represents employment, P represents production, t is a time trend, μ is the error term (assumed to follow a first-order autoregressive process), and α, the β's and θ are parameters to be estimated.[8] The β's in this equation capture the response of employment to changes in output. For example, the sum of β_0 through

---

[7]The one exception that we know of among studies using Japanese data is Sterling 1984.

[8]We could have estimated an equation containing levels, rather than differences, of the employment and production terms. We did begin by fitting levels equations, but the estimated errors in these equations were such as to suggest that the underlying process generating them was very close to a random walk. Because of this and data considerations described below, we adopted the differenced specification shown in equation 6–1.

β_4 (i.e., the coefficients on the lead, the current, and the first three lagged production terms) captures the cumulative effect on employment over three months of a one-time decline in production. Our specification allows production to affect employment with a lag of up to one year. We assume that other factors affecting employment, such as productivity trends and changes in relative factor prices over the estimating period, are adequately captured by the constant term and the time trend.[9] Equations with hours per worker or total hours in place of employment on the lefthand side can be interpreted similarly.

In addition, rather than estimating the β_i's freely, we constrain them to lie along a third-order polynomial in i. That is, we assume that the β_i's can be written in terms of four underlying parameters:

$$\beta_i = \phi_0 + \phi_1 i + \phi_2 i^2 + \phi_3 i^3 \qquad (6\text{-}2)$$

where the ϕ's are the parameters we actually estimate. We impose no end-point constraints on the ϕ's.[10]

It should be recognized that the parameters we estimate may be influenced not only by the institutional constraints that are operative in a particular setting but also by the production structure (the industry composition of output, the engineering technologies in use, and so on) and by expectations concerning future demand.[11] In comparing U.S. and Japanese adjustment patterns, we implicitly assume that the structure of production and the structure of the demand for output are reasonably similar in the two countries. We will return to this issue when we discuss our empirical results.[12]

Note that information on the net accession rate derived from labor turnover statistics can also be used to estimate the employment version of equation 6–1. Given a change in the level of production, employers alter the level of employment

[9]Including a constant plus a time trend in a difference equation is equivalent to including a time trend plus its square in a levels equation. If, for example, productivity growth over a given time period were to reduce the labor input required to produce any given output, that would reduce the constant term in our estimating equation; a slowing in the rate of productivity growth would raise the coefficient on our time trend.

[10]The point estimates of the cumulative effects of changes in output on employment derived from the Almon lag models are almost identical to those derived from the corresponding unconstrained models. In equations for average and total hours, unconstrained models yield somewhat larger short-term responses than the Almon lag models for the United States but very similar results for Japan.

[11]As noted by Hamermesh (1990a), cross-country differences in the distribution of demand shocks across establishments associated with a given change in aggregate demand conditions are another possible source of differences in employment and hours elasticities estimated using aggregate data. Addressing this aggregation issue would require establishment-level data, which we do not have. While we cannot rule out the possibility that aggregation bias has affected our results, there is no obvious reason to believe that any such bias should have affected our U.S. and Japanese estimates differently.

[12]For more detailed discussions of the assumptions underlying alternative specifications and of the interpretation of the finite lag model we have chosen to estimate, see Sims 1974; Nickell 1986; and Abraham and Houseman 1989b.

through some combination of changes in accessions and changes in separations. For example, if output declines, an employer may curtail hiring (reduce the accession rate) and also lay off workers (increase the separation rate). The net change in employment will reflect both actions. Using the approximation that the change in ln(employment) equals the net accession rate, equation 6–1 can be rewritten as:

$$ACCRATE_t - SEPRATE_t = \alpha + \sum_{i=0}^{13} \beta_i \Delta \ln P_{t+1-i} + \theta t + \mu_t \quad (6\text{-}3)$$

where $ACCRATE$ represents the gross accession rate, $SEPRATE$ represents the gross separation rate, and the other terms are as previously defined. If there are problems with the available employment data, as turns out to be the case for Japan, this equation may actually perform better than the corresponding equation based on employment data.

Data

In the analysis that follows we make use of monthly data on employment, hours, and production for the U.S. manufacturing sector and on employment, gross accessions, gross separations, hours, and production for the Japanese manufacturing sector. The analyses reported here are for the manufacturing sector as a whole. We also carried out similar analyses for each of fifteen disaggregated industries in the manufacturing sector; the results of these disaggregated analyses are reported in an appendix available from the authors.[13] Because we were able to obtain only seasonally adjusted production series for Japan, we used seasonally adjusted series throughout. Except as otherwise noted, all of our analyses cover the 1970:1 through 1985:12 time period.

The employment and hours data for the United States come from the employer payroll survey sent to a stratified random sample of establishments each month. The data from this survey permit us to construct not only an overall employment series but also separate employment series for production versus nonproduction workers and for male versus female workers. The survey also yields information on average paid weekly hours for production workers. The published data from this survey are not broken down by establishment size.

The labor input data for Japan are derived from a similar employer survey, the Monthly Labour Survey, sent to a random sample of establishments with five or more employees. This survey covers all workers who are employed on an employment contract of at least one month's duration or who have worked at least eighteen days during each of the previous two months.[14] It yields information on

[13]The fifteen disaggregated industries are food; textiles; apparel; lumber; pulp and paper; chemicals; rubber; stone, clay and glass; iron and steel; nonferrous metals; fabricated metals; nonelectrical machinery; electrical machinery; transportation equipment; and precision machinery.

[14]The definitions given in note 5 imply that the employer-provided data we use include temporary employees but may not include day laborers. In 1984, day laborers accounted for about 2 percent of employment in Japanese manufacturing (see Japan Ministry of Labour 1986).

employment, gross accessions, and gross separations for the covered work force as a whole. The same information is collected separately for production and nonproduction workers and for male and female workers in establishments with thirty or more employees. Similarly disaggregated data on average monthly hours are also available for these establishments. For establishments with five to twenty-nine employees, data are not collected separately for production and nonproduction workers. Except when we look explicitly at patterns of adjustment by size of establishment, the results we report for Japan are based on data for establishments with thirty or more employees.[15]

While the U.S. and the Japanese surveys are otherwise quite similar in concept, there is an important difference in the quality of the employment data derived from them. In the United States, month-to-month movements in all of the employment series we have used are generated using the "link relative" method, which exploits information on the percentage change in employment in establishments that report their employment in both months, and the series are rebenchmarked to population totals annually. The Japanese employment data just described are simply published each month as they become available and are never revised subsequently. Because there are significant month-to-month changes in the sample of reporting establishments, the Japanese employment series are far noisier than the corresponding U.S. series.[16] Each month, however, in addition to reporting their end-of-month employment, establishments responding to the Japanese Monthly Labour Survey are asked to report their accessions and separations. We use this information to calculate the gross monthly accession rate and the gross monthly separation rate at the responding firms. The Japanese employment models are then estimated using equation 6–3 rather than equation 6–1, with the net accession rate rather than the change in ln(employment) as the dependent variable. This approach avoids the problems associated with using employment data based on different samples in different months.[17]

Another difference between the U.S. and Japanese surveys is that the U.S. survey asks for information on paid hours, while the Japanese survey asks for information on actual hours. We discuss the implications of this difference in definition when we report our results.

Finally, the estimation carried out for this paper required monthly data on production. For the United States, we use the monthly industrial production

---

[15]Models fit using data for establishments with five or more employees, rather than thirty or more employees, in cases in which this was possible, yielded findings that were very similar to those we report.

[16]Eiji Shiraishi of the Japan Ministry of Labour brought this problem to our attention. The Ministry of Labour does publish an index of employment in establishments with thirty or more employees that it considers suitable for use in time-series analysis, but no similar indexes are constructed for employment by occupational category, sex, or establishment size.

[17]The use of the net accession rate, rather than the change in ln (employment), to fit our Japanese employment equations had very little effect on the estimated coefficients, but the standard errors in the models using the net accession rate were much smaller.

index constructed by the Federal Reserve Board. Where available, information on physical output serves as the basis for this index. Information on energy usage is generally the preferred proxy for the level of production activity where actual output data are unavailable. In some cases, however, person-hours are used to gauge the level of production activity. For manufacturing as a whole, movements in person-hours proxy for movements in about 19 percent of total output. This feature of the underlying data should be kept in mind as we discuss the results. We do not, however, believe it poses a serious problem for our estimates. For a number of disaggregated manufacturing industries the weight given to person-hours in the construction of the production index is negligible. In the equations that we fit for disaggregated manufacturing industries, the qualitative findings concerning cross-country differences in adjustment are not sensitive to the degree to which hours were used in constructing the Federal Reserve Board production index.

The corresponding Japanese series, the Industrial Production Index, is constructed by MITI based on reports from random samples of firms in a variety of market segments concerning their production of several thousand commodities.

Empirical Results

The first part of our empirical work contrasts the overall pattern of employment and hours adjustment in U.S. and Japanese manufacturing. The second part focuses on differences in employment and hours adjustment across groups within each country and addresses the question of whether a disproportionate share of the burden of adjustment is borne by certain groups.

Production Structure and Demand in U.S. and Japanese Manufacturing

Our central objective in this study was to learn about the effects of the U.S. and Japanese industrial relations systems on employment and hours adjustment. This effort is complicated by the fact that, as noted above, different production structures and different expectations concerning future demand across the two countries might also lead to differences in the pattern of employment and hours adjustment. Thus, an important question is whether U.S. and Japanese employers have been operating in similar environments. If these environments have been sufficiently similar, then it is reasonable to ascribe differences in the responsiveness of employment and hours to the operation of the two countries' labor market institutions rather than to differences in the structure of production or in expectations concerning future demand.

Our major concern with respect to the structure of production was whether differences in the adjustment of aggregate manufacturing labor input to changes in aggregate manufacturing output between the United States and Japan might reflect differences in the composition of the manufacturing base in the two-

TABLE 6-1. *Growth and Cyclicality of Manufacturing Production in the United States and Japan*[a]

	Growth	Cyclicality
United States		
1970–77	.0025	.056
1978–85	.0016	.055
1970–85	.0024	.058
Japan		
1970–77	.0023	.066
1978–85	.0034	.032
1970–85	.0031	.054

[a]The numbers reported in this table were derived from regressions of seasonally adjusted monthly l*n*(production) on a time trend. "Growth" is the time trend coefficient from this regression; "cyclicality" is the standard deviation of the regression residuals.

countries. Although in this paper we report only estimated employment and hours elasticities for manufacturing as a whole, as noted earlier, we have also estimated similar equations for fifteen disaggregated manufacturing industries. The fact that these estimates display patterns very similar to those for manufacturing as a whole suggests that differences in the structure of production between the United States and Japan do not explain the findings reported in this paper.

In theory, differences in the demand conditions prevailing in U.S. and Japanese manufacturing might influence our results. Table 6-1 presents measures of growth and cyclicality in the two countries' manufacturing output during the full 1970–85 period and during the two subperiods 1970–77 and 1978–85.[18] From 1970 to 1977, trend growth in manufacturing production was quite similar in Japan and the United States and the variability of production was actually somewhat greater in Japan. The similarity in demand conditions in the two countries over the 1970–77 period reflects the fact that the manufacturing sector in each country experienced a severe recession in 1974 and 1975, followed by strong recovery. During the 1978–85 period, however, manufacturing output grew much more rapidly in Japan than in the United States and the variability of manufacturing production around its trend was substantially smaller in Japan. Differences in these measures of demand conditions over the 1978–85 period are capturing the fact that while Japanese manufacturing output was stagnant in the early 1980s, U.S. manufacturing output dropped sharply during the 1982 recession that affected the U.S. economy.

Thus, looking at data for the 1970–77 period, when demand conditions in the two countries were relatively comparable, is one way of checking any conclusions concerning the effects of differences in the two countries' industrial relations

[18]At the end of 1977, both countries were experiencing strong growth following the 1974–75 recession, so that our cutoff represents a similar point in the business cycle for the two countries. Given that our estimating strategy requires a substantial number of observations, it also seemed sensible to break the data at the midpoint of the full period so that neither subperiod was too short.

TABLE 6-2. Employment and Hours Adjustment in U.S. and Japanese Manufacturing, 1970–85

	One month	Three months	Six months	Twelve months
Employment				
U.S.	.314[a]	.580[a]	.664[a]	.758[a]
	(.023)[b]	(.028)	(.032)	(.045)
Japan	.015	.074	.141	.207
	(.011)	(.024)	(.032)	(.045)
Production employment				
U.S.	.430[a]	.763[a]	.845[a]	.920[a]
	(.029)	(.035)	(.040)	(.075)
Japan	.025	.118	.211	.277
	(.013)	(.026)	(.033)	(.020)
Average production hours				
U.S.	.224	.270	.202	.115
	(.043)	(.051)	(.057)	(.044)
Japan	.188	.282	.251	.104
	(.068)	(.082)	(.085)	(.094)
Total production hours				
U.S.	.661[a]	1.036[a]	1.046[a]	1.037[a]
	(.052)	(.061)	(.069)	(.078)
Japan	.210	.371	.409	.374
	(.073)	(.090)	(.094)	(.128)

[a]Difference between U.S. and Japanese adjustment significant at the 0.05 level or better.
[b]Numbers in parentheses are standard errors.

systems drawn from analyses for periods that include the late 1970s and early 1980s, when demand conditions were less comparable. That our results are very similar for all three time periods we examine gives us confidence that the qualitative differences we observe between the United States and Japan reflect differences in the two countries' industrial relations systems and not in prevailing demand conditions.

Employment and Hours Adjustment: An Overview

Tables 6–2 and 6–3 provide an overview of labor adjustment in U.S. and Japanese manufacturing. In light of the possible sensitivity of our results to the time period selected, we present separate estimates for the full 1970–85 period, reported in table 6–2, and for the subperiods 1970–77 and 1978–85, reported in table 6–3. Estimates of one-, three-, six-, and twelve-month elasticities are presented for total employment, production employment, average production-worker hours, and total production-worker hours.

The pattern of both total employment and production employment adjustment

TABLE 6-3A. *Employment and Hours Adjustment in U.S. and Japanese Manufacturing, 1970–77*

	One month	Three months	Six months	Twelve months
Employment				
U.S.	.323[a]	.598[a]	.663[a]	.717[a]
	(.032)[b]	(.037)	(.043)	(.084)
Japan	.026	.100	.170	.241
	(.016)	(.028)	(.035)	(.071)
Production employment				
U.S.	.426[a]	.764[a]	.822[a]	.847[a]
	(.039)	(.046)	(.052)	(.055)
Japan	.041	.154	.252	.322
	(.018)	(.031)	(.036)	(.030)
Average production hours				
U.S.	.154	.219	.174	.095
	(.050)	(.056)	(.064)	(.078)
Japan	.211	.290	.294	.100
	(.100)	(.117)	(.116)	(.146)
Total production hours				
U.S.	.574[a]	.981[a]	.995[a]	.939[a]
	(.063)	(.071)	(.081)	(.115)
Japan	.204	.400	.478	.380
	(.105)	(.123)	(.123)	(.160)

[a]Difference between U.S. and Japanese adjustment is significant at the 0.05 level or better.
[a]Numbers in parentheses are standard errors.

is strikingly different in the two countries. In the estimates for all three time periods, U.S. manufacturing employment responded quickly and substantially to changes in production, whereas in Japan there was little adjustment until six to twelve months after the change. Moreover, the magnitude of both total employment adjustment and production employment adjustment was significantly greater in the United States than in Japan over all time horizons.[19]

In contrast, the adjustment of average production-worker hours was quite similar in the two countries. In both the United States and Japan, there was a large and immediate response of average hours to changes in production, and none of the estimated average hours elasticities was significantly different across the two countries. As noted above, however, the hours data for the United States measure paid hours, while the hours data for Japan measure actual hours worked.

[19]The test used to determine the statistical significance of U.S.-Japanese differences was computed as the difference between the estimated elasticities for the two countries divided by the square root of the sum of the variances of these elasticities. Under the assumption that the error terms in the U.S. and Japanese equations are uncorrelated, this test statistic has an asymptotic normal distribution. We use the same test for cross-time period comparisons.

TABLE 6-3B. *Employment and Hours Adjustment in U.S. and Japanese Manufacturing, 1978–85*

	One month	Three months	Six months	Twelve months
Employment				
U.S.	.325[a]	.583[a]	.692[a]	.842[a]
	(.031)[b]	(.040)	(.045)	(.045)
Japan	−.005	.014	.057	.079
	(.014)	(.025)	(.033)	(.060)
Production employment				
U.S.[c]	.452[a]	.798[a]	.858[a]	1.009[a]
	(.042)	(.048)	(.054)	(.061)
Japan[c]	.005	.056	.097	.125
	(.021)	(.032)	(.040)	(.047)
Average production hours				
U.S.	.272	.302	.213	.119
	(.080)	(.100)	(.110)	(.154)
Japan	.149	.249	.205	.146
	(.103)	(.145)	(.168)	(.210)
Total production hours				
U.S.	.741[a]	1.094[a]	1.108[a]	1.162[a]
	(.097)	(.121)	(.134)	(.168)
Japan	.203	.250	.197	.292
	(.113)	(.160)	(.185)	(.225)

[a]Difference between U.S. and Japanese adjustment is significant at the 0.05 level or better.
[b]Numbers in parentheses are standard errors.
[c]Because of difficulties in computing standard errors for the Almon lag model, the numbers in this row are derived from an unconstrained finite lag model.

One might expect the adjustment of actual hours to changes in production to be greater than that of paid hours. For example, employers may be able to schedule vacation time during slack periods, in which case actual hours worked would adjust but paid hours would not. Although we do not know the empirical importance of the difference in definition, we can conclude that average hours in Japanese manufacturing adjust no more, and possibly less, than in American manufacturing. Total production-worker hours elasticities are without exception significantly larger in the United States than in Japan. Again, these differences are, if anything, understated.

As already noted, demand conditions in U.S. and Japanese manufacturing were most similar during the 1970–77 subperiod. During the 1978–85 subperiod, Japanese manufacturing output grew more rapidly and was less cyclically volatile than in the earlier subperiod, while U.S. manufacturing output grew less rapidly and was no less cyclically volatile. The point estimates of the relevant table 6–3 coefficients imply that U.S. employment and hours generally adjusted somewhat more to changes in production during the later subperiod than during the first part of the 1970s, while Japanese employment and hours generally adjusted less.[20] Thus, the magnitude of the divergence between the U.S. and the Japanese adjustment pattern is somewhat sensitive to the period considered. Importantly, however, our qualitative findings are not.

The characterization that Japanese industry relies relatively more on adjustment of average hours while U.S. industry relies relatively more on employment adjustment is certainly accurate. For example, from table 6–2, the adjustment of production employment levels accounts for about two-thirds of the total production-labor input adjustment over a one month time horizon in the United States; in Japan, the adjustment of production employment levels accounts for only about 10 percent of the total production-labor input adjustment over the same time horizon.

Our estimates do not indicate, however, as some researchers have concluded, that average hours adjustment in Japan compensates for the lack of employment adjustment. In both the short and medium term, the adjustment of total production–labor input in Japanese manufacturing is substantially less than that in American manufacturing.

Who Adjusts? Intracountry Differences in Employment Stability

The results of the preceding section may mask significant variation in employment and hours adjustment and corresponding differences in the stability of employment across groups in each country. In the final part of the analysis, we compare labor adjustment by broad occupational category and by sex for both the United States and Japan. In addition, for Japan we look at differences in employment adjustment by establishment size. In this section we present only estimates using data for the entire 1970–85 period. We have, however, also estimated equations using data for the 1970–77 subperiod and for the 1978–85 subperiod, and the qualitative nature of our conclusions generally are not sensitive to the time period selected.[21]

Production versus Nonproduction Worker Adjustment

Table 6–4 compares estimates of one-, three-, six- and twelve-month elasticities of production and nonproduction employment within both U.S. and Japanese

---

[20]For the United States, only the twelve-month production employment elasticity difference is statistically significant at the 0.05 level. For Japan, both the three- and six-month employment elasticity differences are significant. Our results for Japan are consistent with those reported by Muramatsu (1983). On the basis of Koyck models fit for various subperiods, he concludes that employment adjustment was greater following the first oil shock than during either earlier or later subperiods.

[21]The one exception concerns comparisons of male and female employment adjustment in the United States. While employment elasticities for U.S. women are significantly greater than those for U.S. men over the 1970–77 period, they are insignificantly different over the 1978–85 period.

TABLE 6-4. *Production versus Nonproduction Employment and Average Hours Adjustment in U.S. and Japanese Manufacturing, 1970–85*

	One month	Three months	Six months	Twelve months
United States				
Production employment	.430[a]	.763[a]	.845[a]	.920[a]
	(.029)[b]	(.035)	(.040)	(.075)
Nonproduction employment	.031	.140	.231	.370
	(.017)	(.025)	(.031)	(.050)
Japan				
Production employment	.025	.118[a]	.211[a]	.277[a]
	(.013)	(.026)	(.033)	(.020)
Nonproduction employment	.001	−.020	−.018	.059
	(.012)	(.024)	(.031)	
Production average hours	.188[a]		.251[a]	.104
	(.068)	(.082)	(.085)	(.094)
Nonproduction average hours	.059	.144	.172	.072
	(.076)	(.093)	(.097)	(.111)

[a]Difference between production and nonproduction adjustment is significant at the 0.05 level or better.
[b]Numbers in parentheses are standard errors.

manufacturing. It also presents estimates of average hours elasticities for Japanese production and nonproduction workers. As expected, U.S. production employment elasticities are uniformly significantly larger than those for nonproduction employment.[22]

Quite different patterns are evident in Japan. The one-month elasticity estimates for production and nonproduction employment are insignificantly different both from zero and from each other. The labor input of production workers is somewhat more responsive than that of nonproduction workers in the very short run, but this largely reflects the adjustment of average hours rather than of employment. The production employment elasticity does increase steadily over longer time horizons, but the nonproduction employment elasticity remains insignificantly different from zero. By three months out, the production employment elasticity is significantly larger than the nonproduction employment elasticity.

Nonetheless, the differentials in employment adjustment between production and nonproduction workers are much smaller in Japan than in the United States. Given that the lifetime employment system in Japan tends to be extended to blue- and white-collar employees alike, we would expect this result.

[22]To determine the statistical significance of these differences, we used seemingly unrelated regression techniques to estimate unconstrained and constrained versions of the production and nonproduction worker equations. In the constrained versions, we required that the one-, three-, six-, or twelve-month elasticities, as appropriate, be the same for the two groups. This approach permitted us to construct chi-squared statistics for hypothesis testing. The same approach was used to test the statistical significance of the other within-country differences reported below.

TABLE 6-5. Male versus Female Employment and Average Hours Adjustment in U.S. and Japanese Manufacturing, 1970–85

	One month	Three months	Six months	Twelve months
United States				
Male employment	.296[a]	.541[a]	.626[a]	.743
	(.022)[b]	(.027)	(.031)	(.028)
Female employment	.347	.667	.754	.786
	(.031)	(.041)	(.049)	(.079)
Japan				
Male employment	.004[a]	.023[a]	.059[a]	.133[a]
	(.010)	(.022)	(.029)	(.040)
Female employment	.050	.193	.323	.381
	(.019)	(.035)	(.043)	(.076)
Male average hours	.143	.261	.279[a]	.152[a]
	(.069)	(.085)	(.088)	(.113)
Female average hours	.164	.187	.111	−.035
	(.079)	(.096)	(.099)	(.114)

[a]Difference between male and female adjustment is significant at the 0.05 level or better.
[b]Numbers in parentheses are standard errors.

Interestingly, the elasticity point estimates for production workers in Japan are insignificantly different from those of nonproduction workers in the United States. Stated somewhat differently, production workers in Japan enjoy a degree of employment stability that is similar to that enjoyed by nonproduction workers in the United States.

Male versus Female Adjustment

Table 6–5 reports one-, three-, six-, and twelve-month employment elasticity estimates for men and women in U.S. and Japanese manufacturing. Average hours elasticities by sex for Japan are also reported. In the United States, the female employment elasticities are uniformly greater than the male employment elasticities, significantly so for the one-, three-, and six-month time horizons.

In the Japanese manufacturing sector, employment adjustment is much larger among females than among males, especially beginning with the three-month elasticity. All male-female differences in the Japanese employment elasticities are statistically significant. The higher employment elasticities for women in Japan reflects their higher representation as part-time and temporary workers, who are more vulnerable to contract termination. From three months onwards, however, the adjustment of average hours for men is somewhat larger than for women; the six- and twelve-month differences are statistically significant. Thus, it appears that the lower adjustment of male employment is partly compensated for by the greater adjustment of average hours for men. That the average hours for women respond less to changes in demand may reflect in part the fact that, until 1986, tight legal restrictions limited their overtime work.[23]

Because production and nonproduction worker employment elasticities are so different in the United States, estimated male-female differentials are likely to be sensitive to the distribution of men and women across occupations. Unfortunately, the establishment data source we are using does not provide data on male and female employment separately by occupation. Information from other sources, however, suggests that differences in the distribution of men and women between production and nonproduction jobs are unlikely to explain our finding that employment elasticities are higher for women than for men.[24] The same problem in disentangling the effects of occupation and sex on labor adjustment exists for Japan, though the fact that production and nonproduction employment elasticities are more similar implies that it cannot explain much of the male-female differential in Japan.[25]

Although female employment in Japan adjusts more than male employment, the employment elasticities reported in table 6–5 nonetheless imply that the employment elasticities for Japanese women are significantly less than the employment elasticities for either American men or American women. This suggests that Japanese women enjoy greater employment stability than either American men or American women as a group. An important caveat to this conclusion, however, is that we do not look separately at particular groups of workers—those in part-time, temporary, and day laborer positions—that are predominantly female. While women, on average, enjoy strong job security, certain groups of female workers may well provide an important margin for adjustment.

Adjustment by Establishment Size

To examine the relation between establishment size and employment adjustment directly, we estimated separate employment elasticities for establishments with 500 or more employees, 100 to 499 employees, 30 to 99 employees, and 5 to 29 employees. The production variables on the righthand side of our estimating equations measure percentage changes in production for the entire industry, not

[23]Specifically, women were prohibited from working more than 2 hours of overtime in any day, 6 hours in any week, or 150 hours in any year. We thank Eiko Shinozuka and Machiko Osawa for bringing this to our attention.

[24]Tabulations of the May 1979 Current Population Survey indicate that a slightly higher proportion of men than of women in U.S. manufacturing were employed in production jobs (69.8 percent versus 62.6 percent), where production jobs were defined to include craft, operative, laborer, and service positions. On the basis of broad occupation alone, then, one would expect male employment elasticities to be higher than female employment elasticities.

[25]During 1979, about 76 percent of women in Japanese manufacturing were production workers, compared to 63 percent of men. This difference alone would have led one to expect only a 0.003 difference between the one-month female and male employment elasticities; over twelve months, the predicted difference would be only 0.029. The actual differences reported in table 6–5 are much larger than the differences one would expect based simply on differences in production versus nonproduction status.

TABLE 6-6. *Employment Adjustment by Size of Establishment in Japanese Manufacturing, 1970–85*

	Current	Three months	Six months	Twelve months
Establishments with 500	−.005	.023	.072	.168
or more employees	(.014)[a]	(.032)	(.042)	(.050)
Establishments with	.023	.115[b]	.197[b]	.294[b]
100–499 employees	(.014)	(.031)	(.040)	(.048)
Establishments with	.027	.084	.149	.180
30–99 employees	(.016)	(.022)	(.025)	(.029)
Establishments with	.019	.066	.107	.127
5–29 employees	(.013)	(.018)	(.020)	(.023)

[a]Numbers in parentheses are standard errors.
[b]Difference between adjustment for this size class and the largest size class is significant at the 0.05 level or better.

for the individual size class. Consequently, differences in employment adjustment by establishment size may result either from differences in personnel practices, taking output as given, or from differences in the variability of production by establishment size.

The results in table 6–6 do reveal some differences in employment adjustment by establishment size. The distinction appears primarily between establishments in the largest size class—those with 500 or more employees—versus all other size classes. Employment adjustment is generally greater in the three smaller establishment size classes than in the largest, although many of the differences between the top size class and the others are not statistically significant and the twelve-month employment elasticity for establishments with 5 to 29 employees is actually less than that for establishments with 500 or more employees. A comparison of the three smaller size classes, however, shows that employment elasticities generally decline as establishment size falls. It is nonetheless interesting that the relatively slower adjustment in the largest establishment size category coincides with the fact that women are particularly underrepresented in establishments with 500 or more employees.

Conclusion

Japanese workers appear to enjoy, on average, considerably greater job security than American workers. Consistent with previous work, we find that employment levels in Japanese manufacturing adjust much less to changes in production than do U.S. employment levels. Contrary to some previous work, however, we find that the adjustment of average hours is about the same in the two countries. Consequently, the adjustment of total labor input in the Japanese manufacturing sector is also significantly less than that in U.S. manufacturing. Thus, Japanese hours are not sufficiently flexible to offset any of the short-term costs of providing employment security borne by Japanese employers.

Weitzman (1984) and Freeman and Weitzman (1987) have suggested that the bonus system renders compensation considerably more flexible in Japan than in the United States. The relative responsiveness of total labor costs to changes in production in the United States and Japan is something we plan to examine in future work. At this point, it would be premature to conclude that the strong job security characterizing Japanese labor markets imposes costs on employers even in the short run. In addition, Japanese internal labor markets are often characterized as more flexible than American internal labor markets in the sense that Japanese employers have more freedom to reassign workers within the firm.[26] Such flexibility is likely to enhance productivity and may be viewed as a substitute for managerial flexibility in hiring and firing.

Although the stability of employment, on average, is greater in Japan than in the United States, the variation in employment and hours adjustment across groups of workers within each country is considerable. In the United States, the burden of work force adjustment falls primarily on production workers. In Japan, differences between production and nonproduction employment adjustment are relatively small. Both production and nonproduction workers enjoy strong employment security compared to that of production workers in the United States. This may be a result of the changes in industrial relations in Japan after World War II that equalized social relations between blue- and white-collar workers. Such equalization has never occurred in the United States.[27]

In Japan, the burden of adjustment to demand shocks is widely believed to be borne disproportionately by workers in small establishments and by casual workers, who are predominantly women. We find only limited support for the contention that employment adjustment is greater in smaller establishments. The differences between the adjustment patterns of male and female employees appear to be more important. Female employment adjusts much more than male employment, particularly over horizons of three months or more. This finding is consistent with the fact that women comprise the bulk of part-time and temporary workers in manufacturing and, secondarily, are concentrated in smaller establishments.

In sum, in both the United States and Japan, the degree of employment security varies widely across groups, resulting in some overlap between the two countries. In the United States, the employment of nonproduction workers is, in practice, roughly as stable as that of overall employment in Japan. Yet in Japan, among the groups we examined, there is no group whose employment adjusts as much to changes in demand as that of production workers in the United States. In Japan, female workers and to some extent workers in small establishments do bear a disproportionate share of the burden of employment adjustment, but employment of these groups is still less responsive to changes in demand than that of U.S. production workers.

A caveat to this last conclusion is necessary: we could not independently

---

[26]For a recent discussion, see Koike 1984.
[27]We owe this observation to Konosuke Odaka.

examine adjustment patterns for part-time, temporary, and day workers, who are predominantly women. The pattern of adjustment for part-time and temporary employees is likely to be considerably different from that for regular, full-time workers, and the fact that a disproportionate number of women are part-time and temporary workers may well underlie the male-female differentials we report for Japan. Moreover, our data exclude day laborers, although they comprise less than 5 percent of the women employed in the manufacturing sector. Nevertheless, our evidence strongly suggests that Japanese women, on average, enjoy much greater stability of employment than does the average American worker.

7
Why WARN? The Impact of Recent Plant-Closing and Layoff Prenotification Legislation in the United States

Ronald G. Ehrenberg and George H. Jakubson

In July 1988, Congress passed the Worker Adjustment and Retraining Notification Act, which requires employers with one hundred or more employees to provide workers, the state government dislocated worker unit, and local government officials with sixty days' written advance notice before they shut down or make large-scale layoffs. Although legislation calling for advance notice had been active in Congress every year since 1979, 1988 represented the first year that advance notice legislation passed both houses of Congress, and President Reagan, although philosophically opposed to the legislation, bowed to election-year political pressure and did not veto it.

WARN went into effect on February 4, 1989. It requires covered employers to give sixty days' notice of a plant closing or of a layoff that is planned to last at least six months that involves either five hundred or more workers or at least one-third of the employer's work force. Coverage is not universal, however. In addition to not covering small employers, employers are exempted for a number of reasons. Employers are exempted, for example, if they are actively seeking ways to avoid the shutdown (such as trying to find a buyer for the business), if business circumstances that could not be "reasonably foreseen" occur, if a natural disaster directly caused the shutdown or mass layoff, if the employer relocated the business within a "reasonable" commuting distance of its previous location and offers employees jobs at the new location, if the workers to be displaced were hired with the understanding that their employment was limited to the duration of a particular project, or if a planned layoff of less than sixty days was extended because of "unforeseeable" circumstances. In all circumstances, the burden of proof is on the employer to demonstrate that an exemption is warranted.

Penalties for failure to provide the required advance notice include back pay and benefits for each displaced worker for each day of violation and a fine of $500 per day for failing to notify local governments. The determination of whether an

A substantially shorter version of this paper that contained no references appeared as Ehrenberg and Jakubson 1990.

employer who has failed to provide the required notice is covered by WARN or is exempted from the requirement for one of the above reasons is to be made by a federal district court only after a suit has been filed by employees, a union, or a local government. Unlike other forms of labor market legislation such as the Fair Labor Standards Act (governing minimum wages, overtime premium, and child labor) and the Occupational Safety and Health Act, the U.S. Department of Labor has no enforcement authority under WARN.

WARN was passed only after a decade of strenuous debate. We can now look back and address a number of issues it raised. What benefits did its proponents think would arise from the notice legislation, and what costs did its opponents think there would be? What public policies toward advance notice do other nations have? Did displaced workers in the United States receive advance notice before the passage of WARN? What do we know empirically about the effects on workers and firms of the provision of advance notice? What has experience under WARN taught us? Finally, what research issues need to be addressed to decide if WARN is a good idea, and what alternative public policies might help facilitate the provision of advance notice to displaced workers?

Hypothesized Benefits and Costs

Proponents of advance notice legislation argue that notice provisions ease displaced workers' shock and facilitate their search for alternative sources of employment or training. Advance notice to government agencies would allow them time to mobilize their resources to assist displaced workers. Indeed, a companion piece of legislation to WARN, the Economic Dislocation and Worker Adjustment Assistance Act (EDWAA), specifically required that the U.S. Department of Labor fund programs for states to aid dislocated workers and that each state create a state dislocated worker unit (DWU) with the capability of responding rapidly to plant closings and large-scale layoffs.

Advance notice would also allow employers, workers, unions, and local governments to work together to see if ways exist to prevent the plant closing or layoffs. Options might include wage concessions on the part of workers, tax concessions on the part of local government, restructuring of the work environment to improve productivity, or seeking new ownership, including possibly employee ownership.

To the extent that advance notice facilitates workers' transition to new jobs or helps avert worker displacement, proponents argue that it benefits local communities as well as individual workers. Plant shutdowns and massive layoffs place extra demands on communities for social services as the stress induced by unemployment causes an increased incidence of physical and mental ailments. These demands arise at the same time local sales and property tax revenue are reduced because of the fall in community members' incomes caused by the loss of jobs and the decline in property values that would result (Bluestone and Harrison 1982).

Opponents of advance notice legislation argued that it would restrict the free mobility of capital and have a number of other adverse effects on firms. They argued that it would increase worker turnover and decrease productivity in that those productive workers with the best opportunities elsewhere would leave and the morale of remaining workers would suffer. They said it would also decrease the likelihood that buyers of the plant's product would place new orders, that banks would supply new credit, that suppliers would continue to provide services, and that the firm could sell the plant to potential buyers. (The latter explains one of the exemptions under WARN.) In addition, advance notice might depress corporate stock prices. Finally, by effectively increasing the cost of reducing employment, it would encourage firms not to expand operations or to substitute overtime hours for additional employment (McKersie 1982).

Critics often stress that the government should encourage firms to provide advance notice for workers about to be displaced; what they object to is making notice mandatory. Proponents respond that in the absence of mandatory advance notice very few displaced workers actually receive such notice; evidence we cite below suggests the proponents are probably correct.

In evaluating the case for advance notice legislation, it is important to stress that an employer does not bear the full social cost of the plant shutdown or mass layoff for two reasons. On the one hand, because the U.S. unemployment insurance system is financed by an "imperfectly experience-rated" payroll tax, an employer's unemployment insurance payroll tax payments will increase by less than the unemployment insurance benefits the employer's displaced workers receive. On the other hand, an employer typically does not take into account the costs that a mass layoff or plant shutdown imposes on the community.

Proponents of advance notice legislation argue that by implicitly increasing the "cost" of plant closings or mass layoffs, employers will be discouraged from taking such actions. Critics, of course, stress that anything that implicitly or explicitly increases labor costs will encourage the flight of jobs overseas.

Advance Notice Legislation before WARN

Most European nations have legislation that calls for advance notice when employees are to be laid off. As table 7–1 indicates, when an individual's employment is terminated, the length of notice required in these countries typically depends on whether the individual is a white-collar or a blue-collar employee and on his or her length of service with the firm. Typically, in cases when large-scale layoffs or plant shutdowns are contemplated, the legislation also calls for advance notice to be given to unions and the government and for the employer to negotiate with employees and the government over whether the displacement can be averted. Often the legislation requires severance pay for displaced workers, and some countries, such as Sweden, have detailed programs of labor market services, including retraining, job placement, public works jobs, and wage subsidies, to facilitate labor market adjustments. In many European countries, establishments with fewer than one hundred employees are exempt from advance notice requirements, perhaps because the government does not want to add to the costs of small

TABLE 7-1. *Requirements for Advance Notice for Termination of Employment in European Countries, 1989*[a]

Country	Minimum length of service	Employer notice
Austria	Blue collar	2 weeks
	White collar	
	< 2 years	1 month
	2–5 years	2 months
	5–15 years	3 months
	15–25 years	4 months
	> 25 years	5 months
Belgium	Blue collar	
	< 6 months	1 week
	6 mos.–20 yrs.	4 weeks
	> 20 years	8 weeks
	White collar	
	< 5 years	3 months
	5–9 years	6 months
	> 9 years	6 months plus 3 months per each 5 years of service over 9
Denmark	Blue collar	Set by collective bargaining
	White collar	
	< 6 months	1 month
	6 months–2 years, 9 months	3 months
	2 years, 9 months–5 years, 8 months	4 months
	5 years, 8 mos.–8 years, 7 months	5 months
	> 8 years, 7 months	6 months
France	6–24 months	1 month
	> 24 months	2 months
Greece	Blue collar	Set by collective bargaining
	White collar	
	1 year	1 month
	1–4 years	2 months
	4–6 years	3 months
	6–8 years	4 months
	8–10 years	5 months
	> 10 years	5 months plus 1 month per year of service over 10 up to a maximum of 24 months
Ireland	13 weeks–2 years	1 week
	2–4 years	2 weeks
	5–9 years	4 weeks
	10–14 years	6 weeks
	15 years or more	8 weeks

TABLE 7-1. (continued)

Country	Minimum length of service	Employer notice
Luxembourg	Blue collar	
	up to 5 years	4 weeks
	5–10 years	8 weeks
	more than 10 years	12 weeks
	White collar	
	up to 5 years	2 months
	5–10 years	4 months
	more than 10 years	6 months
Malta	1–12 months	1 week
	1–2 years	2 weeks
	2–5 years	4 weeks
	5 years or more	8 weeks
Netherlands	All	1 week + 1 week per year of service over age 21 (to a max. of 13) + 1 week per year of service over age 45 (to a max. of 13) up to a max. of 26 weeks
Norway	< 5 years	1 month
	5–9 years	2 months
	10 years, age 50+	4 months
	10 years, age 55+	5 months
	10 years, age 60+	6 months
Portugal	See note b	2–3 months
Spain	< 1 year	1 month
	1–2 years	2 months
	> 2 years	3 months
Sweden[c]	Age 25–29	2 months
	Age 30–34	3 months
	Age 35–39	4 months
	Age 40–44	5 months
	Age 45 and over	6 months
United Kingdom	1 month–2 years	1 week
	2–11 years	1 week per year of service
	12 or more years	12 weeks
West Germany	Blue collar	
	all employees	2 weeks
	5–9 years (worked over age 35)	1 month
	10–19 years (worked over age 35)	2 months
	20 yrs. or more (worked over age 35)	3 months

TABLE 7-1. *(continued)*

Country	Minimum length of service	Employer notice
West Germany	White collar	
	all employees	1 month
	5–8 years (worked over age 25)	3 months
	8–10 years (worked over age 25)	4 months
	10–12 years (worked over age 25)	5 months
	12 years or more (worked over age 25)	6 months

Source: Authors' interpretation of material in issues of the *European Industrial Relations Review* between May 1985 and November 1989.
ᵃThese notice requirements govern termination of an individual's employment. In some countries additional provisions govern notification of unions and governments when collective dismissals are contemplated.
ᵇNotice required only if two or more workers in companies with fewer than fifty employees or five or more workers in companies with more than fifty employees are dismissed.
ᶜNo statute; typical collective bargaining provision.

businesses (which typically have high failure rates) or because of the belief that shutting down a small business does not have a substantial negative effect on a community.

As table 7–2 indicates, in Canada, both federal and provincial legislation require advance notice. The notice required for individual terminations typically depends on an individual's prior service with the employer. In cases of anticipated plant shutdowns or large-scale layoffs, the length of notice required is longer—typically exceeding the sixty-day notice required by WARN.

Before the passage of WARN, advance notice legislation in the United States was much more modest. Debate about such legislation seriously began with the deep recession of the mid–1970s. The large number of plant closings and permanent layoffs in major manufacturing industries since then increased interest. As has often been the case with other forms of government regulation of conditions of employment in the United States, action by states preceded federal action.

As of early 1988, there was no federal law and only a few state laws relating to advance notice. Three states—Maine, Wisconsin, and Hawaii—required advance notice of plant shutdowns (with size class exemptions). Maine also required one week's severance pay per year of service for workers with more than three years of tenure. The penalties for noncompliance were low in Maine ($500 per establishment) and Wisconsin ($50 per employee) but high in Hawaii (three months' wages and benefits per laid-off worker). Connecticut did not require advance notice, but did require nonbankrupt firms to maintain health insurance and other benefits for up to 120 days for workers unemployed because of plant shutdowns. Massachusetts, Maryland, and Michigan all had voluntary programs in which firms were urged to provide advance notice and/or to continue benefits. Finally, South Carolina "required" employers to give workers two weeks' notice before shutting down but only in situations in which employees were required to give advance notice before quitting.

TABLE 7-2. *Notice Requirements for Termination of Employment in Various Jurisdictions of Canada, January 1, 1988*[a]

	Individual termination		Mass terminations	
Jurisdiction	Minimum length of service	Employer notice	Number of employees	Employer notice
Federal	3 months	2 weeks	≥ 50	16 weeks
Alberta	3 months–2 years	1 week	No special legislation	
	2 years–4 years	2 weeks		
	4 years–6 years	4 weeks		
	6 years–8 years	5 weeks		
	8 years–10 years	6 weeks		
	10 years or more	8 weeks		
British Columbia	6 months–2 years	2 weeks	No special legislation	
	≥3 years	Number of weeks equal to years of service to maximum of 8 wks.		
Manitoba	>2 weeks	1 pay period	50–100	10 weeks
			101–300	14 weeks
			>300	18 weeks
New Brunswick	6 months–5 years	2 weeks	≥25 *if* they represent at least 25% of employer's work force	4 weeks
	≥5 years	4 weeks		
Newfoundland	1 month–2 years	1 week	50–199	8 weeks
			200–499	12 weeks
	≥2 years	2 weeks	≥500	16 weeks
Nova Scotia	3 months–2 years	1 week	10–99	8 weeks
	2 years–5 years	2 weeks	100–299	12 weeks
	5 years–10 years	4 weeks	≥300	16 weeks
	≥10 years	8 weeks		
Ontario	3 months–1 year	1 week	50–199	8 weeks
	1 year–3 years	2 weeks	200–499	12 weeks
	3 years or more	No. of weeks equal to years of service to a max. of 8 weeks	≥500	16 weeks
Prince Edward Island	3 months	1 week	No special legislation	
Quebec	3 months–1 year	1 week	10–99	8 weeks
	1 year–5 years	2 weeks	100–299	12 weeks
	5 years–10 years	4 weeks	≥300	16 weeks
	≥10 years	8 weeks		

TABLE 7-2. (continued)

| Jursidiction | Individual termination | | Mass terminations | |
	Minimum length of service	Employer notice	Number of employees	Employer notice
Saskatchewan	3 months–1 year	1 week	No special legislation	
	1 year–3 years	2 weeks		
	3 years–5 years	4 weeks		
	5 years–10 years	6 weeks		
	≥10 years	8 weeks		
Northwest Territories	No notice provisions		No special legislation	
Yukon Territory	6 months	1 week	25–49	4 weeks
			50–99	8 weeks
			100–299	12 weeks
			≥300	16 weeks

Source: Canadian Master Labor Guide, 1989.
[a]In some cases, employee notice of intent to terminate employment is also required. The federal provisions apply to federal employees and to employees in regulated industries. Provincial regulations apply to both public and private employees with certain exemptions. These exemptions are for both temporary layoffs of specified durations and for certain industries. Some laws also require severance pay. Generally, the penalty for failure to provide the required notice is payment of the employees' regular wages for the specified period.

Before WARN, displaced workers in the United States may have received advance notice of a pending layoff or plant shutdown if they lived in a state in which such notice was required, if a collective bargaining agreement required notice, or if an employer voluntarily chose to provide notice. What fraction of displaced workers actually received advance notice under these circumstances? Three employee-based surveys have recently collected such information. These were the Survey of Displaced Workers (SDW), supplements to the January 1984, January 1986, and January 1988 Current Population Surveys (CPS), the monthly national probability sample of the population from which our unemployment and labor force statistics are derived. These supplements covered workers who were displaced during the 1979–83, 1981–85, and 1983–87 periods respectively.

Table 7–3 presents data on the proportion of displaced workers in these surveys who received advance notice or expected layoffs. For the purpose of this table, displaced workers are defined as persons who permanently lost or involuntarily left a full-time wage and salary job in which they had been employed for at least three years. These data, presented in the first three rows of the table, suggest that more than half the workers displaced during the 1979–87 period did receive advance notice or expect their layoff. Thus, at first glance, it may appear that a substantial fraction of displaced workers in the United States did receive advance notice before WARN.

One must caution, however, that the question "Did you receive advance notice or expect layoff?" does not distinguish between receipt of formal written notice and the situation in which a worker simply could "see the handwriting on the

TABLE 7-3. *Proportion of Displaced Workers Who Received Advance Notice or Expected Layoff in the January 1984, January 1986, and January 1988 CPS Displaced Worker Supplements*

Received advance notice or expected layoff	
January 1984 Survey (workers displaced in 1979–83)	.56
January 1986 Survey (workers displaced in 1981–85)	.55
January 1988 Survey (workers displaced in 1983–87)	.58
Received written advance notice	.20
Received written notice of less than one month	.06
Received written notice of one to two months	.05
Received written notice of two or more months	.07
Received written notice but failed to report length	.02

Source: Authors' calculations from U.S. Bureau of Labor Statistics 1985 and 1987 and tables from a forthcoming bulletin covering the 1983–87 period.

wall" because his or her employer was in trouble. Similarly, it provides no information on the length of advance notice that was received; this is a crucial shortcoming in that the effectiveness of advance notice policies in preventing displacements and easing displaced workers' transitions back to employment presumably depends partially on how far in advance notice is given.

Fortunately, the January 1988 SDW, which covered workers displaced during the 1983–87 period, specifically asked displaced workers if they received formal written advance notice. If individuals answered in the affirmative, they were also asked whether the notice was less than one month, one month to less than two months, or two months or more. The answers to these questions are tabulated in the bottom rows of table 7–3.

Quite strikingly, only 20 percent of these displaced workers reported receiving written advance notice. Moreover, most reported receiving written notice of relatively short duration. Indeed, only 7 percent of the displaced workers reported receiving written notice two or more months before their impending displacement. Hence, before the passage of WARN, only a small fraction of displaced workers actually received the sixty days' written advance notice of displacement that WARN now requires. Two recent studies of employers who laid off a substantial number of workers, one conducted by the U.S. Bureau of Labor Statistics and the other by the U.S. General Accounting Office, confirm this conclusion (see Addison 1991).

Does Providing Advance Notice Matter?

Studies of the effects of legally mandated, collectively bargained, or voluntarily provided advance notice before the passage of WARN have been of two types. The first type looked at the effects of advance notice on employment-related variables at the national or community level. One study that used aggregate data from twenty-three countries over the 1956–84 period found weak evidence that advance notice requirements increase the fraction of the population that is employed but decrease their average weekly hours (Lazear 1987). The author attributed these findings to the fact that many nations with advance notice laws exempt part-time employees and thus encourage employers to substitute part-time for full-time employees.

WARN was in fact designed to reduce the possibility of such substitution. Although part-time employees who work fewer than twenty hours a week are not counted under WARN in determining whether a firm has at least one hundred employees and thus is required to give advance notice of displacement, part-time employees who are displaced from covered firms are required to receive notice under WARN.

Another study examined the effects of plant closings in Maine in a period before the enactment of that state's law. It found that voluntary provision by a firm of at least one month's advance notice to its displaced workers significantly reduced the impact of the closing on the local area's unemployment rate in the month of the closing (Folbre, Leighton, and Roderick 1984). While this result may be due to more rapid reemployment of displaced workers in the presence of advance notice, the authors also found that advance notice was associated with a significant reduction in the size of the local labor force in the month of the closing. This latter result may reflect either labor force withdrawal or outmigration (and possibly reemployment elsewhere); they were unable to ascertain which had occurred.

The second, and by far more numerous, type of studies examine the effects of advance notice on individual displaced workers. For example, one early study of thirty-two plant closings in the United States in the late 1950s and early 1960s found that voluntarily provided advance notice rarely led to increased quit rates or decreased productivity by workers (Weber and Taylor 1963).

More recently, numerous authors, including ourselves, have drawn inferences about the empirical effects of advance notice from analyses of the January 1984 and January 1986 SDW data (Ehrenberg and Jakubson 1988, 1989; Addison and Portugal 1986, 1987a, 1987b; Howland 1988; Podgursky and Swaim 1987a, 1987b; Swaim and Podgursky 1990). On balance, these studies suggest that the provision of advance notice significantly increases the likelihood that a displaced worker will not experience any unemployment. That is, advance notice does provide time for some soon-to-be-displaced workers to find new jobs before their date of displacement. But, in contrast, these studies also suggest that once an individual experiences any unemployment, the presence of advance notice has no effect on his or her ultimate duration of unemployment. Thus, advance notice seems to help only if individuals can find employment before being displaced.

Moreover, receipt of advance notice appears, for the most part, to have no effect on subsequent earnings once a displaced worker is reemployed. Finally, among the people in the SDW who received advance notice, there was no evidence that a firm's most productive workers were more likely to quit before the displacement date, thereby disrupting the firm's operations in its final weeks.

All of these conclusions were based on analyses of the 1984 and 1986 SDW data in which respondents were asked if they "received advance notice or expected layoff." Data from the January 1988 SDW, summarized in table 7–3, suggest that most people who responded affirmatively probably did not receive formal written notice and that those who did primarily received notice of relatively short duration. Recent analyses of the 1988 SDW data suggest that formal written notice increases the likelihood that an individual will experience no spell of unemployment but that the magnitude of the effect of advance notice is smaller than when the broader definition of notice found in the 1984 and 1986 studies was used (Ruhm 1989; Addison and Portugal 1989). Moreover, written notice of at least sixty days lowered the probability of experiencing unemployment by a greater amount than written notice of a shorter duration (Nord and Ting 1991).

Together, these studies suggest that written advance notice per se does not determine a worker's success at finding reemployment after displacement but rather whether, based on the worker's general perceptions of the likely future of the employer, the worker has made efforts to search for new employment. Written advance notice will matter only if it substantially provides new information to the worker on his or her future employment prospects and only if it is of sufficiently long length to give the worker time to conduct a serious job search before being displaced.

Early Experiences under WARN

WARN has only recently come into effect and it is too early to do a formal evaluation of the law. Conversations with U.S. Department of Labor personnel and staff at the state DWUs in a number of states, however, provide several insights into how it is faring. First, compliance with WARN appears to be high. Unlike many other protective labor laws, enforcement of WARN takes place through suits filed in individual federal district courts, not through an office in the U.S. Department of Labor. As such, there is no central receiver of complaints of noncompliance and one has to search hard to obtain evidence. State DWUs, as well as the U.S. Department of Labor, receive numerous inquiries from unions and employees who feel they should have received advance notice, but often it appears that the employers were not required to file because the establishment was small or the size of the layoff exempted them from the law.

Indeed, WARN appears to be providing numerous employment opportunities for lawyers, who often appear to be advising their employer-clients to behave conservatively. As a result, even employers who are not legally required to provide advance notice are often doing so. For example, of the 167 advance notifications received by Pennsylvania's DWU from the time of WARN's enactment though January 9, 1990, only 117 were from employers who were legally required to provide notice. Put another way, about 30 percent of the notifications received were not required under the law. (This pattern was not observed, however, in at least one of the other states contacted.)

Why would employers who did not have to comply with WARN do so? One possibility is that the debate over the passage of the law raised their consciousness of what a "good employer" is. A second possibility is that the law is so complex and so ambiguous that they are simply trying to protect themselves. The penalties for noncompliance are so high (up to sixty days' back wages and benefits) that many employers may be deciding that it is cheaper to comply than to risk being found guilty of a violation.

As a result, although a number of individuals and unions have indicated to state and federal personnel that they intend to file suits for noncompliance, the number of suits actually filed appears to be very small. As of early January 1990, state DWU personnel in a number of northeastern and midatlantic states knew of no lawsuits being filed in their states, and the solicitor's office of the U.S. Department of Labor knew of only eight to ten cases in progress. While it is possible that the cost of pursuing lawsuits is discouraging complainants from filing claims, on balance it appears that compliance with WARN is high. This should be contrasted with the relatively high noncompliance rates for the minimum wage and overtime pay premium provisions of the Fair Labor Standards Act, even though the penalties for noncompliance and the likelihood of being identified as a noncomplier are quite low.

Second, contrary to popular opinion, WARN is not affecting solely or even primarily manufacturing employers. For example, statistics from the second half of 1989 indicate that only 27 percent of the notifications in Pennsylvania were from employers in manufacturing. Similarly, during the same period, less than 40 percent of the displaced workers covered by notifications in New York State came from manufacturing; the majority had been employed in wholesale trade, retail trade, finance insurance and real estate, or service sector jobs. While public debate over advance notice legislation in the United States was precipitated by concern over the declining manufacturing base, WARN affects a much larger range of industries.

Third, WARN per se does not affect a substantial share of permanently laid-off workers in the United States. During the February 1, 1989, to December 31, 1989, period, the first eleven months in which WARN was in effect, there were 127 advance notifications in New York State, involving 22,822 workers. During the same period of time there were 657,247 new claims filed for unemployment insurance benefits and 490,889 first payments made to unemployment insurance recipients in the state. The difference between the number of new claims filed and first payments reflects individuals who were determined to be ineligible for benefits (i.e., those who were dismissed for cause or quit their jobs rather than being laid off) and those laid-off workers who found new jobs within a week.

Even if we ignore the fact that some workers covered by WARN notifications may have found jobs within one week of their displacement (prior studies suggest that about 10 percent of them likely would), it is clear that workers involved in WARN notifications are only a small fraction of all new unemployment insurance recipients in the state. Indeed, during the eleven-month period in question, they represented approximately 4.6 percent (22,822/490,889 × 100) of the state's new unemployment insurance recipients. Even if half these recipients were on temporary layoff waiting to be recalled by their employers, less than 10 percent of permanently displaced workers due to layoffs or plant shutdowns in New York State received advance notice under WARN.

This percentage is low for two reasons. First, as noted above, small firms are not covered by the law, and there are numerous exemptions under WARN. Second, WARN covers only plant shutdowns and mass layoffs. Unlike the laws prevailing in Canada and many European countries, advance notice for layoffs of individuals or small numbers of employees is not required under WARN.

Implications for Future Research and Public Policy

Empirical studies suggest that advance notice may well facilitate labor market adjustments by allowing displaced workers to find employment before their date of displacement. Advance notice appears to reduce the probability that displaced workers will suffer any spell of unemployment and thus may well moderate temporary increases in area unemployment rates. Moreover, virtually all of the studies include as receiving "advance notice" notice of very short duration and thus the results in these studies may well understate the effects of mandated notice of longer duration accompanied by the other supportive services that WARN calls for. Nor did the individual- based data used in most of the studies permit analyses of whether advance notice of pending displacements lead to actions (e.g., reorganization, wage concessions, employee ownership) that help avert displacements.

Although opponents of advance notice cite the potential costs of such policies, empirical studies have found no evidence that advance notice causes the most productive workers to leave the firm or that the productivity of the remaining workers suffers. Moreover, save for one study that used aggregate international data, no studies have provided systematic empirical evidence on the adverse effects of advance notice that opponents have enumerated (Lazear 1987).

While at first glance this discussion suggests support for WARN, several cautions are in order. First, the effects of voluntary provision of advance notice in situations where workers expect impending displacement anyway may be very different from the effects of mandated advance notice in situations where the impending displacement is completely unexpected by workers.

All of the research conducted for the United States has used data that predated WARN. Future research will need to analyze data from subsequent years' versions of the SDW that cover periods when WARN was in effect. Since WARN requires advance notice only for large-scale displacements in large firms, researchers will have to take care to distinguish the effects of WARN from the effects of being displaced as part of a large-scale displacement from a large firm. In addition, to estimate adequately the effects of advance notice per se will require researchers to try to model what displaced workers' expectations of displacement would have been in the absence of advance notice. Put another way, researchers will need to estimate whether formal advance notice actually communicates new information to workers.

Second, the observation that the voluntary provision of advance notice appears to reduce the probability that a displaced worker will suffer any unemployment does not necessarily imply that mandated advance notice will increase employment and decrease unemployment rates. Indeed, one can conceive of situations in which displaced workers compete for a fixed number of vacant positions that only a fraction of them can obtain. Advance notice gives those workers who receive notice an advantage; it increases their probability of finding one of these jobs. If the number of vacant positions is truly fixed, however, by necessity the probability that workers who failed to receive notice will find jobs would have to go down. In this case, the gains to those workers who received notice would come solely at the expense of those workers who failed to receive notice. There would be no social gains from advance notice in that, on average, it would not influence aggregate employment levels and/or unemployment rates.

Studies that use individual-based data sets, such as the SDW, cannot test for the possibility of such displacement effects. The only study of U.S. data that addressed this issue did find evidence that voluntary provision of advance notice led to smaller temporary increases in area unemployment rates (Folbre, Leighton, and Roderick 1984). The one cross-country study of international data, however, found no positive effects of mandated advance notice on aggregate employment levels and unemployment rates (Lazear 1987). Clearly, more studies that focus on the effects of advance notice on area economic outcomes are needed.

Suppose for a moment that all voluntarily provided advance notice actually does is "reshuffle" jobs among displaced workers from those people who fail to receive notice to those people who do receive it. In fact, evidence of such reshuffling might strengthen the case for legislation like WARN if the people who receive notice voluntarily are the ones least in need of such assistance. For example, if before WARN high-wage, unionized workers were more likely to receive notice than comparably skilled, lower-wage nonunion workers (which some data suggest was the case), implementation of WARN would allow the latter a "better shot" at competing with the former for the available jobs when they are displaced. One thus might be in favor of WARN because of its potential redistributive effects, even if one believes it will have no net effect on aggregate employment or unemployment.

Third, it is important when designing a policy intervention like WARN to be clear about the source of public concern. If the major concern is the costs imposed on a local community by a plant closing or large-scale layoff, then public policy should specifically address this concern. While such a concern may argue for advance notice legislation, in this case exemptions from notice requirements should be based on the size of the displacement relative to the local labor market not on the absolute sizes of the displacement and the employer, as is currently done under WARN. In contrast, if the source of the concern is the private costs workers suffer from displacement, then requirements for advance notice of individual displacements and/or severance pay provisions, similar to those that exist in many European countries, might be worth considering.

Indeed, it is worth reemphasizing that the data presented here suggest that only a small proportion of permanently displaced workers in the United States actually receive advance notice of their displacement under WARN. The major reason for this is that WARN exempts small employers and small-scale or individual layoffs at large employers. To the extent that one believes that advance notice is a desirable policy, one might also consider adopting policies that provide incentives for employers to provide advance notice voluntarily for exempted employees. For example, the federal government could provide incentives to firms to provide such notice by funding a share of the unemployment benefits received by notified workers and/or by reducing the corporate profit tax rates of firms that voluntarily provide advance notice to displaced workers.

Finally, well-designed research is needed to address more adequately issues relating to the macro labor market effects of WARN, including whether advance notice of impending displacement helps prevent displacement from occurring, as proponents of the legislation often assert. Moreover, since so much of the research has focused on the potential benefits of advance notice legislation, subsequent studies of WARN might also focus on research issues that have concerned opponents, namely those relating to the potential costs of the legislation.

8
Employment Effects of Worker Protection: Evidence from the United States

James N. Dertouzos and Lynn A. Karoly

The economic system in the United States has always been characterized by labor market flexibility. American business managers have been relatively unencumbered in dismissing poor performers or adjusting the labor force in response to exogenous changes in product demand, technological change, or the competitive environment. In the past, the U.S. system was the envy of European business managers, who attributed a variety of their own economic ills, including high costs, unemployment, and slow growth, to a series of worker protection regulations adopted during the 1960s and 1970s.[1] As a result, several countries, including the United Kingdom, Germany, France, Italy, and Spain, have recently introduced legislation that would relax the legal restrictions on employers.[2]

At the same time that workplace restrictions are being eased in Western Europe, the prevailing trends in the United States are moving in the opposite direction. During the 1980s, a series of judicial rulings placed important limitations on the ability of managers to terminate employees. This paper investigates the labor market consequences of these legal changes. We begin with a brief description of the new employment liabilites for wrongful termination. We then analyze state-

---

[1] For a description of these regulations and a discussion of their claimed effect on business in Western Europe, see International Organization of Employers 1985. See also OECD 1986a for a review of the rather sparse empirical evidence. More recently, Burgess (1988) found that unfair dismissal provisions and redundancy payment provisions have reduced business flexibility in Great Britain. Also, Abraham and Houseman (1989a, 1989b) offer some evidence that U.S. employers adjust more rapidly to output shocks than do their Japanese and West German counterparts.

[2] Although the specifics vary from country to country, most of the proposals relax the legal standards in the area of dismissal protection and/or create loopholes that provide increased managerial discretion in adjusting employment. For example, some of the new codes facilitate the use of fixed-term contracts or temporary employees. See Buechtemann 1990 for a summary of recent legislative proposals for change.

level employment data and provide estimates of the aggregate impact of the new legal restrictions.

Decline of Employment at Will

There is no doubt that there has been a dramatic change in the U.S. legal environment in the last decade with respect to employment law. The prevailing employment-at-will doctrine, a feature of the common law for nearly a century, provided considerable labor market flexibility. It has been eroded, however, by a series of new legal doctrines recognized by the state courts. Before the recent judicially recognized exceptions, the application of the at-will rule was limited to private sector employees without a fixed-term contract who were not covered by a collective bargaining agreement. In addition, a variety of federal and state statutes, such as the National Labor Relations Act and Title VII of the Civil Rights Act, placed restrictions on the ability of employers to invoke the at-will rule.

The new wrongful-termination doctrines are typically divided into three legal theories: the implied contract exception, the public policy exception, and the covenant of good faith and fair dealing. In the case of the first exception, the courts have held that an employee is no longer "at will" when the employer has made explicit or implicit statements that place limits on the ability of the employer to terminate the employment relationship. For example, the evidence of an employment contract has been based on oral statements at the time of the hiring, on written statements in policy manuals, and on the circumstances of the employment relationship, such as longevity of service. In contrast, the public policy doctrine prohibits employers from terminating even at-will employees when the firing violates some public policy as represented, for example, in statutes or regulations. Thus, employers have been held liable for terminating employees who refused to violate a law or who exercised a statutorily protected right. The third doctrine represents the greatest increase in employer liability in that it can imply that employees must always be fired for cause. The doctrine of good faith and fair dealing has been recognized in a more limited form, requiring the existence of an employment contract, and more broadly as a theory applicable to all employment relationships.

Each of the fifty states can be characterized by which of the three legal theories, if any, have been adopted by the judiciary. In addition, because of the differences in the remedies available to a successful plaintiff, it is also important to distinguish states by whether the doctrine represents a tort cause of action (where both compensatory and punitive damages are available) or a contract cause of action. Based on an examination of the precedent-setting cases, we were able to characterize the wrongful-termination environment in each of the fifty states.[3]

Table 8–1 shows the number of states that had adopted various wrongful-termination doctrines in 1980 and 1989. We have also tabulated the number of

[3]For details, see Dertouzos and Karoly 1992.

TABLE 8-1. *Number of States Recognizing Wrongful-Termination Doctrines,*
1980, 1989

	Doctrine			Remedy		At least one doctrine	All three doctrines
	PP	IC	GF	Tort	Contract		
1980	16	7	3	14	9	13	1
1989	40	36	9	38	37	45	8

PP=public policy, IC=implied contract, GF=covenant of good faith and fair dealing.

states that adopted either a tort or a contract remedy. Judging from the figures in table 8–1, there was a virtual landslide of cases in the 1980s, as almost every state recognized at least one of the new doctrines. For instance, in 1980, only thirteen states recognized one of the new legal doctrines. By 1989, forty-five states had recognized at least one. Furthermore, all three of the new legal doctrines were available to employees in eight states, and at least two doctrines were recognized in another twenty-five.

Despite the almost universal acceptance of the new common-law theories, very few state benches have been willing to recognize the most liberal versions of the new doctrines. In 1989, only nine states recognized the good-faith and fair-dealing doctrine. Moreover, with the 1988 California Supreme Court decision in *Foley v. Interactive Data Corp.*, only two states now treat the good faith doctrine as a tort remedy, thereby allowing the plaintiff to claim punitive as well as compensatory damages.

Data

We analyzed state-level data describing annual employment outcomes between 1980 and 1987. Table 8–2 briefly outlines the basic trends and patterns in the level and composition of employment and a measure of output, the gross state product (GSP). The state average for total nonagricultural employment over this time period was more than 1.9 million, ranging from 169,000 to nearly 12 million. On average, employment levels grew about 1.6 percent annually. Of this total, the manufacturing sector represented about 20 percent of total nonagricultural employment, though this percentage varied widely from state to state. The service and retail trade industries averaged 21.1 and 17.3 percent of total state employment respectively. For wholesale trade and the finance, insurance, and real estate sector, the percentages were slightly more than 5 percent. Again, the industrial mix exhibited significant variation across states. Over the time period, the service industry appears to have exhibited the largest growth in employment.

In estimating the impact of the wrongful-termination doctrines on the labor market, we characterized each state's legal environment by year using two methods. The first method, based on the three legal doctrines, uses the following classification: (1) a narrow public policy exception; (2) an implied contract or good-faith contract exception; and (3) a broad public policy or good-faith tort

TABLE 8-2. *Employment and Gross State Product, 1980–86*

	State average	Sample range Min.–Max.	Average 1980	Average 1986
Total employment[a]	1,857	169–11,658	1,782	1,955
Percentage of total				
Manufacturing	20.4	2.2–34.4	20.2	17.5
Service	21.1	13.4–44.2	19.1	22.6
Wholesale trade	5.5	1.7– 8.5	5.6	5.3
Retail trade	17.3	8.3–22.6	16.9	17.9
Finance and insurance	5.5	3.4– 9.6	5.2	5.8
Total gross product[b]	64,329	5,396–452,586	59,511	70,211
Percentage of total				
Manufacturing	20.1	3.0–43.2	20.2	21.2
Service	14.0	6.7–33.9	14.4	15.0
Wholesale trade	6.4	1.9– 9.5	6.4	7.1
Retail trade	9.5	4.4–12.9	9.4	10.2
Finance and insurance	14.7	8.7–20.9	15.1	15.0

[a]Total nonagricultural employees, in thousands.
[b]Total nonagricultural gross state product in millions of 1982 dollars.

exception. These three categories range from the most narrow to the most broad legal theories. For instance, the narrow public policy exception applies only when the employee is terminated contrary to some public policy expressed statutorily, thereby making its application to employee discharge quite limited. States that have recognized the broader public policy doctrine (where public policy may be defined by statutes, legislation, administration rules, or even codes of ethics) or the good-faith tort remedy fall in the most liberal category. These three categories are not mutually exclusive; a state may recognize two or more of these classes of doctrines at the same time.[4]

We also characterized states on the basis of the legal remedies associated with the wrongful-termination doctrines, identifying those states that recognized a tort remedy or a contract remedy. Since tort doctrines allow the plaintiff to claim punitive damages as well as damages for pain and suffering, we expected that the availability of a tort remedy would have a larger impact on labor market outcomes. By using these two ways of characterizing the legal environment, we were able to investigate the impact of the legal doctrines themselves, as well as the effect of the remedies associated with the doctrines.

General Estimating Framework

Our general approach was to estimate a model that assumed that annual employment level in state *i* during year *t*, E_{it}, had the following functional form:

[4]Several states have also reversed earlier decisions that recognized a particular doctrine. Our classification scheme recognizes such reversals.

$$\log(E_{it}) = \beta_0 + \beta_1 \log(GSP_{it}) + \beta_2[\log(GSP_{it-1})] \qquad (8\text{-}1)$$
$$+ \sum_{k=2}^{50} \lambda_k S_{ki} + \sum_{j=1}^{6} \alpha_j Y_{jt} + \delta X_{it} + \gamma W_{it} + u_{it}$$

where S_{ki} are fifty dichotomous variables equal to one indicating a given state; Y_{jt} are dichotomous variables equal to one indicating the year; GSP_{it} represents gross state product, in 1982 dollars, in year t; X_{it} is a vector of other possible control variables; W_{it} are variables indicating the presence of wrongful-termination doctrines; and u_{it} is a random disturbance term.

The state location variables were included to control for a variety of state-specific influences that remain constant over time. Persistent differences in state demographics, occupational composition, or prevailing workplace traditions are examples of such factors, which are unmeasured but likely to be important. The time-trend variables, representing individual year effects, were included to allow for systematic changes affecting all states, such as the influence of technological innovation, fluctuations in the cost of capital, the influence of international markets, or changes in federal statutes regarding worker rights.

The GSP is included as a measure of aggregate labor demand and is assumed to be predetermined by exogenous factors such as consumer income, relative prices, and population.[5] This implies that fluctuations in employment due to factors such as employment liability will be the result of changes in input utilization rather than the production level. For example, firms can maintain output and still reduce employment by substituting capital or by increasing the hours or work intensity of remaining workers.

To allow for labor adjustment costs, the change in GSP (in logarithmic form) was included as an explanatory variable. If firms are unable to reduce or expand the work force instantaneously in response to changes in product demand, a transition period will be necessary before firms are able to achieve the "optimal" level of labor. For a given level of production, employment will be lower during periods of growth and higher during periods of decline.[6]

Effects of Liability on Aggregate Employment Levels

To avoid potential biases associated with the simultaneous determination of the legal environment and employment outcomes, we first estimated a logit

---

[5]This approach is standard in the literature (see Burgess 1988, Abraham and Houseman 1989a, and Hamermesh 1990a). As Quandt and Rosen (1989) demonstrate, more complicated estimation techniques that treat output as endogenous are not likely to produce superior results. Indeed, our own estimates based on substituting predicted values of GSP (using instrumental variables such as aggregate daily newspaper circulation, household income, and population) were invariably the same.

[6]Other formulations allowing for more complex patterns of adjustment failed to explain significantly more of the variation in employment; nor did they alter our estimates of the effects of wrongful-termination doctrines. We describe some of these generalizations to the more simple model below.

model of the probability that a state has a particular wrongful-termination doctrine or remedy at time *t*. The predicted values from this first-stage estimation were then used in the second-stage estimation of the employment equation. To illustrate the first-stage findings, table 8–3 shows the coefficient estimates for the probability that a state has a contract doctrine (column 1) or a tort doctrine (column 2).[7]

The findings indicate that the probability of having one of the various wrongful-termination doctrines is strongly correlated with a number of state characteristics. For instance, states with a right-to-work law, an indicator of a conservative attitude toward labor, are less likely to have either a tort or a contract wrongful-termination doctrine. Likewise, the degree of unionization, another possible indicator of the state's attitude toward labor, is positively related to the probability of having a contract or a tort remedy. Further, the higher the fraction of neighboring states that have recognized the doctrine, the more likely the state is to have the doctrine, although this effect is nonlinear. This result suggests that, to some degree, there may be spillover effects from one state to another. A decline in the unionization rate, a possible indicator of an increase in the demand for common-law protection against unjust dismissal, increases the probability of having a tort or a contract remedy. Finally, the effect of changes in lawyers per capita and changes in the unemployment rate are mixed, while the party of the state's governor has no significant effect.

Table 8–4 reports the regression results for the level of total nonagricultural employment. These simple versions allow for shifts in the level of employment due to prevailing unjust dismissal doctrines. The models control for fixed differences between states and for trends over time.[8] The level and change in aggregate GSP were included, but this version does not allow for systematic differences in the industrial mix across states.[9] The three alternative specifications differ only in their characterization of the legal environment.

In all three cases, the estimated coefficients for GSP suggest that, in the long run, employment increases with production but not in direct proportion. For model 1, the results indicate that a 10 percent increase in production would result in about a 6.6 percent increase in employment.[10] In the short run, firms will be unable to respond immediately to the increase in aggregate demand and the employment changes are likely to be lower. In fact, the estimated coefficient or

---

[7]See Dertouzos and Karoly 1992 for further details on the estimation method, including the estimates for the models predicting the three legal doctrines.

[8]Unless otherwise stated, all estimated models include state dichotomous variables. Most of the fifty coefficient estimates were significantly different from zero. Not allowing for fixed effects invariably increased the magnitude of the coefficient for GSP to about 1.0 and led to instability in the estimates of other effects, including those for the legal environment.

[9]Using this simple version facilitates interpretation of results. As documented below, introducing a variety of complexities does not alter the nature of the estimates.

[10]This result is consistent with several alternative explanations, including economies of scale, increased reliance on overtime or work intensity with output expansion, or relative inelasticity of labor supply.

TABLE 8-3. *Predicting the Status of the Legal Environment Using the Two-Way Legal Classification: 1980–87 Maximum Likelihood Logit Estimates (coefficient standard errors in parentheses)*

Variable	Contract	Tort
Intercept	−0.574	−4.060[a]
	(0.732)	(0.753)
Year = 1981	−0.799	0.572
	(0.627)	(0.573)
Year = 1982	−0.242	0.667
	(0.581)	(0.542)
Year = 1983	0.731	0.696
	(0.516)	(0.503)
Year = 1984	1.573[a]	1.054[b]
	(0.514)	(0.502)
Year = 1985	1.982[a]	1.734[a]
	(0.581)	(0.567)
Year = 1986	2.057[a]	2.082[a]
	(0.551)	(0.542)
Year = 1987	2.220[a]	2.647[a]
	(0.575)	(0.580)
Right-to-work state	−1.641[a]	−0.644[b]
	(0.350)	(0.321)
Percentage change in lawyers per capita	−37.529[a]	44.590[a]
	(14.154)	(12.958)
Percentage neighboring states recognizing doctrine [c,d]	0.053[a]	0.027[b]
	(0.013)	(0.013)
Percentage neighboring states recognizing doctrine, squared	−0.0005[a]	−0.0005[a]
	(0.0001)	(0.0001)
Percentage unionized[c]	0.020	0.080[a]
	(0.024)	(0.025)
Change in percentage unionized[c]	−0.125	−0.223[b]
	(0.113)	(0.110)
Change in percentage unemployed[c]	−0.567[b]	0.236
	(0.260)	(0.255)
Republican governor[c]	−0.097	0.146
	(0.290)	(0.263)
−2 log likelihood	397.42	431.75
Chi-square	150.83[a]	122.13[a]
N	400	400

[a]Different from zero at the 1 percent significance level.
[b]Different from zero at the 5 percent significance level.
[c]Variable lagged three years.
[d]Percentage of states recognizing the doctrine refers to contract doctrines for col. 1 and tort doctrines for col. 2.

TABLE 8-4. *Effects of Liability on Total Employment (coefficient standard errors in parentheses)*

Independent variable	Model 1	Model 2	Model 3
Log (GSP)	.663 [a]	.673 [a]	.644 [a]
	(.020)	(.020)	(.020)
Log (GSP growth)	−.385 [a]	−.390 [a]	−.383 [a]
	(.037)	(.037)	(.037)
Time trends			
1981	.004	.003	.004
	(.004)	(.004)	(.004)
1982	−.013 [a]	−.014 [a]	−.013 [a]
	(.004)	(.004)	(.004)
1983	−.001	−.004	−.001
	(.005)	(.004)	(.005)
1984	.018 [a]	.012 [b]	.017 [a]
	(.006)	(.006)	(.006)
1985	.018 [a]	.006	.016 [b]
	(.007)	(.007)	(.008)
1986	.018 [a]	.006	.016 [b]
	(.008)	(.008)	(.008)
1987	.032 [a]	.019 [b]	.031 [a]
	(.009)	(.009)	(.010)
Court doctrine[c]			
Tort	−.029 [a]	—	−.025 [b]
	(.011)		(.012)
Contract	−.018 [d]	—	−.014
	(.011)		(.011)
Broad PP or GF (tort)	—	−.021 [d]	−.011
		(.012)	(.012)
IC or GF (contract)	—	−.014	—
		(.010)	
Narrow PP	—	.002	—
		(.009)	
R-squared	.999717	.999715	.999717

PP=public policy, IC=implied contract, GF=covenant of good faith and fair dealing.
[a]Different from zero at the 1 percent significance level.
[b]Different from zero at the 5 percent significance level.
[c]Predictions based on logistic models of the status of the law using uncensored data.
[d]Different from zero at the 10 percent signficance level.

elasticity estimate of -.385 for the measure of GSP growth implies that the percentage increase will be only 2.8 during the same calendar year.[11]

Because of cyclical economic influences, the time-trend variables do not display a smooth pattern but suggest that employment has been rising relative to GSP

[11]The short-term elasticity, defined as the percentage change in employment divided by the percentage change in current-year GSP, is computed as .663 − .385, or .278.

since 1980. This could reflect demographic developments, changing labor force participation of population segments, or evolving production technologies. Empirical evidence presented below indicates that the aggregate trend may be due to changes in the industrial mix of the U.S. economy.

In all three specifications, well more than 99.9 percent of the sample variation in the measure of total employment can be explained by the included explanatory variables. Even after purging the variation explained by the fixed-state effects and the time trends, more than 80 percent of the remaining variance is explained by the GSP and court doctrine measures. The differences between the models' explanatory power are not significant, but the tort-contract distinction between jurisdictions (model 1) appears to be slightly more important than differences based on the good-faith, implied contract, and public policy causes of action.

In the first set of results, the coefficient estimates indicate that aggregate employment averages 2.9 percent lower in years following a state's recognition of tort damages for wrongful termination. This estimate is significantly different from zero at the 1 percent level.[12] For states recognizing contract damages, the effect is 1.8 percent, though imprecision in the estimate makes one less confident that this is statistically significant. These estimates can be viewed as incremental effects, so that states recognizing both tort and contract causes of action will have about 4.7 percent lower employment.[13]

In model 2, the doctrinal distinctions were based on whether or not the state jurisdiction recognized the good-faith tort or broad public policy, implied contract or good-faith contract, or narrow public policy exceptions to employment at will. This characterization did not distinguish between tort and contract causes of action. Although qualitative results were similar, the estimated effects were less significant, and the overall explanatory power of the model was lower. Although low significance of the individual estimates preclude making strong conclusions, states with the good faith tort or a broad public policy doctrine appear to have about 2.1 percent lower employment. Employment in years subsequent to the adoption of implied contract exceptions falls by an average of 1.4 percent. The narrow public policy distinction did not have a significant effect.

Model 3 combines the significant doctrinal distinctions of the other versions. The results are consistent with those of model 1. Although the states recognizing the covenant of good faith and fair dealing may have a slightly lower employment

---

[12]The use of predicted rather than actual values for the status of the tort law means that the reported standard errors are slightly biased in a downward direction. Our calculations indicate, however, that the bias is, at most, 30 percent. This adjustment would not alter the relevant coefficients significantly. In addition, efficiency gains from a GLS estimation technique that controls for heteroskedasticity and autocorrelation serves to reduce standard errors by even more than 30 percent. Considering both effects, the reported significance in table 8–2 understates the statistical precision of the estimates.

[13]Strictly speaking, the percentage difference is not exactly equal to the coefficient in a logarithmic model. As Kennedy (1981) demonstrates, for any coefficient estimate b, the expected percentage difference is given by $exp(b - .5 \, var(b))$, where $var(b)$ is the estimated variance of the coefficient. For changes smaller than .1, the coefficient estimate is a close enough approximation.

level, it appears that the availability of tort damages is the driving factor behind the change in business behavior.

We generalized these models in a variety of ways but found that the basic results were unchanged. A variable measuring the percentage of the work force that was unionized was insignificant as were levels of GSP lagged for more than a single period.[14] We allowed the speed of adjustment to vary as a function of whether the economy was experiencing an expansion or contraction, to change over time, or to be affected by the degree of unionization. The interaction terms were insignificant in each case. Finally, we found that wrongful termination doctrines did not significantly affect the speed of adjustment. For aggregate employment, interactions between predicted measures of doctrine probabilities and the growth in GSP were invariably insignificant.[15]

Even though our estimates of doctrinal effects on employment levels are stable with respect to alternative specifications, we remained concerned that our aggregate analysis could well obscure micro-level differences between firms and industries.[16] To examine this possibility, we extended our basic framework to control for differences in industrial composition over time and across states. In regressions reported in table 8–5, we included measures of the levels and growth in the industry-specific GSPs for four groups: services, retail trade, wholesale trade, and the financial, insurance, and real estate sectors. The manufacturing, construction, and transportation industries remain absorbed in the total GSP measure.

The results strongly indicate that there are significant differences between industrial sectors. For example, long-term employment in the service, wholesale, and retail trade industries is more responsive to changes in GSP than are other industries that are absorbed in the total GSP measure. This result can be attributed to the labor intensity and, perhaps, the absence of pronounced scale economies in these industries. In contrast, the financial, insurance, and real estate industries have the lowest labor intensity of all the industrial sectors. Thus, it is not surprising that expansions in this group's GSP had a smaller effect on aggregate employment. Adjustment speed appears to be different in the wholesale trade and financial sectors. For the wholesale trade industry, a large percentage of the increase in employment does not occur until the second year. In contrast, the finance and insurance sector appears to adjust more rapidly than other industry groups.

The estimated effects of the wrongful-termination doctrines are consistent with

[14]This suggests that most labor market adjustments occur within a year following an exogenous change in the optimal level of labor.

[15]As further tests of robustness, we tried to replicate the results using a variety of alternative models and econometric methodologies. For example, we obtained similar results using court doctrine predictions based on models of changes rather than the status in court doctrines. For these models, tort doctrines were found to be associated with a 5 percent fall in employment following their adoption. In addition, we estimated a "difference" model that evaluated the change in employment between 1980 and 1987 as a function of the changes in explanatory variables over that same period of time. Again, the estimates were similar.

[16]For example, Hamermesh (1989a) discusses some of the aggregation biases that could occur if fixed or marginally decreasing costs of adjustment exist.

TABLE 8-5. *Employment Effects of Employer Liability, Controlling for Industry Effects (coefficient standard errors in parentheses)*

	Model 1[a]
Log (GSP)	
Total GSP	.346 [b]
	(.057)
Services	.147 [b]
	(.048)
Retail trade	.091 [c]
	(.050)
Wholesale trade	.125 [b]
	(.029)
Finance and insurance	−.084 [b]
	(.023)
lOG (Growth in GSP)	
Total GSP growth	−.222 [b]
	(.055)
Services growth	−.025
	(.067)
Retail trade growth	−.005
	(.067)
Wholesale trade growth	−.107 [b]
	(.037)
Finance and insurance growth	.102 [b]
	(.024)
Time trends	
1982	−.011 [c]
	(.006)
1983	−.009
	(.008)
1984	.011
	(.009)
1985	.006
	(.010)
1986	−.001
	(.012)
Court doctrine	
Tort	−.031 [b]
	(.011)
Contract	−.018 [c]
	(.010)
Broad PP and GF (Tort)	−.009
	(.011)
R-squared	.99984

PP = public policy, GF = covenant of good faith and fair dealing.
[a]Court doctrine predictions based on logistic models of the status in the law using uncensored data.
[b]Different from zero at the 1% significance level.
[c]Different from zero at the 10% significance level.

the results obtained from the specification that did not control for differences in the industrial mix. Recognition of the tort cause of action for unjust dismissal appears to be associated with a 3 to 4 percent drop in employment compared with jurisdictions in which businesses retain unrestricted rights to fire workers at will. As before, the recognition of an implied contract and the covenant of good faith and fair dealing with punitive damages has a smaller, barely discernible effect on decision making by firms.

Conclusions

Our econometric analysis of state-level employment outcomes provides strong evidence that wrongful-termination doctrines have had a significant effect on business decision making. Following the adoption of the most liberal tort versions of the covenant of good faith and fair dealing and the broad public policy exceptions to employment at will, we observe that employment levels drop significantly.

The emergence of wrongful-termination doctrines appears to be quite costly. But whether or not these changes are desirable depends on the existence of compensating benefits to employees, firms, or society at large. Clearly, some workers will benefit from the enhanced job security. In addition, the legal system might provide some compensation (and future deterrence) in isolated cases of egregious employer behavior. Limitations on manager discretion in firing employees could be more generally efficient, however, benefiting firms as well. For example, the threat of litigation may provide a convenient rationalization for increased micro-management of mid-level executives. From a corporate perspective, such oversight may be optimal even in the absence of potential liability; however, the legal considerations diffuse possible resentment and dissension on the part of middle managers whose human resource decisions are more closely monitored.

Firms may already have incentives to adopt job security provisions and mechanisms to protect employees against mistreatment.[17] If so, what role can the legal system play in enforcing justice in the workplace? One might argue that it provides a "backup" in cases when irrationality prevails or individual managers make decisions that are not aligned with corporate interests. The legal system thereby reduces uncertainty about the enforceability of the implicit agreement and enables management and labor to reap the mutual benefits of a long-term employment relationship.

Of course, there are circumstances in which long-term incentives are not aligned. Firms may not bear the full social cost of their decision to terminate an employee. For example, if workers develop knowledge and skills that are not transferable to other firms, the employer may not bear the loss of this human capital investment when the decision to terminate is made.[18] Finally, if a worker

---

[17]See Dertouzos and Quinn 1985.

[18]Hamermesh (1987) develops this point theoretically and provides some evidence that the sunk costs of firm-specific human capital can be worth thousands of dollars, thereby driving a large wedge between the private and social costs of dismissal.

is unemployed for any length of time, subsidies such as unemployment insurance are only partially funded by the previous employer. Thus, potential liabilities raise the private cost of termination and, theoretically, can make them more consistent with the social costs, thereby inducing more efficient decision making.[19]

This discussion makes it clear that any judgment about the efficacy of unjust dismissal restrictions cannot be made without additional case study analysis of individual firms and microeconomic data describing the internal decision-making process of corporate management. With aggregate information, it is not possible to identify the source of the implied cost increases or to judge whether or not they are desirable. Even if we were able to document the particular behavioral responses, any evaluation of these changes would depend crucially on whether or not firms already have sufficient incentives to provide "optimal" amounts of job security. If they do not, one must then determine whether the resulting changes are too big, too small, or the right kind.

---

[19]Ehrenberg and Jakubson (1988) cite this as a potential justification for recent statutory provisions that are meant to discourage large-scale layoffs.

9
Pressures and Prospects for Employment Security in the United States

Paul Osterman

In a perhaps desperate effort to regain the initiative against the Japanese, General Motors recently established an independent unit—the Saturn Corporation—and charged the union and management with developing a new automobile from scratch. The degree of joint decision making and cooperation between the two parties was unprecedented as they worked together on design, factory layout, work practices, choice of outside suppliers, and the myriad of other elements required to create a new car.

A new industrial relations system was created as the multiple job classifications and work rules of the old system were eliminated. At the core of this system is a commitment to employment security. The language of the labor contract reads: "Saturn recognizes that people are the most valuable asset of the organization. . . . Accordingly, those Saturn members who are eligible for job security, as defined below, shall not be laid off except in situations which . . . are due to unforseen or catastrophic events or severe economic conditions." The eligible workers are the top 80 percent in terms of seniority. The remaining 20 percent constitute a buffer for the firm.

Saturn is a source of great hope for both sides at General Motors. Does this move toward flexible internal labor markets and employment security represent the beginning of a transformation of employment relations in this country? Or does the sad story of Fiero foretell a different outcome?

At the General Motors factory in Pontiac, Michigan (which produced the new Fiero sports car), an extensive team production system was established, and the union was fully involved in production planning and given extensive data on the plant's financial performance (data that is usually closely guarded). This plant was

This paper is a revised version of an earlier paper prepared jointly with Thomas A. Kochan (Osterman and Kochan 1990).

subject to GM's national agreement, which contained a commitment that no plant would be closed for the duration of the contract.

While the Fiero plant opened with much the same hope as Saturn's did, the story of Fiero ended somewhat differently. Instead of closing the plant, which the contract forbade, GM "idled" the plant "temporarily" and laid off all the employees. This semantic distinction was upheld by an arbitrator. These events provide plenty of reason to be cautious about the prospects for innovation in employment security in the United States.

These two examples illustrate the dilemmas confronting the United States. There are substantial and important pressures to increase the level of employment security in the American labor market, yet it is very difficult for any individual firm to maintain such a policy in the face of adverse demand shocks. A few firms have done so but the list is short.

The next section of this paper describes pressures for enhanced employment security and those working in the opposite direction. I then provide some case study evidence and conclude that, without substantial public policy assistance, the prospects for employment security in the United States are mixed at best. The final section discusses the public policy context.

Before turning to these themes, it is important to clear up one possible misunderstanding. Labor force surveys indicate that a substantial minority of American workers already seem to enjoy considerable employment continuity. For example, Hall (1982) estimates that after the age of thirty-five, 40 percent of the labor force is in jobs that will last for twenty years or more. On the face of it, this is not all that different from the Japanese pattern of lifetime employment for this important minority of the labor force.

One qualification is that this pattern varies considerably by gender (as it does in Japan) and occupation. Second, many observers (albeit with less than adequate evidence) believe that average job tenure is falling as the labor market becomes more volatile. These are not the most serious problems with the analogy, however.

There are two crucial concerns. First, in the United States, long-term employment is always at risk. Firms that provided secure jobs in the past can, and often do, alter course. As a result, even if employees manage to retire without having lost their jobs (and hence have become part of Hall's 40 percent), they are nonetheless insecure throughout their careers (the ax may fall anytime), and this insecurity engenders the kinds of behaviors (described below) that employment continuity is intended to overcome.

Second, the long employment tenures Hall and others identified are the result of behaviors that an explicit policy of employment continuity is designed to avoid. For example, a component of the blue-collar labor force at a given company probably do have reasonably secure jobs, but they gained this security by establishing work rules, seniority restrictions, and the like that are increasingly dysfunctional. Hence, the de facto "employment security" that the data reveal does not lead to the benefits that such an outcome is intended to provide since, ironically, the security is the result of quite different behavior. Other nations achieve internal flexibility by having an explicit policy of employment protection "up front" and thus avoid forcing the labor force to achieve protection through bargaining and shop-floor control.

Framework for Thinking about Employment Security

Variability in a firm's environment is a fact of life. What is at stake in a discussion of employment security is how firms respond to, or seek to absorb, that variability. One strategy is the "hire and fire" option. While the "fire" component often receives the greatest notice, the "hire" action implies that companies rely on the external labor market (as opposed to extensive internal training or job ladders) to provide new skills. An alternative strategy is to let the wage structure absorb environmental uncertainty by, for example, sufficiently reducing the wages of workers with those skills and in occupations whose demand has fallen so that they can remain employed under the new conditions. This, of course, is the traditional economics view of the function of wages and lies behind recent calls for increased wage flexibility and profit sharing.[1] Alternatively (or in a complementary way), a firm may seek to train its labor force to the point that its skills are broad enough that the firm can internally redeploy labor in response to changing conditions. This strategy is useful in dealing with shifts in skill requirements and technologies but less adequate for coping with changing levels of demand and hence may be combined with a "core-periphery model." Finally, a firm may attempt to gain partial control over its environment by improving its product development, production, and marketing efforts and in turn linking them more closely to its human resource policies.

What the foregoing suggests is that employment security is best viewed as an element of an organization's set of human resource policies. In turn, human resource policies are part of an even broader set of business and production strategies and policies. For a number of reasons, these human resource, or internal labor market, policies are under reconsideration and there are important pressures in the direction of heightened employment security.

American firms are seeking to shift their internal labor market systems away from the traditional system of narrow job definitions and rigid work rules and toward much more flexible arrangements. Indeed, the United States is an outlier with respect to both Europe and Japan in terms of the rigidity of its shop-floor systems.

The major pressure comes from efforts to reconstitute internal labor markets. The core[2] firms in the American labor market have traditionally organized work

---

[1] See, for example, Weitzman 1985.

[2] This term is used loosely to exclude what might be termed secondary labor patterns. That is, we are not interested here in understanding the low-wage/high-turnover sector in which many youth, immigrants, minorities, and women find themselves. This sector of the labor market is, of course, of central importance to issues of poverty and low income.

according to the logic of one of two dominant models that I will call the industrial model and the salaried model. Our image of what work is like and how it must be changed are reflections of the strengths and weaknesses of these two paradigms.

The industrial model represents the manner of organizing blue-collar work that became the norm as a result of the unionization drives of the Great Depression and that was solidified in the era of postwar prosperity.[3] In this model, work is organized into a series of tightly defined jobs with clear work rules and responsibilities attached to each classification. Wages are attached to jobs and hence an individual's wage is determined by his or her classification. Management's freedom to move individuals from one job to another varies from situation to situation, but typically both promotions and lateral shifts are limited by seniority provisions and by requirements that workers agree to the shift. Finally, there is no formal job security; management is free to vary the size of the labor force as it wishes. When layoffs occur, however, they are generally organized according to reverse seniority.

Although the structure of this model emerged from the spread of unionism, it should not be construed as limited to such situations. Because of fear of unions, government pressures for uniformity,[4] the growth of large firms using mass-production technologies, and imitation, the model spread throughout the economy.[5] Hence, a survey of nonunion firms found that seniority-based promotion and layoff systems were extremely common even in the absence of formal contracts (Abraham and Medoff 1984).

This model has a strong internal logic. Because wages are attached to jobs, it is necessary that the jobs be carefully defined so that there is common understanding concerning who is doing what work and hence is entitled to what wage. Similarly, while the system provides no overall job security (management can vary the size of the work force at will), individual security is based on a bumping system grounded in seniority, and for that system to be effective, careful job classifications are necessary.

The system has the overwhelming value of creating security for workers in the face of an environment where the long-term trend in demand is growing but cyclical fluctuations can be expected to produce significant dislocation. Thus, this system established individual property rights to highly valuable jobs and the value of the jobs increased with one's seniority. There are, of course, costs to this model, notably the difficulty of altering work organization in the face of changing technology or other pressures. This difficulty arises because of the logic of the system itself and because that logic takes on a moral legitimacy over time that adds to its weight. For a long time, however, these difficulties have seemed minor compared to the logic and stability of the industrial model. One reason for this was that an

---

[3]For a historical account of the emergence of this model, see Jacoby 1985a. The classic description of this way of structuring internal labor markets is found in Doeringer and Piore 1971.

[4]For example, unemployment insurance is structured to encourage layoffs and to discourage part-time employment.

[5]For an account of the spread that links it to more general institutions of macroeconomic "regulation," see Piore and Sabel 1984.

expanding product market made stability and predictability the key strategic human resource management concerns. Flexibility in deployment and sometimes even cost were of second order concern to management in this market environment. We will see shortly that the priorities attached to these human resource objectives are changing in response to product market and technological changes that increase the importance of flexibility in the deployment of human resources.

Most labor economics and industrial relations research has emphasized blue-collar work and consequently it is more difficult to describe the salaried internal labor market model. Understanding the model is important, however, for three reasons: it describes the employment pattern of large numbers of workers; it extends beyond salaried work to a number of innovative blue-collar employment settings; and some of its characteristics represent the direction in which management is trying to push work in general.

The salaried model combines a more flexible and personalistic set of administrative procedures with greater commitment to employment security. Although individuals have job descriptions, much as industrial employees have work rules, these descriptions are not intended to have legal or customary force. They are subject to revision by superiors, and employees are prepared to take on new activities as demanded. By the same token, the clearly defined job ladders and promotion sequences that characterize industrial settings are absent.

Flexible career lines and job descriptions are consistent with another aspect of this employment system, the greater role of individual considerations in wage setting. There is considerably greater scope for merit considerations in pay setting, and the wages of two individuals in the same job can vary considerably. Put differently, the pay system of industrial settings, in which the dominant consideration is job assignment, is far less prevalent in the salaried model.

If rigid job classifications and reliance on nonpersonalistic procedures are the key to job security and worker acquiescence in the industrial system, what plays a comparable role in the salaried model? What closes the salaried model is employment security. In the classic salaried model, individuals, once they pass a probationary period, can expect long-term employment with the firm. Unlike the industrial model, in which it is explicitly understood that the firm will adjust the size of the labor force in response to product market conditions or technological change, the implicit promise in the salaried system is that layoffs simply will not occur or the firm will be strenuous in its effort to avoid them.

This latter point, that absolute promises are not necessary, is important because without it the scope of the salaried model would be limited. What is crucial is that employees are sufficiently convinced of the sincerity of the firm's commitment to employment stabilization that they are willing to provide the degree of flexibility that is the firm's reward in the system. I will refer to the "security pledge," but this is merely a shorthand for sufficient employer commitment to employment stabilization to obtain employee consent. Exactly what that level of security is will vary from situation to situation depending on the nature of the industry, the firm's history, and other variables.

What is being "bought," then, is commitment, and the exact price will vary from situation to situation. The nature of the bargain is clear, however, as is the distinction between the salaried and the industrial model.

The salaried model clearly characterizes much white-collar work. The career patterns of most managers and many professionals who work in bureaucracies are accurately captured by the model. The salaried model is not simply another way of describing white-collar work, however. There have always been a few American firms that have stood outside the mainstream industrial model for their blue-collar workers. For example, in the 1920s the exception was termed welfare capitalism and represented an effort to develop an alternative to unions, and in the postwar period a few firms such as IBM applied the model in a blue-collar setting.

What changed in the 1970s and 1980s is that models that were isolated curiosities moved into the mainstream of American thinking. Faced with examples of other nations that have, through varying routes, achieved what looks like the salaried model, American companies—from General Motors to Corning Glass—began to rethink their employment practices. The leading innovative edge in American human resource management came to be represented by the many firms that attempted to achieve greater internal flexibility by, among other changes, enhancing employment security. These changes were initiated in the growing nonunion sector (which, in a reversal of the early postwar pattern, became the source of most innovation in employment systems) and subsequently have spread into portions of the union sector. The question, of course, is whether these transformations are sustainable. I will address this question below.

A second source of pressure, albeit more narrow, to move to heightened employment security comes from the interaction of new technologies and training systems. New technologies alter and increase the skill level required of blue-collar workers by placing a premium on abstract reasoning and computer-based skills. The same technologies also require workers to undertake broader tasks than in the past (i.e., they require more flexible internal deployment of labor than is often possible under existing work rules) (for a review of the literature on this topic, see Osterman 1989). All of these changes exert pressure to have a more deeply trained labor force, yet American firms tend to undertrain their employees.

It is well known from standard human capital models that high turnover will inhibit firms from providing training. The high turnover—or risk of high turn-over—associated with the absence of employment security does indeed appear to have this consequence. By all accounts, U.S. firms tend to undertrain the labor force, particularly blue-collar workers. This is true despite the considerable publicity given to "corporate classrooms" and private sector training.

The consequence of the limited training provided by firms is demonstrated dramatically by comparisons of productivity of comparable technologies in different settings. Studies of Germany and Japan show that for the same technical setup, productivity is much higher outside the United States and that the chief difference appears to be the human resource systems, including training (Jaikumar 1986; Krafcik 1988).

Indeed, despite the widespread belief that private sector training is so extensive that it rivals the formal education system, evidence suggests that employers provide too little training to blue-collar workers. According to a recent Conference Board study, only 18 percent of manufacturing firms provide nonexempt workers with training programs, whereas 33 percent provided such programs for managerial employees and 28 percent offer programs to sales and marketing workers (Osterman 1985:53).

Another survey, by the Bureau of National Affairs, provided similar but more startling results. Sixty percent of firms surveyed provided courses for managers, and 50 percent provided courses for professional and technical workers, but only 18 percent provided courses for nonexempt employees (BNA 1985b:37). Additional evidence on this point comes from a content analysis of training courses offered to firms by outside vendors. Only 14 percent of the more than fifteen hundred courses surveyed served other than clerical or managerial employees (Sonnenfeld 1985:302).

According to both surveys, small firms provided much less training than large ones. This is a common observation and is troubling because there is good evidence that small firms are a source of disportionate job creation and technical innovation. Yet, because these firms lack extensive internal promotion systems and career paths, they are unable to train and often to retain the skilled labor they need. In short, if firms wish to increase the amount of training they provide—and they are under pressure to do so—then greater levels of employment continuity are part of the solution.

A final source of pressure for employment security comes from changing demographics. The American work force is going to grow slowly (from a rate of 2.9 percent a year in the 1970s to 1 percent a year in the 1990s); the average age of the work force will increase as the number of sixteen- to twenty-four-year-old workers falls by 2 million by the year 2000. These developments have two consequences. First, the number of flexible and mobile young workers will fall. Second, as the number of middle-aged employees rises the typical concerns of this group—stability and security—will place pressure on firms (and society) to meet their expectations. In some sense then, the "tastes" of the labor force with respect to the trade-off between employment security and mobility will shift toward security.

Countervailing Pressures

The foregoing described the pressures that are pushing firms to increase employment security. There are, however, pressures being exerted in the opposite direction.

A number of writers have pointed to what they characterize as the dissolution of internal labor markets (e.g., Noyelle 1987). By this they mean the increasing tendency of firms to subcontract work to external organizations, the increased use of temporary and contingent employees, and the growing importance of training in external general purpose institutions such as schools.

While it is true that the use of contingent employment has increased, it is not clear how to interpret this development. In many settings employers use contingent workers to provide a buffer to a core labor force that is granted increased employment security. In these instances, the rise of contingent employment has mixed, not wholly negative, implications for employment security.

The evidence on other aspects of this issue is also mixed. Many analysts believe that the average size of firms is decreasing for a variety of reasons. Several streams of research suggest that increased size is associated with formal internal labor markets (see Osterman 1990) so that, by inference, as firm size falls one would expect that the ties that bind workers to firms would diminish. While the logic is clear, it is less clear how important the point is. Although average firm or establishment size has decreased, the magnitudes involved do not appear very large (Sengenberger and Loveman 1987). What we lack is an understanding, either empirical or theoretical, of how large a decrease in size is necessary before internal labor market characteristics start to shift.

Perhaps the most important countervailing pressure against increased employment security is the widespread perception that the environment is simply too unstable, and employment continuity too costly, to permit firms to establish such policies. Substantial layoffs in previously protected sectors (e.g., white-collar work in autos or telecommunications) are evidence here. Of course, these layoffs are often accompanied by generous severance packages, much more generous than is typically offered to blue-collar workers, but nonetheless the environment has become more insecure for a class of previously protected employees.

More fundamental is evidence that the leading-edge nonunion employers in the United States perceive themselves to be under increasing pressure. These are the firms that since the mid–1970s have been the source of most of the innovation in human resource policies. With their emphasis on enhanced communication with employees, employee involvement in the production decisions, performance-based pay, and employment continuity, these firms have in many respects been the U.S. answer to the Japanese challenge. Indeed, so successful have these companies been that many unionized companies find themselves imitating nonunion internal labor market and personnel policies. One by one, these firms (e.g., Polaroid, Eastman-Kodak, Hewlett-Packard, Advanced Micro-Devices) have turned away from employment security. Even more ominously, firms with an almost ideological commitment to employment security, such as IBM, Delta Airlines, and Digital Equipment Corporation, find themselves under intense pressure to reconsider their policies. These developments raise serious questions about the long-term viability of employment security.

Two Case Studies

To pursue these themes further and to provide greater texture, I turn now to two cases. First, I look at a large leading edge nonunion firm. Second, I examine events in the traditional unionized automobile industry.

Employment Security at Digital Equipment Corporation (DEC)

DEC is a nonunion high-technology firm with a long-term commitment, established by its founder, to employment security.[6] Virtually all staff described this as one of the key "values" of the company. Several years ago, however, the policy came under severe pressure from two sources. First, DEC found itself drifting toward becoming a high-cost producer as technical change reduced unit labor requirements while staffing remained high. Second, sharp downturns in the product market resulted in several disastrous quarters. In response, the firm initiated a "transition" process. The goals of this effort were somewhat confused. In part, it was aimed at rebalancing the labor force by altering occupational distribution, and in part it was intended simply to reduce employment levels. It was also part of a larger effort to shift DEC's manufacturing strategy to reduce inventories and upgrade the priority given to controlling costs as opposed to achieving large production volumes on short notice. Regardless, the overriding purpose was to reshape the firm's human resource profile without resorting to layoffs.

Under the transition process, individuals were "selected" if there was surplus staff in their location. In situations in which an entire line was shut down, all employees were selected. In other cases, specific people were selected by inverse performance ratings. Once selected, a person was exposed to various counseling and orientation sessions, given a chance (with company assistance) to find a new job in the firm, and provided with support for an outside job search. Retraining was offered to persons who could locate a job elsewhere in the firm. White-collar labor (so-called indirect labor) could turn down only one job offer elsewhere in the firm regardless of location, but blue-collar workers were not required to relocate. If, after a given period of time, a person could not find a job elsewhere in the firm or a job she or he wanted outside the company, he or she was placed in a pool and was expected to accept temporary work, part-time assignments, community service, and the like while continuing to search. In several locations, the company also offered incentive resignation plans when the pools threatened to become too large.

The reason that this case is useful is that it provides lessons concerning the possibilities and limits of employment security policies at the firm level. The following seem to be the most important conclusions:

1. *The policy entails very substantial resources and other organizational costs. Only a firm that is highly committed to such a policy is likely to undertake it.* I have been unable to quantify the costs of the program, but they are clearly high. They include corporate staff who oversaw the program and collected data on it (at least four full-time staff for a two-year period); staff in each plant (at least one and often more) who managed the program locally; substantial attention required of

---

[6]For a more detailed case study of DEC's employment security problems, see Osterman et al. 1988.

line managers in selecting, counseling, and seeking to place individuals involved in the program; training costs; incentive retirement expenditures; and—undoubtedly very large—the continued salaries of individuals involved in the program who remained on the payroll as they looked for other work either inside the firm or outside the firm. A year and a half into the program several hundred people were still in "hold" status, collecting salaries but generally not contributing to the firm.

Some of the costs of the program were certainly offset by the gains. At the concrete level, DEC saved on unemployment insurance taxes and recruitment costs. At the more abstract level, DEC was clearly organized along the lines of the salaried model and, as would be expected, executives rationalized the policy by referring to the positive impact on the morale of employees who were not directly involved. The problem, however, is that these benefits are very abstract. Either they are costs that are saved, and hence influence the bottom line only indirectly or over the long run, or they are benefits that, when they do appear, are difficult to attribute to the policy. By contrast, the costs are very real, visible in the short run, and quite attributable.

The conclusion is that it is, and will be, difficult to convince a cost-conscious firm to enter into such a policy and commitment. In this case, DEC had a long-standing commitment based on the philosophy of the founder. The basic thrust was not at issue, only how to implement it.

2. *Even with a high level of commitment, the firm cannot provide employment security.* Despite the large expenditure of resources and extremely powerful company culture aimed at maintaining the security pledge, in the end the firm was forced to rely on devices that shifted insecurity into the external labor market. Although no layoffs were implemented at the time of the study, and in this sense the formal definition of security was maintained, the firm did withdraw employment from seventeen hundred temporary and contract employees (they represented 30 percent of the total reduction). The firm also provided incentive retirements to more than a thousand workers. More recently, the company has in fact laid off some employees.

The elimination of temporary and contract employment was clearly a layoff in the economic sense of the term even though the firm maintained that these workers were not regular employees. The incentive retirement case is more difficult since the individuals voluntarily participated. Nonetheless, there was no doubt a concern that failure to participate would lead to adverse consequences (either layoffs or transfers to unacceptable locations), and some fraction of these separations must be seen as layoffs with a one-time buyout of the previous employment security commitment. In any case, despite the commitment of resources (and the underlying health of the product market), the firm was unable to maintain employment levels internally and had to shed labor. The subsequent fate of those who left is no longer of concern to the firm and, if anything, becomes a matter of public policy. Firms on their own cannot stabilize employment.

3. *Those regular employees who did leave the company as a result of the transition process were better equipped to do so than equivalent workers who experience tradi-*

tional layoffs. These people were provided counseling, job search assistance, had some control over the timing of their exits, and were often given a financial cushion.

Recent Union-Management Initiatives: The Case of the Auto Industry

With relatively few exceptions, the unionized sector has traditionally followed the hire-and-fire approach to employment security for blue-collar occupations.[7] The system of multiple and highly detailed job classifications, each with its own wage rate, and the seniority rules governing the deployment of individuals across these jobs serve as a major component of the "job control unionism" model described earlier. As is now well known, this model has been under severe attack in recent years as employers and unions search for ways to respond to market and technological changes that demand greater flexibility in the use and deployment of labor while at the same time reducing costs in a environment of heightened international and domestic competition (Kochan, Katz, and McKersie 1986). The U.S. auto industry has been at the center of this transformation process both because it has been particularly hard hit by changes in its competitive environment and because its internal labor market system so fully embodies the features of the traditional system.

The United Auto Workers and the major auto firms pioneered in introducing a variety of job security provisions into their contracts in the 1950s and the 1960s designed to cope with cyclical unemployment. The most important of these provisions is the Supplementary Unemployment Benefits (SUB) program. Companies were required to contribute a given amount of money for each hour worked into a fund that workers could draw on to supplement their government unemployment insurance benefits during times of layoff. Over the years, SUB benefits were expanded to provide up to 95 percent of take-home pay. SUB provisions were accompanied by a variety of severance pay plans, early retirement benefits, and related income security protections. Since the auto industry experienced a steady rate of expansion over these years, most of the attention was focused on protection against cyclical rather than structural changes in the industry or the economy. There was, however, an informal but unwritten agreement that new technology would be phased into operations gradually so as to avoid layoffs.

Employment and product demand for U.S. auto producers peaked in 1978. Since then, employment has been falling as a result of increased imports, changes in technology, and other reasons. The first major change in the contractual relationships governing employment security came in the 1982 negotiations with the introduction of the concept of a guaranteed income stream (GIS).

The GIS guaranteed jobs to workers affected by a plant closing who had fifteen or more years' seniority, provided the workers were willing to accept a transfer to another location. Those who were covered but chose not to transfer were eligible

[7]This section was prepared by Thomas A. Kochan.

for a severance payment of 50 percent of their annual earnings for up to fifteen years or until their normal retirement date. In 1982, Ford and GM also agreed to establish joint human resource centers with the UAW, funded originally at five cents per work hour (subsequently raised to ten cents) to provide training, job counseling, and related labor market services to laid-off auto workers (Katz 1985).

As the UAW company centers evolved, their scope of training activities greatly expanded to such areas as safety and health training, training for local union leaders, and a variety of other activities designed to supplement but not subsidize or replace the "normal" training activities of the companies. For example, in addition to jointly sponsored training efforts, GM estimates that in 1986 it spent approximately $60 million on work force training as part of a $300 million technological retrofitting and upgrading of one plant.

In 1984, negotiations between the UAW and Ford and GM added a jobs bank to their employment security package. The jobs bank provided that no worker with more than one year's seniority would be laid off because of technological change, outsourcing, or corporate restructuring. The trade-off for this employment commitment was that the companies retained a free hand in making outsourcing and technological change decisions. Employees were not guaranteed jobs in the event of market fluctuations or changes in demand for their products. Employees displaced by the covered events were provided training and transfer options where jobs were available and were placed on a seniority list for recall as new openings became available. They were not required to terminate employment with the company, however, if no jobs were available.

In 1987, Ford, GM, and the UAW essentially closed the circle by linking current and future employment security to a commitment from the union to accept flexibility in work organization. In essence, the parties put in place a plant-level decision-making process to complete their conversion from the industrial to the salaried model. The 1987 agreements specify "guaranteed employment levels" for each plant based on the current employment levels. Employees may still be laid off temporarily in response to reductions in product demand; however, the companies may not lay off current employees or permanently reduce employment levels because of technological change, outsourcing, or other managerial decisions. Instead, a gradual reduction in the guaranteed employment levels for each plant occurs with the "two-for-one" rule. That is, the guaranteed employment level is reduced by one for every two workers who retire. This attrition rate can be accelerated to a "one-for-one" ratio if plant management and the local union negotiate a special early retirement or other voluntary severance package.

To make these new agreements work, the company and the union have established joint plant-level committees. These groups examine the full range of financial and other managerial information needed to assess the economic performance and competitive prospects for the plant and recommend changes in technology, work practices (including expanded use of team forms of work organization), and related human resource policies.

The comprehensive nature of these employment guarantees and adjustment provisions clearly place strong pressures on the company and the union to adjust their other internal labor market practices in ways that depart from the job control model. It is not surprising, therefore, that both Ford and GM are making efforts to reduce job classifications, adopt team forms of work organization, and reduce the number and levels of supervisors in their organizations. Recently, Chrysler has begun a major effort to do the same. What is less clear, however, is how far the parties have gone in modifying these internal labor market practices in existing facilities. The evidence to date suggests that the biggest changes in existing facilities occurred when the plant was threatened with permanent closing or loss of a significant portion of its work. The more common pattern in existing facilities seems to be gradual, piecemeal movement toward a more flexible internal labor market system as new technology or other major changes in the plant are introduced (Katz, Kochan, and Keefe 1987). The 1987 GM and Ford agreements now put pressure on the parties to adopt this new model across all existing plants.

If these auto industry examples are representative of future developments, we are likely to see more complete adoption of the salaried model in settings where labor and management jointly plan or negotiate the terms of employment for completely new facilities and continued efforts to move gradually away from the job control model in existing union facilities as new technology is introduced. In either case, we are likely to see expanded attention to the employment security and/or adjustment provisions needed to make these changes acceptable to workers and their union leaders.

While these efforts go quite far in protecting workers in specific facilities against managerially controlled shocks to their security, they do not provide an iron-clad employment guarantee. Employees will continue to be at risk to product market changes or industrywide developments. In the case of the auto industry, the biggest future risk to the employment security of U.S. workers is likely to come from the effects of overcapacity. Current estimates from the MIT International Motor Vehicle Program are that in 1990 the capacity of U.S. auto plants exceeded product demand by 4.2 million vehicles (more than 30 percent of the total U.S. market for autos).

What this suggests is that company or plant-specific job banks and adjustment programs may be insufficient. Indeed, the recent layoffs in the auto industry, cited earlier, suggest that while contractual innovations will help ease the pain of job loss for many workers, such loss is nonetheless unavoidable.

Evolution of Policy

As already noted, there is good reason to believe that in both the nonunion and union sectors attempts by private firms to reform internal labor markets and introduce higher levels of employment security are under pressure and may have run out of steam. This raises the question of what role if any there is for public policy.

Public policy can help enlarge the scope of employment security in one of three broad ways:

1. Legislation may restrict firms' options with respect to layoffs.

2. A training system may enhance the skills and flexibility of incumbent employees, hence reducing the likelihood that they will be laid off. In addition, the training combined with the job placement system may speed reemployment of workers who do lose their jobs.

3. Public policy may support and diffuse internal labor market systems and human resource policies that are conducive to employment security.

The legislative restriction approach is thought to characterize some European countries much better than the United States. Perhaps surprisingly, there has, however, been some movement in this direction in America. In the last year of the Reagan administration, a weak law on plant closing was passed,[8] and, while not particularly effective, few would have predicted passage of any such legislation. In addition, the long-standing American doctrine of employment at will (under which workers can be fired for any reason other than explicitly forbidden ones such as race and sex or union organizing) is under challenge, and state courts throughout the nation have begun to impose restrictions on employers' abilities to fire individual workers. These restrictions are usually based on one of three exceptions: public policy exceptions (the person was acting in the public interest, for example by reporting environmentally unsound practices), implied contracts (e.g., statements made in personnel handbooks), or—least commonly—general principles of good faith and fair dealing.

These cases are important and in some states may well lead to legislation as states attempt to place limits on the size of awards (Montana has already passed a law in response to court action). (For a description of recent developments, see Krueger 1991).

It is not clear, however, that these developments should be considered as enhanced employment security as I have been using the term. These court decisions have applied to the firing of individuals, not to larger-scale layoffs due to product market conditions, technological change, business policy, or the like. It is conceivable that restrictions on employment at will represent the opening wedge of more general restrictions, but that is very far from certain and indeed seems unlikely.

The second policy approach is to have a strong employment and training system; Sweden stands as the model. The United States is clearly not following this path.

Most of the public job training system is income targeted and linked to the welfare system. It provides remedial education and very limited job training. The success of these programs is limited (Osterman 1988a). There are some funds provided for training dislocated workers—the classic clients of the Swedish system—but the effort is minimal. In 1988, federal expenditures totaled $246 million for Title III dislocated workers programs (General Accounting Office 1990).

---

[8] The law is weak in that there are a number of exemptions. For example, an employer is exempt if he or she believes that the firm's competitive position would be endangered by announcing a forthcoming layoff or if it is engaged in capitalization.

In addition, the U.S. Employment Service (the U.S. equivalent of the Swedish AMS) is largely ineffective. The Employment Service (ES) has long been regarded as unable to fill any but menial jobs. It is hard to exaggerate the consistency with which employers complain that the service fails to screen workers and that whenever it lists a vacancy it sends them large numbers of unqualified applicants. For their part, job applicants claim that good jobs are rarely listed with the service and that when they are listed they are not filled with service referrals. Statistical evaluations confirm these impressions (Johnson, Dickinson, and West 1985).

The ES suffers from the same fundamental ill that plagues the training system: the system was not conceived and designed to provide genuine service to the private economy. Instead, it has been largely tied to the transfer system. For many years it has been a mechanism to enforce the job search requirement for the receipt of unemployment insurance benefits: recipients had to satisfy officers of the ES that they were looking for work, and in practice that meant ritualistically calling the ES for referrals. This gave the system its basic character. In recent years, the service has also been used to enforce work requirements for the receipt of welfare payments.

A third approach is to undertake efforts with two objectives: first, to provide some support to firms such as DEC that wish to provide employment security so that they are not as isolated as they are now, and, second, to deploy public policy to diffuse internal labor market models that place greater emphasis on employment continuity. One element of supporting firms is clearly to strengthen the employment service and job training system. Beyond this, however, additional steps are at least conceivable. Much of the regulatory framework governing the labor market is premised on full-time "regular" employment being the norm. The expansion of various contingent arrangements poses a challenge to this framework and may undermine some of the protections (particularly in the area of benefits such as health care or training). It seems appropriate to begin to rethink whether to reduce incentives for contingent employment and/or how to provide contingent employees with protections comparable to those of other workers.

The first step in constructing an informed policy in this area would be to develop a database that can track the labor market experiences of contingent workers over an extended period of time. Beyond this, there is a disturbing gap in our understanding of how public policy interacts with private decision making and what levers are available to policy makers. Instead of a useful model or theory of how public policy can encourage the diffusion of private practices, we have only a series of historical lessons. For example, it is clear that the National Labor Relations Act and the War Labor Board helped diffuse the postwar industrial relations system model. This success obviously owed a great deal, however, to intense grass-roots pressure. The legislation drew upon existing practices (but, it is important to note, not on all existing practices) and provided a framework within which those pressures could be played out.

A somewhat different case, equal employment opportunity laws, points to the possibility of a successful regulatory and, at least potentially, punitive framework. Again, these policies were clearly enacted in a climate made somewhat fertile by the civil rights movement. We also have examples of failures, for example, the weak private response to the federal government's efforts to promote work humanization and quality of work life initiatives during of the 1970s and efforts to encourage private systems of unemployment insurance in the 1920s.

A reasonable conclusion would seem to be that local experiments and a degree of grass-roots support are necessary for effective diffusion. At the same time, public policy is not passive in that it can select or legitimate specific models and affect the costs associated with particular practices. "Best-practices" models can be identified and supported with public funds, and efforts can be made to disseminate knowledge of these practices. Having said this, it is obvious that developing a deeper understanding of how government policies help diffuse private practices remains an important topic for future research.

Conclusion

I have not reached a very optimistic conclusion concerning the prospects for employment security in the United States. This is ironic because in many respects the time is very propitious. Most important, for the reasons developed in this paper, the constituency for enhanced security is growing beyond traditional groups. American firms are rethinking their competitive strategy, and a strong minority articulates the view that tranformed human resource management systems that entail higher levels of employment security are the best strategy. There is a constant refrain in the business press and from business leaders that a deeper commitment to training is required. In addition, as already noted, it is possible to point to specific developments, such as plant-closing legislation.

The problem, however, is that it is not clear that these transformed human resource management systems are really taking hold. Indeed, many firms that have moved in this direction are under intense pressure. It is hard to see a substantial public commitment to diffusing these changes and supporting those firms that engage in them, and without such a commitment it is very uncertain whether the reforms can prevail.

The explanation for the acknowledgment of the problem but the weakness of the solution lies, I think, in two characteristics of American labor markets. The first is the weakness of the union movement, and the second is the long-standing aversion to government intervention in private employment practices. Taken together, these characteristics imply that there is little organized pressure for change, that there is little policy attention paid to the problem, and that the academic community has little to offer in the way of workable models of how to influence private employment practices.

Experiments in new forms of worker representation are under way in the United States. In addition, the growing concern with the undertraining of the core labor force has generated new interest in national training policy. Finally, interest in reforming internal labor markets does remain high. Hence, there are signs that enhanced employment security is not a hopeless cause, but there is a very long way to go.

Germany

10

Protection against Unfair Dismissal in West Germany: Historical Evolution and Legal Regulation

Rolf Birk

The right to protection against unfair dismissal in the Federal Republic of Germany is not easy to comprehend. As in most other European countries, there is no clear-cut concept of employment security underlying German dismissal law. A distinctive feature, however, is the priority given to employment security in the sense of the maintenance of the employment relationship as opposed to mere financial compensation for unjustified job loss. In addition to dismissal protection, employment security in Germany encompasses protection against unilateral modifications of the conditions of employment, such as pay, occupational status, and assigned work tasks. In other words, neither the continuation nor the contents of the employment relationship are considered to be solely at the employer's discretion but, rather, are viewed as based on mutual contractual agreement.

Since its very beginning, protection against unfair dismissal in Germany has essentially been regulated by the legislator, whereas collective bargaining agreements at both industry and firm levels have played a subordinate role. Until now, in only a relatively few cases have German trade unions negotiated terms concerning protection against unfair dismissal (the only important exception being collectively negotiated special safeguards for older workers). More frequently, legal standards have been extended through firm-level agreements and negotiated procedures.

This paper provides a brief overview of the historical evolution of German unfair dismissal law and then outlines some core elements of the current system of unfair dismissal protection. In my concluding remarks, I point out some future challenges for German labor law based on a comparison of rival models of dismissal protection.

Historical Evolution

Legal protection against unfair dismissals was first introduced in Germany by the Works Council Act of 1920. The emphasis of the act was not so much on individual job security, however, as on collective participation by workers' representatives (works councils) in the procedure of termination. According to sections 84ff. of the act, legal protection against dismissal was tightly bound to the objection or approval of the works council. The protection of the individual employee thus depended entirely on the commitment and the goodwill of the works council. An employee who wished to contest a dismissal first had to complain to the works council. If the works council accepted the worker's protest, the latter was entitled to sue the employer before a labor court. If the worker prevailed, the employer could choose between reinstatement of the plaintiff or a severance payment compensating the worker for his or her job loss. The recognized reasons justifying a dismissal were essentially the same as they are today. I discuss these reasons below.

In January 1934, the Works Council Act of 1920 was replaced by the Act on the Reorganization of National Labor, by which the national socialist government abolished the works councils. The substance of the old concept of protection against unfair dismissal continued to exist, but its collective component was removed along with the introduction of the so-called leadership principle in labor relations.

It was not until 1947 that the Allied Control Council suspended Nazi labor law. The following years witnessed a growing legal insecurity and fragmentation. Some of the newly established *Laender* (states) referred to the earlier law of the Weimar Republic, while others enacted their own legislation. As a result, protection against unfair dismissals was granted either collectively through codetermination by the works councils or through individual rights established by legislation. Alternatively, the courts, for instance in the British "zone," tried to fill the statutory vacuum by the application of the principle of loyalty and good faith as set out in the Civil Code.

The law against unfair dismissals as it exists today is based on the Dismissal Protection Act of 1951, which restored legal unity in the newly founded Federal Republic. The 1951 Dismissal Protection Act bears the traces of a compromise between employers and unions (the so-called Hattenheim draft) that improved individual rights and reduced the collective component in dismissal protection. This concept of individual rather than collective protection was modified somewhat in 1972 through the Amended Works Constitution Act (*Betriebsverfassungsgesetz*), which again strengthened the collective component by establishing mandatory consultations with the works council before each dismissal.

Core Elements of Current Unfair Dismissal Law

Any outline of the German dismissal law and its legal structure must begin by explaining its basic concept of dismissal. In principle, the employer can terminate the employment relationship only by showing "just cause"; in the absence of just cause, the dismissal is considered invalid and the employment relationship continues. This rather radical version of just cause distinguishes German dismissal law from that of many other European countries. "Unjustly" dismissed employees retain all their rights in the employment relationship, and it is considered the employer's fault if the employer fails to accept the labor service offered by the unlawfully dismissed employee.

Ex ante Prevention of Unjustified Dismissals

Legal dismissal protection sets in, however, before the express notice of termination by the employer. The prime objective of the Dismissal Protection Act is to prevent dismissal in cases in which no substantial reason is given. An essential element in unfair dismissal protection, therefore, is the legal limitation and definition of what is to be considered "just cause" for dismissal. The definition of "good" or "just" cause for dismissal makes it clear that the law does not intend to establish any absolute safeguard against employment termination. Only in exceptional cases does the law exclude ordinary (i.e., nondisciplinary) dismissals altogether, as in the case of pregnant women or elected members of the works council, for example.

The Dismissal Protection Act does not apply to enterprises with fewer than six regularly employed employees (excluding apprentices). The legislator did not want to burden small businesses with social responsibilities beyond their scope.[1] To be entitled to legal protection against unjust dismissal, the act further requires a minimum tenure of at least six months in the firm. The law thus refers both to the establishment (number of employees) and to the firm as a whole (tenure). The firm (and not the establishment) is also the point of reference in cases of dismissal due to organizational and operational changes.

Just Cause

German unfair-dismissal law further allows job terminations only if they are "socially justified." This concept of social justification applies to each dismissal for economic reasons, regardless of whether it involves one or more workers. Collective redundancies are treated by the law as merely involving several individual dismissals.

The principle of social justification in German dismissal law recognizes three basic legitimate grounds for dismissals: (1) termination as a result of incapacity or poor performance of the worker, (2) dismissal for misconduct by the worker, and (3) termination for economic reasons including operational requirements of the establishment. Termination based on incapacity of the worker is justified if the worker is no longer in possession of the necessary physical and mental capac-

---

[1] The exclusion of small businesses employing fewer than six workers from statutory dismissal protection has recently been reaffirmed by the federal Supreme Court.

ities required to perform the job, regardless of whether this incapacity has been caused by the worker or not. Dismissals because of long and/or frequent sickness are recognized in principle but have been subject to strict control by the labor courts.

Terminations for misconduct on the part of the worker occur more frequently. The law recognizes all violations of contract by the employee as misconduct justifying dismissal.

Terminations for economic reasons are justified only if they are seen as vital to the economic objectives of the undertaking and cannot be avoided by reasonable alternative technical, organizational, or economic measures taken by the employer. The interest of the individual employee in job security ranks only second if the economic circumstances of the undertaking require a reduction of the work force. By this priority rule, both legislator and labor courts have acknowledged the need for quantitative, structural, and qualitative adjustments. These adjustments may be necessary because of external factors, such as a recession or a decline in the demand for the firm's products, or internal factors, such as technical changes in the production process and necessary reorganizations of work, including ration- alization measures. A crucial regulation regarding collective redundancies is the requirement that the workers affected be selected according to "social" criteria ("procedures of social selection"). The Dismissal Protection Act has left these criteria unspecified, but they have been laid out in rulings of the federal labor court.

The law thus leaves economic decisions about personnel requirements and necessary work force reductions to the discretion of the employer. Only the external and internal factors leading to the entrepreneurial decision and the consequences arising from it for the individual worker are subject to judicial control (see fig. 10–1).

Procedural Regulation

The concept of individual rights and remedies against unfair dismissals under- lying the Dismissal Protection Act is complemented by the right of the works council to be consulted by the employer before each dismissal. According to the Amended Works Constitution Act of 1972, the employer is obliged to inform the works council of impending dismissals (for economic or other reasons) and to give workers' representatives the opportunity to comment and thereby influence the decision of the employer. If the employer fails to inform the works council, the dismissal is considered null and void. If the works council objects to a planned dismissal and the worker decides to contest its justification through a labor court, the employment relationship continues until the court has settled the conflict (see fig. 10–2).

A further crucial element in German dismissal law is the so-called principle of reasonableness or adequacy. According to this principle, dismissals for economic reasons are permissible only if there is no possibility of further employment in the enterprise or in the firm at large. This implies that the employer has to offer

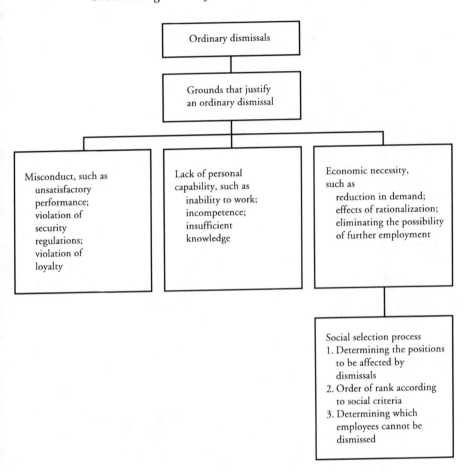

Source: Oechsler 1988:400.

FIGURE 10–1. *"Just-Cause" and "Social Selection" Requirements in German Dismissal Law*

the worker alternative employment within the firm even if this involves a change in the terms of employment or attempt to prevent redundancies through the introduction of work sharing.[2] According to the same principle, dismissals for reasons of misconduct by the worker are lawful only if the employer has given the employee adequate prior warnings that his or her behavior may result in dismissal. Finally, before dismissing a worker on grounds of personal incapacity or bad health, the principle of adequacy requires the employer to undertake all reasonable efforts to prevent the job loss for the worker (e.g., by retraining or

---

[2]The obligation to introduce short-time work (work sharing) to prevent otherwise necessary dismissals has been disputed by some labor courts.

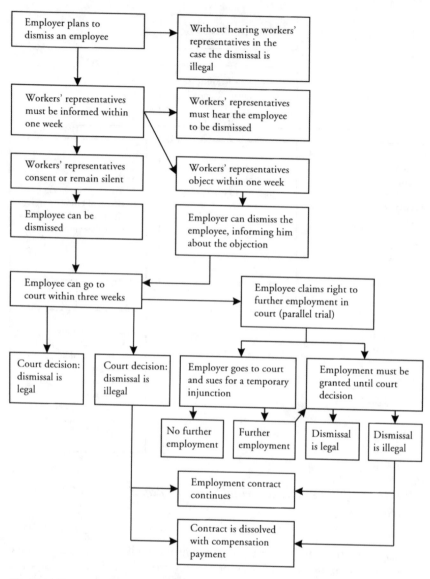

Source: Oechsler 1988:404.

FIGURE 10–2. Procedures and Remedies in German Dismissal Law

reassigning the worker to a different job in the enterprise or by waiting for the results of medical care, including health cure, and rehabilitation measures).

Remedies

The priority of employment security over mere compensation for job loss in German dismissal law is evident further in that there is no general legal obligation to make severance payments in the case of dismissals. Mandatory severance payments are restricted to special circumstances, such as when the worker prevails in court but refuses to continue the employment relationship or when severance payments have been negotiated between management and the works council in the context of a social plan accompanying major work force reductions or work reorganizations.

Whereas German dismissal law emphasizes the ex ante prevention of dismissals through procedural rules and norms, legal control of compliance with these rules and the justification of the dismissal takes place only ex post, that is, if the employee decides to contest his or her dismissal through a labor court. Thus, legal proceedings essentially depend on the initiative of the individual worker. The risk of permanent job loss inherent in ex post judicial control of the justification of dismissals, especially if court proceedings extend over longer time periods, has been substantially reduced, however, through the right of continued employment during court litigation under the Amended Works Constitution Act of 1972. Labor court rulings have also made the act apply in principle to workers dismissed by firms without elected works councils and therefore not covered by the Works Constitution Act. Data for 1989 show that close to three-quarters (72 percent) of all labor court cases dealing with dismissals (not including appeals) in (West) Germany were, in fact, settled within three months.[3]

A further important feature of the law against unfair dismissals is the close relationship of material and procedural law. An employee may claim protection against unfair dismissal by filing a suit against the employer within three weeks of receiving notice of his or her termination. If the employee fails to take action within this period, the right to litigate against the dismissal is forfeited and the dismissal remains effective.

If the employee prevails, the labor court declares the dismissal to be socially unjustified and void; consequently, the employment relationship is regarded as persisting and the employer is liable for back wages. Although reinstatement or continuation of employment is the prime target of German dismissal law, the prevailing worker (not the employer, except in the case of managerial or executive staff) may plead for a dissolution of the employment relationship if prolonged cooperation with the employer would involve social strains and therefore appears unreasonable. If the request for dissolution is granted by the court, the employer has to pay an indemnity to the worker, taking into consideration age, tenure, the individual reemployment probability of the worker, the loss of entitlements (e.g., to firm-specific pension benefits) involved with the job loss, as well as the economic situation of the firm. Maximum indemnity has been set by the courts at twelve months' salary but may be increased up to eighteen months for workers aged fifty-five or older with at least twenty years of tenure.

If the labor court finds the dismissal to be socially justified and therefore effective, the employment relationship is considered terminated at the end of the legal or contractually agreed-on prenotification period or, in cases of continued employment during legal procedings, by the time of the court decision.

[3]Cf. Bundesminister fuer Arbeit und Sozialordnung 1990:103.

Conclusion

Viewed in an international comparative context, German dismissal law can be said to be in a moderate position between the extremes of more or less unregulated employment-at-will systems and highly regulated systems involving substantial employment guarantees. Hiring and firing are not completely at will (i.e., at the employer's discretion as in the U.S. nonunionized sector) (see Gould, chap. 5), but neither does German labor law recognize lifetime employment guarantees, as have frequently been assumed to govern the employment relationship in large Japanese corporations (see Koike 1987a; Inagami 1988). German dismissal protection thus certainly belongs to those models of employment security that provide only relative protection against unfair (i.e., unjustified) employment terminations. Of the other major European countries, Italy, France, and the United Kingdom adhere to a similar model of relative employment protection. There are many differences in detail, however, reflecting the specific historical evolution of labor law in each of these countries. Unlike German law, for example, most other European systems of employment security do not render unjust or unfair dismissals void but instead offer the unjustly fired employee a choice between reinstatement (i.e., resumption of employment with their previous employer) or compensation for the job loss (for a comparative overview, see Becker and Etzel 1986:391ff.; International Labor Office 1985:77ff.).

A rough classification of the main European systems of dismissal protection can be undertaken with regard to the method of protection and its legal consequences. There are three basic types of protection, which differ mainly in the relative importance of their individual and collective components: (1) employment security through individual protection against unfair dismissal, requiring legal action by the individual employee (Germany); (2) individual protection mediated through collective workers' representatives at the firm level (Austria); and (3) protection through the threat of collective industrial action by the workers (United Kingdom and Italy). There are also three legal remedies for unjustified terminations: (1) payment by the employer of an indemnity or severance allowance (Belgium and France); (2) the choice of reinstatement in the old job or severance pay as compensation for the job loss (Italy and United Kingdom); and (3) annulment of the dismissal and continuation of the employment relationship (Germany).

In recent years the German model of employment security has been facing serious challenges. The strong legalistic approach taken toward employment security in Germany has been criticized for reducing labor market flexibility. To overcome this deficiency, critics of the established model have called for a strengthening of collectively negotiated procedures and arbitration systems at firm or industry level. The rapid increase in fixed-term work contracts that are not subject to dismissal protection has raised the question of whether it is desirable from a sociopolitical view to maintain the established system's strong orientation toward permanent (i.e., indefinite) employment arrangements. Notwithstanding these challenges, protection from unfair dismissal constitutes an integral component of a social market economy.

11
Employment Security and Efficiency: Assumptions in the Current Debate and Empirical Evidence for West Germany

Friedrich Buttler and Ulrich Walwei

From the beginning of the period of high unemployment in OECD countries, labor market institutions and regulations were said to have both a direct and, via other economic variables influencing structural change, an indirect negative impact on employment. The debate on the importance of institutions and regulatory constraints for the functioning of labor markets constitutes one aspect of the current general discussion on deregulation. Supporters of deregulation stress that market rigidities stem from the regulations. Deregulation of labor markets is expected to improve the ability and willingness of employers and employees to adjust to changing economic circumstances. Opponents of deregulation claim that labor market institutions serve to protect employees. The debate on deregulation of the labor market thus reflects the basic conflict between efficiency and equity goals long known to economic theory.

Labor market institutions cannot be subject to a general assessment with regard to the above-mentioned goals; they each require a detailed economic analysis. This paper summarizes the most important pros and cons of dismissal protection, which has been one of the core issues in the debate on labor market deregulation.

Dismissal protection increases employers' transaction costs by limiting their behavioral options. Layoff restraints, by increasing the fixed costs of labor, are said to conflict with social protection goals by reducing firms' overall employment capacity. The idea of social protection underlying employment security regulation is said to focus primary attention on the interests of actual job holders, but social protection, in contrast, should be motivated by equity goals for the total work force. It aims to stabilize income, status, and work standards. The assumption in the debate that employment security policies conflict with efficiency goals needs further consideration. In doing so, the peculiarities of the employment relationship and the differences between labor markets and commodity markets have to be taken into account. In the case of labor market imperfections, dismissal protection may under certain circumstances exert a positive influence on allocative efficiency. The stability of an employment relationship, supported by dismissal protection, may be an important stimulus for an employee's willingness to show loyalty, motivation, and adaptability and thus commitment to a firm's goals.

The underlying viewpoint of the above argument is that not all elements of employment relationships should be flexible at the same time. Limitations on numerical flexibility via stabilization of employment contracts (supported by dismissal protection legislation) may be a precondition for employees to react with high functional flexibility to new challenges due to changes in external markets and internal organization. This viewpoint therefore assumes a regime that is based on high employment security, high wages, and high productivity, in contrast to one based on mere wage competition in order to clear the labor market. A mix of both regimes can be observed in the Federal Republic of Germany, whereas the latter regime is predominant in the United States. The co-existence of both regimes in one country, within an industry, or in an enterprise is the subject of theories of labor market segmentation.

We start this paper by characterizing the economically significant main components of dismissal protection and listing the important arguments of the current debate. Subsequently, we focus on four aspects that have played a prominent role in the current debate: employment, productivity, the flexibility of the labor market, and the insider-outsider problem. Some of our assumptions will be exemplified by referring to the situation in the Federal Republic of Germany, where employment protection is said to be high compared to other European countries and in particular to the United States (Emerson 1988a).

Components of Dismissal Protection

Dismissal procedures differ in many details among European countries. Dismissals are allowed in principle, but the employers' prerogative to dismiss at will is reduced by legal just-cause standards (e.g., criminal acts, gross misconduct, incapacity, redundancy) and by the role of third parties (e.g., trade unions, works councils, and courts). Dismissals for economic reasons are often set out in extensive detail and involve statutory procedures, periods of notice, and minimum amounts of compensation (Emerson 1988a).

In the Federal Republic of Germany the dismissal of an employee is valid only if it can be justified in accordance with a catalog of recognized grounds for dismissal (e.g., misconduct, personal insuitability, operational reasons). In addition, periods of notice—laid down in the Civil Code and in collective agreements—have to be taken into account. Furthermore, some groups of employees (e.g., handicapped persons, expectant mothers) enjoy additional employment protection. Moreover, the works council has the right to be heard by the employer before each dismissal. Finally, there are special regulations relating to mass dismissals, which require that an announcement be made to the local labor office and that works councils be consulted. In the case of mass dismissals, a social compensation plan (*Sozialplan*) is obligatory under certain circumstances (for a more detailed description, see Birk and Buechtemann, chaps. 10 and 13).

Critique

Regulations that raise the costs of firing staff and thus the opportunity costs of hiring may be thought of as having the following negative impacts on employers, employees, and the labor market at large:

1. Procedural constraints and severance costs add an element of fixed costs to labor costs. At the time of recruitment, expenses for dismissal or delays are potential costs, although they can be anticipated by a firm considering the probability of dismissal. This probability depends on the chances of the firm finding itself with excess labor at some future date. Such anticipated costs could reduce the demand for labor and encourage capital-for-labor substitution (Gavin 1986).

2. The lower probability of dismissal, caused by the existence of employment protection, may have an adverse effect on work effort because of the difficulty of sanctioning shirking workers. Moreover, negative productivity effects could arise if there is an unwarranted labor surplus in the enterprise or if wrong recruitment decisions cannot be reversed (Molitor 1986).

3. Extensive dismissal protection may reduce fluctuation in employment and unemployment. Thus, the flexibility of the labor market could be reduced and structural change in the economy hindered.

4. A reduced fluctuation in employment may also imply relatively poor chances for "outsiders" (e.g., unemployed persons or persons who have interrupted gainful employment) to be reintegrated into the labor market. Using this line of argument, dismissal protection is frequently said to lead to an unjust distribution of existing jobs (Zoellner 1978). Thus, Reuter (1982) claims that regulations aimed at protecting disadvantaged groups in the labor market failed because in the final analysis they worked against the reemployment opportunities of precisely those groups they were intended to protect.

Economic Effects of Dismissal Protection

Employment

Variations in the employment level of an economy depend on recruitments and dismissals by firms. To judge the impact of employment protection regulations on decisions concerning recruitment and dismissal, a transaction cost analysis may be helpful (Williamson 1985).

In the employment relationship, transaction costs arise because employing persons in enterprises requires expenditures for internal coordination in addition to direct wage costs (e.g., costs for search, training, vocational adjustment, and termination of employment contracts). These costs are generally independent of the duration of the employment contract. They are to this extent fixed costs of employment.

The existence of fixed costs of employment is an important reason for the efficiency of long-term relationships. Fixed costs of employment have the character of investments in the employment relationship. These investments represent a capital stock that is productive only as long as the employment relationship continues. Amortization of the investment is linked to continuity of the prerequisites. First, there has to be an interest in amortization of fixed costs during the current contract. Second, fixed costs are definitely lost if the relationship is terminated (Crawford 1988).

Transaction costs in the form of fixed costs of employment influence not only the duration of employment relationships but also decisions of employers regarding recruitments and dismissals. Costs of dismissal protection together with other fixed costs of employment tend to decrease recruitments (Schellhaass 1984; Long and Siebert 1983; Nickell 1978). Whether this leads to a lower level of overall employment cannot be answered before the effects of employment protection on both hiring and firing decisions are taken into consideration.

The existence of transaction costs renders not only recruitments more difficult but also dismissals. Whereas recruitments are hindered because of the fixed-cost character of transaction costs, dismissals are impeded by the irreversibility of those costs (Bellmann and Buttler 1989). Dismissals will not be attractive for the employer as long as transaction costs in the form of fixed costs of employment are not amortized and marginal productivity covers at least part of the sunk costs.

More freedom of dismissal through deregulation would reduce termination costs as part of total transaction costs. This would make both recruitments and dismissals easier. Nevertheless, average employment and unemployment would perhaps be the same over the business cycle because more dismissals in recessionary periods would be followed by more recruitments in periods of recovery (Franz 1989; OECD 1986b). Severance costs and procedural constraints (imposed by regulations of dismissal protection) will therefore cause higher employment in periods of weak demand (Gavin 1986). Consequently, dismissal protection can be seen as having an anticyclical effect.

There is another argument suggesting that the employment effects of the costs of dismissal protection will not necessarily be negative. As will be argued in the following section, the costs of dismissal protection may be interpreted as investment-causing productivity gains induced by the stabilization of the employment relationship. In this case the potential costs of the termination of the employment contract must be set against the productivity incentives arising from dismissal protection. The resulting employment effects will be ex ante uncertain.

Productivity

To a certain extent, dismissal protection may improve employees' commitment to work. By supporting stable employment relationships, dismissal protection may under certain conditions ensure high labor productivity. This can be explained by the economics of team production; in other words, by the economics of the firm.

Team production is profitable if there is a difference between its output and the total output of all team members working individually. The additional return team production yields compared to individual production depends inter alia on the team members' work commitment.

Employees often have considerable opportunities for varying their work effort or for shirking. This is because of job idiosyncrasies and peculiarities in employment contracts. The latter result from the use of human labor as a productive factor. Labor as a productive factor cannot be separated from the worker (Marshall 1920; Schruefer 1988). The employer is entitled to use the worker's performance only in the production process (Cheung 1983; Edwards 1981). This is why an "overlap" of disposition spheres occurs between the user and the owner of labor. As a consequence, employment contracts remain to a certain extent unspecified with regard to performance (Reich and Devine 1981). They merely offer a frame to be filled by the employer's managerial dispositions. Concrete contents and the intensity of work performance (= effort) remain ex ante undetermined. This is not necessarily a disadvantage for the employer, for he or she can handle labor input more flexibly if specifications of employment contracts are incomplete. In addition, control and/or incentives are necessary to secure high performance. For this reason, dismissal protection should ensure only employment security and not job security. Whereas employment security makes functional flexibility (i.e., internal mobility) possible, job security does not.

Insufficiently specified employment contracts lead to asymmetries of information between contractors regarding mutual implicit obligations (e.g., promise of performance, promise of career, permanent employment). To ensure work outcomes like those agreed on in a work contract, it would be necessary either to reorganize the work process tayloristically to ensure performance control or, if this were not profit maximizing, to stimulate readiness for cooperation with job incentives. "Investments in trust" are therefore necessary to create a spirit of cooperation (Wintrobe and Breton 1986).

Stable employment relationships will be essential whenever costs and benefits of investments in the employment relationship are spread over time. Game theory has shown that readiness for cooperation is negatively influenced by ex ante limitations of relationships (e.g., fixed-term contracts) (Axelrod 1984; Walwei 1990a). In this respect unlimited contracts are favorable. Dismissal protection thus stabilizes expectations toward permanent employment, reduces transaction costs due to asymmetries of information, and stimulates cooperative behavior. This is not true in cases where costs and benefits of investment can be ex ante specified to be realized within the same fixed term. In such a case the labor relationship adopts the characteristics of a commission contract or contract for services.[1]

This assumption has been confirmed by a range of literature. Some efficiency wage models assume a positive relationship between labor productivity on the one hand and wage levels, including job satisfaction, on the other (Yellen 1984; Stiglitz 1987). Dismissal protection can also be seen to be a prerequisite for the

---

[1]In a commission or service contract one party undertakes to bring about a particular result and the other party, a customer, promises to pay for it.

functioning of seniority rules (Lazear 1979; Bellmann 1986). Last-in/first-out rules for dismissals may generate additional productivity.

By extending the Shapiro and Stiglitz model of unemployment as a worker discipline device, Levine (1989:902) shows that dismissal protection policies prevent negative external effects:

> The private calculation of the costs of a dismissal policy ignores an externality that occurs when a firm fires a worker. When a dismissed worker is replaced, the hiring rate increases. The increased hiring rate reduces the expected duration of unemployment for workers at other firms to maintain a sufficient cost of job loss to motivate their workers. At the margin, it always increases efficiency to provide a greater level of employment security (for example, require more evidence before firing a suspected shirker) than the privately efficient contract provides.

This argument refers to the overall economic efficiency of dismissal protection policies and is not concerned with firm productivity only.

In sociological literature employment security is also interpreted as favoring loyalty and the dedication of employees to a firm's objectives (see, for example, Akerlof 1984a). Piore (1986) claims that on the one hand employment security encourages a firm to invest in training and thereby upgrades the productivity of the employee. On the other hand, there are positive productivity effects caused by the greater willingness of workers to accept technological change and internal job mobility.

The productivity argument holds especially for activities relying on complex teamwork (on "relational" teams, see Williamson 1985), high skills, and variable technology. It is less significant where jobs are simple to learn and easy to supervise. In the first category of jobs, employment protection will be relatively more beneficial and less costly than in the latter case (Emerson 1988a).

Given the conditions just described, ex ante unlimited employment may be a basic requirement for efficient contracts. In this context, regulations preventing dismissal at will (e.g., legal protection against unfair dismissal) are significant in strengthening employee commitment. In addition, dismissal protection legislation is advantageous (compared to individual contractual arrangements) because it reduces transaction costs. Each worker and firm need not negotiate conditions separately with respect to dismissal protection (Savarese 1980).

At the same time, it has been argued that employment security may lessen work effort. The employee may reduce his or her effort to a minimum as defined by regulations or jurisdiction regarding dismissal due to misconduct. Especially if the costs of monitoring work performance are high, job tenure requires supplementation through additional effort incentives and through the efficient selection of job applicants.

Incentives to increase work effort could include seniority wages, profit sharing, or reasonable prospects of promotion within the firm. If the firm's personnel policy is based on stable employment relationships, the careful screening of job applicants will gain in importance. Firms have to ensure that applicants are able to do the job and to work hard. For this reason, firms may choose different approaches. They could raise their screening costs to recruit more effective employees. Furthermore, firms could have longer probationary periods to give them time to examine newly hired employees' work commitment. Such a probationary arrangement could be an initial period of a permanent contract (with a lower degree of dismissal protection) or a fixed-term contract (not involving any dismissal protection) with the prospect of a permanent contract if the employee proves efficient. Alternatively, firms could fill some of their vacancies only with tried and tested persons already employed in the firm (recruitment from the internal labor market).

The German Employment Promotion Act (*Beschaeftigungsfoerderungsgesetz*) permits fixed-term contracts of up to eighteen months without the requirement of a "legitimate reason" for the fixed term. Thus, firms can test the workers' ability during a comparatively long period of probation. Prolonged probation periods in the form of initial fixed-term employment do not, however, necessarily increase total employment (see Buechtemann, chap. 13).

Labor Market Flexibility

Information about labor market flexibility can be provided by data on fluctuation in both employment and unemployment. As we mentioned above, dismissal protection stabilizes employment levels and reduces fluctuations in employment. A high fluctuation in employment would cause not only social hardships on the part of workers but substantial increases in fixed turnover costs (hiring and training costs on the part of firms. In contrast, modest fluctuations in both employment and unemployment would indicate that there are relatively poor chances for outsiders to be reintegrated into employment and that matching problems could arise.

In spite of the fact that German dismissal protection has been said to be extensive, fluctuation in employment seems to be remarkably high. According to the employment statistics of the Federal Employment Agency, the annual turnover rate of employees subject to social security contributions remained close to 28 percent from 1984 to 1988. Average job duration was a little more than 3.5 years during this period.

Overall figures for labor turnover have to be supplemented by information on the variation in job durations. In a longitudinal analysis, Cramer (1986) found substantial variations in employment stability by gender, age, nationality, and level of skill. Stable employment is more prevalent among men than among women and among German workers than among foreign workers. Further, workers with vocational training enjoy more stable employment than those without such training (table 11–1).

Fluctuations in unemployment have also been considerable in Germany. Despite relatively constant levels of unemployment (between 1.87 and 2.33 millions in 1989), 3.95 million persons left unemployment in 1989 while 3.81 million employees joined the unemployment register. Nearly one-third (30 percent) of all entrants into unemployment (53 percent of all previously employed entrants)

TABLE 11-1. Share of Stable Employment (Continuously Employed between 1976 and 1981) in Germany

Social Groups	Neither vocational training nor upper secondary school leaving certificate[a]	Vocational training, but no upper secondary school leaving certificate	No vocational training, but upper secondary school leaving certificate	Vocational training and upper secondary school leaving certificate	Higher education		All skill levels
					Nonuniversity type	University type	
Men							
Germans							
< 30 years	49.9	51.4	20.3	40.8	43.6	35.2	49.3
30–50 years	63.0	74.5	76.2	64.3	75.9	57.9	70.9
>50 years	50.5	59.2	72.3[b]	69.9	66.3	71.0	57.0
Non-Germans							
<30 years	30.7	36.1	17.6[b]	—	38.3[b]	25.7	32.0
30–50 years	43.0	43.3	—	43.9[b]	40.8[b]	29.4	42.7
>50 years	42.4	50.6	—	—	—	—	44.6
Women							
Germans							
<30 years	44.8	44.7	33.2	40.0	27.8[b]	22.7	43.7
30–50 years	47.4	50.6	47.3[b]	52.9	37.4	26.8	48.7
>50 years	59.2	62.0	68.6[b]	68.9[b]	61.5[b]	65.7[b]	60.5
Non-Germans							
<30 years	30.7	33.3	26.1[b]	36.4[b]	—	25.0[b]	31.0
30–50 years	36.2	41.3	—	—	—	30.0	36.7
>50 years	46.5	34.2[b]	—	—	—	—	44.0
Total	48.3	56.4	33.1	50.6	54.9	41.0	52.3

Source: Cramer 1986:249.

[a]Includes persons whose qualifications are unknown.

[b]Includes not more than one hundred but more than thirty persons.

TABLE 11-2. *Inflow into Unemployment by Mode of Termination of Employment Contract*

	Mode of termination			
Year[a]	By employee (quits)	By employer (permanent layoffs)	By mutual agreement	End of fixed-term contract
1984	19.2	63.7	4.3	12.8
1985	18.1	64.2	3.6	14.0
1986	20.0	61.5	3.4	15.1
1987	19.7	60.2	4.0	16.1
1988	22.8	56.3	4.6	16.3
1989	25.5	53.4	5.4	15.7

Source: Federal Employment Agency 1990:719.
[a]Figures refer to a two-week observation period (each May or June).

resulted from dismissals by the employer (table 11–2). Another 9 percent (16 percent of all those previously employed) entered unemployment after the expiration of a fixed-term contract. The growing proportion of voluntary job leavers (quits) among the unemployed since 1988 reflects the improvement in the overall labor market situation.

These fluctuations suggest that dismissal protection in Germany in practice helps neither to preserve jobs nor to prevent unemployment. Recall that the governing rule is freedom of dismissal limited by legal or collectively bargained constraints. Moreover, to a certain degree, dismissal protection has hampering effects on fluctuation because it prevents ad hoc employment adjustment.

Insider-Outsider Problem

One of the main criticisms of established systems of dismissal protection is that they protect permanently employed incumbent workers and disregard the interests of outsiders (i.e., the unemployed). It is said that employment protection causes inequality in both employment opportunities and unemployment risks.

Investigating the reemployment opportunities of different groups, Meyer (1989) argues that dismissal protection discriminates against unemployed workers whose productivity is low if the collectively negotiated wage structure does not offer wage levels that make it profitable to hire them. Unskilled young workers, severely handicapped persons, certain groups of women, and older persons belong to these disadvantaged groups. Such persons are usually protected by special layoff restraints that may add to their discrimination in the labor market. Employers consequently can be expected to be, ceteris paribus, more reluctant to hire from these groups the more their special rights cause additional dismissal costs. This argument can be examined using data on employment and unemployment of severely handicapped persons in West Germany. Severely handicapped persons are protected to a larger extent than other groups of workers. They cannot be

TABLE 11-3. *Average Completed Duration of Unemployment (in months)*[a]

Year	Unemployed with health problems	Unemployed without health problems	All unemployed
1985	10.3	6.4	6.8
1986	10.2	6.2	6.7
1987	10.2	6.3	6.7
1988	10.1	6.3	6.7
1989	11.1	6.1	6.7

Source: Federal Employment Agency 1990:711.
[a]Figures refer to a two-week observation period (each May or June).

dismissed without previous agreement by local authorities (Section 12 of the Act for the Severely Handicapped).

The unemployment rate of severely handicapped persons is above average, having increased from 11.6 percent to 12.6 percent over the period 1983–89, during which the general unemployment rate fell from 8.6 percent to 7.3 percent. Severely handicapped persons also bear a higher risk of *remaining* unemployed. Their average completed duration of unemployment was ten and eleven months during the period 1985–89, whereas the average duration for persons without health problems was close to five months (see table 11–3). The data also show that severely handicapped persons have a lower chance of getting reemployed following unemployment (see table 11–4).

At the same time, severely handicapped persons who are employed bear a lower risk of *becoming* unemployed. Between 1985 and 1989, the share of severely handicapped persons among all newly unemployed persons remained nearly constant (between 3.2 and 3.3 percent), whereas the share of severely handicapped persons within the total labor force was close to 4 percent (Federal Employment Agency 1990:713).

The insider-outsider argument emphasizes that regulations aimed at achieving dismissal protection increase the risk of remaining unemployed. But, as the reported figures show, those regulations reduce the risk of becoming unemployed and improve the competitiveness of socially disadvantaged persons.

The latter is also true of social selection criteria applicable in the case of dismissals for economic or operational reasons (see Birk, chap 10). The rule requires that younger, better trained persons be laid off first. Their reemployment opportunites can be assumed to be compararively high (Von Stebut 1982). In addition, special dismissal protection regulations in favor of certain disadvantaged groups such as older workers ensure that those persons facing reemployment difficulties in the external labor market will not be the first to lose their jobs when the economy declines.

The effects of dismissal protection on job distribution are therefore ambiguous. Assessment depends on whether persons are employed (insiders) or unemployed (outsiders). In general, however, it is questionable whether dismissal protection in favor of certain groups is of particular significance for the structure of employment and especially for the actual amount of long-term unemployment. Other

TABLE 11-4. Rates of Outflow from Unemployment to Employment[a]

Year	Severely handicapped unemployed	All unemployed
1985	53.5%	73.6%
1986	55.9	73.0
1987	51.2	68.1
1988	50.3	67.8
1989	47.2	59.2

Source: Federal Employment Agency 1990:712.
[a]Subsequent reemployment as percentage of total outflow from unemployment based on data for a two-week observation period (each May or June).

factors may be more important in influencing the emergence of long-term unemployment (e.g., the expected productivity of certain employees).

One further question in this context is important: should firms bear the additional labor costs caused by the employment of disadvantaged persons and of the regulations protecting these groups? These costs, especially for small and medium-sized enterprises, could weigh heavily. If the employment of disadvantaged persons and their special protection against dismissal are deemed socially desirable, then society as a whole instead of individual firms should bear the additional labor costs. Adequate forms of subsidies (e.g., wage-cost subsidies) financed by the state budget should be considered.

Conclusions

German dismissal protection regulations do not prohibit dismissals as such. Dismissals are necessary to facilitate employees' and employers' adaptation to changing conditions inside and outside the firm. It therefore must be possible to terminate employment contracts.

Although German law explicitly permits dismissals, each dismissal has to be grounded in just cause. Notice periods, just-cause requirements, and procedural constraints make it more costly to adapt the number of workers to fluctuations in demand. Dismissal protection ensures a fair balance between the contracting parties by assigning certain rights (dismissal protection) to the employee. At the same time, dismissal protection does not need to run counter to firms' objectives. Recall the positive effects of permanent employment relationships on commitment to work and thus on productivity.

The effects of dismissal protection on the distribution of jobs (insider-outsider problem) are ambiguous. Assessing regulations in favor of certain target groups depends on whether certain persons are employed or unemployed. Negative distributional effects of dismissal protection can be neglected only if there is no overall deficit in jobs. To preserve a comparatively low risk for disadvantaged groups of becoming unemployed and to reduce the risk of remaining unemployed, additional measures to improve the reemployment of such persons should be examined. For example, in the case of severely disabled or elderly persons, this could mean wage-cost subsidies, settling-in allowances, special training programs, and more effective placement services.

Finally, the lack of information certainty about a firm's legal position is causing unnecessary transaction costs. This was the finding of an empirical analysis conducted by Buechtemann and Hoeland (1989). The authors found that in the case of fixed-term contracts additional recruitments resulted from the better predictability of the legal consequences created by the Employment Promotion Act. The costs caused by judicial overcomplexity are an obstacle to the advantageous effects of dismissal protection. It should be examined whether legal uncertainty could be reduced by a more precise specification of legal reasons for dismissal instead of complicated jurisdiction.

12
Employment Security and Efficiency Reconsidered: A Comment on Friedrich Buttler and Ulrich Walwei

Wolfgang Franz

The preceding paper provides a comprehensive and informative account of the institutional regulations concerning dismissal protection in Germany and a thoughtful overview of its possible economic effects. Indeed, high and persistent levels of unemployment in Europe have often been attributed to a lack of flexibility in European labor markets compared to, for instance, the seemingly high flexibility in the United States. Specifically, the well-documented, longer average job tenure of workers in Germany compared with that of workers in the United States is regarded as standard evidence that there is less labor mobility in Germany because of direct restrictions on labor turnover, such as employment security laws.

Increasing Legal Uncertainties

Casual experience with dismissal protection sometimes makes it easy to accept this view. Let me quote one extreme example.[1] Two years ago the second senate of the German Federal Labor Court had to decide on the following case. Between February 1984 and October 1985 (roughly 600 days), a worker who was a substitute member of the works council of a large firm came late to shift work on exactly 104 days. He received several oral warnings and, between May 1984 and October 1985, five written warnings, two of them with the threat of dismissal. But the worker continued to be unpunctual. The firm consulted the works council which, of course, objected to his dismissal (he was a substitute member of the works council). Finally, the firm dismissed him for shirking and the Federal Labor

---

[1] The example is from Ruethers 1989a:15 and Ruethers 1989b:10. The judgment referred to above has not remained uncontested. In a very recent case the Federal Labor Court decided that repeated tardiness may justify the dismissal of an employee *regardless* of the adverse impact on the production process (see *Bundesarbeitsgericht 2 AZR 375/90*, decision of January 17, 1991).

Court had to decide whether the dismissal was justified. The Federal Labor Court refused to approve of the dismissal and remanded for a new trial in which the firm had to prove that the dismissed worker's behavior had caused a concrete impairment of the production process.

This decision represents new developments in jurisdiction. It is, of course, tempting to be cynical or satirical, but the major conclusion to be drawn from this example is the following. In addition or in contrast to the statements made in Buttler and Walwei's paper, it may not be the laws themselves that protect against dismissals but the growing uncertainty by firms about the developments in jurisdiction and the possibility of an imposition of further protections by labor court rulings. It is easy to imagine firms refraining from filing a suit if it involves long legal proceedings and if the result is highly uncertain. Firms may switch to more capital-intensive production.

Structural Impact of Employment Protection and Labor Market Mismatches

An informed discussion about dismissal protection requires an evaluation of the quantitative impact of these inflexibilities. Unfortunately, a close look at the data on the aggregate number of unemployed persons cannot accomplish this. If employment protection reduces inflows into unemployment on the one hand and increases unemployment duration on the other, reflecting reduced outflows because of the smaller number of hires (see the contribution by Flanagan, chap. 4), then the net impact on the size of the unemployed pool may be negligible. The laws and/or their extension by court jurisdiction affect the structure of employment and unemployment, however, by raising total labor costs and by changing the ratio of fixed to variable labor costs. Presumably, the difficulties in firing will lead to more careful screening of job applicants when the firm is hiring. In my view, Buttler and Walwei focus a little too much on the job tenure of skilled workers. There is every reason to argue that in the case of skilled workers both sides—the employer and the employee—are interested in long-lasting relationships because of, for instance, the existence of transaction costs. It is the handicapped and/or less skilled workers or workers whose productivity is difficult to identify who bear the major burden of this protection.

The econometric evidence on labor demand functions is unique in showing that there is a nonnegligible inverse relationship between employment and fixed labor costs. Put differently, the greater choosiness of employers because of difficulties in firing shirking workers creates an increasing mismatch between labor demanded and labor supplied. A well-known economic tool to check whether this fits the data is the Beveridge curve, (i.e., the relation between vacancies [v] and unemployment [u]). Figure 12-1 shows the u/v curve for the Federal Republic of Germany from 1962 to 1988, using corrected data for vacancies. Such a correction is required because official vacancy figures include only those vacancies that are reported to the labor office (i.e., roughly one-third). In the absence of

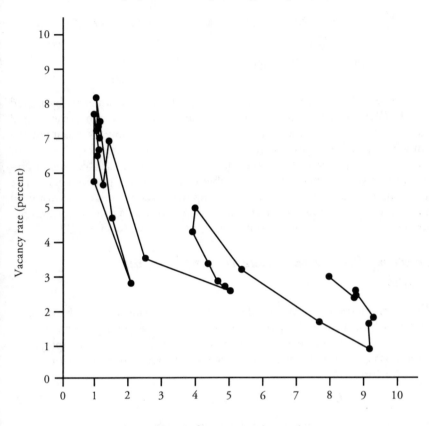

FIGURE 12–1. Beveridge Curve for the Federal Republic of Germany Using Corrected Data for Vacancies

any other reliable data, I have divided the number of officially notified vacancies by the fraction of all job placements through the labor office. This fraction is in turn approximated by the ratio of cumulated inflows of vacancies during one year to the sum of all new hires during the same year. The figure suggests an outward shift of the Beveridge curve, indicating greater maladjustment in the labor market. As I have shown elsewhere, this shift is confirmed by econometric estimates of the u/v curve.[2] If increased employer choosiness is the reason for this outward shift of the Beveridge curve, the cyclically adjusted duration of vacancies should have risen. The following regression represents a crude attempt to disentangle cyclical and trend movements of the duration of officially reported vacancies (DV):[3]

[2] See Franz 1991 for more details.
[3] T-values are in brackets; p denotes the first-order autocorrelation coefficient.

$$DV_t = 4.88 - 1.43 * UR_t + 0.499 * TIME \qquad (12\text{–}1)$$
$$(2.4) \quad (4.8) \qquad\qquad (2.8)$$
$$R^2 = 0.901 \quad DW = 2.20 \qquad p = 0.420$$
$$(1.6)$$

where UR refers to the aggregate unemployment rate instrumented by lagged values of UR and vacancy rates. In contrast to other countries such as the United Kingdom,[4] the average duration of vacancies increases over time. Without putting too much emphasis on this result, the significant positive time trend does not contradict the employer-choosiness explanation since other variables such as regional and/or skill mismatches were unable to explain this phenomenon. The next relevant question is whether increased employer choosiness is due to dismissal protection. Here one should be careful in drawing too hasty a conclusion; another econometric exercise casts some doubts on this hypothesis (see fig. 12-1).

Increasing Mismatches Due to Employment Protection?

This econometric experiment is designed to investigate whether the inability of firms to adjust their work force is more of a problem in (West) Germany than in the United States and, therefore, able to explain differences in unemployment between both countries. Consider the following stripped-down model of a labor demand function:

$$\ln E_t = (1 - \lambda) \ln E^*(Z)_t + \lambda \ln E_{t-1} \qquad (12\text{–}2)$$

where E stands for employment and Z is a vector of explanatory variables such as factor prices, output, and the like. More important is the adjustment of actual employment E to its desired level E^*, captured by the partial adjustment process incorporated in equation 12-2. Hamermesh (1988) has estimated such an equation for the United States for the 1973–85 period based on quarterly data and obtained a coefficient $l = 0.983$ as compared to $l = 0.881$ for the Federal Republic of Germany over the same period, also using quarterly data. This rate is even lower, indicating a somewhat faster adjustment to the desired level in Germany than in the United States.

Moreover, splitting the time period for Germany into two subperiods yields coefficients $l = 0.846$ for 1972–78 and $l = 0.829$ for 1979–85; the difference between the two periods is not statistically significant.[5] More revealing is an equation in which the number of employees E is replaced by person-hours (i.e., the product of the number of employees and average working time per employee). While Hamermesh (1988) estimates only a minor reduction of the coefficient for such a version ($l = 0.932$), the coefficient for Germany is now $l = 0.483$. Whatever the merits of such an exercise, it is not obvious that employers in

[4]See Jackman, Layard, and Pissarides 1989.
[5]See Franz 1989 for details.

Germany face greater difficulties in adjusting their work force compared with employers in the United States. The contrast is more pronounced if the flexibility in adjusting working time via short time or overtime work is taken into account. The reasons for higher unemployment must therefore be sought in other quarters. Here our judgment is in agreement with the views expressed by the other contributors to this volume who deal with the German situation.

13

Employment Security and Deregulation: The West German Experience

Christoph F. Buechtemann

I n Germany, as in most other European countries, employment security regulations have come under increasing attack since the early 1980s by business
associations' representatives, economists, and legal experts. Under the traumatic impression of costly work force reductions in the wake of the oil price
recessions of 1974–75 and 1981–82 and in the face of growing economic uncertainties, legal employment protection regulations and collectively bargained job
security provisions have come to be widely regarded as institutional rigidities
hampering work force adjustment, increasing fixed labor costs, reducing the
allocative efficiency of labor markets, and thus accounting, at least in part, for
persistently high levels of unemployment and sluggish employment growth (see
Long and Siebert 1983; Soltwedel 1984; Dichmann 1988; Schellhaass 1990;
Soltwedel et al. 1990:134ff.). Consequently, many policy advisers have advocated
a relaxation, if not partial abolition, of existing legal layoff and dismissal restraints
as a way to combat high unemployment and stimulate job creation (see Reuter
1985; Kronberger Kreis 1986; Walter 1988; Sachverstaendigenrat 1990). Put
simply, the arguments of the proponents of a deregulation of employment security
provisions rest on two underlying assumptions:

The first assumption is that both statutory and collectively bargained employment protection regulations have a strong *genuine* impact on firms' adjustment
behavior and employment decisions. This assumption reflects a view of employment security provisions as exogenously imposed institutional constraints that are
more or less incompatible with microeconomic efficiency.[1]

---

[1] Schotter (1986:116ff.) has called this the "rules view" of institutions, as opposed to the
"behavioral view," which looks at social institutions "not as sets of predesigned rules but rather as
unplanned and unintended regularities of social behavior (social conventions) that emerge 'organ-
ically'" (118).

The second assumption is that the facilitation of external work force adjustments through hiring and firing, as postulated under the American employment-at-will doctrine, would consequently increase the allocative efficiency of labor markets. This assumption reveals an archaic conception of the functioning of labor markets as in principle akin to that of the classical spot-market type.[2]

Despite the absence of empirical evidence to support either of these notions and the policy recommendations derived from them, many European governments during the 1980s relaxed legal restrictions on layoff and dismissals and/or widened existing "loopholes" within the established system of employment security provisions (e.g., by facilitating the conclusion of fixed-term contracts or reducing legal barriers toward the use of labor supplied by temporary work agencies) (see Emerson 1988a; OECD 1989a). In (West) Germany this step was taken with the 1985 Employment Promotion Act (EPA), which in addition to introducing new regulations in the area of part-time work and job sharing, brought a relaxation of employment protection regulations for newly established small enterprises,[3] extended maximum periods for the use of agency workers,[4] and reduced legal restrictions on the conclusion of fixed-term contracts.[5] Among these legal changes, the relaxation of legal restraints on the conclusion of fixed-term contracts certainly has been the most important and most controversial new regulation enacted by the EPA. By this measure, which after an initial experimental period (1985–89) was prolonged for another six years until the end of 1995, the government hoped to exert a positive impact on firms' hiring decisions in the face of persisting uncertainties about future labor demand.

In the following section of this paper I will give a brief overview of the scope and range of employment security regulations in Germany and review the available empirical evidence with regard to their allegedly detrimental impact on firms' work force adjustment and hiring decisions. I then present some core findings of an empirical evaluation of the new temporary work regulations enacted by the

[2]The assumption that only external labor market transactions are efficient underlies large parts of the labor economics literature; it implies that "although market outcomes may be judged as distributionally unsatisfactory, any governmental intervention in this market is likely to decrease rather than to enhance efficiency" (Cohen and Wachter 1989:245).

[3]The EPA partly exempted such enterprises from the obligation to set up a social plan in the case of major work force reductions or production reorganizations and changed the mode of calculation of the minimum number of employees required for the application of the Dismissal Protection Act (*Kuendigungsschutzgesetz*) of 1951.

[4]The maximum period for individual missions under the Agency Workers Act (*Arbeitnehmerueberlassungsgesetz*) was extended from three to six months.

[5]The legislative changes introduced by the EPA concerning the conclusion of fixed-term contracts are described in more detail later in this paper. In addition to the new regulations brought by the EPA, the Federal government in 1985–86 introduced further legislative changes relaxing dismissal protection for disabled workers (*Schwerbehindertengesetz*) and reducing restrictions on the conclusion of temporary work contracts in universities and other publicly funded research institutions (*Gesetz ueber befristete Arbeitsvertraege mit wissenschaftlichem Personal an Hochschulen und Forschungseinrichtungen*).

EPA. I conclude with a summary of the results and some policy conclusions with regard to the competitive challenges confronting industrial countries in the decade ahead.

Range and Impact of Employment Protection in West Germany

The Legal Framework

From an international comparative perspective, (West) Germany certainly has a highly elaborate system of layoff and dismissal restraints.[6] Judging by the results of a survey by the International Organization of Employers (IOE 1985, quoted in Emerson 1988a:791) Germany ranks second (behind France) among those European countries in which the legal obstacles to the termination of employment contracts are deemed "fundamental."

Unlike others European countries, such as Italy and the United Kingdom, where statutory employment protection was introduced in the 1960s and 1970s, the foundations of the German system of employment protection were laid as early as the 1920s. During this formative decade of German labor law, the works councils were first granted limited co-determination rights in cases of unjustified and unduly harsh dismissals (1920); firms were obliged to introduce short-time working (work sharing) to prevent or at least "stretch" major work force reductions and plant closings (1920–23); special statutory prenotification periods were introduced for older white-collar employees (1926); and special laws were enacted to protect handicapped workers as well as pregnant women against ordinary job dismissals (1920–1927). Significantly, the introduction of these rudimentary employment security regulations coincided with the establishment of Germany's first unified system of mandatory unemployment insurance (see Syrup 1957:176ff.; Preller 1978:349ff.).

This basic framework of employment security was considerably extended and supplemented by collective agreements during the 1950s, 1960s, and 1970s (for details, see Weller 1969; Lutz 1987:219ff.; Buechtemann and Stille 1992). Today, employment protection in Germany is regulated by a comprehensive system of laws, court decisions, and collective agreements that covers the overwhelming majority of the labor force.

By law, all except disciplinary (or "extraordinary") dismissals and layoffs generally require advance notification, the periods of which increase with seniority and have been frequently extended by collective agreements (see Bispinck 1990). The core regulations of German dismissal protection are laid down in the Dismissal Protection Act of 1951 (as amended in 1969), which covers all workers permanently employed for more than six months in establishments with at

---

[6]For a more detailed account, see Sengenberger 1982; Oechsler 1988; Birk, chap. 10.

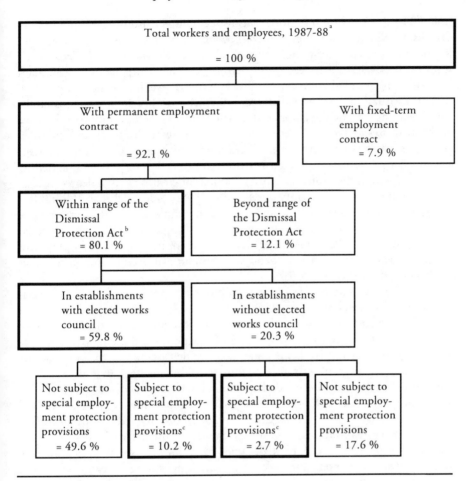

Total workers and employees, 1987-88[a]

= 100 %

With permanent employment contract

= 92.1 %

With fixed-term employment contract

= 7.9 %

Within range of the Dismissal Protection Act[b]
= 80.1 %

Beyond range of the Dismissal Protection Act
= 12.1 %

In establishments with elected works council
= 59.8 %

In establishments without elected works council
= 20.3 %

Not subject to special employment protection provisions
= 49.6 %

Subject to special employment protection provisions[c]
= 10.2 %

Subject to special employment protection provisions[c]
= 2.7 %

Not subject to special employment protection provisions
= 17.6 %

Source: Representative WZB telephone survey, 1987–88.

[a] Excluding public servants, military personnel, and apprentices (n = 4,930).

[b] Employed in establishments with at least six workers on a regular basis and with tenure exceeding six months.

[c] Forty-five years or older with at least twenty years of tenure with present employer or disabled under the Disabled Workers Act (Schwerbehindertengesetz).

Figure 13-1. Range of Employment Protection Provisions in the Federal Republic of Germany, 1987–88

least six employees,[7] roughly 80 percent of the total dependent work force (see fig. 13–1). Under the act, all dismissals and layoffs must be grounded in *"just*

[7]Apprentices and marginal workers whose weekly working time does not exceed ten hours are not counted. These groups were excluded from the count by the Employment Promotion Act, thus increasing the number of small establishments not covered by statutory dismissal protection.

cause."[8] In the case of job terminations for economic reasons, just cause implies that dismissals could not be prevented through alternative measures, such as work sharing or internal reassignment and retraining of the workers affected. In the case of collective layoffs for economic reasons, the law further requires redundant workers to be selected according to "social criteria," such as seniority, personal economic situation, and individual reemployment prospects. Further restrictions have been imposed by the labor courts, which during the past four decades have established strict standards, especially for individual dismissals on personal grounds such as malperformance, misconduct, bad health, and frequent absenteeism, that go far beyond the basic dismissal protection originally intended by the legislator and, therefore, have been blamed for creating a high degree of legal unpredictability and uncertainty (see Ruethers 1986; Soltwedel et al. 1990:28ff.). As a rule, both law and court decisions require the employer to make all reasonable efforts to prevent job terminations. In the case of unjustified dismissals or violations of procedural rules, the worker may sue for continuation of the employment relationship or for monetary compensation through a labor court (for more details on this point, see Birk, chap. 10).

In addition to statutory regulation, employment protection in Germany has a strong collective component. Under the amended Works Constitution Act of 1972, all layoffs and dismissals have to be explicitly or implicitly approved by the firm's works council. In the case of disapproval, the employment relationship continues until a labor court has decided on the justification of the dismissal. The range of this rule is illustrated by the fact that in 1987–88 roughly 60 percent of the dependent labor force[9] qualified for statutory employment protection and were employed in establishments with an elected works council (see 13–1). In the case of major work force reductions (as during major work reorganizations), the works council is further entitled to demand the negotiation of a social plan designed to minimize social and economic hardships for the workers affected, for example, by setting up early retirement schemes or granting seniority-graded severance payments.[10] Finally, if unavoidable collective layoffs exceed a certain proportion (6 to 10 percent) of the firm's work force, the firm must notify the local labor office, which may delay them for up to a month and mandate the introduction of short-time working in the meantime.

---

[8]Accepted reasons for "ordinary" dismissals are misconduct, unsatisfactory work performance, unjustified absence from work, violation of safety regulations, lack of personal capability, or bad health involving long or frequent absenteeism, as well as economic necessity due to lack of demand or technological reorganization. Personal misconduct may also justify an "extraordinary" dismissal; in this case the employee may be fired "at once" (i.e., without the regular pronotification period).

[9]Excluding public servants and apprentices.

[10]The total number of social plans negotiated during a year is not known. The proportion of persons receiving benefits from a social plan among the registered unemployed amounted to roughly 60,000 (3 percent of all unemployed) in September 1984 (see Hemmer 1988:105). The total number of employment terminations involving a social plan can be assumed to be significantly higher (200,000–250,000 per year, or 15–16 percent of all employment terminations).

These general regulations have been supplemented by special protective provisions for certain categories of workers, such as women before and following childbirth, employees on parental leave, severely handicapped workers, drafted employees during compulsory military service, and elected members of the works council. Termination of workers belonging to these categories is limited to extraordinary cases and in most cases is subject to prior approval by local authorities. Collective agreements have furthermore ruled out "ordinary" (i.e., nondisciplinary) dismissals of older workers after they reach a certain age (forty-five to fifty-five years) and minimum tenure (fifteen to twenty years). Such agreements, which originated in the 1960s (see Boehle and Lutz 1974) and were significantly expanded throughout the 1970s, today cover more than 13 percent of the dependent work force or roughly 50 percent of all workers aged forty-five and older (see Warnken and Ronning 1990). Adding tenured (i.e., lifetime) civil servants, handicapped workers, as well as persons on parental or military leave, the total number of workers enjoying more or less absolute employment protection in (West) Germany amounts to an estimated 4.8 million, or 23 percent of the country's total dependent workforce (see fig. 13–1).

The picture is incomplete without mentioning a series of supporting measures and provisions, such as Germany's comprehensive insurance-based work-sharing scheme, which greatly reduces workers' earnings losses from short-time work[11] and which thus has to be seen as an important public subsidy for firms' labor hoarding.

Germany's various public early retirement schemes, which partly date back to the 1950s but were significantly expanded during the 1970s and 1980s, have created selective "outlets," offering a socially acceptable way around the relatively strict employment safeguards that apply to the majority of older workers.

Last but not least, firms have been permitted to resort to temporary help supplied by temporary work agencies or to hire workers on fixed-term contracts, provided that labor demand is temporary in nature and the contracts do not exceed legally defined maximum periods.[12]

The range of these supporting measures and regulations can be illustrated by the following data:

Even during the economically prosperous period 1985–87, roughly 11 percent of all private firms, employing 20 percent of all workers in the private sector, had temporarily introduced work sharing involving short-time wage compensation out of the unemployment insurance fund.[13]

During the same period almost one out of five (19 percent) of all job termi-

---

[11]In the case of a 20 percent (40 percent) reduction in weekly working time, workers on work-sharing schedules still achieve on average 96.5 percent (86.4 percent) of their previous full-time net earnings because of short-time working compensation (see Flechsenhaar 1980:97ff).

[12]For a more detailed description of German temporary work regulations, see Buechtemann and Quack 1989.

[13]During the recession year 1975, not less than 46 percent of all firms in the manufacturing sector employing fifty or more workers had short-time working schedules (Friedrich and Spitznagel 1981:27).

nations in the private sector were due to the expiration of a fixed-term employment contract.[14]

One out of three workers retiring at the age of fifty-five or older between 1984 and 1987 did so through special early retirement schemes.[15]

Given the complexity and wide range of employment protection regulations in Germany, it seems highly plausible to assume that both labor law and collective agreements, though "cushioned" by selective exemptions (e.g., small firms) and supportive measures (e.g., early retirement schemes), have indeed imposed substantial restrictions on firms' freedom to dismiss workers for economic as well as noneconomic reasons. From the viewpoint that external work force adjustments necessarily imply a higher degree of adjustment efficiency, it would seem only logical to infer that the widening of existing loopholes within this tightly knit system of employment security safeguards would have a significant impact on firms' firing and hiring decisions. This assumption has been guiding not only the hopes of the proponents of deregulation but, ironically, the fears of its critics, particularly the unions, as well.

Impact of Employment Security Regulations on Personnel Policies

Employment stability and worker turnover. In the current flexibility debate, employment security provisions have been frequently cited as an important factor accounting for the prevalence of long-term job attachments and relatively long average tenures in (West) Germany as compared to other OECD countries, especially the United States (see Schmidt 1985; OECD 1986b). In fact, in the postrecession year 1985, close to two-thirds (65 percent) of all workers in Germany had been continuously employed with their current employer for more than five years versus 40 percent in the United States, 58 percent in France, and 52 percent in the United Kingdom. Forty-two percent in Germany had been with their current employer for more than ten years. Likewise, job retention rates in Germany were found to be significantly higher than in the United States, particularly among younger age groups (see Bellmann and Schasse 1988; Schasse 1991), revealing an overall high degree of job stability that comes close to that prevailing in Japan (see Hashimoto 1990a:249ff.).

In seeming contradiction to these findings, other studies have found the Ger-

---

[14]Unlike the situation in other European countries such as France or the United Kingdom, the supply of temporary workers through licensed temporary work agencies under the 1972 Agency Workers Act (*Arbeitnehmerueberlassungsgesetz*) has played only a minor role in the German labor market. Even at its peak in 1989, the total number of persons hired from temporary work agencies did not exceed 94,000 or 0.36 percent of the total dependent work force; not more than 3 to 4 percent of all job terminations are due to the end of "missions" of agency workers (see Buechtemann and Quack 1989).

[15]Not counting premature exits into retirement due to invalidity (see Buechtemann and Stille 1992).

man labor market to be relatively fluid in terms of total worker turnover and annual job separation rates. Indeed, official social security statistics show roughly 5.5 million job accessions and almost the same number of job separations each year, equaling annual hiring and job separation rates of 27 and 29 percent respectively (1988),[16] which appear to be inconsistent with the popular notion of Eurosclerosis (Giersch 1985).

The emerging picture of a relatively high degree of external labor mobility and worker turnover is reaffirmed by the results of a representative survey of establishments in the private sector (see Buechtemann and Hoeland 1989:96ff.). Over the two-year period May 1985 to April 1987, the 2,392 firms investigated reported a total of 32,000 new hires and 31,000 job terminations, equaling an annual hiring separation rate of roughly 13 percent of the average stock of workers employed at the beginning of the observation period.[17] The overwhelming majority (83 percent) of all job terminations and new hires reported were indeed accounted for by mere worker turnover that did not involve any lasting net changes in the size of the firms' work forces.

At first sight, high employment stability coupled with high worker turnover seems puzzling, but a closer look at the firm-level data provides an explanation. Worker turnover is highly concentrated in a small minority of high-turnover firms. Whereas the majority (62 percent) of firms in the German private sector are characterized by highly stable work forces with low worker turnover that averaged no more than 3.7 percent of the work force per year, half of all job terminations and new hires were accounted for by only 19 percent of all firms in the private sector, whose average annual worker turnover amounted to 27 percent. The latter group of high-turnover firms consisted largely of small and medium-sized enterprises in construction, food processing, and rather low-skill service industries (hotel and catering; transportation; body care and cleaning services) and thus presents a strong contrast to the high degree of job stability found especially in the expanding mechanical engineering and higher-skill service industries.[18] This suggests that industry and firm-specific characteristics (i.e., endogenous factors) rather than merely institutional factors account for the observed high degree of job stability on the one hand and the high worker turnover among a minority of firms on the other hand. The findings indicate that aggregate turnover data are hardly adequate for measuring labor market flexibility; nor do such data allow any conclusions with regard to the relative impact of employment security regulations.

[16]Excluding apprenticeship contracts but including accessions and terminations due to business setups and firm closings. For a detailed analysis on the basis of longitudinal data, see Cramer 1986 and Cramer and Koller 1988.

[17]These rates are significantly lower than those reported by the Federal Employment Agency in that they do not include hirings and job terminations within the public service, in agriculture and forestry, or in private establishments with less than five employees and do not include job accessions and terminations in the course of business setups and closings.

[18]The latter include banking and insurance, legal services, economic consulting, business services, health care, and education.

Firms' use of dismissals and layoffs. The firm-level data collected in our survey also contain information about the mode of job separation. As shown in table 13–1, dismissals accounted for no more than 26 percent of all reported job separations by the firms in our survey. The majority of job separations were accounted for by voluntary quits (39 percent), the expiration of fixed-term employment or apprenticeship contracts (25 percent), and job terminations by mutual agreement or on reaching early or regular retirement age (10 percent). Annual dismissal rates,[19] on average, do not exceed 3.5 percent of the work force and thus can be seen to play only a minor part in total worker turnover. Table 13–1 further shows that even among firms with a declining work force over the observation period, the average share of dismissals in all job separations remained well under 30 percent and the annual dismissal rate did not exceed 8 percent of the work force. These findings are consistent with previous studies that unanimously found a strong tendency among German firms to avoid layoffs in economic downturns as long as possible and to exhaust all other measures of "soft" work force reduction (hours adjustment, natural attrition, worker buyouts, early retirement) before resorting to layoffs (for a review, see Hotz-Hart 1989; Pick 1988).

As in the case of total worker turnover, layoffs and dismissals were strongly concentrated among a small minority of firms adhering to an intensive hire-and-fire personnel policy. Close to half of all involuntary job terminations were accounted for by no more than 13 percent of all firms in the private sector. The annual dismissal rate of these firms amounted to some 25 percent of their work force compared to only 0.8 percent among the remaining 87 percent of all firms. The small group of hire-and-fire firms again largely consisted of small establishments in the construction and rather low-skill service industries and were characterized by a high proportion of unskilled and semiskilled workers among their work force, a relatively high share of labor costs in total production costs, and major fluctuations in business activity because of volatile product demand and irregular orders. It is worth noting that it was by no means exclusively the shrinking firms with declining work forces that adhered to a pattern of adjustment involving frequent dismissals. In fact, the majority (55 percent) of the hire-and-fire firms showed stable or even growing employment levels during the observation period. Equally worth noting, the hire-and-fire firms complained much more frequently (59 percent) than the remaining firms (31 percent) about difficulties in attracting adequate job applicants. This indicates that, from the firms' point of view at least, adjustment through massive external worker turnover does not necessarily involve a higher degree of adjustment efficiency (see fig. 13–2).

The mere existence of a minority of firms that adhere to an intensive hire-and-fire policy is certainly apt to challenge the notion that more or less universally applying employment security provisions has made external work force adjustments through dismissals prohibitively costly in Germany.[20] This, in turn, raises

---

[19]That is, dismissals and layoffs as a percentage of all workers employed at the beginning of the period.

[20]Eighty-six percent of the hire-and-fire firms were employing six or more workers and thus fell into the range of statutory employment protection under the Dismissal Protection Act.

TABLE 13-1. *Stock of Employees, Hires, and Job Separations in Private Sector Firms, According to the Development of the Total Work Force, May 1985–April 1987*

	All firms in the private sector (n = 2,004)	Firms with strongly increasing work force (> 15%) (n = 335)	Firms with slightly increasing work force (<15%) (n = 423)	Firms with stable work force (+/–1%) (n = 541)	Firms with slightly declining work force (< 15%) (n = 449)	Firms with strongly declining work force (> 15%) (n = 253)	Total declining firms (> 1%) (n = 702)
Total number of workers employed, May 1985	94,461	8,515	30,124	14,585	33,196	8,040	41,236
Total number of hires, May 1985–April 1987	25,457 (=100%)	5,895 (=100%)	9,177 (=100%)	2,848 (=100%)	5,956 (=100%)	1,538 (=100%)	7,494 (=100%)
Total number of separations, May 1985–April 1987	24,994 (=100%)	3,271 (=100%)	7,208 (=100%)	2,843 (=100%)	7,863 (=100%)	3,804 (=100%)	11,667 (=100%)
Dismissal by employer	26.1%	35.8%	18.2%	26.2%	22.6%	40.6%	28.5%
End of apprenticeship contract	4.7%	2.1%	3.1%	3.8%	5.8%	7.9%	4.9%
End of fixed-term contract	20.0%	19.9%	31.5%	15.2%	18.1%	6.5%	10.8%
Voluntary quits	38.9%	36.1%	39.3%	45.7%	39.2%	34.7%	28.5%
Retirements and deaths	10.3%	6.7%	8.2%	9.0%	14.2%	10.2%	9.7%
Annual dismissal rate	3.5%	6.8%	2.2%	2.6%	2.7%	9.6%	8.0%

Source: Buechtemann and Hoeland 1989:100 (representative firm survey in the private sector, April–June 1987).

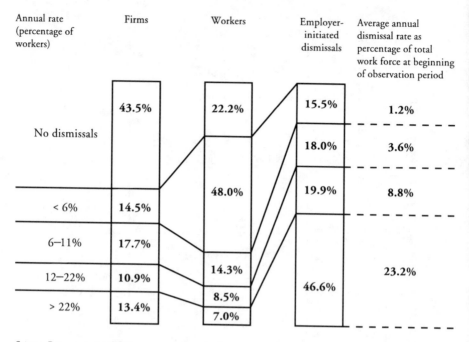

Source: Representative WZB company survey in the private sector, 1987 (n = 2,392).

FIGURE 13-2. *Worker Dismissals in the Private Sector of the Federal Republic of Germany, May 1985 to April 1987*

doubts as to whether the high degree of employment stability observed for the vast majority of firms in the private sector can be attributed to exogenously imposed institutional layoff and dismissal restraints.

   Impact of dismissal protection on firms' firing and hiring behavior. Skepticism as to whether exogenously imposed employment security regulations have had a strong genuine impact on firms' manpower policies is further suggested by the results of earlier research that focused on the issue in greater detail. According to this evidence, actual prenotification periods of dismissals and layoffs in 1978, on average, lasted no more than thirty-eight days (twenty-four days for blue-collar workers but eighty-three days for white-collar employees) (Falke 1983). Voluntary or mandatory severance payments (including those negotiated under a social plan)[21] were involved in only 8 percent of all involuntary job terminations

---

[21]Severance payments in the context of a social plan negotiated under the Works Constitution Act accounted for nearly half (47 percent) of all cases of severance payments or 3.8 percent of all dismissals in private industry (see Falke et al. 1981:132ff.). The average amount of severance payments under a social plan tend to be higher than those paid in individual dismissals not involving a social plan. According to Hemmer (1988), severance payments in the context of a social plan exceeded DM 10,000 per worker in almost 60 percent of the cases investigated over the period 1980–85.

and on average amounted to no more than two monthly gross wages, the median payment hardly exceeding one month's gross earnings (Falke et al. 1981:132ff.).

No more than 3.3 percent of all dismissals and layoffs intended by private sector managers in 1978 (8 percent of all dismissals and layoffs in firms with an elected works council) were, in fact, disapproved of by the works council (see Hoeland 1983).

Only a small proportion (8 to 9 percent) of all involuntary terminations actually end up in a labor court.[22] The majority of successful suits result in mere financial compensation rather than actual reinstatement,[23] which, on average, amounted in 1978 to no more than 0.56 percent of a monthly gross wage per year of seniority (see Falke 1983:37ff.).

The actual costs of firing workers appear to be considerably lower than might be inferred from merely looking at the tightly knit regulatory framework governing dismissals in Germany.

The low costs involved in actual dismissal cases may, however, reflect mere selection effects, that is, that firms abstain from dismissals in those cases in which the costs imposed by legal or collectively bargained employment security regulations would exceed certain tolerable thresholds (see also Gavin 1986). In this case the actual direct dismissal costs would grossly underscore the total economic costs of dismissal protection. Let us remember that the genuine intention of dismissal laws is to prevent rather than to merely "tax" dismissals. Both the actual dismissal behavior of firms and the direct costs involved in these cases may therefore tell only part of the story.

At first sight the assumption that job security regulations exert a deterrent impact on firms' dismissal decisions appears to be supported by the results of a longitudinal survey of newly hired workers. As summarized in table 13–2, the actual probability of involuntary job loss appears to be inversely related to the degree of legal employment protection. The highest risk of job loss is observed for workers hired on fixed-term contracts that expire without any notice by the employer, followed by workers hired on a permanent basis in small firms with less than six employees (i.e., outside the range of statutory dismissal protection under the Dismissal Protection Act). More than one out of four (26.6 percent) of the former and one out of eight (13 percent) of the latter actually lost their jobs involuntarily during the six-month period following the initial survey. A significantly lower risk of job loss is shown for workers within the range of statutory employment protection. No more than four out of one hundred permanently hired workers with a tenure exceeding six months and in firms employing six or more workers actually experienced job loss during the subsequent six-month period. This share is once again much lower (1.5 percent) among permanently hired workers in establishments with an elected works council. As such, however,

---

[22] Calculated on the basis of data on annual dismissal cases supplied by the Federal Ministry of Employment and Social Affairs.

[23] Actual reinstatement in the job occurred in not even 0.4 percent of all litigation cases or only 0.03 percent of all dismissals in 1978 (see Falke et al. 1981:959ff.).

TABLE 13-2. *Job Separation Rates of Newly Hired Workers and Employees in the Federal Republic of Germany, 1987–88*

Type of employment at the time of the initial survey	Number of cases (weighted)	Termination by the employer[a]	Voluntary quits	Continuously employed with same employer
		During six months following the initial survey		
Total newly hired workers[b]	3,077	11.3%	12.6%	76.1%
Hired on fixed-term contract	816	26.6%	16.6%	56.8%
Hired on permanent contract	2,261	5.8%	11.2%	83.0%
In firms with fewer than six employees	318	12.9%	13.0%	74.1%
In firms with six or more employees	1,943	4.3%	10.3%	85.4%
With tenure exceeding six months	1,162	4.1%	8.2%	87.7%
In firms with an elected works council	662	1.5%	4.8%	93.7%

Source: Representative WZB Longitudinal Survey of Workers and Job Seekers, 1987–88.
[a]Including expiration of fixed-term contracts.
[b]With tenure not exceeding two years at the time of the initial survey.

these data do not allow any conclusion with respect to the genuine impact of employment protection in that the differential in job loss probability may be largely explained by other variables such as firm size or the skill level of the jobs involved. Multivariate analyses of the firm survey data reported above have indeed shown that the mere existence of a works council has no statistically significant impact on firms' firing behavior when other variables such as firm size, industry, skill level of the work force, and demand fluctuations are controlled for.

Doubts as to whether employment security regulations have a strong deterrent impact on firms' dismissal behavior are further raised by direct evidence from firm surveys and company case studies. According to these studies, personnel managers—in their own words—have been able to realize almost all intended layoffs and dismissals without incurring major financial and/or legal difficulties. The majority of personnel managers did not perceive statutory employment security regulations to be major obstacles to necessary employment terminations (see Falke et al. 1981:151ff.; Buechtemann and Hoeland 1989:272ff.). This is consistent with studies that have shown labor-hoarding practices in the German manufacturing sector during economic downturns to be motivated primarily by firms' concerns about maintaining their qualified work force and avoiding high search, recruitment, and training costs in the following upswing; that is, by *economic* considerations rather than by *institutional* factors such as the existence of legal or collectively bargained layoff restraints (see Nerb et al. 1977; Friedrich and Spitznagel 1981:30ff.). Similarly, a survey of 186 medium-sized firms conducted in late 1983 (i.e., at the peak of the OPEC II recession) found that, for the majority of the firms, employment security regulations were attributed to have no influence on company decisions (see Kayser and Friede 1984:38).

What is true with regard to *firing* should be all the more true with respect to *hiring*. According to studies carried out in the late 1970s (Falke et al. 1981:156) and the late 1980s (Buechtemann and Hoeland 1989:272ff.), only a small minority (19 percent) of firms, most of which indeed had been recently facing major work force reductions, indicated that employment protection regulations had some impact on their hiring decisions. If such an impact was mentioned, in most cases it referred to the *quality* of their new recruits rather than to the *number* of new hires. Consistent with this, other studies have found that it is primarily lack of product demand that most German firms perceived to be the essential barrier to increasing their work forces, whereas institutional factors, such as legal layoff and dismissal restraints, seemed to play only a subordinate role in firms' hiring decisions (see Nerb 1978:77ff.; Koenig and Zimmermann 1985). In fact, in a Europeanwide survey of manufacturing firms carried out in 1985 and replicated in 1989, "insufficient flexibility in hiring and shedding labor" was mentioned by German firms only fifth (after "insufficient demand," "foreign competition," "skill shortages," and "high non-wage labor costs") as a reason for not hiring more workers, whereas, for example, it ranked first in France and Italy (see Nerb 1986:71ff; Hofmann, chap. 25). In Germany, firms do not appear to perceive legal job security regulations as a major constraint on their work force adjustment behavior. The available microevidence thus suggests that the genuine impact of employment security regulations on firms' firing and hiring decisions has been frequently overstated in the current debate on labor market flexibility.

Nor is there firm macroevidence to support the view that employment security regulations have greatly affected firms' work force adjustment behavior. Recent studies using aggregate data for the manufacturing sector (Maurau and Oudinet 1988; Franz 1989; Hotz-Hart 1989) have shown that employment elasticities to variations in industrial output are rather large in Germany and, in fact, come close to those in the United States, thus significantly exceeding the employment elasticities found for France, Italy, and even the United Kingdom, where legal layoff and dismissal barriers are said to be substantially lower than in most other European countries (see Emerson 1988a).

Time-series analyses of ten manufacturing industries in Germany over the period 1963–87 found no evidence of an intertemporal slowdown in work force adjustment that could "support the hypothesis that hiring and firing has become more difficult and that total employment has become more inflexible over time" (Kraft 1988:13). Quite the contrary, in seven out of the ten industries investigated, the speed of work force adjustment had increased compared to the 1960s and early 1970s.

The latter finding is consistent with historical microevidence showing that the majority of German firms were adhering to a personnel strategy of work force stabilization and low external worker turnover during the early 1960s, long before job security regulations were expanded by law, court rulings, and collective agreements (see Lutz and Weltz 1966; Lutz 1987). In this light, the extension of employment security provisions during the late 1960s and 1970s appears to have been largely a mere ex post codification and legal universalization of de facto standards and practices that had previously evolved "endogenously" with the development of internal labor markets in wide parts of the economy (see also Lutz, chap. 26).

Taken together, the empirical evidence largely fails to support the theoretically derived notion that employment protection has had a significant deterrent effect on firms' firing and hiring behavior. The high degree of employment stability observed for the vast majority of German firms in the private sector seems to reflect other than merely institutional factors, such as firms' economic interest in maintaining a qualified, loyal, and highly motivated work force and in avoiding high transaction costs and productivity losses associated with a hire-and-fire strategy. Conversely, the finding that, in the absence of strong institutional dismissal restraints, the majority of firms had a high degree of job stability whereas the finding that the minority of firms adhering to a hire-and-fire strategy had frequent personnel problems, appear to challenge the common notion that adjustment through the external labor market is necessarily optimal in terms of adjustment efficiency. This conclusion, in turn, raises doubts as to whether the promotion of external work force adjustment through the selective relaxation of existing layoff and dismissal restraints is likely to affect vital parameters of firms' personnel policies and thus to have a genuine stimulating impact on job creation.

Impact of Deregulation: The 1985 Employment Promotion Act

Facilitation of Fixed-Term Employment

Fixed-term employment contracts are by no means a new phenomenon in the German labor market. Empirical studies from the 1970s and 1980s show that fixed-term job arrangements have always played an important part in firms' adjustment to variations in business activity and the management of periods of peak demand. Until 1985, however, the Federal Labor Court, in order to avert an evasion of legal dismissal protection regulations, had in a long history of case rulings restricted the conclusion of fixed-term contracts to a set of clearly defined "legitimate" cases, such as seasonal work, replacement of temporarily absent permanent employees, temporary help in periods of peak demand, carrying out of special tasks that are temporary in nature, and employment in the context of trainee programs or public job creation schemes. At the same time, the Federal Labor Court had always strictly ruled out economic uncertainty as a legitimate reason for hiring workers on a temporary basis; in such cases fixed-term contracts would be disallowed and treated as permanent engagements (i.e., involving all legal obligations concerning protection from unfair dismissal).

By the new regulations of the Employment Promotion Act, these restrictions were largely suspended. Through the abolition of the requirement of a legitimate reason for the conclusion of fixed-term contracts up to a maximum duration of eighteen months,[24] the EPA has explicitly legalized fixed-term contracts in cases of uncertainty about future labor demand. In so doing, the government hoped that firms would be induced to hire additional workers rather than pay overtime premia to their core work forces. In fact, the abolition of the requirement of a legitimate reason amounted to a carte blanche for the use of fixed-term contracts in those cases that would have been considered illegal before the EPA, including to prolong the probationary period for newly hired workers beyond statutory limits.

The EPA's new temporary work regulations certainly fall short of recent deregulation measures in other European countries and have to be considered a moderate political compromise between the proponents of a more thorough deregulation of employment protection (see, for example, Kronberger Kreis 1986) and its opponents, headed by the unions. Instead of directly relaxing legal dismissal and layoff restraints as, for example, the French and British governments have done (see Maurau and Hyman, chaps. 19 and 16, respectively), the EPA affects job security only indirectly, by encouraging fixed-term hires that do not require any notice on the fixed date of expiration. This has two important implications with regard to the EPA's potential effects on firms' staffing decisions. First, in that the new temporary work regulations refer primarily to the *hiring* process, they can be assumed to display their strongest momentum in an economic recovery when firms are hiring additional staff; and second, by restricting the maximum duration of contracts concluded under the EPA to eighteen months and excluding the option of a subsequent renewal for another fixed-term period, the new regulations refer to short-term job arrangements only, thus reinforcing rather than weakening the principle of seniority inherent in most employment security provisions. These limitations of the new temporary work legislation must be borne in mind when interpreting the empirical results about the EPA's actual impact on firms' hiring (and firing) decisions reported below.

Use of Fixed-Term Contracts

Despite fears expressed by the unions that the new regulations would initiate an erosion of the hitherto predominant "standard employment relationship," fixed-term work contracts in Germany still account for only a small share of overall employment (1987–88: 7.9 percent).[25] As in most other European coun-

---

[24]Or twenty-four months in the case of newly set-up enterprises employing not more twenty workers.

[25]The empirical evidence reported below is based on a representative survey of 2,392 firms in the private sector, a representative survey of 1,968 placement officers of the Federal Employment Agency, a longitudinal survey of 6,468 employed and unemployed workers, and in-depth case study interviews with personnel managers in 30 manufacturing firms. For a detailed description of the design and findings of the study, see Buechtemann and Hoeland 1989.

TABLE 13-3. *Workers on Fixed-Term Employment Contracts in the Federal Republic of Germany, 1984–88*

	1984 (EC LFSS)	1985 (MZ)	1986 (MZ)	1987 (MZ)	1988 (MZ)
Workers and employees total[a] (in 1,000s)	19,375.1[b]	19,577.6	19,979.8	19,948.7	20,431.0
	= 100%	= 100%	= 100%	= 100%	= 100%
On permanent working contract (including agency workers)	18,461.8[b]	18,224.0	18,423.3	18,612.2	18,992.0
	95.3%	93.2%	92.2%	93.3%	93.0%
On fixed-term contract (including public job creation programs)	765.8[b]	1,080.8	1,230.2	1,105.0	1,193.0
	4.0%[c]	5.6%[c]	6.3%[c]	5.6%[c]	5.8%[c]
Type of employment contract not specified	148.5	272.8	326.3	231.5	367.0
	0.8%	1.4%	1.6%	1.2%	1.2%

Source: Federal Statistical Office; EC Labour Force Sample Survey (LFSS) 1984; *Mikrozensus* (MZ) 1985, 1986, 1987, 1988; special tabulations on behalf of WZB.
[a]Excluding public servants, apprentices, and persons in compulsory military/community service.
[b]Estimate.
[c]Proportion of fixed-term workers among all workers with specification of type of employment.

tries, however, the number of workers in Germany who are employed on a fixed-term basis increased considerably during the 1980s in both absolute and relative terms (1984–88: + 350,000/ + 46 percent; permanent employment: + 442,000/ + 2.4 percent). In fact, more than 44 percent of the total increase in dependent employment between 1984 and 1988 took place in the form of temporary (i.e., fixed-term) jobs (see table 13–3). Contrary to expectations, however, this increase in fixed-term employment occurred largely between 1984 and 1985, *before* the EPA's new regulations came into effect in May 1985. This indicates that the growing number of temporary work arrangements was accounted for by other than merely regulatory factors, such as cyclical variations in the demand for temporary help for coping with peak workloads or structural changes in labor supply and demand (for a discussion of these factors, see Buechtemann and Hoeland 1989:8ff.). The implications of this trend for labor market dynamics become apparent when the perspective is shifted toward labor market *flows.* Under current labor market conditions, more than one-third (36 percent) of all newly hired workers in the private sector start their jobs on fixed-term contracts.[26]

Despite the large proportion of fixed-term engagements among all newly started jobs, fixed-term employment is still largely concentrated in a small proportion of

---

[26]In the public sector this share amounted to more than 50 percent. See Buechtemann and Hoeland 1989:42ff.

all enterprises in the private sector.[27] In fact, two out of three (67 percent) German enterprises in the private sector made no use of fixed-term employment contracts during the first two years after the new regulations of the EPA came into force, although the majority (80 percent) of these firms hired new personnel during the observation period. These *nonuser firms* consisted largely of small and medium-sized enterprises[28] with rather skilled work forces, little fluctuation in product demand, and low worker turnover. The primary reason they gave for not using temporary work contracts was that they were "exclusively interested in stable, long-term employment relationships." While other motives were hardly mentioned at all, this reason was mentioned by 83 percent of the nonusers, representing not less than 50 percent of all enterprises in the private sector.

The remaining third (33 percent) of all private sector firms that did make use of fixed-term contracts can be split into two contrasting subgroups according to the intensity of their use of fixed-term contracts. More than half of these firms (or 18 percent of all firms in the private sector) could be classified as *moderate users* of fixed-term contracts; that is, the large majority (74 percent) of their new recruits were still hired on a permanent basis. These firms were predominantly medium-sized and larger enterprises in the manufacturing sector employing an average of 121 workers and accounting for about 40 percent of all new hires in private industry. They were further characterized by a relatively skilled work force,[29] and, on average, showed a clear trend toward expansion of personnel over the period May 1985 to April 1987.

The remaining 15 percent of private sector firms can be classified as *intensive users;* on average they hired more than 74 percent of their new recruits on a fixed-term basis and thus accounted for more than 70 percent of all fixed-term contracts concluded in private industry. This small group of intensive users consisted largely of smaller enterprises[30] characterized by relatively strong fluctuations in product demand due to irregular orders,[31] high worker turnover, a relatively high share of wage costs in total production costs, a rather low-skilled work force, and a clearly negative trend in overall employment during the observation period (see fig. 13–3).

Fixed-term job arrangements are thus highly concentrated in a small group of firms making substantial use of them. Moreover, fixed-term contracts are strongly concentrated within certain job categories. As predicted by human capital theory (see Abraham 1988), the majority (70 percent) of temporary jobs in the private

---

[27]The following results relate to the use of fixed-term employment contracts in the private sector only (excluding agriculture and forestry).

[28]On average, they employed twenty-three workers at the time of the survey.

[29]More than two-thirds (67.2 percent) of their work forces consisted of skilled workers and employees.

[30]Ninety percent did not employ more than fifty workers; on average, these firms employed sixty-nine workers at the time of the survey.

[31]Seasonal workload was mentioned by only a minority of these firms as a reason for fluctuations in business activity.

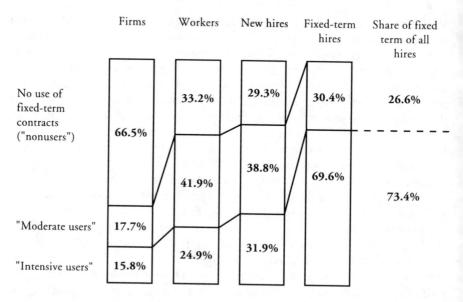

Source: Representative WZB company survey in the private sector, 1987 (n = 2.392).

FIGURE 13-3. Use of Fixed-Term Contracts by Firms in the Private Sector of the Federal Republic of Germany, May 1985 to April 1987

sector were found to require neither vocational skills nor any training on the job. Whereas skilled workers in most cases (80 percent) are still hired on a permanent basis, reflecting firms' interest in keeping these workers for longer periods and avoiding premature quits, unskilled workers have a less than 50 percent chance of being given a permanent contract under current labor market conditions.

The findings reported so far refer to total fixed-term employment independent of its legal basis and therefore do not permit any conclusions regarding changes in recruitment behavior due to the new regulations of the EPA. As expected, the evidence shows that since 1985 the majority (78 percent) of user firms actually intensified their use of fixed-term hires (26 percent) or used fixed-term contracts for the first time (52 percent). The large part of the overall increase in fixed-term employment, however, was in firms that had used fixed-term contracts before 1985. Likewise, in those firms that *intensified* their use of or used fixed-term contracts *for the first time* since the EPA, the change in recruitment behavior was accounted for by an array of heterogeneous factors, such as cyclically growing demand for temporary help, new working time regimes, and growing variations in business activity due to a reduction in inventories and an increase in production to order. Among these factors, the legal facilitation of fixed-term contracts through the EPA has, at most, played a subordinate role.

The importance of cyclical and structural rather than regulatory factors in the recent increase in temporary job arrangements is further affirmed by the type of fixed-term contracts concluded by private sector firms. Of these contracts, 93 percent conformed to the rules and criteria set up for fixed-term contracts by the Federal Labor Court long before the EPA came into force. In other words, most of these contracts were covered by one of the legitimate reasons defined by the rulings of the labor courts (85 percent) and/or did not exceed a maximum duration of six months (70 percent), up to which fixed-term contracts had always been legal without any further restrictions. In total, only 7 percent of all fixed-term contracts, accounting for less than 2 percent of all new hires in the private sector, did not conform to these criteria and therefore have to be considered genuine contracts concluded under the new regulations of the EPA. Again, these genuine contracts were concentrated in a small minority of not more than 4 percent of all firms, employing hardly 10 percent of all workers in the private sector. In contrast to the majority of user firms, these firms consisted largely of medium-sized and larger enterprises in rather low-skilled service industries, including retail,[32] that reported little variation in business activity but a high degree of uncertainty about future labor demand. In most cases these firms, which on average hired 60 percent of all their new recruits on a fixed-term basis, already made substantial use of fixed-term appointments before the EPA.

Despite intensive government propaganda extolling the benefits of the new regulations, the overwhelming majority (96 percent) of firms in the private sector have obviously ignored the additional options offered by the EPA, primarily because they were "exclusively interested in long-term employment relationships." Evidently most firms do not consider external work force adjustment through hiring and firing superior in terms of efficiency to other (internal or external) forms of adjustment. Only at first sight does this conclusion appear to be contradicted by the finding that, according to the personnel managers in the firms surveyed, about one-quarter (26 percent) of all fixed-term employment contracts in the private sector had been formally concluded with explicit reference to the new regulations of the EPA. Even in those firms that had hired personnel on a fixed-term basis with explicit reference to the EPA, 90 percent of all fixed-term appointments were found to be covered by one of the traditionally accepted legitimate reasons and/or did not exceed six months in duration (i.e., conformed with the more restrictive regulations in force before the EPA). The reason these firms nevertheless explicitly referred to the EPA when concluding "traditional" fixed-term contracts has to be seen primarily in the EPA's simplification of contractual procedures (i.e., no requirement of a "legitimate reason" to be mentioned in the contract) and the ensuing reduction in legal uncertainty (no arbitration risks) (see Buechtemann and Kraft 1992). Indeed, both the simplification of contractual procedures and the reduction of firms' legal uncertainty involved with the judge-made law that characterized the "old regime" must be considered the primary effects of the EPA (see Buechtemann and Hoeland 1989:239ff.).

That firms have largely ignored the impulse intended by the EPA is further highlighted by their responses regarding their motives for using the new temporary

---

[32]This category again includes hotels, catering, transportation, cleaning, body care, and personal services other than health care and education.

work regulations. The prime motive for concluding fixed-term contracts under the EPA has clearly been shown to be the possibility of optimizing on-the-job screening of newly hired workers without facing dismissal restrictions in the case of lack of ability or weak performance. This motive was classified as "very important" by more than one-third (39 percent) of all firms hiring with explicit reference to the EPA and by roughly half (48 percent) of all firms making genuine use of the extended options provided by the EPA, reflecting an overall increase in skill requirements and growing choosiness with regard to the skill level of job applicants.[33] The high importance attached to prolonged worker screening is further shown by the fact that the majority (55–56 percent) of workers hired under the EPA were given a permanent contract by their firms on the expiration of their fixed term, compared to only 25 percent of those hired for a fixed term under the "old regime" (see Buechtemann and Hoeland 1989:331ff.).

By contrast, the ability to adapt labor more flexibly to variations in business activity appears to be of only secondary importance from the firms' point of view. This motive, which has been at the core of the arguments put forward by the proponents of deregulation, was considered "very important" by only one in four (25 percent) firms making explicit use of the EPA and not even one in six (16 percent) firms concluding genuine EPA contracts. The latter, in fact, accounted for not more than 0.6 percent of all firms in the private sector. The widely shared assumption that firms would use the new options opened by the EPA to resort to a hire-and-fire strategy of intensified external workforce adjustment appears to have little basis in reality.[34] Most firms evidently do not share the orthodox notion that an increase in external labor turnover is likely to increase adjustment efficiency, once again indicating that factors other than dismissal protection legislation must account for the observed prevalence of long-term employment relationships in Germany.[35]

A similar picture emerges with respect to the political "calculus" of substituting additional fixed-term hires from the external labor market for overtime work by the core work force. The motive of reducing overtime hours of the stably employed work force by hiring additional workers on a fixed-term basis was deemed "very important" by only 16.5 percent of the firms hiring temporary workers with explicit reference to the EPA and by only 10 percent of the firms making genuine use of the new regulations, the latter amounting to a mere 0.4 percent of all firms in the private sector. Consistent with both the results of previous research for (West) Germany (see Weidinger and Hoff 1984; Brinkmann et al. 1986:42ff.) and theoretical assumptions proposed by Ehrenberg and Schumann (1982:37ff.), the corridor within which firms are capable and willing to substitute additional

---

[33]That employers have intensified their screening endeavors with respect to occupational and social skills was reaffirmed by the answers given by the 1,968 placement officers surveyed in the context of the same study. See Buechtemann 1989b.

[34]For a similar conclusion with respect to the prolongation of the waiting period for protection against unfair dismissal in the United Kingdom, see Evans et al. 1985:62.

[35]For a similar conclusion with respect to the United Kingdom in the late 1970s, see Daniel and Stilgoe 1978.

workers for hours appears to be relatively narrow. This, of course, has important implications with regard to the employment effects attributable to the EPA.

Employment Impact of the EPA

The starting point for assessing the immediate employment impact of the EPA's new temporary work regulations were again those 7 percent of all fixed-term contracts that we have referred to as *genuine* EPA contracts. Of these roughly 110,000 fixed-term contracts concluded in the private sector each year,[36] only about one in five (21.7 percent or 25,000 per year) were in fact classified by the firms as "additional" hires that would probably not have occurred without the new regulations of the EPA. Additional fixed-term hires due to the EPA thus account for not more than 1.5 percent of all fixed-term contracts concluded in the private sector or at most 0.5 percent of all new hires in the private sector. Evidently, the legal facilitation of fixed-term contracts has had hardly any seizable impact on employers' willingness to take on additional staff. The remaining 80 percent of all genuine fixed-term hires indeed have to be considered as largely representing "substitution effects": this means that these workers most probably would have otherwise been given a permanent contract from the beginning. Such cases of mere substitution of fixed-term for permanent contracts accounted for roughly 65 percent (or roughly 75,000 per year) of all *genuine* contracts concluded under the EPA during the observation period and thus amounted to almost three times the volume of its direct employment effects in terms of additional hires attributable to the EPA. Still, compared to the hopes and fears expressed by the EPA's proponents and opponents, both effects must be considered rather marginal in that the actual use of the new possibilities provided by the EPA has been limited to a small number of cases (2 percent of all new hires) and to a small minority (4 percent) of all firms in the private sector.

In the medium term, however, the modest additional hiring effects instigated by the EPA tend to be largely offset by a higher speed of work force adjustment, which can be shown to arise from its immediate substitution effects. Over time, workers hired on a fixed-term contract under the EPA were found to face a significantly higher risk of redundancy than workers hired on a permanent basis from the beginning, even when controlling for the skill level of the jobs (see Buechtemann and Hoeland 1989:340ff.; Buechtemann 1989b). This finding is also reflected in the results of our firm survey: whereas, on average, almost two-thirds of all workers hired on the basis of the EPA were subsequently taken into permanent employment by their firms, this share amounted to not more than 20 percent in firms with an overall declining work force during the observation period. Our findings thus lend strong empirical support to the assumption made by Bentolila and Bertola (1990) that a relaxation of legal dismissal restraints, while having hardly any impact on firms' *hiring* behavior, may in fact have a sizeable positive effect on their *firing* decisions. Taking both their intended effects (addi-

---

[36]Data again refer to the first two years after the EPA came into force (May 1985–April 1987).

tional hiring) and their unintended effects (substitution) into consideration, the short-term *net employment impact* of the EPA's new temporary work regulations must be regarded as negligible despite the overall favorable economic climate prevailing during the observation period. In the medium term, however, particularly in the event of an economic downturn, its marginal positive employment impact is most likely to be reversed into a negative one because of the observed substitution effects and the ensuing enhanced redundancy risks for the workers affected.

At least with respect to (West) Germany, the empirical evidence shows the widely shared expectation, that liberating firms from strict employment security regulations through the "loophole" created by the EPA would have a strong genuine impact on their hiring decisions, to be unjustified. This conclusion is consistent with comparable evidence from other countries (see, for example, Bjoerklund and Holmlund 1987; Elbaum et al. 1986; Maurau, chap. 19). At the same time, our findings make clear that a relaxation of legal dismissal restraints may well induce moral hazard effects in terms of more rapid work force reductions in the case of a sudden decline in demand. In the medium and long run, one would therefore expect, on balance, a reduction rather than an increase in total employment because of a "deregulation" of employment security.

"More Employment through Less Employment Security": A Realistic Policy Agenda for the 1990s?

Judging by the empirical evidence, the theoretically derived assumption that legal employment protection regulations have put a severe restraint on firms' staffing policies, preventing them from carrying out necessary work force adjustments, seems to be largely unfounded, at least with respect to the Federal Republic of Germany. Likewise, the experience of the German Employment Promotion Act has so far disproved expectations that a relaxation or partial abolition of institutional layoff and dismissal restraints would have a significant impact on firms' hiring decisions and thereby stimulate job creation.

Instead, the findings presented above have shown (West)Germany to be characterized by a relatively high degree of employment elasticity over time as well as considerable external labor turnover, contradicting the popular notion of Eurosclerosis. At the same time, however, both external labor turnover and more pronounced dismissals were found to be strongly concentrated in a small minority of firms adhering to an intensive hire-and-fire policy. The overwhelming majority of German firms, by contrast, exhibit a high degree of employment stability, little external worker turnover, and very low dismissal rates. This pattern has been especially pronounced within the sucessfully expanding mechanical engineering and higher-skill service industries.

The finding that only a small minority of firms adhere to an intensive "hire-and-fire" policy certainly challenges the view that universally applying job security provisions have made external work force adjustments prohibitively costly for firms and therefore are likely to account for the high degree of employment stability and low worker turnover observed among the large majority of firms in the private sector. Both the prevalence of stable, long-term employment relationships and the fact that most firms in the private sector have refrained from using the new options offered by the EPA's temporary work regulations are likewise apt to cast doubts on the "orthodox" assumption that an increase in external labor turnover is likely to increase adjustment efficiency. Consequently, it appears that endogenous economic factors and efficiency considerations rather than exogenously imposed layoff and dismissal restraints account for the high degree of employment stability observed in the overwhelming majority of firms in (West) Germany. The latter evidently prefer an adjustment strategy involving a high degree of internal or functional flexibility in the framework of stable, long-term employment arrangements to external flexibility involving frequent dismissals and short-term hires.

Given (West) Germany's overall economic setting, such an adjustment strategy that relies on a high degree of internal rather than external flexibility may also be superior in terms of macroeconomic efficiency. This is evident from the characteristics of those firms that adhere to a hire-and-fire strategy of external work force adjustment. This group was found to consist largely of smaller and medium-sized enterprises in the construction and low-skill service industries, with high labor costs, a comparatively low-skilled work force, a high incidence of personnel problems (especially skill shortages), and a declining employment trend. Judging by their characteristics and job creation performance, these firms hardly represent the type of firm that is likely to sustain (West) Germany's international competitiveness and to ensure full employment in the years to come (see Streeck 1991).

By contrast, successful, expanding enterprises in the manufacturing and higher-skill service industries were found to be characterized by low worker turnover and very low dismissal rates,[37] a low incidence of fixed-term hires, a significantly higher-skilled work force, and a marked trend toward employment expansion (see Buechtemann and Hoeland 1989:123).

In an environment of enhanced economic uncertainties, rapidly changing patterns of product demand, and high-speed technological innovation, the short-term availability of a broadly trained, "polyvalent," and flexible corporate human capital reservoir is likely to become more and more important in providing the kind of micro- and macro-flexibility required to cope with the increased competitive pressures faced by highly industrialized, high-wage economies (see Sengenberger 1987; Piore 1986; Bruno 1987). This is illustrated by the considerable expansion of firms' further training efforts and expenditures during the past decade. According to data from the official annual population survey (*Mikrozensus*), the number of workers participating in firm-based further training measures doubled between 1980 and 1988 (see Buechtemann and Stille 1992). During the same period total expenditure by private enterprises for further training (including training on the job) quadrupled, reaching an estimated 2.9 percent of

---

[37]Most of the worker turnover in these firms was, in fact, accounted for by voluntary quits rather than by employer-initiated separations.

the total wage bill in 1988 (see Weiss 1990). Likewise, most firms have considerably increased their skill requirements when hiring new personnel from the external labor market, thus, of course, further reducing the reemployment prospects of the swelling ranks of unskilled workers among the long-term unemployed (see Buechtemann 1989b). With increasing turnover costs (hiring costs and investments in human capital), firms' interest in external work force adjustments can be expected to decline still further, whereas their interest in measures supporting internal adjustments to quantitative and qualitative demand variations, such as flexible working-time regimes and work-sharing schemes or the expansion of publicly provided training facilities and infrastructure, is likely to increase.

Further deregulation of employment protection, by contrast, would most probably benefit only a small minority of firms that adhere to a strategy of external work force adjustment and is therefore unlikely to result in any additional employment effects in the short run. In the medium or long run, however, further relaxation of job security provisions may well—as shown by the experience of the German Employment Promotion Act—induce unintended moral hazard effects in terms of more rapid workforce reductions during economic downturns, that is, increase firms' firing propensity and, on balance, result in a reduction rather than an increase in total employment. "More jobs through less employment protection" does not appear to be a realistic and successful policy agenda for meeting the competitive challenges of the 1990s and beyond.

14
Eurosclerosis Reconsidered: Employment Protection and Work Force Adjustment in West Germany

Kornelius Kraft

The preceding paper by Christoph Buechtemann offers a detailed exposition of the development of labor market legislation in West Germany during recent years. This paper addresses the change in the speed of employment adjustment. The costs of reducing a firm's labor force have been increased, a significant part of the work force is protected against dismissals, and the risk of possible legal proceedings serve to make redundancies more expensive. Clearly, the intensification of worker protection laws leads to expectations of a decline in employment flexibility. In addition to institutional reasons for a slowdown in the speed of employment adjustment, economic arguments point to a decline in adjustment dynamics. Finally, even if labor adjustment is slower, this does not necessarily mean there are only negative welfare effects.

Buechtemann has pointed to firms' endogenous interest in long-term employment relationships as an important reason for the failure of the Employment Promotion Act to stimulate job creation. This argument is certainly true of skilled workers. To compete internationally, German firms have to offer technologically advanced products, and to produce these goods, they need highly skilled employees who have both general and firm-specific skills. It is well known that if firm-specific skills are required, employment adjusts more slowly to changes in environmental conditions than it otherwise would. It is possible that the need for specific skills has been increasing. An argument in support of this view is the speed of technical progress, implying an increased demand for training on the job to accommodate to the specific technology. Buechtemann presents some evidence that training on the job has greatly increased in recent years. Given the greater

Financial support by the Deutsche Forschungsgemeinschaft is gratefully acknowledged.

importance of firm-specific skills, employment should have become less flexible. Consequently, the assumption was that work force adjustment to changes in output would be less pronounced.

Over the past ten to fifteen years, the ratio of skilled to unskilled workers has increased. In general, short-term slumps in demand led to fewer redundancies among skilled workers, who thus faced a lower risk of job loss and dismissal than unskilled workers. Hence, there were obvious economic (neoclassical) reasons to expect a slower adjustment of employment regardless of the legal framework.

An opposing force is the increase in unemployment. Every discharge for cyclical reasons implies an assessment of the costs involved in recruiting an adequately skilled worker when the economy recovers. A relatively high unemployment rate eases recruitment, and therefore the speed of adjustment of employment should increase.

In contrast to Buechtemann, I am convinced that some dismissals are conducive to efficiency. The efficiency wage theory developed by Shapiro and Stiglitz (1984) explains unemployment as caused by insufficient information on employees' performance. Dismissals may be viewed as a punishment device for shirking. The punishment consists of income losses due to unemployment and the risk of being reemployed under worse conditions or in low-wage firms. But the threat of dismissal is credible only if it is executed from time to time. To put it differently, some dismissals may be necessary to keep performance at a high level.

Lazear's agency theory (Lazear 1979, 1981) on the reasons for the observed increase in remuneration with age works only if a person is fired for insufficient performance, however defined. In the later years of the employment relationship, the wage exceeds productivity. These deferred payments will work as an incentive mechanism, however, only if insufficient performance is punished by dismissal before the worker reaches seniority.

If the theories of Shapiro, Stiglitz, and Lazear accurately characterize internal labor markets, legal dismissal restraints are likely to have an adverse effect on efficiency.

Empirical Test

In the following section I report some of the results of a simple econometric test concerning employment adjustment in the Federal Republic of Germany. This test can be understood as complementing the analysis reported in the preceding paper. It is an investigation of the changes in the speed of adjustment from 1970 to 1987. The data basis consists of twenty-one West German manufacturing industries. The test procedure is based on a simplified version of the error correction model. Using the following empirical model, I analyzed whether the lag parameter changed during the above time period and, if so, why.

$$dN_t = \mu(\Theta\, X_{t-1} - N_{t-1}) + e_t \qquad (14\text{--}1)$$

In this equation, X characterizes desired employment, N stands for employment, dN denotes the change of employment over time, and μ, which has a value between zero and one, indicates the speed of adjustment to the desired employment level. This is a simplified version of the error correction model; the explanatory variables in first differences are omitted. The dependent variable is the change in employment of the industry under consideration. As usual, the optimal number of workers is explained by some economic variables called X. In this respect, I use the production level as a proxy for product demand and the wages of each industry as explanatory variables. The variable *WAGE* is the nominal remuneration per employee divided by the inflation rate since the product price of each industry was not always available. As in many countries, the wage rate is available only as an average of the basic wage and overtime premia:

$$w = w_b H_s + (1 + z) w_b (H - H_s) \qquad (14\text{--}2)$$

with z denoting the overtime premium, w_b the basic wage, H working time, H_s standard working time; w is the calculated average value. The use of this figure may lead to a bias in that the payment of overtime premia in a "good" state of demand and the change in employment are most likely to be correlated. To correct for this possible deficiency, equation 14–2 is solved for w and, in that no reliable information concerning z is available, the minimum value that has to be paid, 0.25, is set into equation 14–2.

To proxy for other reasons for changes in labor demand, such as technical progress, a trend variable and its square are added. In this connection the most interesting parameter is the adjustment coefficient μ. Usually this parameter is assumed to be constant, exactly the opposite of what is of interest here. This parameter is therefore explained using economic variables.

The crucial variable is the time trend. A significant coefficient of this variable would suggest that employment has become less flexible over time. A second variable is a dummy called *T85*, which has unit value during the years 1985–87 and is zero otherwise. By this it is tested whether the Employment Promotion Act has led to a faster adjustment of labor.

In addition to these variables, other potential effects are considered. One such variable is unionization, measured as the ratio of employees who are members of a union (*UNION*). In general, unions aim at employment stabilization and thus one might find an effect of unionization on employment adjustment. German labor law gives unions and their representatives at firm level considerable information and veto rights, which may well lead to a slowdown in employment adjustment. In addition, I considered the impact of one union in particular. The variable *IGM* has the value 1 if the metalworkers' union IG Metall is bargaining in an industry. This union is well known for its relatively aggressive behavior and for being the leader in annual wage negotiations. The variable tests whether a difference to other unions is measurable.

A variable of obvious relevance in the given context is the unemployment rate. It is expected that in times of relatively high unemployment the number of workers is more rapidly adjusted than otherwise in that it is relatively easy to find and hire adequately skilled employees when the economy recovers. Unemployment is measured as a ratio, not a percentage, and its highest level is 0.092. Finally, a

TABLE 14-1. *Determinants of the Speed of Adjustment*

c	β_0	β_1	β_2	β_3	β_4
−.16	.30	−.004	−.03	.02	−.015
(−2.78)	(3.16)	(−1.24)	(−2.42)	(1.76)	(−2.40)
β_5	θ_1	θ_2	ϕ_1	ϕ_2	
.05	.99	−.89	.03	−.0009	
(3.44)	(19.12)	(−3.03)	(4.62)	(−5.63)	

D-W = 1.95.
T-values are in parentheses; n = 357.

constant term is added. All continuous variables are expressed in logarithmic values. This specification leads to the following econometric model:

$$dN_t = c + (\beta_0 + \beta_1 TREND + \beta_2 T85 + \beta_3 UNION_t$$
$$+ \beta_4 IGM + \beta_5 UNEMP_t) *(\Theta_1 OUTPUT_{t-1} \qquad (14\text{-}3)$$
$$+ \Theta_2 WAGE_{t-1} - N_{t-1}) + \phi_1 TREND$$
$$+ \phi_2 (TREND)^2 + e_t$$

Given the way this model is specified, a positive coefficient of one of the adjustment parameters points to an increase in adjustment speed. Obviously, this relation is nonlinear, so estimation by OLS is inapplicable. The method used is maximum likelihood. The results are presented in table 14–1. It turns out that the trend is insignificant in the lag term. Hence, there is no evidence that employment has become less flexible over time. Moreover, the coefficient of the variable *T85* has the wrong sign and is significant. This result implies a slowdown in employment adjustment since the 1985 Employment Promotion Act went into force.

Surprisingly, unionization has no effect, whereas the IG Metall dummy is significant. In industries in which this union bargains, employment is more slowly adjusted than in other industries. Nobody familiar with industrial relations in Germany and with the behavior of IG Metall in particular will be surprised by this result.

The expected and significant effect of unemployment deserves attention. In times of high unemployment, labor is adjusted more quickly to changes in output and wages. Most likely this is because of the lower costs of hiring workers when demand is recovering.

Finally, the variables *OUTPUT* and *WAGE* each have the expected impact on labor demand. The wage-employment elasticity is rather high, but not of an unusual magnitude.

Conclusion

My analysis supports Buechtemann's empirical results. On the one hand, the Employment Promotion Act has had no measurable positive effect on employment flexibility. On the other hand, if the reason for this result is that firms are more concerned with maintaining employment stability, then we could expect adjustment speed to decrease over time regardless of the legal framework. This is not the case, however, if we control for the influence of a number of variables.

One possible reason for the persistence of considerable employment flexibility in the presence of increased adjustment costs may be that hours are less variable as labor and hours per worker are to some extent substituted. Usually it is assumed that the adjustment of hours is costless. The number of overtime hours per worker fell significantly, however, during the 1970s and 1980s (see Brinkmann et al. 1986) and thus total hours became less flexible. One speculative explanation might be that unions attempted to reduce the number of overtime hours. Nevertheless, the relation of hours flexibility to employment adjustment is an interesting topic for future research.

United Kingdom

15
Employment Protection and Labor Relations: The Regulatory Model of Job Security in the United Kingdom

Brian Bercusson

This paper describes a model of the legal framework of employment protection regulations and job security provisions (dismissal and layoff restrictions) in the United Kingdom. As the title indicates, the subject is conceived in terms of both employment protection and labor relations. This juxtaposition reflects a major tradition of labor law thinking in Great Britain that divides labor law into individual employment protection law and collective labor relations law. In the following outline of the core elements characterizing the system of employment security regulation in the United Kingdom, I intend to deviate from this tradition and, instead, as I have substantiated in greater detail elsewhere (Bercusson 1982), to emphasize the tight nexus and close interaction of statutory (individual) dismissal protection, collective bargaining, and government policies, particularly in the area of employment policy and social security in determining what is frequently, in an attempt at simplicity, referred to as the law of job security.

Labor Relations: Procedures and Substance

Legal concepts and industrial relations institutions and procedures may fail to convey the substance of employment protection. The terms and conditions of employment of most employees in Britain are still determined by collective agreements. Attention to statutory and other legal standards has to take account of the substantive content of collective agreements. Naturally, attention should be paid to the procedural mechanisms of union recognition, collective bargaining, and industrial action. But equal attention should be paid to the level of substantive protection offered.[1] For example, the technique of incorporating collectively

[1] As Hyman puts it: "Workers do not admire collective bargaining simply as an elegant ritual. They value trade unionism . . . as a mechanism for maintaining and improving the conditions of

agreed standards into individual contracts of employment has received relatively little attention, even though the legal consequences of collective agreements fall mainly on the individual employer and employee. The attention that has been paid has a procedural bias: the difficulty identified is that of establishing which collective agreement in a complex structure of bargaining is to be incorporated, particularly when there are conflicting agreements. There is the separate problem, however, of the suitability of the substantive content of agreements to be translated into individual contractual rights. Some substantive provisions may transfer easily into contracts of employment (e.g., terms on wages, hours, holidays, sick pay, and so on). But, increasingly, important parts of collective agreements present difficulties in translating them into individual contractual rights: job evaluation schemes, disciplinary rules and procedures, disputes procedures, redundancy procedures, productivity agreements, union recognition and facilities agreements, and so on.[2]

Functional Distinctions in the Law on Job Security

A systematic analysis of the regulation of job security through employment protection law and labor relations requires that a number of distinctions be made. These functional distinctions overcome some of the deficiencies of the conventional model of British labor law and its categorical division between individual employment law and collective labor law. These distinctions are consistent with the application chosen in the following account of classical techniques of comparative labor law. The functional approach emphasizes that the comparison of different national legal rules and institutions must subordinate the formal legal classification to a search for functional equivalence. The same approach applies to the analysis of the formal classification of employment protection law regulating job security.

It is suggested that in analyzing the British law on employment security (and for the purposes of comparative analysis of other countries' employment protection laws), a functional differentiation is necessary between at least three broad categories of terminations arising out of different circumstances: (1) diminution in the quantity of work; (2) changes in the work obligation, including reorganization of the enterprise; and (3) misconduct, ill health, and incompetence. This classification is still inadequate insofar as the rubric of employment protection law artificially excludes from consideration the law of social security and in particular unemployment benefits, which is crucial to understanding the operation of the legal protection of job security.

---

their working lives. ... [There are dangers in assigning] primacy to the parties to collective bargaining and to the procedural arrangements in which they participate, and only secondary importance to the substantive outcome of their relationship. ... The mere participation in job regulation may of course be wholly compatible with the stagnation or deterioration of material conditions" (1978:33–34).

[2]For examples of judicial decisions related to this problem, see Benedictus and Bercusson 1987:503–10.

In the remainder of this paper I present an account of British employment protection law in the area of job security. The paper is organized within the framework of the alternative model of employment protection, taking into account the substance of collective practice and using functional categories. Only the substance of the law is as developed in the conventional legal model.

The Law on Job Security and Decline in the Quantity of Work

The problem of diminution in the quantity of work may be dealt with by employers terminating contracts of employment with due notice, but the adverse consequences are not confined to workers.[3] The loss of a cohesive work force and the antagonism bred by such actions affect management's interests as well. One result has been the negotiation of collective agreements laying down detailed rules applicable in circumstances in which there is a reduction in the availability of work. These include rules on income maintenance (e.g., guaranteed pay) and work sharing (e.g., bans on overtime).

The problem has gradations, beginning with relatively small reductions in work, rising to substantial amounts lost, and finally to wholesale loss of jobs. Each of these problems has been subject to legislative attention: respectively, the law on guarantee payments, the law on redundancy through layoffs or short-time working, and the law on unfair dismissal, redundancy consultation, and redundancy payments. Additional provision is made by social security law on unemployment benefits and subsidies to employers retaining workers on short time. This area has been particularly fruitful in the establishment of links between legislation and collective bargaining.

Contract law. The obligations of the employer under the contract of employment when there is too little work are sometimes ambiguous. For example, what is the position when there is too little work but there is a contract with an agreed wage for a forty-hour week?[4] Such ambiguities may be accounted for by negotiations leading to collective agreements guaranteeing wages, but even these give rise to legal uncertainties as to the rights and obligations of the employer and the employees.[5]

Employment subsidies. The problem of too little work and consequent un-

---

[3]The material in this section is developed in Benedictus and Bercusson 1987:106–51.

[4]See *Hanson v. Wood (Abingdon Process Engravers)* (1968), Industrial Tribunal Reports 46 (Q.B.D.), in which the employees were dismissed when they refused their employer's demand that they work and be paid for only 32.5 hours instead of 40 hours weekly because of a reduction in trade.

[5]Compare *Powell Duffryn Wagon Company Ltd. v. House* (1974), Industrial Tribunal Reports 46 (N.I.R.C.), in which the employees were laid off but the employer refused to pay the guaranteed minimum wage, and *Neads v. CAV Ltd.* (1983), Industrial Relations Law Reports 360 (Q.B.D.), in which, when a dispute occurred between the employer and employees in another department, the employer purported to lay off Neads, who nonetheless continued to work at part of his job unaffected by the dispute, although the employer refused to pay him for the period.

employment has led to government intervention, the main thrust of which has been to provide subsidies to those affected: employers and workers. A significant feature of this legal form of employment protection is that judicial policy making is largely ousted. Policy is implemented through the administration of the social security system or other public agencies (before its demise, the Manpower Services Commission).

Guarantee payments for workers. Before 1975, an employee who was temporarily suspended from work (laid off) had to absorb the cost, except insofar as he or she could recoup something from the state (unemployment benefit) or from the employer (guaranteed pay, usually by virtue of a collective agreement). The Employment Protection Act 1975 altered this arrangement by placing some of the burden on the employer. An employer who lays off a worker or puts him or her on short time must continue to pay normal wages for a limited period. The wages payable are subject to a very low maximum, however, and wages are payable for a maximum of only five days in any three-month period. Failure by the employer allows for a complaint to an industrial tribunal. In practice, through changes in the regulations on unemployment benefits, the state effectively transferred the burden of paying unemployment benefits to the employer, leaving workers with the arduous task of enforcing payment through the industrial tribunals.[6]

Wage subsidies for employers. These have taken a variety of forms. A few of the most important can be presented as illustrations of this technique of employment protection. The Temporary Employment Subsidy Scheme (TES), introduced on August 18, 1975, and closed on March 31, 1979, was by far the largest single measure introduced between 1975 and 1979 to protect employment. Gross spending on TES totaled over £500 million sterling. The cumulative total of employees who were supported by TES at any time represented more than 6 percent of all employees in manufacturing and some 2.5 percent of all employees in Great Britain. During the three and a half years it was available, 8,787 applications were approved, involving 540,266 jobs. At any one time TES was typically supporting around 150,000 jobs and keeping about 100,000 employees off the unemployment register. Provided the employer was prepared to defer an impending redundancy affecting ten or more workers in an establishment, the firm might qualify for a subsidy of £10 a week for each full-time job maintained. The subsidy was payable for a maximum of one year. A requirement was introduced for all firms to present a restructuring plan if they wanted to receive the subsidy for more than six months. The industrial distribution of TES was remarkable: the textiles, clothing, and footwear industries accounted for 43 percent of the jobs covered, although these industries comprise less than 4 percent of total employment in the United Kingdom and less than 10 percent of all private sector employees.[7]

---

[6]The provisions are now in the Employment Protection (Consolidation) Act 1978, sections 12 et seq. For comment on the interaction with social security law, see Bercusson, "Annotations to Section 12," in Drake and Bercusson 1981.

[7]For details on other schemes, see Metcalf 1982. The implications of schemes of this kind for labor law are explored in Freedland 1980.

More recently, large-scale wage subsidies have taken the form of training schemes for young people. The Youth Training Scheme (YTS) was introduced in April 1983 and offered training mainly to sixteen- and seventeen-year-old dropouts. It consisted of work experience and off-the-job training (for at least thirteen weeks) provided in 1985–86 through some 5,800 managing agents (including employers, industrial training boards, employers' associations, and private training companies) and sponsors (voluntary groups and local authorities). Managing agents were paid £2,050 per trainee (from September 1984), from which they paid each trainee £1,312.50 (£26.25 a week for fifty weeks) as a tax-free allowance. The remaining £737.50 were for training costs and the agent's fee. In 1985–86, nearly 400,000 young people participated in YTS, and the Manpower Commission bore costs in excess of £800 million annually. Payments through YTS effectively subsidized a substantial proportion of employers' wage costs for trainees.

Redundancy. Redundancy dismissal resulting from too little work has not been the subject of comprehensive and systematic legal regulation. The legal rules are scattered over legislation and common law on redundancy payments, unfair redundancy dismissals, consultation procedures with trade unions and employees, time off to look for work in a redundancy situation, and so on. Here the legal rules are organized so as to set out the legal model comprising key aspects of the redundancy problem encountered in practice, usually in the following chronological order: preventing redundancy; redundancy consultations; selection for redundancy; redundancy notice and time off to look for work; and redundancy payments.

The law on each of these aspects can be contrasted with industrial practice manifest in collective agreements. Collective industrial practice poses a challenge to the British legal model of employment protection law. First, there is the policy question of whether such practice is best left alone, untrammeled by legal supervision or enforcement procedures. But also, does British labor law have adequate techniques and institutions to play a constructive role? For example, is the common law of contract flexible enough to cope with the obligations laid down in these agreements? Are courts and tribunals competent to deal with conflicts in this sphere involving not only individual workers and employers but also trade unions, work groups, and related employers?

Definition of redundancy. There is a legislative definition of redundancy in the Employment Protection (Consolidation) Act 1978 (EPCA, section 81[2]):

> For the purposes of this Act an employee who is dismissed shall be taken to be dismissed by reason of redundancy if the dismissal is attributable wholly or mainly to
> (a) the fact that his employer has ceased or intends to cease, to carry on the business for the purposes of which the employee was employed by him, or has ceased or intends to cease, to carry on that business in the place where the employee was so employed, or
> (b) the fact that the requirements of that business for employees to carry out work of a particular kind, or for employees to carry out work of a particular kind in

the place where he was so employed, have ceased or diminished or are expected to cease or diminish.

This definition is also applicable to unfair redundancies (EPCA section 57[2][a] by virtue of section 153[2]). As a matter of policy, the decision of an employer to declare a redundancy could be challenged: the employer's motivation as a causal factor in the dismissal following cessation could be questioned, or, when this motivation is linked, as it usually is, with a judgment of the economic "requirements of the business," the rationality of that judgment could be tested.

In fact, the subjective business discretion of the employer declaring a redundancy is rarely questioned by the courts. In one case, employees declared redundant challenged the employer's assertion that the factory was not economically viable. The industrial tribunal queried whether they could go into policy decisions of a company's board of directors on trading and economic matters. On appeal to the Employment Appeal Tribunal, the court reiterated that "there could not and cannot be any investigation into the rights and wrongs of the declared redundancy."[8]

In another case, the industrial tribunal seemed to demand accounts or figures from the employer demonstrating lack of economic viability. The Employment Appeal Tribunal repudiated this approach: "There is no special obligation on the employer's side to establish the existence of some economic or accountancy state of affairs which would, as it were, justify the declaration of a state of redundancy."[9]

The statutory definition, however, does assume the existence of a set of facts. On a claim for a redundancy payment, a statutory presumption exists that the reason for the dismissal is redundancy (EPCA section 91[2]). Unfair dismissal cases, where such a presumption does not operate, highlight the need for facts to prove that a redundancy situation does exist.

In most cases, the closing of a plant is held to be a redundancy situation. In less desperate circumstances, however, the industrial tribunals have experienced some difficulties when one or more employees were dismissed from an enterprise that continued to operate.

Many dismissals follow changes at work or major reorganizations, alleged to cause the redundancies. Others reflect the policy issues already referred to: challenges to the employer's motivation for the dismissals, particularly when this follows a judgment on the economic rationality of the business's requirements. The "fact that the requirements of that business for employees to carry out work of a particular kind . . . have ceased or diminished" involves a judgment weighing employment, wages, prices, and profits. Various cases illustrate the policy dilemmas facing the courts when they are pushed to question employers' judgments, for example, whether the business was "overstaffed" or whether workers who left

---

[8] *Moon v. Homeworthy Furniture (Northern) Ltd.* (1976), Industrial Relations Law Reports 298 (E.A.T.), per Kilner Brown J.

[9] *H. Goodwin Ltd. v. Fitzmaurice* (1977), Industrial Relations Law Reports 393 (E.A.T.), per Phillips J.

refusing a reduction in wage rates imposed by an employer in difficulty were dismissed for redundancy reasons.[10]

Preventing redundancies. Surveys reveal the use of many different techniques prescribed by collective agreements between employers and trade unions to avoid redundancies. These include retirement of those over pension age; limitations on recruitment, overtime, and subcontract work; replacement of casual and temporary labor; redeployment; retraining; and short-time working.[11]

Laws aimed at avoiding redundancies began with the provision under the original Redundancy Payments Act 1965 whereby the employer could avoid liability to make a redundancy payment by offering the employee "suitable alternative employment" (now EPCA, section 84). But there was no legal obligation on the employer to do so. The beginnings of such an obligation were introduced by the Industrial Relations Code of Practice 1972.[12] Tribunals are obliged to take the code into account, and the code (paragraph 45) encourages management to seek to avoid redundancies by such means as restrictions on recruitment, retirement of employees beyond normal retiring age, reductions in overtime, short-time working to cover temporary fluctuations in staffing needs and re-training or transfer to other work.

The code (paragraph 46) also advises management to

(vi) consider introducing schemes for voluntary redundancy, retirement, transfer to other establishments within the undertaking, and a phased rundown of employment; ... (vii) offer help to employees in finding other work in co-operation, where appropriate, with the Department of Employment, and allow them reasonable time off for the purpose.

Redundancy dismissals can be held unfair unless employers act reasonably under the circumstances (EPCA, section 57[3]). It is up to tribunals and courts to adopt the policy laid down in the code. Each case involves a policy choice: will the court use the code to require employers to take steps to prevent redundancies, or not?[13]

These decisions deal with the requirement to consider measures to avoid or prevent redundancies developed from the statutory "reasonableness" test in the law of unfair dismissal (EPCA, section 57[3]). Collective agreements requiring such measures have already been cited.

A combination of the statutory requirements with those of collective agreements could have been a powerful model of employment protection in redundancy

---

[10]See *Hindle v. Percival Boats Ltd.* (1969), 1 All England Reports 836 (Court of Appeal); *Chapman v. Goonvean and Rostowrack China Clay Co. Ltd.* (1973), Industrial Cases Reports 310 (Court of Appeal).

[11]See, for example, the survey of 110 redundancy agreements and schemes in *Bargaining Report* 33 (May-June 1984), published by the Labour Research Department.

[12]For the legal effect of this code, see the Trade Union and Labour Relations Act 1974, schedule 1, paragraph 3; Employment Protection Act 1975, schedule 17, paragraph 4(1).

[13]For some important and interesting precedents, see *Vokes Ltd. v. Bear* (1974), Industrial Cases Reports 1 (N.I.R.C.); *Williams v. Compair Maxam Ltd.* (1982), Industrial Relations Law Reports 83 (E.A.T.).

situations. Such a combination might seem to be indicated by EPCA, section 59(b), which declares a dismissal unfair if the employee "was selected for dismissal in contravention of a customary arrangement or agreed procedure relating to redundancy." Unfortunately, the courts have restricted this requirement to selection procedures in the narrowest sense: breaches of agreements with respect to other than the direct selection of the person to be made redundant were held not to be covered by this provision. The courts preferred to retain their discretionary power to decide whether the employer had acted reasonably under EPCA section 57(3), even when the collective agreement was violated.[14]

Redundancy consultations. There is a clear link between the taking of measures to avoid redundancy and redundancy consultation, for only consultation with the employees affected and their trade union representatives can ensure that alternatives to redundancy are thoroughly explored. Collective agreements have improved upon the statutory requirements in the Employment Protection Act 1975 (EPA), which provide that employers should consult trade unions over redundancy proposals a minimum of thirty or ninety days before dismissals are to take place (if redundancies are involved). Surveys of collective agreements with guaranteed minimum consultation periods have revealed requirements of two to twelve months.

There are two principal legal sources that require consultation before redundancies may be implemented: The first such source is EPA section 99, which requires consultation with trade unions. The origins of this legal obligation lie in EEC Council Directive 75/129 of February 17, 1975. The provisions raise a number of difficulties when applied to complex industrial relations circumstances. Who are the trade union representatives at different levels? What if the employer is not a single independent entity but a unit in a complex organization involving a holding company and a number of subsidiaries? At what level in the decision-making process of this larger economic unit does the obligation come into being? When is a trade union "recognized" so as to require the employer to consult it? Each of these questions raises sensitive issues of policy that tribunals have had to consider.[15]

The second legal source is the Industrial Relations Code of Practice 1972 (paragraphs 44–46), which stipulates that management should consult employees or their representatives in redundancy situations. This code has been invoked as one source for interpreting the "reasonableness" obligation (EPCA, section 57[3]) in cases of dismissals as including an obligation to consult. Thus, failure to consult over redundancies may be so unreasonable as to make the subsequent dismissal unfair. Nonetheless, the courts are reluctant to relinquish their discretion to decide upon the required timing and content of the consultations. In each case the tribunal measures what the employer has done against the sole legal criterion of reasonableness.

---

[14]The case that established this point is *McDowell v. Eastern British Road Services Ltd.* (1981), Industrial Relations Law Reports 482 (E.A.T.).

[15]For decisions on these and other issues, see Benedictus and Bercusson 1987:128–35.

Selection for redundancy. When measures to avoid redundancy have not succeeded and consultations have not led to alternatives, the invidious task of selection for redundancy arises. A review of 110 redundancy schemes and job security agreements concluded that "while a number of schemes do mention factors such as timekeeping and attendance records as criteria for selection, the most common methods are volunteers, early retirement and last-in-first-out."

Section 59 of the Employment Protection (Consolidation) Act requires adherence to such arrangements or procedures, though the courts' determination of what constitutes such arrangements or procedures raises questions of policy related to bargaining structures and processes, particularly the identification and recognition of custom and practice. Where there is no customary arrangement or agreed procedure, the reasonableness requirement of EPCA section 57(3) has been invoked in two ways to fetter management's subjective discretion in selecting who is to be made redundant. The first fetter concerns the criteria used by the employer in making the selection. The emphasis here is on "objective" criteria. The second fetter concerns the standard of reasonableness that the employer is required to satisfy in applying these criteria (the standard of the "reasonable employer" applied in unfair dismissal claims generally). The cases reveal conflicts of opinion as to how closely the tribunals should examine the criteria used by the employer in the selection process and how strictly application of these criteria should be queried.

Redundancy notice and time off to look for work. There is no special legal provision for redundancy notice. The statutory minimum of one week after four weeks' employment generally applies. Although this increases by one week for each year of employment to a maximum of twelve weeks' notice after twelve years of service (EPCA section 49), surveys have found that many agreements improve on this.

Workers about to be made redundant are entitled under legislation to "reasonable" time off to look for work at the "appropriate" hourly rate (EPCA section 31). Maximum liability for the employer is stipulated at two-fifths of the workers' weekly pay. Again, surveys disclose that a number of schemes improve on this.

Redundancy payments. The redundancy payments legislation (now EPCA sections 81–120) requires employers to pay compensation to workers dismissed by reason of redundancy. Compensation is calculated as a multiple of a week's wages and the number of years of continuous employment with the employer (up to a maximum of 20 years and 1.5 weeks' pay; the maximum weekly pay is fixed annually after a review by the secretary of state). Failure to make the payment entitles the employee to complain to an industrial tribunal. Again, surveys have found a number of schemes that improve on this, often up to four times the statutory provision.

The original legislation also set up a redundancy fund financed through employers' national insurance contributions, whereby an employer making a redundancy payment can claim a rebate from the fund. The Wages Act 1986, however, restricted the right to a rebate to those employers with nine or fewer employees.

The Law on Job Security and Changes in the Work Obligation

The concept of a fixed definition of tasks performed by the worker is at odds with the employer's need for flexibility to meet the changing requirements of production.[16] Trade unions have accepted very broad flexibility clauses in many industries but have sought compensation for this concession in terms of job security or income.

Unfortunately, there is no legal concept or category that corresponds to the problem of changes at work. The law is to be found in doctrines of variations in the contract of employment, rules on dismissal for refusal to accept changes, and redundancy claims. Little account is taken of the role played by collective agreements on changes at work. Yet detailed rules and procedures already exist in practice governing changes: status quo clauses, trial periods, training and retraining provisions, procedures for resolving disputes arising from changes, and many other sophisticated mechanisms.

Changes may be proposed by either side, though more often legal disputes arise as a result of changes initiated by the employer. If everybody concerned consents, there will be no dispute and hence no need for court intervention. If there is a dispute, then the law may be invoked. Such disputes present themselves in a number of ways.

Changes of contracts. In practice, changes are often unilaterally imposed by an employer. In law, the obligations in the contract of employment, including the work obligation, can be changed only by mutual consent. Even so, the changes initiated by the employer may be implemented in practice for a period of time before any legal challenge is made (e.g., through proceedings for unfair dismissal or redundancy payments following dismissal). If a tribunal or court finds that the employee did not consent, the unilateral change in the work obligation will be a breach of contract; may constitute a constructive dismissal which is unfair; or may amount to a dismissal for redundancy.

If it is found that the employee did consent, he or she will be bound by the changed obligation. An initial question is, therefore, whether implementation of unilateral changes implies that the employee has consented. For example, in cases in which the employee protested while complying, the judges have sometimes recognized that it might be "unrealistic" in ordinary circumstances for an employee to make a protest.[17] The issue of consent is particularly problematic when the change in the work obligation is informally implemented on the shop floor and challenged much later.

Trial periods under common law and under statute. Under common law, significant change that is unilaterally imposed on an employee may amount to a repudiation by the employer of the contract of employment. The right of the

---

[16]The material in this section is developed in Benedictus and Bercusson 1987:58–92.

[17]Contrast *Jones v. Associated Tunnelling Co. Ltd.* (1981), Industrial Relations Law Reports 477 (E.A.T.), and *DHSS v. Coy* (1985), Industrial Relations Law Reports 263 (House of Lords).

employee to accept the employer's repudiation and terminate the contract may be waived, however. A waiver may also be implied by delay in "accepting" the repudiation (i.e., terminating the contract). The courts have recently developed a "common law trial period." Thus there is now a "reasonable" period during which the worker is entitled to make up his or her mind as to whether to accept the new employment or quit (and claim unfair dismissal or a redundancy payment).[18]

Under the Employment Protection (Consolidation) Act 1978, if there is a dismissal for redundancy (loss of the previous) job but the employee is offered a different but suitable job, there is an automatic statutory four-week period (section 84[3]–[7]). There is then no repudiation. This situation may be difficult to distinguish from the case in which the employee is told he or she must take a new job on pain of dismissal (a repudiatory act), in which case a common-law trial period comes into effect.

The force of the statutory trial period in cases of changes at work is evident from a case in which it was held to override and thus invalidate a collective agreement on redeployment whereby, as part of his contract of employment, the employee agreed to allow changes in his work obligation in the event of redundancy.[19]

Changes and dismissal. Employees risk dismissal if they resist change. Should this occur, the question will arise whether a dismissal for refusal to accept change is fair and whether the employee is entitled to statutory redundancy compensation: the conflict is between the right of management to change the work obligation unilaterally and the right of the worker to adhere to the obligation he or she has accepted. Employment protection depends on the court insisting that an employer demanding work changes compensate the employee who does not wish to accept them and so loses his or her employment.

Unfair dismissal on "economic" grounds. Remarkably, the legislation on protection against unfair dismissal does not explicitly provide for the case of economic dismissals—apart from the case of redundancy or diminution of work. Reorganization of the enterprise, which may require major changes to be imposed on employees, has been dealt with by the courts under the only rubric available in the legislation. Apart from the listed reasons justifying dismissal in EPCA section 57(2) (incapability, ill health, and misconduct), the legislation adds "or some other substantial reason of a kind such as to justify the dismissal" (section 57[1][b]). This has been interpreted by the courts as including as justifications for dismissal "sound, good business reasons," "commercial necessity," and refusal by an employee "to undertake his part in the new reorganization which was beneficial to the efficient running of the company."[20]

---

[18]See *Shields Furniture Ltd. v. Goff* (1973), Industrial Cases Reports 187 (N.I.R.C.); *Turvey v. Cheyney & Son Ltd.* (1979), Industrial Cases Reports 341 (E.A.T.).

[19] *Tocher v. General Motors Scotland Ltd.* (1981), Industrial Relations Law Reports 55.

[20] *Hollister v. National Farmers Union* (1979), Industrial Cases Reports 542 (Court of Appeal); *Bowater Containers Ltd. v. McCormack* (1980), Industrial Relations Law Reports 50 (E.A.T.).

The policy behind the substantive principle that economic dismissals are fair following changes at work resulting from reorganizations implemented unilaterally by management may be contrasted with the policy adopted in the special case of transfers of undertakings between employers under the Transfer of Undertakings (Protection of Employment) Regulations of 1981. Regulation 8(2) provides that "where an economic, technical or organizational reason entailing changes in the workforce of either the transferor or the transferee before or after a relevant transfer is the reason or principal reason for dismissing an employee . . . [the dismissal shall] be regarded as having been for a substantial reason of a kind as to justify the dismissal."

The interpretation of this provision contrasts with that regarding economic dismissals under the unfair dismissal legislation. The court of appeal held:[21]

> It is far from clear that it was the intention of the legislature (or of the EEC Directive 77/187 which required the regulations to be made) that immediately following a transfer the employees of the transferred undertaking could be made to accept new terms of service. The purpose of the directive was "the safeguarding of employees' rights in the event of transfers", and the regulations themselves include in their name the words, "Protection of Employment". Amongst the most crucial rights of employees are their existing terms of service. We are not satisfied that there is a clear statutory intention to ensure that, following a transfer, the transferee company can insist on equating the terms and conditions of the "transferred" employees to those of his existing employees, notwithstanding the fact that such alteration may constitute a detriment to the transferred employees.

The policy justification put forward for finding dismissals unfair in the case of transfer of undertakings would seem to apply with equal force to changes in terms not connected with transfers.

The substantive issue of fairness in the general law of unfair dismissal has been decided by judges in the interests of the employer desiring change. The main restrictions so far placed by the courts are procedural ones. The employer should adopt certain procedures in introducing the change; otherwise, the dismissal will be for a fair reason but may be unreasonably implemented and hence unfair. So, for example, the employer must have and produce evidence that he or she adequately considered the case for and against the reorganization or changes leading to the dismissal; needs to indicate that he or she considered alternatives to dismissing the employee; and should have discussed or consulted with the employee about the changes affecting him or her.[22]

Redundancy and changed work obligations. Statutory protection of employees in redundancy situations depends on the definition of redundancy in EPCA section 81(2)(b): "the fact that the requirements of that business for

---

[21] *Berriman v. Delabole Slate Ltd.* (1985), Industrial Relations Law Reports 305 (Court of Appeal), per Browne-Wilkinson L.J. at 308.

[22] *Banerjee v. City & East London Area Health Authority* (1979), Industrial Relations Law Reports 147 (E.A.T.); *Ladbroke Courage Holidays Ltd. v. Asten* (1981), Industrial Relations Law Reports 59 (E.A.T.); *Orr v. Vaughan* (1981), Industrial Relations Law Reports 63 (E.A.T.).

employees to carry out work of a particular kind have ceased or diminished." There is some division of opinion in the courts as to whether this protection applies to dismissals resulting from changes in the work obligation or wholesale reorganization of the business. From a technical viewpoint, the question is whether it is a requirement of the business for employees or for work that is emphasized. The former allows for protection of employees who are dismissed; the latter protects the business. From a policy viewpoint, the question is whether the employer's interest in the business or the employees' interests in employment or compensation are paramount.

It is well known that redundancy payments have been a major factor enabling employers to achieve reorganization by undercutting collective resistance by the work force. The cases demonstrate that there is no consistent judicial policy on whether reorganization will be facilitated by allowing dismissed employees to claim redundancy payments. Some judges are reluctant to allow such claims, taking the view that the costs involved might deter change. Other judges, aware of employee resistance, have tended to favor allowing redundancy claims in cases of change or reorganization at work, thus undermining collective resistance. The changing industrial relations climate of the 1980s, in a context of high unemployment, has often enabled employers to impose changes and reorganization even without the inducement of redundancy payments.

Collective agreements on changes at work. Many organized workers have gained some control over changes at work by negotiating collective agreements whereby employers have undertaken certain obligations in cases of proposed changes, particularly where new technology is involved. These include provisions containing safeguards on the following matters:[23]

1. anticipating changes: advance notice and information, joint machinery of discussion, consultation, and negotiation;

2. introducing changes: status quo clauses, trial periods, training and retraining, health and safety, and operational conditions;

3. monitoring changes agreed to be introduced in terms of their impact on employees' conditions;

4. job and income security: redundancies, redeployment, and pay; changing job descriptions and job satisfaction;

5. getting the benefits: reductions in work time; pay and productivity.

The Law on Job Security and Misconduct, Ill Health, and Incompetence

The current debate over regulatory models of employment protection and job security has emphasized the situations already analyzed: work force reductions and enterprise reorganizations. Yet the regulatory model purports to cover far more than cases of job insecurity. Indeed, most such models had their origins in the fears over job security arising from cases of ill health, disciplinary penalties

[23]For illustrations from collective agreements, see Benedictus and Bercusson 1987:88–92.

(including dismissal) for misconduct, and alleged incompetence. The models often had to be adjusted when regulation of economic dismissals arrived on the political agenda.

The substantive standards and procedures prescribed by the law were different for each of these "noneconomic dismissal" cases. The jurisprudence is vast and too complex to be covered here.[24] One general point only will be invoked, however, to illustrate the regulatory model: the legal standard of fairness as the "reasonable employer" standard.

Legal protection against unfair dismissal under the Employment Protection (Consolidation) Act 1978 requires that the employer should have a sufficient reason for dismissing an employee and that the employer act reasonably under the circumstances. This raises the issue of whether tribunals and courts are prepared to challenge the actions of management in dismissing employees and, if so, the standards they will invoke to assess management behavior.

Most lawyers have declared that, under the law, far from being empowered to pass judgment on the employer's actions, tribunals must take the part of the employer and ask if, as the employer, the action was reasonable. The tribunal is not to judge as an independent arbiter whether the action was reasonable but whether an employer would think it was. The standard of reasonableness is thus turned into that of a reasonable employer. The only qualification is that the courts may assess management behavior in terms of what is called "good industrial relations practice." The courts have remained reluctant, however, to allow standards of good industrial relations practice to impose limits on their overriding discretion to decide cases on the basis of the "reasonable employer" test.

Conclusion

I have presented this detailed account of British employment protection law because it highlights the importance of the wider legal and institutional framework for analyzing national systems of employment security from an international comparative perspective. Different models of presentation might have been chosen that are both more and less legal-technical, though in all cases they draw on the same legislation. A more legal-technical model would have ignored the relevance of collective bargaining agreements and industrial practice in the regulation of job security. Attention would have focused even more narrowly on the legislative provisions and court decisions used in interpreting and applying those provisions. Analysis would have proceeded by way of classification of the materials under traditional legal headings (common law, statute, and so on), and standards would have been applied to the relevant labor law that are equally applicable to other areas of law: the clarity of the statutory enactments and their interpretation, the consistency and quality of the judicial reasoning, and so forth. To the extent that the relevant law borrows doctrines from other areas of law (contract, tort, criminal, company), it would be analyzed in terms of any changes adopted in the

[24]See generally Benedictus and Bercusson 1987:296–404.

application of these doctrines (e.g., developments in economic torts, use of codes of practice in criminal cases, nature of contracts of employment, employees' interests in company law). There is plenty here to occupy the academic labor lawyer.

From the point of view of policy analysis, however, the contributions of such an approach are limited. Clarity and internal consistency are beneficial, and doctrinal developments may prove valuable. But the starting point of such analysis is the legal material and the focus of attention remains on those materials.

These shortcomings have not prevented many commentators from adopting a critical attitude to labor law, analyzing the policy behind the legal provisions and questioning its adequacy. The approach proposed here merely attempts to push further down that road. Its starting point is that it is necessary to promote awareness of alternative models of employment protection law.

A less legal-technical approach would have undertaken, through established social science techniques, to discover the impact of the statutory law on job security. This would provide information about worker, employer, and union attitudes to the legislation (awareness, ignorance, positive and negative evaluations), the extent of its use (tribunal applications, use in negotiations), and its outcomes (reemployment, compensation, and rejection of complaints). This approach is essential for a contextual understanding of the law on employment and job security. What both these alternative approaches share is a more or less exclusive focus on the statutory rules of employment protection, sometimes supplemented by marginal reference to contractual rules and industrial practice, but only as these affect the statutory rules.

What I have tried to add to these approaches is, first, a functional differentiation among the rules regulating employment or job security according to the circumstances concerned (diminution, change, and reorganization; ill health, incompetence, and misconduct) and, second, an appreciation of the importance not only of the statutory rules of job security but of the provisions of collective bargaining agreements and provisions in other legal domains (economic law in the form of employment subsidies and social security provisions).

This paper has been able to do no more than sketch a comprehensive, context-oriented approach to employment protection law. It is hoped that this sketch may illuminate the comparative debate.

16

Labor Law, the Labor Market, and the State: British Industrial Relations under the Conservatives

Richard Hyman

The purpose of this paper is twofold: to elaborate and explain the distinctive evolution of British approaches to employment protection and to adopt an approach that is at least implicitly comparative, highlighting the "peculiarities of the English" and considering whether there are nevertheless more general lessons to be drawn from the U.K. experience.

Law and Collective Bargaining in Britain

In most countries, the regulation of employment conditions, including the employer's right to hire and fire, is directly shaped by law, whether by constitutional provisions, specific enactments, or both. In Britain, the connection between law and employment regulation is far more indirect and in many respects contradictory. Collective bargaining rather than legal provision is the most important regulatory mechanism for most employees, affecting the conditions and status of nonunionists as well as union members. Historically, collective bargaining has operated as an alternative to detailed legal regulation, and the complex tension between the legal system and industrial relations institutions has resulted in many idiosyncrasies in the nature of employment protection.

Underlying the British judicial system are the principles of common law: the body of rules and assumptions—in some respects a substitute for a written constitution—that are presumed to have existed from time immemorial. The power of the courts to interpret and apply these principles under changing circumstances gives judges the status, in effect, of surrogate legislators. Fundamental to the common law have always been the rights of property, and as a corollary the sanctity of contracts. The right of individual workers to agree to a contract of employment on whatever terms they saw fit and of the employer to be protected against breach of this contract traditionally framed the judicial view of industrial relations. In the nineteenth century, collective efforts by workers to regulate the terms on which they would accept employment, to negotiate as a group or through representatives, or to organize a strike were repeatedly held to constitute illegal conspiracies "in restraint of trade."

The method by which trade unionism and collective bargaining were eventually legalized was not, as in many countries, by establishing a positive right to organize, to bargain, and to strike but by defining an area of industrial relations in which the application of the common-law doctrines of restraint of trade and breach of employment contract was excluded. The key legislative reforms (Trade Union Act 1871, Conspiracy and Protection of Property Act 1875, and Trade Union Act 1906) created a series of negative "immunities," areas of collective activity that were protected from the hostile force of common law.

The manner by which collective barganing was legalized had two important consequences, one specific and one more general. The specific result is that "in strict juridical terms, there does not exist in Britain any 'right' to organize or any 'right' to strike. The law still provides no more than a 'liberty' to associate in trade unions and certain 'liberties' of action by which trade unions can carry out industrial struggle" (Wedderburn 1980:69). Hence, a redefinition of the scope of these immunities (either by judicial creativity or by new statute) that may at first appear narrow and technical can nevertheless have very substantial implications for the legality of trade union action. Many of the legislative initiatives of the Conservative government in the 1980s have been precisely of this character; their cumulative effect has been almost to eliminate the circumstances in which a strike may lawfully be organized. To the extent to which the freedom to apply bargaining power in collective action is an important basis of employment protection—as indeed is the case in Britain—such narrowing of trade union immunities is de facto a means of deregulating the employer.

The more general and more diffuse consequence is a deep-rooted disjunction between collective bargaining and the law. The very notion of a collective contract, of central importance in so many countries, does not exist in Britain; collective agreements are "binding in honour only" and acquire legal relevance only to the extent that their terms are explicitly or implicitly incorporated into the individual employment contracts of those covered. Likewise, trade unions are not traditionally regarded as agents of their members. The individualistic bias of the legal system is no absolute bar (as U.S. experience demonstrates) to the juridification of industrial relations, but in the formative period of large-scale collective bargaining there was a broad consensus among employers, trade unions, and governments in Britain that the law could make little positive contribution to employment regulation.

A century ago the Royal Commission on Labour concluded its massive inquiry by insisting that voluntary agreement between organizations of workers and employers was far preferable to legislation as a method of resolving labor problems, a principle firmly enshrined within public policy in modern Britain. While the "tradition of voluntarism" (Flanders 1974) did not, indeed, preclude some positive labor legislation, the latter was in the main of only secondary importance (Kahn-Freund 1954). The philosophy of collective laissez-faire, as it is often known, was clearly expounded by the Trades Union Congress in its evidence to the Donovan Royal Commission (1966:69): "It is where trade unions are not competent . . . to perform a function, that they welcome the state playing a role in at least enforcing minimum standards, but in Britain this role is recognized as the second best alternative to the development by workpeople themselves of the organization, the competence, the representative capacity, to bargain and to achieve for themselves satisfactory terms and conditions of employment."

Employment Protection under Free Collective Bargaining

The preference for "free collective bargaining" over legal regulation meant that employment protection was not traditionally provided in British labor law. There did indeed exist a tort of "wrongful dismissal," but this merely covered dismissals without whatever period of notice the employment contract prescribed, and without special justification and the only remedy was an award equivalent to the loss of wages during the notice period. "Normally the employer's power of dismissal—summary if there are grounds, or otherwise on short notice—and his power to select those to be dismissed, are in Britain wholly protected by the legal structure erected upon the contract of employment," wrote Wedderburn in the first edition of his labor law text (1965:90). Legislation limiting the employer's right to hire and fire, he continued, "would be a major novelty for our system."

This legal vacuum did not entail that every employer could dismiss at will. Collective pressure through trade unions and the norms of good personnel practice held by many employers, particularly in the public sector, tended to require standards of consistency and fairness in both penal dismissals and the imposition of redundancies. In particular, the dismissal of workplace trade union activists and representatives was likely to provoke forceful resistance wherever collective organization was established. Formal procedures governing discipline, redundancy, and dismissal, however, whether or not they were negotiated with trade unions, were traditionally rare within the private sector (Anderman 1972). In part this was because most trade unionists themselves were reluctant to agree to such procedures, believing that they would compromise their ability to resist in principle any threat to a member's employment.

The norm of legal abstention was significantly qualified by a number of enactments (though scarcely what Towers, in chapter 17, terms a "flood of legislation") in the 1960s and 1970s. The Redundancy Payments Act 1965—passed under a Labour government but drafted by its Conservative predecessor—introduced the principle of compensation for workers with more than two years' continuous employment who were dismissed for reasons of redundancy. The Industrial Relations Act 1971—designed primarily to restrict and regulate trade unions— purported to establish "the right not to be unfairly dismissed by (an) employer." Excluded from this right, among others, were part-time employees, those with less than two years' service, and strikers. When the 1971 act was repealed by the 1974–79 Labour government, these provisions were retained in the new legislation

(Employment Protection Act 1975, Employment Protection [Consolidation] Act 1978). The coverage of legislative protection was extended; in particular, the length of service requirement was reduced to six months and part-timers working more than eight hours a week were brought within the provisions (though a longer service requirement was specified). Since 1979, the eligibility requirements have been made increasingly restrictive, the onus of proof of unfair dismissal has been altered in the employer's favor, and a penalty has been introduced for persisting with claims that preliminary assessment deems futile.

But even before 1979, employment protection was something of a misnomer for the redundancy and unfair dismissals legislation. Rather than establishing a right to work, the law created a right to limited compensation for dismissal in certain circumstances. Any recognition of a property right in employment was negated by the simultaneous specification of procedures for compulsory purchase.

The 1965 Redundancy Payments Act was explicitly concerned with financial compensation for job loss. It defined criteria for eligibility, scales of entitlement, and procedures for the partial refund by the state of redundancy payments made by employers. Rather than protecting jobs, the act was designed to facilitate the imposition of redundancies as a means of encouraging "flexibility in the deployment of labour" (Parker et al. 1971:3). Employee and trade union resistance to redundancy, it was believed, inhibited many employers from labor-saving innovations in technology and work organization. Thus, the aim of the legislation was to legitimize the principle of redundancy and establish a standard procedure for the negotiated restructuring of employment (Fryer 1973).

Whether or not by design, statutory redundancy payments have also created important obstacles to collective employee resistance to job loss, since workers are encouraged to respond to redundancy in terms of an individualistic cost-benefit calculus. Older workers with many years' service may perceive their interests to be very different from those who are entitled to less or no compensation.

Statutory redundancy payments must also be seen against the background of the lack of any right to strike in Britain: an employer is entitled to dismiss workers who strike to resist redundancy (or for any other reason), and the latter then forfeit all entitlement to statutory compensation. Not surprisingly, this right of employers has proved a potent restraint on trade union resistance to collective dismissals.

The law on unfair dismissals does provide a remedy of reinstatement or reengagement as well as financial compensation, but as Towers indicates in chapter 17, the number of cases in which reemployment is recommended is negligible. Further, such an award is ultimately unenforceable: an employer who fails to comply merely becomes liable to additional compensation. Though the rhetoric surrounding the initial enactment did indeed emphasize the need to protect employees against unfair dismissal, reemployment of workers who are unfairly dismissed has always been a "lost remedy" (Dickens et al. 1985). Financial awards or settlements are usually modest: in 1988–89, the median award was only £1732, equivalent to roughly seven times the average weekly wage for full-time adult employees. This is partly because awards are subject to maxima that are themselves relatively low, particularly in the case of low-paid workers with limited service, who are perhaps most vulnerable to unfair dismissal; partly because industrial tribunals are typically parsimonious in the exercise of their discretion. As Dickens et al. conclude (1985:139), "Taken together, the limited use of the re-employment remedy and the way in which compensation is assessed serve typically to set a low price on the unfair deprivation of a job and can have little deterrent value for most employers."

If unfair dismissals legislation in Britain does not realistically act as a means of employment protection, how then should it be interpreted? For Anderman (1986:416), it "can most usefully be viewed as part of an overall public policy of attempting to promote efficient management." The timing of this "major novelty for our system" is significant: the 1960s saw a growing criticism of the fragmentation and informality of industrial relations practices and the opportunism and incoherence of most employers' personnel policies. The consequence, it was argued by such bodies as the Donovan Royal Commission, was an excessive volume of small-scale localized disputes and an endemic inefficiency in management's use of labor. The development of formal disciplinary and dismissals procedures was advocated as an important element in the reform of British industrial relations, and a statutory framework was seen as a necessary stimulus to management. Those employers who followed "good practice" in drawing up clear procedures and applied them consistently would have little to fear from the law.

This has indeed been demonstrated in practice. Complaints of unfair dismissal normally succeed only when an employer has clearly acted arbitrarily, in breach or in the absence of a domestic disciplinary procedure, or when the principles of "natural justice" (allowing the worker to know the alleged offense and to offer a defense) have been disregarded. Tribunals have very limited discretion to stray beyond such procedural questions and probe the substantive reasonableness of a dismissal; they are required "to adopt a standard of fairness which reflects the lower reaches of acceptable managerial practice" (Anderman 1986:424). A wide scope for employer discretion is thus confirmed by the law of unfair dismissal: "the norms to which the tribunals refer are the traditional practices of the exercise of managerial prerogative" (Collins 1982:92). Moreover, as in the case of redundancy payments, the availability of a statutory mechanism of appeal may reduce the prospect of collective resistance to individual dismissals, thus serving to "defuse conflict and undermine the solidarity of organised labour" (Collins 1982:86). To the extent that this occurs, the law on unfair dismissals may actually make it easier for an employer to discharge an unwanted employee.

It is not surprising, therefore, that, although many employers (and Conservative politicians) believe that the legislation of the 1960s and 1970s significantly reduced the ability to dismiss workers, there is no serious evidence that in practice it acted as a restraint on employment flexibility (Daniel and Stilgoe 1978). Whatever the pretensions of the initial legislators, the claim to have established a system of employment protection was largely rhetorical. In this respect, there was very little for the Thatcher government to deregulate, and, not surprisingly, the claim that it dismantled major statutory barriers to business turns out to be a matter of ideology as much as substance.

Employment protection and collective bargaining in the 1980s. This brings me back to my starting point: in Britain, collective bargaining rather than labor law has been the main source of whatever employment protection exists; and it is in this area that the initiatives of the Thatcher government have had their greatest effect.

The reduction of "trade union power" was an explicit objective of the Conservative government elected in 1979. The means adopted to achieve this aim include six major statutes designed to regulate and restrict union organization and industrial action; the rejection of the processes of tripartite concertation established in previous decades; and the encouragement of mass unemployment as a source of discipline in labor markets. In the course of a decade, union membership has fallen from 13.3 million to 10.3 million, representing a reduction in density from roughly 55 to 40 percent. How far this substantial— but far from catastrophic— numerical decline has entailed a loss of influence and bargaining power is a contentious, and perhaps ultimately unanswerable, question (Hyman 1989; Kelly 1988; McIlroy 1988). One reason is that developments in British industrial relations in the 1980s have displayed great diversity, a reflection both of contrasting sectoral and regional trends in employment and unemployment and of segmentation in labor markets. This helps explain why real incomes increased on average by some 25 percent during the decade, despite the highest levels of unemployment in half a century.

It follows that the relationship between collective bargaining and labor market dynamics has varied according to context. One useful distinction is between private manufacturing, public employment, and private sector services. In the former, a massive restructuring of employment occurred in the early 1980s, with a widespread process of closings and contractions, resulting in a loss of a quarter of all jobs. Particularly hard hit were those traditional sectors of male manual work where trade unionism was most strongly entrenched.

Though trade unions were thrown on the defensive, few employers—in marked contrast to their U.S. counterparts—pursued an active process of deunionization. In general, the density of unionization and the coverage of collective bargaining remained stable in this sector throughout the 1980s. What is less clear is how far the substantive influence of unions within collective bargaining was diminished.

Arguably, a process of "concession bargaining" has occurred, not—as in North America—over pay but over the organization of production. Unions—or groups of trade unionists on the shop floor—have often been forced to cede the job controls that were a traditional feature of industrial relations in British manufacturing. In particular, unions have been obliged to agree to schemes of technical innovation and work reorganization that have substantially reduced employment levels. Their main influence has been restricted to the form and timing of job loss. More specifically, collective bargaining has tended to encourage a process of controlled contraction through voluntary redundancy, early retirement, and "natural wastage." The reduction or elimination of overtime—which in Britain has always been a distinctive source of numerical flexibility—and temporary use of short-time working have been other union-preferred responses to reduced demand for labor. Such negotiated forms of employment restructuring have perhaps maintained relative job security for unionized insiders but at the cost of diminished employment opportunities for new labor force entrants. This may well help explain the disproportionately high levels of youth unemployment in Britain in the 1980s.

The public sector has been a major target for Conservative initiatives, on the grounds that "public sector monopolies" are both inherently inefficient and an incentive to irresponsible trade union power. One response has been a program of privatization encompassing such public utilities as gas, electricity, water, and telecommunications, as well as a range of other nationalized industries. Local authorities and the health service have been obliged to seek private tenders for a range of services traditionally performed by directly employed staff. Regulations that in the past ensured a monopoly for public enterprise (e.g., postal services, municipal transport, docks) have been modified or abolished, allowing competition from the private sector. In those areas of public employment that have otherwise survived unscathed, rigid budgetary controls—and a succession of strategic managerial appointments—have resulted in challenges to established employment practices and hence a far harsher climate for industrial relations.

The implications of these changes for employment protection have been mixed. The new priority for "commercial" as opposed to "social" considerations has caused a drastic contraction of employment in such nationalized industries as steel and coal, reinforcing regional imbalances especially in long-term unemployment. In the more profitable of the privatized industries, traditional industrial relations procedures—including those regulating dismissals—have been largely sustained. Here, too, protection for insiders has resulted. Compulsory competitive tendering has undoubtedly exposed some particularly vulnerable groups of workers (e.g., women in cleaning and catering) to the mercies of cost cutting and anti-union employers. Even among relatively core groups of employees in some public services, there has been a move toward "atypical" forms of employment. Overall, then, government policies toward the public sector have caused some deregulation of institutionalized employment protection, but the aggregate effect is probably not dramatic.

Finally, the main area of employment expansion in the 1980s was in private services. This is by no means a homogeneous category— including at one extreme financial and professional services with some of the highest-paid occupational groups in the country, at the other such services as catering, retail, and cleaning, with predominantly low-paid and female employees. This sector has contributed substantially to the growth of women employed part time: at the end of 1989, women represented 48 percent of the total employed work force, and of these, 42 percent worked part time (fewer than thirty hours a week). Private services have also provided much of the growth of self-employment, now more than 3 million workers.

In some cases, self-employed status is a mechanism whereby an employer can hire dependent workers while escaping the legal obligations normally associated with dependent employment. The Conservative government's encouragement of service sector growth as the archetype of an "enterprise economy" has interacted with its systematic efforts to impede collective organization by employees. Since the assault on "trade union power" has borne most heavily not on strongly unionized sectors but on those that have always presented difficulties for trade union organization, the consequence has been to increase the proportion of the labor market in which collectively bargained forms of employment protection are weak or nonexistent. It may reasonably be concluded that current British government policies lead inevitably to the expansion of what Gorz (1989) has described as a vulnerable, oppressed "servile class."

Conclusion

Labor law has never been a significant source of employment protection in Britain. Accordingly, it is misleading to regard the desire by the late Thatcher government to dismantle statutory regulation as a major factor in the restructuring of the British labor market. Rather, it is those policies that have directly or indirectly reduced the influence of collective bargaining that have most clearly affected the patterns of employment protection. The effects have been complex and uneven, but the aggregate outcome is clearly a significant expansion of that segment of the labor market in which a vacuum of regulation exists. The principle of "subsidiarity," one might suggest, here generates particularly unattractive social consequences.

Can any general lessons be drawn from the British experience in the 1980s? Though the United Kingdom represents an extreme case, processes of collective negotiation—whether centralized or decentralized, formal or informal—are important in many other countries in conditioning management decisions on recruitment and dismissal and the forms of contracts offered to workers. Whatever view is taken of the mechanisms of employment protection—as a general support for employee interests or a particularistic benefit for insiders at the expense of outsiders—it is clear that institutional as opposed to statutory regulation can be a major influence on labor market dynamics and that the relationship between the two can be of crucial importance. Likewise, the process of deregulation involves a complex interconnection between law and social control. A narrow legalistic analysis of employment protection is therefore inadequate, though more so in some countries than others. If the conclusion is that we require a particularly sophisticated conceptual and theoretical apparatus for the understanding of labor market dynamics, this should not be bad news for those in our own distinctive labor market.

17

Employee Protection Policy, the Labor Market, and Employment: The U.K. Experience

Brian Towers

B y the early 1980s, the Thatcher government's intention to induce a decisive shift away from the consensus, interventionist policies of its predecessors was apparent. All policies were to be broadly subordinated to the needs of economic policy, which was to be pursued in the context of a return to the free markets that were believed to have been associated with the United Kingdom's economic transformation in the nineteenth century. The labor market attracted particular attention on the grounds that—as claimed by the government and its supporters—it inhibited the pursuit of enterprise, efficiency, high productivity, and competitive unit labor costs and, in consequence, contributed to unemployment. The underperformance of the labor market was largely attributed to the excessive regulation and inflexibility arising from collective bargaining practices, trade union activities, and employment protection legislation. It followed that a program of labor market deregulation in its widest sense would contribute significantly to the achievement of economic goals and the maximization of employment opportunities.

This paper is concerned only with the effects of regulation (and deregulation) on employment rather than the wider issue of the relationship between free markets and economic performance. The paper is divided into four sections. In the first two I describe the evolution of employment protection in the United Kingdom and the weakening of that protection in the years up to and after 1979. The third section reviews the rationales for government policy in the light of empirical research into labor markets and the effects of employment protection. The final section reviews the arguments presented and offers some conclusions.

Employment Protection before 1979

Employment protection in the United Kingdom has traditionally been implemented by two means: direct legislation and the processes of collective bargaining.

Collective bargaining supported by a framework of legal immunities for trade unions (established by the Trade Disputes Act 1906) has been the route long preferred by the parties to industrial relations and successive governments. The role of legislation has been to provide protective "floors" where collective bargaining has little or no influence. Especially in the 1960s and 1970s, the legislative floors were progressively strengthened through the provision of new, individual employment rights. In the area of pay, the United Kingdom developed a mix of statutory bodies and procedures. These provided defenses against low pay and supported claims based on comparisons between different groups. The most notable of these bodies were the wages councils, and the use of pay comparisons was given a statutory procedure under schedule 11 of the 1975 Employment Protection Act. A similar prop to pay comparability applied to workers employed by companies having contracts with central and local government. The Successive Fair Wages Resolutions of the House of Commons (i.e., a simple majority of members, the first in 1891 and the last in 1946) guaranteed, though without the force of law, that workers on public sector contracts would be paid no less than their counterparts in their specific trade or industry taken as a whole.

Nonetheless, the history of government attempts to influence the level of pay settlements for its own and other employees it has preferred to work goes with rather than against the grain of collective bargaining. Its frequent recourse to counterinflationary policies up to 1979 normally was sought within a voluntary context and retreated into statutory compulsion only following failure to reach agreement or because the voluntary approach was ineffective even with agreement. Indeed, government has always preferred to implement policy at arm's length through permanent agencies, standing commissions, review bodies, and specially appointed committees.

The dual nature of the instruments of employment protection in the United Kingdom and the shifting and occasionally uneasy relationship between the two largely explain the piecemeal and ad hoc development of one of these instruments—statutory employment protection. Yet an overall, historical pattern can be identified. Kahn-Freund (1983) suggests three "layers" of development up to 1979. The first, established in the nineteenth century, sought through the Factories Acts to protect the health and safety of workers against the rigors of laissez-faire capitalism and, by separate legislation, to prevent employers from avoiding the cash payment of wages (i.e., "trucking").

The second layer related to wages. The earlier, preindustrialization involvement of the state in setting the level of wages finally succumbed to free market ideology in 1824, when London magistrates lost their power to fix the wages of silk weavers in Spitalfields (Bayliss 1962). State involvement in wage fixing did not reemerge until the last quarter of the nineteenth century following campaigns exposing low pay and degrading conditions in the "sweated" trades. The first House of Commons Fair Wages Resolution of 1891 was followed by the Trade Boards Act of 1909, which introduced statutory powers to fix minimum wages in low-paying industries without trade union organization. The boards were converted to tripartite wages councils in 1945. Their powers to set minimum rates were extended in a series of further statutes to include piecework, overtime rates, holiday pay, and holiday entitlements.

The third layer of protection moved beyond wages to the wider employment relationship, beginning with the Contracts of Employment Act (1963) and the Redundancy Payments Act two years later. In 1971, the Conservative government's Industrial Relations Act introduced protection against arbitrary dismissal through the already-existing industrial tribunals—the products of the 1964 Industrial Training Act. The 1971 act was repealed by the succeeding Labour administration, but it retained and extended the scope of the industrial tribunals in the EPA of 1975. In the same act, it extended its influence into the employment relationship with provisions for maternity leave and maternity pay. At the same time, it gave legislative support to the trade unions in advancing their protective functions. The independent Advisory Conciliation and Arbitration Service (ACAS), established under the EPA, was given statutory duty to promote collective bargaining through a statutory recognition procedure available to trade unions.

In addition to the EPA and the Employment Protection (Consolidation) Act (which in 1978 brought together earlier legislation in a more coherent form), parallel laws were enacted with direct implications for the employment relationship. These included measures to promote equal pay (1970), improve health and safety at work (1974), and limit sex and race discrimination (1975 and 1976).

The growth of legislative protection of employment was mainly concentrated in the period 1974–78, under the Labour government, but not exclusively so. The 1959–64 Conservative government began the legislative process, and the unfair dismissals provisions of the Conservative's 1971 act have remained in place, albeit with a narrowing of their scope and effectiveness.

Weakening of Employment Protection: 1979–90

While the differences between government polices up to and after 1979 are often exaggerated (MacInnes 1987), there was undoubtedly a much stronger emphasis in the latter period on the subordination of employment and industrial relations policies to economic policy. Economic policy had two strands: the control of inflation through the instrument of the money supply and the progressive deregulation of product and labor markets, although the second strand did not become fully manifest until after the Conservatives' second election victory of 1983 and the quiet relaxation followed by the de facto abandonment of the monetary strategy after 1985. The deregulation of product markets was primarily sought through the privatization program of selling off state-owned industries and transferring public sector services to the private sector. The deregulation of labor markets was approached through weakening the instruments of employment protection.

The long and virtual consensus (although with differing emphases) between the parties over the need to extend employment protection was in large measure rejected by the three Thatcher governments after 1979. Its legislative program (supported by its policies as a public sector employer) was directed primarily

TABLE 17-1. Unemployment in the United Kingdom, December 1979–89

Year	Number (1,000s)	Percentage
1979	1,261	5.2
1980	2,100	8.6
1981	2,764	11.5
1982	3,097	12.8
1983	3,079	12.8
1984	3,219	13.4
1985	3,273	11.8
1986	3,229	11.6
1987	2,696	9.6
1988	2,047	7.3
1989	1,639	5.8

Source: Department of Employment.

toward reducing the trade unions' ability to protect their members under a system of supportive collective bargaining rather than toward taking up the floor of employment protection legislation laid down over the previous thirty years. This process was, in practice, limited, however, and in certain respects individual rights were advanced.

Measures against the Trade Unions

The government's intention to weaken the trade unions, and by implication the process of collective bargaining, was materially assisted by economic policies associated with the rapid growth of unemployment in the early 1980s and its maintenance at historically high levels throughout most of the decade (table 17–1). Furthermore, net employment growth in the recovery from the 1980–81 recession centered on the rapid expansion of private sector services while employment continued to decline in production and construction (table 17–2).

The restructuring illustrated in table 17–2, which was welcomed by the government as a necessary economic development, was the principal explanation for the rapid fall in trade union membership in both absolute and relative terms from the peaks of 1979. The consequent erosion of the trade unions' influence, bargaining power, and confidence was reinforced by the government's legislative program and policies to reduce the employment protection functions of the unions. This program and associated policies covered trade union recognition, the decentralization of collective bargaining, the removal of the closed shop, the placing of limits on the scope of industrial action, and the use of ballots to regulate both the conduct of industrial action and internal trade union organization.

Trade union recognition. Under the 1975 Employment Protection Act, independent trade unions were given a unilateral statutory procedure to seek recognition. This statutory procedure was abolished by the government in 1980, although a voluntary procedure through ACAS was retained. Hence, in the 1980s,

TABLE 17-2. Job Creation in the United Kingdom, 1981–89

Category of worker	1981 (1,000s)	1985 (1,000s)	1989 (1,000s)	Change 1981–89
All employees	21,386	20,920	21,931	+2.5%
Agriculture and fishing	343	321	280	−18.4
Production and construction	7,900	6,830	6,577	−16.7
Services	13,142	13,769	15,074	+14.7
Wholesale and retail distribution	3,163	3,186	3,336	+5.5
Hotels and catering	930	1,027	1,091	+17.3
Banking, insurance, and finance	1,712	2,039	2,588	+51.2
Public administration	1,844	1,862	1,909	+3.5
Education	1,559	1,557	1,710	+9.7
Medical and other health services	1,247	1,301	1,426	+14.4

Source: Department of Employment data from June of each year.

there was a reversal to the pre–1975 position (i.e., British employers were not by law required to recognize or bargain with trade unions and could withdraw recognition previously granted). Since 1980 there has been a decline in the growth of recognition agreements, although this may have had more to do with trade union weakness than with the abolition of the statutory procedure. When the procedure was in force, it was rarely used, although the unions had less need of a statutory route in the 1970s than in the 1980s, when conditions were much less favorable to the recognition process (Towers 1989).

Decentralization. Since the mid–1980s, the government has taken a strong line against national pay bargaining at industry and company levels. It has been viewed as both inflationary and insensitive to local labor market conditions. It has already been abolished in the nationalized water industry, soon to be privatized; reduced in importance in civil service pay negotiations; and strongly advocated in local government and bargaining arrangements for teachers' pay. The private sector seems to be following the government's example. Recent evidence suggests an acceleration of a long-established trend away from multiemployer, industry level bargaining toward single-company bargaining at group and/or plant level (Palmer 1990). Well-publicized developments in major industries such as banking, railways, docks, and steel have attracted imitators. In the main, however, the decentralization process has been closely associated with the reduction in the bargaining strength of the trade unions.

The closed shop. Even as late as the 1989 Employment Act, the government did not take the step of formally banning the closed shop; it simply withdrew the statutory immunities that gave closed shops legal protection. The 1989 Employment Bill, however, which became law in 1990, abolished trade union membership as a condition of employment.

Industrial action. Under British common law, virtually all industrial action is illegal (i.e., in breach of contract). The "right" to take industrial action has been protected since the 1906 Trade Disputes Act by statutory immunities designed to prevent court action by employers against workers involved in industrial disputes.

In 1982, these immunities were significantly narrowed to exclude political as opposed to trade disputes. In 1984, majority ballots were required to guarantee immunity for official industrial action, although under the 1988 Employment Act, individual trade union members, even under a majority vote, can still refuse to strike without risking disciplinary action by their unions and have recourse to a new commissioner for the rights of trade union members. The balloting rules were extended to unofficial industrial action in 1990 through a requirement for unions formally to repudiate such action, leaving trade union members open to dismissal by their employers.

During disputes themselves, the option of supportive secondary action has now been abolished, and through legal decisions and police practice, picketing is effectively restricted to a maximum of six persons. Additionally, during or after the disputes, employers now have the power to dismiss those involved on a selective basis without risking an action for unfair dismissal at an industrial tribunal.

Ballots and trade union organization. The government's procedure for balloting has been applied to areas beyond industrial action. All members of union national executives and their senior officers are now subject to reelection by secret ballot at least five times each year. Since 1984, unions must also ballot every ten years to retain their political funds. Previously, under the 1913 Trade Union Act, there was no requirement to ballot at regular intervals.

This comprehensive, so-called step-by-step legislation (six statutes from 1980 to 1990) is potentially far-reaching in its effects. Employers are required to initiate action for alleged breaches of the law by trade unions, but there is evidence they are reluctant to do so (Evans 1986). Furthermore, the balloting requirements do not seem to have hampered recourse to official action, and ballots are now used routinely to strengthen unions' negotiating positions. On the potential constraints placed on unofficial action via ballots or union repudiation, it is possible that employers will wish to avoid counterproductive legal action. It is also possible that the attempt to undermine the unions' political funds through ten-yearly balloting has resulted in affirmative votes in every union, and a number of other unions set up political funds for the first time. More generally, these examples indicate how industrial relations legislation can be limited in its effects by the practical imperatives of collective bargaining. In the case of the United Kingdom, it may also be that government influences employer behavior more effectively by setting an example or merely exhorting a view than by legislating. The banning of independent trade unions (and subsequent dismissal of some members) at the Government Communications Head Quarters (GCHQ) in 1984 may have influenced the rising (though still limited) incidence of derecognition in the late 1980s. The trend toward decentralization of collective bargaining may also have been stimulated by strong government advice and example. It is also likely that the government's key role in the defeat of the National Union of Mineworkers in 1984–85 both weakened other trade unions' resolve and stiffened so-called macho management stances.

In general, the limited influence of industrial relations legislation (or its unintended consequences) on the behavior of management and trade unions may help explain the equally limited impact of employment protection legislation. I will return to this issue later in the paper.

Deregulation

The employment protection legislation of the Thatcher government has been deregulatory in two main respects. First, it has been its general intention to limit, and in some cases remove, what it sees as restrictive statutory individual rights, even though in certain cases the regulatory process has been advanced, in part because of the impact of European Community legislation on the United Kingdom. Second, employment protection legislation has removed most of the statutory regulation of pay.

Limiting individual rights. The route to the implementation of statutory individual rights lies in the system of tribunals established in 1964. The jurisdiction of the tribunals includes compensation for redundancy, claims for equal pay, redress for race and sex discrimination, and a limited number of occupational health and safety matters. The work of the tribunals was, and is, dominated, however, by unfair dismissal claims, which consistently account for at least 70 percent of all cases. Since 1979 the rules regulating unfair dismissal claims have been subject to two major changes. The length of the continuous employment period before a claim can be brought has been extended from six months to two years. There has also been a change in the responsibility for the burden of proof. Responsibility formerly lay with the employer, but it now rests equally with the dismissed employee. There has been an overall drop in the number of unfair dismissal applications as well as in the number proceeding to tribunal.

Experiences in the area of women's rights have been mixed. Although maternity payments and access to maternity leave have been made more difficult, time off is now available for prenatal care. In 1986, antidiscrimination provisions were introduced, and there is now an important new right to claim equal pay for work of equal value. The specific right derives from European Community legislation and has recently been underpinned by a number of significant legal decisions in the courts. More recently, in the Employment Act 1989, most legislation that discriminates against women in employment and training has been removed, including the ban on working in quarries and in mines. Women are also eligible to receive statutory redundancy payments up to the same age limit as men, normally sixty-five. The 1989 act also removes restrictions on the hours, including on night work, that young people over school-leaving age may work. They are also now permitted to engage in street trading.

The gains for women have been implemented by the government through positive regulation and deregulation, although they may have been motivated more by a concern about impending labor shortages than by an enthusiasm for greater equality. This ambivalence was especially evident in the government's reluctance to translate the EC's equal pay provisions into British law. In any event, the measures discouraging discrimination and promoting positive rights for women have been given strong instrumental support by some British employers (notably in banking and retailing), in reaction to the labor scarcity among young people and fears of a major expansion of equal value claims by trade unions.

EC legislation has also extended protection to employment contracts, trade union recognition, and collective agreements following takeovers, mergers, or corporate restructuring under the Transfer of Undertakings (Protection of Employment) Regulations of 1981, although so far this protection has not been viewed as unequivocal in the courts (Towers 1989).

EC legislative pressure has not, however, been the sole explanation for the continuing growth of regulation alongside deregulation. Several British government policy initiatives have significantly advanced the degree of intervention. The prime example is the government's ambitious training programs both for young people (Youth Training Scheme) and adults (Enterprise Training), reflecting the importance of training as a policy issue and the commitment to training by the previous Labour administration.

In certain respects the emphasis on training (especially for young people) initially partly reflected the government's desire to reduce the official level of unemployment. More recently, it has clearly been a reaction to the skilled labor shortage, which is limiting economic expansion, and the unfavorable comparisons regarding training drawn by influential commentators among the United Kingdom, West Germany, France, the United States, and Japan (U.K. Department of Employment 1988).

Training has not been seen as an activity that, in quantity and quality, can be left to the market alone, in spite of the rhetoric. Indeed, it is something of a paradox in relation to training and other examples of intervention that a government that has made a political and economic virtue of deregulation has, in fact, added to the layers of regulation (Lewis 1986). Training may be becoming less exceptional, however. The recently established Training and Enterprise Councils, which are administered by employers, represent a withdrawal from the interventionist training strategy. Even funding, which comes through the Department of Employment, has been cut and looks to be set on a downward course.

The government has also been ambivalent about its intention to abolish the long-established wages councils. These grew out of the trade boards, set up under the act of 1909. The regulatory powers of the councils were progressively extended, and until 1986 they could set piecework and overtime rates, holiday pay and holiday entitlements, as well as basic rates. Under the Wages Act of 1986, the twenty-six councils, still covering 2.5 million workers, were restricted to the setting of a single minimum hourly and overtime rate; young people under twenty-one were removed from their jurisdiction; small businesses were required to be represented on the employers' side; and the councils had to allow for the possible effects on levels of employment in setting rates.

These provisions reflected two key aspects of the government's philosophy and concerns: first, its view that fixing wages above market rates contributed to unemployment, not least that of young people, which remained at high levels

TABLE 17-3. Unemployment by Age in the United Kingdom, 1981–89

Year	Under 18	18–19	20–24	Under 25
1981	8.3	10.2	20.1	38.6
1982	7.5	10.4	19.7	37.6
1983	6.9	11.5	19.7	38.1
1984	6.4	12.2	20.8	39.4
1985	5.9	11.2	21.4	38.5
1986	5.5	10.0	21.1	36.6
1987	4.9	9.0	20.4	34.3
1988	4.5	8.4	20.0	32.9
1989	4.0	8.1	20.6	32.7

Source: Department of Employment data from January of each year.

throughout the 1980s (table 17–3); and second, its belief that small businesses were the driving force for competitiveness and job creation. Yet, faced with significant employer resistance, the government has recently drawn back from its original intention to abolish the councils completely.

Deregulating pay. The government's firm rejection in 1979 of the almost continuous income policies of the previous twenty years was demonstrated by early action against the statutory and institutional remnants of the Callaghan government. The comparability principle was weakened by the 1980 repeal of schedule 11 of the 1975 EPA, which had given trade unions the right to seek a legally enforceable award against employers through the Central Arbitration Committee. The same fate befell the Clegg Comparability Commission as it repeatedly disappointed the government by failing to make advances toward reconciling the long-established comparability principle with the revived doctrine of market forces. The government also acted against the pay regulation machinery of much older provenance. Fair wages (i.e., the industry's "going rate") for workers on public sector contracts had been guaranteed by successive House of Commons resolutions since 1891. A House resolution of 1982 abruptly overturned its predecessors.

Rationales for Policy

Official British thinking in the area of employment protection has been influenced by what Standing has termed (1986b:5) the "new orthodoxy of economic theory," that is, that greater flexibility in labor markets (parallel to product, capital, and financial markets) will allow them to "clear" at lower levels of unemployment growth. This search for greater flexibility requires the removal (or at least a significant limiting) of imperfections and rigidities, in particular, employment protection legislation and the capacity of trade unions to inhibit the cold, beneficial showers of market forces. The British government has, in a recent and important white paper, pointed to what it calls three "barriers to employment": poor industrial relations; excessive pay increases and inflexible pay arrangements;

and the inadequate supply of trained people. It has undertaken to remove these barriers through a "sustained program of deregulation in the labor market to secure the flexibility we need for employment growth" (U.K. Department of Employment 1988:19).

Interestingly, as Rosenberg (1989b:13) has pointed out, what were once termed rights under employment protection legislation have been converted into rigidities. Similarly, as has been frequently observed by British commentators, in the case of trade unions, their statutory protections or "immunities" have become "privileges." This redefinition completes the neoclassical perspective, which is then free to inform the rationales for policy and its implementation. But this perspective is not limited to one dimension: it reaches down to the level of the firm. As Rosenberg (14) again puts it: "The role of the state is clear—deregulate the labor market in order to eliminate the rigidities and approach a purely 'competitive' labor market. This will directly increase wage and numerical flexibility. It will indirectly lead to more functional flexibility by weakening unions, thus increasing the freedom of employers to reorganize the work process in order to increase efficiency."

While British policy toward the labor market is clear in its intentions, it is not always consistent and can be charged with unrealism. Inconsistency, for example, in the case of the government's approach to employment protection legislation, which combines deregulation with increasing regulation, need not be a problem. Policy contradictions are not necessarily a handicap toward the achievement of a mix of policy goals for which different instruments are appropriate. Policies may be at best futile, however, or at worst counterproductive if they are informed by mistaken assessments of the actual functioning of institutions and social processes or guided by unrealistic objectives regarding their removal or reform. In particular, the official vision of how labor markets function has doubtful validity on the basis of well-established empirical research. Furthermore, the government's own commissioned research throughout the 1980s consistently frustrates the view that employers are handicapped in their freedom to pursue flexible employment strategies by employment protection legislation.

Labor Markets and Their Reform

In policy discussions about labor markets, the terms "deregulated," "competitive," and "flexible" are frequently used both interchangeably and without clear meaning. In *Employment for the 1990s* (1988), it is implicitly assumed that deregulation will lead to greater labor market flexibility. This follows of course, only if it is assumed that deregulation will remove the rigidities and imperfections that inhibit the flexible processes supposedly attached to competitive labor markets that will be released after deregulation. If regulation exists in the context not of competition but of permanently segmented labor markets, then deregulation may simply remove protection from the most disadvantaged (i.e., "deregulated labor markets are not synonymous with competitive labor markets") (Rubery et al. 1989).

Nor does deregulation mean what it says in the legal sense. Some labor lawyers have recently pointed out that the removal of statutory protection through deregulation can simply restore regulation in its traditional form (i.e., through common law). For example, United Kingdom statutory employment protection applies only to employees with contracts of employment who meet minimum weekly hours and length of service qualifications (e.g., sixteen hours and two years' service for unfair dismissal protection). The "flexible labor force" of the self-employed, homeworkers, and young people in government training schemes are excluded. This narrow scope of statutory protection leaves large numbers of flexible workers and others subject to the uncertainties of the common-law rules regulating the employment relationship (Lewis 1986:14ff.). Further, this flexible labor force is not static. Recent estimates from research undertaken by the Department of Employment concludes that it comprises one-third of the labor force, that it has been growing rapidly over the 1980s, and that it is likely to keep growing into the 1990s (Hakim 1987).

Nor is flexibility a concept that has meaning only in this wider context. In recent years analysts have given considerable attention to labor flexibility within organizations. In the United Kingdom, work in the "flexible firm" (Atkinson 1987) has attracted widespread interest and controversy (Pollert 1987).

There is also a growing body of detailed empirical, international research that reports wide national variations in the pursuit of flexible labor goals (Standing 1986b and 1988b; de Neubourg 1990). A recent study by Brunhes for the OECD (1989a) identifies five forms of "enterprise labor flexibility" in the context of three national "models"—the Japanese, the American, and the Western European. This work reveals the viability, in different contexts, of combining employment protection with flexibility through an appropriate mixture of different means (i.e., the enterprise itself, the external labor market, and legislation).

None of this suggests the need for a seamless garment of flexibility and deregulation running from the enterprise to the external labor market as assumed by the neoclassical thinking influencing British policy. Neither is the neoclassical argument research-based. It is now a noncontroversial finding that the British labor market is divided into primary and secondary segments preventing market clearing across the labor market as a whole (Craig et al. 1982) and that this condition may be in its essentials a permanent one. Thus, although recent empirical research suggests that "simple dualist theories" do not match the evidence of multisegmented markets with some movement between the segments, the labor market remains structured "so as to perpetuate the enduring advantages and disadvantages of identifiable groups of workers" (Burchell and Rubery 1990).

The problems that arise when important areas of public policy are informed not by sound, empirical research but by unworldly theorizing are not confined to the United Kingdom, of course, but they certainly constitute a serious impediment to policy success in the United Kingdom as elsewhere. Furthermore, the current minimal impact of empirical labor market research on policy is reflected by the limited influence of research initiated, and funded, by the British government itself into the effects of employment protection legislation.

TABLE 17-4. Unfair Dismissal Cases and Outcomes in the United Kingdom, 1975–89

Year	Cases (1,000s)	Settled	Withdrawn	To tribunal
1975	24.4	34.1%	24.0%	41.9%
1976	36.6	35.4	20.3	44.2
1977	39.2	38.4	20.6	41.0
1978				
1979	39.8	40.4	23.1	36.5
1980	38.2	47.4	22.6	30.0
1981	43.8	40.0	24.8	35.1
1982	41.5	42.0	25.7	32.3
1983	38.6	43.6	23.8	32.6
1984	36.2	47.6	21.9	30.5
1985	35.4	50.9	23.8	25.3
1986	44.2	54.2	20.9	24.8
1987	39.0	63.3	16.3	20.4
1988	35.2	67.0	14.7	18.4
1989	34.9	70.0	13.1	16.9

Source: Advisory, Conciliation, and Arbitration Service annual reports.

Employment Protection Legislation: Research Evidence, 1979–89

The first phase of Thatcherite economic policy put great stress on small firms as an ingredient in the revival of enterprise, economic growth, and job creation. In the case of employment protection legislation, it was believed that its impact was greatest on small firms. The definition of a small firm poses problems. The seminal Bolton Report (1971) used two hundred or fewer employees for manufacturing, twenty-five or fewer for construction, and a turnover of less than £50,000 for retailing. Evans et al. (1985) defined small as under fifty employees. The argument was that the legislation adds to employment costs via recruitment, supervision, discipline, and freedom to dismiss, inhibiting numerically flexible responses to changes in labor market conditions (Evans et al. 1985). It was also believed that the earnings of young people relative to adults had a negative effect on their employment, thereby explaining the high levels of unemployment among youth. In 1981, those under twenty-five constituted 38.6 percent of total unemployment. By 1984, the figure stood at 39.4 percent and although it fell in the second part of the 1980s, it remained as high as 32.7 percent in 1989 (table 17–4).

The Department of Employment commissioned several surveys throughout the late 1970s and 1980s to examine the impact of the legislation on small firms. Clifton and Tatton-Brown (1979) found that employment protection legislation had not had a negative impact on small-firm employment, although it had induced employers to exercise more care in recruiting workers. This study confirmed earlier research by the Policy Studies Institute (Daniel and Stilgoe 1978) for large firms. Research published in 1985, also by the Department of Employment (Evans et al. 1985), in which firms with fewer than fifty employees made up 64 percent of the sample, found that firms' hiring and dismissal behavior was only marginally influenced by employment legislation and that both managers and their employees had minimal knowledge of the legislation.

These findings were confirmed by another Department of Employment study published in 1989 (Scott et al.). This research found that employment legislation was a matter of indifference and insignificance to small firms; no more than 7 percent identified it as a problem. Further, recalling the finding of Evans et al. (1985), according to which the primary explanation for indifference was ignorance of the regulations in force, legislation was not attributed any importance with respect to staffing policies.

Ignorance of the legislation was also an important finding of independent 1982 research (Ford 1982) that studied the employment effects of wages councils, unfair dismissal, redundancy payments, employment contracts, and maternity leave. This research also confirmed that few firms file claims under the legislation and concluded that "in general the literature consistently highlights the contrast between lack of knowledge and experience of the legislation, and the emphatic beliefs in its detrimental consequences" (42).

Research into the effects of earnings levels on the employment of young people has attracted widespread academic interest given its policy importance and in the context of the debate on the role of wage councils in setting statutory minimum wage rates. Marsden and Richardson (1986) contrasted the relatively high unemployment of young people after the 1979 recession with the lower figures that prevailed in the 1930s, when the earnings of young people were lower as a proportion of average earnings and employment protection hardly existed. They concluded that the employment costs of young people do influence their employment share and that reducing their pay would improve their job prospects, although this could be at the expense of adult workers, particularly in a nonexpansionary period. They rejected arguments for the abolition of wages councils, however, on the grounds that the effect could be to replace adult workers by young people at lower rates of pay.

Marsden and Richardson's views had been confirmed earlier in an econometric study for the Department of Employment (Wells 1983), which, using data for the period 1969–81, found that the employment of young people under eighteen years is reduced by increases in their average earnings relative to those of adults. A later Department of Employment survey (Roberts et al. 1989) examined the employment effect on young people's employment prospects of the Youth Training Scheme and of the Young Workers' Scheme (YWS). The YWS was introduced in 1982. Employers were offered subsidies if their wage rates for sixteen year olds were set below the prescribed levels under the scheme. This research found that for a large majority of employers the schemes made no difference with regard to the number of young people actually employed and that firms' hiring decisions were largely conditioned by traditional influences—gender, reluctance to change working practices, and the low priority given to training.

The consensus of the research in the 1980s that the great majority of employers do not adjust their employment policies in response to employment legislation was seen as conclusive even among leading neoclassical economists with the ear of the Thatcher government (Minford 1985). The government acted on the belief, however, especially in relation to small businesses, that employment protection was a negative influence on employment. Government action concentrated on two areas: unfair dismissal rules and procedures and the wages councils. The qualifying period for unfair dismissal was, as we have seen, extended to two years in 1985 and the burden of proof on the employee was given equal weight to that of the employer. The negative effect upon the number of unfair dismissal cases proceeding to tribunal hearing was immediate (table 17–4). Thus, the government-sponsored research demonstrated that small firms had been given help they did not require.

Review and Conclusions

Policies that seek to improve job security and establish minimum working conditions for those in employment, either through legislation or the promotion of collective bargaining, do not have, or need, economic or employment rationales. They can be pursued for social or political reasons even if negative employment consequences can be demonstrated. A century ago the Anti-Sweating League, in its campaigns that led to the Act of 1909, and the trade boards—the progenitors of the present wages councils—argued that even if setting minimum rates of pay to protect workers and their families would lead to fewer jobs, the jobs were not worth saving if the low wages attached to them were insufficient to take workers and their families out of poverty and degradation (Bayliss 1962). The loss of employment argument was ignored by Winston Churchill at the Board of Trade and did in fact prove to have little, if any, substance. The argument does, however, stubbornly remain a century later and again despite evidence to the contrary.

There is an absence of empirical evidence in United Kingdom conditions that employment protection policies have a significant negative impact on employment opportunities. This evidence is drawn from the Department of Employment's own surveys, which have been subjected to careful examination in a study by the International Labor Organization. The conclusion was the same: "What does seem to be happening is that employment protection is being provided for only a shrinking proportion of the labor force, possibly to those who least need it and only to a small number of those who have the greatest employment security. As such, its relevance as an explanation of high unemployment is surely minimal" (Standing 1986b:63).

This skepticism can be extended to the special case of youth unemployment, in which the evidence that the number of lost jobs rose because their pay was too high relative to that of adults was sufficiently tentative and limited to be discounted. Nor is there evidence to justify the claims of positive benefits to small companies from deregulation. Much of the government's case relates to unfair dismissal. Dismissal cases are concentrated in small companies, but this is likely to be because they lack satisfactory dismissal procedures compared to large organizations.

Unfair dismissals also need to be kept firmly in perspective relative to all dismissals. One reported but dated estimate (Lewis 1989:319) of the total annual number of dismissals in the United Kingdom is 3 million, including redundancies. Redundancies in Great Britain, based on Department of Employment figures, rose from 187,000 in 1979 to a peak of 532,000 in 1981 and then fell steadily to 104,000 in 1989. An estimate of 2.5 million dismissals, discounting redundancies at the highest figure for the 1980s, suggests that unfair dismissal cases (table 17–3) amounted to 1.8 percent of all individual dismissals in 1981. Only about one-sixth actually go on to a tribunal, where no more than one-third win their cases, and of these only 1 percent get their jobs back. Nonetheless, unfair dismissal cases dominate the work of industrial tribunals, which are the main agencies for handling all forms of complaints under the employment protection legislation of the past thirty years. It is not at all surprising that all the survey research sponsored by the Department of Employment from 1979 to 1989 supports the statistical picture that employment protection legislation is of negligible interest to small firms.

The legislation is also narrow in its coverage. As we have seen, it largely excludes the growing "flexible labor" force (self-employed, part-timers, temporary workers), one-third of the whole, on which the government places such emphasis in its policy. These workers have at best minimal employment protection, and about two-thirds are female (Hakim 1987). It is in this unprotected segment of the labor force that market adjustments in pay and conditions are most likely to occur (i.e., outside the protected segments in full-time, permanent employment). It is also in the flexible labor force—mainly among women and young workers—that efforts to promote unionization and collective bargaining have the greatest potential and present the greatest problems. Some employers—especially in retailing and banking—are beginning to respond to the labor shortages among young people with significant improvements in pay, an extension of parallel full-time benefits, and the tailoring of working time to meet the needs of married women.

While current labor market research on segmentation suggests that labor markets are more likely to be multisegmented and to have some movement between the segments rather than being rigidly dualistic, these findings still remain far from the assumptions of the neoclassical model. If it is generally true that the market segments composing the supply of labor are "likely to be relatively stable over time and associated with interactive relationships between [the] individuals' past work history, their current labor market position and their attitudes towards their current jobs and expectations of the future" (Burchell and Rubery 1990:42), then deregulatory policies, assuming the holy verities of the neoclassical model, are likely to be ineffective or simply to place greater burdens on those already disadvantaged.

The labor market model that seems to have most influenced United Kingdom policy makers in the 1980s is that of the United States. Brunhes et al. (1989:22) stress the high degree of external mobility in the U.S. labor market. Yet it is of interest in terms of "traditional" and "flexible" employment that the proportionate split in the United States is similar to that in the United Kingdom and differs little from that of the EC as a whole (Hakim 1987). Furthermore, though the employment-at-will principle of American law regulating the contract of employment eases the ability of employers to dismiss individual employees, there is evidence of a slow erosion of that principle. Forty-four states have now developed one or more common-law exceptions, although only one (Montana) has legislated on wrongful discharge (Gould, chap. 5). There is, of course, another national model available to the U.K. government that has a high degree of employment protection, a similar culture, and an overall economic performance much superior to that of the United Kingdom and the United States and that has been sustained over a long time: that of West Germany.

Government policies and legislation, of course, have a much smaller impact than is commonly supposed or governments claim. For example, collective bargaining in the United Kingdom, on the frequently repeated authority of ACAS, has not been seriously eroded in spite of the government's six major pieces of legislation, its own strong stance toward the public sector as a major employer, and a constant stream of exhortation and advice: "Collective bargaining still remains, directly or indirectly, the prime determinant of the terms and conditions of employment for the majority of people at work" (ACAS 1990:18).

At the level of the enterprise, large or small, much takes place that is influenced by powerful external pressures, of which the government is only one and may be the least important. For example, while the U.K. government has frequently commended policies to increase labor flexibility in internal as well as external labor markets, corporate researchers repeatedly report the significance of other determinants, such as heightened international competition, technological change, growing acquisition and merger activity, and significant changes in the requirements of their customers. Even then, there is evidence that radical approaches to labor flexibility are not all that widespread and that the process of change and diffusion may be slowing down (Incomes Data Services 1990). Additionally, and this may be of wider significance for government policy, enterprises pursuing these radical policies normally do so in a much wider context, often including a strong commitment to job security. Of course, more often than not these enterprises in the United Kingdom are of Japanese or U.S. origin.

In the case of large U.S. corporations, Osterman (chap. 9) has suggested that a shift may be taking place from the "industrial" to the "salaried" model (i.e., from rigid job classifications, pay structures, and hire and fire to flexible job classifications, individual pay, and job security). Here the key trade-off is flexibility for security, although widespread progress toward the salaried model is contingent on supportive labor market policies from government toward employers and employees, not least a major commitment to training. This may be a more equitable and solidly based prescription for labor market change than that currently on the table in the United Kingdom.

France

18
Workers' Protection and the Regulation of Labor Relations in France during the 1980s

Antoine Lyon-Caen

I t is hardly surprising in a country like France, with its allegedly high level of legal "guaranteeism," that the persistence of high unemployment and the specter of aging production capacities have caused critics to denounce labor law as acting as a brake on modernization and as a factor of institutional "sclerosis" in the economy.

This denunciation, which was vehement among certain employer groups particularly in the late 1970s and early 1980s, has acquired a vitalist tone that may be summed up by the saying, "If you want the sap to run, you first must weed out the dead wood." In more prosaic terms, this reproach has in various guises nourished and given momentum to a political program that basically rests on two propositions: protective regulations above all involve costs for enterprises; and if the aim is employment promotion and modernization of the economy, one must start by dismantling regulations and reducing the density of legal protections in order to cut labor costs.

What has followed from this program? Has it been translated into the system of French labor law, that imposing body of legal regulations governing working conditions and industrial and labor relations?

Before analyzing this question, we must be aware of some limitations. The first limitation relates to the period under consideration: the political change that occurred in 1981, when socialists and communists, joined for the first time in postwar France to form a parliamentary majority, went hand in hand with a comprehensive project to establish industrial democracy in French labor relations. At that time it was inconceivable that the legal changes announced would entail any erosion or reduction in protective regulations for workers. Yet the legal reforms that were to follow between 1981 and 1985 by no means all involved a reinforcement or extension of workers' protection. Moreover, an analysis of the past decade of French labor legislation provides useful insights not only because the first phase (1981–85) can teach us many lessons but also because the subsequent years witnessed significant political changes (a conservative majority from 1986 to 1988, then the reelection of a socialist government in 1988) that help in answering a further question: to what extent are changes in labor legislation dependent on changes in government majorities?

The second limitation concerns the very object of our analysis: the complexity and multiplicity of legal regulations—the important role they have played in the current political debate in France—and spatial restrictions induce me to limit my attention to the level of legislation. This may suggest that labor relations in France are essentially regulated by law. Such an impression would be highly misleading, however, in that it is primarily the social partners (i.e., union and employer confederations) and the immediate labor market parties themselves that transform and implement legal regulations into practice.

Given these general limitations, I can formulate my central hypothesis: the legal changes that have taken place in France during the past ten years have increased the flexibility of labor utilization by reducing the amount of direct, substantive restraint on management and by strengthening the collective bargaining element in the implementation of labor regulation,[1] yet without thereby affecting the fundamental balance between capital and labor, the establishment and maintenance of which has traditionally been the core objective of labor legislation.[2] In the subsequent sections of this paper I will substantiate this hypothesis from two angles, first, by taking a closer look at the source of labor regulation, namely, the role and intentions of the legislator, and, second, by analyzing the contents and substance of labor legislation enacted in the 1980s.

Role of Labor Legislation

Put simply, labor legislation during the past ten years was guided by two basic inspirations: the first, which prevailed during the initial years (1981–85), conceives labor law as strengthening workers' rights and thereby acting as a vehicle toward industrial democracy (*citoyenneté dans l'entreprise*). This was the guiding philosophy underlying the "Arroux laws,"[3] enacted between 1981 and 1983, which increased workers' protection against employers' abuses of their disciplinary power, strengthened workers' voice in matters concerning working conditions (act of August 4, 1981), and mandated equal opportunities for men and women in the workplace (act of July 13, 1983). The object of these laws and of the whole legislative package of which they are a part[4] was to transform the existing "code of labor relations" into a "code of economic democracy." This approach reflects a traditional vision of labor law as, by extending workers' rights and protections,

---

[1] These two lines of development have been poignantly described by Jeammaud (1986) as "the law of flexible labor" on the one hand and "the flexible law of labor" on the other.

[2] With regard to this balance (which should not be confounded with equality), see Lyon-Caen and Jeammaud 1986.

[3] Named after the labor secretary in office between 1981 and 1983.

[4] Essentially the law of collective bargaining and of collective firm-level representation as well as the law on occupational safety and health.

a core element of political democracy at large. What deserves consideration in the current context, however, is not so much the appeal to general political ideals but its reference to economic efficiency. Besides promoting industrial democracy, the extension of workers' rights in the early 1980s was presented as a road toward liberating idle resources that could not be mobilized within a rigid setting of persistent asymmetries between capital and labor, unbalanced disciplinary powers in the hands of employers, and narrow job demarcations. Knowledge, innovative capacities and the search for new forms of work organization necessary to overcome the economic crisis could only be activated if supported by law. "Industrial democracy as a remedy for the crisis-stricken economy" was the motto underlying the emerging new "legal economism" of the early 1980s (see Jeammaud 1983).

But even if external circumstances brought an early end to the underlying political program, French labor legislation has nonetheless preserved its sensitivity to the economic implications of workers' rights in labor relations. In fact, the change in political power that took place in 1986 had practically no consequences with regard to the legal innovations enacted between 1981 and 1983 by the preceding Socialist government. Nor have subsequent repeated legal changes concerning "atypical" (or contingent) employment arrangements (particularly temporary work) (see Maurau, chap. 19), questioned the principle of equity and nondiscrimination in labor relations, regardless of whether they were born out of a liberal spirit (1986) or were designed to promote employment growth (1990).

The second intention underlying the labor legislation of the 1980s was to find ways to influence the functioning and job creation performance of the labor market. Most legislative efforts explicitly aimed at modifying legal barriers toward reducing unemployment. The tendency was clear: the enactment of new regulations or the modification of existing laws were conceived as purely instrumental in achieving goals beyond the law itself. Examples include the various legal changes that have taken place since 1985 in the area of "atypical" employment and the various measures introduced for promoting the reemployment of job seekers, particularly youngsters, women, and the long-term unemployed. Such legislative action, based mostly on statistical evidence, implies a high degree of regulatory instability, in that it constantly needs to be adapted to changing labor market conditions. The consequence has been a growing density and steady proliferation of state interventions into the labor market.

Another important trait of French labor legislation since the beginning of the 1980s has been the legal promotion of collective negotiations, which drew its justification from the relatively weak status of collective bargaining in France, the political intention to inject more democratic elements into labor relations, and the search for regulatory models that would allow more flexible adaptation to varying product market conditions. Diverse means were used to encourage negotiations: strengthening the rights of trade unions as well as workers' representation at the firm level; direct promotion of collective bargaining, notably by establishing legal obligations to bargain at firm and industry levels; and increasing the scope for collectively bargained standards.

The latter method reflects the new relationship between the law and collective bargaining. In fact, from 1982 onward, legislation recognized the possibility that collectively bargained terms could deviate from legal standards in a way not necessarily favorable for employees. Since 1982, this possibility of negotiating "derogatory agreements" (*accords derogatoires*) has been gradually expanded to cover the whole area of working time (duration and schedules) without, however, being extended to other aspects of working conditions.

Today hardly anyone would disagree that collective bargaining has gathered momentum under the influence of these legal developments. The annual reports by the Labor Ministry's labor, employment, and vocational training departments provide unambiguous evidence of this new contractual activity.[5] The surge in collective bargaining has not in any way been accompanied by a decline in legislative activity, however. It is this co-existence of regulation through law and collective bargaining that calls for some further explanation. One point that attracts attention is the trend toward "prenegotiating the law." Let us look at four examples.

The directive of January 16, 1982, on working time, which had the force of law, was to spawn "derogatory" agreements. It basically replicated a cross-sector agreement of July 1981. The law on continuing vocational training enacted on February 24, 1984, substantiated a cross-sector agreement of October 1983 on measures promoting youth employment. The act of December 30, 1986, relating to dismissal procedures, which abolished the much-criticized public authorization for economically motivated dismissals, did no more than codify, with few exceptions, the results of a national cross-sector agreement dating from October 20, 1986. Finally, the latest revision of the law governing "precarious" (i.e., contingent) employment contracts (fixed-term and temporary employment) through the act passed on July 12, 1990, simply adds weight to a prior national cross-sector agreement of March 30, 1990.

This process of prenegotiating the law is the outcome of diverse impulses. The public authorities look to the agreements between the "social partners" to discover substance and justification for legal reforms, as if, confronted with social relations that are rather difficult to govern, they show their willingness to trade legislative "sovereignty" for a certain degree of social consensus. But this concern for social consensus has taken place within a context of trade union pluralism and conflicting interests, and it has been rare for all the trade union confederations[6] to sign these regulatory agreements at once. Unable to achieve unanimous support for proposed reforms, the government regards legislation as an essential relay. It should be noted, however, that this procedure of collective prenegotiation and subsequent universalizing legislation commonly applies to areas traditionally governed by state regulations that, in order to function more efficiently, need to be modified.

If state legislation has continued to grow despite the surge in collective bargaining, this is partly because the legislation was intended to adjust the existing

---

[5]See annual reports published by La Documentation Française in Paris.

[6]France has five national, cross-sectoral union confederations representing workers' interests: the CGT, the CFTC, the CGT-FO, the CGC-CFE, and the CFDT.

legal framework to economic exigencies and firms' efficiency considerations and because collective bargaining cannot possibly cover every aspect of the adjustment process. It is therefore up to the legislator to devise and offer regulatory models as a quid pro quo for an alleviation of financial and social burdens on business. This has, in fact, been the preferred route for ensuring a multiplicity of work and employment patterns while at the same time maintaining basic protections for workers. Besides, collective bargaining is necessarily selective in that it cannot fully represent those social groups whose vulnerability has been accentuated by ongoing trends toward labor market fragmentation and for whose protection, therefore, special legal safeguards and legislative measures have to be devised.

Young people in search of first jobs, the long-term unemployed, and older workers threatened by corporate restructuring and reorganization have typically been the target groups of special employment policies based on administrative and legislative action. Although French trade unions, with their traditionally broad local, occupational, and cross-industry foundations, have recently appeared to be more willing to integrate the interests of these vulnerable groups into their bargaining agendas, experience shows that it has been the state that has primarily propagated the notion of "fragile constituencies" and has developed "positive discrimination" measures in their favor.

Last but not least, the proliferation of state legislation is certainly also due to the increasing regulation of collective bargaining itself, which can be seen as the price paid for the very limited credit generally given to collective bargaining in France. Legal regulation of collective bargaining has been required not only to promote collective bargaining as such and to establish procedural norms for collective negotiations but also, and above all, to enhance both parties' confidence in their negotiated agreements and to define the boundaries of collective bargaining, particularly with regard to the possibility of negotiating "derogatory" terms not necessarily to the benefit of workers. The most poignant example relates to the regulation and organization of working time. Although legal working-time standards have remained in force, deviations from these standards (e.g., extensions of the reference period for calculating average weekly working time, the individualization of working-time schedules, and the organization of special weekend shifts) have been legally permitted, but in each instance permission has been tied to special legal injunctions, such as mandatory topics for collective negotiation or legal guarantees of representative and participatory rights for the parties involved.[7] To the extent that the various components of working time have become negotiable, the amount of such accompanying legislation has expanded. This trend of the French system, at the heart of which is a quest for greater diversity through collective bargaining solutions that has necessitated an increase in concomitant

---

[7]Under the pluralist French trade union system, any representative union may, within legally defined limits, negotiate regulations that are then binding on all employees independent of union membership (universal validity of labor contracts). To prevent incursions on workers' interests, the law provides for a right to object to certain agreements on the part of the union representing the majority of workers in the enterprise (i.e., the union that obtains more than 50 percent of the votes in company elections); such an objection renders union contracts invalid.

legislative interventions, makes clear that flexibility is by no means incompatible with or necessarily inimical to workers' protection.

At the same time, the above reveals the complexity of the interrelationship between flexibility and regulation in France. If, as Gaudu (1986:361) has claimed, "the French way to flexibility is through expanding regulation," it is because regulation not only has played an important role in promoting "industrial democracy" but above all has been vital in broadening the scope for collective negotiations and establishing minimum standards, rules, and procedures for the implementation of alternative ways of hiring and terminating workers.[8] This example shows that legal regulation is by no means always prescriptive in nature. It can also take the form of regulatory offers, leaving room for alternative options, and/or, by setting disincentives, indicate a preference for one option over the other, or it may confine itself to establishing procedural rules and "arenas" for collective negotiations about the most suitable practices between the labor market parties themselves.

Contents of Labor Legislation

Looking back further to the second half of the 1970s, we can identify two trends in French labor legislation. The first was a trend toward progressive, legal "standardization" of employment and working conditions. Several factors were essential in contributing to this trend: a broad and realistic view of factual worker subordination taken by the courts, a general affirmation of the principle that the indefinite employment contract should be and remain the standard, the retention of a dense fabric of regulations governing working time and the preservation of close links between working hours and pay, as well as, of course, a growing emphasis on principles of nondiscrimination. The second trend was toward stabilization of employment relationships, reflecting the grown importance attached to seniority systems and the increasingly complex rules and procedures governing employee terminations, which had induced a substantial rise in firms' dismissal costs.

The 1980s by no means challenged these trends from the very beginning. Quite the contrary, one of the declared aims of the socialist reform program drawn up in 1981 was to set a limit on the expansion of "precarious" employment practices and to curb the tendency toward the "externalization" of labor through subcontracting and thereby to reestablish a higher degree of uniformity and "collectivity" in labor relations. After stricter regulations concerning temporary and fixed-term employment were enacted in early 1982, however (for details see Charraud, chap. 20), the aim of restricting atypical (or nonstandard) employment soon dropped

---

[8]Workers can be terminated or sent into early retirement. Nowadays, employee termination covers various procedures involving diverse protective provisions. For example, any employee threatened with dismissal for economic reasons must be offered retraining measures. If the employee accepts the offer, the employment contract is terminated "by mutual agreement," but this does not imply any relinquishing of compensation entitlements that are due in the case of regular dismissals. Likewise, complex regulations were introduced in 1987 to facilitate early retirement.

in priority on the political agenda, although it did not fall into oblivion. The political imperatives had changed and, henceforth, the preponderant political mottos have been "controlled diversity" and "adaptation to structural change."

Controlled Diversity of Employment Arrangements

The quest to incorporate diversity into the legal fabric of labor relations runs like an unbroken thread through the institutional evolution of the past decade. The models of alternative work patterns and nonstandard employment arrangements protected by labor legislation grew steadily in range and number, with the public debate focusing primarily on contingent models of the duration and organization of working time. In particular, legislative activities increasingly reflected the growing multiplicity of forms of employment. A brief list will suffice.

Alongside the permanent employment contract, which is still the normative pillar of common law, we have witnessed the emergence of noncontractual forms of employment as they characterize, for example, the legal status of participants in further training measures (*stagiaires*), who do not enjoy the same rights as regular employees. Only recently (law of December 1989), the legislator has taken steps to reintegrate such forms of noncontractual employment into the body of employment law by assimilating their legal status to that of atypical employment contracts, which have existed, for example, in the context of apprenticeship training.

The relative increase in such atypical employment arrangements combining work and training (*contrats formation-emploi*), which are legally derived from the old contract of apprenticeship, provided the second route toward the diversification of employment that occurred during the 1980s.

A third factor in the spread of contingent employment was the rapid increase in "flexible employment contracts," although not every type of such arrangement prompted an equally dense web of legal regulations and protections. These include fixed-term contracts and labor hired from temporary work agencies (regulations on temporary work date back to 1979), part-time employment, and so-called intermittent employment contracts that is, indefinite work contracts containing provisions for temporary interruptions (systematized since 1986), as well as employment contracts with intermediary agencies (regulated since 1987).

It would be misleading to say that the legal codification of these nonstandard forms of employment reflected any attempt to reverse the preceding trend toward standardization of the conditions of employment or to dismantle the dominant model of permanent, full-time employment that had evolved from it. In fact, the aim of legislative activities regarding contingent work during the 1980s was not only to incorporate the diversity in work patterns but also and primarily to control it. Here, again, a short typology takes the place of a more thorough analysis (for this, see Maurau, chap. 19).

First and foremost, controls were imposed by laying down the essential conditions and criteria under which each of these contingent employment arrangements may be used. Thus, the latter are not functionally equivalent or interchangeable, except maybe in the case of fixed-term contracts and labor hired from temporary work agencies.[9] The course legislation took during the 1980s is interesting in this respect: the initial restrictive policy of the early 1980s gave way to a gradual relaxation of restraints from 1985 on, which was followed by a return to a more restrictive policy in 1990.

Control can also be exerted through direct administrative interventions, for example, when firms apply for public subsidies or for exoneration from social costs (e.g., social security contributions). In special cases (e.g., "intermittent work contracts"), the task of curbing the spread of atypical employment arrangements has been left largely to the collective bargaining process: the use of such contracts is permitted only if it is provided for by a collective bargaining agreement.

Finally, while diversity in employment patterns has been encouraged by legislation, it has, at the same time, been limited by a sensible balance of deviations from common-law principles on the one hand and antidiscrimination provisions on the other. The aim of preserving this balance can be seen to underly not only most of the surging legislative activities in the area of labor law but also, and even more so, the vehement debates, particularly within the judiciary.

Adaptation to Structural Change

Employment stability remains a prime concern of social policy and labor law. Gradually, however, this preoccupation with employment stability is giving way to a stronger consideration of the need for adaptation. The trajectory of this shift in principles is rather complex. Let us look as three aspects of this development.

The body of new regulations relating to firm-level personnel management provide the first illustration of how change has become a value of its own in recent labor law legislation. In fact, recent labor legislation, most of it merely reiterating regulations stipulated in collective agreements, makes only vague hints about the mode of firm-level implementation. But given these at best casual hints, judges, in the hope of resisting changes negotiated through collective bargaining, have whittled down to almost nothing whatever rights and entitlements employees may attempt to deduce from their individual employment contracts.

Based on the argument that the terms established by collective bargaining agreements do not form part of individual work contracts, the bargaining parties have been more or less free to withdraw from and deny employees benefits and protections that previous agreements had granted them. This stance, justified by the need to adjust employment conditions and compensation patterns to economic and technological change, has been adopted and extended by the judiciary to include traditional practices that have always been an important source of firm-level labor regulation: an employer may at any time revoke hitherto adhered-to practices, and workers do not possess any leverage in their contracts to demand

---

[9]That they have in fact been viewed as complements rather than equivalents or substitutes is shown by Charraud in this volume (chap. 20).

that formerly applied conditions of pay and employment be preserved (see Savatier 1986; Deprez 1988; Langlois 1989).

A further example of how the quest for adaptation to changing market conditions and pressures to increase productivity has found its way into labor legislation is seen in the diversification of working-time schedules and the new role attributed to collective bargaining in establishing and implementing new working-time models. Yet another example of how economic efficiency criteria have been integrated into labor legislation are the transformations undergone by the law governing work force reductions.

Between 1975 and 1986, French dismissal law contained provisions requiring the prior authorization of dismissals for economic reasons by local labor authorities (*inspecteurs du travail*). This procedure provoked bitter criticism from employers. Whatever the truth in this criticism, the provisions were based largely on two considerations: the first was that firms should be prevented from using economically motivated work force reductions to upgrade the skill level of their work force through mere worker substitution; and the second was that any firm conducting major work force reductions involving dismissals should, within its means, provide some kind of compensation to the workers affected.

When the *autorisation administrative* of collective dismissals was finally abolished in 1986, virtually the last major legal obstacle to quantitative work force adjustments was removed. Although the removal of such obstacles may have been one reason underlying the legal change, there was another, frequently neglected dimension, which is evident in recent government initiatives and developments in collective bargaining: the abolition of collective dismissal procedures has stimulated the emergence of regulations concerning *qualitative* work force adjustment and "skills management." This has been accompanied by the introduction of a series of preventive measures, such as the establishment of a workers' right to reskilling[10] in the case of impending redundancies (enacted in August 1989); by a legal obligation on firms to draw up so-called adaptation plans in the case of technological reorganizations; by a legal requirement that there be regular company employment forecasts; and by the authorization of public agencies to provide financial support for measures by firms to prevent work force reductions.

Since 1989, a number of exemplary company agreements have instituted regulations in this spirit designed to organize what has come to be called anticipatory personnel management. Moreover, the judiciary, in a somehow praetorian manner, have begun to regard all redundancies announced in the name of restructuring production as illegal as long as firms have not submitted a plan for personnel adaptation.

What then do we discover if we seek a coherent interpretive framework that integrates all of these diverse developments? We perceive an as yet hesitant attempt to replace quantitative work force adjustment by more qualitative skills manage-

---

[10]In that reskilling takes place outside the firm and the firm merely has to bear some of the financial costs during retraining, this right cannot be seen as a serious constraint on firms' personnel practices.

ment, an attempt to preempt problems arising from dequalified labor and skill losses by anticipating developments and preventing skill mismatches. In other words, we encounter a new tendency toward replacing the hitherto prevailing model of quantitative employment stability with a model that emphasizes qualitative adjustments through labor mobility and human capital development.

Time will show if this emerging new model can be put to practice on a broader basis or if it will remain limited to a handful of champion firms and if current modes of labor regulation and prevailing conceptions of worker protection require further revisions. Whatever the case, the result will most likely add additional fuel to the heated debates of experts.

Concluding Hypotheses

The developments described above have been associated with a profound transformation of the nature of French labor legislation. This calls for some further interpretation that I will present in the form of two concluding hypotheses.

The first hypothesis refers to the historical roots and evolution of French labor legislation. Throughout the wider area of labor relations, state legislation has always played a major role. This would seem to be the outcome of a long-standing political contract that has persisted throughout variable states of the economy. In the framework of this political contract, which was molded in the late nineteenth century, legislation is seen as an instrument in the hands of government to establish and maintain a balance between capital and labor as well as between various categories of workers. Correcting market outcomes through redistribution has been the underlying rationale of social legislation (see Ewald 1987).

Yet legislation is the product of parliamentary (i.e., political) activity only in a very formal sense, which leads to my second hypothesis: modern labor legislation is in fact essentially shaped by a fairly limited circle of high-ranking representatives and functionaries from business and trade union organizations who, though seldom deeply investigated, are the real architects of labor law. In their "judicial culture" (see Lyon-Caen 1989:1) we would doubtlessly find some explanations for recent developments in labor legislation. These architects' paramount role in legislation demands justification as well as measures to ensure adequate democratic participation. They have to take into consideration the potential effects legal regulations may have on vital parameters of the functioning of labor markets. The fact that the impact of legislation thus becomes measurable in terms of its efficacy in achieving its political objectives implies that there is a constant need for reevaluation, rectification, and readjustment. The architects of law also have to take into consideration the concern for social consensus, which seems to explain the increasing triadic side by side nature of "prenegotiated laws," experimental decrees (i.e., "sunset legislation"), and the legislative proposition (rather than imposition) of regulatory models to the immediate labor market parties.

While focusing on recent developments in labor legislation and their underlying political objectives and justifications, we must not lose sight of ongoing overall economic and social developments. Workers have to be integrated in firms. This requires preparing them for continuous adaptation, mobility, and further training, rather than merely promising them an illusionary stability. When firms must cut their work forces, workers have to be reemployed elsewhere. It is certainly better to have employment with diminished guarantees than to be excluded from employment altogether.

French labor law is, in its way, a prisoner of its own history and architects, but that does not prevent it from undergoing notable transformations; far from it.

19

Regulation, Deregulation, and Labor Market Dynamics: The Case of France

Guy Maurau

The search for flexibility has promoted a broad spectrum of different forms of employment in France and, above all, a challenging of the guarantees attached to the dominant form of employment: dependent employment on the basis of an indefinite work contract.[1] Economic requirements have without doubt served to justify the emergence of such flexible forms of employment. But, as in other countries, this development has been shaped by the overall institutional framework and its particular impact on the labor market at large. I will first consider French labor legislation and the legal system covering labor relations in France. Once I have identified the nature of the relationship between labor market dynamics and labor market regulation, I will present and analyze the steps taken by the French government in 1985–86 toward deregulation. The examination of their possible impact will raise some questions about the efficacy of such measures in achieving their declared objectives.

The Labor Market and Regulation

When analyzing the labor market, consideration must be given to the respective positions and roles of legislation, industry-level collective bargaining, and negotiated procedures at the firm level. Two basic concepts of collective bargaining arrangements appear to be at odds in the current labor relations literature: the "transactional" concept, according to which collective agreements are a means of exchange between employers and trade unions involving mutual concessions; and the "protective" concept, according to which collective agreements serve to improve workers' relative position. Which of the two concepts is adequate depends on the sociohistorical setting and each country's labor market organization thus

[1] On this point compare Maurau and Okba 1986–87; Maurau 1988; and Maurau and Oudinet 1988. See also the bibliography at the end of each of these articles.

reflects "the philosophy and the culture of the society in which collective bargaining is taking place" (Javillier 1986:59).[2]

In France, statutory provisions and regulations occupy a privileged position in labor relations. Their declared intention is "to limit the powers of the employer in order to protect wage and salary earners and to recognize, to their benefit, the latter's subjective rights vis-à-vis their employer" (Lyon-Caen and Jeammaud 1986:19). Labor legislation is seen as a core element in "mediating the relations between the classes," whereas the role of provisions stemming from collective bargaining seems to be of secondary importance.

Since the beginning of the 1980s, however, public authorities have aimed at "more directly promoting collective negotiations particulary within the firm" (Lyon-Caen and Jeammaud 1986:29). The dominant concept underlying collective bargaining has shifted from being protective to being more transactional: "The classic form of 'redistributive' negotiations (designed to improve the rights and benefits of workers vis-à-vis minimum statutory requirements) is gradually being replaced by 'integrative' negotiations; this leads to 'quid pro quo' agreements, the most tangible results of which tend to correspond to employers' expectations" (Lyon-Caen and Jeammaud 1986:38–39).

This first characteristic of the institutional setting of the French labor market therefore refers to the relationship between legislation and collective bargaining. It is helpful to take a closer look at the concept of employment underlying French labor legislation: "the concept . . . of employment is the subject of major legal formalization in such a way that the law or practitioner in the field of labor legislation makes a relatively clear distinction between occupational activity, considered as dependent employment, and an activity which does not come under the category of (dependent) employment" (Merle 1989:26). The quotation draws attention to the distinction between dependent employment and other types of work relations and to the role of the former as a standard or model. Therein lies perhaps one of the main reasons for the often impassioned debates on the "erosion" of the "standard employment relationship" through the creation of "new" or "atypical" forms of employment. As Merle has stated, "innovation in the forms of employment is frequently perceived as involving the risk of attacking the model, of eroding labor legislation or, at worst, of helping to aggravate 'underemployment' " (1989:26).

From the mid–1970s on, growing economic uncertainties and the increasing constraints imposed by external competition on a slow-growth economy have led enterprises to call for a relaxation of protective regulations for employees as stipulated in the provisions covering dependent employment. These protective regulations cover a broad area ranging from employment stability, redundancy guarantees, and the maintainance of purchasing power through unemployment benefits to social protection in the widest sense. The French debate on atypical employment (*formes particulières d'emploi*) has to be seen against this background. Firms have come to regard standard employment as a burden, as an obstacle

---

[2]The terms *transactionnelle* and *protectrice* are used by Javillier (1986).

inhibiting necessary employment adjustments to variable labor demand, and as an impediment to necessary wage adjustments. By workers and trade unions alike, any relaxation of protective regulations can only be seen as a challenge to past labor achievements and a deterioration of the relative position of labor.

Furthermore, all economic agents have attached considerable importance to a statutory definition of dependent employment and atypical work. According to an EC survey conducted in 1985, 53 percent of all industrial firms in France expected a positive impact on employment from a relaxation of legal restraints on fixed-term contracts and temporary work, compared to only 27 percent in the United Kingdom (see Emerson 1988a; Elbaum 1988). In the same way, on the basis of a study by the Conseil National du Patronat Français (CNPF or National Council of French Employers) undertaken in early 1984, its then president, Yvon Gattaz, concluded that the abolition of certain regulatory constraints and parafiscal taxes would lead to the creation of 471,000 additional jobs, more than 400,000 of which would be created in the year immediately following implementation. One condition would have to be met, however: employers would have to be certain that these changes in employment relations were to be permanent.

Economic necessity for the one group, erosion of labor legislation for the other, the statutory and regulatory provisions concerning employment contracts have been at the center of the political and social debate for many years. The importance generally attributed to statutory and regulatory provisions obliged public authorities to take steps to codify firms' allegedly new employment practices. But new in this context is very relative: from the beginnings of industrialism in the nineteenth century, there have been very diversified forms of employment. The progressive elaboration of legal norms for atypical forms of employment (act 1–3–1972 on temporary employment, act 12–27–1975 on part-time employment, and act 1–3–1979 on fixed-term contracts) reflects first and foremost the need for a pragmatic management of labor relations: "To adapt the regulations to the new demands of the production system while avoiding opening the door to massive deregulation, the destabilizing effects of which on social relations and on labor market dynamics could prove greater than the gains to be made in terms of flexibility" (Merle 1989:30).

This desire for compromise while maintaining the statutory approach raises several issues. Employers have shown remarkable legal ingenuity in circumventing and evading protective regulations, for instance, by subcontracting work usually undertaken by wage and salary earners. Nevertheless, we should not a priori reject the preventive virtues of legislation. Thus, one might argue that the statutory approach has helped maintain a minimum consensus.

Legislation Promoting External Flexibility

Without going all the way back to the early 1970s and to the first legislative steps taken toward regulating atypical (contingent) employment, I shall focus on the reforms made during the 1980s. In fact, the coming into power of a socialist government in 1981 led in the area of labor legislation to a rupture in the

TABLE 19-1. *Number of Wage and Salary Earners in France, 1982–85*

	April-May 1982	March 1983	March 1984	March 1985
Full-time, permanent dependent employment	11,754	11,576	11,289	11,071
Agency workers	127	113	103	113
Fixed-term contracts	306	263	256	315

Source: Enquête d'Emploi.
Workers in state and regional authorities are not included.

previously prevailing favorable trend toward maximum flexibility. Thus, the presidential ordinances of February 5, 1982, on fixed-term contracts and temporary employment (i.e., workers supplied through temporary work agencies) were based on three principles:

1. Common law covers permanent contracts. The ordinances give the precise details of the grounds on which temporary work may be used.

2. In principle, it is not possible to conclude fixed-term contracts or to hire agency workers for more than six months or to use them to fill permanent positions.

3. All workers holding temporary jobs have the right to the same wages and benefits as workers hired on a permanent contract.

These ordinances led in 1982 and 1983 to a noticeable decline in the growth of temporary work arrangements (table 19–1).

The continued increase in unemployment forced public authorities from 1985 on to modify regulations defining dependent employment and the legal guarantees attached to it in order to enhance labor market flexibility. These first steps toward deregulation are important because they reveal a new approach on the part of the government.

In May 1985, collective agreements were signed covering temporary work agencies. This signaled the desire of temporary employment agencies to provide social guarantees and thus to improve their public reputation. These agreements were followed by the act of July 25, 1985, which created much more flexible conditions for the use of temporary workers than those specified by the 1982 ordinance. The law extended the maximum duration of temporary assignments beyond six months and prolonged the list of justified reasons for hiring temporary staff. Apart from granting more liberal statutory provisions, the main impact of the law was to be seen in its symbolic character: for the first time, a socialist government recognized the importance of temporary employment for labor market dynamics (see, for example, TECSA Conseil 1989).

The turning point in the legal regulation of atypical employment, marked by the ordinances of 1982, was but a temporary one. If the ordinances made the use of temporary work more difficult, they were merely reiterating a basic principle in French labor relations: the public nature of regulation. This had been elaborated progressively in order to increase steadily the minimum protection afforded to wage and salary earners. The underlying objective was "to assimilate as far as possible atypical forms of employment to the standard employment relationship" (Pelissier 1985:537) in terms of both individual and collective rights.

The assertion of equal rights for atypical and regular employees did not prevent the growing use of atypical work, however. Legislation had to be adapted to practices that were becoming increasingly widespread. Hence, the presidential decree no. 85–399 of April 3, 1985 (introduced before the act of July 25, 1985) stipulated that persons registered as unemployed for more than twelve months with the national employment agency (ANPE) could be hired on a fixed-term contract for an extended maximum duration of twenty-four months without the requirement of a particular reason for not hiring on a permanent basis. The law of July 1985 thus reflects a general development that had begun earlier. Nonetheless, this stage is important for two reasons: it crowns the development whereby labor legislation based on statutory or regulatory provisions must endeavor as far as possible to achieve a compromise between two conflicting demands, that is, to permit a transformation of labor relations while at the same time keeping at bay the disadvantages inherent in uninhibited competition. A general consensus appears to be emerging and gaining ground concerning the role of labor legislation.

The legal reform drafts of 1986 thus have to be seen in the context of a general development that had already begun both in the sphere of actual economic behavior and the sphere of labor legislation. What is new is their simultaneity: in a relatively short time several reform drafts were introduced that all aimed to increase labor market flexibility and to adapt legislation to economic needs. Legal reforms took place in three major areas: the obligation to obtain administrative permission to dismiss workers on economic grounds was abolished, restrictions on temporary work were loosened, and the introduction of more flexible working times was facilitated.

The first measure has without doubt attracted the most attention. Moreover, it is the one French employers most favored. In the CNPF study mentioned above, close to three-quarters (72 percent) of the assumed total employment impact of the new regulations was attributed to the abolition of the public authorization for laying off workers for economic reasons. The actual reform was undertaken in several steps, and efforts were made to involve the social partners (i.e., trade unions and employers' representatives). First, the act of July 3, 1986, obviated the need to obtain official permission for layoffs in the case of work force reductions involving fewer than ten workers. Second, the national interindustry agreement of October 20, 1986, envisaged the creation of retraining contracts (*contrats de conversion*) for large-scale redundancies.[3] Finally, the act of December 30, 1986, reformed all statutory provisions concerning the dismissal of staff for

---

[3]Two confederations refused to sign this agreement: the CGT (General Labor Confederation) and the CGC (General Confederation of Managerial Staff).

economic reasons and abolished all requirements to obtain official permission before dismissing staff on economic grounds.

Furthermore, the procedures were made much simpler. In the case of individual redundancies, the legally required procedure remained the same regardless of the reason for the redundancy, the size of the company, and the tenure of the employee: a mandatory interview must be held with the worker before notification, and the firm has to inform the authorities of individual dismissals only ex post.

For smaller-scale collective redundancies involving fewer than ten employees over a thirty-day period, the same procedural requirements were introduced as for individual redundancies. For larger-scale redundancies involving ten or more employees over a period of thirty days, a slightly more complicated procedure was enacted requiring prior consultations with the works council and verification of procedural compliance by the authorities. The requirement of an official verification of the economic grounds for the dismissals was abolished, however. The whole procedure must be completed within a maximum period of thirty days.

The main legal innovation regarding atypical work was introduced by the ordinance of August 11, 1986, on contingent employment (*travail différencié*). In addition to the creation of a new type of seasonal employment contract ("intermittent work"), the ordinance brought about two major innovations: a firm no longer has to give reasons for using temporary workers from agencies or workers hired on a fixed-term basis, and the maximum period for temporary work arrangements was generally extended to two years. Beyond doubt, these changes amounted to a dilution of hitherto prevailing legal standards, thus completing a development that had already been under way.

The current socialist government—as of July 1990—has enacted a further legal reform of atypical employment that at first sight appears more restrictive than the 1986 regulations[4] but in fact does not fundamentally challenge the possibility of relatively free use of atypical work arrangements.

The preparation of legislation regarding working hours proved to be more difficult. After overcoming a series of obstacles, the final act could not be passed until on June 19, 1987. In fact, the first hurdle was taken in February 1986 with the vote on the Delabarre act, enabling "variations" in weekly hours tied to the twofold condition of a reduction in average weekly hours and the drawing up of a company or sector agreement. Here too the objective was to legally codify practices that were already widespread. The act of 1987 legalized these practices by obviating the restrictive conditions imposed by the Delabarre act.

The main impact of this large-scale package of measures has been first and foremost psychological. The reforms reflect already existing practices considered necessary to improve labor market performance. It should also be noted that above

---

[4]The new law reduces the maximum duration for single or multiple temporary work arrangements to twelve to eighteen months (in exceptional cases twenty-four months) and limits the use of temporary workers to certain situations such as temporary work load, seasonal work, or anticipated total abolition of the job.

all these measures cover "external" or numerical flexibility. It is true that the act of June 19, 1987, provides for a quite liberal internal adaptation of working hours to production needs, but recent French legislation stresses first and foremost external flexibility (i.e., adjustment of the size of the work force). This explains the reforms of redundancy procedures and temporary work regulations. We can now ask whether these deregulation measures have actually influenced firms' behavior and have led to changes in labor market performance.

Deregulation, Firms' Personnel Policies, and the Labor Market

We can attempt to answer the question by analyzing time-series data describing labor market performance or by drawing on recent firm survey evidence. The available national labor market data help us locate the phenomena in a wider context.

The act of July 3, 1986, also put an end to the possibility of directly compiling statistical time series on economically motivated dismissals. The Ministry of Employment and Social Affairs was requested to publish the results of a survey on the effects of this law during the third quarter of 1986. The study that was finally submitted is far from satisfactory, however. The months of July, August, and September are not representative as far as labor turnover (hiring and firing) is concerned. Furthermore, the study fails to take into account the response lag after the law went into effect so that the reliability of the results is doubtful. Given these shortcomings, the study concluded that the act of July 3, 1986, had only a minor impact: "The volume and the structure of redundancies during the third quarter of 1986 are close to those observed for the third quarter of 1985" (Perreaux 1987).

Nevertheless, we have access to monthly figures on people registering as unemployed with the national employment agency (ANPE) after having been laid off for economic reasons. Up to the enactment of act of July 3, 1986, their numbers correlated relatively well with the official figures for redundancies (see Marchand and Martin Le-Goff 1987:9). The latter suggest a large increase in dismissals for economic reasons: "The econometric estimates indicate a monthly figure of around 40,000 redundancies (seasonally adjusted), i.e., similar in scope to the 35,000 officially authorized redundancies per month during the second quarter of 1985." This increase at the end of the second quarter of 1986 seems to be consistent with statistics on employment fluctuations in enterprises employing more than fifty workers: the number of dismissals for economic reasons rose by 17 percent from September to November 1985 as it did during the same months in 1986 (Marchand and Martin Le-Goff 1987).

Table 19–2 refers to inflows into registered unemployment by previous labor force status and type of separation from the last job and covers the period from 1984 to 1987. The data confirm that there was a slight increase in dismissals for economic reasons in 1986 (+ 3.5 percent) and 1987 (+ 3.1 percent). The more promising state of the French economy and the ensuing improvements in the

TABLE 19-2. *Inflows into Registered Unemployment in France by Reason, 1984–88*

Reason	Total 1984 (in 1,000s)	Change 1984/1985	Total 1985 (in 1,000s)	Change 1986/1985	Total 1986 (in 1,000s)	Total 1987 (in 1,000s)	Total 1988 (in 1,000s)	Change 1987/1986	Change 1988/1987
Economic redundancy	549.7	+2.7%	564.3	+3.5%	584.1	602.0	547.6	+3.1%	−9.0%
Other reason for redundancy	327.5	−2.2	320.4	+5.9	339.2	339.0	344.9	−0.1	+1.8
Resignation	283.6	−11.1	252.1	−0.4	251.0	236.7	243.1	−5.7	+2.7
End of fixed-term contract	1,307.1	+8.4	1,416.4	+14.2	1,617.3	1,729.4	1,822.2	+6.9	+5.4
End of temporary employment (agency work)	182.6	+4.7	191.2	+7.8	206.1	209.9	229.5	+1.8	+9.4
First-time entrant to unemployment	606.0	−1.8	595.3	+4.3	620.8	550.2	553.4	−11.4	+0.6
Reentrant to unemployment	318.5	−2.7	309.8	+0.5	311.4	271.2	313.6	−12.9	+15.7
Other	123.4	+11.9	138.1	+6.9	147.6	152.0	201.4	+3.0	+32.5
Total	3,698.4	+2.4	3,787.6	+7.7	4,077.5	4,090.2	4,255.7	+0.3	+4.0

Source: ANPE.

TABLE 19-3. Developments in Dependent Employment, 1982–88 (in thousands)

	April-May 1982	March 1983	March 1984	March 1985	March 1986	March 1987	March 1988
Full-time, permanent dependent employment[a]	11,754	11,576	11,289	11,071	10,861	10,765	10,685
All forms of nonstandard employment (practical training, part-time employment, temporary employment, fixed-term contracts)	1,999	2,009	2,078	2,333	2,663	2,775	2,971
Participants in on-the-job training	59	57	48	57	103	157	188
Trainees in state and local authorities	15	14	20	95	195	187	178
Temporary employment (agency workers)	127	113	103	113	128	122	164
Fixed-term contracts	306	263	256	315	389	478	538
Wage and salary earners							
Full-time	16,441	16,303	15,937	15,879	15,890	15,840	15,872
Part-time	1,536	1,609	1,706	1,867	2,075	2,078	2,166

Source: INSEE. Enquêtes d'Emploi.
[a]Excluding employees of state and regional authorities.

labor market have reversed this trend, however, and led to a decline in dismissals for economic reasons (− 9 percent) in 1988. It seems that in late 1986 and 1987 firms indeed used the less restrictive regulations to lay off a larger number of workers, who were then replaced by more suitable workers (the number of people reentering the work force increased by 6.1 percent in 1987 and by 4.9 percent in 1988). This trend is even more surprising inasmuch as the increase in economically motivated dismissals during that period was particularly pronounced in firms with fewer than ten workers where procedural requirements had been abolished altogether. Before looking more closely at the respective impact of economic fluctuations and legislation on labor market performance, I shall present some evidence on the changes in the use of temporary work.

The first statistical series in this field stem from population surveys. They refer to specific times of the year (usually March–April), allowing us to identify the relative share of different forms of employment among the work force at large (see table 19–3).

The data confirm the various forms and increasingly diversified pattern of employment: a decline in the number of regular jobs by more than a million in six years, a large increase in "work-and-training" contracts (contrats formation-emploi) among younger workers, and a continuing increase in temporary and fixed-term jobs. Even if the growth of the latter had been temporarily stopped by the ordinances of 1982, they started to increase again in 1984, and the legislative measures of 1985 and 1986 merely served to fuel this growth. We must recognize a certain efficacy of these measures, however. The net change in temporary jobs was 13.3 percent in 1986, − 4.7 percent in 1987, and 34.4 percent in 1988. The corresponding figures for fixed-term contracts were 23.5 percent in 1986, 22.9 percent in 1987, and 12.6 percent in 1988. Initially, it was mainly fixed-term employment that accounted for the total increase in atypical work.

The analysis of the structure of temporary jobs sheds some light on the reasons enterprises make use of them. Temporary workers hired from temporary work agencies and those hired directly on fixed-term contracts do not seem to be easily interchangeable. Agency workers are mostly men; workers in construction and industry (particularly in heavy industry) are overrepresented among them. By contrast, in the case of fixed-term contracts, the tertiary sector is dominant, with an overrepresentation of women. This basic structure has changed little up to now, but recent years have witnessed an increase in temporary work among higher-skilled workers: "We are now witnessing the introduction of temporary jobs in executive positions. From a few hundred in 1987, this figure rose to several thousand in 1988. The figures for temporary jobs in middle management have also strongly increased (by 50 percent). Normally engineers and technicians are the groups most attracted to these jobs" (Charraud and Guergoat 1989).

This leads us to investigate in more depth the reasons for using this type of employment. The results reveal a strong influence of the business cycle. In fact, at the beginning of an economic recovery recruitments are normally made in the form of atypical work (i.e., fixed-term contracts or agency work). Figure 19–1 shows that "the majority of hires are for nontraditional jobs. Of all workers hired during the past three years, one in two has an atypical job, whereas six years earlier the proportion was only one in three" (Cézard and Heller 1988:17). Younger people are affected most by this practice, particulary young women under thirty, who account for almost two-thirds of all temporary workers.

As far as the inflow into unemployment is concerned, the number of persons coming from a fixed-term contract increased from 35.3 percent in 1984 to 42.8 percent in 1988. During the same period the share of previous agency workers among the newly registered unemployed increased from 4.9 percent to 5.4 percent.

These flow data are probably an indication of lasting changes in the labor market. Since the early 1980s, hiring practices appear to have changed considerably, with 1984 being a key year (see table 19–4): for every 1,000 workers employed at the beginning of 1984, there were 193 recruitments during the following twelve months (212 in 1983), only 54 of whom were on a permanent basis (73 in 1983). The number of fixed-term recruitments per 1,000 wage and salary earners was 113 in 1984 (106 in 1983). The majority of *new* employees are given fixed-term jobs.

Considerations of this kind based on time-series data enable us to focus more directly on firm practices. The increase in economic uncertainty and foreign competition reinstated the concept of flexibility in employment. Firm and establishment surveys enable us to distinguish between internal flexibility, which involves adjusting the work volume without altering the size of the work force

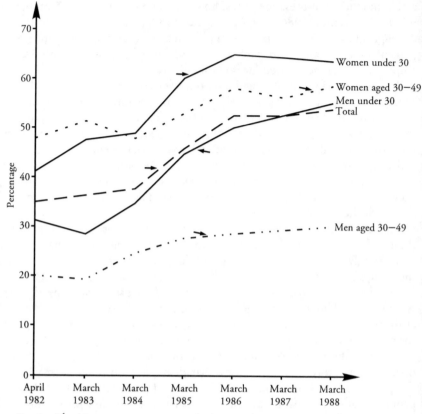

Source: *Enquête d'Émploi.*

[a] Number of wage and salary earners who have been with the company for less than three months on a part-time basis, in practical training, or on a temporary or fixed-term contract basis as a proportion of the total number of persons who have been with the company for fewer than three months.

FIGURE 19-1. Proportion of Recently Hired Wage and Salary Earners in Atypical Jobs in France

(variations in working hours or reorganization of work), and external flexibility, which involves adjusting the size of the work force to changes in production and demand (by making workers redundant or offering temporary jobs). Against this background we are seeking to identify the possible influence of the new legislation on the behavior of enterprises. We have access, among other things, to the results of a special study conducted by the Ministry of Employment in addition to quarterly time-series data on firms' hiring and firing behavior (see Gasnier 1989). A total of 13,828 undertakings, each with more than ten workers on their payroll, were covered by the special study. They took part in nine quarterly surveys between April 1985 and April 1987. These data are complemented by a special survey by the TECSA Conseil involving interviews with fifty-one firms using temporary

TABLE 19-4. *Recruitment by Kind: Fixed-Term and Temporary Engagements (number of recruitments per 1,000 wage and salary earners present at beginning of period)*

	Fixed-term employees				Agency workers				Total recruitments			
	Industry	BPW[a]	Services	Total	Industry	BPW[a]	Services	Total	Industry	BPW[a]	Services	Total
1983	79.4	75.4	165.8	106.9	48.4	76.9	119.4	73.1	149.7	103.1	334.1	212.1
1946	81.7	80.0	172.2	113.1	31.8	61.8	91.4	54.5	132.0	174.5	301.6	193.7

Prepared by D. Depardieu and M. C. Laulhe on the basis of DMMO studies.
[a]Building and public works.

workers, and with some temporary work agencies as well as representatives from trade unions and the Ministry of Employment.

It would seem that most French companies make little use of the possibilities for internal flexibility, for instance, by varying the length of working hours. According to one study, only 28.3 percent of the firms had introduced variable working hours between April 1985 and April 1987. Because of the design of the survey methods used, this figure may underestimate the use of flexible scehdules, especially in small and medium-sized enterprises: "The fact remains that the length of working hours is not the primary tool for adjusting employment to meet demand fluctuations" (Gasnier 1989:98). The study by the TECSA Conseil comes to the same conclusion: "In the majority of cases observed there does not appear to be any marked degree of flexibility in internal employment structures, nor, more importantly, do executives look on this as a major vehicle for flexibility" (TECSA Conseil 1989:52). The TECSA study offers the following information: overtime accounts for only 1 to 2 percent of total hours worked, flexible working hours seem to be too difficult to manage.

We should perhaps attempt to identify the real reasons underlying the limited use of internal flexibility and for the limited impact of legal provisions aimed at increasing working-time flexibility. Like Merle, I believe the answer may lie in the peculiar features of the French employment system: constraints inherent in the French system of labor relations, the lack of adult training schemes, and the deficit in public assistance in the case of excess labor (for example, short-time working subsidies or early retirement programs). All these circumstances have encouraged firms to turn to the external labor market (work force substitutions or adjustment of the number of employees to the needs of production) rather than make efforts to adapt the employed work force on a longer-term basis (Merle 1989:29).

With regard to external flexibility, priority has been given to the possibility of laying off staff, particularly for economic reasons, and the increased use of fixed-term and temporary work arrangements. As far as dismissals are concerned, the available data allow us to determine quite exactly the immediate impact of the new legislation during the second quarter of 1986. Although this impact should not be disregarded, the main emphasis should be on the influence of the business

cycle (recall that the number of people registered with ANPE as job seekers on
the grounds of economic dismissal fell by 9 percent in 1988 because the labor
market situation improved overall). Moreover, and this factor influenced the
creation of atypical jobs, companies had to reorganize and lay off large numbers
of workers during the first half of the 1980s. For the firms involved, this had been
a major traumatic experience that they did not want to repeat at any price. In the
eyes of management, the redundancy programs had failed. Managers saw them
as having had an adverse impact on the social climate in their enterprises, by
running counter to the values they were asking their employees to uphold (TECSA
Conseil 1989:27). Furthermore, personnel managers may have been afraid that
the liberalization of redundancy legislation would lead to a surge in labor court
litigation. This would be a further explanation for priority given to temporary
work arrangements.

I have noted that all the available indicators stress the importance of fixed-term
contracts and agency work at times when the general economic climate is characterized by increasing uncertainty. According to evidence from labor force surveys, the number of fixed-term personnel increased from 306,000 to 611,000
between 1982 and 1989 (+99.7 percent) and the number of agency workers
from 120,000 to 234,000 (+82.8 %). The restrictive legislation of 1982 no
doubt temporarily slowed down this development, but 1984 heralded renewed
growth in atypical jobs. The main surge in temporary work occurred *before* the
legislative changes of 1985 and 1986.

The two studies mentioned (Gasnier 1989; TECSA Conseil 1989) emphasize
the need for analytical firm-level research. The TECSA study distinguishes between three factors that could explain the recourse to temporary jobs. First, there
are the *structural factors* peculiar to the individual firm (its social tradition or
product market environment). Companies engaged in seasonal activities have to
make more use of this kind of employment. The choice between fixed-term
contracts and agency workers may depend on the tradition within the company
or even its system of values.

Second, there are *"climatic" factors* linked to the experiences of the company
and the development of its economic environment during recent years. It should
be remembered that the traumatic effects of large-scale redundancies up to the
mid-1980s may have resulted in a stronger recourse to fixed-term and temporary
arrangements, at least in the beginning of the subsequent economic recovery.
Permanent contracts are offered only if the employment situation is seen as stable.
If the company is still committed to reducing its work force, use of atypical
arrangements may constitute a "safety valve." Furthermore, any increase in economic uncertainties cannot but encourage companies to move in the same direction (i.e., to offer jobs involving little or no employment protection).

Third, and finally, there are *opportunity factors* linked to the immediate economic situation and peculiar to each company. Some companies, for example,
use atypical jobs as a recruitment tactic. Thus, "there will be a greater volume of
atypical jobs in the company during the period of recruiting additional staff"
(TECSA Conseil 1989:46).

Is it possible to distinguish between different types of firms based on the factors that influence their flexibility decisions? Choices may depend first and foremost on purely economic considerations. In this case, fixed-term contracts may appear advantageous, at least in the short run, but the higher costs of temporary workers hired from agencies may be justified by the fact that these workers normally entail fewer difficulties for the user enterprise. In other cases, it is the social climate in the company that will benefit. Pressure to integrate the holders of fixed-term contracts into the permanent work force is greater than in the case of agency workers. Hence, the former will be used uniquely in the prerecruitment phase.

In reality, and this does not help in our analysis, the diversity of factors at play explains the great degree of heterogeneity in the behavior of companies and the difficulties involved in identifying the genuine impact of deregulation. I should try to establish a typology, however. The study by TECSA Conseil (1989) indicates that firms with cyclically varying working hours also "made greater and more diverse use of workers on fixed-term contracts, a category that has grown to the detriment of stable employment. In these establishments, the number of permanent personnel had, in fact, declined more than in other production units." This no doubt explains the development of dualism in the labor market.

One criterion for distinguishing between firms with different recruitment practices would be the existence or nonexistence of variations in the length of working hours for cyclical reasons. Firms mentioning such variations use recruitment on a fixed-term basis more often than firms with fixed working hours and those with variable working hours for structural reasons (for example, the reorganization of work or production). Firms with hours variations for cyclical reasons also make more frequent use of agency workers; this is true for 40 percent of these firms (compared to 37.7 percent of firms with fixed working hours and 36.5 percent of firms without any variations in weekly working time).

One explanation for the differences could be economic constraints. Firms that vary the length of working hours for cyclical reasons are often involved in seasonal or variable activities and make more use of different forms of flexibility than the others do. Firms that vary working hours for structural reasons are going through a difficult phase of reorganization and hire very few new people. Finally, the situation is no doubt easier for establishments with fixed working hours. They do not make use of atypical jobs except in periods of rising labor demand to achieve "flexibility in management and lower costs."

This preliminary conclusion requires some supplementary remarks. First of all, workers on fixed-term contracts and agency workers are not easily interchangeable. The latter have relatively short-term tasks, particularly in heavy industry. The former involve higher direct recruitment costs and must be given longer-term assignments, which may even lead to permanent employment (one in two workers initially hired on a fixed-term basis later enters permanent employment, compared to one in three agency workers). Even if atypical employment may act as a "bridge" into stable employment in some cases, it may also mark the beginning of a process

TABLE 19-5. *Proportion of User Firms and Proportion of Employees with Temporary (Agency and Fixed-Term) Contracts in the Total Work Force and among Wage and Salary Earners in User Firms in France, 1989*

Size of firm	Proportion of user firms	In total work force	Among wage and salary earners of user firms
		Proportion of wage and salary earners with temporary contracts (agency workers and workers on fixed-term contracts)	
10–49 wage and salary earners			
Fixed-term contracts	45.6%	4.2%	8.3%
Agency workers	8.3	0.7	6.5
Total	—	4.9	—
50–199 wage and salary earners			
Fixed-term contracts	71.1	4.6	—
Agency workers	24.1	1.3	4.7
Total	—	5.9	—
200–499 wage and salary earners			
Fixed-term contracts	80.9	3.9	4.7
Agency workers	41.5	1.5	3.4
Total	—	5.4	—
> 500 wage and salary earners			
Fixed-term contracts	83.3	2.4	2.7
Agency workers	59.6	1.3	1.0
Total	—	3.7	—
All institutions			
Fixed-term contracts	50.7	3.8	5.4
Agency workers	12.0	1.1	3.4
Total	—	4.9	—

Source: INSEE, *Premières synthèses*, October 1989, no. 2.

toward instability or even long-term unemployment. Second, the use of temporary work arrangements increases with the size of the undertaking (see table 19–5). Perhaps a larger-sized undertaking is more able to manage the diversified forms of jobs. Finally, it seems that the increase in atypical forms of employment coincides with an overall economic recovery. This has been the case since 1985 and more particularly since 1987.

There appears to be a set of very diverse, parallel factors that are responsible for the growth in atypical job arrangements and that have to be seen in the context of persisting high unemployment. The genuine impact of new legislation designed to encourage the use of atypical employment and to relax regulatory restraints can be determined only with difficulty. The economic actors, however, have attached considerable importance to the legislative changes. The measures introduced in 1985 and particularly in 1986 have been interpreted as creating greater freedom as far as redundancies and atypical jobs are concerned. Compounding the issue is the special nature of French labor market regulation, in which legislation plays a more prominent role than do collective agreements. If we want to promote regulation through collective agreements because it appears more adaptable to the diverse flexibility needs of firms, new economic challenges will emerge (the question of cost) and new social claims will be raised.

20
The Impact of Temporary Work Legislation in France, 1980–1989

Alain Charraud

As described in more detail in the preceding chapters, French legislation relating to the use of fixed-term contracts and labor provided by temporary work agencies was repeatedly amended during the past several years, first in 1982, then in 1985 and 1986, and most recently in July 1990. On the first occasion this was to curb abuses in the use of "precarious" work and to improve the protection afforded the workers concerned. In 1985 and 1986, legislative changes were introduced in view of the persistently high unemployment, with the aim of introducing a higher degree of flexibility into the regulations of the 1982 law, which was considered to be excessively restrictive. While the 1982 act appears to have checked recourse to these two types of employment, it appears that the two laws that followed merely echoed a widespread tendency toward a growth in temporary jobs.

That there has been an increase in temporary jobs is undeniable, and its influence on the stability of and imbalances within the labor market has been commented on extensively, from both theoretical and empirical perspectives (e.g., Boyer 1986a; Brunhes et al. 1989; Elbaum 1988). The links between temporary employment and political endeavors to tighten or relax legislation have not, however, to my knowledge, formed the focus of extensive analysis.

My aim in this paper is to examine in greater detail these links over the 1980–89 period. This preliminary study is mainly empirical and focuses primarily on trends in temporary work supplied through temporary work agencies. The development of fixed-term contracts relates as much, as we shall see, to legislation concerning publicly funded employment programs (job creation measures) as to that immediately promoting temporary work. What is more, in the case of agency

This paper presents the preliminary findings of a research report produced by Jean-Marie Fournier and Jean-Claude Guergoat for the Employment Policy Division of the Ministry of Labor's Studies and Statistics Department.

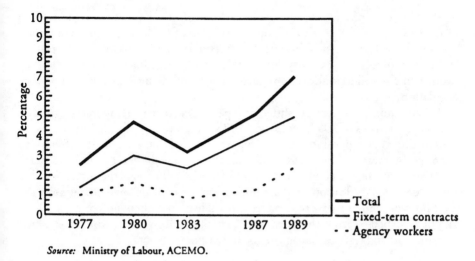

Source: Ministry of Labour, ACEMO.

FIGURE 20–1. Temporary Jobs as a Proportion of Total Dependent Employment in France, April 1977 to April 1989

work, it is more feasible to carry out a detailed econometric analysis of the effects of legislation. This analysis shows that the 1982 regulations had a very marked restrictive impact (a drop of approximately one-third in temporary work), while the 1985 and 1986 laws seem to have had only negligible effects.

Development of Fixed-Term Contracts (FTC) and Employment Policy

Between 1980 and 1983, the proportion of fixed-term contracts in total employment declined after having increased significantly during the preceding years. From 1984 until 1990, this proportion increased continuously (see fig. 20–1). If we want to identify the effects of legislation on this trend, we need to look at monthly or quarterly data on temporary work; such data were not available before 1985. What is more, after 1985, the growth in fixed-term contracts is due in part to state-funded job creation programs in the context of public policies designed to reduce youth unemployment. Thus, between 1985 and 1988, the number of persons in "alternance training" (work-and-training contracts [*contrats formation-emploi*]) increased from 110,000 to almost 320,000, of which approximately 80 percent were on fixed-term contracts. If we compare these figures to those for total fixed-term employment, which increased from roughly 300,000 in 1985 to about 600,000 in 1989, we can see that it is impossible to study the impact of legislation on temporary employment separately from the effects of public youth employment schemes and, more recently, public programs promoting the reemployment of unemployed adults. Furthermore, recent research has demonstrated that state-subsidized employment has in many cases replaced nonsubsidized jobs.

Unlike the case of fixed-term employment, we do have quarterly figures going back for more than twenty years on the volume of labor hired from temporary work agencies (expressed as annual full-time equivalents). In addition, job creation policies are unlikely to have any direct effects on the medium-term trend in agency work, which could cloud the observable effects of changes in temporary work legislation.

I shall examine in turn the different types of recourse to temporary work that the successive laws of 1982, 1985, and 1986 sought to modify, analyze the short- and medium-term developments arising from these laws, and, finally, attempt to account, by means of an econometric model, for these different types of recourse to temporary labor. The objective is to provide as full an explanation as possible and even a quantification of the genuine impact of legislative changes on the evolution of temporary work. The results will lead to a discussion of what effects might be expected from the most recent change in legislation, which has aimed at reintroducing restrictions on the use of temporary labor.

Legislation by Successive Amendments

During the 1980s, French legislation on the hiring of personnel through temporary work agencies (henceforth referred to as temporary employment) underwent two major changes that to a certain extent pointed in opposite directions. First, the decree of February 1982 sought to remedy abuses of the law by tightening regulations on temporary employment. The law restricted the use of temporary staff to two circumstances: replacement of an absent employee and an exceptional or transitory work load. Furthermore, it introduced protection that sought to give temporary employees the same social rights in terms of salaries, fringe benefits, working conditions, and access to facilities.

Second, the July 1985 act and the ensuing regulations of August 1986, passed in a climate of high unemployment (in 1985, the unemployment rate reached 10 percent), introduced a degree of flexibility into the restrictions imposed by the 1982 law. Under pressure from firms pushing for greater flexibility in personnel management, two new circumstances in which recourse to temporary staffing was permissible were introduced in 1985: occasional or seasonal demand and temporary staffing needs during restructuring.

Nevertheless, all the social benefits enacted in 1982 were retained. The temporary contract could now be renewed within a maximum term of twenty-four months, regardless of circumstances.

With the 1986 law, a further, and in some ways final, step toward enhancing flexibility was taken. The list limiting the circumstances in which the use of temporary staffing was permissible was, in effect, abolished. Since then, only the official definition of temporary employment can provide protection against abuse: the contract has to be drawn up for a specific job, which must not be part of the regular, ongoing activities of the firm. In that this definition applied to fixed-term contracts as well as to agency work (temporary employment), the two previously separate laws were thereby brought into line. Temporary employment thus joined

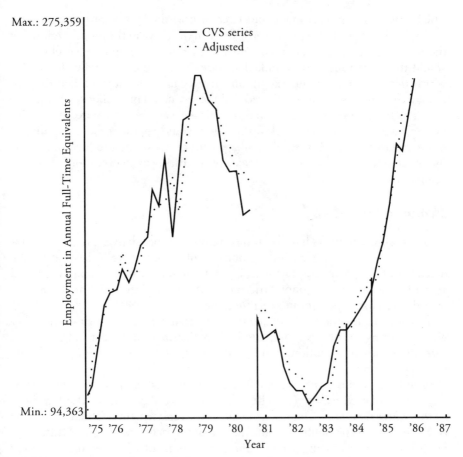

Max.: 275,359

— CVS series
· · · Adjusted

Employment in Annual Full-Time Equivalents

Min.: 94,363

'75 '76   '77   '78   '79   '80   '81   '82   '83   '84   '85   '86 '87

Year

FIGURE 20-2. Evolution of Temporary Work (Agency Work) in France since 1975

fixed-term employment as the main tool available to firms to adjust their employment levels to fluctuations in demand and restructuring requirements.

Trends in Temporary Employment (Agency Work)

The research findings on the nature of contracts signed between temporary work agencies and user firms enable us to estimate the quarterly volume of temporary employment (in annual full-time equivalents) for the period 1975–89. Adjusted for seasonal variations, these data illustrate the general trend (fig. 20–2). They are not, however, sufficient to enable us to draw definitive conclusions about the effects of the successive legal changes. The 1982 law does indeed seem to have brought about a drop in the use of temporary staff, but this trend had already begun earlier (in the second quarter of 1980). As for the 1985 and 1986 laws, they were enacted during a period of very fast growth starting in mid-1984, which was so strong that one could refer to it as the "temporary employment boom." Nevertheless, there is no vertical rise in the curve in the months following the implementation of these regulations. Variations in temporary employment would therefore appear to be linked to variations in the economic climate for which they are, to a certain extent, an early signal. Thus, the sudden drop in temporary employment in 1980 preceded the second oil price shock, whereas the rise from 1984 onward preceded an economic recovery. Furthermore, the continuous growth in temporary work up to 1989 would appear to be a response to more structural changes: the tight management of stocks and production and the use of temporary staff to carry out major restructuring in an ever more uncertain economic environment.

Econometric Model

So far, all my remarks have been qualitative and speculative. To gain a better understanding of the extent and significance of the effects of legislation on the dynamics of temporary employment, I have tried to evaluate the trends described above by means of an econometric model that takes into account the factors considered most important in explaining the trend.

To construct the model, I isolated the three main reasons for hiring temporary workers during the observation period: (1) replacement of absent staff, (2) need for staff because of exceptional work loads, and (3) need for temporary staff during restructuring.

In addition to these three reasons, three variables enable us to assess the relative importance of each reason: (1) The volume of paid employment (NEt) in those sectors where temporary employment allows the replacement of absent staff (that is, all sectors except public administration and agriculture), (2) the difference between actual employment levels and the amount of labor required to meet exceptional production demands: $NE^*t - NEt$; and (3) investment (It) relating to restructuring. This enables us to hypothesize that the volume of temporary labor needed to replace absent employees is $aNEt$, where $0 < a << 1$.

Similarly, the quantity of temporary staff required to remedy a shortfall in staffing in relation to production plans would be $b(NE^*t - NEt)$, where $b < 1$ if we assume only a partial difference.

Finally, $C It + d$ stands for the requirements of temporary staff linked to the restructuring process. A model accounting for these factors can therefore be expressed by the following equation:

$$TTt = aNEt + b(NE^*t - NEt) + cIt + d \qquad (20-1)$$

Supposing that firms' production hypotheses are in line with a Cobb-Douglas type function with complementary production factors, constant economies of scale and an elasticity of production factors of less than 1, the model can finally be expressed as follows:

$$TTt = a0 + a1\ It + a2\ Qt + a3\ NEt + St \qquad (20-2)$$

where Qt: gross internal market production and

$$t\text{:white noise } [E(\Sigma t) = 0;\ v(\Sigma t = \sigma;\ cov(\Sigma t, \Sigma t') = 0] \qquad (20\text{-}3)$$

This simple expression of the model presumes a series of strong hypotheses that I shall not deal with here in detail since they pertain to standard neoclassical economic theory. In particular, the step from short-term balance to long-term trends is achieved through capital-labor substitution. Over a short period of time, the model assumes the capital coefficient to be constant.

If we want to remove desired production levels from the model, we must assume that firms make rational hypotheses, that is:

$$Q^*t = E(Qt/Inf(t)) = Qt + Vt \qquad (20\text{--}4)$$

where E stands for the expectation of Qt in $t - 1$; $Inf(t)$: information in $t - 1$ about t.

Of course, the underlying neoclassical framework is extremely reductionist, but it does have the merit of allowing the effects of legislation to be introduced in a simple manner. To account for the three successive changes in legislation, it is sufficient to introduce indicators into the regression for each of the periods identified in the study. The indicator has the value of 1 if it is present in the given period and 0 if not. Its coefficient, if significant, indicates an upward movement on the right side of the regression. The model is expressed as:

$$TTt = a0 + a1\ NEt + a2\ Qt + a3\ It$$
$$+ b1\ leg\,82 + b2\ leg\,85 + b3\ leg\,86 + Ut \qquad (20\text{--}5)$$

where

$Leg\,82 = 1$ if tS [82:2; 85:3], 0 if not.
$Leg\,85 = 1$ if tS [85:4; 86:3], 0 if not.
$Leg\,86 = 1$ if tS [86:4; 89:4], 0 if not.

Expressed in this way, the coefficient for the first period (1975–82) is the constant $a0$ and each of the coefficients $b1$, $b2$, and $b3$ gives the variation observed in relation to this first period.

The legislative changes, in fact, had their effect in the quarter preceding their inclusion in the model.

Results

We shall not dwell on the convergence difficulties of the model, which are linked to the fact that I am operating a regression on seasonally adjusted figures, which gives rise to an auto-correlation of the remainders. If I use a standard least squares procedure, I can finally obtain a calculation method that converges. Whatever method is used, the $R2$ for the regressions is very high (of the order of 0.95) and the coefficients are all highly significant.

The coefficient for the 1982 legislation is extremely negative, confirming the depressing effect of the law on the temporary work market. If we take a confidence interval equal in size to the average divergence, we can estimate the drop in the trend for temporary employment after 1982 to amount to the equivalent of

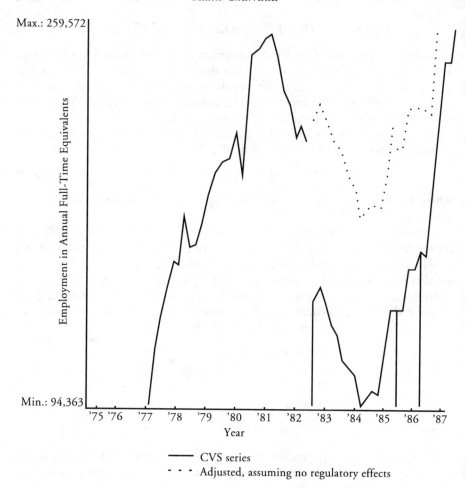

FIGURE 20-3. *Evolution of Temporary Work (Adjusted) in France in the Absence of Legislative Changes*

between sixty thousand and eighty thousand annual full-time jobs (that is, a fall of approximately one-third).

The other two coefficients are also negative but not to the same degree. The tests of the hypothesis do not allow us to state that they are significantly different. As a first hypothesis, therefore, we must conclude that the 1985 and 1986 laws, aimed at encouraging the use of temporary work, did not have any significant genuine effect on the upward trend in temporary employment.

We are not in a position to reject the hypothesis that these laws may have had a marginally stimulating effect, of the order of ten thousand jobs in annual full-time equivalents if the difference between the coefficient for the 1982–85 period and for the 1985–86 and 1986–89 periods are taken to be significant (see figs. 20–3 and 20–4).

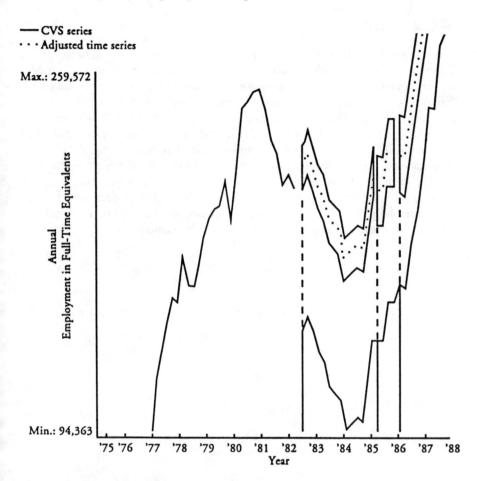

FIGURE 20–4. Evolution of Temporary Work (Adjusted) in France, including Hazard Estimate

The restrictive effects of the 1982 legislation did not, however, prevent temporary employment agencies and the firms they serve from adapting, for, as we note, from 1984 onward there was a surge in temporary employment. Thus, it appears as if the 1985 and 1986 laws were enacted to enable legislation to catch up with what had already been happening and perhaps to give a nudge in the right direction. In fact, these laws gave legal status to practices that apparently already existed in certain sectors: use of temporary staff as a form of parallel management of certain labor categories within the restructuring process or as a flexible management tool to respond to cyclical demand fluctuations, in what firms feel to be an uncertain economic environment with persisting labor market tensions.

What Next?

Although the 1985 and 1986 laws did not genuinely affect trends in temporary employment in any significant way at the time under investigation, they enabled the employment growth in temporary work to last longer than might have been expected, if one takes into account the vigorous upturns in 1987, 1988, and 1989 (approximately 200,000 jobs created in 1988–89, 90,000 in 1987). In this respect, the enactment of a new, more restrictive law in July 1990 should have put a halt to the upward trend in temporary employment. The most recent data show a "spontaneous" stabilization that might be attributable to the economic upturn and the creation of more stable (i.e., permanent) jobs. Furthermore, the gross figures for monthly temporary employment contracts show a decline in January and particularly in August 1989, precisely when the new restrictive legislative reform was at issue. This might be a case of "early warnings."

Italy

21
Employment Protection and Labor Relations in Italy

Tiziano Treu

Traditionally, the Italian industrial relations system has given great attention to the issue of job security (often to the detriment of flexibility). This focus results from the convergent effects of legal regulation and collective bargaining, both of which seek to apply rigid measures to protect workers from the various forms of employment reduction.[1] The Italian system has employed almost the complete typology of measures aimed at employment security known in industrialized countries. The main measures can be categorized in three groups.

The first group includes remedial measures intended to act as a deterrent to work force reduction and to the same extent reduce its effects on employees. These include advance notice, which is required in all cases of discharge but to a varying extent (from one week to six months, depending on the employee's seniority and category), and a length-of-service allowance, which is a lump-sum payment due in all cases of employment termination and equivalent to one month's salary per year of service. This is considerably more than in other countries.

The second group includes procedural and substantive requirements directed at prohibiting the arbitrary use of the employer's power to dismiss workers both individually and collectively. These requirements are similar to those in most countries; dismissals generally require just cause or justified reason. The control of the latter is stricter than in most other countries, however, since article 18 of Act 300/1970 empowers a judge to order reinstatement with back pay if an employee is unjustly discharged (an employer who does not abide by the judge's order is obliged to pay regular wages up to the time of actual reinstatement,

[1]For general information on Italian industrial relations and labor law, see Treu 1982.

particularly in those areas of the country where the discharged employee faces difficulty in finding another job). The effectiveness of this provision has been considerable, indeed greater in some respects than expected. Recent research indicates that more than 40 percent of such judicial orders lead to actual re-instatement.

The rigidity of these provisions has been "compensated," however, by their limited coverage: they do not apply to enterprises employing fewer than sixteen employees (six in agriculture). In firms employing fewer than thirty-five employees, the judge can grant only an indemnity to unjustly discharged employees.

Given the fragmented structure of the Italian economy, this limited coverage excludes a considerable percentage of the work force (more than one-third) from protection. This has tended to reinforce the dual nature of the Italian labor market. For this reason, the Italian system of employment security has been repeatedly challenged, lately with success. Under the pressure of a referendum to abrogate the limited coverage of individual dismissal protection, an act was passed that extended monetary compensation in cases of unjust dismissal to small-firm em-ployees (May 11, 1990, no. 108).

The Workers' Statute (Act 300/1970) does not include provisions for dismissal, a fact that reflects the traditional view that external controls of the grounds for collective dismissal are incompatible with the discretionary powers of the employer in a free enterprise system to assess and decide on the economic requirements of the enterprise. The courts have always held, however, that a worker dismissed because of collective work force reductions is entitled under Act 604 and Act 300 to appeal to the labor court to have the justification for the dismissal reviewed as if it were an individual dismissal for an alleged "objective" reason—at least after the conciliation procedures usually established by collective agreements have failed.

It also has been assumed that the courts cannot review the justification of the collective dismissal as such; they can only determine whether the dismissal of the individual employee necessarily followed from the firm's decision to reduce the size of its staff. Some courts and writers have questioned the social justification of employers' decisions on the ground that such dismissals should be used only as a last resort after other measures have been taken to avoid them. The important role of the judiciary in guaranteeing protection to individual workers in the case of collective dismissals has been reinforced by the practice of the collective bar-gaining parties and the administrative authorities, who also tend to apply the principle that dismissals should be a measure of last resort.

The third set of measures, less traditional and indeed rather peculiar to the Italian system, is intended not to limit the employer's power directly but to prevent collective dismissals in particular. These legislative measures provide for wage compensation to the employee in the case of layoff and short-time working to be paid out of a special social security fund called the Cassa Integrazione Guadagni (CIG, or the Wage Compensation Fund). The purpose of this legislation was to permit, in specified circumstances, derogation from the traditional labor and civil law rules, under which the employer had, except in cases of "force majeure," to pay regular wages if he or she wished to layoff workers temporarily or to employ them on short time instead of resorting to dismissals.

From its original limited scope, the use of the CIG was progressively extended during the 1970s in many respects: with respect to the conditions of intervention (not only temporary enterprise difficulties but also sectoral or local economic crises, industrial restructuring, reorganization or reconversion of the undertaking are now included); the definition of entitled beneficiaries (originally limited to blue-collar workers in industry, the CIG has been partially extended to white-collar workers and other sectors); the level of compensation, which has been unified at 80 percent of the gross pay for the hours not worked, and the maximum duration of benefits. Originally limited to thirteen weeks, benefits have been prolonged to nine months and in the case of enterprise reorganization for an indefinite period of time (i.e., as long as the reorganization lasts, which is monitored by ministerial authority). Authorizations have been granted all but automatically, with the consent and under the pressure of both social parties. In fact, the latter usually found recourse to the CIG the easiest solution insofar as it allows the firm numerical flexibility at practically no cost to the enterprise or to the workers concerned.

Because of this legal extension and the rather lenient public authorization practice, during the 1970s the CIG became the major instrument of public income protection for workers in the face of industrial restructuring and, indirectly, the major instrument of employment security. The number of lost work hours compensated by the CIG grew steadily throughout the late 1970s and early 1980s and reached its peak in 1984, from whence it declined to 758 million hours in 1984, 660 million hours in 1985, 594 million hours in 1986, 491 million hours in 1987, and 385 million hours in 1988. Because of the insufficiency of the social partners' contributions, financing of the CIG has been shifted largely onto the state budget.

Until the late 1970s, all these legislative measures were reinforced, with considerable success, by a union practice directed at controlling the use of staff at enterprise levels. The consultation procedure provided by law in the case of layoffs often amounted to actual bargaining. In cases of particularly serious economic difficulties, public mediation, public financial assistance, or even direct takeover of a firm by state-controlled entities (GEPI) contributed to overcoming firms' crises, again with the goal of job protection.

Practice in the Late 1970s

Beginning in the second half of the 1970s, a slow modification in the mix of employment protection measures becomes apparent. Both public authorities and social partners experienced difficulties in coping with the serious restructuring process affecting Italian (and European) industry by merely traditional job protection techniques. A first reaction in Italy was to apply more intensively than in the past a set of "defensive" measures directed toward concentrating protection on the core labor force, redistributing work among them, and supporting a "soft" expulsion of old workers from the labor market. Recruitment freezes, overtime reduction, and internal transfers were the first and easiest measures adopted, usually through collective bargaining. Rotation in layoff and working-time reduction followed; the latter in particular became a major union demand advanced (not only in Italy) with various objectives. In practice, working-time reduction has been possibly more effective in sheltering incumbent workers from the impact of reduced labor demand than in actually redistributing work at large (i.e., to the benefit of the unemployed).

Early retirement began to be widely subsidized through new legal provisions: By Act 115 of 1968, industrial workers made redundant due to restructuring in the context of an officially recognized local or sectoral crisis were entitled to a special indemnity equal to their seniority-graded pension benefits after reaching the age of fifty-seven (men) or fifty-two (women) (i.e., three years before regular retirement age) and after having paid pension contributions for at least fifteen years.

Another fairly common measure has been to encourage workers to accept early retirement by means of financial incentives. Enterprises in sectors severely affected by the economic crisis (e.g., the textile industry) have resorted extensively to this measure, usually on terms negotiated with the unions. The financial incentives are bargained on a case-by-case basis and usually are paid out of the general budget of the enterprise in the form of an increased length-of-service allowance.

In spite of their growing use, the measures indicated so far have not led to a reduction in redundancies in the sectors most severely hit by the economic crisis. Extraordinary legislation has therefore been enacted for the steel industry, permitting early retirement for employees over fifty years of age (Act 863/1984).

Other measures such as Act 675/1977 have been introduced to promote the mobility of workers affected by industrial crisis and restructuring. This act is intended to favor the direct passage of redundant employees from declining enterprises affected by economic crisis, restructuring, or reconversion to expanding enterprises, provided that they were receiving public financial aid or operate in the same industrial sector and area (as defined by the same administrative order certifying the state of crisis). The latter group of enterprises is prevented from resorting to the free labor market and must give priority in hiring to workers made redundant by firms of the former category who are on a special list at the regional labor offices. Act 675 also grants benefits to workers willing to be relocated through this procedure: a special installation allowance, reimbursement of travel and household moving expenses, as well as assistance with administrative formalities and housing.

In practice, however, the effects of this legislation have been totally disappointing, largely because of the inefficiency of the public labor offices that have been unable to apply the procedure, and the negative impact of the rigid recruitment requirements. Act 264 of 1949, still in force, allows recruitment only through the public labor offices and, thus, seriously limits the direct passage of workers from one firm to another. The law even imposes strict limits on the right of the employer to name the workers he or she requests from the offices (so-called request by number and qualification).

Impact of the Employment Measures

The value of all of these measures has been widely debated. Criticism has been growing in Italy as elsewhere concerning the excessive rigidity of labor market institutions, including the particularly excessive employment security regulations. According to the critics, this rigidity has not only inhibited firms' adaptability and economic efficiency but has contributed to a "blockade" of labor mobility and worker turnover, thereby protecting the existing work force at the cost of foreclosing job opportunities for newcomers (see Auer, chap. 23).

Indeed, labor turnover (total exits plus total entries), showed a marked decline from the end of the 1960s, when the level was similar to that observed in other countries, to the end of the 1970s (see Dell'Aringa 1981:79ff.; Martini 1979:66ff.). But the explanation of this trend remains controversial. Many authors have doubted that the reduction in hirings can simply be explained as a reaction by employers to legally imposed dismissal restraints (see Frey 1978; Garonna 1984). Instead, it has been assumed that the explanation for this trend lies in the interaction of different institutional or political factors. Some have emphasized the increased rigidity imposed on the labor market by trade union practices, particularly after the 1969 "hot" industrial relations autumn or, specifically, the restrictions on the employer's power to dismiss workers introduced by the Workers' Statute in 1970 (see Modigliani-Tarantelli 1979:205ff.). Others have pointed to the wide use of CIG-financed temporary layoffs in lieu of permanent dismissals, a practice promoted by trade unions in that period (see Dell'Aringa 1981:89). Others have tried to show the influence of such variables as the segmentation of the labor market or the role of small firms (see Valentini 1981:193ff.) and of the relatively large number of unpaid family and home workers in Italy, who are highly concentrated in certain sectors and regions.

No simple explanation appears to be satisfactory. Clearly, the influence of legal restrictions on dismissals as such should not be overstated. A closer analysis indicates that the secular decline in the dismissal rate—as in labor turnover in general—tends to be inversely correlated with firm size, thus confirming the importance of this variable. But the overall decrease in worker mobility and dismissal rates during the period 1967–77 was proportionately higher in small firms than in larger ones. In fact, the relative reduction in dismissal rates was highest in enterprises with fewer than nine employees. This contradicts the notion that dismissals should have become largely impossible in firms with thirty-five or more workers (i.e., where most legal dismissal restraints apply) and should have remained fairly easy in smaller firms that are excluded from legislation (see Scarpat-Pizzuto-Ferrari 1984[2]).

---

[2]This study showed that no decisive correlation existed over the period 1966–77 between the

An econometric analysis of labor mobility for the period 1965–77 has convincingly shown the particular function of income-protected layoffs as an anticyclical measure. The use of CIG is certainly influenced by the cycle, but it is also linked to political and social decisions. In fact, in 1974–75, it doubled in one year. Its effects have been important in bringing about a balanced reduction in labor mobility, particularly dismissals, in the low phase of the cycle and, indirectly, in hirings during the following upswing, given the connection between the two flows. The same trend could be tested for more recent years (after 1980), when use of the CIG more than doubled and then reached a maximum in 1984 (see Tronti, chap. 22).

The same analysis seems to confirm the important role of small firms (and small versus large firm segmentation) in all aspects of worker mobility: quits (given the type of workers who are more inclined to mobility: immigrants, marginal workers, and such and who are overrepresented in smaller firms), hirings, particularly small firms' greater use of seasonal hirings, and dismissals, given the less rigid dismissal restraints applying in small firms.[3]

Other institutional factors of rigidity that have contributed to reducing mobility in different sectors and types of employment include the legal restrictions on temporary work, union opposition to part-time employment, and, more generally, the presence of barriers (differentials in wages, working conditions, and recruitment methods, as well as special protective legislation for women) between different segments of the labor market, that is, between industry and the tertiary sector, between the public and private sectors, and between self-employment and dependent employment (see Martini 1979).

Though it is not possible to draw definitive conclusions from these studies, several interpretations and policy conclusions seem to be persuasive. The importance of institutional factors in addition to cyclical elements can hardly be denied. A general influence comes from the climate of industrial relations, which has favored increasing resistance to labor mobility, especially involuntary job separations, particularly in sectors with higher rates of unionization (i.e., medium-sized and larger firms). More than exerting direct effects as such, legal dismissal protection seems to be an expression or consequence of a more complex social phenomenon. Use of the CIG, itself an expression of the same social policy, appears to have played a significant anticyclical role that in many respects serves both enterprise flexibility and employment security by preserving the internal labor market (see Garonna 1984:114ff.).

Some negative consequences of the limited flexibility of the Italian labor market have also become increasingly evident, however, particularly in a period of slow growth and no job creation. One is the reduced overall turnover in unemployment, especially the increase in the duration of unemployment and the high

---

trend in industrial conflict and the rate of dismissals. The same negative results have been reached by analyzing data on absenteeism related to the size of firms.

[3]Difficulties involved with geographical mobility (e.g., availability of housing facilities) have been found to be another relevant variable in this context (see Valentini 1981).

percentage of first entrants such as young adults) among the unemployed (see Auer, chap. 23).

Italy in the early 1980s had the lowest percentage of dismissed workers and the highest share of first labor market entrants among the unemployed. The reduced labor mobility between sectors combined with pronounced labor market segmentation between core and marginal workers has concentrated flexibility pressures on marginal and unemployed workers and thus has tended to increase the importance of marginal labor, with potentially perverse effects. The traditional system, which favored extensive use of CIG, has certainly accounted for Italy's relative success in reducing mass dismissals and alleviating the impact of work force reduction on the core of the working population. To some extent this system has allowed large sectors of Italian industry to adjust with relatively low social and economic costs. But signs of deterioration have become clearly visible in the functioning of the CIG itself. Not only has static income protection usually prevailed over the CIG's original objective of supporting personnel restructuring and enterprise reconversion, but the CIG has also proved inadequate in preventing the heavy work force reductions that have occurred in Italian industry and that have been implemented by means of both massive early retirement and the freezing of recruitment (the annual rate of hiring in manufacturing reached a low of 8 percent in the early 1980s).[4]

New Industrial Relations Practices in the 1980s and "Bargained" Flexibility

Major policy changes emerged during the 1980s as part of general modifications in the overall socioeconomic and political climate. These changes had two main goals: to make the labor market more flexible and to make industrial relations practices more innovative. Both goals are common in most industrialized countries, but some specific traits of the Italian solution are worth mentioning.[5]

Fairly common measures aimed at flexibility were introduced by the Italian legislature: increased incentives for part-time work, wider possibilities for the use of fixed-term employment contracts (first for young workers on the basis of so-called work-and-training contracts, later for all workers), a relaxation of hiring restrictions (through a partial abolition of the system of administrative hiring lists), and a relaxation of legal restraints on the employment of women (particularly in night work and jobs involving physical strains). These measures have been, though only cautiously, accepted by the major Italian trade union confederations.

A further specific aspect of the Italian system is that while the need for more flexibility has been recognized by all parties, the employer is not allowed total discretion in staffing decisions. Under the laws outlined above, the implementation of flexibility measures has been subject to collective negotiations, usually

---

[4]The number of persons entering early retirement between 1980 and 1985 has been estimated at 134,000 (an average of 26,800 a year) or 12 percent of all persons retiring over the period.

[5]For more details, see Treu 1985:29ff.

coupled with public control by the institutions involved in labor market regulation (labor offices, tripartite labor commissions). This reflects a more general orientation of Italian labor policy that is shared by the government and trade unions: the basic choice of the Italian government has not been one of laissez-faire or of market liberalization, which would be impracticable given the political and social conditions of the country. Instead it has promoted concerted flexibility of the labor market.

Tripartism at the macroeconomic level (expressed in central agreements on wage indexation and other general labor relations policy issues) is paralleled by tripartism at the micro (enterprise) and meso (territorial) levels, directed toward improving labor mobility and productivity. In the specific field of employment flexibility, union involvement has produced uneven results because of the diversity of labor market conditions and employer attitudes (in Italy, as elsewhere, employers have been gaining the initiative as never before in firm-level labor relations). The opportunity for the union to bargain over the conditions and implementation of flexibility, however, varies with union strength, the general character of labor relations at the territorial and enterprise level, as well as previous labor-management traditions and attitudes. The outcomes on these issues therefore reflect the overall "dualisms" of the Italian scenario: mainly those between small and medium-sized or large firms, between southern and northern regions, and between manufacturing and the service sector. Successful collective bargaining and tripartism over flexibility is thus by no means a general pattern; largely unregulated areas (particularly at the periphery of the system) have developed side by side with collectively regulated areas of the economy.

In total, a positive adjustment attitude, or a more cooperative, coordinated approach to the flexible use of personnel, has been gaining ground among the social partners. This is true not only with regard to employment security and worker mobility, where recent legislation has supported the trend toward negotiated flexibility, but also in other areas such as geographical mobility, working time, and wages. Flexible forms of working time and wages, particularly productivity bonuses, have become a common object of enterprise bargaining since 1985.

The positive attitude taken by the unions in this regard has been strongly influenced by another aspect of Italian labor legislation, namely that the overall trend toward negotiated flexibility has not been accompanied by an erosion of the traditional protection of employees from unfair and unjustified dismissals. The recourse to the CIG has recently declined because of the overall improvement in economic and labor market conditions, but it is still available for firms to cushion economic hardships arising from industrial restructuring. The legal restrictions on employers' power to discharge workers (Act 604/1966 and Act 300/1970) have resisted all the assaults of critics over the years. Recent legislation has even extended protection against unjustified dismissal to firms employing fewer than fifteen workers, and in some sectors (e.g., small artisan firms) this extension of protection was anticipated by collective agreements. Thus, the high degree of stability of the typical or "standard" employment relationship has remained a central feature of the Italian labor relations system.

The combination of a high degree of legal protection with the more recent developments outlined above demonstrated that the preferred policy followed by both government and unions has been one of bargained internal flexibility and external stability—at least with regard to the "official" labor market.[6] So far, this policy seems to have worked to the benefit of both parties, workers and employers. Its inherent utility may be enhanced within the framework of less conflictual and more cooperative industrial relations as they recently have been developing in many sectors of the Italian economy.

Evaluation and Conclusion

Whereas cooperative arrangements can easily be implemented and sustained with regard to the stably employed core work force, the liberalization of hiring regulations has particularly affected young workers. Over the past ten years, the normal mode of labor market entry for young workers has been through work-and-training contracts (i.e., fixed-term contracts), which have been strongly subsidized and supported by national and regional legislation. Between 1985 and 1988, the number of young workers hired on such contracts totaled more than 1.2 million. Together with apprenticeship contracts, these two-year contracts have by far been the most common fixed-term employment arrangements. The large majority of these contracts (95 percent according to employers' sources) have been subsequently transformed into indefinite employment contracts.

These data suggest that work-and-training contracts are favored by employers in that they allow a long period of probation for young workers and a rotating "entry" labor force at low cost, which may then be selectively integrated into the stable, core work force. Less frequent are ordinary fixed-term contracts, the number of which has been rather limited because of union opposition (precise figures are not available, but the total number yearly is probably not more than 100,000). The use of part-time contracts has also increased but less rapidly than expected: the share of part-time workers still does not exceed 6 to 7 percent of the total work force. Apparently, employers refrain from offering part-time jobs because of their uncertain and possibly unfavorable social security implications, particularly with regard to old age pensions.

The current framework of labor law and industrial relations shows a marked evolution from the scenario of the 1970s. The rigid protective legislation on various aspects of the labor market and the strict job-to-job control exercised by the unions have given way to bargained flexibility both in the shaping of the employment relationship and in other aspects of staffing utilization. Within this evolving framework of bargained flexibility, unions and employers have widely adopted a practice of cooperative labor relations based on a quid pro quo of greater internal flexibility and mobility for the guarantee of job security and possibly

---

[6]Internal flexibility is also favored in other respects (e.g., by court rulings, which recently have adopted a less rigid interpretation of the limits set by article 13, Act 300/1970, on worker transfers and internal reassignments).

stronger union involvement in firm-level decision making. In this respect, Italian labor relations seem to be shifting from traditional conflictual pluralism toward informal joint negotiation over various aspects of labor regulation, including labor flexibility. This pattern has for a long time been successfully practiced in major European and Scandinavian countries. The success of these countries in terms of both their economic and employment performance has been much discussed. Such discussions involve the relative importance of the participatory model of labor relations in a setting of increasing work force skills and public commitment to a full-employment policy.

The meaning of "successful employment policy" needs to be specified, particularly as the term applies to the core labor force, where labor flexibility and job security are positively joined, and to atypical or peripheral forms of employment, whose flexibility by definition excludes employment security and participation.

Many observers believe that the new pattern of participative flexibility in labor relations has contributed to improving the international competitiveness of the Italian economy, which indeed has showed fairly good results in the last few years. It also seems to have helped reactivate the Italian labor market.

Although precise analyses have not been conducted recently, signs of reactivation are indeed visible. The rate of hiring has increased, though mainly through work-and-training contracts, and the same appears to be true of overall labor turnover and worker mobility. In most areas of northern and central Italy, employment levels have improved considerably, to the point of reaching what is considered full employment. Some areas, in particular the South, are still affected by structural unemployment, however, and the scope of atypical employment in these areas has remained high. Comparative analyses might convince us that the permanence of peripheral work in depressed labor market areas is the price for the positive linking of internal flexibility and external employment security in the more prosperous core segments of the labor market. But the question remains, What is a "fair price"? How much of the periphery for a stable core? How much disparity in working conditions and job security?

These issues will probably not be solved by either the industrial relations system (whether conflictual or cooperative) or legislation (whether protective or deregulatory) alone. Their solution calls for a range of public policies promoting economic growth and employment. The Italian system has been traditionally defective in this respect. The strong protective orientation of Italian labor legislation has not been matched by active and effective personnel and training policies.

Considerable public funds have been allocated by both national and regional authorities to support various employment and training programs, particularly for young people and recently for the long-term unemployed. These programs have been poorly administered, however, because of the lack of institutions capable of adequately monitoring the diversified sectors of the labor market and of distributing the funds according to needs. The quality if not the quantity of vocational training leaves much to be desired for the same reasons, particularly in the critical areas of new professions. Public coordination of research efforts and of technological know-how, as well as its diffusion among employers and em-

employees, is similarly defective. Flexibility and cooperation between labor and management at the level of individual enterprises are probably necessary conditions to promote economic efficiency and at the same time maintain employment security. But they certainly are not sufficient.

Innovations are necessary in the public policy domains mentioned above: better coordination of training programs for improving the long-term accumulation of human capital within the enterprise; more coordination of programs promoting research and development and, in general, more effective employment policies. Only a combination of such policies can activate a cycle of innovation, growth, and work force quality conducive to improving performance in both production and employment.

Policies are also needed to support the difficult experiments initiated by unions and employers that are aimed at moving away from conflictual short-term relations toward long-term cooperative efforts in the field of personnel and wage policies. As indicated above, Italian unions have, much more than in the past, come to accept and support a national objective of flexibility and competitiveness, including some wage restraint. To some extent they have been convinced to follow this path by the legal assurances that employers will not abuse flexibility. Much less clear is the degree of involvement the unions will be allowed in other critical aspects of management, such as technological innovation and career and skill development. Even less clear is the extent to which they will be able to improve their relative position in the existing but inefficient tripartite institutions handling vocational training and labor market mobility. The latter two issues will be critical to successfully implementing social agreements directed toward improving Italy's overall economic and job creation performance.

22
Employment Security and Labor Market Segmentation: Economic Implications of the Italian Cassa Integrazione Guadagni

Leonello Tronti

In the geography of labor protection, Italy occupies a very prominent place. Its ranking could be thought of as at one extreme of a line connecting the United States and Western Europe. Italy is probably endowed with the most developed set of legal and policy instruments for labor protection. This peculiar characteristic of the Italian employment relations system exerts its influence on the way it works as well as on the performance of the economic system at large.

The reasons for Italy's highly protective attitude toward labor can be traced to cultural, social, and historical causes. The attitude permeates the constitution of the republic itself (1948), to the point that article 1 states that "Italy is a democratic Republic, founded on labor" and article 4 encharges the republic with the task of acknowledging to all citizens the right to work and of enacting "the conditions for making that right effective."

It is only within this general framework that the Cassa Integrazione Guadagni can be understood. Created in 1941 through a collective agreement to compensate workers on temporary work reductions or layoff, it soon became a fundamental instrument for the management of industrial working time. Unique to Italy, this instrument has played a crucial role in the restructuring and adjustment process that has allowed the Italian industrial sector to recover from the two oil shocks and the dramatic social turbulences of the 1970s.

The objective of this paper is to sketch the evolution of this instrument and of its economic functions, as well as to provide some elements for the assessment of its economic effects on industrial macro-level performance, employment, and wages. The last section is devoted to the presentation of the main features of the reform recently approved by the Italian Parliament, aimed at imposing limitations and introducing innovations into the scheme (Act no. 223/91).

Birth and Development of the CIG

Origins (1941–63)

The first appearance of the Cassa Integrazione Guadagni was in the form of a collective agreement between unions and firms in the industrial sector (13.6.1941), geographically limited to the northern area of the country. The agreement, establishing a compensation to workers for wage losses due to cuts in working time, was spurred by a widespread expectation of reductions in some sectors of industrial production in connection with the state of war. The necessities of war caused production increases in some firms at the expense of others, but industrial firms, if granted some compensation for the costs involved, were willing to keep their workers employed and ready to work so as to meet regular production needs as soon as recovery started again (François-D'Harmant and Brunetta 1987; Arrigo 1990).

The new scheme initially applied only to temporary reductions in working time (i.e., labor hoarding in firms compelled to reduce operations). The allowance granted to workers originally amounted to 75 percent of their hourly wage rate, and was paid for each hour reduced below their standard forty-hour week. Funding was provided directly to the CIG by all industrial employers through a 5 percent levy on their total wage bill. The agreement also included a ban on dismissals and was complemented by the institution of a special benefit for workers on leave.

In 1945, the 1941 agreement was extended to the whole country, and the CIG became a general institution for industrial workers. The amount of the benefit was reduced to two-thirds of the hourly wage rate for all hours lost in the range of twenty-four to forty hours per week. In 1947, the CIG was extended again, to cover temporary layoffs (i.e., reductions to zero hours). Valid causes for application were all events outside the employer's and/or employee's control. The maximum duration of benefits was limited to three months, and workers for whom a rapid recall could not be expected were excluded altogether.

In this first period, the scheme underwent a few sectoral extensions that did not affect its main economic meaning as a financial support for labor hoarding and temporary layoffs, although they were an early signal of its future development. In 1955–56, the CIG was extended to the cotton industry, which was undergoing a publicly recognized sectoral crisis. In 1963, the construction industry was included to provide for work cuts caused by bad weather and other causes beyond the control of the employer; the construction industry's fund, however, was organized under a separate administration (the still-existing Gestione Edilizia of CIG).

Extending the CIG in Many Directions (1964–77)

The second period was characterized by a more intense use of the CIG, particularly during the recessions of 1964–65, 1970–71, and 1974–75 (see fig. 22–1).

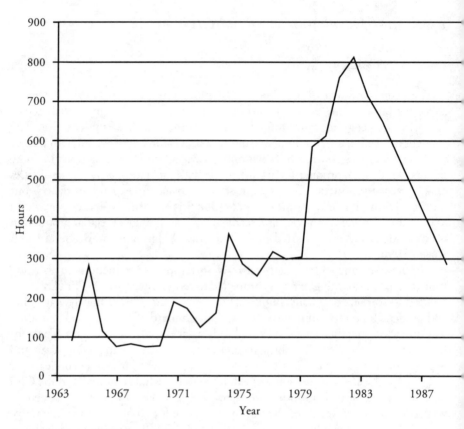

Source: INPS.

FIGURE 22-1. CIG Dynamics
(Total CIG-conceded hours in millions)

The scheme was subject not only to quantitative growth but to repeated broadening of its scope and change in its economic significance.

The first major modification was the introduction of the extraordinary intervention in 1968 (Cassa Integrazione Straordinaria or CIGS; Act no. 1115/68). This new department within the CIG fund was established to deal with temporary reductions in work load and with longer-term work force adjustments triggered by such events as sectoral and local economic crises; restructuring and reorganizing processes; reconversions (Riconversione Industriale; Act no. 464/72) due to changing products and markets; employment crises (i.e., mayor adjustments of "socially relevant" firms, whose operations strongly affect other firms in the region [Act no. 675/77]).

Through the introduction of CIGS, the original scope of the program was widely extended and the CIG began to fulfill a number of new economic functions in addition to subsidizing labor hoarding and temporary layoffs. These can be summarized as follows (see table 22–1): (1) disguising dismissals to defuse industrial conflict, which had dramatically increased following the "hot" autumn of 1969; (2) absorbing social shocks resulting from both social conflict and economic as well as technological disequilibria, either inside or outside the firm; (3) public subsidizing of corporate restructuring or reorganization, that is, enabling firms to "externalize" the opportunity costs of labor retraining and to have the whole economic system pay for it.

Such a profound transformation, from a merely temporary labor-hoarding subsidy to a large-scale industrial restructuring support system, required the creation of a new institutional framework to manage it. To make the complex decisions involved with the extended coverage of the scheme and to ascertain the eligibility of firms for its benefits, new bodies were established. The first such body was the interministerial committee, which sets guidelines for industrial policy (Comitato Interministeriale per il Coordinamento della Politica Industriale or CIPI; Act no. 675/77). It has also been charged with evaluating the economic conditions of firms applying for CIGS. The second body was made up of the Regional Employment Commissions (Commissioni Regionali per l'Impiego) and the Central Employment Commission (Commissione Centrale per l'Impiego), which guide redundant workers toward new jobs (Act no. 675/77). The establishment of these bodies implied a basic change in the Italian industrial relations structure toward tripartite decision making: the commissions each include representatives of the trade unions, of employers' organizations, and of the government (regional and/or Ministry of Labour). Such "concerted action" proves effective mainly at the regional level.

Along with the scope and institutional setup of the CIG, the benefits were also changed. Since 1968, it has compensated workers at a rate of 80 percent of their contractual hourly wage rate. The actual working time of the worker may vary from zero to forty-four hours per week; the CIG replaces 80 percent of their pay for the difference between the time actually worked and the standard working time (forty-four and subsequently forty hours per week).

Also during this period, a parallel institution was created to take care of collective redundancies caused by plant closings. It is called the Special Unemployment Benefit (Disoccupazione Speciale or DS), and it pays collectively fired workers 66 percent of their previous wages for a maximum period of 180 days (Act no. 1115/68). The DS was the first form of income maintenance for the unemployed of some economic weight introduced in Italy. Previously, workers relied on private agencies and social ties (family, firm, church, and so on) during economic distress.

In conjunction with the DS, "mobility lists" were created (Act no. 675/77), designed to enroll workers threatened by redundancy for reemployment on comparable economic terms in geographical proximity to their previous jobs.

Explosion during the 1980s

In the 1980s, the Italian industrial sector underwent a process of profound restructuring and reorganization, caused by the heavy impact of the two oil price shocks on an economy highly dependent on imports of raw materials. This restructuring process was heavily financed by the CIG. In 1981, the number of

TABLE 22-1. *Ordinary and Extraordinary CIG Interventions*

	Ordinary Intervention		
Objectives	*Premises*	*Possible conditions for intervention*	*Legal assumptions*
Stabilization of production in the presence of periodic fluctuations. Mediation by public authorities on the criteria for sharing costs of dealing with these periodic difficulties.	Interventions of a social welfare nature. Compulsory contributions from the firm involved. The provincial INPS committee is competent to grant the intervention.	Unforeseen situations that have an effect on salaries due to: reduction or suspension of production for company reasons; transitory situations that are not the fault of the company; temporary market conditions. These unforeseen situations can affect both the employer and the employee.	On a different level from normal contractual risk sharing; the intervention of the public authorities shifts the question of typical industrial risk costs outside the area of labor relations, and this is independent of the need to establish responsibilities.

Extraordinary Intervention

Objectives	Premises	Possible conditions for intervention	Other characteristics
To encourage labor mobility within the terms of the law on industrial reconversion.	Rather complex area, since it has links with transformations, redimensionings, and closings.	Intervention in favor of workers in firms undergoing restructuring or reconversion, who will not be taken on again.	State assistance for companies in different situations of industrial tranformation.
To manage employment crises from a point of view that goes beyond single companies or geographical areas.	Possible areas of conflict with the company's right to manage the concern.	Specific conditions for intervention: maintenance of the staff during periods of economic crisis. maintenance of fictional employment in case of unresolvable economic crises; in support of operations aimed at labor mobility (for example, the activity of GEPI); fitting in with labor mobility schemes;	Acquisition by the companies of flexible margins in employment and working hours, with the state taking care of the cost.
Earnings integration does not necessarily have to be temporary.		helping discharged workers when there are no immediate solutions to the problem of alternative work.	

Source: François-D'Harmant and Brunetta 1987.

hours lost and compensated by the CIG amounted to 578 million, or close to 4 percent of total industrial hours. This explosion continued through 1984, when CIG-compensated hours reached their maximum of 816 million hours, or 7 percent of total hours in the industrial sector. From 1985 on, applications to the CIG began to decline noticeably, with the number of hours paid falling at an average annual rate of about 20 percent (table 22–2).

During the 1980s, the CIG also underwent qualitative changes, the first being a radical modification of the formula for calculating the level of benefits; benefits eligibility was extended to only a few, very specific cases. The CIG also began to be used in a new way: as a tool for income maintenance and financial assistance for reemployment.

In 1980, a fundamental step was made toward making the CIG less attractive to workers by imposing a ceiling on the monthly amount payable under the "extraordinary" regime (Act no. 427/80). The maximum amount was fixed at 600,000 lire, and a new mechanism was introduced for its automatic adaptation to inflation: as of January 1 of each year, it was to rise by only 80 percent of the increase in the cost-of-living allowance (the so-called Scala Mobile) awarded in the previous year. Through this change, the benefit lost its peculiar feature of being totally indexed to wages and became more similar to a partially indexed lump-sum benefit (fig. 22–2). Besides setting a limit on the economic impact on public budgets caused by the explosion of applications, this modification undermined the possibility of collusion between firms and unions in the use of the CIG and gave a clear signal to redundant workers to search for new jobs.

At the same time, there was a further attempt to fit the requirements and circumstances of particular firms (e.g., Unidal, a publicly owned food company, or Standa, a big department store) and sectors, such as journalists or catering firms working for companies in crisis (the so-called tailored CIG), to the CIG. The CIG also became an instrument for maintaining the income of construction workers in the Mezzogiorno region. Construction workers made redundant after the completion of public contracts henceforth could apply for benefits if the local labor market offered few alternative employment opportunities but there was the prospect of new public investments. In such cases they can be put under the CIG for up to a maximum period of twenty-four months (a limit often circumvented in one way or another). The program can also be used to support reemployment and job creation initiatives by specific public firms as well as efforts by discharged workers to found their own businesses (the so-called Marcora Law).

Economic Role of the CIG

The CIG undeniably provided considerable assistance between 1978 and 1983, during the period of industrial restructuring in Italy (Barca and Magnani 1989). Such a comprehensive program could well assume a broad range of functions as heterogenous as subsidizing labor hoarding and temporary layoffs, preventing and "disguising" permanent dismissals, social shock absorption, longer-term high-

TABLE 22-2. CIG in the Industrial Sector: Hours paid (in 1,000s), 1979–88

	1979	1980	1981	1982	1983	1984	1985	1986	1987	1988
Gestione ordinaria										
Ordinary intervention	59,005	109,338	189,015	193,205	229,250	198,280	121,708	101,667	88,783	62,576
Extraordinary intervention										
Blue collars	133,772	124,764	282,598	332,379	412,953	489,974	455,011	430,517	345,365	282,306
White collars	12,835	11,089	29,961	37,726	48,613	58,139	57,096	53,366	42,729	35,270
Total	205,612	245,191	501,574	563,310	690,816	746,393	633,815	585,550	476,877	380,152
Gestione edilizia	93,946	61,946	76,171	56,981	55,702	70,104	82,816	61,806	56,970	39,966
Grand total	299,558	307,137	577,745	620,291	746,518	816,497	716,631	647,356	533,847	420,118

CIG costs, 1960–89 (in billion liras)

1960	1965	1970	1975	1980	1981	1982	1983	1984	1985	1986	1987	1988	1989
2	52	44	285	945	1.824	1.724	3.451	1.917	3.931	4.129	3.367	2.882	2.031

Unemployed previously employed, 1972–89 (in 1,000s)

1972	1980	1981	1982	1983	1984	1985	1986	1987	1988	1989
224	210	215	281	352	466	468	501	547	537	507

———— Nominal.
    +   At 1989 prices.
Source: INPS.

FIGURE 22-2. CIG Hourly Benefits

level income maintenance, as well as the promotion of reemployment and business setups of redundant workers.

For the workers themselves, the CIG offers the privileged condition of being able to combine a regular though somewhat lower wage payment with income from "unofficial" work (in Italy, two-thirds of all atypical employment is attributable to second jobs) or a substantial annuity of leisure. Despite this, some surveys have shown that workers perceive the CIG as a danger signal regarding the future of their jobs and therefore as spurring them to search for new jobs. In this case the CIG can be viewed as a program providing time and money for job searching (Schenkel 1990).

Above all, the CIG has proved to be a flexible instrument for subsidizing work force adjustments in both quantitative and qualitative terms (layoffs and retraining) as well as enhancing working-time flexibility. At the end of a CIG intervention (in particular, of the Extraordinary program), the firm has fewer workers, and those who remain will have a different skill and age composition (i.e., fewer blue-collar and fewer older workers).

As to the relative weight of the economic functions described above, we find for 1980–87 the following distribution for all firms using CIGS: the majority (88.4 percent) were in crises, restructuring, or reorganizing; only 7.9 percent were ceasing operations; and 1.1 percent were participating in special work-sharing schemes (*Contratti di solidarietà*). The remaining cases were in local and/or sectoral crises (2.6 percent) and were excluded from the benefit in 1988.

Geographically, 21 percent of all the companies under the CIG were in Milan, Turin, or Naples. The share of compensated hours in total employment is greater in the South, however, than in the North, as is the percentage of Extraordinary CIG hours of all hours conceded. Furthermore, the decline of Extraordinary CIG began in the South in 1986, one year later than in the North.

Despite the sudden fall in the number of conceded hours after 1984, the CIG still remains at a very high level (comparable to that of 1980) in the northern Italian city of Milan (Del Boca and Rota 1990). This persistence of high CIG levels is contrasted by a strong decline in industrial employment and a rather high level of industrial capacity utilization in Milan. Part of this seeming paradox is explained by the fact that, while longer-duration programs have declined rapidly, the average duration has been decreasing only very slowly. Another important factor is the shift in the gender composition of benefit recipients. In Milan, women show a tendency to remain under the CIG, while male workers are moving out of it. Between 1985 and 1987, the percentage of male workers under the CIG fell from 72.6 percent to 58.3 percent, while the percentage of females rose from 27.4 percent to 41.7 percent.

Furthermore, there has recently been a shift toward smaller enterprises among the firms applying for CIG benefits. Many large firms have completed their reorganization, whereas small and medium-sized firms no longer seem to enjoy their traditional flexibility advantages (see Bank of Italy 1990). The greater numerical flexibility enjoyed by small firms will be significantly reduced by the extension of the just-cause principle for dismissals to firms with fewer than fifteen employees (Act no. 180/90).

On a more general level, Padoa-Schioppa (1988) has recently attempted to analyze the economic role of the CIG in theoretical terms. Viewing the CIG as an institutional arrangement for work sharing with an institutionally fixed wage-replacement rate and comparing it to a system of nominally fixed unemployment benefits as given in other European countries, Padoa-Schioppa shows that ceteris paribus the CIG is associated with lower employment levels and higher profits. The argument, though presented convincingly, applies only to the period preceding the CIG "explosion" during the early 1980s. As we have seen, in 1980 a ceiling was imposed on the monthly unit benefit, causing a virtual halt in the CIG's growth in real terms. Ever since, the ceiling has had the effect of making the CIG look all the more similar to a partially indexed lump-sum benefit in proportion to the hours not worked and as such resembling standard unemployment benefits (fig. 22–2).

But the difficulties involved in assessing the economic role of the CIG overall are not limited to theoretical assessments. To a large extent they also apply to empirical analyses. Any empirical evaluation is impaired by the fact that during the 1980–87 period industrial employment went through a dramatic crisis that resulted in the loss of some 1 million jobs as well as a substantial decline in output growth (in 1986, industrial output in real terms almost equaled its 1980 level).

In the presence of such drastic changes, hypothetical scenarios of how things would have developed in the absence of the CIG appear at least questionable.

Profit Maintenance versus Crowding Out

One methodological approach to assessing the economic role of the CIG is to divide the argument into two separate steps. The first step would aim at analyzing the economic long-term effect on profits, investment, and growth. The crucial point in this analysis lies in the evaluation of the balance between a "crowding-out effect" on private investment and a "profit-maintenance effect," engendered by lowering the actual wage rate.

A very similar issue has recently been addressed by Giavazzi and Spaventa (1989). Their conclusion is that the CIG (as well as other employment protection and job creation schemes) may well have created a transfer flow from wages and taxes in general to profits and that such a flow has been essential in funding industrial reorganization while at the same time minimizing adjustment costs (in terms of employment and output losses), thus contributing to the very good long-term economic performance of Italy as compared to, for example, that of Great Britain. In their rather optimistic paper, Giavazzi and Spaventa are not interested in estimating the crowding-out effect implied by the financing of such social shock absorbers as the CIG, early retirement programs, and so forth, since their focus is the positive longer-term aspects outlined above. Looking more closely at the current performance of the Italian economy, however, one notes that, while the impression of a strong and vital economic system is undeniable, the burden of the huge public debt still weighs heavy and has contributed to a slowdown in economic growth (see Beenstock 1990). Further, Italy's international competitiveness in many traditional areas (mechanical engineering, tools, business machines) has shown continuous signs of weakness.

In conclusion, a cost-benefit evaluation of the effects of the CIG on the macroperformance of the economic system, questionable as it may be, should probably be less optimistic than Giavazzi and Spaventa suggest, even if the recent recovery in Italy has been remarkable.

Employment Protection versus Turnover Freezing

A second step in assessing the CIG's economic impact would have to focus on its employment consequences by examining another crucial trade-off, that between the protection the CIG offers to the employed and the obstacles it raises to the employment (or reemployment) of the unemployed (above all by slowing down labor turnover). The employment protection effect can be appreciated by looking at table 22–3, which compares the dynamics of workers under the CIG with that of permanently displaced workers. The data show that only a very small portion of the employment shock associated with the crisis and the ensuing reorganization phase resulted in actual unemployment, while almost all of it was absorbed by the CIG.

TABLE 22-3. *Dynamics of Workers in CIG[a] and Official Number of Unemployed with Previous Employment (Base year: 1967 = 100)*

Year	(A) Dynamics of workers in CIG	(B) Dynamics of officially unemployed with previous employment	B/A
1967	100.00	100.00	100.00%
1968	101.43	92.99	91.68
1969	94.29	78.96	83.74
1970	97.14	69.87	71.93
1971	265.72	72.47	27.27
1972	240.00	58.18	24.24
1973	181.43	64.42	33.51
1974	225.72	50.39	22.32
1975	498.58	63.64	12.76
1976	408.57	65.97	16.15
1977	364.29	54.55	14.97
1978	464.29	54.55	11.75
1979	428.58	58.18	13.58
1980	438.58	54.55	12.44
1981	825.72	55.84	6.76
1982	885.72	72.99	8.24
1983	1067.15	91.43	8.57
1984	1165.72	121.04	10.38
1985	1024.30	121.56	11.87
1986	924.29	130.13	14.08
1987	762.86	142.08	18.62
1988	600.01	139.48	23.25
1989	401.43	131.69	32.81

Source: INPS, ISTAT.
[a]Number of workers in CIG is estimated as the ratio of total conceded CIG hours to maximum yearly time payable under CIG.

The data also show a parallel decline in industrial job accessions and job separations until the use of CIG reached its maximum in 1983–84. From then on, industrial hiring and firing began to increase once more. At the aggregate level, one should therefore expect to find some link between the CIG and hiring and firing dynamics that the decline in the use of the CIG coincides with increasing labor mobility and turnover. This conclusion is substantiated by the results of two quantitative studies of the statistical links between the CIG, industrial hirings, and employment (tables 22–4 and 22–5). Table 22–4 shows that the CIG has played a remarkable role in depressing industrial hirings. Over the 1972–88 period, a 1 percentage point growth in total compensated CIG hours resulted in a 0.75 percent decline in industrial hirings.

If, however, we model employment with reference to CIG utilization (table 22–5), we find only a slight (if any) confirmation of the role played by the CIG

TABLE 22-4. CIG and Labor Turnover,[a] 1972–88

$\overline{R}^2$	SEE	D-W	Intercept	CIG	Employment	Exits
.7878	13.05%	2.21	1367.2	−.70324	−.15722	.68358
			(3.170)	(−5.543)	(−2.556)	(2.969)

Source: ISTAT, national accounts. Turnover estimates are based on ISTAT, Big Industrial Companies'
Survey. Within parentheses: t-tests.
[a]Estimated equation is a linear regression of total entries in industry over (1) total conceded CIG hours; (2)
standard labor units in industry (employees only); (3) total exits from industry.

in cutting the volume of industrial labor input. The variable is statistically significant, but the negative elasticity of employment to CIG can only reach the value of 0.06: the impact of productivity and demand (as approximated by GNP) prove far more substantial. The alleged genuine negative impact of the CIG on overall industrial employment appears even more questionable if one bears in mind the dramatic changes in industrial employment that occurred in the period under examination. If CIG has had any impact, it has been on working time rather than employment. In fact, the program has been shown to substitute to some extent for absenteeism: increasing CIG utilization favors tight discipline of working time, bringing it under stricter control by the employer (Schenkel 1990).

To conclude, the empirical evidence suggests that the effect of the CIG on employment has not been to squeeze or enhance but rather "freeze" employment. Hirings as well as firings (but not other kinds of job separations) have been frozen, so that turnover has slowed down drastically. Those employed have thus been able to preserve their jobs. The cost of such protection was paid by those outsiders who otherwise would have found a job in industry; a considerable part of this group consists of youngsters who face great difficulty in finding equivalent jobs in other sectors, even if the latter were expanding rapidly. The CIG's freezing of such entries into industrial employment is therefore likely to account for some portion of Italian youth unemployment.

Wage Protection

The issue of the economic role of the CIG may also be tackled from a different perspective, namely, that of insider-outsider theory and segmentation theory, by showing the program's role in maintaining wage rate dynamics by creating temporary layers in the industrial labor market. As we have seen, the CIG can be interpreted as an instrument with which to protect insiders from being discharged and to avoid their substitution by outsiders. For this model to fit well, real wages must show at least downward stickiness if not continuous growth, despite high unemployment or changes in other variables affecting wage determination.

In fact, during the years of the CIG explosion, the industrial labor market in Italy experienced a high degree of segmentation as a result of a new quadripartite

TABLE 22-5. *CIG's Role in Employment Determination,*[a] *1972–88*

	$\bar{R}^2$	SEE	D-W	Intercept	CIG	Productivity	Demand
				7201.2	−.92920	−.38102	.17917
With CIG	.9735	.78%	1.87	(37.974)	(−7.286)	(−11.477)	(8.575)
				7991.9		−.32659	.11926
Without CIG	.8751	2.02	1.09	(23.654)	—	(−4.647)	(2.858)

Source: ISTAT, national accounts. Within parentheses: t-tests.
[a]Estimated equation is a linear regression of standard labor units in industry (employees only) over (1) conceded CIG hours; (2) productivity (industrial added value at constant prices per total labor unit); (3) GNP at constant prices.

hierarchy created by the program itself. This hierarchy can be summarized as follows:

At the bottom of the ladder are individually discharged workers and unemployed outsiders (i.e., new entrants or reentrants) who are kept out of work because of the slowdown in industrial hiring and the bleak employment prospects in other sectors.

The second layer consists of previously employed workers who are now on the mobility lists of the labor offices. They will probably get a new job since they are in a priority position with respect to vacancies.

The third layer consists of workers receiving CIG benefits—the part of the labor force that is working less than standard work time, in some cases even under a "zero-hours" regime. They get paid less than regular wages, but are still employed and have all their rights, even if their jobs may be endangered in the medium term.

At the top of the hierarchy are workers who are safe and secure in their jobs. They felt assured enough to bargain 3.4 percent real wage increases per year (1975–84) despite economic turbulence and social unrest.

Unfortunately, even if this model seems to fit the Italian case, statistical evidence provides only partial confirmation of the CIG's alleged effects on wages. Table 22–6, which presents the results of a wage equation for industry and three other sectors, shows that during 1972–88 the CIG played a statistically significant role in the determination of the industrial wage rate but only a small part in trend deviations. As a matter of fact, a 1 percentage point change in CIG utilization corresponded to a change of just 0.11 percent in both nominal and real wage rates.

This result is due to the higher variability of the CIG's rate of change around its trend and to its frequent fluctuation from positive to negative values (fig. 22–3). Certainly, the inclusion of the CIG along with other independent variables provides a better explanation of the industrial wage rate, and the CIG wage equation for industry fits better than any wage equation for the other sectors. Far more relevant, however, is the role of productivity. By itself, the CIG at best helped prevent the wage rate from falling, but it does not account for its rise. This

TABLE 22-6. CIG's Role in Wage Determination,[a] 1972–88

	$\bar{R}^2$	SEE	D-W	Intercept	CIG	Productivity	Employment
Industry	.9995	2.04%	2.05	−100.96	.24739	.43737	1.44974
(with CIG)				(−4.783)	(9.254)	(54.157)	(4.728)
Industry	.9966	4.30	0.51	−38.25	–	.43988	.60304
(without CIG)				(−.721)		(20.533)	(.776)
Transports	.9924	3.99	0.95	−7.71	–	.40594	.96810
				(−1.233)		(13.537)	(1.434)
Sales	.9968	3.61	0.89	0.55	–	.44572	−.37345
				(.151)		(15.565)	(−.163)
Banks and insurance	.9870	6.44	1.97	1.19		.38521	−.80590
				(.350)		(13.817)	(−.549)

Source: ISTAT, national accounts. Within parentheses: t-tests.
[a]Estimated equation is a linear regression of gross wage rate over: (1) conceded CIG hours; (2) productivity (industrial added value per total labor unit); (3) standard labor units in industry (employees only).

is clearly shown by the opposite dynamics of CIG utilization and the wage rate after 1984.

Reforming the CIG

Having set forth the main elements of an inevitably complex assessment of the economic effects of such a complex employment protection instrument as the CIG, it may be worth noting that the Italian Parliament has recently reformed the CIG profoundly. An extensive reform draft had been in existence since 1985 and under closer examination for at least two years. After many adjustments and separate approvals of a few abridgements (renewals of CIG benefits, ordinary unemployment benefits, and such), a final single text was approved by Parliament (Act no. 223/91).

Such a thorough reconsideration of the CIG program has several aims, which together are expected to correct the two major defects: the CIG's excessive costs and its depressing effect on labor mobility. The analysis presented in this paper confirms the relevance of such a correction to the better functioning of the CIG.

Among the new features are stricter time limits on benefit entitlement, a limitation of firm eligibility to participate in the program; new ceilings on the benefits paid to workers; more experience rating of employers' contributions; an extension of coverage in cases other than economic crisis, the so-called public contracts CIG;[1] an extension to new sectors (industrial craftmanship; smaller wholesale and retail firms employing between two hundred and one thousand employees) and new beneficiaries (industrial white collars, beforehand protected only by CIGS); and the creation of a new, separate institutional arrangement for

[1]That is, if a public contractor has to cut working hours as a consequence of payment delays by public authorities.

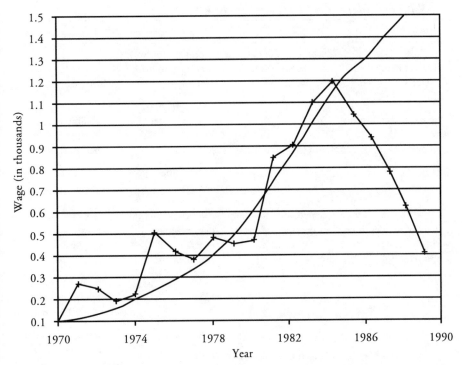

Source: INPS, ISTAT.

FIGURE 22-3. CIG and the Wage Rate (Money wage rate: 1970 = 100)

managing horizontal labor mobility (*Mobilità*). Reductions in the unit cost of the scheme to the taxpayer are expected to come from higher contributions and stricter experience rating, as well as from new time, eligibility and benefit limitations. Labor mobility is to be facilitated by the new Mobility Fund, which is designed to put an end to the "disguised dismissal" function of CIG while taking over its income-maintenance and re-employment and self-employment financing functions (see table 22–7).

More generally, the reform is intended to build up a new, unified framework, linked to other active labor policy instruments and institutions, such as vocational training and guidance, employment registration offices, early retirement schemes, apprenticeship, on-the-job training contracts, and so on. The reform, in the tradition of bi- and trilateral concerted action back to the first agreement on the Scala Mobile in January 1983, is also intended to improve the quality of Italian industrial relations by facilitating and promoting worker solidarity and a strategic coordination between unions and employers.

TABLE 22-7. *Major Features of the CIG Reform*

Extensions	Limitations	Social Concertation	New Instruments
CIG too extended to white-collar workers.	Exclusion from CIGS of firms with fewer than 15 employees.	Incentives for work sharing ("Solidarity Contracts").	Creation of *Mobilità*:
Extension to craftsfirms with over 15 employees.	Ceiling on all benefits.	Employment of workers under CIG in socially useful jobs.	abolition of Special unemployment benefit (DS);
Extension to sales firms with 200–1,000 employees.	Higher application costs to employers: doubling of the contributions for CIGS after 12 months' use.	Contribution shelters in case of union-firm concertation on the reorganization program and employment.	higher contributions to employers (additional 5%);
			incentives for firms hiring workers under *Mobilità*;
			incentives for self-employment;
CIG for delayed payments of public contracts (construction, industry).	Obligation for firms to provide a reorganization program, to be approved by CIPI, for all applications to CIGS.		for older workers in *Mobilità*, benefits up to retirement age.
	New time limits for CIGS: two to four years or no more than three years total over five in case repetition.		
	Applications both to CIG and CIGS no longer admitted.		

Methodological Note

Statistical tests in the paper (tables 22–5, 22–6, and 22–7) are based on the following equations:

$$nfl = f(Cig, xfl, N) \tag{22-1}$$

$$N = g(Cig, Y^*, \pi^*) \tag{22-2}$$

$$w = h(Cig, \pi, N) \tag{22-3}$$

Where

nfl = entries in industry;
Cig = total CIG hours conceded;
xfl = exits from industry;
N = industrial employment;
Y^* = GNP at constant prices;
π^* = industrial productivity at constant prices;
π = industrial productivity at current prices;
w = nominal gross wage rate.

This simple recursive model, aimed at assessing only the short-period effects of CIG on employment, labor turnover, and the wage rate, has been estimated through linear regressions by substituting N, as predicted by equation 22–2, into equations 22–1 and 22–3.

23
Sequences in Rigidity and Flexibility and Their Implications for the Italian Labor Market

Peter Auer

My subsequent remarks, originally conceived as a comment, draw heavily on the preceding papers by Leonello Tronti and Tiziano Treu. The simple argument I want to put forward and discuss is the following: creating rigidities in one part of the labor market necessitates the creation of institutional flexibility buffers in other parts to allow for work force adjustment. Once such a flexibility arrangement is working in some parts of a national labor market (in Italy's case mainly the industrial labor market), it is likely to lead to rigidities in other parts of the labor market, which eventually have to be coped with by instituting additional flexibility arrangements. There seems to be an open-ended sequence of rigidity and flexibility.

To develop this argument for the Italian case (the French case would certainly be another interesting example), I assume that there is a link between two "sets" of rigidity and flexibility arrangements. The first set consists of the dismissal protection established through the 1970 Workers' Statute, which was enacted following the "hot" autumn of 1969 (rigidity), and the Cassa Integrazione Guadagni (flexibility). In that the latter was introduced in 1941, my sequential argument seems not to hold. It was after the introduction of the Workers' Statute, however, that the CIG was altered profoundly to allow for more massive downward adjustment of the labor force. (In its original version of 1941, the CIG was created as a flexibility device to allow for numerical downward adjustment in the face of the dismissal ban during war production; see Garonna 1989.) The second set of rigidity/flexibility arrangements consists, on the one hand, of the employment rigidity created for new entrants precisely because of the first set of rigidity/flexibility arrangements and the introduction of employment training contracts and, on the other hand, the so-called "placement by name" (*chiamata nominativa*) to cope with it.

The argument developed so far is very general and an oversimplification of the complexities and subtleties of the Italian labor market. It might well be that reduced exits and the problems of entry arising therefrom occur in very different parts of the labor market (the one in the industrial sector dominated by large firms, where the rigidity/flexibility arrangements exert their influence; the other in the small-firm sector of industry or the service sector, which are only partially covered by the arrangement) and that, therefore, no direct connection at all exists between exit restrictions in the industrial sector and youth unemployment (which in large part is synonymous with first-entry unemployment).

Rigidity and Flexibility: The Workers' Statute and the CIG

Treu points to the fact that, although the Workers' Statute of 1970 (Act 300/1970) was designed to cope only with individual dismissals, it functions also as a deterrent for collective dismissals in that collectively dismissed individuals have the right to appeal to the courts. The probability of prevailing in court appears to be high: more than 40 percent of verdicts result in reinstatement. But other regulations may also have some influence on dismissals, such as those governing advance notice and severance pay, the latter of which is particularly high in Italy. It should be noted that severance payments in Italy are actually a deferred payment in that they are due also in the case of voluntary quits. Severance payments could have some deterrent effect on mass dismissals, however, in that heavy costs could occur suddenly that would not be spread over time as in the case of voluntary quits.

Although the absence of state regulation dealing with collective dismissals and major redundancies in Italy was criticized by the European Commission in the early 1980s, Italian dismissal protection seems quite substantial and has indeed been criticized for imposing rigidities on the labor market. This is not the place to discuss in detail whether the regulations themselves have had a considerable influence on employers' behavior and have made it impossible to "simply" dismiss or whether the strength of the trade unions in the early 1970s had such an effect. Recalling the labor unrest of the 1970s, however, I note that the combined effect of regulations and trade union strength resulted in a powerful dismissal protection regime. At that time, jobs in some large Italian enterprises began to be seen as the property of imcumbent workers, and this property right involved internal job as well as external employment security.

The important point is that Italian firms were coping with this rigidity as the Cassa Integrazione Guadagni, an already-existing buffer for flexibility, was being amended and used extensively. As Garonna (1987) has shown, the CIG has, in principle, a double function: *ordinary* intervention to cope with work force adjustment vis-à-vis cyclical variations in economic activity, and *extraordinary* intervention, designed to cope with major structural adjustments. In practice, it is hard to distinguish between these two functions. The main distinction between the ordinary and the extraordinary branch of the CIG seems to be one of costs, duration, and procedures: ordinary CIG is based on employers' contributions, and benefits are temporary in duration and easily obtainable; extraordinary CIG is state financed, and there are indefinitely prolongable benefits but complex procedures. Hours not worked are fully compensated by the CIG, and the reduction of working hours in both regimes can be partial (short-time working) or total (layoff).

Methodologically, it may not be sufficient to assume a link between the rigidity of dismissal protection and the flexibility arrangements of the CIG only because of the different timing of their introduction; but coincidences are obvious. Indeed, the CIG had existed for a long time when the Workers' Statute was introduced in 1970, and some basic changes (introduction of the extraordinary intervention to cope with sectoral and local crises) were undertaken in 1968. But changes so as to permit companies to adjust employment levels massively with substantial subsidies from the state were introduced in 1972 and 1975, and the total hours paid by the CIG have risen (with some cyclical variation) ever since, reaching a peak in 1983–84 (see the figures presented by Tronti, chap. 22).

Thus, the flexibility of the CIG obviously permitted work force adjustment despite dismissal protection. As workers even on total layoff (zero work hours) continue to be formally employed by their firm, open unemployment has been prevented.

The question remains, however, how these specific rigidity/flexibility arrangements have affected the labor market. There is some evidence that the low risk of job loss in such a protective institutional setting could entail a higher unemployment risk for outsiders, namely, youth seeking first employment (see table 23–1).

Low Risks for Insiders

Recent evidence on the risk of job loss involving subsequent unemployment shows, not surprisingly, a particularly low risk in those sectors of the Italian economy where the CIG has been heavily used. In 1987, about 28 percent of all CIG hours occurred in the metal manufacturing and engineering sectors (Schenkel 1989). In 1988, the risk of job loss with subsequent unemployment in this sector was 0.4 in Italy[1] as contrasted with 1.0 in France, 0.9 in Germany, and 1.2 in the United Kingdom (OECD 1990a).

If one looks at the structure of unemployment in Italy and compares it to that of other European countries, the risk of job loss with subsequent unemployment seems to be very low indeed. In 1987, the share of persons among the unemployed who previously worked was only 20 percent in Italy, as compared to 67 percent in (West) Germany. That this is more than a merely temporary deviation in the structure of Italian unemployment from the structure found in other countries is evident in table 23–1. In Italy since the 1970s, the swelling ranks of the unemployed have been filled not by job losers, as in other countries, but rather by

[1]The risk of job loss is calculated by dividing the percentage of unemployed in the sector by the percentage of workers who were working in the sector one year earlier. A risk index of 1 is equal to the OECD average; a lower rate shows a lower-than-average risk (see OECD 1990a).

TABLE 23-1. Job Losers as a Percentage of Total Unemployment

	1983	1988
France		
Job loss less than three years ago	47.6%	49.5%
Adjustment[a]	57.5	64.7
Germany[b]		
Job loss less than three years ago	32.8	36.6
Adjustment[a]	42.8	52.6
Italy		
Job loss less than three years ago	19.5	21.5
Adjustment[a]	25.8	28.7
Sweden		
Total job losses	61.0	47.2
Adjustment[c]	67.7	56.0
United Kingdom[d]		
Job loss less than three years ago	42.2	31.1
Adjustment[a]	51.8	47.5
United States		
Total job losses	41.8	33.4
Adjustment[b]	51.4	44.9

Source: OECD Employment Outlook 1990:50.

[a]Adjustment is calculated by adding to the unemployed who lost their job less than two or three years ago in EC countries the job losses that occurred more than two or three years ago, estimated by multiplying the total number of cessations of employment more than two or three years ago respectively by the percentage of recent job losses in total recent cessations.

[b]1984 instead of 1983.

[c]This adjustment is calculated by adding to the job losers the job losses suffered by reentrants. This share is estimated at 42.5 percent on the basis of the average figures known for Sweden between 1983 and 1988.

[d]1987 instead of 1988.

young adults facing an entry problem. As a report of the Italian Labor Ministry puts it: "Despite the serious consequences of technological innovation and restructuring in terms of job destruction, modern unemployment consists much more substantially in jobs not found than in jobs lost" (Ministero del Lavoro e della Providencia Sociale 1988:214).

This has not always been the case. A historical perspective shows that a marked change in the distribution of the unemployed occurred in the 1970s. Whereas in the 1950s and 1960s, unemployment due to prior job loss (if we disregard problems related to that definition and take the figures collected by the central Italian statistical office for granted) reached about 40 to 50 percent of total unemployment in Italy, during the 1970s, it declined—with some cyclical fluctuation—in absolute as well as relative terms. Between 1970 and 1980, the number of job losers among the unemployed declined by 27 percent, whereas the number seeking first employment rose by about 100 percent and the number of those trying to reenter the labor market rose by 50 percent. In 1980, only 211,000 of the 1,684,000 unemployed had been previously employed, that is a

TABLE 23-2. *Unemployment in Italy by Categories (in thousands)*

Year	Unemployed	First entrants	Other job seekers
1959	715	461	354
1969	304	459	397
1970	269	449	393
1971	279	435	395
1972	262	568	466
1973	248	515	540
1974	194	488	429
1975	245	509	472
1976	254	601	565
1977	210	690	638
1978	210	787	563
1979	224	859	603
1980	211	882	591
1981	215	989	691
1982	281	1,156	615
1983	352	1,292	620
1984	477	1,167	746
1985	481	1,250	740
1986	501	1,296	814
1987	547	1,354	931

Source: Ministero del Lavoro et della Providencia Sociale 1988:214.

share of only 12.5 percent (see table 23–2). Then, during the 1980s, the picture changed: from 1980 to 1987, the number of previously employed among the unemployed rose by 159 percent, whereas the number of first-time job seekers and reentrants rose by only 53 percent and 60 percent respectively, so that one might speak of a reemergence of *classical unemployment* in the deregulation period of the 1980s.

Barriers for Outsiders

It is the period of the 1970s up to the early 1980s, therefore, during which the rigidities probably had their strongest impact in preventing massive labor shedding. Even today, however, the majority of the Italian unemployed are under twenty-five years of age, and most are first-time job seekers. Among the European countries, only Spain has a higher youth unemployment rate (see table 23-3). In Italy, young women have a particularly high unemployment rate, whereas unemployment among adult males is comparatively low.

Regional factors also affect the distribution of unemployment. Young females in the South have an unemployment rate higher than 50 percent, whereas adult males in the northern and central regions have an unemployment rate of less than 3 percent.

Employment protection through the CIG is heavily geared toward the indus-

TABLE 23-3. Unemployment Rates in Europe[a]

	West Germany	France	Italy	United Kingdom
	Males and females			
1985	7.3	10.3	9.4	11.5
1986	6.5	10.4	10.6	11.5
1987	6.4	10.6	11.0	10.6
1988	6.4	10.4	12.4	8.7
	Under 25 years			
1985	10.5	26.1	31.5	18.6
1986	7.7	25.0	33.8	18.4
1987	7.0	23.8	33.5	15.8
1988	6.4	22.2	35.4	12.2
	25 years and over			
1985	6.4	7.1	4.7	9.3
1986	6.2	7.5	5.6	9.5
1987	6.2	8.1	6.2	9.1
1988	6.4	8.2	7.5	7.7
	Males			
1985	6.3	8.5	6.2	11.8
1986	5.5	8.5	7.2	11.9
1987	5.3	8.3	7.4	11.0
1988	5.3	7.8	8.2	9.1
	Under 25 years			
1985	9.8	23.0	25.1	19.9
1986	6.7	21.7	28.2	19.4
1987	6.4	19.6	28.3	16.6
1988	6.0	17.6	29.7	13.1
	25 years and over			
1985	5.5	5.9	3.0	9.5
1986	5.2	6.3	3.5	9.8
1987	5.1	6.4	3.8	9.5
1988	5.1	6.2	4.4	8.0
	Females			
1985	8.8	12.7	15.4	11.0
1986	8.2	12.8	16.9	11.0
1987	8.0	13.5	17.3	10.1
1988	8.1	13.6	19.7	8.2
	Under 25 years			
1985	11.4	29.4	39.1	17.1
1986	8.8	28.5	40.4	17.2
1987	7.6	28.1	39.7	14.7
1988	7.0	26.8	42.0	11.2

TABLE 23-3. *(continued)*

	West Germany	France	Italy	United Kingdom
		Females		
		25 years and over		
1985	7.9	8.8	8.3	9.0
1986	8.0	9.2	9.8	9.0
1987	8.1	10.3	10.8	7.3
1988	8.4	10.8	13.3	7.3

Source: Eurostat 1988:182.
[a]Standardized for comparison.

trial sector (Schenkel 1989), which explains the low percentage of open male unemployment in the prime age groups. Since northern and central Italy are more industrialized than the South (36 percent industrial employment compared to 23 percent), the absolute number of CIG hours compensated has been higher in the northern and central regions (about two-thirds in 1987).

Rigidity/Flexibility Arrangements and Labor Market Entry

Do the very specific rigidity/flexibility arrangements of the Italian industrial labor market help explain Italy's high-entry unemployment? The argument is simple: the special rigidity/flexibility arrangements, where adjustment is made in a sort of closed system, do not allow youngsters to enter the core industrial labor market. Unfortunately, we have no sophisticated model able to analyze such relationships. My discussion of the topic is therefore be conjectural. What we lack is flow data on the labor market, which alone could provide information about mobility patterns.

Maurau and Oudinet (1988) have studied employment elasticities in four European countries (Germany, France, the United Kingdom, and Italy) over the period 1960–83. They found Italy to exhibit the weakest long-term elasticity of industrial employment: a reduction of 10 percent in production leads to a subsequent reduction in employment of only 3 percent. Italy also had the weakest long-term elasticity of working hours to changes in production.

All I have said about the low mobility and unemployment structure points to the fact that Italy has something like a closed industrial labor market, where numerical flexibility is not achieved by external labor shedding but rather by labor hoarding or "disguised dismissals" via the CIG. Studies of labor market flexibility in Italy therefore cannot ignore the number of workers and hours compensated by the CIG. Taking this into account, one can assume that mobility patterns within this closed system exhibit a rather high degree of flexibility.

But the flexibility provided by the CIG does not seem to spill over to the external labor market, however, and therefore possibly presents an entry barrier to new industrial jobs, as Tronti acknowledges (chap. 22). Of course, I speak of a period in which net additional hirings were low because of the crisis and industrial firms seemed to have sufficient flexibility through the CIG and did not often have to resort to the external labor market for hiring. Probably other features of the Italian labor market, such as the rigid placement system, whereby the unemployed are ranked according to criteria such as length of unemployment, their income situation, and so on (special lists for certain qualifications do, however, exist), have had an additional negative effect on hiring. Under this regime, firms are obliged to hire workers according to their administrative ranking and not according to the firms' needs. Intensive use of the CIG in such cases seems to be much more efficient in coping with adjustment problems.

During the last years, however, some changes have been introduced into the system, and it seems like a bureaucratic irony that a departure from the rigid ranking requirement (the so-called *chiamata nominativa*—the hiring by name and not only by imposed rank order) has been announced as a measure of active labor market policy.

Disconnected Exit and Entry Restrictions?

Exit restrictions and entry problems for first-time job seekers may occur (and do occur) in different segments of the labor market. I have already pointed to the regional and gender dimension of the CIG (the *cassaintegrati* are disproportionately men from the industries of the northern and central regions, whereas the unemployed facing entry problems are disproportionally women from the South).

One has to add the enterprise size dimension. Looking at data on labor market policies specially designed to cope with the entry problem (such as work-and-training contracts—*contratti formazione-lavoro*—as well as the *chiamata nominativa*), one can see that the majority of participants find work in small firms (with up to forty-nine employees) that only rarely make use of the CIG. The service sector, where the CIG is not as widely used as in the industrial sector, accounts for about 40 percent of the participants in work-and-training contracts (Ministero del Lavoro et della Providencia Sociale: 1988). These figures do not say, however, whether youth would have joined the ranks of industrial core workers in the absence of the specific rigidity/flexibility regime. One could argue that it is precisely because of the closed system in the industrial core sectors that the effect of labor market policies on the hiring policies of large industrial firms is only marginal. But the figures might also tell us that labor market entry generally occurs largely in sectors and firms not covered by the special rigidity/flexibility arrangements. Under such an assumption, their impact on labor market entry would be far less dramatic.

More research is needed to effectively address the question of whether the rigidity/flexibility regime characterizing the Italian industrial labor market is a major cause of Italy's high-entry unemployment. That it is a major cause is not supported by all the facts. It seems that the problem of the CIG is not primarily one of hindering entries but of disguising exits at a rather high cost for the state and the taxpayer. The 1991 reform (which cut benefits, introduced employer contributions, reduced the duration of CIG compensation, and allowed external mobility for persons on total layoff in the CIG) appears to be a response to this problem. Coping with the entry problem of young people requires different measures, such as the work-and-training contracts. Moreover, in the absence of a proper unemployment insurance system, the CIG acts as a functional equivalent to unemployment benefits and thus fills an important gap in the Italian system of social protection. It can be amended substantially only if there is a thorough institutional reform of the Italian labor market.

Part III

The Future of Labor Market (De)Regulation in Industrialized Countries

24
Labor Regulation in an Era of Fragmented Flexibility

Guy Standing

For those concerned with labor questions, the 1980s were ugly. Not only were the levels of unemployment awful, but labor fragmentation accelerated almost everywhere. We are likely to look back on the 1980s as the decade in which disgracefully little attention was paid to the growing inequalities associated with labor developments and the reformulation of labor policies. It is this fragmentation that will shape labor policies in the 1990s.

The theme of this paper is that, as a general tendency, labor regulations in the 1980s moved from being collective and protective to being individualistic and promotional. This reflected and perhaps accelerated the growth of labor fragmentation. In that context, there are two possible directions labor regulation could take in the 1990s, when the difficulty will lie in combining collective security with individual flexibility.

The 1980s: Era of Individualistic Regulation

It is surely incorrect to see the 1980s as simply a decade of deregulation, although this was a rhetorical theme of the dominant supply-side and libertarian economic orthodoxy of the decade. Undoubtedly, the preceding period had been one of extensive growth of labor security, promoted in part by protective, collective regulations. To assess recent trends, it may help to reiterate the seven dimensions of labor security that developed in the 1950s, 1960s, and early 1970s:

1. labor market security—preserved in the commitment to full employment;
2. employment security—preserved or strengthened by regulations designed to protect workers from arbitrary dismissal and to impose costs on employers wishing to cut employment without due notice;
3. job security—accepting and legitimating practices by which groups of workers could retain a niche in the production process, a defense against rapid development of the technical division of labor;

4. work security—regulated protection of occupational health and safety, often with the onus of proof of safety on employers;
5. income security—protection of vulnerable groups through minimum wage mechanisms, collective bargaining, and "progressive" fiscal welfare;
6. labor reproductive security—a social commitment to underwrite the costs of education and skills development and the social productivity of the work force and potential work force, through subsidized schooling, training, health facilities, and so on;
7. labor process security—laws and regulations enhancing the political and economic role of trade unions and other "corporatist" institutions designed, ostensibly at least, to protect the collective interest of workers.

In many countries, all seven forms of labor security were eroded in the 1980s to varying degrees. The erosion took various forms but was probably due primarily to the fragmentation of the working population into increasingly distinctive categories with very different degrees of labor security.

Before turning to that, it seems useful to reiterate some conceptual distinctions. There are protective regulations, designed to prevent adverse insecurities being visited on groups of workers. There are promotional regulations, designed to create an environment in which certain forms of activity can and will occur. There are restrictive regulations, which prevent groups of workers from acting in certain ways that might be to their advantage. There are paternalistic regulations, designed to "guide" workers in certain directions that the government believes, or claims to believe, is in their interest. And there are fiscal regulations, designed to shape labor supply or the pattern of employment in certain ways, such as by subsidizing low pay or altering the relative costs of employing low-skilled or part-time workers. When commentators refer to labor deregulation, they seem to be referring primarily to the first type of regulation.

In the 1980s, there was *explicit* deregulation, in the form of derogation of all four types of regulation that were geared to collective, solidaristic protection, and there was *implicit* deregulation, that is, an erosion of regulatory protection by means other than legislative change. Although few governments adhered strictly to the extreme libertarian, supply-side agenda of the 1980s, most were dragged along in the general direction.

An essential part of the Chicago school of law and economics, which underlay the supply-side orthodoxy of the 1980s, is that protective regulations can be justified only if they demonstrably promote economic efficiency. For adherents of this school, there is a prima facie presumption that such regulations create more harm than good. Yet an essential part of the libertarian agenda is that individualistic labor regulations should displace collective, protective regulations, the twin justification being the desire to promote individual property rights and the belief that decentralized, individualized labor relations would ensure that markets would "clear" and unemployment fall (or rise) to its "natural" rate, as determined by frictional and structural characteristics of the labor market. According to this perspective, the gradual extension of individualized contracts of employment—to which we might give the rather ungainly name of contractualization—would impose behavioral norms on workers based on individualistic, common-law principles. The courts could be relied on to rule against collective interventions by reference to freedom in the labor market. Unions could indulge in fanfare flag-waving negotiations every two or three years, when collective framework contracts were up for renegotiation. But ideally, by the tenets of those steering down this libertarian path, this would become atavistic to the point of marginal relevance. Company employee associations (along the Japanese model perhaps) could grow. To the extent that industrial or craft unions persisted, they would be constrained to the point of being agents of management as much as agents of redistribution, let alone anything more radical.

By the end of the 1980s, large parts of the libertarian agenda were well on the way to being realized. Individualization of employment contracts has extended down the pay and occupational status scales, and one suspects that such contracts have become more comprehensive as the practice has spread. There is also ample evidence of an erosion of collective, protective regulations. Implicit deregulation has been occurring because of (1) nonimplementation of protective regulations; (2) inadequate resources and personnel devoted to the task of policing existing regulations, especially bearing in mind the increased need given the greater variety of labor relations; (3) the erosion of the capacity to resist among those denied their rights to protection; (4) a growing and cultivated sense of ambiguity among potential beneficiaries about the validity of such rights; and (5) an increasing loss of entitlement by virtue of their labor status.

A major cause of the fifth form of implicit deregulation has been the drift from regular full-time wage employment; major causes of the third and fourth forms have been deunionization (or, more likely, nonunionization), chronic unemployment, and growing inequality. Yet perhaps the biggest single factor in the implicit deregulation of the 1980s was less tangible: fear changed sides. Whereas in the 1960s employers led in introducing practices ahead of regulations—implicit regulation—to avoid the threat of disruption, in the 1980s they led deregulation in the confident belief that the door was open, that others were going through it, and that resistance was enfeebled.[1]

Explicit deregulation has come about because of the repeal of protective laws, whether wholly or, more commonly, by the creation of selective or "targeted" rather than universal rights, sometimes by the creation of loopholes in the legislative framework. Rights per se have been eroded by the tightening of conditionality, protection being made more selective, and the onus of proof of right being shifted to the workers and made more costly to pursue. Examples of explicit deregulation include the emaciation of the wages councils in the United Kingdom

---

[1]Although it is hard to substantiate, one senses that the more intensive international competition and the pressure to conform to low-cost practices have contributed to the implicit deregulation and intensification of work. In that context, a recent comparison of labor practices in two plants of an American multinational concluded that productivity in the Columbus, Ohio, plant was much higher than in the U.K. plant, partly because there was no scaffolding in the former, partly because there was bell-to-bell working with no time lost at meal or tea-break times, no coffee breaks, no canteen, no employment security, and all practices were preserved by an "open shop" labor policy, excluding unions, so that workers were allocated work as and when management saw fit.

and legislation in the Federal Republic of Germany permitting unions and employers to derogate from working-time legislation. There have been numerous cases in most of Europe, North America, and elsewhere testifying to the underlying trend.

Although there has been both implicit and explicit deregulation of protective and collective institutions and mechanisms, it would be misleading to characterize this as simple deregulation. Pro-individualistic regulations have been displacing pro-collective regulations.[2] For the supply-side libertarian, the 1980s might be seen as a transitional era, between one based on collective regulation to one of individual contractualization. In the process, it is somewhat ironic that those pressing for deregulation have typically done so by reference to the need to restore full or near-full employment. Whereas the old orthodoxy was that regulations were to protect workers in employment, the latter-day orthodoxy is that regulations should be judged by whether or not they enable more people to obtain employment. For instance, an act was passed in Belgium in March 1987 permitting firms to extend working hours beyond the standard if doing so had positive employment effects. Elsewhere, lower "recruitment" wages have been sanctioned and encouraged by fiscal measures, ostensibly to boost job creation.

As for implicit deregulation, it has surely been extensive with the growth of more flexible employment, both in the functional sense (reducing job security and employment security) and the external sense, with the shift from protected, full-time wage labor to less secure forms of labor relations, through the relative growth of small-scale units, outsourcing, subcontracting, and casualization. If one accepts that these trends represent the outcome of longer-term managerial, cost, and technological considerations (boosted by new technologies and the changing international division of labor) rather than a passing period of recession and adjustment, then one can reasonably argue that conventional forms of protective regulation geared to labor security will be increasingly bypassed—avoided rather than evaded—in the 1990s.

There is no space here to document these points in any detail, but before turning to a consideration of one of the rapidly developing regulatory responses to the partial collapse of the old "social democratic" regulatory system, it may be useful to conceptualize the labor fragmentation that has perhaps been the outstanding feature of labor market developments in the past decade.

Labor Force Fragmentation

The 1980s was a period of growing inequality almost everywhere.[3] The available data understate the extent to which inequality has grown, but they also understate

---

[2]For example, fiscal incentives have been introduced to encourage the growth of personal pensions and others to boost individualistic profit-related pay.

[3]For instance, in the United Kingdom—admittedly an extreme example, but by no means alone in terms of the general trend—various respectable estimates have suggested that income inequality was greater in 1989 than in 1889, the year of Charles Booth's first reliable earnings survey in the country.

the extent to which income insecurity—or potential inequality—has grown. We know that nominal and real-wage flexibility have increased and that this trend has been in part a euphemism for the ability of firms to lower real wages and more easily widen or change wage differentials. For instance, a survey of employers by the United Kingdom's Confederation of British Industry in May 1989 found that in the previous three years those firms reporting that it was easy to increase wage differentials had risen from one-third to over one-half, while those reporting that it was hard to do so had fallen from one-third to a little more than one-quarter (CBI 1989:14, table A7).

Besides the considerable evidence on wage differentials—and even in relatively egalitarian countries such as Sweden wage differentials stopped narrowing in the late 1970s and probably widened in the 1980s (for a review, see Standing 1988b, chap. 3)—there are very good reasons for believing that inequality has grown much more than conventional income and earnings data suggest. One reason is that tax changes and changes in relative prices of items consumed by the rich and poor—due partly to supply-side deregulation of rents, transport, and so on—have widened the inequality of living standards. Another reason is statistical; more of the income of high-income earners are not being measured, and more of the lowest-income earners are being omitted from surveys, sometimes because employers do not record them, giving an inflated average for the low-paid categories. Another reason is that growing numbers of lower-income workers lack private or state benefits.[4] Another reason is the "postcapitalist" nature of many employment relations and the ongoing process of class fragmentation. It is this latter process that I wish to stress. Any conceptualization of fragmentation will be questionable and must depend in part on one's analytical objectives. But it is surely essential to have an image of the various strata to which regulatory frameworks would have to apply. After all, one of the presumptions of the social consensus welfare state of the postwar era was that the labor force was unfragmented, the norm being a male full-time wage worker in regular, protected employment with a dependent wife who was either inactive or only peripherally in the labor force. In the 1990s, by contrast, labor regulation and distribution policy have to take account of something like the following pattern of fragmentation.

There are seven strata, each defined by its distinctive relation to regulatory policies. At the top is an *elite*, characterized by its internationalization and increasing detachment from the labor process beneath it. At the very peak are a handful of rapacious individuals who are crazed by the pursuit of their nth billion dollars. Below are some very wealthy groups which are detached from national regulatory frameworks. Essentially, they are "capitalist employees" who earn much of their income through profit sharing, the acquisition of subsidized shares, and a growing range of fringe benefits, some of which have a full value way in excess of any taxable, monetized value. Thus, executives increasingly rely on "performance-

---

[4]For one recent and rather different attempt, see Runciman 1990. For another approach, which seems to be based on wage levels, stability of employment, and demographic characteristics, see Burchell and Rubery 1990.

related" bonuses. In 1989, these accounted for 20 percent of management salaries in Britain, beyond which were numerous perks that had been growing relative to other sources of income (see CBI 1989:5). In the United States, senior executives on average receive more than half their total income in nonsalary form. Those in this elite have income security and other forms of labor security to the extent that they want it. Much of their power lies in the concealed way their income and wealth accumulate, essentially legally. It is hardly comforting that the main drawback for those in this elite is that their lifestyle is intense and fraught with stress, which ultimately threatens their hold on their status and control.

The next stratum consists of what might be called *proficians*. These are nominally independent "consultants" and self-employed specialists. The expansion in the number of such workers in the past decade has been a spectacular feature of the pursuit of "flexible specialization," about which so much has been written. Key characteristics of the members of this stratum are their relative youth, their frenetic work style, and their self-satisfaction. In general, they have little labor security but remind us of Tawney's tadpoles—most are dying but some are becoming smug, croaking frogs—except that a far larger proportion seem to thrive because they have taken advantage of enterprise flexibility and the advantage to firms of using flexible specialists for short-term purposes and thus avoiding overhead costs.

Whether the growth of this stratum will continue into the 1990s is hard to predict. Their "market price" may decline and enterprises may find that, as the cost of such workers comes down, it is more advantageous to reintegrate these functions in-house. More likely, the external status granted to the proficians will preserve their semiautonomy. Thus, these two aspects should create a monetized wedge that could be shared by workers and firms who both value the flexibility and autonomy that the more distant working relationship entails.

A key aspect of the elite and profician strata is that they tend to be beyond the welfare state and other regulatory institutions; they have access to privatized benefits and neither contribute to nor gain entitlement or social security benefits. This elitist detachment leads them to give political support to the transformation of the welfare state from what Richard Titmus called the institutional, redistributive model to the selective, residual model. They have been subject to implicit deregulation, but except in crisis, they are unlikely to be very worried about it.

These first two labor strata represent the upper echelons of "popular capitalism," though the term "overclass" is probably a misnomer.[5] The point is that they are part of the fragmented labor structure, not outside it. Below them are *state bureaucrats*, senior functionaries who seem oriented increasingly to serving the interests of the upper strata and who retain the range of labor security they obtained in the expansive times of the 1960s and early 1970s. In some countries they may have lost some security and been affected by the erosion of protective

---

[5]Townsend (1990) seem to have a combination of these two strata in mind when he describes the overclass.

regulations, but it is hard to gain a clear picture of the seriousness of that erosion; one suspects that they have lost job security and employment security.

A fourth stratum might be called the *capitalist worker* stratum. It consists of those almost randomly fortunate wage workers who, through share payments or access to successful profit-sharing schemes, accumulate savings that allow them to set themselves up in some petty full-time or part-time business or to live off dividends. Numerically the group may represent only a tiny fraction of the work force, but it is ideologically rather important. Overall, they have gained income security and may have less need for employment or labor market security and so be less inclined to oppose implicit or explicit deregulation of those forms of security. One would expect them to be critical of labor process security since it is based on solidaristic principles and oppose mechanisms for promoting income security through redistribution and institutional protection of those at the lower end of the labor market.

Fifth down the labor process ladder is the old *proletarian* stratum, made up mainly of unionized male workers in regular wage employment. This was the Beveridge and Bismarckian norm for the national insurance social security system. For well-known reasons, their numbers have been declining numerically and have had their labor security eroded in various ways. They have been a major source of the growth of the bottom stratum. In general, they have tended to lose income security, job security, work security, labor market security, and, most crucially, labor process security. Part of their declining bargaining strength and lost social cohesion has occurred because of the erosion of job security (as distinct from employment security), stemming from technological change and a series of concessions to management on job demarcation.[6] If wages are tied to job or task assignments and workers are forced to concede the right to job retitling and rebundling to the will of management, then wage flexibility will be increased. Thus, for example, data from the regular CBI employer surveys in the United Kingdom indicate that in the past decade between one-quarter and one-third of all pay settlements included concessions on working arrangements (CBI 1989:6, 13). This implies a reduction not only in job security but in income security.

This stratum has also lost employment security for similar reasons and has been threatened by two-tier or multiple-tier employment contract and wage structures, which may be transitional phenomena en route to flexible labor relations. They have also been affected by working-time flexibility. This might be beneficial for both employers and workers, but unless such flexibility is regulated by collective bargaining, as is still the rule in Italy and Germany, it will be insecure and subordinated flexibility on the employers' terms, as was the case with the abolition of restrictions on night work and weekend work. In sum, one can hypothesize

---

[6]In the United Kingdom, the 1987 ACAS survey found that in the previous three years one-third of all companies covered had relaxed demarcations to allow production workers to do maintenance tasks, and more than one-fourth had relaxed them to allow one craftsworker to do the work of others (ACAS 1988a).

that a growing proportion of this stratum is in a precarious position, more likely to be moved across job categories without the labor security for which they fought so successfully in previous eras. As their labor insecurity grows, they will swell the sixth stratum.

The sixth stratum is what might best be called the *flexiworker* stratum. In many countries it has grown enormously in recent years, encompassing many forms of "nonregular" wage labor and other precarious labor statuses made more vulnerable by the explicit and implicit deregulation of the time. One is tempted to subdivide this heterogeneous category, but what the various groups have in common is an absence of any labor security, most of all labor process security. Whereas the proletarian stratum has increasingly been expected to be functionally flexible (i.e., to lose its crucial job security), flexiworkers are also labor-status flexible, likely to shift between wage and nonwage forms of employment, sometimes combining activities, sometimes not.

Official labor force classifications are often hard to apply. Euphemisms are almost amusing. We have seen the emergence of "permanent temporaries," "self-employed employees," and "in-house workers." Some firms maintain workers on temporary contracts for many years; some employment agencies put workers on permanent contracts as temporaries, guaranteeing them a retainer and employment status but not any particular job or income.

The resultant fragmentation can have grim effects that highlight the underlying insecurity. Recently there was a wretched court case in the United Kingdom in which fishermen who had been working for a firm for twenty years or more were deemed to have failed to satisfy the condition that to be entitled to redundancy benefits workers must have been in regular employment for at least two years. As their work in the period immediately preceding their redundancy had become irregular, the required spell or regular employment continuity had been broken, resulting in their loss of entitlement. The fishermen had become flexiworkers without knowing it.

Flexiworkers need not be unskilled in a technical sense. Thus, the spread of telecomputing or remote work often involves computational skills. But they are likely to have no employment security and little or no labor process security, in that they are isolated from the work process, ignored in promotions, easily dismissed, and unlikely to identify with industrial or craft unions.

Apparently, telecomputing has also become a mechanism for geographical decentralization and even for extending the international division of labor. Some firms have set up regional centers in which "out-workers" assemble to work for part of the time. The New York Life Insurance Company, having had difficulty in retaining trained staff in its U.S. offices, set up an office in Ireland, where it sends insurance claim forms to be processed and sent back to New York. Remote working has even been used as a form of regional policy to shift jobs to high-unemployment areas without the need to shift the plant or offices if the firm wants to remain in a strategically placed central location. The United Kingdom's National Economic Development Council launched information technology work centers in five inner cities for precisely this purpose. In short, by such methods, capital remains concentrated while labor becomes more fragmented and decentralized.

Typically, flexiworkers are in and out of jobs, whether full time or part time, and are paid wages or income in some other form. Rarely are they in jobs long enough to earn entitlement to occupational welfare, social security, or even privatized insurance benefits, let alone long enough to develop the confidence to join or form unions.

Some of the characteristics of the growth of flexiworkers are too well known to warrant repetition. One trend is worth stressing, however: large parts of the employment function itself may be in the process of being contracted out to intermediaries—labor-only agencies or "employee-leasing" companies (the more popular term in the United States). Such contracting out takes many forms, including the "turn-key" provision of work teams of complementary groups. I anticipate a lucrative profession mushrooming in the 1990s—employment contract lawyers who will bargain for many workers, as agents do for football players and actors, over not only salaries and benefit packages but also such matters as employee loan arrangements between companies (a growing practice in Japanese firms, apparently), zero-hours contracts, maximum and minimum working-time contracts, on-call contracts, and annual hours contracts.

Symbolic of the moves toward employee subcontracting was the recent abolition of Britain's national dock labor scheme, whereby dockers had obtained some income and employment security through a registration system that had helped maintain minimum wages and regulated training and skill standards. For more than fifty years, this symbol of decasualization had been preserved; now the prospect of labor auctions, wage undercutting, and market clearing is back. It is only one of many such moves.

Temporary employment agencies have grown for secretaries, contract cleaners, building workers, hotel kitchen staff, security service workers, maintenance workers, electronics production workers, and numerous others. Some labor-only employment agencies have become multinational enterprises, and in some cases they have become monopsonist-monopolists with strong rent-acquisition possibilities. Already there is an International Confederation of Temporary Work Firms, which recently reported that the number of workers in the EC on temporary contracts had grown by 15 to 20 percent a year in the 1980s. This rate is expected to grow after 1992 when the EC becomes a single market. Apparently, the growth has been greatest in the Netherlands, France, Germany, the United Kingdom, and Belgium. The European Commission's concern for "social dumping" is leading to consideration of new regulations, but the European Court of Justice's decision in March 1990 authorizing Spanish and Portuguese firms to transport their own temporaries to work for them in other parts of Europe seems to open the door to further expansion.

One can paint these developments as benign or malign. The modern libertarian would contend that competition will force the agencies to provide incentives for workers to stay with them, and there may indeed be some stabilization of employment in such agencies, which will decide on their allocation to firm X or Y, with pensions, sick pay, paid leave, and the rest. This will entail low levels of job security, however, in that such workers will be shifted at the will of intermediaries and the firms to which they are contracted. This is *subordinated* flexibility, which is a threat to occupation by its incessant insecurity and casualization at the point of production. Skills that will be fostered include mobility; those underdeveloped will include a broad understanding of specific production processes.

In recent years there has been a proliferation in the variety of employment contracts, many of which are characterized by employment insecurity that identifies flexiworkers. Some contracts cover specific groups of workers; some reflect prevailing production or management strategies. In ILO enterprise-level labor flexibility surveys, we have been probing how to disaggregate labor statuses. The experience has highlighted the inadequacy of dualistic vocabulary. The term "temporary," for instance, covers a wide spectrum of usefully distinctive contractual relations. Here is not the place to go into the distinctions or their implications, but just listing the main forms of contracts highlights the fragmentation process:

1. casual, typically for day work, in which there is no oral or written contract;
2. temporary, fixed-term, oral agreements, with no retention, either for (a) stop-gap work or (b) job work;
3. temporary, fixed-term, oral, on a continuing basis, either for 2a or 2b;
4. temporary, fixed-term, written contracts, as for 2a or 2b;
5. temporary, age limited (e.g., for youths aged sixteen to nineteen or for preretirement);
6. apprenticeship contracts, with or without assurance of subsequent employment;
7. trainee or probationary, of specified or unspecified duration;
8. adaptation contracts, for posttraining practical purposes;
9. temporary contracts for first-time job seekers, as in Germany;
10. job-sharing contracts;
11. employment orientation contracts, particularly for youth;
12. solidarity contracts, involving shared cuts in wages and working time in recessions;
13. variable-time contracts, in which the length of the working day or week is adjusted to meet the firm's requirements;
14. part-time contracts, also involving features of other forms of contracts;
15. regular, full-time contracts.

This list is scarcely exhaustive and excludes forms of dependent "self-employment." Flexiworkers fit into most of the first fourteen categories, and while most of those have always existed, it is their growth that is striking. The scope for employment insecurity and income insecurity in this "contractual fragmentation" is considerable, even though the diversity provides potential flexibility for firms and workers that could be advantageous for either or both. Labor process security is minimal because such workers have no social space into which to bond cohesively. Moreover, such flexiworkers typically lack entitlement to occupational welfare or insurance-based state welfare. Some groups may have access to some benefits, some to others, but the dominant picture is one of exclusion or inadequacy of entitlement. Ironically, of course, they have a greater need for such benefits because they lack labor security in most of the respects outlined earlier. This means they are always under threat of sinking into the seventh stratum.

This stratum, which seems to have grown enormously in some countries in the 1980s, has attracted various epithets, the most popular and controversial being underclass or lumpenproletariat.[7] The former term seems to have stuck, despite criticisms, and has been treated as a conservative instrument by writers such as Charles Murray, who have presented it as a segment of the population who lack a work ethic and are dependent on welfare to the point where they need to be rehabilitated.[8] But liberals too have sentimentalized its growth, often failing to criticize the productive, technological, and labor structures that generate lumpen components.

One might best describe this stratum as detached, since the defining characteristic is a loss of attachment to regular economic activity, often involving long-term or chronic recurrent unemployment and an equally chronic need for state transfers from outside the national insurance schemes. The loss of labor security by those in the old proletarian stratum and the absence of labor security among flexiworkers, particularly in the form of entitlement to social security, means that the potential source of growth of the detached stratum has itself boomed in the 1980s.[9]

To a certain extent, it is from this group that the state can draw low-paid labor to help create wage and employment flexibility in other strata. But perhaps its main social impact is as a major source of fear for those workers who are unwilling to become subordinately flexible.

Detachment, social exclusion, and marginalization have become popular terms in recent debates on labor market developments. The Fordist system may have broken down, but if it has, it has done so not just because mass production based on regular wage labor has shrunk but because the regulatory framework has become dysfunctional, given that more of the population of advanced industrialized countries have become detached from productive society, that is, detached as workers. Consumer capitalism depends on workers consuming mass-produced products, and increasingly most people's identities are tied only to consumption

---

[7]For a review, see Auletta 1982.

[8]Conservatives attribute the growth of the underclass to individual behavioral failings coupled with the welfare system, which together make it hard or impossible for members of this stratum to enter the economic mainstream. Liberals tend to attribute their exclusion to employers' refusal to hire certain groups. One question in the debate is whether such individuals would take jobs if offered them. But a more fundamental issue is structural. What produces and reproduces such a detached social-labor stratum? A labor market that depends on subordinated flexibility and certain types of flexibility may generate a larger detached stratum than one based on strict hierarchies of jobs or on alternative social divisions of labor.

[9]For instance, in the United States, the proportion of those who became unemployed who had unemployment insurance benefits fell from more than 40 percent in the 1970s to about 33 percent in 1989. Even the number of job losers receiving unemployment insurance (UI) benefits has fallen, partly because there has been a change in the type of jobs subject to unemployment, partly because UI benefits are now taxed, reducing the incentive to claim; partly because there has been an increase in the level of earnings necessary for entitlement to regular UI benefits in many states; partly because of a tendency to disqualify workers if they quit jobs rather than penalize them temporarily; partly because states have means-tested UI benefits; and partly because of moves to workfare.

and their status as consumers, not to production and their work status. This applies to most of the labor fragments, none of which are easily organizable to pursue a coherent strategy of labor process security because they have no collective identity. It has almost reached the stage when one cannot envisage collective class action anymore, only sectional action, for instance, on ethnic, age, or gender issues.

Detachment is complex. Many are formally detached from productive society, as in the case of the long-term unemployed and many of those in "labor market schemes." Others are behaviorally detached even though they are employed, such as many flexiworkers, who have little employment security and thus little access to nonwage components of "working-class" income, such as earnings-related benefits that, as in Germany, were built up as incentives to continuity of employment. Historically, the social insurance welfare system has had a regulatory function, with earnings-related mechanisms expected, first, to increase productivity through incentive and workers' commitment effects, and, second, to raise the firms' expected return to investment in training. But if the labor process is not generating the sort of employment for which such regulations can function to raise efficiency, then one can anticipate attempts to revise the system to secure a more effective regulatory framework.

Labor process fragmentation erodes the integrative capacity of both Beveridge and Bismarckian social security systems. They were conceived primarily to foster productivity while ensuring income security for the working population and their dependents. In many respects, they have become means of weakening labor process security, because that depends crucially on the existence of common interests, and means of undermining labor market security, because that depends on workers having effective freedom in the labor market, which has been corroded by "poverty traps," "unemployment traps," work test rules, and so on. The more complex the system, the more one can expect the regulatory objectives to be dominant. Moreover, as argued elsewhere, with labor flexibility and fragmentation, the social security's contributory base tends to shrink and benefit entitlement tends to become narrower and more fragile. Yet many of those advocating more flexibility in labor and product markets also contend that welfare encourages and strengthens behavioral dependency. It is in that spirit that governments have shifted toward more "targeting"—greater use of means tests, tighter conditionality for benefits, tighter behavioral monitoring, and the promotion of "welfare pluralism." In many countries one sees a strong trend toward some variant of workfare, defined as the payment of benefits conditional on predetermined employment-related activity. In the United States, so often the pattern setter, the number on workfare increased by more than 60 percent in one year. We are creeping to workfare now, but it is scripted to play a major role in the libertarian cinema of the 1990s.

Related to workfare is another trend associated with the growth of subordinated flexibility, the changing role of training. This trend stems from the perceived need to raise productivity. The basic supply-side view is that to raise skills, wage differentials need to widen and be more individualized. But along with more flexible payment systems, ostensibly designed to promote productivity, there has been a trend toward what might be called "trainingitis," which derives from the erosion of skill in the traditional sense of that term. The more occupations are split into jobs, the more labor statuses are flexible, and the more lower labor strata grow, the greater the role one can expect to be allocated to job and labor market training. In various European countries the state role in such training has grown enormously, and one possibility is that a growing proportion of the population will have work "careers" consisting of flexible combinations of short-term jobs preceded and succeeded by training and retraining. This pattern could lead to workers having a whirlwind of jobs interspersed with training. There is talk of an "active society" for the 1990s based on benign presentations of this twilight zone of intermittent training and productive activity. But workers obliged to shift from pillar to post in a fashion determined by some regulatory body are hardly likely to lead the way to the acta vita.

In sum, if the libertarian, supply-side path to labor flexibility persists, the following characteristics seem likely:

1. a contractualization of the labor process, with pro-individualistic regulations constraining collective action;
2. welfare pluralism, with the state as fall-back, "safety-net" provider, with privatized benefits for the upper strata and voluntary private services to fill the gaps left by an incomplete insurance system (a model presented as "the caring society" in the Netherlands: see de Neubourg 1990);
3. privatization of social policy as well as of economic spheres;
4. workfare replacing means-tested and universal transfer payments for the employable;
5. more policing of welfare "scroungers";
6. greater police presence in civil society to control the losers in an aggressively competitive economic environment;
7. a neocorporatist state based on an overt employer-government alliance in place of tripartism, with trade unions shrinking or shackled by legislation and their own fragility in flexible labor markets.

As stated, these characteristics are exaggerated, but they are sufficiently present as trends to suggest that the search for alternatives would be reasonable.

Toward Cooperative Flexibility

There is a nucleus of an alternative scenario in corporatist traditions kept alive in the Nordic region in the 1980s, but we would have to combat a critical limitation of the Nordic models. An essential element of any viable alternative must be the avoidance of labor fragmentation and income insecurity. Yet the danger is that critics of the dominant trend toward subordinated flexibility will continue to give primacy to labor market security and employment security. Although both are valuable and should be seen as instrumental to the promotion of other rights, neither is what could be called a meta-right, that is, an ultimate social objective. Treating them otherwise ultimately undermines their political legitimacy.

The error of the old "laborist" model surely lies in a faulty syllogism: there is a right to work; all rights imply duties; therefore, there is a duty to labor. One could give countless examples of unfortunate deductions from this line of reasoning. To give just one minor example, a recent international meeting of trade unionists concluded that the answer to the inadequacy of social security provision associated with the growth of more flexible forms of employment was more full-time jobs (OECD 1989c:7). But one may guess that full-time wage labor is neither desired by the majority nor desirable on efficiency or equity grounds. If full-time wage employment is treated as a meta-right, then one must favor market-clearing wages, whatever they may be, and a compromise on various other forms of labor security, notably labor process and work security.

Full employment is always possible. But it is neither an effective means of overcoming labor fragmentation nor any longer a reliable means of reversing the growing inequalities and erosion of labor process security. That recognition is needed if policy reform is to relate to current realities without drifting into some atavistic cul de sac, such as the mass creation of "public sector jobs."

Fortunately, in some European economies, alternative strategies are taking shape. We may be in an era of social experimentation in the course of which partial reforms will be pieced together to create the basis for a much more flexible lifestyle by the end of the twentieth century. This vision must surely be of a social structure in which labor process security and income security are guarded and enhanced as meta-rights.

Such reforms are taking various complementary directions, and one feels that they would fuse more successfully and sooner if we could articulate the social and labor structure we would like to create. Here it might be useful merely to outline the reforms that could possibly shape an alternative path to labor flexibility.

First and foremost, unless organizations can be revived to represent the collective voice of the vulnerable segments of society, notably those in the sixth and seventh strata, the necessary impetus to sustainable, nonsubordinated flexibility will not emerge or will be dissipated. This is why the evolving structure and strategy of unions and their regrouping are crucial, particularly the possibility of community unions to replace industrial or craft unions. A variant has been called associational unionism, the theme being that the union would represent workers who would otherwise not be constantly in the same trade or industry.

If workers are "postcapitalist" in the sense of not being in stable wage labor, they will be uncommitted to industrial unionism, just as flexiworkers can scarcely be expected to be committed to craft unionism, besides being hard to organize or to retain as union members. But neither will community unionism flourish if the organization is merely an agency for job placements, advisory services, personal loans, and a source of social security for their members, even though these functions are desirable. If that is all unions become, the state or private commercial firms will always compete, forcing them to become individualistic entities. Only if unions are constantly concerned with the primary problem of the era, redistribution, will they develop a pivotal role. There are signs that moves to redefine communal solidarity are stengthening and that economic democracy, as well as political and industrial democracy, will be high on the agenda in the 1990s. Without economic democracy, one can see no alternative to the subordinated flexibility sketched earlier.

Perhaps more advanced in practice is the application, as well as theoretical discussion, of experimental policies to promote flexible lifestyles that actually build on the fragmenting tendencies in the labor process. Many of these policies are double-edged in that they could be either converted into instruments to intensify subordinated flexibility or integrated with other policies to promote a more cooperative, egalitarian flexibility.

If there are more part-time employment slots and there is a need to respond more speedily to economic restructuring—perhaps as a result of more rapid and pervasive technological innovation—then it makes little sense to hope to buck the trend. It makes much more sense to facilitate flexible work patterns on terms workers desired. This is one reason for foreseeing an era of social experimentation. One sees the outlines of what could be a social dividend route to flexibility, called that because it is based on redistributing the economic surplus in ways other than by wage income and welfare. This would also give precedence to the right to work over the right to employment, bearing in mind that a right to do something can exist only if there is a matching right not to do it.

Something like a social dividend approach is crystalizing in the various experimental policies and institutional developments taking place in some parts of Europe. One thinks of the sabbatical year and time bank debates in Sweden and Finland, solidarity contracts in Belgium, partial retirement schemes, career break and parental leave arrangements, the *revenue minimum d'insertion* in France, wage earner funds, renewed interest in profit sharing, the renewed growth of cooperatives in Italy and elsewhere (including the former Soviet Union, in a big way), industrial districts in Baden-Wuerttemberg and in Italy and elsewhere, and so on.[10] Experimentation is the order of the moment. Thus, old ideas about time banks have been repackaged as less radical reforms. And in Finland, for instance, a government committee has proposed the phased introduction of one-year sabbaticals for all workers, giving them the right to periodic breaks from their main labor force activity (Leija, Santamaki-Vuore, and Standing 1990:chap. 6). Partial retirement schemes and the removal of arbitrary notions about the age of retirement are widely regarded as cautious steps in the direction of lifetime flexibility, especially in the context of the aging of European workers, though such schemes can be, and have been, easily turned into sources of inequity and discrimination unless they are developed in the appropriate institutional context.

There is also constructive discussion of unconditional income transfers, or citizenship income grants. These would decouple labor market status and behavior from income security and facilitate flexible combinations of productive and reproductive activities, helping in the process to legitimize the black economy and

---

[10]In the United States as well, lifestyle flexibility may be back on the agenda. A recent survey for the Employment Benefit Research Institute found that about 80 percent of Americans thought there should be parental leave and about 50 percent thought it should be paid leave.

encourage the growth of the informal economy. As long as governments lack the courage or vision to promote the genuine right to income security, that is, unconditional, universal, and individual, the potential for flexible specialization will be restricted. Basic security from deprivation as a citizenship right will be a necessary condition. It will not be the only one, for to create an environment of cooperative flexibility will require labor process security, to prevent the vulnerable in the lower labor strata from being detached and to combat the oppressive potential implicit in contract law replacing collective regulation of labor relations. There must be institutions and regulations to provide the safeguards against the structural inequalities that market mechanisms by themselves are bound to produce and intensify. That is why work security and payment system security (including minimum wage protection) will remain essential components of any regulatory framework. Ultimately, however, the institutional structure for developing labor process security will be far more significant than regulations. New forms of unions, new forms of collective agency and voice, and new meanings of solidarity will need to emerge.

Conclusion

Events in Eastern Europe have given the issues discussed here new poignancy. A bogeyman has been removed, and after a year or two debates about the direction of social policy may become decidedly more progressive as a consequence. Fears about social dumping, raised by the rhetoric of 1992, will have to be addressed even more urgently. The market-oriented orthodoxy is promoting subordinated flexibility everywhere, but in the wings is an emerging paradigm of flexibility based on cooperation and security. For it to succeed, it is essential that the means for recovering and extending labor process security be strengthened. Craft unions are almost anachronistic in societies where trades or crafts are ephemeral. Industrial unions are enfeebled by the multinational, multi-industrial nature of modern conglomerates. There must be moves downstream so that unions represent the aspirations and needs of all the groups in our fifth, sixth, and seventh labor strata.

The only way for such organizations to emerge as restructuring organizations is by diminishing fear and insecurity. For this to occur, there will have to be a shift in the social security system in the direction of decoupling the labor market from the provision of income security. If one sees the existing welfare system as increasingly a regulatory device rather than as a device for effectively and equitably combating poverty, marginalization, and social exclusion, then it deserves a radical revision.[11] That surely is one of the two keys to cooperative, secure flexibility, the other being economic democracy in some form.

At present, the fragmentation of society is such that political democracy and

---

[11]If one defines liberty negatively as the absence of coercion, then the welfare state has tilted in the direction of reducing liberty. Traditionally, the welfare state has been defended as promoting positive liberty by providing the basis for individual choice in conditions of security. In labor market terms, at least, positive liberty has not been promoted very effectively in recent years.

the existing welfare institutions are far more likely to cement the socioeconomic divides than to reduce the marginalization of flexiworkers and detached groups. A simple majority can almost always be mobilized politically to limit the rights and security of vulnerable minorities. But enabling large numbers to make the transition out of the bottom three strata, let alone disintegrating the artificial fragmentation of the labor process, is scarcely feasible unless the institutional basis of income provision and work organization is revised.

This paper has deliberately not speculated on the sociodemographic fragmentation that could be expected to accompany different forms of labor fragmentation. This is a limitation that other papers in this volume have partially redressed. Surely, women have predominated in the flexiworker stratum in most countries, just as middle-aged and older men have been the principal losers in the erosion of labor security in the old proletarian stratum. In some societies, workfare-type options are likely to be targeted at women and ethnic minorities, in others at youth and immigrants. In most societies, the new forms of labor fragmentation are likely to intensify interhousehold inequality because of the high probability of joint entry into specific labor strata by husbands and wives or partners. But these are speculations that need to be addressed in the light of more detailed analyses of labor fragmentation.

In sum, an alternative approach to the supply-side libertarian route will have to be based on the promotion of the meta-rights of labor process security and income security, which are the necessary conditions for positive liberty. If democracy is to become a reality in the 1990s rather than a rapidly debased term, institutions and regulations will need to evolve to promote three complementary forms—political democracy, industrial democracy (through codetermination to ensure work security, occupational security, protective regulations, and so on), and economic democracy (through institutional mechanisms to redistribute economic surplus, citizenship income dividends, and so on). This would effectively reverse the traditional social democratic and socialist agenda, since, rather than nationalizing the means of production, it would accept the privatization of the management and ownership functions while socializing the surplus. The form of this alternative democratic framework is still far from clear, but the contours are beginning to take shape.

25

Institutional Barriers to Job Creation: Views and Expectations of Firms and Workers in the European Community

Claus Hofmann

In a survey of employees and firms in the industrial and retail sectors of the European community conducted in mid-1989, the European Commission tried to obtain information on the labor market. The data help improve our knowledge of labor market adaptability and adjustment efficiency and the range of labor market policy instruments.

The ad hoc surveys were amended to the regular monthly business and consumer surveys conducted on behalf of the European Commission. Results were obtained from eleven member states (Denmark did not participate in the extension of the enterprise survey; Luxembourg did not take part in the consumer survey).

In this paper, I will comment on some results of the surveys that indicate there are still obstacles to employment creation.

Considering that EC countries enjoyed a record increase in employment during the 1980s because of an economic upswing that lasted for almost a decade, unemployment has been persisting at remarkably high levels. In addition, labor force participation is low in most EC countries compared to Scandinavian countries, the United States, or Japan. Thus, the EC still has a great employment potential to be exploited conducted on behalf of the European Commission. The fundamentally improved growth conditions and the favorable prospects opened up by the completion of the internal market, the catching-up process of the less favored countries, the creation of the Economic and Monetary Union, and now the integration of Central and Eastern Europe into the world economy may create favorable conditions for the EC to exploit this underutilized employment potential. Clearly, removing institutional barriers hampering the full utilization of labor resources has to be a prime policy concern.

Employment Plans in the Industrial and Retail Sectors

In 1990–91, industrial companies planned, on average, to employ more qualified workers, most of them on a full-time basis. Only in the Federal Republic of Germany and the Netherlands did industrial firms plan to expand the number of skilled part-time jobs. And in all the member countries except for Greece, Ireland, and Portugal, industry intended, on average, to reduce both full-time and part-time jobs for unskilled workers. These results once again underline the fact that the lack of occupational skills considerably increases workers' risks of becoming and remaining unemployed. According to the survey results, the slight increase in industrial employment will continue into the future.

The projected overall increase in employment in the retail sector is somewhat more pronounced. Here, too, the increase is expected to be mainly in skilled jobs, but both full and part time. Retailers are less optimistic concerning the future of unskilled full-time employment, which is likely to decline in some of the countries, notably Belgium, France, and the Netherlands.

Reasons for Not Increasing the Work Force

A core question in the industry survey referred to potential barriers to hiring more workers. As in a previous survey carried out on behalf of the EC Commission in 1985 (see Nerb 1986), firms were asked to rank ten possible reasons for not increasing their work force, according to their importance in their hiring decisions. Most firms put "present and expected levels of product demand" at the top of the list, as they had done four years earlier. Compared to 1985, however, the percentage of firms considering this reason "very important" decreased slightly, presumably reflecting the overall improvement in the economic situation. In Italy, the Netherlands, and the United Kingdom, lack of demand was mentioned more often than in the other countries, probably because of a slight weakening in the economy, notably in Italy and the United Kingdom.

The second most important reason for the reluctance to hire was, as it had been in 1985, "insufficient profit margins due to domestic and foreign competition." In France, the United Kingdom, and the Federal Republic of Germany, this reason was mentioned less frequently on average than in other countries in the EC.

The third most important reason, as in 1985, was "high nonwage labor costs." Compared with the EC average, more respondents in Belgium, Spain, the Netherlands, and Germany mentioned nonwage labor costs, while those in the United Kingdom said they played only a subordinate role in recruitment decisions.

A similar picture emerges with regard to "insufficient flexibility in hiring and shedding labor." This reason ranked fourth for the EC as a whole. As already shown by the survey four years earlier, lack of flexibility in hiring and firing is rated particularly high in Italy, the Netherlands, and Spain, whereas it is much less of a deterrent to increasing the work force in France, Germany, and particularly in the United Kingdom.

"Rationalization and/or the introduction of new technologies" continues to rank fifth as an obstacle to increasing employment, whereas "shortages of adequately skilled job applicants" has gained in relative importance. By 1989, this reason had moved up to sixth place, compared with eighth in 1985. The "high level of direct wage costs" and "other costs" are still in seventh and eighth place respectively, while "insufficient productive capacity" increased slightly in importance and now ranks ninth. The present high levels of capacity utilization in industry appear to be causing no insurmountable difficulties regarding further expansion of employment.

Similar results emerge for the retail sector. Here, too, "present and expected levels of product demand" was ranked first and "insufficient profits due to non-wage labor costs" ranked second. Both factors were rated as "very important" by 41 percent of the retailers. "Insufficient profits due to high wage and salary levels" ranked third, followed by "insufficient profit margins due to competition." The shortage of adequately skilled applicants ranked fifth among retailers in all countries as a reason for not hiring additional staff (table 25–1).

Variation in Operating Hours and Employment Creation

In the face of increasing capital costs per worker and the growing importance of capacity shortages at given high levels of capacity utilization, the issue of business operating hours has gained importance in the public debate on employment policies. Longer operating hours are seen as a way to increase output and employment without increasing capital stocks. Extending business hours may therefore substantially reduce the costs of creating additional jobs.

On average, the contractually agreed-on workweek of full-time industry employees in the EC is thirty-nine hours. Whereas the standard workweek of full-timers has been reduced in recent years in Belgium, Germany, France, and the United Kingdom, full-time employees in Greece, Spain, Ireland, and Portugal still work a standard week of forty hours or more; Portugal ranks at the top with an average forty-four-hour workweek.

By contrast, industrial businesses operated sixty-six hours per week on average in the EC. There are strong variations between countries, however, ranging from fifty-three hours in Germany to seventy-seven hours in Belgium. Long operating hours were also found in the United Kingdom (seventy-six hours), the Netherlands (seventy-four hours), and Italy (seventy-three hours). Part of the cross-country variation in operating hours is likely to be accounted for by differences in industrial structure, firm size, and use of shift work (table 25–2).

It is interesting in this context to look at the evolution of operating hours over the past five years. On balance, operating hours in the EC have decreased. The Netherlands, France, and the United Kingdom are the only countries where they clearly show a net increase. For 1990–91, industrial firms in Belgium, Greece,

TABLE 25-1. *Reasons for Not Increasing Employment Levels in Industrial Firms in Selected EC Countries, 1989**

Reason	Germany				France				United Kingdom				Italy				Spain			
	A	B	C	D	A	B	C	D	A	B	C	D	A	B	C	D	A	B	C	D
Current and expected demand for products	52	54	54	42	42	39	45	34	72	70	70	65	53	50	54	79	41	33	50	48
Insufficient profit margin due to competition	47	45	43	40	50	50	48	33	43	49	42	43	55	51	47	68	53	49	56	72
Insufficient profit margin due to nonwage labor costs	39	53	51	49	61	55	50	45	32	25	21	19	64	65	60	48	61	64	50	48
Lack of adequately skilled job applicants	48	49	43	43	47	40	43	27	56	49	40	35	40	42	45	46	25	25	30	34
Rationalization/introduction of new technologies	34	40	45	46	34	45	48	61	30	35	27	44	53	54	62	61	23	20	21	24
Insufficient production capacities	11	12	15	8	14	11	12	8	22	19	10	18	19	17	10	31	15	8	13	9
Insufficient flexibility in hiring and firing labor	44	47	38	39	51	43	43	47	32	30	33	22	54	52	60	67	53	51	47	42
Insufficient profit margin due to wage costs	48	44	42	36	24	19	21	19	36	35	36	24	38	39	30	42	32	35	32	29
Increase in subcontracting work	10	12	11	9	21	19	18	18	14	9	7	13	23	25	22	17	11	12	14	24
Insufficient profit margin due to other costs	27	24	27	25	18	23	23	16	29	31	25	20	45	39	36	69	37	32	42	49

Source: EC labor market survey, 1989.

*Percentages represent proportion of firms classifying item as "very important" or "important."

A=firms with fewer than 200 workers; B=firms with 200–499 workers; C=firms with500–999 workers; D=firms with 1,000 or more workers.

TABLE 25-2. *Working Hours and Operating Hours of Industrial Firms in the EC*

	Average operating hours per week[a]							Contractually agreed working hours of full-time employees[b]						
	under 40	between 40 and 60	between 60 and 80	between 80 and 120	120 and over	no reply	average hours	under 35	between 35 and 38	between 38 and 40	between 40 and 42	over 42	no reply	average hours
Belgium	27	15	20	19	19	0	77	3	54	40	2	0	1	37
Denmark	25	48	18	5	2	2	53	0	56	43	1	0	0	38
Germany	45	24	3	9	18	1	64	9	2	3	79	7	0	40
Spain	23	38	9	14	14	2	69	3	6	13	69	7	2	40
France	28	24	15	16	13	4	69	1	11	81	4	1	2	39
Ireland	19	61	2	5	12	2	61	4	4	13	78	2	0	41
Italy	11	50	5	20	14	0	73	–	–	–	–	–	–	39
Netherlands	20	37	5	12	26	0	74	1	20	42	33	4	0	39
Portugal	10	80	3	4	3	0	54	–	–	–	–	–	–	44
United Kingdom	18	34	13	13	21	1	76	1	50	36	8	2	4	37
EC	22	40	13	12	12	2	66	1	37	45	14	2	2	39

Source: EC labor market survey.
[a]Percentage of all industrial firms.
[b]Percentage of all workers.

France, Italy, the Netherlands, and the United Kingdom planned to lengthen their operating hours. The three most important obstacles to longer hours were reported to be the terms in collective agreements, insufficient demand, and legal restrictions. Italian and German firms particularly consider the terms in collective agreements to be an obstacle to increasing capital utilization through longer business hours.

One of the main ways of dissociating working hours and operating hours is to increase the use of shift work. Seventy percent of all industrial firms in the EC reported using shift work; 29 percent had two shifts, 23 percent had three shifts, and 17 percent had four or more shifts. A low incidence of shift work in the Federal Republic of Germany reflects in large part the lower operating hours there.

Again, a similar picture is revealed for the retail sector. Compared to the average thirty-nine hour workweek of employees, businesses in the EC's retail trade are open an average of fifty-three hours per week. Averages vary widely from country to country, however, ranging from forty-five hours in Spain (weekly working time: forty-three hours) to fifty-eight hours in the United Kingdom (weekly working time: thirty-nine hours).

A comparison of shop hours and full-time working hours shows the extent to which working hours and operating times have already become dissociated. The United Kingdom is in the lead. Weekly shop hours, on average, are nineteen hours longer than the working hours of a full-time employee. In France, the difference is almost as large (eighteen hours). The discrepancy is less extreme in Belgium (thirteen hours) and the Netherlands (twelve hours), while the Federal Republic of Germany ranks at the other end of the spectrum (nine hours). As is to be expected, in the two countries with the lowest proportion of part-time workers (Spain and Portugal), shop hours and contracted working hours reveal the least discrepancy.

The answers show that in recent years most retailers in the EC, particularly in France, Italy, and the United Kingdom, have increased the hours in which they are open. Hours in Belgium and the Federal Republic of Germany have declined slightly, however.

Restrictions on business hours vary across countries. Retailers were given ten possible reasons for not being able to increase their hours. Administrative or legal constraints were mentioned first. This reason ranks at the top in Italy, the Netherlands, and France. Lack of customer demand was frequently cited; this was also the main reason for not taking on additional workers. These two reasons are the ones most frequently mentioned by British retailers. The costs of reorganization, company and collective agreements, and the lack of qualified applicants, in declining order of importance, were given as other reasons for not extending business hours.

Working-Time Preferences of Workers

The results of the Community-wide survey of workers and employers carried out in mid–1989 indicate that most workers in the EC would prefer shorter working hours than those specified in their employment contracts. On average the contractually agreed-on working time was thirty-six hours per week, whereas the preferred working time was thirty-five hours a week. On average, actual and preferred working times were not far apart.

In addition to wanting shorter hours, workers are still surprisingly ready, within certain limits, to work more flexible hours. In 1989 (as in 1985), 52 percent of workers were in favor of more variable working hours if working hours were at the same time reduced. Since 1985, the proportion of workers objecting to more flexible working hours has remained unchanged at 44 percent. Workers in Europe indicate a great readiness (61 percent) to start work earlier or finish later, which would enable individual working hours to be dissociated from company operating hours. With this kind of arrangement, the same capital stock could provide more jobs, and capital utilization could be increased considerably.

Workers are less eager to work on weekends. The survey results show that a rather high proportion of workers (44 percent) are still willing to work on Saturdays, but few are prepared to work on Sundays (21 percent were prepared to work on Sundays compared to 20 percent who actually do). Likewise, a considerable minority would consent to regular night work (21 percent compared to 14 percent who actually do so).

The increasing dissociation of working times and business operating hours is likely to increase the scope for a further expansion of part-time work. Currently, the proportion of part-timers averages 15 percent in the EC as a whole, though there are wide variations between countries (e.g., 2 percent in Greece compared to 27 percent in the Netherlands). The survey shows that 22 percent of full-time workers would prefer a part-time job to their current full-time job. If these workers shifted to part-time work, it would open up work opportunities to other job seekers. On average, however, 37 percent of part-time workers are seeking a full-time job, evidence that there has been an increase in "involuntary" part-time work in recent years.

In that workers are ready to work shorter hours (mainly by changing from full to part-time employment), a purely arithmetical calculation reveals that a considerable volume of work (5 percent) is available for additional employment if existing institutional and noninstitutional barriers to the realization of individual working-time preferences were removed.

Conclusions

The survey results reported above show that there is considerable scope for more flexibility in meeting workers' preferences for shorter and more flexible working hours on the one hand and the requirement of firms for a high degree of capacity utilization on the other. Realization of this potential would spur a nonnegligible expansion of both output and employment. Capacity utilization in industry could be enhanced by up to 30 percent through a reorganization of operating hours, not considering night shifts or Sunday work. On the side of the employed workers themselves, there do not seem to be as many barriers to realizing this potential as the public debate frequently leads us to believe. It is up to legislators and particularly the social partners to explore these possibilities.

26
Economic Change, Internal Labor Markets, and Workers' Protection: Toward an Agenda for the 1990s

Burkart Lutz

S tructural change is inextricably linked to economic growth. This has been common knowledge since at least the days of Schumpeter. This basic realization has been confirmed many times since it was first formulated, the most recent example being a negative one, the stagnation of the economies in the Eastern Bloc, where so far all the mechanisms of "creative destruction" in an economy have been missing. Nobody disputes the fact that the production and employment structures of an economy constantly have to adapt to shifts in demand, to the consequences of differential increases in productivity, and to changes in the international division of labor. The discussion of how this adjustment should proceed is a highly controversial one, however, all the more so since there has been a marked decline in the growth rate in most highly industrialized nations since the mid-1970s.

Quest for Deregulation

In economic policy debates since then, one position in particular has been vigorously advocated (and occasionally has exerted a strong influence on policy makers). This position identifies itself with the catchword "deregulation." Without too great a risk of oversimplification, the underlying structure of the thought behind it can be expressed in two hypotheses: one significant reason for the persistently slow economic growth in many Western economies and the resulting underemployment is that their production and employment structures fail to adapt sufficiently; and the main cause of this failure is assumed to consist in an excessive regulation of employment and the labor market with the aim of protecting workers' interests.

The consequences derived from these hypotheses are obvious. They can be expressed in the form of a simple equation:

Less regulation = more growth = more employment.

If we reverse this equation, then greater protection of employment relationships goes hand in hand with increased unemployment, less growth, and less prosperity. With statutory and/or contractual regulations stabilizing wages and making it more difficult to dismiss employees, trade unions and their political associates on the Left have, it is argued, lured employees into a trap, the enormous effects of which are contrary to their original intentions. In the final analysis, it is in the interests of employees to rid themselves of this trap, if necessary by smashing the "excessive" power of trade unions.

Arguments such as these, which have dominated public opinion and government policies in major Western industrial nations from time to time, stem from rudimentary premises about how the labor market functions and are incompatible with most of the evidence. It seems far more realistic to assume the following: First, the long-term stabilization of employment within the framework of institutionally screened internal labor markets does not reduce the adaptability of the production structure in many enterprises; on the contrary, it may even enhance adaptability, at least under certain, by no means exceptional, conditions.

Second, in internal labor markets certain adjustment mechanisms may be effective if they are founded on the long-term upgrading of the skills of the work force (which in turn is able to generate a considerable potential for additional productivity increases and innovation).

Third, the "internalization" of structural change and adjustment has its limitations, which cannot be overcome by dismantling the regulations as such but only by complementary regulation aimed at strengthening vocational training and promoting "professional" labor market structures.

Given the cursory nature of this paper, I take the liberty of tendering a few empirical facts and theoretical considerations that support these three theses, without claiming completeness or the provision of extensive evidence.[1]

Emergence of Internal Labor Markets and Employment Stabilization

The rapid economic growth that all European industrial nations experienced from the early 1950s to the mid–1970s was accompanied by a radical structural change in the modern industrial and service sectors of the economy. One need recall only the decline of traditional industries such as textile and coal, which employed hundreds of thousands of people directly after World War II and were replaced by completely new industrial sectors, sometimes within a single decade. This structural change did not create any particular adjustment problems for the bulk of the economy, however, since it could rely on a massive labor supply from the traditional sectors and the subsistence economy (family workers and housewives).

[1]More evidence is provided in my two books, Lutz 1984 and Lutz 1987.

To the extent that—sooner or later, depending on the country and the pace of economic growth—this inflow of labor dwindled and growth depended more and more on increases in labor productivity at given employment levels (a process termed intensive accumulation by regulation theorists), structural change had to be accomplished internally (i.e., within the limits of constrained labor supply and demand). The consequence of this change was an enormous increase in adjustment pressure that persisted even when economic growth slowed down temporarily.

Following the logic of the promulgators of deregulation, firms in such a situation would have had to want to facilitate exchange with the external labor market. In the Federal Republic of Germany at least, the sparse empiricial evidence suggests the exact opposite, namely, a growing "internalization" of firms' employment policies in the course of the 1960s. This meant, above all, the exclusion of marginal workers, increased efforts to stabilize regular staff, and the creation of stable patterns of internal upward mobility, even where the majority of workplaces had previously been staffed largely through recruitment from the external labor market.

This increasing orientation toward the use of internal labor markets was certainly not imposed, at least not in the Federal Republic of Germany, by political regulation or collective bargaining agreements. Quite the opposite; labor and social legislation tended to neglect seniority rights and protection against dismissal until the late 1960s. It was not until then that the legislative and contractual protection of the individual employment relationship began to be extended. This appears, however, to have been primarily an adjustment of legal norms to the widespread practice of ensuring de facto employment security to regular employees within the structures of internal labor markets and was indeed seen as such by contemporary observers. The internalization of labor markets, which began in the 1960s, must therefore have been based on strong company self-interest rather than on exogenously imposed restraints.

What is more, a comparison of the large industrial nations leads to the same interpretation: an unequivocal negative correlation between the degree of normative protection and the stability of employment relationships on the one hand and the dynamics of economic development on the other is completely out of the question. If there is a correlation at all, it is in the other direction than the one assumed in the current flexibility or deregulation debate.

Structural Adjustment and Skill Demands

A second thesis I want to put forward, based mainly on theoretical arguments but founded on empirical evidence, emphasizes the issue of qualification and competence. It seems highly plausible that the "new" conditions for growth emerging during the 1960s, which may be summarized in a convenient formula as the transition from extensive to intensive accumulation, have created a marked increase in and/or a far-reaching shift toward the need for workers to possess technical and organizational skills. The considerably more capital-intensive means of production have become more complex and complicated and their underutilization even more expensive; new production processes of an increasingly "systemic" nature have been gaining ground and demanding comprehensive control; new technologies have been moving in everywhere; new and technologically more sophisticated products are appearing more and more quickly on the trail of their predecessors, and so on.

In principle, firms can cope with the resulting increase in the demand for qualifications and skills in three ways:

According to the first and to a certain extent classical method, the existing work force is supplemented or even replaced by new, appropriately skilled workers recruited from the external labor market.

According to the second method, the firm ensures that the incumbent work force acquires the necessary additional skills (e.g., through further training, intensified on-the-job training, and so on);

According to the third method, the firm attempts to make the necessary new skills available not, as in the first two cases, by increasing the skills of the work force but rather by incorporating "skills" into their technological and organizational structures.

The first method, in which the firm's employment policy relies on the quantitative and qualitative capacity of the external training system to provide the skills needed, would seem to be the less practicable in the short and medium term the "newer" the necessary skills are and the more urgent the need for them is. Especially in the 1960s, this method was effectively precluded to large sectors of European industry because it usually takes many years for the effects of innovations in national training systems to show in the labor market.

The second method presupposes that long-term, secure employment should be offered, at least to employees who are supposed to acquire new skills. (The old argument as to the reason for employers' interest in a relatively protected internal labor market has lost none of its weight even if it has become unfashionable.)

But even the third method, that of incorporating new skills into technological and organizational structures, is largely incompatible with high worker turnover since it exposes firms to the volatility of the external labor markets. In fact, a large number of firms seem to have opted, for good reasons, for a combination of the second and third methods.

To the extent that companies, of their own accord, install relatively protected internal labor markets (which are then further protected by legislation and/or collective agreements), they undoubtedly incur a loss of quantitative employment flexibility. But by using long-term, stable employment relationships for developing new skills continuously and comprehensively and not depending on the external labor market and the external training system, firms gain new potential for action and innovation in other dimensions and as a result are far better equipped to react to the constraints and opportunities of structural change with strategic answers instead of simple ad hoc adjustment.

The development of continental European industry (and perhaps Japanese industry as well) over the past twenty years supplies sufficient evidence to support the above argument.

Strategic Flexibility as an Alternative to Deregulation

It is not difficult to demonstrate—and with this I introduce my third thesis—that, at least from an overall economic perspective, even a lasting increase in the strategic flexibility and innovation potential of an average firm through the development of highly specific skills within the framework of internal labor markets cannot cope with every type and every pace of structural change. Technological developments of a disruptive nature or far-reaching changes in demand extending beyond sector boundaries cannot be met solely by existing enterprises.

The high degree of credibility occasionally granted to deregulation arguments can be explained quite plausibly by the fact that trends in socioeconomic development that make it necessary for the work force to show considerable mobility beyond the boundaries of sectors and companies have gained enormous momentum since the mid–1970s. No one disputes that in such a situation the strong internalization of labor markets and employment patterns may become dysfunctional and cause considerable losses in overall economic efficiency. Nevertheless, an answer is needed that does not simply discount the macro- and microeconomic advantages of internal labor market arrangements (being able to rely quickly on large reserves of skills) as a simple dismantling of given employment protection rules might involve. Rather, a response is needed that allows substantially more voluntary mobility in the external labor market while maintaining the same or an even higher level of skills among the work force. This mobility should be motivated and driven by individual cost-benefit calculations rather than by exogenously imposed mobility constraints.

Such an answer quite obviously consists in making the first method described above (the provision of skills through the external labor market) more practicable on a broader scale even in times of rapid structural change. Above all else, it implies a massive expansion of professional labor markets and of professional training necessary to fuel this expansion; in other words, labor markets in which clearly defined and structured skills that, should the need arise, yield high productivity in variable business contexts after short periods of familiarization, are in supply and demand. Apart from the German-speaking countries, however, which still exhibit occupational and professional labor markets on a large scale, such labor markets are found only among formally trained, that is to say, academically trained, personnel.

This is certainly not a coincidence. Professional labor markets cannot be created by the much-hailed spontaneous effects of market forces. They are highly "artificial," highly vulnerable creations whose existence and ability to function require far more conscious political planning, regulation, and control than the mere legal codification and protection of internal labor markets, the alleged inefficiency of which has been at the core of the arguments put forward by proponents of deregulation.

Recognizing the obvious limitations of coping with structural change by relying solely on the mechanisms of internal labor markets, the simple alternative of "more" or "less" regulation of labor markets appears to be misplaced, unrealistic, and deceptive. The essential questions are, What different forms of regulation are capable of providing the flexibility needed in the short and long run? What are the normative and institutional implications of such a new mode of regulation? What demands would it make on public and private resources, and which strategies might best bring about the transition from the current state to the new one? The war cry of the promulgators of deregulation has fortunately not brought about any far-reaching changes in existing regulatory systems in most Western European industrialized countries. Nevertheless, from a historical perspective, it did have one dramatic effect: it prevented these really urgent and difficult questions from being asked, not to mention seriously answered.

27
Coordinated Flexibility: The Future of Labor Market Regulation

Günther Schmid

T he task of an epilogue to a book such as this one is not to summarize, applaud, or criticize the preceding papers but to complement the extensive analyses presented by providing some conceptual arguments that delineate the horizons for future research and policy approaches. I shall do this by presenting some final hypotheses on how future policies could support coordinated flexibility, involving a complementarity of employment security and labor market flexibility, with the latter denoting "high adjustment capacities to structural change." Such a policy would have to be guided by the cybernetic principle of "requisite variety" (Ashby 1970:207) in combination with such "civilized constraints" as social (or income) security, free choice of profession, free spatial mobility, and social justice or "fairness" standards.

Coordinated flexibility thus points far beyond mere job or employment security, taking into account the conclusion of many of the contributors of the preceding papers that employment security, whatever its definition and mode of implementation, has to be seen and analyzed within the institutional framework of the labor market at large. Labor market institutions and respective policy interventions, in turn, have to reflect the variety in the socioeconomic environment of firms and households (the latter being frequently neglected in labor economics) and to take into account the existence of such civilized constraints as the human limits and conditions of problem solving.

Requisite variety combined with civilized constraints—this is my basic assumption—requires concentrating on *functional* flexibility rather than merely on *numerical* flexibility. Workers' protection, if properly designed, can then be interpreted as a set of institutional constraints inducing firms (and workers) to follow an adjustment strategy of functional flexibility, which, as shown by Lutz in this volume, does not necessarily constitute an antithesis to, but may in fact be a necessary prerequisite for, efficient numerical flexibility (but not vice versa).

The distinction between functional and numerical flexibility can be illustrated by another distinction that is reflected in the seminal work of Jon Elster (1979), namely, that between "local" and "global" maximizers, going back to Leibniz, who saw man as being uniquely capable of *reculer pour mieux sauter*. Or, as Schumpeter stressed, the maximal exploitation of present possibilities (e.g., firing) may often be an obstacle to the maximization of new and future possibilities (e.g., creating a loyal, highly motivated, and polyvalent labor force). The following examples may illustrate the general idea.

Cyclical demand variety could be managed by the provision of collectively organized funds for wage replacement for employees working reduced hours so as to bridge greater fluctuations in demand. An example is the short-time working compensation scheme in Germany (integrated into the unemployment insurance fund), which enables firms to maintain their skilled work force through periods of slack demand and overcapacity. The scheme could be improved and extended in many ways, especially by upgrading unskilled and semiskilled workers during phases in which employees work reduced hours.

Life-cycle supply variety could be managed by providing collectively organized funds for wage replacement to cover such recurrent life-cycle variations in the labor supply as parenthood, care for the elderly, social work, sabbaticals, and educational leaves. An example is part-time unemployment benefits (recently introduced for limited target groups in Germany and already fairly widespread in Sweden) for full-time employees who reduce their working time and take part-time general educational or vocational training courses. Another example is the parenthood allowance (*Elternschaftsgeld*). There are many more forms of such public-private mixes in working-time regimes, especially in the public sector (the right to part-time work under specified circumstances) and on a private basis for privileged employees in large private companies. The general model here is employment security combined with a greater number of ways to vary labor supply. Labor productivity can be affected positively as well as negatively. In the latter case, suitable flexible arrangements of work organization have to be invented that may have to be supported by public policy.

Occupational variety could be strengthened by deregulating occupational segregation due to barriers to vertical and horizontal vocational mobility by, for example, opening universities to all citizens independent of their formal schooling. This strategy increases employment security indirectly by increasing the potential for mobility. It also supports employers' willingness to give up old-fashioned jobs, and it reduces self-destructive competition for university credentials.

Social variety could be supported by collective wage-compensation funds for the less productive labor force (e.g., disabled people). This strategy increases employment security for targeted groups without putting the burden on the individual firm. While average individual productivity may decrease, per-capita real income may increase because of the increased utilization of personnel resources. Sweden, for example, has low growth rates for average productivity, one reason being that country's comparatively high integration of economically marginal groups. But Sweden has almost the same real-income-per-capita growth rates as West Germany.

Infrastructural variety could be increased through the modernization of public infrastructure, that is, by increasing public investment in telecommunications, transport, energy conservation, recycling, environmental protection, business services, educational services, urban renewal, and so on. Employment security is thereby provided in two ways: directly by public job creation and indirectly through improvement in the competitiveness and performance of enterprises and national or international economies. David Aschauer of the Chicago Federal Reserve Bank has calculated that a dollar of public investment produces more output today than a dollar of private investment and that private profitability would rise by 2 percentage points–say, from 10 percent to 12 percent—if investments in the infrastructure were merely brought back to the U.S. levels of 1981 (see Aschauer 1989). As in the United States, public investment declined dramatically in West Germany during the 1980s.

Protecting workers without negatively affecting the labor market's dynamics requires moving one step backward to take two steps forward. The institutionalization of this strategy is extremely difficult, but it can be accomplished in many ways. The papers in this volume provide insights into how to move closer to this goal. They also show that we cannot lean back in our chairs; further research needs to be done.

References

Abraham, K. G. 1983. "Structural/Frictional vs. Deficit Demand Unemployment: Some New Evidence." *American Economic Review* 73: 708–24.

————. 1988. "Flexible Staffing Arrangements and Employers' Short-Term Adjustment Strategies." In *Employment, Unemployment and Labour Utilization,* edited by R. A. Hart, 288–311. Boston: Unwin Hyman.

Abraham, K. G., and **S. N. Houseman.** 1989a. "Job Security and Work Force Adjustment: How Different Are U.S. and Japanese Practices?" *Journal of the Japanese and International Economies* 3: 500–521.

————. 1989b. "Employment Security and Labor Adjustment: A U.S.-German Comparison." University of Maryland. Mimeo.

Abraham, K. G., and **J. L. Medoff.** 1983. *Length of Service, Terminations, and the Nature of the Employment Relationship.* NBER Working Paper no. 1086. Cambridge, Mass.: National Bureau of Economic Research.

————. 1984. "Length of Service and Layoffs in Union and Nonunion Work Groups." *Industrial and Labor Relations Review* 38 (Oct.): 87–97.

Adams, C. D., and **T. Coe.** 1989. *A Systems Approach to Estimating the Natural Rate of Unemployment and Potential Output for the United States.* IMF Working Paper 89/89. Washington, D. C.: International Monetary Fund.

Addison, J. T. 1989a. "The Controversy over Advance Notice Legislation in the U.S." *British Journal of Industrial Relations* 27 (July): 235–63.

————. 1989b. "Job Rights and Economic Dislocation." In *Micro-economic Issues in Labor Economics: New Approaches,* edited by R. Drago and R. Perlman, 130–54. New York: Harvester-Wheatsheaf.

Addison, J. T., ed. 1991. *Job Displacement: Consequences and Implications for Policy.* Detroit: Wayne State University Press.

Addison, J. T., and **A. C. Castro.** 1987. "The Importance of Life-Time Jobs: Differences between Union and Non-Union Workers." *Industrial and Labor Relations Review* 40 (April): 393–405.

Addison, J. T., and **B. T. Hirsch.** 1989. "Union Effects on Productivity, Profits and Growth: Has the Long Run Arrived?" *Journal of Labor Economics* 7 (Jan.): 72–105.

Addison, J. T., and **P. Portugal.** 1986. "The Role of Unemployment Insurance in White and Blue-Collar Unemployment Duration following Displacement." University of South Carolina. Mimeo.

———. 1987a. "The Effect of Advance Notification of Plant Closing on Unemployment." *Industrial and Labor Relations Review* 41 (Oct.): 3–16.

———. 1987b. "Job Displacement, Relative Wage Changes and Duration of Unemployment." University of South Carolina. Mimeo.

———. 1989. "Advance Notice and Unemployment: New Evidence from the 1988 Displaced Worker Survey." University of South Carolina. Mimeo.

Adler, J. N. 1989. "Settling Wrongful Termination Actions: A Practical Approach." *Industrial Relations Law Journal* 2 (1): 18–25.

Advisory, Conciliation and Arbitration Service (ACAS). 1988a. *Labour Flexibility in Britain: The 1987 ACAS Survey.* London.

———. 1988b. *Redundancy Arrangements: The 1986 ACAS Survey.* ACAS Occasional Paper no. 37. London.

———. 1990. *Annual Report 1989.* London.

AFL-CIO. 1987. "Executive Council Statement on 'The Employment-at-Will Doctrine.'" Mimeo.

Akerlof, G. A. 1984a. *An Economist's Book of Tales.* Cambridge: Cambridge University Press.

———. 1984b. "Labor Contracts as a Partial Gift Exchange." In *An Economist's Book of Tales,* 145–74. Cambridge: Cambridge University Press.

Akerlof, G. A., and **B. G. Main.** 1981. "An Experience-Weighted Measure of Employment and Unemployment Durations." *American Economic Review* 71 (Dec.): 1003–11.

Akerlof, G. A., and **J. L. Yellen.** 1986. "Introduction." In *Efficiency Wage Models of the Labor Market,* edited by G. A. Akerlof and J. L. Yellen, 1–21. New York: Cambridge University Press.

Amendola, M., and **J. L. Gaffard.** 1988. *The Innovative Choice: An Economic Analysis of the Dynamics of Technology.* Oxford: Basil Blackwell.

Anderman, S. D. 1972. *Voluntary Dismissals Procedure and the Industrial Relations Act.* London: PEP.

———. 1986. "Unfair Dismissals and Redundancy." In *Labour Law in Britain,* edited by R. Lewis, 415–47. Oxford: Basil Blackwell.

Anthony, D. 1985. "Japan." In *Managing Workforce Reduction: An International Survey,* edited by M. Cross, 91–129. London: Croom-Helm.

Aoki, M. 1984. "Aspects of the Japanese Firm." In *The Economic Analysis of the Japanese Firm,* edited by M. Aoki, 3–43. Amsterdam: North Holland.

———. 1988a. *Information, Incentives, and Bargaining in the Japanese Economy.* New York: Cambridge University Press.

———. 1988b. "A New Paradigm of Work Organization: The Japanese Experience." WIDER Working Paper no. 36.

———. 1990. "Toward an Economic Model of the Japanese Firm." *Journal of Economic Literature* 28 (March): 1–27.

Armstrong, E. G. A. 1971. "Wages Councils, Retail Distribution and the Concept of the 'Cut-off.' " *Industrial Relations Journal* 2 (Autumn): 9–21.

Arrigo, G. 1990. "Un bilancio della CIG verso la riforma." In *Rapporto '89: Lavoro e politiche della occupazione in Italia*, edited by the Italian Ministry of Labor, 471–81. Rome: Poligrafico dello Stato.

Ashby, W. R. 1970. *An Introduction to Cybernetics.* London: Chapman & Hall.

Atkinson, J. 1987. "Flexibility or Fragmentation? The United Kingdom Labour Market in the Eighties." *Labour and Society* 12 (Jan.): 87–106.

———. 1989. "Four Stages of Adjustment to the Demographic Downturn." *Personnel Management* 21 (Aug.): 20–24.

Atkinson, J., and **N. Meager.** 1986. "Is Flexibility Just a Flash in the Pan?" *Personnel Management* 18 (Sept.): 26–30.

Auer, P., and **C. F. Buechtemann.** 1990. "La dérégulation du droit du travail: Le cas de la libéralisation du recours aux contrats de travail à durée déterminée. L'expérience de l'Allemagne Fédérale et de la France." In *Chroniques internationales du marché du travail et des politiques d'emploi, 1986–1989*, edited by P. Auer et al., 179–90. Paris: La Documentation Française.

Auer, P., et al. 1991. *Labor Force Adjustment to Structural Change: Experiences in Germany, France, Sweden and the United Kingdom.* Report on behalf of the EC Commission. Berlin: Wissenschaftszentrum.

Auletta, K. 1982. *The Underclass.* New York: Random House.

Axelrod, R. 1984. *The Evolution of Cooperation.* New York: Basic Books.

Ayres, R. A. 1985. "A Schumpeterian Model of Technological Substitution." *Technological Forecasting and Social Change* 27: 375–83.

Azariadis, C., and **J. Stiglitz.** 1983. "Implicit Contracts and Fixed Price Equilibria." *Quarterly Journal of Economics* 48: 1–22 (Suppl.).

Bacot, M., et al. 1977. *La legislation relative à la protection de l'emploi et son impact sur les politiques des entreprises.* Paris: Centre d'Études de l'Emploi.

Bank of Italy. 1990. *Relazione generale sul 1989.* Rome.

Barca, F., and **M. Magnani.** 1989. *L'industria italiana fra capitale e lavoro: Piccole e grandi imprese dall'autunno caldo alla ristrutturazione.* Bologna: Il Mulino.

Barron, J. M., and **J. Bishop.** 1985. "Extensive Search, Intensive Search, and Hiring Costs: New Evidence on Employer Hiring Activity." *Economic Inquiry* 23 (July): 363–82.

Barron, J. M., J. Bishop, and **W. C. Dunkelberg.** 1985. "Employer Search: The

Interviewing and Hiring of New Employees." *Review of Economics and Statistics* 67 (1): 43–52.

Bastone, E., and **S. Gourlay.** 1986. *Unions, Unemployment and Inflation.* Oxford: Basil Blackwell.

Bayar, A. 1987. "Labour Market Flexibility: An Approach Based on a Macrosectoral Model for Belgium." *Labour and Society* 12 (1): 37–53.

Bayliss, F. J. 1962. *British Wages Councils.* Oxford: Basil Blackwell.

Becker, F., et al. 1986. *Gemeinschaftskommentar zum Kuendigungsschutzgesetz und sonstigen kuendigungsschutzrechtlichen Vorschriften.* 2d ed. Neuwied: Luchterhand.

Becker, G. 1975. *Human Capital.* 2d ed. Cambridge, Mass.: National Bureau of Economic Research.

Becker, J. M. 1972. *Experience Rating in Unemployment Insurance: An Experiment in Competitive Socialism.* Baltimore: Johns Hopkins University Press.

———. 1981. *Unemployment Insurance Financing: An Evaluation.* Washington, D.C: American Enterprise Institute.

Bednarzik, R. W. 1983. "Layoffs and Permanent Job Losses: Workers' Traits and Cyclical Patterns." *Monthly Labor Review* 106 (Sept.): 3–12.

Beenstock, M. 1990. "Saving, Investment and Growth in the Industrialized Countries: An Econometric Investigation." Paper presented at the Villa Mondragone Conference, Rome, July.

Bellace, J. R. 1983. "A Right of Fair Dismissal: Enforcing a Statutory Guarantee." *University of Michigan Journal of Law Reform* 16: 207–31.

Bellmann, L. 1986. *Senioritaetsentlohnung, betriebliche Hierarchie und Arbeitsleistung.* Frankfurt: Campus.

Bellmann, L., and **F. Buttler.** 1989. "Lohnstrukturflexibilitaet—Theorie und Empirie der Transaktionskosten und Effizienzloehne." *Mitteilungen aus der Arbeitsmarkt- und Berufsforschung (Mitt AB)* 22 (2): 202–17.

Bellmann, L., and **U. Schasse.** 1988. "Employment Tenure in the U.S. and the Federal Republic of Germany." Discussion paper no. 123. Department of Economics, University of Hanover.

Benassy, J. P. 1982. *The Economics of Market Disequilibrium.* Boston: Academic Press.

Benassy, J. P., R. Boyer, and **R. M. Gelpi.** 1979. "Régulation des économies capitalistes et inflation." *Revue economique* 30 (May): 397–441.

Benedictus, R., and **B. Bercusson.** 1987. *Labour Law: Cases and Materials.* London: Sweet and Maxwell.

Ben-Ponrath, Y. 1980. "The F-Connection: Families, Friends, and Firms and the Organization of Exchange." *Population and Development Review* 6 (1): 1–30.

Bentolila, S., and **G. Bertola.** 1990. "Firing Costs and Labor Demand: How Bad Is Eurosclerosis?" *Review of Economic Studies* 57 (2): 381–402.

Bercusson, B. 1979. *The Employment Protection (Consolidation) Act 1978.* London: Sweet and Maxwell.

Bertola, B. 1990. "Job Security, Employment, and Wages." *European Economic Review* 34: 851–86.

Bertrand, H. 1989. "Modèles d'emploi européens: Convergence au divergence?" Report for the EC Commission. Mimeo.

Bessy, C. 1987. "Analyse sectorielle des licenciements economiques sur la période 1980–1985." *Travail et emploi* 31 (March): 37–45.

Bird, D. 1990. "Redundancies in Great Britain: A Review of Statistical Sources and Preliminary Results from the 1989 labour force survey." *Department of Employment Gazette,* Sept., 450–54.

Bishop, J. 1990. "Job Performance, Turnover, and Wage Growth." *Journal of Labour Economics* 8 (3): 363–86.

Bispinck, R. 1990. *Kuendigungsfristen und Kuendigungsschutz in Tarifvertraegen.* Elemente qualitativer Tarifpolitik no. 13. Duesseldorf: WSI.

Bjoerklund, A., and **B. Holmlund.** 1987. "Worker Displacement in Sweden: Facts and Policies." Paper presented at the American Economic Association meetings, Stockholm, December.

Blanchard, O. J., and **L. H. Summers.** 1987. "Hysteresis in Unemployment." *European Economic Review* 31: 288–95.

———. 1988. "Beyond the Natural Rate Hypothesis." *American Economic Review* 78 (May): 182–87.

Blanchard, O. J., et al. 1987. "Employment and Growth in Europe: A Two-Handed Approach." In *Restoring Europe's Prosperity: Macroeconomic Papers from the Center for European Policy Studies.* edited by O. Blanchard et al., 95–123. Cambridge, Mass.: MIT Press.

Blanchflower D. G., and **A. J. Oswald.** 1988. "Internal and External Influences on Pay Settlements." *British Journal of Industrial Relations* 36 (Nov.): 363–70.

Blanchflower, D. G., A. J. Oswald and **M. D. Garrett.** 1990. "Insider Power in Wage Determination." *Economica* 57 (226): 143–70.

Blank, E. C. 1989. "Mobility and Wage Growth of Male Household Heads." *Applied Economics* 21: 475–85.

Bloch, L., and **J.-P. Puig.** 1986. "Baisser les salaires réels, réduire les sureffectifs industriels: Deux aspects de la flexibilité de l'emploi." *Economie et statistique* 191 (Sept.): 3–20.

Blondel, D. 1986. "De la flexibilité de la main-d'oeuvre comme mode de régulation à la valorisation de la ressource humaine comme déterminant de la croissance." Paper presented at the ASFE colloquium, Paris, September.

Bluem, N. 1984. "Das Beschaeftigungsfoerderungsgesetz 1985." *Wirtschaftsdienst* 9: 419–22 (Suppl.).

Bluestone, B., and **B. Harrison.** 1982. *The Deindustrialization of America: Plant Closings,*

Community Abandonment, and the Dismantling of Private Industry. New York: Basic Books.

Boehle, F., and **B. Lutz.** 1974. *Rationalisierungsschutz-abkommen.* Stuttgart: Otto Schwarz.

Boldt, G., et al. 1958. *Die Stabilitaet des Arbeitsverhaeltnisses nach dem Recht der Mitgliedstaaten der EGKS."* Luxembourg: EGKS.

Bolt, J. E. 1983. "Job Security: Its Time Has Come." *Harvard Business Review* 6: 115–23.

Bolton Report. 1971. *Report of the Committee of Enquiry on Small Firms. Cmnd 4881.* London: HMSO.

Booth, A. L. 1987. "Extra-Statutory Redundancy Payments in Britain." *British Journal of Industrial Relations* 25: 401–19.

Booth, A. L., and **M. Chatterji.** 1989. "Redundancy Payments and Firm-Specific Training." *Economica* 56 (4): 505–21.

Boré, C., and **J.-C. Guergoat.** 1989. "Les mouvements de main d'oeuvre et l'intérim." *Dossiers statistiques du travail et de l'emploi* 51 (Aug.): 37–40.

Bosch, G. 1985. "West Germany." In *Managing Workforce Reduction: An International Survey,* edited by M. Cross, 164–98. London: Croom-Helm.

———. "Hat das Normalarbeitsverhaeltnis eine Zukunft?" *WSI-Mitteilungen* 39 (3): 163–76.

Bowles, S., and **R. Boyer.** 1990. "Labour Market Flexibility and Decentralization as Barriers to High Employment? Notes on Employer Collusion, Centralized Wage Bargaining and Aggregate Employment." In *Labour Relations and Economic Performance,* edited by R. Brunetta and C. Dell'Aringa, 325–52. Basingstoke: Macmillan.

Boyer, R. 1979. "Wage Formation in Historical Perspective: The French Experience." *Cambridge Journal of Economics* 3 (March): 99–118.

———. 1981. "Les transformations du rapport salarial dans la crise: Une interprétation des aspects sociaux et économiques." *Critiques de l'economie politique* 15–16 (April-June): 185–228.

———. 1983. "Wage Labor, Capital Accumulation, and the Crisis: 1968–1982." *Toqueville Review* 5 (Spring-Summer): 136–63.

———. 1986a. "Informatisation de la production et polyvalence . . . ou comment une flexibilité peut en cacher une autre." *Formation emploi* 14 (April-June): 6–21.

———. 1986b. "La relation salariale entre théorie et histoire." In *Le travail: Marchés, règles, conventions,* edited by R. Salais and L. Thevenot, 295–312. Paris: Economica.

———. 1986c. *"Théorie de la régulation: Bilan, critique, perspectives."* Paris: La Découverte. (American ed., 1990. *The Regulation School.* New York: Columbia University Press.)

———. 1987. "Labour Flexibilities: Many Forms, Uncertain Effects." *Labour and Society* 12(1): 107–25.

———. 1988a. "Is a New Socio-Technical System Emerging?" Paper presented at the conference "Structural Change and Labor Market Policy," Arbetslivscentrum, Var Gard, June.

———. 1988b. *The Search for Labor Market Flexibility.* Oxford: Clarendon Press.

———. 1989a. "L'impact du marché unique sur le travail et l'emploi: Une comparaison des approches macroéconomiques et des recherches en économie du travail." Paper presented at the inaugural conference of the Association Européenne des Economistes du Travail, Turin, September.

———. 1989b. "New Directions in Management Practices and Work Organisation." Paper presented at the OECD conference "Technical Change as a Social Process: Society, Enterprises and the Individual," Helsinki, December.

———. 1989c. "The Transformations of the Capital Labor Relation and Wage Formation in Eight OECD Countries during the Eighties." Paper presented at the international symposium "Making Economies More Efficient and Equitable, Factors Determining Income Distribution," Tokyo, November.

———. 1989d. "The Transformations of Modern Capitalism. By the Light of the Regulation Approach and Other Political Economy Theories." Paper presented at conference, Comparative Governance of Economic Sectors, Bellagio, May-June.

———. 1989e. "Politiche, economiche e uscita della crisi." *L'industria,* Inglo, Septembre: 415–52.

———. 1990a. "The Capital and Labor Relations in OECD Countries: From the 'Golden Age' to the Uncertain Nineties." Paper presented to the WIDER project "The Transformation of the Capital Labor Relations," Paris.

1990b. "The Impact of the Single Market on Labour and Employment." *Labour and Society* 15(2): 109–42.

———. Forthcoming. *La seconde transformation: Trajectoires du capitalisme contemporain.* Paris: Economica.

Boyer, R., ed. 1986. *La flexibilité du travail en Europe.* Paris: La Découverte.

Boyer, R., and B. Coriat. 1986. "Technical Flexibility and Macro Stabilisation." *Ricerche economiche* 40 (Oct.-Dec.): 771–835.

Boyer, R., and J. Mistral. 1978. *Accumulation, Inflation, Crises.* 2d ed. Paris: Presses Universitaires de France.

Boyer, R., and A. Orlean. 1990. "Convention salariale: Du local au global, l'exemple fordien." CEPREMAP. Mimeo.

Boyer, R., and P. Petit. 1988a. "Science, Technique et Croissance Economique." Paper presented at the international OECD seminar "Science, Technology and Growth," Paris, June.

———. 1988b. "Technical Change, Cumulative Causation and Growth: An Exploration of Some Post Keynesian Theories." Paper presented at the international OECD seminar "Science, Technology and Growth," Paris, June.

———. 1991. "Kaldor's Growth Theories: Past, Present, and Prospects." In *Nicholas*

Kaldor and Mainstream Economics, edited by E. J. Nell and W. Semmler. London: Macmillan.

Boyer, R., and **B. Reynaud.** 1988. "Flexibilité salariale: Les arguments du libéralisme à l'épreuve des théories microéconomiques modernes." In *AFSE Colloque Annuel.* Paris: Nathan.

Brinkmann, C., et al. 1986. "Ueberstunden: Entwicklung, Strukturen und Bestimmungsgroessen." *Beitraege zur Arbeitsmarkt- und Berufsforschung (BeitrAB)* 98.

Brown, C., and **M. Reich.** 1989. "When Does Union-Management Cooperation Work? A Look at NUMMI and GM–Van Nuys." *California Management Review* 32 (Summer): 26–44.

Brown, J. N., and **O. Ashenfelter.** 1986. "Testing the Efficiency of Employment Contracts." *Journal of Political Economy* 94 (June) 540–87.

Brown, S. P. 1987. "How Often Do Workers Receive Advance Notice of Layoffs?" *Monthly Labor Review* 110 (June): 13–17.

Brown, W., and **S. Wadhwani.** 1990. "The Economic Effects of Industrial Relations Legislation since 1979." Discussion Paper no. 376. Centre for Labor Economics, London School of Economics.

Brown, W., et al. 1981. *The Changing Contours of British Industrial Relations.* Oxford: Basil Blackwell.

Brunhes, B., J. Royot, and **W. Wassermann.** 1989. *La flexibilité du marché du travail: Nouvelles tendances dans l'entreprise.* Paris: OECD.

Bruno, S. 1987. "Micro-Flexibility and Macro-Rigidity: Some Notes on Expectations and the Dynamics of Aggregate Supply." Mimeo.

Buchele, R. 1983. "Economic Dualism and Employment Stability." *Industrial Relations* 22 (3): 410–18.

Bué, J. 1989. "Les différentes formes de flexibilité." *Travail et emploi* (3): 29–35.

Buechtemann, C. F. 1984. "Der Arbeitslosigkeitsprozess: Theorie und Empirie strukturierter Arbeitslosigkeit in der Bundesrepublik Deutschland." In *Arbeitslosigkeit in der Arbeitsgesellschaft,* edited by W. Bonss and R. Heinze, 53–105. Frankfurt: Suhrkamp.

———. 1987a. "Abschied vom Dauerarbeitsverhaeltnis?" Paper presented at SAMF workshop, Hamburg, June.

———. 1987b. "Befristete Beschaeftigung: Entwicklungstendenzen im internationalen Vergleich." *Internationale Chronik zur Arbeitsmarktpolitik* 28: 10–11.

———. 1989a. "Beschaeftigungsfoerderung durch Erleichterung befristeter Arbeitsvertraege: Arbeitsmarktwirkungen des Beschaeftigungsfoerderungsgesetzes aus der Sicht der Arbeitsvermittlung." *Arbeit und Beruf* 40 (12): 379–85.

———. 1989b. "More Jobs through Less Employment Protection? Evidence for West Germany." *Labour* 3 (Winter): 23–56.

———. 1990. "Kuendigungsschutz als Beschaeftigungshemmnis? Empirische Evidenz fuer die Bundesrepublik Deutschland." *Mitteilungen aus der Arbeitsmarkt- und Berufsforschung* 23 (3): 394–409.

————. 1991. "Current and Emerging Labor Markets: Western Europe and North America." Paper presented at the International Conference on Migration and Emigration from the Former Soviet Union, November, RAND Corp., Santa Monica, Calif.

Buechtemann, C. F., and **K. Burian.** 1986. "Befristete Beschaeftigungsverhaeltnisse: Ein international-vergleichender Ueberblick." *Internationale Chronik zur Arbeitsmarktpolitik* 26: 4–8.

Buechtemann, C. F., and **A. Hoeland.** 1989. "Befristete Arbeitsvertraege nach dem Beschaeftigungsfoerderungsgesetz 1985 (BeschFG 1985). Ergebnisse einer empirischen Untersuchung i.A. des Bundesministers fuer Arbeit und Sozialordnung." In *Forschungsberichte*, vol. 183, edited by the Federal Ministry of Labor and Social Affairs (BMA). Bonn: BMA.

Buechtemann, C. F., and **K. Kraft.** 1992. "*Employment Effects of 'Deregulation': An Econometric Test.*" RAND Corp., Santa Monica, Calif. Mimeo.

Buechtemann, C. F., and **N. Meager.** 1991. *Leaving Employment: Patterns in EC Countries.* Discussion paper FSI–1991. Berlin: WZB.

Buechtemann, C. F., and **S. Quack.** 1989. " 'Bridges' or 'Traps'? Non-standard Employment in the Federal Republic of Germany." In *Precarious Jobs in Labor Market Regulation: The Growth of Atypical Employment in Western Europe,* edited by G. Rodgers and J. Rodgers, 109–48. Geneva: International Labour Office.

————. 1990. "How Precarious is 'Non-standard' Employment? Evidence for West Germany." *Cambridge Journal of Economics* 14 (3): 315–30.

Buechtemann, C. F., and **F. Stille.** 1992. *Unemployment and Labour Market Flexibility: Federal Republic of Germany.* Report prepared on behalf of the International Labour Office (ILO). Berlin and Geneva: ILO.

Bulow, J. I., and **L. H. Summers.** 1986. "A Theory of Dual Labor Markets with Applications to Industrial Policy, Discrimination and Keynesian Unemployment." *Journal of Labor Economics* 4 (July): 376–414.

Bundesminister fuer Arbeit und Sozialordnung. 1990. "Arbeits- und Sozialstatistik: Taetigkeit der Arbeitsgerichte." *Bundesarbeitsblatt* 7/8 (July/Aug.): 254–60.

Burchell, B., and **J. Rubery.** 1990. *Segmented Jobs and Segmented Workers: An Empirical Investigation.* ESRC Social Change and Economic Life Initiative Working Paper no. 13. Oxford: ESRC.

Bureau of National Affairs. 1985a. *Employee Discipline and Discharge.* PPF Survey no. 139. Washington, D.C.: BNA.

————. 1985b. *Personnel Policies Forum* 140. Washington, D.C.: BNA.

————. 1989. *Without Just Cause: An Employer's Practical and Legal Guide on Wrongful Discharge.* BNA report no. 103. Washington, D.C.

————. 1990. *Daily Labor Report,* Feb. 6, A8-A9.

Burgess, S. M. 1988. "Employment Adjustment in UK Manufacturing." *Economic Journal* 98 (March): 81–103.

Burgess, S. M., and **S. Nickell.** 1990. "Labour Turnover in UK Manufacturing." *Economica* 57 (2): 295–317.

Burtless, G. 1983. "Why Is Insured Unemployment So Low?" *Brookings Papers on Economic Activity* (1): 225–49.

———. 1987. "Jobless Pay and High European Unemployment." In *Barriers to European Growth: A Transatlantic View,* edited by R. Z. Lawrence and C. L. Schultze, 105–68. Washington, D.C.: Brookings Institution.

Business Week. 1980. Special issue, "Reindustrializing America." April.

Buttler, F. 1987. "Vertragstheoretische Interpretation von Arbeitsmarktinstitutionen." In *Arbeitsmaerkte und Beschaeftigung: Fakten, Analysen, Perspektiven,* edited by G. Bombach et al., 203–24, Tübingen: J. C. B. Mohr.

Calmfors, L., and **J. Driffill.** 1988. "Bargaining Structure, Corporatism, and Macroeconomic Performance." *Economic Policy* 5 (April): 14–61.

Capelli, P. 1985. "Plant-Level Concession Bargaining." *Industrial and Labor Relations Review* 39 (Oct.): 90–104.

Carter, S. B. 1988. "The Changing Importance of Life-Time Jobs, 1892–1978." *Industrial Relations* 27 (3): 287–300.

CBI. 1989. "Pay, Performance and Inflation." Memorandum from the Confederation of British Industry to the National Economic Development Council, London, Oct. 18.

Centre d'Etude des Revenues et des Couts (CERC). 1989. *Les structures de salaires dans la Communaute Economique Européenne.* Paris.

CEPREMAP-CORDES. 1977. *Approches de l'inflation: L'exemple français.* Research report no. 22. Paris. Mimeo.

Cézard M., and **J. L. Heller.** 1988. "Les formes traditionnelles d'emploi salarié déclinent." *Economie et statistique* 215 (Nov.): 15–23.

Challier, M. C. 1986. "Travail atypique et flexibilité de l'emploi." *Revue française des affaires sociales* 40 (Jan.-March): 77–95.

Chan-Lee, J., D. T., Coe, and **M. Prywes.** 1987. "Microeconomic Changes and Macroeconomic Wage Disinflation in the 1980s." *OECD Economic Studies* 8 (Spring): 121–57.

Charraud A., and **J.-C. Guergoat.** 1989. *Le développement des emplois temporaires.* Initial Summaries no. 2. Paris: Ministry of Labour.

Cheung, S. N. S. 1983. "The Contractual Nature of the Firm." *Journal of Law and Economics* 26: 1–23.

Choffel, P., P. Cuneo, and **F. Kramarz.** 1988. "Les modalités d'adaptation après le premier choc pétrolier." *Economie et statistique* 213 (Sept.): 33–40.

Choffel, P., and **O. Garnier.** 1988. "Articulation des marchés internes et externes du travail: Aspects dynamiques." In *Structures du marché du travail et politiques d'emploi,* 256–70. Paris: Syros.

Clasen, L. 1983. "Tarifvertraege: Geringere Abschluesse." *Bundesarbeitsblatt* 4: 11–19.

Clifton, R., and **C. Tatton-Brown.** 1979. *Impact of Employment Legislation on Small Firms.* Department of Employment Research Paper no. 6. London.

Coase, R. H. 1983. "The Problem of Social Cost." In *Law, Economics, and Philosophy: A Critical Introduction with Applications to the Law of Torts,* edited by M. Kupperberg and C. Beitz, 13–40. Savage, Md.: Rowman & Littlefield.

Coe, D. T. 1985. "Nominal Wages, the NAIRU, and Wage Flexibility." *OECD Economic Studies* 5 (Autumn): 87–126.

Cohen, G. M., and **M. L. Wachter.** 1989. "An Internal Labor Market Approach to Labor Law: Does Labor Law Promote Efficient Contracting?" In *Proceedings of the Forty-first Annual Meeting of the IRRA,* edited by B. D. Dennis, 243–50. Madison, Wisc.: Industrial Relations Research Association.

Cohen, M. S., and **A. R. Schwartz.** 1980. "U.S. Labor Turnover: Analysis of a New Measure." *Monthly Labor Review* 103 (Nov.): 9–13.

Collins, H. 1982. "Capitalist Discipline and Corporatist Law." *Industrial Law Journal* 11: 78–93, 170–77.

Cooper, R. W. 1987. *Wage and Employment Patterns in Labour Contracts: Microfoundations and Macroeconomic Implications.* Chur, Switzerland: Harwood Academic Publishers.

Cooter, R. D. 1991. "Economic Theories of Legal Liability." *Journal of Economic Perspectives* 5 (Summer): 11–30.

Cooter, R. D., and **D. L. Rubinfeld.** 1989. "Economic Analysis of Legal Disputes and Their Resolution." *Journal of Economic Literature* 27: 1067–97.

Cooter, R. D., and **T. Ulen.** 1988. *Law and Economics.* Glenview, Ill.: Scott, Foresman.

Corbel, P., et al. 1986. "Les mouvements de main d'oeuvre en 1985." *Economie et statistique* 193–194 (Nov./Dec.): 17–26.

Craig, C., et al. 1982. *Labour Market Structure, Industrial Organisation and Low Pay.* Cambridge: Cambridge University Press.

———. 1985. *Payment Structures and Smaller Firms: Women's Employment in Segmented Labour Markets.* Department of Employment Research Paper no. 48. London.

Cramer, U. 1986. "Zur Stabilitaet von Beschaeftigung: Erste Ergebnisse der IAB-Stichprobe aus der Beschaeftigtenstatistik." *Mitteilungen aus der Arbeitsmarkt- und Berufsforschung (MittAB)* 2: 243–56.

Cramer, U., and **M. Koller.** 1988. "Gewinne und Verluste von Arbeitsplaetzen in Betrieben: Der 'Job Turnover'-Ansatz." *Mitteilungen aus der Arbeitsmarkt- und Berufsforschung (MittAB)* 3: 361–77.

Craswell, R., and **J. E. Calfee.** 1986. "Deterrence and Uncertain Legal Standards." *Journal of Law, Economics and Organization* (2): 279–303.

Crawford, V. P. 1988. "Long-Term Relationships Governed by Short-Term Contracts," *American Economic Review* 78 (6): 485–99.

Curme, M. A., et al. 1990. "Union Membership and Contract Coverage in the United States, 1983–1988." *Industrial and Labor Relations Review* 44 (Oct.) 5–12.

Curtin, E. A. 1970. *White Collar Unionization.* Studies in Personnel Policy no. 220. New York: National Industrial Conference Board.

Daniel, W. W. 1978. "The Effects of Employment Protection Laws in Manufacturing Industry." *Department of Employment Gazette,* June, 658–61.

———. 1981. "A Clash of Symbols: The Case of Maternity Legislation." *Policy Studies* 2 (Oct.): 74–85.

———. 1985. "The United Kingdom." In *Managing Workforce Reduction: An International Survey,* edited by M. Cross, 67–90. London: Croom-Helm.

Daniel, W. W., and N. Millward. 1983. *Workplace Industrial Relations in Britain: The DE/PSI/SSRC Survey.* London: Heinemann.

Daniel, W. W., and E. Stilgoe. 1978. *The Impact of Employment Protection Laws.* London: Policy Studies Institute.

Darby, M. R., J. C. Haltiwanger, and **M. W. Plant.** 1986. *The Ins and Outs of Unemployment: The Ins Win.* NBER Working Paper no. 1997. Cambridge, Mass.: National Bureau of Economic Research.

Davis, L., and **D. North.** 1971. *Institutional Change and American Economic Growth.* New York: Cambridge University Press.

Davis, S., and **J. Haltiwanger.** 1989. "Gross Job Creation, Gross Job Destruction, and Employment Reallocation." University of Chicago. Mimeo.

———. 1991. *Gross Job Creation, Gross Job Reduction, Employment Relocation.* NBER Working Paper no. 328. Cambridge, Mass.: National Bureau of Economic Research.

Deaton, D. 1984. "The Incidence of Dismissals in British Manufacturing Industries." *Relations Industrielles* 39: 61–65.

de Broucker, P. 1988. "Stabilité de l'emploi et flexibilité du marché du travail: aperçu de l'OCDE." In *Structures du marché du travail et politiques d'emploi,* 151–63. Paris: Syros.

Del Boca, A., and **P. Rota.** 1990. "Special Earnings Short-Time Compensation in Milan." In *Report '89: Labor and Employment Policies in Italy,* edited by Italian Ministry of Labor, 464–70. Rome: Poligrafico dello Stato.

Dell'Aringa, C. 1981. *L'agencia per la mobilitá della manodopera.* Milan: V.P.

Demsetz, H. 1972. "Wealth Distribution and the Ownership of Rights." *Journal of Legal Studies* 1 (July): 223–32.

de Neubourg, C. 1990. *Unemployment and Labour Market Flexibility: The Netherlands.* Geneva: International Labour Office.

Deprez, J. 1988. "La part faite à l'idée de negotiation dans la theorie juridiques des usages d'entreprise." *Droit social,* 57–67.

Dertouzos, J. N. 1988. "The End of Employment-at-Will: Legal and Economic Costs." RAND Corp. Santa Monica, Calif. Mimeo.

Dertouzos, J. N., E. Holland, and **P. Ebener.** 1988. *The Legal and Economic Consequences of Wrongful Termination.* Report no. R–3602-ICJ. Santa Monica, Calif.: RAND Corp.

Dertouzos, J. N., and **L. A. Karoly.** 1992. *Labor Market Responses to Employer Liability.* Report no. R 3989-IC. Santa Monica, Calif.: RAND Corp.

Dertouzos, J. N., and **T. Quinn.** 1985. *Bargaining Responses to the Technology Revolution: The Case of the Newspaper Industry.* Report no. R–3144-DOL. Santa Monica, Calif: RAND Corp.

Dertouzos, M. L., et al. 1989. *Made in America: Regaining the Productive Edge.* Cambridge, Mass.: MIT Press.

Dichmann, W. 1988. "Arbeitsmarktverfassung und Arbeitsmarktflexibilitaet." *Beitraege zur Wirtschafts- und Sozialpolitik,* vol. 162. Cologne: Deutscher Instituts-Verlag.

Dickens, L., M. Hart, M. Jones, and **B. Weekes.** 1981. "Re-employment of Unfairly Dismissed Workers: The Lost Remedy." *Industrial Law Journal* 10: 160–75.

Dickens L., et al. 1984. "The British Experience under a Statute Prohibiting Unfair Dismissal." *Industrial and Labor Relations Review* 37 (July): 497–514.

———. 1985. *Dismissed. A Study of Unfair Dismissal and the Industrial Tribunal System.* Oxford: Basil Blackwell.

Diekmann, J. 1985. "Betriebliche Wirkungen regulativer Arbeitsmarktpolitik." *Sozialer Fortschritt* 34 (2): 35–39.

Disney, R., and **E. M. Szyszcak.** 1984. "Protective Legislation and Part-Time Employment in Britain." *British Journal of Industrial Relations* 22 (March): 78–100.

Doeringer, P., and **M. Piore.** 1971. *Internal Labor Markets and Manpower Analysis.* Lexington, Mass.: Heath.

Dombois, R. 1986. "Sozialstaatliche Schutzregelungen und einzelbetriebliche Flexibilitaet: Beschaeftigungspolitik der Rieckmers-Werft von 1954–1985." *Arbeit und Betrieb* 15 (Oct.): 36–69.

Dombois, R., et al. 1982. "Vom Heuern und Feuern zur stabilen Mindestbelegschaft— Drei Jahrzehnte betrieblicher Beschaeftigungspolitik eines Schiffbauunternehmens." *Mehrwert* 23 (Sept.): 7–35.

Dore, R. 1986. *Flexible Rigidities: Industrial Policy and Structural Adjustment in the Japanese Economy.* Stanford: Stanford University Press.

———. 1987. *Taking Japan Seriously: A Confucian Perspective on Leading Economic Issues.* Stanford: Stanford University Press.

Dormont, B. 1988. "Une analyse comparative sur données d'entreprises des ajustements de l'emploi dans la crise en France et en RFA." In *Structures du marché du travail et politiques d'emploi,* 164–75. Paris: Syros.

Dornbusch, R. 1986. "Unemployment: Europe's Challenge for the '80s." *Challenge* 29 (Sept.–Oct.): 11–18.

Drake, C. D., and **B. Bercusson.** 1981. *The Employment Acts: 1974–1980.* London: Sweet and Maxwell.

Dumenil, G., and **D. Levy.** 1989. "Micro Adjustment Behavior and Macro Stability." *Seoul Journal of Economics* 2(1): 1–37.

Dunne, T., M. Roberts, and **L. Samuelson.** 1989. "Plant Turnover and Gross Employment Flows in the U. S. Manufacturing Sector." *Journal of Labor Economics* 7 (1): 48–71.

Edwards, R. 1981. *Herrschaft im modernen Produktionsprozess.* Frankfurt: Campus.

Ehrenberg, R. G. 1985. *Workers' Rights: Rethinking Protective Labor Legislation.* NBER Working Paper no. 1754. Cambridge, Mass.: National Bureau of Economic Research.

Ehrenberg, R. G., and **G. H. Jakubson.** 1988. *Advance Notice Provisions in Plant Closing Legislation.* Kalamazoo, Mich. W. E. Upjohn Institute.

———. 1989. "Advance Notification of Plant Closing: Does It Matter?" *Industrial Relations* 28 (Winter): 60–71.

———. 1990. "Why WARN?" *Regulation* (Summer): 39–46.

Ehrenberg, R. G., and **P. L. Schumann.** 1982. *Longer Hours or More Jobs? An Investigation of Amending Hours Legislation to Create Employment.* Ithaca, N.Y.: ILR Press.

Elbaum, M. 1988. "Les attentes des entreprises vis-à-vis de la flexibilité ont jusqu'ici peu influé sur l'emploi." *Economie et statistique* 206: 13–31.

Elbaum, M., and **M. Tonnerre.** 1986. "La procédure de licenciement économique: Delais, influence sur les décisions de gestion du personnel et devenir de l'entreprise." *Dossiers statistiques du travail et de l'emploi* 19 (Feb.): 5–28.

Elbaum, M., et al. 1986. "La suppression de l'autorisation administrative de licenciement: Des emplois ou des chomeurs?" Mimeo.

Eliasson, G. 1986. "Innovation Change, Dynamic Market Allocation and Long-Term Stability of Growth." Paper presented at the Conference on Innovation Diffusion, Venice, March.

———. 1989. "Modelling Long-Term Macro-Economic Growth as a Based, Path-Dependent, Experimentally Organized Economic Process: The Swedish Micro-to-Macro Model." Paper presented at the International OECD Seminar "Science, Technology and Economic Growth," Paris, June.

Elster, J. 1979. *Ulysses and the Sirens: Studies in Rationality and Irrationality.* Cambridge: Cambridge University Press.

Emerson, M. 1987. "Comment to D. Metcalf." In *The Fight against Unemployment: Macroeconomic Papers from the Center for European Studies,* edited by R. Layard and L. Calmfors, 77–82. Cambridge, Mass.: MIT Press.

———. 1988a. "Regulation or Deregulation of the Labour Market: Policy Regimes for the Recruitment and Dismissal of Employees in the Industrialised Countries." *European Economic Review* 32 (4): 775–817.

———. 1988b. *What Model for Europe.* Cambridge, Mass.: MIT Press.

Epstein, R. 1984. "In Defense of the Contract at Will." *University of Chicago Law Review* 51 (Fall): 947–82.

European Economic Commission. 1987. "Adaptation of Firms: Commission Memorandum on Internal and External Adaptation of Firms in Relation to Employment." *European Industrial Relations Review* 163 (8): 21–36.

Eurostat. 1988. *Employment and Unemployment.* Luxembourg.

Evans, S. 1987. "The Use of Injunctions in Industrial Disputes, May 1984–April 1987." *British Journal of Industrial Relations* 25 (Nov.): 419–35.

Evans, S., et al. 1985. *Unfair Dismissal Law and Employment Practice.* Department of Employment Research Paper no. 53. London.

Ewald, F. 1987. *L'état providence.* Paris: Grasset.

Eymard-Duvernay, F. 1985. "Schemas d'analyse de la flexibilité." Centre d'Études de l'Emploi. Paris. Mimeo.

Fair, R. C. 1985. "Excess Labor over the Business Cycle." *American Economic Review* 75 (1): 239–45.

Falke, J. 1983. "Kuendigungspraxis und Kuendigungsschutz in der Bundesrepublik Deutschland." In *Kuendigungspraxis, Kuendigungsschutz und Probleme der Arbeitsgerichtsbarkeit,* vol. 45, *Beitraege zur sozialwissenschaftlichen Forschung,* edited by R. Ellermann-Witt et al., 13–43. Opladen: Westdeutscher Verlag.

Falke, J., et al. 1981. *Kuendigungspraxis und Kuendigungsschutz in der Bundesrepublik Deutschland,* vol. 47, *Forschungsberichte,* edited by the Federal Ministry of Labor and Social Affairs (BMA). Bonn: BMA.

Favereau, O. 1989. "Irréversibilités et institution: Les problèmes du passage micro/macro." Paper presented at the international seminar "Irréversibilités dans les modes de croissance," EHESS, Paris, June.

Fay, J. A., and J. L. Medoff. 1985. "Labor and Output over the Business Cycle: Some Direct Evidence." *American Economic Review* 75 (4): 638–55.

Federal Employment Agency. 1990. *Amtliche Nachrichten der Bundesanstalt fuer Arbeit* 38 (5): 647–760.

Fels, J., and E. Gundlach. 1990. "More Evidence on the Puzzle of Interindustry Wage Differentials: The Case of West Germany." *Weltwirtschaftliches Archiv* 126 (3): 544–60.

Fels, G., and G. M. von Furstenberg, eds. 1989. *A Supply-Side Agenda for Germany: Sparks from the United States, Great Britain, European Integration.* Berlin: Springer Verlag.

Fishel, D. R. 1984. "Labor Market and Labor Law Compared with Capital Markets and Corporate Law." *University of Chicago Law Review* 51: 1061–77.

Fisher, I. [1933] 1965. *The Theory of Interest.* Reprint. New York: Augustus M. Kelley.

Fitoussi, J. P., and J. Le Cacheux. 1989. "Une théorie des années quatre-vingt." *Observations et diagnostics economiques: Revue de l'OFCE* 29 (Oct.): 117–60.

Flanagan, R. J. 1987a. "Efficiency and Equality in Swedish Labor Markets." In *The Swedish Economy,* edited by B. P. Bosworth and A. M. Rivlin, 125–84. Washington, D. C.: Brookings Institution.

————. 1987b. "Labor Market Behavior and European Economic Growth." In *Barriers to European Growth: A Transatlantic View*, edited by R. Z. Lawrence and C. L. Schultze, 175–211. Washington, D.C.: Brookings Institution.

————. 1987c. *Labor Relations and the Litigation Explosion.* Washington, D.C.: Brookings Institution.

————. 1988. "Unemployment as a Hiring Problem." *OECD Economic Studies* 11 (Autumn): 123–54.

Flanagan, R. J., D. W. Soskice, and L. Ulman. 1983. *Unionism, Economic Stabilization, and Incomes Policies: European Experience.* Washington, D.C.: Brookings Institution.

Flanders, A. D. 1974. "The Tradition of Voluntarism." *British Journal of Industrial Relations* 12: 352–70.

Flechsenhaar, H. R. 1980. *Kurzarbeit als Massnahme der betrieblichen Anpassung.* Frankfurt: Verlagshaus Harry Deutsch.

Folbre, N., J. Leighton, and M. Roderick. 1984. "Plant Closings and Their Regulation in Maine, 1971–1982." *Industrial and Labor Relations Review* 37 (Jan.): 185–97.

Ford, J. 1982. "Who Breaks the Rules? The Response of Small Businesses to External Regulation." *Industrial Relations Journal* 13 (Autumn): 40–49.

Foulkes, F. K. 1980. *Personnel Policies in Large Non-Union Companies.* Englewood Cliffs, N. J.: Prentice-Hall.

————. 1989. "Employment Security: Developments in the Non-Union Sector." In *Proceedings of the Forty-first Annual Meeting of the IRRA*, edited by B. D. Dennis, 411–17. Madison, Wisc.: Industrial Relations Research Association.

François-D'Harmant, A., and R. Brunetta. 1987. "The Cassa Integrazione Guadagni." *Labour* 1 (1): 15–57.

Franz, W. 1989. "Beschaeftigungsprobleme auf Grund von Inflexibilitaeten auf Arbeitsmaerkten?" In *Beschaeftigungsprobleme hochentwickelter Volkswirtschaften*, vol. 178, *Schriften des Vereins fuer Socialpolitik NF*, edited by H. Scherf, 303–40. Berlin: Duncker und Humblodt.

————. 1991. "Match and Mismatch on the German Labor Market." In *Mismatch and Labour Mobility*, edited by F. Padoa-Schioppa, 105–35. Cambridge: Cambridge University Press.

Freedland, M. 1980. "Leaflet Law: The Temporary Short-Time Working Compensation Scheme." *Industrial Law Journal* 9.

Freeman, C. 1989. "The Nature of Innovation and the Evolution of the Productive System." Paper presented at international OECD seminar "Science, Technology and Economic Growth," Paris, June.

Freeman, R. B., and J. L. Medoff. 1984. *What Do Unions Do?* New York: Basic Books.

Freeman, R. B., and M. L. Weitzman. 1987. "Bonuses and Employment in Japan." *Journal of the Japanese and International Economies* 1 (June): 168–94.

Frey, B. 1978. "Ristrutturazione-riconversione industriali e mobilitá del lavoro." *Tendenze dell'occupazione* 7–8: 1–10.

Freyssinet J. 1987. "Promesses et déconvenues de la droite." *Les temps modernes* 496–97 (Nov.-Dec.): 209–23.

Friedman, S., and **L. Fisher.** 1989. "Collective Bargaining and Employment Security." In *Proceedings of the Forty-first Annual Meeting of the IRRA*, edited by B. D. Dennis, 418–29. Madison, Wisc.: Industrial Relations Research Association.

Friedrich, W., and **E. Spitznagel.** 1981. *Beitraege aus der Arbeitsmarkt- und Berufsforschung (BeitrAB)*, vol. 49, *Wachstum, Beschaeftigung und Investitionstaetigkeit im Verarbeitenden Gewerbe.* Nuremberg.

Fryer, R. H. 1973. "Redundancy, Values and Public Policy." *Industrial Relations Journal* 11 (4): 2–19.

"GAO Report Finds Productivity Center's Accomplishments Limited." 1978. *Daily Labor Reporter*, May 26, A5–A6.

Garber, S. 1989. "The Reserve-Labor Hypothesis, Short-Run Pricing Theories, and the Employment-Output Relationship." *Journal of Econometrics* 42 (2): 219–46.

Garen, J. E. 1988. "Empirical Studies of the Job Matching Hypothesis." In *Research in Labor Economics*, edited by R. G. Ehrenberg, 9:187–224. Greenwich, Conn.: JAI Press.

Garonna, P. 1984. *L'economia della Cassa Integrazione.* Padua: CIEUP.

———. 1989. "La CIG: Instrument de politique industrielle ou sociale?" In *La flexibilité en Italie*, edited by M. Maruani, E. Reynaud, and C. Romani, 131–42. Paris: Syros.

Gasnier C. 1989. "La flexibilité du travail: Résultats d'enquêtes." *Travail et emploi* 39: 97–101.

Gaudu, F. 1986. "L'emploi dans l'entreprise privée: Essai de théorie juridique." Thesis, University of Paris I.

Gavin, M. K. 1986. "Labor Market Rigidities and Unemployment: The Case of Severance Costs." International Finance Discussion Paper. Board of Governors, Federal Reserve, Washington, D.C. Mimeo.

General Accounting Office. 1987. *Plant Closings: Information on Advance Notice and Assistance Provided Dislocated Workers.* Report to Congressional Committees O HRD 87–105. Washington, D.C.

———. 1990. *Dislocated Workers: Expenditures under Title III of the Job Training Partnership Act.* Washington, D.C. February.

Gennard, J. 1986. "Job Security: Redundancy Arrangements and *Practices* in Selected OECD Countries." OECD, Paris. Mimeo.

Gennard, J., and **C. Lockyer.** 1985. *Job Security, Redundancy Arrangements and Practices: The Case of the United Kingdom.* Paris: OECD.

Genthon, V., and **P. Maroni.** 1989. "Moins de licenciements économiques, davantage de préretraites et de conventions de conversion." *Dossiers statistiques du travail et de l'emploi* 51 (Aug.): 41–45.

Gerlach, K., and **U. Schasse.** 1990. "Labor Market Effects of Quits and Dismissals." In *Conference Papers of the Second European Association of Labor Economists Conference* IIb: 455–64.

Giavazzi, F., and L. Spaventa. 1989. "Italy: The Real Effects of Inflation and Disinflation." *Economic Policy* 8 (April): 24–54.

Giersch, H. 1985. "Eurosclerosis." Kiel Discussion Papers no. 112. Kiel Institute for World Economics, Kiel, Germany. Mimeo.

Gloeckner, W. H. 1985. "Das Arbeitsrecht im Zeichen der Wende." *Die Neue Gesellschaft* 32 (9): 814–21.

Glyn, A. 1988. "Contraction and Expansion: The Divergence of Private Sector and Public Sector Unionism in the United States." *Journal of Economic Perspectives* 2 (Spring): 63–88.

Goldberg, V. 1980. "Bridges over Contested Terrain: Exploring the Radical Account of the Employment Relationship." *Journal of Economic Behavior and Organization* 1 (Sept.): 249–74.

———. 1984. "A Relational Exchange Perspective on the Employment Relationship." In *Firms, Organization, and Labor,* edited by F. H. Stephen, 127–45. New York: St. Martin's Press.

Gorz, A. 1989. *Critique of Economic Reason.* London: Verso.

Gottschalk, P., and T. Maloney. 1985. "Involuntary Terminations, Unemployment, and Job Matching: A Test of Job Search Theory." *Journal of Labor Economics* 3: 109–23.

Gould, W. B., IV. 1984a. *Japan's Reshaping of American Labor Law.* Cambridge, Mass.: MIT Press.

———. 1984b. "Protection from Wrongful Dismissal." *New York Times,* Oct. 22, A21.

———. 1984c. "Reflections on Wrongful Discharge Litigation and Legislation." *Arbitration.*

———. 1986. "The Idea of the Job as Property in Contemporary America: The Legal and Collective Bargaining Framework." *Brigham Young University Law Review* 4: 885–915.

———. 1987–88. "Stemming the Wrongful Discharge Tide: A Case for Arbitration." *Employee Relations Law Journal* 13 (Winter): 404–25.

———. 1988. "Job Security in the United States: Some Reflections on Unfair Dismissal and Plant Closure Legislation from a Comparative Perspective." *Nebraska Law Review* 67 (28): 42–47.

Gould, W. B., IV, et al. 1984. "To Strike a New Balance: A Report of the Ad-hoc Committee on Termination-at-Will and Wrongful Discharge, Appointed by the Labor and Employment Law Section of the State Bar of California." *Labor and Employment Law News,* Feb. 8.

Greenwood, J. A. 1972. "On the Abolition of Wages Councils." *Industrial Relations Journal* 3 (4): 30–42.

Gregory, R. G., and W. F. Foster. 1982. "A Preliminary Look at Some Labor Market Dynamics in Australia, Japan, and North America." Paper presented at the Conference on Japanese and Australian Labor Markets, Australian National University.

Gross, H., et al. 1987. *Arbeitszeitstrukturen im Wandel: Ergebnisse einer aktuellen Repraesentativumfrage zu den Arbeitszeitstrukturen in der Bundesrepublik Deutschland. Arbeitszeit '87*, edited by Ministerium fuer Arbeit, Gesundheit und Soziales des Landes NRW. Dusseldorf.

Gross, H., and C. Thoben. 1989. "Daten zur Ueberstundenarbeit." Kurzbericht no. 2. ISO Institut, Cologne.

Grubb, D. 1986. "Topics in the OECD Phillips Curve." *Economic Journal* 96 (March): 55–79.

Guigni, G. 1987. "Juridification: Labor Relations in Italy." In *Juridification of Social Spheres: A Comparative Analysis of the Areas of Labor, Corporate, Antitrust, and Social Welfare Law*, edited by G. Teubner, 191–208. Berlin and New York: de Gruyter.

Haber, S. E. 1983. "A New Method for Estimating Job Separations by Sex and Race." *Monthly Labor Review* 106 (June): 20–27.

Hakim, C. 1987. "Trends in the Flexible Workforce." *Department of Employment Gazette* 95 (Nov.): 549–60.

———. 1990. "Core and Periphery in Employers' Workforce Strategies: Evidence from the 1987 E.L.U.S. Survey." *Work, Employment and Society* 4 (2): 157–88.

Hall, R. 1982. "The Importance of Lifetime Jobs in the U.S. Economy." *American Economic Review* 72 (Sept.): 716–24.

Hall, R., and E. Lazear. 1984. "The Excess Sensitivity of Layoffs and Quits to Demand." *Journal of Labor Economics* 2 (2): 233–57.

Hamermesh, D. S. 1986. *The Demand for Workers and Hours and the Effects of Job Security Policies: Theory and Evidence*. NBER Discussion Paper no. 2056. Cambridge, Mass.: National Bureau of Economic Research.

———. 1987. "The Costs of Worker Displacement." *Quarterly Journal of Economics* 102 (Feb.): 51–75.

———. 1988. "The Demand for Workers and Hours and the Effects of Job Security Policies: Theories and Evidence." In *Employment, Unemployment, and Labor Utilization*, edited by R. A. Hart, 9–32. Boston: Unwin Hyman.

———. 1989a. "Labor Demand." Michigan State University. Typescript.

———. 1989b. "Labor Demand and the Structure of Adjustment Costs." *American Economic Review* 79: 674–89.

———. 1989c. "What Do We Know about Worker Displacement in the U.S.?" *Industrial Relations* 28 (Winter): 51–59.

———. 1990a. "Aggregate Employment Dynamics and Lumpy Adjustment Costs." *Carnegie Rochester Conference Series on Public Policy* 33: 93–130.

———. 1990b. "Unemployment Insurance Financing, Short-Time Compensation and Labor Demand." In *Research in Labor Economics*, edited by R. G. Ehrenberg, 11: 241–69. Greenwich, Conn.: JAI Press.

Hanami, T. A. 1982. "Japan." In *Workforce Reductions in Undertakings: Policies and*

Measures for the Protection of Redundant Workers in Seven Industrialized Market Economy Countries, edited by E. Yemin, 167–85. Geneva: International Labor Organization.

Harrison, B. 1984. "Plant Closures: Effects to Cushion the Blow." *Monthly Labor Review* 107 (June): 41–43.

Hart, R. 1987. *Working Time and Employment.* Boston: Allen and Unwin.

Hashimoto, M. 1981. "Firm-Specific Human Capital as a Shared Investment." *American Economic Review* 71 (June): 475–82.

———. 1990a. "Employment and Wage Systems in Japan and Their Implications for Productivity." In *Paying for Productivity: A Look at the Evidence*, edited by A. S. Blinder, 245–95 Washington D. C.: Brookings Institution.

———. 1990b. *The Japanese Labor Market in a Comparative Perspective with the United States.* Kalamazoo, Mich.: W. E. Upjohn Institute.

Hashimoto, M., and J. Raisian. 1988. "The Structure and Short-Run Adaptability of Labor Markets in Japan and the United States." In *Employment, Unemployment and Labor Utilization*, edited by R. A. Hart, 314–40. Boston: Unwin Hyman.

Heiner, H. 1988. "Imperfect Decisions and Routinized Production: Implications for Evolutionary Modelling and Inertial Technical Change." In *Technical Change and Economic Theory*, edited by G. Dose et al. London: Pinter Publishers.

Hemmer, E. 1988. *Sozialplanpraxis in der Bundesrepublik: Eine empirische Untersuchung.* Cologne: Deutscher Instituts-Verlag.

Hoeland, A. 1983. "Das Verhalten von Betriebsraeten in der Kuendigungssituation." In *Kuendigungspraxis, Kuendigungsschutz und Probleme der Arbeitsgerichtsbarkeit*, vol. 45, *Beitraege zur sozialwissenschaftlichen Forschung*, edited by R. Ellermann-Witt et al., 67–84. Opladen: Westdeutscher Verlag.

Hofmann, C., et al. 1991. "Developments in the Labor Market in the Community— Results of a Survey Covering Employers and Employees." *European Economy* 47 (March): 7–49.

Holmlund, B. 1986. "A New Look at Vacancies and Hirings in Swedish Industry." Mimeo.

Holzer, H. H. 1987. "Hiring Procedures in the Firm." In *Human Resources and the Performance of the Firm*, edited by M. M. Kleiner et al., 243–94. Madison, Wisc.: Industrial Relations Research Association.

———. 1990. "Wages, Employer Costs and Employee Performance in the Firm." *Industrial and Labor Relations Review* 43 (Feb.): 147–64.

Hooper, P., and K. A. Larin. 1989. "International Comparisons of Labor Costs in Manufacturing." *Review of Income and Wealth* 35 (Dec.): 335–55.

Horvath, F. W. 1982. "Job Tenure of Workers in January 1981." *Monthly Labor Review* 105 (Sept.): 34–36.

Hosios, A. J. 1986. "Layoffs, Recruitment, and Interfirm Mobility." *Journal of Labor Economics* 4 (4): 473–502.

Hotz-Hart, B. 1989. *Modernisierung von Unternehmen und Industrien bei unterschiedlichen industriellen Beziehungen.* Bern: Haupt.

Hounshell, D. A. 1984. *From the American System to Mass Production, 1800–1932.* Baltimore: Johns Hopkins University Press.

House of Commons (HC) Select Committee on Employment. 1985. *Report on Wages Councils.* HC no. 254. London: HMSO.

Houseman, S. 1991. *Industrial Restructuring with Job Security: The Case of European Steel.* Cambridge, Mass.: Harvard University Press.

Howland, M. 1988. *Plant Closings and Worker Displacement: The Regional Issues.* Kalamazoo, Mich.: W. E. Upjohn Institute.

Hsing, Y. 1989. "Testing for the Flexible Employment Elasticity Hypothesis: Application of an Expanded Box-Cox Model to U.S. Manufacturing." *Quarterly Review of Economics and Business,* 29 (Summer): 96–107.

Huber, P. W., and **R. E. Litan, eds.** 1991. *The Liability Maze.* Washington, D. C.: Brookings Institution.

Hyman, R. 1978. "Pluralism, Procedural Consensus and Collective Bargaining." *British Journal of Industrial Relations* 16 (1): 16–40.

————. 1989. *The Political Economy of Industrial Relations: Theory and Practice in a Cold Climate.* London: Macmillan.

Ichniowski, C., and **D. Lewin.** 1987. "Grievance Procedures and Firm Performance," In *Human Resources and the Performance of the Firm,* edited by M. Kleiner et al., 159–93. Madison, Wisc.: Industrial Relations Research Association.

Inagami, T. 1988. *Japanese Workplace Industrial Relations.* Japanese Industrial Relations Series no. 14. Tokyo: Japan Institute of Labor.

Incomes Data Services. 1990. *Flexibility at Work.* Study no. 454.

Institut der deutschen Wirtschaft. 1990. "Der Arbeitsmarkt." *Informationsdienst des Instituts der deutschen Wirtschaft,* Jan. 11, 3.

Instituto Centrale di Statistica. *Annuario di statistica del lavoro.* Various volumes.

International Organization of Employers, ed. 1985. *Adapting the Labour Market.* Geneva.

Jackman, R., R. Layard, and **C. Pissarides.** 1989. "On Vacancies." *Oxford Bulletin of Economics and Statistics* 51: 377–94.

Jacoby, S. N. 1982. "The Duration of Indefinite Employment Contracts in the United States and England." *Comparative Labor Law* 5 (Winter): 85–128.

————. 1984. "The Development of Internal Labor Markets in American Manufacturing Firms." In *Internal Labor Markets,* edited by P. Osterman, 23–69. Cambridge, Mass.: MIT Press.

————. 1985a. *Employing Bureaucracy.* New York: Columbia University Press.

————. 1985b. "Progressive Discipline in American Industry: Its Origins, Development, and Consequences." *Advances in Industrial and Labor Relations* 3: 213–60.

————. 1990a. "The New Institutionalism: What Can It Learn from the Old?" In *The Economics of Human Resource Management,* edited by D. J. B. Mitchell and M. A. Zaidi, 172–90. Cambridge, Mass.: Basil Blackwell.

————. 1990b. "Norms and Cycles: The Dynamics of Non-Union Industrial Relations in the United States, 1897–1987." In *New Developments in the Labor Market: Toward a New Institutional Paradigm,* edited by K. G. Abraham and R. B. McKersie, 19–56. Cambridge, Mass.: MIT Press.

Jacoby, S. N., and D. J. B. Mitchell. 1990. "Sticky Stories: Economic Explanations of Employment and Wage Rigidity." *American Economic Review* 80 (May): 33–37.

Jaikumar, R. 1986. "Post-Industrial Manufacturing." *Harvard Business Review,* Nov.–Dec. 69–76.

Japan Ministry of Labour. 1986. *1984 Yearbook of Labour Statistics.* Tokyo.

Javanovic, B. 1979. "Job Matching and the Theory of Turnover." *Journal of Political Economy* 89 (5): 972–90.

Javillier, J.-C. 1986. "Ordre, juridique, relations professionnelles et flexibilité: Approches comparatives internationales." *Droit social* 1: 56–65.

Jeammaud, A. 1983. "Les lois Auroux: Plus de droit ou un autre droit?" *Critiques de l'economie politiques* 23–24 (April/Sept.): 223–43.

————. 1986. "Flexibilité: Le procès du droit du travail." In *Flexibilité du droit du travail: objectif ou realité,* 23–54. Paris: Editions Legislatives et Administratives.

Jefferson, M. 1990. "The Effects of Equal Value Claims on Businesses." *Industrial Relations Journal* 21 (Spring): 7–13.

Johnson, T., K. P. Dickinson, and R. West. 1985. "An Evaluation of the Impact of ES Referrals on Applicant Earnings." *Journal of Human Resources* 20 (Winter): 117–38.

Joll, C., et al. 1983. *Developments in Labor Market Analysis.* London: Allen and Unwin.

Jorgenson, D. W., and J. A. Stephenson. 1967. "The Time Structure of Investment Behavior in U. S. Manufacturing, 1947–1960." *Review of Economics and Statistics* 99 (Feb.): 16–27.

Kahn, C. 1985. "Optimal Severance Pay with Incomplete Information." *Journal of Political Economy* 93: 435–50.

Kahn-Freund, O. 1954. "Legal Framework." In *The System of Industrial Relations in Great Britain,* edited by A. D. Flanders and H. A. Clegg, 42–127. Oxford: Basil Blackwell.

————. 1983. *Labour and the Law.* 3d ed. London: P. Davies and M. Freedland.

Katz, H. 1985. *Shifting Gears.* Cambridge, Mass.: MIT Press.

Katz, H., T. Kochan, and W. Keefe. 1987. "Industrial Relations and Productivity in the U.S. Auto Industry." In *Brookings Papers on Economic Activity, Special Issue on Microeconomics,* 3:685–715. Washington, D.C.

Katz, L. F., and L. H. Summers. 1989. "Industry Rents: Evidence and Implications."

In *Brookings Papers on Economic Activity: Microeconomics:* 209–90. Washington, D.C.: Brookings Institution.

Kaufman, R. 1979. "Why the U. S. Unemployment Rate Is So High." In *Unemployment and Inflation: Institutionalist and Structuralist Views,* edited by M. J. Piore, 155–69. White Plains, N.Y.: M. E. Sharpe.

Kayser, G., and **C. Friede.** 1984. *Wirkungsanalyse der Sozialgesetzgebung.* Bonn: Institut fuer Mittelstandsforschung.

Kelly, J. 1988. *Trade Unions and Socialist Politics.* London: Verso.

Kennedy, P. E. 1981. "Estimation with Correctly Interpreted Dummy Variables in Semilogarithmic Equations." *American Economic Review* 71 (Sept.): 801–24.

Keynes, J. M. 1973. *The Collected Writings of J. M. Keynes.* Vol. 7, *The General Theory of Employment, Interest and Money.* London: Macmillan.

Klauder, W. 1989. "Arbeitsmarkt und Ausscheiden aelterer Arbeitnehmer aus dem Erwerbsleben: gegenwaertige und zukuenftige Tendenzen und Probleme." *Sozialer Fortschritt* 38 (4): 85–95.

Kochan, T. A., H. Katz, and **R. B. McKersie.** 1986. *The Transformation of American Industrial Relations.* New York: Basic Books.

Kochan, T. A., D. P. McDuffie, and **P. Osterman.** 1988. "Employment Security in a Changing Environment: A Case Study of Digital Equipment Corporation." *Human Resource Management* 27: 121–44.

Kochan, T. A., and **R. B. McKersie.** 1989. "Future Directions for American Labor and Human Resource Policy." *Relations Industrielles* 44 (1): 224–44.

Koenig, H., and **K. F. Zimmermann.** 1985. *Determinants of Employment Policy of German Manufacturing Firms: A Survey-Based Evaluation.* Discussion Paper no. 302–85. Mannheim: Institut fuer Volkswirtschaftslehre und Statistik, University of Mannheim.

Koike, K. 1984. "Skill Formation Systems in the U. S. and Japan: A Comparative Study." In *The Economic Analysis of the Japanese Firm,* edited by M. Aoki, 47–75. Amsterdam: North Holland.

———. 1987a. "Human Resource Development and Labor Management Relations." In *The Political Economy of Japan,* edited by K. Yamamura and Y. Yasuba. Vol. 1, *The Domestic Transformation,* 289–330. Stanford: Stanford University Press.

———. 1987b. "Japanese Redundancy: The Impact of Key Labor Market Institutions on the Economic Flexibility of the Japanese Economy." In *Labor Market Adjustments in the Pacific Basin,* edited by P. T. Chinloy and E. W. Stromsdorfer, 79–101. Boston: Kluwer-Nijhoff.

———. 1990. "Intellectual Skill and the Role of Employees as Constituent Members of Large Firms in Contemporary Japan," In *The Firm as a Nexus of Treaties,* edited by M. Aoki et al., 185–208. Newbury Park, Calif.: Sage.

Kokkelenberg, E., and **D. Sockell.** 1985. "Union Membership in the United States, 1973–81." *Industrial and Labor Relations Review* 39 (4): 497–543.

Kolstad, C. D., et al. 1990. "Ex-Post Liability for Harm versus Ex-Ante Safety Regulation: Substitutes or Complements?" *American Economic Review* 80 (Sept.): 888–901.

Koshiro, K. 1984. "Lifetime Employment in Japan: Three Models of the Concept." *Monthly Labor Review* 107 (Aug.) 34–35.

Krafcik, J. 1988. "High Performance Manufacturing: An International Study of Auto Assembly Practice." MIT International Motor Vehicle Program. Mimeo.

Kraft, K. 1988. "Sind die Beschaeftigungsverhaeltnisse in der Bundesrepublik ueber Zeit inflexibler geworden?" In *Zeitschrift fuer Betriebswirtschaft (ZfB), Ergaenzungsheft* 2: 7–15.

———. 1991. "The Incentive Effects of Dismissals, Efficiency Wages, Piece Rates, and Profit Sharing." *Review of Economics and Statistics* 73 (Aug.): 451–59.

Kravaritou-Manitakis, Y. 1988. *New Forms of Work: Labour Law and Social Security Aspects in the European Community.* Dublin: European Foundation for the Improvement of Living and Working Conditions.

Kronberger Kreis, W. Engels, et al., eds. 1986. *Mehr Markt im Arbeitsrecht.* Vol. 10, *Schriftenreihe des Kronberger Kreises,* Bad Homburg.

Krueger, A. B. 1988. "The Evolution of Unjust-Dismissal Legislation in the U.S." Princeton University Industrial Relations Section. Mimeo.

———. 1991. "The Evolution of Unjust Dismissal Legislation in the United States." *Industrial and Labor Relations Review* 44 (4): 644–60.

Krueger, A. B., and L. H. Summers. 1988. "Efficiency Wages and the Inter-Industry Wage Structure." *Econometrica* 56 (March): 259–93.

Kuechle, H. 1990. "Kuendigungsvorschriften im europaeischen Vergleich." *WSI-Mitteilungen* 43 (June): 392–400.

Lafont, J., D. Leborgne, and **A. Lipietz.** 1982. *Redéploiement industriel et espace économique: Une étude inter-sectorielle comparative.* Paris: CEPREMAP.

Langlois, P. 1989. "Les usages." In *Les transformations du Droit du travail,* 285–98. Paris: Dalloz.

Langlois, R. M. 1986. "Rationality, Institutions, and Explanation." In *Essays in the New Institutional Economics,* edited by R. M. Langlois, 225–55. Cambridge: Cambridge University Press.

Layard, R. 1986. *How to Beat Unemployment.* Oxford: Oxford University Press.

Layard, R. and L. Calmfors, eds. 1987. *The Fight Against Unemployment.* Cambridge, Mass.: MIT Press.

Layard, R., and **S. Nickell.** 1985. *The Causes of British Unemployment.* Discussion Paper no. 204. London: Center for Labour Economics, London School of Economics.

———. 1986a. "The Performance of the British Labour Market." Discussion paper no. 249. London: Centre for Labour Economics, London School of Economics.

———. 1986b. "Unemployment in Britain." Discussion Paper no. 240. London: Centre for Labour Economics, London School of Economics.

Lazear, E. P. 1979. "Why Is There Mandatory Retirement?" *Journal of Political Economy* 87: 1261–84.

———. 1981. "Agency, Earnings Profiles, Productivity, and Hours Restrictions." *American Economic Review* 71 (Sept.): 606–20.

———. 1987. "Job Security and Unemployment." Hoover Institution, Stanford University. Mimeo.

———. 1988. "Employment-at-Will, Job Security, and Work Incentives." In *Employment, Unemployment, and Labor Utilization*, edited by R. A. Hart, 39–61. Boston: Unwin Hyman.

———. 1990. "Job Security Provisions and Employment." *Quarterly Journal of Economics* 105 (Aug.): 699–726.

Leborgne, D. 1987. *Vers de nouvelles formes d'organisation et de concurrence?* Report CGP-CEPREMAP. Paris: CEPREMAP.

Leibenstein, H. 1976. *Beyond Economic Man: A New Foundation for Microeconomics.* Cambridge, Mass.: Harvard University Press.

Leija, R., T. Santamaki-Vuore, and **G. Standing.** 1990. *Unemployment and Labour Market Flexibility: Finland.* Geneva: International Labour Office.

Leonard, A. S. 1988. "A New Common Law of Employment Termination." *North Carolina Law Review* 66: 631–86.

Leonard, J. 1987. "In the Wrong Place at the Wrong Time: The Extent of Frictional and Structural Unemployment." In *Unemployment and the Structure of Labor Markets*, edited by K. Lang and J. Leonard, 141–63. New York: Basil Blackwell.

Leslie, D. L. 1989. "Economic Analyses of Labor Law." In *Proceedings of the Forty-first Annual Meeting of the Industrial Relations Research Association*, edited by B. D. Dennis, 227–35. Madison, Wisc.: Industrial Relations Research Association.

Letts, S. J. 1989. "Cox versus Resilient Flooring Division of Congoleum: An Attempt to Clarify Wrongful Termination under California Law." *Industrial Relations Law Journal* 2 (1): 66–72.

Levine, D. J. 1989. "Just-Cause Employment Policies When Unemployment Is a Worker Discipline Device." *American Economic Review* 79: 902–5.

———. 1991. "Just-Cause Employment Policies in the Presence of Worker Adverse Selection." *Journal of Labor Economics* 9 (3): 294–305.

———. 1992. "Demand Variability and Work Organization." In *Democracy and Markets: Problems of Participation, Democracy, and Efficiency*, edited by S. M. Bowles, H. Gintis, and B. Gustafsson. Cambridge: Cambridge University Press.

Levine, D. J., and **L. D'Andrea-Tyson.** 1990. "Participation, Productivity, and the Firm's Environment." In *Paying for Productivity: A Look at the Evidence*, edited by A. S. Blinder, 183–243. Washington, D. C.: Brookings Institution.

Lewis, P. 1981. "Employment Protection: A Preliminary Assessment of the Law of Unfair Dismissal." *Industrial Relations Journal* 12 (March-April): 19–29.

———. 1986. "The Role of the Law in Employment Relations." In *Labour Law in Britain*, edited by R. Lewis, 3–43. Oxford: Basil Blackwell.

———. 1989. "Unfair Dismissal and Tribunals." In *A Handbook of Industrial Relations Practice*, edited by B. Towers, 319–44. London: Kogan Page.

Lilien, D. 1980. "The Cyclical Pattern of Temporary Layoffs in U.S. Manufacturing." *Review of Economics and Statistics* 62 (Feb.): 24–31.

Lindbeck, A., and D. Snower. 1986. "Wage Setting, Unemployment, and Insider-Outsider Relations." *American Economic Review* 76: 235–39.

———. 1988a. *The Insider-Outsider Theory of Employment and Unemployment.* Cambridge, Mass.: MIT Press.

———. 1988b. "Job Security, Work Incentives, and Unemployment." *Scandinavian Journal of Economics* 90 (4): 453–74.

Litan, R. E., and C. Winston. 1988. *Liability: Perspectives and Policy.* Washington, D.C.: Brookings Institution.

Long, N. V., and H. Siebert. 1983. "Lay-Off Restraints and the Demand for Labour." *Zeitschrift fuer die gesamte Staatswissenschaft* 139: 612–24.

Lundvall, B. A. 1989. "Innovation, the Organized Market and the Productivity Slow-Down." Paper presented at the international OECD seminar "Science, Technology and Economic Growth," Paris, June.

Lusterman, S. 1986. *Corporate Training.* New York: Conference Board.

Lutz, B. 1984. *Der kurze Traum immerwaehrender Prosperitaet.* Frankfurt: Campus.

———. 1987. *Arbeitsmarktstruktur und betriebliche Arbeitskraeftestrategie: Eine theoretisch-historische Skizze zur Entstehung betriebszentrierter Arbeitsmarktsegmentation.* Frankfurt: Campus.

———. 1989. "Normality, Crisis, or Stagnation: Reflections on the Current State of Capitalist Economies." In *Political Regulation in the "Great Crisis,"* edited by W. Vaeth, 13–23. Berlin: Sigma.

———. 1991a. "The Contradiction of Post-Taylorist Rationalization and the Uncertain Future of Industrial Work." In *Technology and Work in German Industry*, edited by N. Altmann et al. Frankfurt: Campus.

———. 1991b. "Education and Job Hierarchies: Contrasting Evidence from France and Germany." In *Technology and Work in German Industry*, edited by N. Altmann et al. Frankfurt: Campus.

Lutz, B., and F. Weltz. 1966. *Der zwischenbetriebliche Arbeitsplatzwechsel: Zur Soziologie und Soziooekonomie der Berufsmobilitaet.* Eschborn: RKW.

Lutz, B., et al. 1973. *Arbeitswirtschaftliche Modelluntersuchung eines Arbeitsmarktes.* Eschborn: RKW.

Lyon-Caen, A. 1989. "Changement politique et changement du droit du travail." In *Les transformations du droit du travail*, 1–10. Paris: Dalloz.

Lyon-Caen, A., and **A. Jeammaud.** 1986. *Droit du travail, democratie et crise.* Arles: Actes Sud.

McCarthy, W. 1981. "What Can We Do about Unemployment?" *Industrial Relations Journal* 12 (Nov.-Dec.): 5–9.

McCormick, B., and **G. P. Marshall.** 1985. "Minimum Wages and Unemployment: The Reform of the Wages Councils." *Industrial Relations Journal* 16 (Winter): 38–46.

McIlroy, J. 1988. *Trade Unions in Britain Today.* Manchester: Manchester University Press.

MacInnes, J. 1987. *Thatcherism at Work.* Milton Keynes: Open University Press.

Mackay, D. I., et al. 1971. *Labour Markets under Different Employment Conditions.* London: Allen and Unwin.

McKersie, R. 1989. "Comment." In *Proceedings of the Forty-first Annual Meeting of the Industrial Relations Research Association,* edited by B. D. Dennis, 439–44. Madison, Wisc.: Industrial Relations Research Association.

McKersie, R., ed. 1982. *Plant Closings: Public or Private Choices?* Washington, D.C.: Cato Institute.

Maddison, A. 1982. *Les phases du développement capitaliste.* Paris: Economica.

Makeham, P. 1980. *Youth Unemployment.* Department of Employment Research Paper no. 10. London.

Manes, C., and **D. Rosenbloom.** 1985. "Terminating At-Will Employees: Rethinking the Statutory Approach," Ph. D. diss., Harvard Law School.

Mansfield, E. 1988. "Industrial R&D in Japan and the United States: A Comparative Study." *American Economic Review* 78: 223–28.

Marchand. O. 1989. "Emploi, offre de travail et chômage dans les principaux pays développés: Les effets de la crise." *Economie et statistique* 220 (April): 35–45.

Marchand O., and **E. Martin-Le-Goff.** 1987. "Stabilité de l'emploi mais reprise du chômage en 1986." *Economie et statistique* 198 (April): 3–13.

Marks, D. 1984. "Incomplete Experience Rating in State Unemployment Insurance." *Monthly Labor Review* 107 (Nov.) 45–52.

Marsden, D. 1986. *The End of Economic Man? Custom and Competition in Labor Markets.* New York: St. Martin's Press.

Marsden, D., and **R. Richardson**, eds. 1986. "Youth Employment: A Symposium." *British Journal of Industrial Relations* 24 (March): 83–102.

Marshall, A. 1920. *Principles of Economics: An Introductory Volume.* 8th ed. London: Macmillan.

Martini, M. 1979. *La mobilità del lavoro in Lombardia, Italia e nei paesi europei.* Milan: ReR.

Maruani, M., E. Reynaud. and C. Romani, eds. 1989. *La flexibilité en Italie.* Paris: Syros.

Maume, D. J., Jr. 1991. "Child-Care Expenditures and Women's Employment Turnover." *Social Forces* 70 (2): 495–508.

Maurau, G. 1988. "Formes d'emploi et flexibilité: Une comparaison France/Royaume-Uni." *La note de l'IRES* 15: 1–10.

Maurau, G., and **M. Okba.** 1986–87. "Précarisation, désindexation et flexibilité: Un essai d'analyse du cas européen." *La note de l'IRES* 10 (Oct.): 3–16 and 11 (Jan.): 18–28.

Maurau G., and **J. Oudinet.** 1988. "Précarité et flexibilité: Un essai de comparaison des industries européennes." *La note de l'IRES* 18: 4–17.

Mendelsohn, S. R. 1989. "Wrongful Termination Litigation in the U.S. and Its Effect on the Employment Relationship." OECD Working Party on Industrial Relations. Mimeo.

Merle, V. 1987. "Transformations du marché du travail et transformation de l'intervention publique." *Les temps modernes* 496–97 (Nov.–Dec.): 233–53.

———. 1989. "Les nouvelles formes d'emploi en France." *Travail et emploi* 39: 25–31.

Merrilees, W., and **R. Wilson.** "Disequilibrium in the Labour Market for Young People in Great Britain." Manpower Research Group Discussion Paper no. 10. University of Warwick.

Metcalf, D. 1982. *Alternatives to Unemployment: Special Employment Measures in Britain.* Report no. 610. London: Policy Studies Institute.

———. 1987a. "Labour Market Flexibility and Jobs: A Survey of Evidence from OECD Countries with Special Reference to Europe." In *The Fight against Unemployment: Macroeconomic Papers from the Center for European Studies,* edited by R. Layard and L. Calmfors, 48–76. Cambridge, Mass.: MIT Press.

———. 1987b. "Trade Unions and Economic Performance: The British Evidence." In *Labour Relations and Economic Performance,* edited by R. Brunetta and C. Dell'Aringa, 283–303. Basingstoke: Macmillan.

Meyer, D. 1989. "Der Bestandsschutz im Arbeitsverhaeltnis als oekonomisches Gut. Ansaetze zu einer effizienten Regelung," *Jahrbuch fuer Nationaloekonomie und Statistik* 206 (3): 208–24.

Miller, R. 1971. "The Reserve Labor Hypothesis." *Economic Journal* 81 (March): 17–35.

Millward, N., and **M. Stevens.** 1987. *British Workplace Industrial Relations, 1980–1984: The DE/ESRC/PSI/ACAS Surveys.* Aldershot: Gower Press.

MIMOSA. 1990. "Mimosa, une modélisation de l'économie mondiale." *Observations et diagnostics economiques: Revue de l'OFCE* 30 (Jan.): 137–98.

Minford, P. 1985. *Unemployment: Cause and Cure.* Oxford: Basil Blackwell.

Ministère du Travail. 1981. *Rapport sur le droit des travailleurs.* Paris: La Documentation Française.

Ministère du Travail, de l'Emploi et de la Formation Professionnelle. 1988. "Politiques d'emploi." In *Structures du marché du travail et politiques d'emploi,* 49–87. Paris: Syros.

―――. 1989. *Le recours au travail temporaire et à durée determinée et ses conséquences sur le marché du travail.* Parliamentary report. Paris: Ministère du Travail, de l'Emploi et de la Formation Professionnelle.

Ministère du Travail, de l'Emploi et de la Formation Professionnelle, ed. *Statistiques du travail.* Various volumes.

Ministero del Lavoro e della Previdenza sociale. 1988. *Report 1987: Labour and Employment Policies in Italy.* Rome.

Mintzberg, H. 1978. "Patterns in Strategy Formation." *Management Science* 24 (9): 934–48.

Mitnick, B. M. 1980. *The Political Economy of Regulation.* New York: Columbia University Press.

Modigliani-Tarantelli, P. 1979. "Structural and Transitory Determinants of Labor Mobility: 'Hold's' Conjecture and Italian Experience." *BNL Quarterly Review,* Sept., 205–18.

Molitor, B. 1986. "Sozialpolitik in der Marktwirtschaft." *Ordo* 37: 559–71.

Mosley, H. 1991. "Evaluation of Employment Protection Regulation: Policy Regimes of Employment Security in France, Germany, Italy and the United Kingdom." Report prepared for the Commission of the European Communities. Wissenschaftszentrum Berlin fuer Sozialforschung. Mimeo.

Mumford, P. 1975. *Redundancy and Security of Employment.* Aldershot: Gower Press.

Muramatsu, K. 1983. *The Analysis of the Japanese Labor Market* (in Japanese). Tokyo: Hakutoushobou.

Naegele, G. 1983. *Arbeitnehmer in der Spaetphase der Erwerbstaetigkeit. Forschungsberichte,* edited by the Federal Ministry of Labor and Social Affairs (BMA). Bonn: BMA.

―――. 1988. "Fruehverrentung in der Bundesrepublik Deutschland." In *Arbeit—Freizeit—Lebenszeit: Neue Uebergaenge im Lebenszyklus,* edited by L. Rosenmayr and F. Kolland, 207–32. Opladen: Westdeutscher Verlag.

Nakamura, J. 1983. "The Role of the Labour Market for Solving the Problem of Stagflation." *Economic Studies Quarterly* 34 (Aug.): 147–55 (in Japanese).

―――. 1984. "Macroeconomic Policy and Employment-Unemployment" (in Japanese). In *Contemporary Unemployment,* edited by K. Koike, 175–200. Tokyo: Dobunkan.

National Conference of Commissioners on Uniform State Laws. 1990. "Draft Uniform Employment-Termination Act." *Individual Employment Rights Manual* 70 (Oct. 22): 21–36.

Neef, A., and **C. Kask.** 1991. "Manufacturing Productivity and Labor Costs in Fourteen Economies." *Monthly Labor Review* 114 (12): 24–37.

Nelson, R. 1989. "First Synthesis of the Presentations and Debates." Paper presented at the international OECD seminar "Science, Technology and Economic Growth," Paris, June.

Nerb, G. 1978. "Beschaeftigungspolitische Verhaltensweisen der Unternehmen—Ergebnisse von IFO-Umfragen." *IFO-Schnelldienst* 18–19: 72–78.

————. 1986. "Employment Problems: Views of Businessmen and the Workforce—Results of an Employee and Employer Survey on Labour Market Issues in the Member States." *European Economy* 27 (March): 13–110.

Nerb, G., et al. 1977. "Struktur, Entwicklung und Bestimmungsgroessen der Beschaeftigung in Industrie und Bauwirtschaft auf mittlere Sicht." *Mitteilungen aus der Arbeitsmarkt- und Berufsforschung (MittAB)* 2: 291–310.

Neumann, G., and **E. Rissman.** 1984. "Where Have All the Union Members Gone?" *Journal of Labor Economics* 22 (April): 175–92.

Nickell, S. J. 1978. "Fixed Costs, Employment and Labour Demand over the Cycle." *Economica* 45: 329–45.

————. 1979. "Unemployment and the Structure of Labour Costs." In *Policies for Employment, Prices and Exchange Rates*, edited by K. Brunner and A. H. Meltzer, *Journal of Monetary Economics* Supplement, 187–222. Carnegie-Rochester Conference Series on Public Policy no. 11.

————. 1982. "The Determinants of Equilibrium Unemployment in Britain." *Economic Journal* 92 (Sept.): 555–75.

————. 1986. "Dynamic Models of Labour Demand." In *Handbook of Labor Economics*, edited by O. Ashenfelter and R. Layard, vol. 1, 473–522. New York: North Holland.

Nickell, S. J., and **S. Wadhwani.** 1989. "Insider Forces and Wage Determination," Discussion Paper no. 334. Centre for Labour Economics, London School of Economics. Mimeo.

Nord, S., and **Y. Ting.** 1991. "The Impact of Advance Notice of Plant Closings on Earnings and the Probability of Unemployment." *Industrial and Labor Relations Review* 44 (July): 681–91.

Noyelle, T. 1987. *Beyond Industrial Dualism.* Boulder, Colo.: Westview Press.

Nutzinger, H. G. 1988. "Employee Participation by Co-Determination, Labor Law and Collective Bargaining." In *Management under Differing Labour Market and Employment Systems*, edited by G. Dlugos et al., 301–12. Berlin and New York: de Gruyter.

O'Donnell, J. 1987. "Brownfields, Transplants, and New Entrants: The Overcapacity Problem." Working paper. MIT International Motor Vehicle Program.

OECD. 1983. *Employment Outlook 1983.* Paris.

————. 1984. *Employment Outlook 1984.* Paris.

————. 1985. *Employment Outlook 1985.* Paris.

————. 1986a. *Employment Outlook 1986.* Paris.

————. 1986b. *Flexibility in the Labour Market: The Current Debate. A Technical Report.* Paris.

———. 1987. *Employment Outlook 1987.* Paris.

———. 1988a. *Employment Outlook 1988.* Paris.

———. 1988b. *Structural Adjustments and Economic Performance.* Paris.

———. 1989a. *Economies in Transition: Structural Adjustment in OECD Countries.* Paris.

———. 1989b. *Employment Outlook 1989.* Paris.

———. 1989c. "The Future of Social Protection." Report on a Meeting of Trade Union Experts Held under the OECD Labour Management Programme, Paris, October.

———. 1989d. "Working Party on Industrial Relations: Social Aspects of New Technologies." MAS/WP3 (89). Mimeo.

———. 1989e. *Les perspectives economiques de l'OCDE* 45.

———. 1990a. *Employment Outlook 1990.* Paris.

———. 1990b. "Manpower and Social Affairs Committee: A New Framework for Labour Market Policies." Draft general report.

———. 1990c. "The Role of Indicators in Structural Surveillance." Working Paper no. 72. Department of Economics and Statistics.

Oechsler, W. A. 1988. "Employee-Severance—Regulations and Procedures." In *Management under Differing Labour Market and Employment Systems,* edited by G. Dlugos et al., 397–410. Berlin and New York: de Gruyter.

Offe, C. 1985. *"Disorganized Capitalism: Contemporary Transformations of Work and Politics.* Cambridge: Polity Press.

Offe, C., and K. Hinrichs. 1984. "Sozialoekonomie des Arbeitsmarktes: Primaeres und sekundaeres Machtgefaelle." In *Arbeitsgesellschaft: Strukturprobleme und Zukunftsperspektiven,* edited by C. Offe, 44–86. Frankfurt: Campus.

Oi, W. Y. 1962. "Labor as a Quasi-Fixed Factor." *Journal of Political Economy* 70 (Dec.): 538–50.

Okun, A. M. 1975. "Inflation: Its Mechanics and Welfare Costs." *Brookings Papers on Economic Activity* 2: 351–90.

———. 1981. *Prices and Quantities: A Macroeconomic Analysis.* Washington, D.C.: Brookings Institution.

Osterman, P. 1985. "White-Collar Employment." In *Challenges and Choices Facing American Labor,* edited by T. Kochan. Cambridge, Mass.: MIT Press.

———. 1987. "Turnover, Employment Security, and the Performance of the Firm." In *Human Resources and the Performance of the Firm,* edited by M. M. Kleiner, 275–317. Madison, Wisc.: Industrial Relations Research Association.

———. 1988a. *Employment Futures: Reorganization, Dislocation, and Public Policy.* New York: Oxford University Press.

———. 1988b. "Employment Systems in the United States: Competing Models and Contingent Employment." Paper presented at Conference, Alternative Forms of Employment, Paris, September.

————. 1989. "New Technology and the Organization of Work: A Review of the Issues." In *The Challenge of New Technology to Labor Management Relations*, edited by D. Mowery and B. Henderson, 5–17. Washington, D.C.: U.S. Department of Labor.

————. 1990. "Permanent Turnover and Internal Labor Markets: A New Approach for Modeling and Measurement." Sloan School of Management. Mimeo.

————. 1991. The Impact of IT on Jobs and Skills," In *The Corporation of the 1990s*, edited by M. S. Morton, 220–43. New York: Oxford University Press.

Osterman, P., and T. A. Kochan. 1990. "Employment Security and Employment Policy: An Assessment of the Issues." In *New Developments in the Labor Market: Toward a New Institutional Paradigm*, edited by K. G. Abraham and R. B. McKersie, 155–82. Cambridge, Mass.: MIT Press.

Osterman, P., et al. 1988. "Employment Security in a Changing Environment: A Case Study of Digital Equipment Corporation." *Human Resource Management* 27: 121–44.

Ott, C. 1972. "Die soziale Effektivitaet des Rechts bei der sozialen Kontrolle der Wirtschaft." In *Zur Effektivitaet des Rechts, Jahrbuch fuer Rechtssoziologie und Rechtstheorie*, edited by M. Rehbinder and H. Schelsky, 3: 345–408. Dusseldorf: Bertelsmann Universitaetsverlag.

Padoa-Schioppa, F. 1988. "Underemployment Benefit Effects on Employment and Income Distribution: What We Should Learn from the System of the Cassa Integrazione Guadagni." *Labour* 2 (2): 101–24.

Palmer, S., ed., 1990. *Determining Pay: A Guide to the Issues*. London: Institute of Personnel Management.

Parker, S. R., C. G. Thomas. N. D. Ellis, and **W. E. J. McCarthy.** 1971. *Effects of the Redundancy Payments Act*. London: HMSO.

Patel, P., and L. Soete. 1987. *The Contribution of Science and Technology to Economic Growth: A Critical Reappraisal of Evidence*. Paris: OECD.

Pelissier, J. 1985. "La relation de travail atypique." *Droit social* 7: 531–39.

Perreaux, P. 1987. "Les licenciements économiques au cours du troisième trimestre 1986." *Dossiers statistiques du travail et de l'emploi*, July, 5–13.

Pick, P. 1988. *Betriebliche Beschaeftigungspolitik und Arbeitsmarktstruktur: Eine theoretische und empirische Untersuchung des betrieblichen Beschaeftigungsverhaltens in der arbeitsmarktpolitischen Problemregion Duisburg/Oberhausen*. Regensburg: Transfer.

Piore, M. J. 1980. "Economic Fluctuations, Job Security, and Labor Market Duality in Italy, France, and the U.S.." *Politics and Society* 9 (4): 379–408.

————. 1986. "Perspectives on Labor Market Flexibility." *Industrial Relations* 25 (2): 146–65.

————. 1988. "Travail, action et metier: L'expérience du travail dans le système de production flexible." Paper presented at colloquium, Logiques d'entreprise et formes de legitimite, Association PROTEE, Paris, January.

————. 1989. "The Evolution of Business Strategy and Low Wage Work in the U.S.."

In *Flexibility and Labor Markets in Canada and the U.S.*, edited by G. Laflamme et al., 163–72. Geneva: International Labour Office.

Piore, M. J., and **C. Sabel.** 1984. *The Second Industrial Divide: Possibilities for Prosperity.* New York: Basic Books.

Podgursky, M., and **P. Swaim.** 1987a. "Duration of Joblessness following Displacement." *Industrial Relations* 26 (Fall): 213–26.

————. 1987b. "Job Displacement and Earnings Loss: Evidence from the Displaced Worker Survey." *Industrial and Labor Relations Review* 41 (Oct.): 17–29.

Pollert, A. 1987. "The Flexible Firm: A Model in Search of Reality." University of Warwick Papers in Industrial Relations no. 19.

Poret, P. 1986. "La formation sectorielle des salaires dans cinq économies européennes: Premiers résultats d'une étude statistique." Document de travail no. 86–7. Direction de la Prévision.

Posner, R. A. 1984. "Some Economics of Labor Law." *University of Chicago Law Review* 51: 988–89.

Preller, L. 1978. *Sozialpolitik in der Weimarer Republik.* Hamburg: Athenaeum.

Pries, L., and **R. Trinczek.** 1989. "Modernization of Manufacture in the FRG: Management Strategies at a Time of Change in Technology, Work Organisation and Personnel Policy." Paper presented at the International OECD conference "Technological Change as a Social Process: Society, Enterprises and the Individual," Helsinki, December.

Pristin, Terry. 1991. "Job Loss Suits Take New Twist." *Los Angeles Times*, Oct. 16, A1.

Quandt, R. E., and **H. S. Rosen.** 1989. "Endogenous Output in an Aggregate Model of the Labor Market." *Review of Economics and Statistics* 71 (Aug.): 394–400.

Raff, D. R. 1988. "Efficiency Wage Theory, the Intra- and Inter-Industry Structure of Earnings." Working paper. Harvard University.

Raff, D. R., and **L. H. Summers.** 1987. "Did Henry Ford Pay Efficiency Wages?" *Journal of Labor Economics* 5 (4): 57–86.

Rebitzer, J. B. 1986. "Establishment Size and Job Tenure." *Industrial Relations* 25 (Fall): 292–302.

————. 1987. "Unemployment, Long-Term Employment and Productivity Growth." *Review of Economics and Statistics* 69 (Nov.): 627–35.

————. 1989. "Long-Term Employment Relationships." In *Microeconomic Issues in Labor Economics: New Approaches*, edited by R. Drago and R. Perlman, 16–33. New York: Harvester-Wheatsheaf.

Rebitzer, J. B., and **M. D. Robinson.** 1990. "Employer Size and Dual Labor Markets." Sloan School of Management. Mimeo.

Reich, M., and **J. Devine.** 1981. "The Microeconomics of Conflict and Hierarchy in Capitalist Production." *Review of Radical Political Economics* 12: 27–45.

Reid, F., and G. Swartz. 1982. *Prorating Fringe Benefits for Part-Time Employees in Canada.* Toronto: University of Toronto Industrial Relations Centre.

Reuter, D. 1982. "Reichweite und Grenzen der Legitimitaet des Bestandsschutzes von Arbeitsverhaeltnissen." *Ordo* 33: 165–99.

———. 1985. "Die Rolle des Arbeitsrechts im marktwirtschaftlichen System—Eine Skizze." *Ordo* 36: 51–88.

Reuter, E. 1988. *The Economic Consequences of Expanded Corporate Liability: An Exploratory Study.* Santa Monica, Calif.: Institute of Civil Justice, RAND Corp.

Roberts, K., et al. 1989. *The Changing Structure of Youth Labour Markets.* Department of Employment Research Paper no. 59. London.

Robertson, M. 1989. "Temporary Layoffs and Unemployment in Canada." *Industrial Relations* 28 (Winter): 82–90.

Romani, C. 1987. *La Cassa Integrazione Guadagni: Réalités juridiques, économiques et sociales d'une institution.* Aix-en-Provence: LEST.

Root, L. S. 1987. "Britain's Redundancy Payments for Displaced Workers." *Monthly Labor Review* 110 (June): 18–23.

Rose-Ackerman, S. 1991. "Regulation and the Law of Torts." *American Economic Review* 81 (2): 54–58.

Rosen, S. 1985. "Implicit Contracts: A Survey." *Journal of Economic Literature* 23: 1144–75.

Rosenberg. S. 1989a. "De la segmentation à la flexibilité." *Travail et société* 14 (Oct.): 387–438.

———. 1989b. "Labour Market Restructuring in Europe and the United States: The Search for Flexibility." In *The State and the Labour Market,* edited by S. Rosenberg, 3–22. New York and London: Plenum Press.

Rosow, J. M., and R. Zager. 1984. *Employment Security in a Free Society.* New York: Pergamon Press.

———. 1988. *Training: The Competitive Edge.* San Francisco: Jossey-Bass.

Rowthorn, B. 1989. "Wage Dispersion and Employment in OECD Countries." Paper presented at the international symposium "Making Economies More Efficient and Equitable, Factors Determining Income Distribution," Tokyo, November.

Rowthorn, R. 1975. "What Remains of Kaldor's Law?" *Economic Journal* 85 (March): 10–19.

Rubery, J., et al. 1989. "Government Policy and the Labour Market: The Case of the United Kingdom." In *The State and the Labour Market,* edited by S. Rosenberg, 23–45. New York and London: Plenum Press.

Ruethers, B. 1986. "Arbeitsrecht und Arbeitsmarkt: Das Problem der Verschraenkung oekonomischer Verhaltensweisen und rechtlicher Rahmenbedingungen." In *Zeugen des Wissens,* edited by H. Maier-Leibnitz, 739–82. Mainz: Hase & Kuehnel.

————. 1989a. "Die Rache des Gutgemeinten." *Frankfurter Allgemeine Zeitung* Nov. 11, 15.

————. 1989b. "Gesteigerter Kuendigungsschutz fuer Bummelanten." *Frankfurter Allgemeine Zeitung,* Aug. 2, 10.

Ruhm, C. J. 1987. "The Economic Consequences of Labor Mobility." *Industrial and Labor Relations Review* 41 (Oct.): 30–49.

————. 1989. "Advance Notice and Postdisplacement Joblessness." Boston University. Mimeo.

Runciman, W. G. 1990. "How Many Classes Are There in Contemporary British Society?" *Sociology* 24 (4): 377–96.

Sachverstaendigenrat. 1990. *Jahresgutachten 1989/90 zur gesamtwirtschaftlichen Entwicklung.* Bundestagsdrucksache 11–5786. Bonn.

St. Antoine, T. 1985. "The Revision of Employment-at-Will Enters a New Phase." *Labor Law Journal* 36: 563–67.

Salop, J., and **S. Salop.** 1976. "Self-Selection and Turnover in the Labor Market." *Quarterly Journal of Economics* 90 (Nov.): 619–27.

Savarese, J. 1980. "Protecting At Will Employment against Wrongful Discharge: The Duty to Terminate Only in Good Faith." *Harvard Law Review* 93 (8): 1816–44.

Savatier, J. 1986. "La révocation des avantages resultants des usages de l'entreprise." *Droit social,* 890–905.

Scarpat-Pizzuto-Ferrari. 1984. "Bilancio delle leggi sul lavoro dopo lo Statuto dei lavoratori." *Quaderni della giustizia* 40 (Oct.): 165–83.

Scase, R., and **R. Goffee.** 1980. *The Real World of the Small Business Owner.* London: Croom-Helm.

Scharpf, F. W. 1987. "Grenzen der institutionellen Reform." In *Jahrbuch zur Staats- und Verwaltungswissenschaft,* edited by T. Ellwein et al. 1: 111–54. Baden-Baden: Nomos.

Schasse, U. 1991. *Betriebszugehoerigkeitsdauer und Mobilitaet: eine empirische Untersuchung zur Stabilitaet von Beschaeftigungsverhaeltnissen in der Bundesrepublik Deutschland.* Frankfurt: Campus.

Schellhaass, H. M. 1984. "Ein oekonomischer Vergleich finanzieller und rechtlicher Kuendigungserschwernisse." *Zeitschrift fuer Arbeitsrecht* 15 (2): 139–71.

————. 1989. "Sozialplaene aus oekonomischer Sicht." *Zeitschrift fuer Arbeitsrecht* 20 (2): 167–207.

————. 1990. "Das Arbeitsrecht als Beschaeftigungshemmnis?" In *Mehr Arbeit durch weniger Recht? Chancen und Risiken der Arbeitsmarktflexibilisierung,* edited by C. F. Buechtemann and H. Neumann, 87–104. Berlin: Sigma.

————. 1991. "Der Bestandsschutz als Technologiesteuer?" *Jahrbuecher fuer Nationaloekonomie und Statistik* 207: 620–25.

Schenkel, M. 1989. "La CIG: Instrument de réduction du temps de travail." In *La* *flexibilité en Italie*, edited by M. Maruani, E. Reynaud, and C. Romani, 143–52. Paris: Syros.

———. 1990. "The Economic Effects of CIG." In *Report '89: Labor and Employment Policies in Italy*, edited by the Italian Ministry of Labor, 459–63. Rome: Poligrafico dello Stato.

Schenkel, M., and **M. Zenezini.** 1986. "Alcuni aspetti della Cassa Integrazione Guadagni: Un'analisi empirica." *Rivista internazionale di scienze sociali* 44 (1): 87–112.

Schettkat, R., and **M. Wagner,** eds. 1990. *Technological Change and Employment: Innovation in the German Economy.* Berlin and New York: de Gruyter.

Schiff, F. W. 1986. "Short-Time Compensation: Assessing the Issues." *Monthly Labor Review* 109 (May): 28–30.

Schlicht, E. 1978. "Labour Turnover, Wage Structure, and Natural Unemployment." *Zeitschrift fuer die gesamte Staatswissenschaft* 134 (4): 337–46.

Schmid, G. 1986. "Flexibilisierung des Arbeitsmarkts durch Recht?" *Aus Politik und Zeitgeschichte* B23/86: 22–38.

———. 1988. *Labour Market Policy in Transition: Trends and Effectiveness in the Federal Republic of Germany."* EFA Report no. 17. Stockholm: EFA.

Schmidt, K.-D. 1985. *Arbeitsmaerkte im Wandel: Auswirkungen fuer die Bildungspolitik.* Kiel: Institut fuer Weltwirtschaft.

Schmitter, P., et al., eds. Forthcoming. *Comparative Governance of Economic Sectors.* New York: Oxford University Press.

Schotter, A. 1986. "The Evolution of Rules." In *Economics as a Process: Essays in the New Institutional Economics*, edited by R. N. Langlois, 117–34. Cambridge: Cambridge University Press.

Schregle, J. 1981. "Comparative Industrial Relations: Pitfalls and Potential." *International Labour Review* 23 (Jan.–Feb.): 15–30.

Schruefer, K. 1988. *Oekonomische Analyse individueller Arbeitsverhaeltnisse.* Frankfurt: Campus.

Schuck, P. H. 1991. "Tort Law and the Public Interest." In *Competition, Innovation, and Consumers' Welfare*, edited by P. H. Schuck. New York: W. W. Norton.

Schultze, C. L. 1985. "Microeconomic Efficiency and Nominal Wage Stickiness." *American Economic Review* 75 (March): 1–15.

Schultze, C. L., and **R. Z. Lawrence, eds.** 1988. *Barriers to European Growth: A Transatlantic View.* Washington D.C.: Brookings Institution.

Schultz-Wild, R. 1978. *Betriebliche Beschaeftigungspolitik in der Krise.* Frankfurt: Campus.

Schupp, J. 1988. "Erwerbsbeteiligung und Arbeitsmarkt." In *Lebenslagen im Wandel: Daten 1987*, edited by H. -J. Krupp and J. Schupp, 88–113. Frankfurt: Campus.

Schwab, S. 1989. "The Economics Invasion of Labor Law Scholarship," In *Proceedings* of the Forty-first Annual Meeting of the Industrial Relations Research Association, edited by B. D. Dennis, 236–42. Madison, Wisc.: Industrial Relations Research Association.

Scott, M., et al. 1989. *Management and Industrial Relations in Small Firms*. Department of Employment Research Paper no. 70. London.

Seghal, E. 1984. "Occupational Mobility and Job Tenure in 1983." *Monthly Labor Review* 107 (Oct.): 18–23.

Selznick, P. 1968. "Law: The Sociology of Law." In *International Encyclopedia of the Social Sciences* 9: 50–59.

———. 1969. *Law, Society, and Industrial Justice*. Washington, D.C.: Russell Sage Foundation.

Sengenberger, W. 1982. "Country Report: Federal Republic of Germany." In *Workforce Reductions in Undertakings*, edited by E. Yemin, 79–106. Geneva: International Labour Office.

———. 1986. "Mangelnde Flexibilitaet auf dem Arbeitsmarkt als Ursache der Arbeitslosigkeit." In *Wege zur Vollbeschaeftigung*, edited by H. J. Krupp., B. Rohwe, and K. W. Rothschild, 91–106. Freiburg: Rombach.

———. 1987. *Struktur und Funktionsweise von Arbeitsmaerkten: Die Bundesrepublik Deutschland im internationalen Vergleich*. Frankfurt: Campus.

Sengenberger, W., and **G. Loveman.** 1987. *Smaller Units of Employment: A Synthesis Report on Industrial Reorganization in Industrialized Countries*. Geneva: International Institute for Labor Studies, International Labor Office.

Shapiro, C., and **J. E. Stiglitz.** 1984. "Equilibrium Unemployment as a Worker Discipline Device." *American Economic Review* 74: 433–44.

Shattuck, C. A. 1989. "The Tort of Negligent Hiring and the Use of Selection Devices: The Employee's Right of Privacy and the Employer's Need to Know." *Industrial Relations Law Journal* 2 (1): 2–17.

Shavell, S. 1984. "Liability for Harm versus Regulation for Safety." *Journal of Legal Studies* 13 (June): 357–74.

Shimada, H. 1986. "Employment Adjustment and Employment Policies: Japanese Experience." Keio University. Mimeo.

Shimada, H., T. Hosokawa, and **A. Seike.** 1982. *An Analysis of Wage and Employment Adjustment Processes*. Economic Planning Agency no. 84 (in Japanese).

Shimada, H., A. Seike, T. Furugori, Y. Sakai, and **T. Hosokawa.** 1982–83. "The Japanese Labor Market: A Survey." *Japanese Economic Studies* 11 (Winter): 3–84.

Shinozuka, E. 1980. "Recent Employment Adjustment according to Firm Size" (in Japanese). In *Analysis of the Contemporary Labour Market*, edited by T. Nakamura and S. Nishikawa, 35–57. Tokyo: Sogo Rodo Kenkyusho.

Shinozuka, E., and **E. Ishihara.** 1976. "Employment Adjustment after the Oil Shock: An International Comparison by a Partial Adjustment Model" (in Japanese). Japan Economic Research Center Discussion Paper no. 17.

Siebert, H. 1989. "Kuendigungsschutz und Sozialplanpflicht—Optimale Allokation von

Risiken oder Ursache der Arbeitslosigkeit." In *Beschaeftigungsprobleme hochentwickelter Volkswirtschaften: Schriften des Vereins fuer Socialpolitik NF*, edited by H. Scherf, 178: 267–86. Berlin: Duncker und Humblot.

Siebert, W. S., and **J. T. Addison.** 1991. "Internal Labor Markets: Causes and Consequences." *Oxford Review of Economic Policy* 7 (1): 76–92.

Simitis, S. 1987. "Juridification of Labor Relations." In: *Juridification of Social Spheres: A Comparative Analysis in the Areas of Labor, Corporate, Antitrust and Social Welfare Law*, edited by G. Teubner, 113–61. Berlin and New York: de Gruyter.

Sims, C. 1974. "Output and Labor Input in Manufacturing." *Brookings Papers on Economic Activity* (3): 695–728.

Sisson, K. 1989. *Personnel Management in Britain.* Oxford: Basil Blackwell.

Slichter, S. H. 1929. "The Current Labor Policies of American Industries." *Quarterly Journal of Economics* 18 (May): 393–435.

Soderstrom, H. T. 1972. "Cyclical Fluctuations in Labor Productivity and Capacity Utilization Reconsidered." *Swedish Journal of Economics.*

Solow, R. M. 1956. "A Contribution to the Theory of Economic Growth." *Quarterly Journal of Economics* 70 (1): 65–94.

———. 1979. "Another Possible Source of Wage Stickiness." *Journal of Macroeconomics* 1 (Winter): 79–82.

Soltwedel, R. 1984. *Mehr Markt am Arbeitsmarkt: Ein Plaedoyer fuer weniger Arbeitsmarktpolitik.* Munich and Wien: Philosophia Verlag.

Soltwedel, R., **et al.** 1990. *Regulierungen auf dem Arbeitsmarkt der Bundesrepublik.* Kieler Studien, vol. 233. Tuebingen: J. C. B. Mohr/Siebeck.

Sonnenfeld, J. 1985. "Demystifying the Magic of Training." In *HRM Trends and Practices*, edited by R. Walton and P. Lawrence, 302–18. Cambridge, Mass.: Harvard University Press.

Sorge, A., and **W. Streeck.** 1987. "Industrial Relations and Technical Change: The Case for an Extended Perspective." Wissenschaftszentrum Berlin Discussion Paper IIM/LMP 87–1.

Spalter-Roth, R. M., and **H. I. Hartmann.** 1990. *Unnecessary Losses: Costs to Americans of the Lack of Family and Medical Leave.* Washington, D.C.: Institute for Women's Policy Research.

Spulber, D. F. 1989. *Regulation and Markets.* Cambridge, Mass.: MIT Press.

Standing, G. 1986a. *Labour Market Flexibility: Cause or Cure for Unemployment?* Public Lecture no. 25. Geneva: International Institute for Labour Studies, International Labour Office.

———. 1986b. *Unemployment and Labour Market Flexibility: The United Kingdom.* Geneva: International Labour Office.

———. 1988a. "Labor Flexibility and Insecurity: Towards an Alternative Strategy." International Labour Office. Mimeo.

————. 1988b. *Unemployment and Labour Market Flexibility: Sweden.* Geneva: International Labour Office.

Statistisches Bundesamt. 1989. *Stand und Entwicklung der Erwerbstaetigkeit: Ergebnisse des Mikrozensus.* Stuttgart: Kohlhammer.

Sterling, W. P. 1984. "Comparative Studies of American and Japanese Labor Markets." Ph.D. diss., Harvard University.

Stewart, M. B. 1991. "Union Wage Differentials in the Face of Changes in the Economic and Legal Environment." *Economica* 58 (2): 155–72.

Stieber, J. 1984. "Most U.S. Workers Still May Be Fired Under Employment-at-Will." *Monthly Labor Review* 107 (May): 34–38.

————. 1985. "Recent Developments in 'Employment-at-Will.'" *Labor Law Journal* (Aug.): 557–63.

Stiglitz, J. E. 1987. "The Causes and Consequences of the Dependence of Quality on Price." *Journal of Economic Literature* 25: 1–48.

Storey, J., ed. 1989. *New Perspectives in Human Resource Management.* London: Routledge.

Strah, B. 1989. *The Politics of De-industrialization.* London: Croom-Helm.

Streeck, W. 1985. "Industrial Relations in West Germany 1974–1985: An Overview." Wissenschaftszentrum Berlin Discussion Paper IIM/LMP 85–19.

————. 1988. "Skills and the Limits of Neo-Liberalism: The Enterprise of the Future as a Place of Learning." Wissenschaftszentrum Berlin Discussion Paper FSI 88–16.

————. 1991. "On the Social and Political Conditions of Diversified Quality Production." In *Beyond Keynesianism: The Socio-economics of Production and Full Employment,* edited by E. Matzner and W. Streeck, 21–61. Aldershot: Edward Elgar.

Streeck, W., et al. 1987. "The Role of the Social Partners in Vocational Training and Further Training in the Federal Republic of Germany." Wissenschaftszentrum Berlin Discussion Paper IIM/LMP 87–12.

Struempel, B. 1989. "Popular Bases of Conflict and Solidarity: A Review of the Evidence from a Decade of Economie Problematique." In *Industrial Societies after the Stagnation of the 1970s: Taking Stock from an Interdisciplinary Perspective,* edited by B. Struempel, 185–207. Berlin and New York: de Gruyter.

Summers, C. 1976. "Individual Protection against Unjust Dismissal: Time for a Statute." *Virginia Law Review* 62: 481–532.

Sundquist's Report. 1988. *New Technologies in the 1990s: A Socio-Economic Strategy.* Report prepared for the OECD by a group of experts under the chairmanship of Ulf Sundquist. Paris: OECD.

Swaim, P., and **M. Podgursky.** 1990. "Advance Notice and Job Search: The Value of an Early Start." *Journal of Human Resources* 25: 147–78.

Sweet, M. L. 1981. *Industrial Location Policy for Economic Revitalization: National and International Perspectives.* New York: Praeger.

Syrup, K. 1957. *100 Jahre staatliche Sozialpolitik, 1839–1939*, edited by J. Scheuble and O. Neuloh. Stuttgart: Kohlhammer.

Szyszcak, E. M. 1986. "Employment Protection and Social Security." In *Labour Law in Britain*, edited by R. Lewis, 360–88. Oxford: Basil Blackwell.

Tachibanaki, T. 1987. "Labour Market Flexibility in Japan in Comparison with Europe and the United States." *European Economic Review* 31 (April): 647–77.

Tarantelli, E. 1973. *Studi di economia del lavoro.* Milan: Guiffre.

———. 1986. *Economia politica del lavoro.* Turin: Utet.

Tarullo, D. K. 1989. "Public Policy and Employment Security." In *Proceedings of the Forty-first Annual Meeting of the IRRA*, edited by B. D. Dennis, 430–38. Madison, Wisc.: Industrial Relations Research Association.

TECSA-Conseil. 1989. "Étude de l'impact et de l'ordonnance du 11 août 1986 sur le travail différencié: Rapport final."

Teece, D. J. 1989. "Technological Development and the Organization of Industry." Paper presented at international OECD seminar "Science, Technology and Economic Growth," Paris, June.

Teubner, G. 1985. "After Legal Instrumentalism? Strategic Models of Post-regulatory Law." In *Dilemmas of Law in the Welfare State*, edited by G. Teubner, 299–326. Berlin and New York: de Gruyter.

———. 1987. "Juridification: Concepts, Aspects, Limits, Solutions." In *Juridification of Social Spheres: A Comparative Analysis in the Areas of Labor, Corporate, Antitrust, and Social Welfare Law*, edited by G. Teubner, 3–48. Berlin and New York: de Gruyter.

Thurow, L. 1985. *The Zero-Sum Solution: Rebuilding a World-Class American Economy.* New York: Simon & Schuster.

Tiano, A. 1988. *Economie du travail.* Paris: Presses Universitaires de France.

Topel, R. H. 1983. "On Layoffs and Unemployment Insurance." *American Economic Review* 73 (Sept.): 541–59.

———. 1985. "Unemployment and Unemployment Insurance." In *Research in Labor Economics*, edited by R. G. Ehrenberg, 7: 91–136. Greenwich, Conn.: JAI Press.

Towers, B. 1987. "Trends and Developments in Industrial Relations: Managing Labour Flexibility." *Industrial Relations Journal* 18 (Summer): 79–83.

———. 1989. "Running the Gauntlet: British Trade Unions under Thatcher, 1979–88." *Industrial and Labor Relations Review* 42 (Jan.): 163–88.

Townsend, P. 1990. "Underclass and Overclass: The Widening Gulf between Social Classes in Britain in the 1980s." Forthcoming in *Sociology in Action*, edited by G. Payne and M. Cross. Basingstoke: Macmillan.

Trades Union Congress. 1966. *Trade Unionism.* London: TUC.

Treu, T. 1982. "Italy." In *Workforce Reductions in Undertakings*, edited by E. Yemin, 141–66. Geneva: International Labour Office.

————. 1985. "Recent Development of Italian Labour Law." *Labour and Society* 10 (1): 27–44.

————. 1987. "Italy." In *International Encyclopedia of Labor Law and Industrial Relations* 2d ed., 1992, edited by R. Blanpain, 212–41. Boston: Kluwer.

Tronti, L., and **R. Turatto.** 1990. "Employment Protection and Labor Market Segmentation: The Fiftieth Anniversary of the Italian 'Cassa Integrazione Guadagni.'" Paper presented at the Second Annual Meeting of the European Association of Labor Economists (EALE), Lund, Sweden, September 20–23.

Troy, K. 1990. *Rethinking Employment Security.* Research Bulletin no. 244. New York: Conference Board.

U.K. Department of Employment. 1988. *Employment for the 1990s.* London: HMSO.

U.S. Chamber of Commerce. 1990. *Employee Benefits, 1989.* Washington, D.C.

U.S. Department of Labor. 1985. *United States–Japan Comparative Study of Employment Adjustment.* Report of the U.S. Department of Labor and the Japan Ministry of Labour, Comparative Research Project on Employment Adjustment. Washington, D.C.

U.S. Department of Labor. Bureau of Labor Statistics. 1985. *Displaced Workers, 1979–83.* Bulletin 2240. Washington, D.C.: Government Printing Office.

————. 1987. *Displaced Workers, 1981–85.* Bulletin 2289. Washington, D.C.: Government Printing Office.

Valentini, C. 1981. *La politica attiva del lavoro in Italia e il problema della mobilitá.* Milan: Universitá Bocconi.

Von Hippel, E. 1988. *The Sources of Innovation.* New York: Oxford University Press.

Von Stebut, D. 1982. *Der soziale Schutz als Regelungsproblem des Vertragsrechts.* Berlin: Duncker und Humblodt.

Vrain, P., and **R. Ardenti.** 1988. "Restructurations et licenciements dans les grandes entreprises." *La lettre d'information du C.E.E..* 9 (Sept.): 1–7.

Wachter, M. L., and **G. M. Cohen.** 1988. "The Law and Economics of Collective Bargaining: An Introduction and Applications to the Problems of Subcontracting, Partial Closure, and Relocation." *University of Pennsylvania Law Review* 136 (May): 1349–1417.

Wachter, M. L., and **O. E. Williamson.** 1978. "Obligational Markets and the Mechanics of Inflation." *Bell Journal of Economics* 9 (Autumn): 549–71.

Wachter, M. L., and **R. D. Wright.** 1990. "The Economics of Internal Labor Markets." In *The Economics of Human Resource Management,* edited by D. J. B. Mitchell and M. A. Zaidi, 86–108. Oxford: Basil Blackwell.

Walter, N. 1988. "The Inflexibility of Labour Market Related Institutions: Some Observations for Germany." In *Management under Differing Labour Market and Employment Systems,* edited by G. Dlugos, et al., 133–42. Berlin and New York: de Gruyter.

Walwei, U. 1990a. "Analyse arbeitsrechtlicher Regelungen am Beispiel des Kuendigungsschutzes." *WSI-Mitteilungen* 43 (June): 392–400.

————. 1990b. *Oekonomisch-rechtliche Analyse befristeter Arbeitsverhaeltnisse*, vol. 139, *Beitraege zur Arbeitsmarkt- und Berufsforschung*. Nuremberg: Institute of Employment Research.

Warnken, J., and **G. Ronning**. 1990. "Activity Structures and the Diffusion of New Technology in the Enterprise." In *Technological Change and Employment: Innovation in the German Economy*, edited by R. Schettkat and M. Wagner, 215–53. Berlin and New York: de Gruyter.

Watanabe, S. 1989. "The Diffusion of New Technologies, Management Styles and Work Organization in Japan: A Survey of Empirical Studies." Paper presented at International OECD Conference, Technological Change as a Social Process: Society, Enterprises and the Individual, Helsinki, December.

Weber, A., and **D. Taylor**. 1963. "Procedure for Employee Displacement: Advance Notice of Plant Shut-Downs." *Journal of Business* 36 (July): 302–15.

Wedderburn of Charlton, Lord. 1965. *The Worker and the Law*. Harmondsworth: Penguin.

————. 1980. "Industrial Relations and the Courts." *Industrial Law Journal* 9: 65–94.

Wedderburn of Charlton, Lord, and **W. T. Murphy, eds**. 1982. *Labour Law and the Community: Perspectives for the 1980's*. London: Institute of Advanced Legal Studies.

Weidinger, M., and **A. Hoff**. 1984. "Mehrarbeit und Mehrarbeitspolitik in der Bundesrepublik Deutschland." Report for the International Labour Office. Mimeo.

Weiler, P. C. 1990. *Governing the Workplace: The Future of Labor and Employment Law*. Cambridge, Mass.: Harvard University Press.

Weiss, A. 1990. *Efficiency Wages: 1990 Models of Unemployment, Layoffs and Wage Dispersion*. Princeton, N.J.: Princeton University Press.

Weiss, R. 1990. *Die 26-Milliarden-Investition: Kosten und Strukturen betrieblicher Weiterbildung*. Cologne: Deutscher Instituts-Verlag.

Weitzman, M. L. 1984. *The Share Economy*. Cambridge, Mass.: Harvard University Press.

————. 1985. *Steady State Unemployment under Profit Sharing*. Department of Economics Working Paper no. 399. Cambridge, Mass.: MIT.

Weller, A. 1969. *Arbeitslosigkeit und Arbeitsrecht*. Stuttgart: Fischer.

Wells, W. 1983. *The Relative Pay and Employment of Young People*. Department of Employment Research Paper no. 42. London: Department of Employment Research.

Westin, A., and **S. Salisbury, eds**. 1980. *Individual Rights in the Corporation*. New York: Random House.

Williams, K. 1983. "Unfair Dismissals: Myths and Statistics." *Industrial Law Journal* 12 (Sept.): 157–65.

Williamson, O. E. 1975. *Markets and Hierarchies: Analysis and Antitrust Implications*. New York: Free Press.

————. 1980. "The Organization of Work: A Comparative Institutional Assessment." *Journal of Economic Organization and Behavior* 1: 39–60.

————. 1985. *The Economic Institutions of Capitalism.* New York: Free Press.

Wintrobe, R., and **A. Breton.** 1986. "Organizational Structure and Productivity." *American Economic Review* 76: 530–38.

Wittman, D. 1977. "Prior Regulation Versus Post-Liability: The Choice between Input and Output Monitoring." *Journal of Legal Studies* 6 (Jan.): 193–211.

Wolf, C., Jr. 1988. *Markets or Governments: Choosing Imperfect Alternatives.* Cambridge, Mass.: MIT Press.

Wolleb, E. 1988. "Mutamenti nei rapporti di produzione nella crisi: Ascesa e tracollo del fordismo in Italia." In *La flessibilita del lavoro in Europa,* edited by R. Boyer and E. Wolleb, 57–79. Milan: Franco Angeli.

Wood, D., et al. 1988. *Employers' Labour Use Strategies. First Repeat of the 1987 Survey.* Department of Employment Research Paper no. 63. London: Department of Employment.

Yellen, J. L. 1984. "Efficiency Wage Models of Unemployment." *American Economic Review* 74: 200–205.

Zarnowitz, V. 1985. "Recent Work on Business Cycles in Historical Perspective: A Review of Theories and Evidence." *Journal of Economic Literature* 23 (June): 523–80.

Zoellner, W. 1978. *Sind im Interesse einer gerechteren Verteilung der Arbeitsplaetze Begruendung und Beendigung der Arbeitsverhaeltnisse neu zu regeln? Gutachten fuer den 52. Deutschen Juristentag.* Munich: Beck Verlag.

Zylberberg, A. 1981. "Flexibilité, incertain et théorie de la demande de travail." *Annales de l'INSEE* 42: 31–52.

Notes on Contributors

Katharine G. Abraham received her Ph.D. in economics from Harvard University. From 1980 to 1987, she held positions at the Sloan School of Management and at the Brookings Institution. Since 1988, she has been a professor of economics at the University of Maryland and a research associate at the National Bureau of Economic Research. Her research focuses on internal labor markets and unemployment. Abraham is the coeditor (with R. B. McKersie) of *New Developments in the Labor Market: Toward a New Institutional Paradigm* and coauthor (with S. N. Houseman) of *Job Security in America: Lessons from Germany.*

Peter Auer holds a Ph.D. in the social sciences from the University of Bremen. Since 1978, he has been a research fellow at the Social Science Center Berlin, where he participated in major comparative projects in the areas of labor market policy and industrial relations. Among Auer's recent publications are *Post-Taylorism: The Enterprise as a Place of Learning Organizational Change* (with C. Riegler) and *Labour Force Adjustment to Structural Change: Experiences in Germany, France, Sweden and the United Kingdom.*

Brian Bercusson holds a Ph.D. from Christ's College at Cambridge University. He has also studied law at the London School of Economics. Since 1986, Bercusson has been a professor of law at the European University Institute, in Florence, Italy. Recent publications include "Fundamental Social and Economic Rights in the European Community," in *Human Rights in the European Community,* and "The European Community's Charter of Fundamental Social Rights for Workers," in *Modern Law Review.*

Rolf Birk received a doctorate in law in 1966 from the University of Erlangen-Nuremberg. From 1975 to 1983, he was a professor of law at the University of Erlangen-Nuremberg and at the University of Augsburg. Since 1983, he has been a professor of law at the University of Trier and director of its Institute for Labour Law and Industrial Relations in the European Community. Birk is coeditor of the *Zeitschrift fuer vergleichende Rechtswissenschaft* and of the *Zeitschrift fuer auslaendisches und internationales Arbeits- und Sozialrecht* and author of *Der gewerkschaftliche Warnstreik im oeffentlichen Dienst* and of *Gesetz zur Regelung kollektiver Arbeitskonflikte—Entwurf und Begruendung* (with H. Konzen, M. Loewisch, T.

Raiser, and H. Seiter), as well as articles on national, international, and comparative labor law.

Robert Boyer graduated from the Ecole Polytechnique, the Ecole Nationale de Ponts et Chaussées, and the Institut d'Etudes Politiques and has studied economics at University of Paris I. He has worked for the Center of Studies on Incomes and Costs (CERC) and for the Ministry of Finance. He is now a senior researcher in economics at CEPREMAP and on the faculty of the Ecoles des Hautes Etudes en Sciences Sociales. His research areas are economic history, macroeconomic modeling, and international labor market comparisons from the viewpoint of the *régulation* approach. Boyer's major publications include *Capitalismes: Fin de siècle, The Regulation School: A Critical Introduction,* and *The Search for Labour Market Flexibility.*

Christoph F. Buechtemann received his Ph.D. in the social sciences from the University of Munich. From 1985 to 1991, he was research coordinator at the Social Science Center Berlin. Since May 1991, he has worked as a senior economist at the RAND Corporation in California. Buechtemann's principal research areas are international comparative research in labor economics, corporate adjustment, and the economics of regulation. His recent publications include (with S. Quack) "Non-Standard Employment: How Precarious Is It? Evidence for West Germany," in the *Cambridge Journal of Economics,* "Does (De-) Regulation Matter?" in *Beyond Keynesianism,* and *Unemployment and Labor Market Flexibility: West Germany* (with F. Stille).

Friedrich Buttler received a Ph.D. in economics from the University of Goettingen in 1967. Since 1973, he has been a professor of economics at Paderborn University and was its president from 1976 to 1987. His main areas of teaching and research are public finance, labor economics, and regional economics. Since 1988, Buttler has been the director of the Institute of Employment Research in Nuremberg.

Alain Charraud received a doctoral degree in social sciences from the University of Paris-Sorbonne in 1975. He was in charge of the national health survey at the Institute National de Statistique et Economie from 1980 to 1985 and then chief editor of its journal, *Economie et statistique.* Charraud is now head of the Employment Policy Studies Division of the Ministry of Labour in Paris. His recent publications include *Le developpement des emplois temporaires* (with J. C. Guergoat).

James N. Dertouzos received his doctorate in economics from Stanford University in 1980. He is currently a senior economist with the RAND Corporation in California. He is on the faculty of the RAND Graduate School and also teaches at the University of California at Los Angeles. Dertouzos's primary areas of research are the economics of human resources, military manpower, and competition in the mass media industries. Recent articles include "Economic Effects of Media Concentration," in the *Journal of Industrial Economics,* and *The Effects of Military Advertising,* a RAND Corporation Monogragh.

Ronald G. Ehrenberg is the Irving M. Ives Professor of Industrial and Labor Relations and Economics, director of research, and director of the Institute for Labor Market Policies at the School of Industrial and Labor Relations at Cornell University. He also is a research associate at the National Bureau of Economic Research and a senior research fellow at the Consortium for Policy Research in Education. He received his Ph.D. in economics from Northwestern University. His research spans such areas as public sector labor markets, wages in regulated industries, the evaluation of labor market programs and legislation, the incentive effects of compensation systems, and resource allocation issues in education.

Robert J. Flanagan has a Ph.D. in economics from the University of California at Berkeley. He is a professor of labor economics at the Graduate School of Business at Stanford University, where he has been on the faculty since 1975. Flanagan has also served on the staffs of the U.S. Council of Economic Advisers and the Organization for Economic Cooperation and Development. Among his recent publications are "Labor Market Behavior and European Economic Growth" in *Barriers to European Growth: A Transatlantic View*, "Compliance and Enforcement Decisions under the National Labor Relations Act," in the *Journal of Labor Economics*, and "The Economics of Unions and Collective Bargaining," in *Industrial Relations*.

Wolfgang Franz is a professor of economics at the University of Konstanz. He received his Ph.D. from the University of Mannheim. After his "habilitation," Franz was a professor at the University of Mainz and later at the University of Stuttgart. He has also been a research fellow at the National Bureau of Economic Research. His research focuses on labor economics and applied macroeconomics. He is coeditor of the Journal *Empirical Economics* and has published in international journals. Franz's most recent book is *Arbeitsmarktoekonomik*.

William B. Gould IV received a law degree in 1961 from Cornell Law School and did graduate work at the London School of Economics in 1962–63. The Charles A. Beardsley Professor of Law at Stanford Law School, he has been a professor there since 1972. Gould is the author of *Japan's Reshaping of American Labor Law* and of *A Primer on American Labor Law* and more recently, of "The Supreme Court and Employment Discrimination Law in 1989: Judicial Retreat and Congressional Response," in the *Tulane Law Review*, and "Judicial Review of Labor Arbitration Awards—Thirty Years of the Steelworkers Trilogy: The Aftermath of AT & T and Misco," in the *Notre Dame Law Review*.

Daniel S. Hamermesh received his Ph.D. in economics from Yale University. He has taught at Princeton University and since 1976 has been a professor of economics at Michigan State University. He has been a visiting faculty member at Dalhousie, Harvard, La Trobe, Australian National, and Gadjah Mada universities. Since 1979, Hamermesh has also been a research associate at the National Bureau of Economic Research. Among his publications are "Labor Demand and the Structure of Adjustment Costs," in the *American Economic Review*; "Sleep and the Allocation of Time," in the *Journal of Political Economy*; *Economics of Work and Pay*; and *Labor Demand*.

Claus Hofmann studied economics at the University of Frankfurt. From 1972 to 1987 he was deputy head of the Economics Division of the German Federal Ministry of Employment and Social Affairs and from 1987 to 1990 an economic adviser at the Commission of the European Communities in Brussels. Since 1990, Hofmann has been head of the Economics Division at the German Federal Ministry for Employment and Social Affairs.

Susan N. Houseman received her Ph.D. in economics from Harvard University. From 1985 to 1989, she was on the faculty of the School of Public Affairs at the University of Maryland. Since 1989, she has been a senior economist at the W. E. Upjohn Institute for Employment Research. Houseman is the author of *Industrial Restructuring with Job Security: The Case of European Steel* and coauthor (with K. G. Abraham) of *Job Security in America*.

Richard Hyman received his Ph.D. from Nuffield College at Oxford University. He is a professor of industrial relations and convenor of graduate studies at the Industrial Relations Research Unit at the University of Warwick. His recent publications include *Strikes*; *The Political Economy of Industrial Relations: Theory and Practice in a Cold Climate* (with W. Streeck); and *New Technology and Industrial Relations*, as well as many articles in leading economics journals.

George H. Jakubson is an associate professor of labor economics at the School of Industrial and Labor Relations at Cornell University. He received his Ph.D. in economics from the University of Wisconsin—Madison in 1983 and joined the ILR school in 1983. He is also a research associate with the Institute for Research of Poverty at the University of Wisconsin. He has done research on the effects of transfer programs as well as econometric methods for the analysis of panel data.

Lynn A. Karoly received her Ph.D. in economics in 1988 from Yale University and is an associate economist at the RAND Corporation. Her research has focused on the distribution of income and wages in the United States and on the economic impact of employment liability. She is currently conducting analyses of migration behavior and military personnel. Recent publications include "Changes in the Distribution of Individual Earnings in the U.S.: 1967–1986," in the *Review of Economics and Statistics*, and "The Trend in Inequality among Families, Individuals and Workers in the U.S.: A 25–Year Perspective," forthcoming in *Uneven Tides: Rising Inequalities in the 1980s*. She is also a member of the faculty of the RAND Graduate School.

Kornelius Kraft received his Ph.D. in economics in 1984 from the University of Kassel. Since May 1992, he has been a professor of economics at the University of Fribourg in Switzerland. From 1980 to 1986, he was a research associate at the Social Science Center Berlin and from 1986 to 1992 lecturer at the University of Kassel. Kraft's major research interests are labor economics, industrial organization, and health economics. Recent publications include "Cooperation, Productivity and Profit Sharing," in the *Quarterly Journal of Economics* (with F. FitzRoy), "Efficiency and Internal Organization: Works Councils in West German Firms," in *Economica*, and "The Incentive Effects of Dismissals, Efficiency Wages, Piece Rates, and Profit Sharing," in the *Review of Economics and Statistics*.

Burkart Lutz holds a Ph.D. from the University of Freiburg, Germany. In the late 1950s, Lutz worked free-lance for a number of German and European firms, trade unions, and research centers, in particular, the Institut fuer Sozialforschung in Frankfurt, and was a member of the steering group for a large-scale international comparative study on the European steel industry. In 1965, he founded the Institute for Social Science Research in Munich, which he codirected until 1990. His more than twenty books and countless articles and essays deal principally with issues of the labor market, work and technology, firm policy, and education and training.

Antoine Lyon-Caen received his doctorate in law from the University of Paris. From 1975 to 1979, he was a professor at the law school of Caen, and since 1979, he has been at the law school of Paris-Nanterre. Since 1988, he has also been a research adviser at the School of Advanced Studies in the Social Sciences. Lyon-Caen's research interests are international comparative research in labor law and industrial relations, and social policies. He is the coauthor (with G. Lyon-Caen) of *International and European Social Law*.

Guy Maurau received his Ph.D. in economics from the University of Paris I in 1972. From 1973 to 1985, he was a lecturer at the University of Rouen and from 1985 to 1988 a senior economist at the Institute des Recherches Economiques et Sociales in Paris. Since October 1988, he has been head of the Department of Economics of the University of Rouen. Maurau's recent publications deal with atypical employment and work force adjustment from an international comparative perspective.

Paul Osterman is a professor of human resources and management at the Sloan School of Management at the Massachusetts Institute of Technology. He received his Ph.D. in economics from MIT. Osterman is the author of three books— *Getting Started: The Youth Labor Market*; *Internal Labor Markets*; and *Employment Futures: Reorganization, Dislocation, and Public Policy*—as well as articles on employment policy, internal labor markets, human resources within firms, poverty, and social policy.

Horst-Manfred Schellhaass received his Ph.D. in economics from the University of the Saarland in Saarbruecken. Since April 1978, he has been a professor of economic theory at the Technical University of Berlin. His principal areas of interest are the economics of employment protection, industrial organization, and the deregulation of the housing market. He is the author of "The Disinterest in Efficient Subsidization" in *Kyklos* and of "Sozialplaene aus oekonomischer Sicht" in *Zeitschrift fuer Arbeitsrecht*.

Günther Schmid received his Ph.D. in political science from the Free University of Berlin. From 1978 to 1990, he was research coordinator and deputy director of the Social Science Center Berlin, where he is now director of the research unit on labor market policy and employment. Schmid is also a professor of political economics at the Free University of Berlin and the author of *Unemployment Insurance and Active Labor Market Policy* (with B. Reissert and G. Bruche), *Labor Market Policy in Transition,* and "Institutional Conditions of Effective Labor Market Policy," in *Beyond Keynesianism.*

Guy Standing is coordinator of Labour Market Research in the employment department of the International Labour Organization. He has a Ph.D. in economics from the University of Cambridge and has done extensive research and field work in Western and Eastern Europe and in developing countries. His books include *Towards Social Adjustment: Labour Market Issues in Structural Adjustment* and *In Search of Flexibility: The New Soviet Labour Market.*

Brian Towers has a Ph.D. from Nottingham University. He cofounded the *Industrial Relations Journal* in 1970 and has been its sole editor since 1972. In 1990, Towers was appointed chair of industrial relations at Strathclyde Business School. His research interests and publications focus on the relationship between economic performance and industrial relations policies and practice.

Tiziano Treu is a professor of labor law at the Catholic University of Milan and president of the Italian section of the International Industrial Relations Association, as well as a member of the organization's executive committee. He is the author of the report on Italy in the *International Encyclopedia of Labor Law and Industrial Relations* and the editor of the book *Labour Relations in the Public Service.*

Leonello Tronti received a laureate in philosophy from the University of Milan. In January 1988, he became research coordinator at the Fondazione G. Brodolini in Rome and in 1990 a lecturer of labor economics at the Università G. D'Annunzio (Teramo) and coeditor of the annual report *Labour and Employment Policies in Italy.* He is the coeditor of *Welfare State and Redistribuzione* (with R. Brunetta) as well as the author of "A Structural Approach to the European Labour Market" (with R. Turatto) in *Labour,* and other academic articles and reports.

Ulrich Walwei received his Ph.D. in economics from the University of Paderborn. Since 1988, he has been a researcher at the Institute of Employment Research in Nuremberg. His research interests are the economics of regulation (particularly labor law), European labor markets, and international comparative research in social and labor law. He is the author (with R. Konle-Seidl and H. Ullmann) of "The European Social Space: Atypical Forms of Employment and Working Hours in the European Community," in the *International Social Security Review,* and of "Fixed-Term Contracts in EC Countries," in *Intereconomics.*

Index